CONTEMPORARY POSTCOLONIAL THEORY

9

CONTEMPORARY POSTCOLONIAL THEORY

A READER

Edited by

Padmini Mongia

Associate Professor of English,
Franklin & Marshall College,
Pennsylvania

A member of the Hodder Headline Group
LONDON • NEW YORK • SYDNEY • AUCKLAND

First published in Great Britain in 1996 by
Arnold, a member of the Hodder Headline Group
338 Euston Road, London NW1 3BH
175 Fifth Avenue, New York, NY10010

Distributed exclusively in the USA by
St Martin's Press Inc.
175 Fifth Avenue
New York, NY10010

British Library Cataloguing in Publication Data
A catalogue entry for this book is available from the British Library

Library of Congress Cataloging-in-Publication Data
A catalog entry for this book is available from The Library of Congress

ISBN 0340 65288 8 (Pb)
ISBN 0340 65289 6 (Hb)

Composition in 10/12 Times by York House Typographic, London
Printed and bound in Great Britain by J W Arrowsmith Ltd, Bristol

CONTENTS

ACKNOWLEDGEMENTS

Various people have helped in different ways with this book. I would like to thank the inter-library loan staff at Franklin & Marshall College; Franklin & Marshall College for funding research; Cookie of the English department there; Luca at the University of Rome, 'La Sapienza' for dealing with countless faxes; Carrie Rentschler for assistance with research; and Gautam Kundu and Samantha Fenno for their comments. Richard I must thank for innumerable and unquantifiable kindnesses and for living much longer with this Reader than either of us planned. My deepest thanks, though, go to my sister, Radhika, and to Jeremy Hawthorn; their interest and work on this volume, from its earliest stages to the final ones, have provided a sustenance and support that I could never properly acknowledge.

Every effort has been made to trace copyright holders of material produced in this book, but if any have been inadvertently overlooked the publishers will be glad to make the necessary arrangements at the first opportunity.

Press, 1994. Reprinted by permission of Indiana University Press.

Barbara Christian, 'The Race for Theory', in *The Nature and Context of Minority Discourse*, eds. Abdul R. JanMohamed and David Lloyd, Oxford: Oxford University Press, 1990. Reprinted by permission of the author and Oxford University Press.

Biodun Jeyifo, 'The Nature of Things: Arrested Decolonization and Critical Theory', *Research in African Literatures* 21 (1990). Reprinted by permission of Indiana University Press.

Chandra Talpade Mohanty, 'Under Western Eyes: Feminist Scholarship and Colonial Discourses', *Boundary 2*, 12.3/13.1 (Fall 1984). Copyright Duke University Press, 1984. Reprinted with permission.

Gayatri Chakravorty Spivak, 'Poststructuralism, Marginality, Postcoloniality and Value', in *Literary Theory Today*, eds. Peter Collier and Helga Geyer-Ryan. Copyright © 1990 by Gayatri Chakravorty Spivak. Used by permission of the publisher, Cornell University Press, and the author.

Dipesh Chakrabarty, 'Postcoloniality and the Artifice of History: Who Speaks for "Indian" Pasts?' *Representations* 37 (Winter 1992). Copyright © 1992 by the Regents of the University of California. Reprinted by permission of the author and the Regents of the University of California.

Paul Gilroy, ' "The Whisper Wakes, the Shudder Plays": "Race," Nation and Ethnic Absolutism', from *There Ain't No Black in the Union Jack*, London: Routledge, 1991. Reprinted by permission of Routledge.

Aijaz Ahmad, 'The Politics of Literary Postcoloniality', *Race and Class* 36.3 (1995). Reprinted with permission from the Institute of Race Relations.

Arif Dirlik, 'The Postcolonial Aura: Third World Criticism in the Age of Global Capitalism', *Critical Inquiry* 20 (Winter 1994). Reprinted by permission of the author and University of Chicago Press.

Ella Shohat, 'Notes on the Post-Colonial', *Social Text* 31/32 (1992). Copyright Porter Institute, Tel Aviv University, 1982. Reprinted with permission.

Sara Suleri, 'Woman Skin Deep: Feminism and the Postcolonial Condition,' *Critical Inquiry* 18 (Summer 1992). Reprinted by permission of the author and University of Chicago Press.

Ruth Frankenberg and Lata Mani, 'Crosscurrents, Crosstalk: Race, "Postcoloniality" and the Politics of Location', *Cultural Studies* 7.2 (May 1993). Reprinted by permission of *Cultural Studies*, the authors, and Routledge.

Rosemary Jolly, 'Rehearsals of Liberation: Contemporary Postcolonial Discourse and the New South Africa', *PMLA* 110.1 (January 1995). Reprinted by permission of the Modern Language Association of America.

INTRODUCTION

Students in a range of disciplines, whether they are studying in Lagos or London, New Delhi or New York, are increasingly confronted with the term 'postcolonial'. At first sight it seems straightforward but problems of definition soon appear. Does the term refer to texts or to practices, to psychological conditions or to concrete historical processes? Or does it perhaps refer to the interaction of all these? Those who find themselves puzzling about such issues should take heart, for such puzzlement suggests *not* that they are failing to grasp what postcolonial theory and criticism involve but rather that they have already begun to engage with the powerful contending forces and disputes which swirl around the term and its uses.

Consider the following two positions. At a conference organized in New York in May 1991 titled 'Critical Fictions', Ama Ata Aidoo commented on the 'postcolonial':

> Perhaps the concept was relevant to the United States after its war of independence, and to a certain extent to the erstwhile imperial dominions of Canada, Australia, and New Zealand. Applied to Africa, India, and some other parts of the world, 'postcolonial' is not only a fiction, but a most pernicious fiction, a cover-up of a dangerous period in our people's lives.[1]

At the same conference, Homi K. Bhabha asserted that 'the term postcolonial is increasingly used to describe that form of social criticism that bears witness to those unequal and uneven processes of representation by which the historical experience of the once-colonized Third World comes to be framed in the West'.[2] Aidoo is concerned that the 'post' in postcolonial fallaciously suggests the installation of regimes of power substantively different from colonial structures, implicitly ones which rectify the unequal global distributions of power. For Bhabha the valence of the 'postcolonial' seems to be that it functions to direct our attention, indeed to 'bear witness', to inequities in modes of representation.

Aidoo, and other writers and critics are troubled by the periodicity the term evokes since it is arguable that the colonial period has been followed by a 'post' – in the sense of after – colonial one. Used with an uncritical emphasis on the 'post', the term does direct attention away from present inequities – political, economic and discursive – in the global system. Other critics, though, read the 'post' in postcolonial as signifying both changes in power structures after the official end of colonialism as well as colonialism's continuing effects, particularly as they are manifested discursively. For them, postcolonial theory is an umbrella term that covers different critical approaches which deconstruct European thought in areas as wide-ranging as philosophy, history, literary studies, anthropology, sociology and political science. In this perspective, the term postcolonial refers not to a simple periodization but rather to a methodological revisionism which enables a wholesale critique of Western structures of knowledge and power, particularly those of the post-Enlightenment period.[3]

Aidoo, however, is not alone in expressing reservations regarding the use of the term and the work produced under its banner. But where her anxiety stems from wanting to keep colonial and contemporary historical realities on the agenda, for others the resistance to postcolonial studies is animated variously by objections regarding the chief sites of its production, the diffuseness of what one might call its 'object of study', and even claims that postcolonial theory is not merely implicated in but strengthens well-established structures of power. Nor indeed is this list exhaustive as postcolonial theory becomes the locus of complex debates and the target of virulent criticisms. Recently, Russell Jacoby berated postcolonial criticism for 'claiming four centuries and most of the planet as its domain'.[4] Arif Dirlik's not entirely facetious response to the question 'When is postcoloniality supposed to have begun?' is to say: 'When Third World intellectuals have arrived in First World academe',[5] and Lorna Goodison wearily asks, 'When is postcoloniality going to end? How long does the post-colonial continue?'[6]

How, then, should we understand the simultaneous disagreement regarding the very validity of postcolonial theory *and* the growth of work that attaches itself to it? One way to settle the matter would be an attempt to define what constitutes postcolonial theory's methodology and its 'object of study'. However, beginning with the very term 'postcolonial' and continuing to the cross-disciplinary critiques that are included under it, a vast range of different and often conflicting interests and concerns jostle for attention. While much contemporary postcolonial theory, particularly in the Anglo-American academy, has a broadly post-structuralist approach, this approach is neither exhaustive of the methods postcolonial theory utilizes nor unique to it. Further, with the growing popularity of 'post' words in the academy as well as the media, the 'postcolonial' has accrued an enormous amount of weighty baggage. Firstly, the term itself operates in at least two different registers at once: it is a historical marker referring to the period after official decolonization as well as a term signifying changes in intellectual approaches, particularly those which have been influenced by post-structuralism and deconstruction. Secondly, in the last ten years, the term has been deployed to replace what earlier went under the names of 'Third World' or 'Commonwealth' literature, to describe colonial discourse analysis, to detail the situations of migrant groups within First World states, and to specify oppositional reading practices. As the term grows in popularity, it consumes specific yet heterogeneous interests. Given the many areas where the term 'postcolonial' defines varied practices, it is no surprise that confusion and criticism often attend its uses and that demands for explanations of just what the 'postcolonial' signifies increase.

Precisely because of the proliferation of postcolonial discourses, demarcating criteria regarding either methodology or object of study is a difficult, even dangerous task. One can do so only by refusing to engage the tension between the divergent perspectives held by Aidoo and Bhabha over the very signification and value of the term postcolonial. Rather than offer prescriptive definitions of what should or does constitute postcolonial theory, I find it more useful to explore and interrogate the arguments of different positions, to see contemporary postcolonial theory as a 'sign that should be interrogated, a locus of contradictions', to borrow Hazel Carby's formulation from a different context.[7] Thus, a productive way to understand postcolonial theory is to attempt to outline how it has come to be formed at certain institutional sites. This allows us to attend to the historically specific contestations and debates within and about the area of inquiry, to map some of the significant connections it bears to other discourses, and to engage and interrogate concepts that it has theorized. Further, this approach has the advantage that the 'meaning' of postcolonial theory is left fluid, while specifying its present formation in particular contexts.

We must bear in mind that what postcolonial theory might mean in one context cannot simply be globalized and forced not only to function for, but be relevant to, intellectuals working in different parts of the world. The selection of essays in this Reader facilitates an exploration and understanding of postcolonial theory in the Anglo-American academy. While necessarily a part of the recent upsurge in postcolonial theory, this Reader also seeks to keep open the questions of its validity and provenance. My aim is not to provide a selection of materials that presents postcolonial theory as a cohesive discourse but instead one that draws students into the current debates to grapple with the contested issues. This selection ensures that we do not slip into a simple understanding of postcolonial theory and thus do an injustice to the constant interrogation and self-reflexivity demanded of it. In many ways, the problems surrounding issues of definition and the purview of postcolonial theory reflect the difficulties of engaging with such notions as representation, identity, agency, discourse and history. In this introduction, I address these issues whilst outlining the formation and contestations of postcolonial theory in the Anglo-American academy.

I

Published in 1978, Edward Said's *Orientalism* is a crucial text for what has become known as postcolonial theory.[8] Said's most influential argument was that Orientalism needed to be understood 'as a discourse ... by which European culture was able to manage – and even produce – the Orient politically, sociologically, militarily, ideologically, scientifically, and imaginatively during the post-Enlightenment period'.[9] His point was not to posit a more 'real' Orient against the one constructed by Orientalism but to draw attention to how Orientalism was implicated in the very structures that determined its conditions of possibility – namely the historical circumstances of European colonialism and imperialism. Said explored both the range of Orientalism and the ways in which it authorized and thereby controlled the Orient. Powerful European conceptions of the Orient determined that it was not a 'free subject of thought or action';[10] Orientalism controlled the nature and shape of knowledge, as well as how it was produced and disseminated. This, as Said argued, was not 'disinterested' knowledge, although much of it certainly operated under that guise. Serving very real material interests, the numerous texts of Orientalism – in philology, ethnography, political science, art and literature – played a vital part in constructing an Orient that allowed for the deployment of specific forms of control over it. Further, by questioning the distinction between 'pure' and 'political' knowledge, and destabilizing the former, Said highlighted the fact that cultural texts play a part in the great game of colony and empire, of race and its deployment, so that the last two hundred years of European imperialism had to be understood vis-à-vis the cultural texts that laid the groundwork for and buttressed the structures of imperialism.

Orientalism spawned an analysis of literary and other texts which foregrounded their imbrication in the social and political worlds of which they were a part. In addition to Said's work, the proceedings of two symposia at Essex University in 1982 and 1984, which were published in the volumes titled *Europe and Its Others*, not only publicized the work of critics such as Gayatri Chakravorty Spivak and Homi K. Bhabha but also underscored the extent to which an analysis of colonial discourse was becoming a legitimate area of inquiry in literary and other studies.[11] The Centre for Contemporary Cultural Studies in Birmingham published the influential volume *The Empire Strikes Back* in 1982.[12] Simultaneously, the first volume of *Subaltern Studies: Writings on South Asian History and Society* that appeared in Delhi, with the specific aim of rectifying the 'elitist bias characteristic of much research and academic work' in South Asian studies, was gaining wider circulation in the Western academy.[13] A special issue of *Critical Inquiry* in 1985 was devoted to the topic ' "Race", Writing, and Difference'.[14] Concurrently, one witnessed fundamental reassessments of modes of knowledge production in a whole range of academic disciplines such as anthropology, history, literary studies and sociology. Thus, even this admittedly selective list of texts points to the range of fields in which issues of race, colony, empire and nationhood were becoming central intellectual concerns even as the very modes of knowledge production and the politics of intellectual work were under scrutiny.

Moreover, these issues were addressed with a new interest in representation and discourse. In a whole host of academic disciplines, attention shifted towards the fluid, contested modes, whereby textual and disciplinary authority was constructed. This 'turn to language' problematized the nature of representation itself and of an assumed linguistic transparency that gave access to a 'reality' that lay outside. Not surprisingly, this attention to the contingency of representation led to analyses both of the ways in which disciplines constructed their own authority as well as of the material circumstances of intellectual production. Whereas an earlier anti-colonial critique had foregrounded Western constructions of the colonizer and colonized, of centre and periphery, and had challenged the dualisms that shaped knowledge in areas such as literature, psychoanalysis and history, these texts remained in many ways dependent on the very structures they were interested in dismantling. Often, then, these texts inverted the structure of binary distinctions – between master and slave, for instance – but without necessarily questioning the validity of the dualism itself. The most significant challenge posed to colonialism, the narrative of nationalism, for instance, while serving a crucial function for decolonization nevertheless relied on the narrative of modernity as progress and accepted the 'universal' value of Enlightenment notions of freedom and democracy. Replacing the grand narrative of which Europe was the norm, nationalism posited the modern nation-state as the new ideal. Postcolonial theory, on the other hand, problematizes the nation-state and its ideologies and reveals the difficulty of conceiving the nation even as an 'imagined community'.[15] It rejects both the 'Western *imperium* but also the nationalist project'[16] and takes as its task the understanding and critique of the 'link between the structures of knowledge and the forms of oppression of the last two hundred years'.[17] The burden of postcolonial theory, therefore, is the burden of Western philosophy, a rethinking of the very terms by which knowledge has been constructed.

The development of postcolonial theory also needs to be understood in terms of new socio-historic pressures. The political concepts that have shaped modern history – democracy, the citizen, nationalism – no longer seem adequate for coping with contemporary realities. The rise of new social movements around such issues as race, gender and ethnicity, have revealed the limits of older conceptions of community, individual and nation.[18] Profound changes such as decolonization, the movements of peoples on a hitherto unmatched scale, and new distributions of global power, have led to instabilities which have revealed that the old narratives of progress and reason are inadequate for addressing contemporary realities and the numerous fractures that attend them. Postcolonial theory has been formed as a response to these pressures even as it offers a means of speaking of them.

Postcolonial theory can be seen as growing out of these questions and the challenges they posed to and within traditional academic disciplines. Gyan Prakash describes postcolonial criticism as critiquing the 'historicism that projected the West as History',[19] where Europe is its theoretical subject. The Subaltern Studies Collective, for instance, intervenes in the production of academic history by attempting a historiography that restores agency to the subaltern classes.[20] Going beyond colonial, nationalist and Marxist historiography, all three of which it sees as problematic since they resort to foundationalist structures, Subaltern Studies offers an anti-foundationalist historiography.[21] In his analysis of subaltern studies as postcolonial criticism, Prakash suggests that postcolonial critique 'does not enjoy a panoptic distance from colonial history but exists as an aftermath, as an after – after being worked over by colonialism'.[22] Postcolonial theory foregrounds the legacy of the Enlightenment and modernity to underscore the significance that this legacy has had for constructing the conceptual foundations of Western thought. Attempting to dismantle Enlightenment certainties, postcolonial theory acknowledges their continuing and residual power. As a result, postcolonial theory offers not some 'pure' alternative but rather stresses that it is always 'after the empire of reason',[23] always after having been worked over by colonialism.

The rise of postcolonial theory in metropolitan academies must also be understood, in part, in terms of the debates that have raged since the 1980s which go under the broad rubric of 'multiculturalism'. The challenges now posed to traditional disciplines and their 'canons' have been built on the space cleared by the struggles of the 1960s and 1970s, primarily those of Black Studies and Women's Studies. Further, the multiplying constituencies of the First World, together with the cross-disciplinary challenges posed by contemporary theory, have created the space for a new opposition. Within this space, postcolonial theory finds a niche in the Western academy.

There is no question that postcolonial theory's provenance is greatest, (although by no means exclusively so), in First World academies. Many critics are troubled by this popularity and some argue that the oppositional stance which marked postcolonial theory until recently seems to be eroding with its growing institutionalization.[24] Further, since the term 'postcolonial' is increasingly used to define marginal constituencies in the First World, critics charge postcolonial theory with absorbing specific, local struggles so that all oppositional discourses, whether they are African-American or Chicana, for instance, are now subsumed under the postcolonial mantle.

This embattled situation might be understood by the fact that in some instances the postcolonial is deployed as a universal structuring formation. Consider the perspective offered by the Australian writers of *The Empire Writes Back*. They use the term postcolonial 'to cover all the culture affected by the imperial process from the moment of colonization to the present day'.[25] Placing the literatures of diverse nations such as India, Sri Lanka, Malaysia, Malta and even the USA on the same register, they suggest that what all these literatures have in common is that they 'emerged in their present form out of the experience of colonization and asserted themselves by foregrounding the tension with the imperial power'.[26] In their search for a stable definition of the postcolonial, Ashcroft, Griffiths and Tiffin's understanding of postcolonial literature raises as many, if not more, problems than it is intended to solve.[27] Their argument has led to vivid and stringent critiques by a host of different voices which have pointed out that such an understanding of the 'postcolonial' flattens and homogenizes the impact of colonialism on different parts of the world. Further, as Aijaz Ahmad puts it, when the terms 'colonial' and 'postcolonial' are used so diffusely, ' "colonialism" ... becomes a transhistorical thing, always present and always in process of dissolution in one part of the world or another'.[28]

If the impact of colonialism is understood as having produced equal and common effects, so that, for instance, the USA shares the same space as Kenya, postcolonial criticism no longer intervenes in Europe's grand narratives of progress and civilization but becomes itself another grand narrative. Socio-historic, cultural and racial differences are elided as colonialism itself becomes a privileged historical marker. The historical fact of European colonialism governs the understanding of specific, local circumstances with the result that all that came before becomes 'precolonial' and everything after 'postcolonial'. The progress narrative that postcolonial theory is interested in critiquing remains firmly in place as the history of the world is re-written in terms of precolonial, colonial and postcolonial stages.[29]

Not surprisingly, such totalizing demands are not restricted to the academy but find a responsive echo in the media as well, where the enormous popularity of 'post' words can hardly be ignored. Consider Pico Iyer's article in the 8 February 1993 issue of *Time* magazine on the so-called 'new world literatures'. Iyer repeatedly refers to the several geographical and cultural locations that postcolonial writers claim as their own; these writers, he says, 'are the creators, and creations, of a new postimperial order in which . . . all countries are part of a unified CNN and MTV circuit, with a common frame of reference in McDonald's, Madonna and Magic Johnson'.[30] While Iyer celebrates the transgressive potential equally available to these new products of the 'postimperial' order, his essay is built on the easy and dangerous conflation of postcoloniality, marginality, postmodernism and cosmopolitanism. It is no doubt true that new technologies of communication and the global movements of peoples strain any simple understanding of location. Nevertheless, to suggest that postcolonial writers share a common frame of reference in some unified (and implicitly equal?) transnational circulation of ideas and cultural products, is to refuse to address the inequities that shape current global relations.

The conflation of the postcolonial and cosmopolitan subject cannot be relegated to the media; its popularity is visible everywhere in the Anglo-American academy as well. It is fuelled to a large extent by the fractured subjectivities of post-structuralist theory. As hybridity, marginality and the diasporic become ever more seductive notions for describing contemporary constructions of conflict-ridden subjectivity, the experience of migration becomes 'emblematic of the fissured identities posited by post-structuralist theory, and hence synonymous with the fractures – epistemic and otherwise – experienced by colonized people'.[31] Bhabha's notion of hybridity, while liberating the analysis of colonial discourse from the binary oppositions between self and other, between the speaking subject and the silent 'native', has also generated a host of problems. On one hand, it enables him to produce an 'autonomous position for the colonial within the confines of the hegemonic discourse'.[32] On the other, Bhabha's celebration of hybridity has led to the privileging of migrancy and exile which ostensibly confer a greater critical edge to the migrant intellectual. As Loomba and Kaul suggest, 'the subject position of the hybrid is routinely expanded into the only political-conceptual space for revisionist enunciation'.[33] Aijaz Ahmad is only one amongst many who take the notion of hybridity to task; he points out the dangers of Bhabha's exploration, an exploration which lends itself to the aspecificity and ahistoricity of a hybrid subject remarkably free of any gender, class or race constraints.[34]

The de-centring of subjectivity in postcolonial theory has raised other problems as well. Critics charge postcolonial theory with only inadequately addressing the agency and indeed resistance of the native. For instance, Benita Parry, in her 1987 essay 'Problems in Current Theories of Colonial Discourse', charges Spivak with being unable to hear the voice of the subaltern and suggests that Spivak's work stems from a 'theory assigning an absolute power to the hegemonic discourse in constituting and disarticulating the native'.[35] Responding in part to her 'Three Women's Texts and a Critique of Imperialism', Parry argues that Spivak, in her reading of Jean Rhys's *Wide Sargasso Sea*, shows a 'deliberated deafness to the native voice where it is to be heard'.[36] For Parry, 'it should be possible to locate traces and testimony of women's voice on those sites where women inscribed themselves as healers, ascetics, singers of sacred songs, artizans and artists, and by this to modify Spivak's model of the silent subaltern'.[37] Parry's essay has generated a host of responses[38] including one from Spivak herself where she points out the dangers of the 'identitarian ethnicist claims of native or fundamental origin'.[39] The issue, though, remains a crucial one that postcolonial theory has yet to work through substantively.

Even as postcolonial theory is charged with evading the specificities of identity, there is a concomitant view that the term postcolonial is 'simply a polite way of saying not-white, not Europe, or perhaps not-Europe-but-inside-Europe'.[40] In this view, postcolonial theory is 'about' the Third World or recently decolonized nations. This understanding of postcolonial theory is in part fuelled by the fact that in the Anglo-American academy we most often encounter texts such as *Orientalism* in courses or settings concerned with 'difference', the Third World, or those attempting to understand the 'Other of the West' instead of those directly concerned with Western philosophy and modes of knowledge production. Ironically, one of Said's major arguments in *Orientalism* was to stress that the discourse of Orientalism, while ostensibly 'about' the Orient, really tells us more about the machinery that produced this discourse. 'My real argument', says Said, 'is that Orientalism is – and does not simply represent – a considerable dimension of modern political-intellectual culture, and as such has less to do with the Orient than it does with "our" world'.[41] We are thus simultaneously alerted to the problematic of representation, the collusion of power and knowledge, and the modes by which disciplines construct their object of study.

One of the effects of this 'marginalization' is the view that postcolonial theory is only produced by authentic, 'native', Third World voices and has resonance only for the migrant constituencies of the First World. Such a view informs Arif Dirlik's argument in his essay 'The Postcolonial Aura'. He ascribes the recent ascendancy of postcolonial theory in the Western academy to the newly held power of Third World intellectuals who have 'arrived' in First World academe. Dirlik's argument resorts to a dangerous essentializing that suggests that identity – understood in terms of race and national belonging – offers transparent access to the kind of critical work that is produced. The effect of such a perspective is that the binary distinctions between the 'West' and the 'rest' are kept firmly in place. And indeed, his formulation is only possible if a large number of First World theorists whose work is decidedly postcolonial are systematically excluded from the equation.

However, the challenges posed by oppositional discourses such as postcolonial theory are not unproblematic. Even as we might celebrate the possibilities made available by such discourses, we need to remain aware of their constraints. In her essay in this volume, Gayatri Spivak also assesses the location of postcolonial studies in the Western academy. She asks us to (re)consider the status of the appellation 'Third World' and the effects that follow from its function to give a 'proper name to a generalized margin'.[42] Alerting us to the term's genealogy and movement from an economic to a culturalist descriptor, she points to how such uses cannot only cover over the complexity and specificity of this 'generalized margin', as a range of 'peripheral' regions come to be clubbed together as the 'Third World', but how, in acceding to such an appellation within the academy, we might participate in 'the construction of a new object of investigation – "the third world", "the marginal" – for institutional validation and certification' and thus become 'complicitous in the perpetration of a "new orientalism"'.[43] Spivak's fear is that the formation of postcolonial theory in the Western academy could well replicate the mode of operation of the discourse of Orientalism, particularly if intellectuals from the Third World readily accept this designation for their work.

Spivak is not alone in her concern about the production of a Third World that suits the interests of the metropolitan centre. In this collection alone, several voices address the historical and institutional constraints on what knowledge is produced and disseminated. Anthony Appiah, for instance, cynically states that 'postcoloniality is the condition of what we might ungenerously call a *comprador* intelligentsia: a relatively small, Western-style, Western-trained group of writers and thinkers, who mediate the trade in cultural commodities of world capitalism at the periphery'.[44] Like the marketing of the hugely successful texts of the Latin American 'boom' of the 1960s and 1970s, the marketing of contemporary 'postcolonial' products is also a success story. Careful exclusion determines which texts circulate and indeed get 'canonized'. Arun Mukherjee warns that those texts valorized in the Western academy as 'postcolonial' are selected because they reflect concerns shared by 'postmodern' ones.[45] In a related, if albeit different, vein Barbara Christian sees contemporary critical theory exercising a hegemony that silences black, feminist voices. In their different ways, all these critics ask for a rigorous and constant attention to intellectual production and its conditions of possibility.

II

The Reader is arranged in three sections with overlapping interests and concerns. The first, 'Shifting Terrains', offers access to different conceptual maps that help the student to anchor approaches critical for contemporary postcolonial theory. These approaches illustrate the difficulty of 'fixing' post-colonial theory even as they offer insights into some of the most contentious issues. Edward Said's *Orientalism* remains a seminal text, not only because it lays the groundwork for contemporary postcolonial theory but also because the issues Said raises remain critical ones today. The selection in this Reader is from Said's Introduction where he spells out his different approaches to Orientalism and lays out the terms of his analysis. The last brief selection is drawn from the section 'Latent and Manifest Orientalism' which forms, in part, the basis of Homi Bhabha's intervention in what he describes as a 'polarity or division at the very centre of Orientalism. It is, on the one hand, a topic of learning, discovery, practice; on the other, it is the site of dreams, images, fantasies, myths, obsessions and requirements' (p. 41). Bhabha argues that Said contains the tension between these two aspects of Orientalism by relying on a binarism that 'enables Europe to advance securely and *unmetaphorically* upon the Orient' (p. 42). As a result, 'there is always, in Said, the suggestion that colonial power is possessed entirely by the coloniser' (p. 42). Instead, Bhabha argues for a radical ambivalence at the heart of colonial discourse which he explores here through an examination of the 'colonial stereotype [as] a complex, ambivalent, contradictory mode of representation' (p. 40). Bhabha's essay thus disrupts the binary distinctions that operate in *Orientalism*.

Appiah's interrogation of the relation between postcolonialism and post-modernism is in part built on the argument that the 'post' in both instances works as a 'space-clearing gesture' in order to create the market for cultural products that offer themselves as 'new'. However, despite the commodifica-tion that marks many postcolonial products, Appiah also offers another sense of the postcolonial – works that go beyond both colonial and nationalist narratives. While postcolonial production remains part of the commodification that is signalled by the 'post' both here and in postmodernism, the postcolonial is also that which critiques both Western rationality and modernity and the post-colonial regimes that followed decolonization.

Stephen Slemon's essay raises an issue that has been extremely troublesome in postcolonial theory – which cultural texts can justifiably claim postcolonial status? Slemon argues for the inclusion of ex-colonial settler literature under the rubric 'postcolonial'. His argument is essentially built around a considera-tion of resistance which is not simply embedded in the text but produced through the interaction between readers and the 'structures of their own culturally specific histories' (p. 73). Slemon therefore argues 'that resistance texts are necessarily double, necessarily mediated, in their social location' (p. 79). Slemon's case for including ex-colonial settler literature is founded on the

> *ambivalence* of literary resistance itself [which] is the 'always already' condition of Second-World settler and post-colonial literary writing, for in the white literatures of Australia, or New Zealand, or Canada, or southern Africa, anti-colonialist resist-ance has *never* been directed at an object or a discursive structure which can be seen as purely external to the self (p. 80).

Slemon's argument steers away from nation-based definitions but is by no means uncontested. In fact, part of his essay is framed as a response to Arun Mukherjee's 'Whose Post-colonialism and Whose Postmodernism?' in which she forcefully argues that including ex-colonial settler literature under the rubric postcolonial is only possible under the sign of postmodernism and only if the place of racial difference in colonial relations is ignored.

Benita Parry's essay continues the exploration of resistance but in the arena of the much maligned discourse of nativism and in particular of Négritude. For Parry, much contemporary postcolonial theory devalues the narratives of anti-colonial struggle as nativist, as 'the narcissistic desire to find an other that will reflect Western assumptions of selfhood'.[46] Arguing for a fresh consideration of Négritude in Fanon's work, Parry suggests that 'the task ... of cherishing and defending against calumniation altered and mutable indigenous forms ... is not the same as the hopeless attempt to locate and revive pristine pre-colonial cultures' (p. 91).[47] Parry concludes with at least 'two cheers for nativism'.

In part, Parry's essay relies on Stuart Hall's wonderfully nuanced notion of identity which negotiates between essentialist and post-structuralist formations. Hall offers two related ways of thinking about identity in 'Cultural Identity and Diaspora'. In the first, cultural identity is defined 'in terms of one shared culture, a sort of collective "one true self" ' (p. 110). This notion, as he points out, played an important role in the anti-colonial struggles of this century and continues to be a 'very powerful and creative force in emergent forms of representation amongst hitherto marginalised peoples' (p. 111). The second position on identity stresses that identities are not fixed but 'subject to the continuous "play" of history, culture and power' (p. 112). From this perspective, identities are not 'grounded in a mere "recovery" of the past' (p. 112). Instead, Hall suggests that 'identities are the names we give to the different ways we are positioned by, and position ourselves within, the narratives of the past' (p. 112). By arguing for these two notions as it were in the same register, Hall is able to argue that the 'play of "difference" within identity' (p. 114) exceeds a binary structure of representation so that 'at different times, in relation to different questions, the boundaries are re-sited' (p. 114). Hall emphasizes the necessity of understanding different notions of identity that remain sensitive to specific locations and moments; he is thus able to argue for a strategic essentialism that has served a crucial role in anti-colonial struggles of the past and continues to do so today.

Finally, Rey Chow's essay 'Where Have All the Natives Gone?' intervenes in one of the most heated discussions in contemporary postcolonial theory: the 'native' as silent object or speaking subject. Here Chow contends with the difficult issue of how to rewrite the space of the postcolonial/native 'in such a way as to refuse the facile turn of sanctifying the defiled image with pieties and thus enriching ourselves precisely with what can be called the surplus value of the oppressed' (p. 124). Chow insists on the commodification of the 'native' but attempts to steer a path between the 'native' as lack and the native as 'the site of authenticity and true knowledge' (p. 140). Finally, Chow arrives at two

important conclusions: first, that 'our fascination with the native, the oppressed, the savage, and all such figures is therefore a desire to hold on to an
unchanging certainty somewhere outside our own "fake" experience' (p. 141).
Second, she argues that the native is an 'indifferent defiled image' (p. 141) as
she continues to stare 'indifferently, mocking our imprisonment within imagistic resemblance and our self-deception as the non-duped' (p. 141).

The next section, 'Disciplining Knowledge', is designed to evoke both the
notion of discipline as a field of study and discipline as a means of exercising
power. Nor indeed are these two meanings of discipline separate. In fact, the
readings in this selection address how discipline – as an academically defined
entity – works to control and regulate what knowledge is produced, how
knowledge is disseminated, and indeed the material consequences of scholarship. Barbara Christian argues that the current race for theory 'has silenced
many of us to the extent that some of us feel we can no longer discuss our own
literature' (p. 149). Many contemporary black feminist critics are coerced, she
says, by the power of contemporary critical theory and by the power of the US
academic machinery which controls grants, funding and jobs, to either produce
what the institutional structure demands or be silenced. In his discussion of the
field of African critical discourse, Biodun Jeyifo makes a point that has a useful
bearing on this discussion as well. He says that 'behind the claims and counter-
claims the "foreign" scholar-critics and "native" claimants of "natural" proprietory rights to critical insight lies a vastly displaced play of unequal power
relations between the two camps' (p. 163). Jeyifo addresses the unequal access
to funding and resources available to African scholars and their Western
counterparts (in terms of geographical and institutional affiliation), in order to
understand the turf battles that are fought between 'native' and 'foreign' critics
of African critical discourse.

Like Jeyifo and Christian, Mohanty's essay addresses the worldliness of
scholarship as all three demand that scholars pay rigorous attention to the
imbrication of academies in socio-economic distributions of world power.
Mohanty addresses one of the most contested areas of feminist scholarship –
the relationship between specific women and their lived histories and Woman
as a signifier. Concerned with the tense relationship between lived experience
and the marker Woman in feminist theory, Mohanty argues that much Western feminist scholarship resorts to positing a singular Third World woman who
is made representative of varied Third World women. She urges feminist
scholars to address their intellectual production, keeping in mind the enormous power of the 'authorizing signature of Western humanist discourse'
(p. 174) and its material consequences.

Gayatri Spivak's essay in this section warns against the production of a new
object of knowledge – the Third World – in the Anglo-American academy.
Like the other essays in this section, Spivak is concerned with the constraining
mechanisms of institutional realities that 'discipline' what knowledge is produced and if and how it is disseminated. Dipesh Chakrabarty's essay also
addresses the enormous weight of Western institutional structures but in the

arena of historiography. Arguing that the disciplinary formation of academic history is inseparable from the story of modernity and its attendant narratives of citizenship, progress and the nation-state, Chakrabarty suggests that History can only replicate the structure of a progress narrative in which Europe was there 'first' and the Third World, for instance, can only follow. Chakrabarty demonstrates that Europe remains the subject of all history whether that history is Indian, Kenyan or Nigerian and recommends an intervention that provincializes Europe, the ' "Europe" that modern imperialism and (third-world) nationalism have, by their collaborative venture and violence, made universal' (p. 240–1). This project is not one which is culturally relativist, for as Chakrabarty stresses 'the point is not that Enlightenment rationalism is always unreasonable in itself but rather ... through what historical process – its reason ... has been made to look "obvious" far beyond the ground where it originated' (p. 241). At the same time, Chakrabarty acknowledges that 'this is a history that will attempt the impossible' (p. 243), given the 'knowledge protocols of academic history' (p. 244) and the monumental weight of established institutions against which a revisionist history needs to struggle.

In a related exploration of the narrative of the nation, Paul Gilroy's chapter from *There Ain't No Black in the Union Jack* studies the 'new racism' in Britain to reveal the collusion between left and right as the 'limits of the nation coincide with the lines of "race" ' (p. 262). Gilroy shows how the politics of race is 'fired by conceptions of national belonging and homogeneity which not only blur the distinction between "race" and nation, but rely on that very ambiguity for their effect' (p. 250). Building his argument on the deployment of race in academic and other discourses, Gilroy demonstrates that national and racial identity are posited as inseparable. Not only is the nation constructed as a homogenous entity, but as Gilroy argues, the 'ethnic absolutism' that informs notions of 'authentic' and 'inauthentic' belonging keeps blacks outside the national community.

Finally, the last section, 'Locating Practice', offers essays that address the production of postcolonial theory in the Anglo-American academy, paying specific attention to the constraining mechanisms of location. The essays by Dirlik and Ahmad are two of the most scathing critiques levelled against postcolonial theory and its sites of production. For both, the interest of the metropolitan academy in postcolonial theory gives cause for alarm as both see contemporary postcolonial theory refusing to address its relation to a global capitalism. Dirlik argues that since much postcolonial theory does not accord capitalism a foundational status, and thus diverges from using traditional Marxism as its primary critical tool and political aim, it has been welcomed into the Western academy.[48] Further, he points out that contemporary postcolonial theory refuses to address its relation to global capitalism and he rightly wonders at this silence. Dirlik's answer – that postcolonial theory 'is designed ... to cover up the origins of postcolonial intellectuals in a global capitalism of which they are not so much victims as beneficiaries' (p. 313) – reduces the import of an issue that has yet to be dealt with substantively.

Aijaz Ahmad, in his essay in this volume, also addresses the relation between academic practice and its site of production. For Ahmad, metropolitan theory is always already contaminated; as far as he is concerned, the fact that many (in fact, Ahmad suggests *all*) postcolonial theorists 'live and do their theorizing' (p. 278) in First World countries leads directly to the ineffectuality of their production. Ahmad is right to demand that attention be paid to the sites as well as the content of intellectual production, but his critique of postcolonial theory, based mainly on its chief sites of production, is troublesome. Situating a disciplinary field in a context is quite different from explaining it away *because* of its context. No doubt the location of students and intellectuals in metropolitan academies is a highly privileged one. But only if the academy is seen as fundamentally apolitical, with all proper resistance lying outside in the realm of a more 'real' politics, can postcolonial theory be seen as fundamentally flawed.

Ella Shohat's essay is an exploration of the 'political significations' (p. 322) of the term postcolonial. Shohat suggests that there are two separate genres of the 'post' which operate with different 'referential emphasis, the first on disciplinary advances characteristic of intellectual history, and the latter on the strict chronologies of history *tout court*' (p. 323). She rightly points out that these different emphases lead to some of the 'conceptual ambiguities of the term' (p. 323). Further, while much work that is produced under the banner of 'postcolonial' attempts to go beyond anti-colonial nationalist critiques, the term itself 'linguistically reproduces, once again, the centrality of the colonial narrative' (p. 328). Furthermore, Shohat argues that the rising ascendancy of the postcolonial, particularly in the United States, not only absorbs other oppositional discourses but that this ascendancy may be explained by the fact that the 'postcolonial' allows a safe distance from confrontation with oppositional groups closer to home.

Sara Suleri reads the multiplying subjectivities of 'othered' women as inseparable from the mechanisms of the metropolitan academy. Her essay explores the 'uneasy selfhood' (p. 337) accorded to the postcolonial woman even as feminist criticism remains troubled by questions of identity formation. In current work that attempts to theorize racial and gendered difference, Suleri rightly points out that 'sexuality is reduced to the literal structure of the racial body, and theoretical interventions within this trajectory become minimalized into the naked category of lived experience' (p. 339). Personal narrative offers the 'only salve to the rude abrasions that Western feminist theory has inflicted on the body in ethnicity' (p. 342). 'Such claims to radical revisionism take refuge in the political untouchability ... accorded the category of Third World Woman, and in the process sully the crucial knowledge' (p. 342) the category still has to offer feminism. Her question: 'What comes first, race, gender or profession?' (p. 340) echoes Appiah's comments referred to earlier on the production of the postcolonial for the West. Postcolonial feminism, Suleri argues, offers an alternative that is 'conceptually parochial and scales down the postcolonial condition in order to encompass it within North American academic terms' (p. 342).

A rigorous attention to the politics of location informs the validity Franken-berg and Mani find in the postcolonial (p. 362). Building on the deployment of a conjuncturalist politics in some contemporary feminist theory, they stress that 'colonial/postcolonial relations [are] ... co-constructed with other axes of domination and resistance' (p. 358); as a result there are 'moments and spaces in which subjects are "driven to grasp" their positioning and subjecthood as "postcolonial"; yet there are other contexts in which, to use the term as the organizing principle of one's analysis, is precisely to "fail to grasp the specific-ity" of the location or the moment' (p. 362). The value of such a perspective lies in the fact that the postcolonial is viewed as a worthwhile position only in terms of the specificities of location. When asked to have a more universal validity, its oppositional force immediately disperses. One such instance is offered by Rosemary Jolly's essay, which demonstrates how postcolonial theory can become a conservative tool when asked to be the overarching formulation for the study of the literature of diverse nations and diverse groups within those nations. As Jolly suggests, the desire to bring South Africa under an already constituted understanding of postcolonial literary theory distorts South Afri-can cultural production in order to fit the predetermined contours of the term.

III

Unlike other Readers on the market, this one is not so much interested in offering a comprehensive mapping of all the areas of debate and discussion as it is in making available a selection of key articles which deal with issues central to an exploration of contemporary postcolonial theory. To my mind, one of the chief uses of a Reader lies in the fact that it makes the task of locating and procuring texts easier for the reader. It therefore matters that the texts made available are not 'partial' or altered to suit the interests of the editor. With the single exception of the selection from *Orientalism* (and for obvious reasons), I have chosen not to edit the materials reproduced. Further, by making available 'whole' texts in their individual contexts, the Reader does not smooth over the concerns and questions that propel each individual inquiry. These essays, therefore, provide access to alternate maps of postcolonial theory that could be created.

Many of the essays in these sections could be categorized differently; the Frankenberg/Mani essay, for instance, could belong just as well to 'Shifting Terrains'; the Spivak piece could easily be placed in 'Locating Practice'. My deliberately large section divisions enable, I hope, the student to consider alternatives to the ones I offer and to see the ways in which issues of gender, ethnicity and location impact on each other as opposed to working within some neat whole of their own. It is inevitable, though, that this introduction contain an apology for the paths not taken and for the constraints produced by the selection I offer. It is partly to offset this fixing and stabilizing of contemporary postcolonial theory that I include an extended (although by no means exhaustive) bibliography.

Notes

1 Ama Ata Aidoo, 'That Capacious Topic: Gender Politics', in Phil Mariani, ed., *Critical Fictions* (Seattle: Bay Press, 1991), p. 152.

2 Homi Bhabha, ' "Caliban Speaks to Prospero": Cultural Identity and the Crisis of Representation', in Mariani, *Critical Fictions*, p. 63.

3 Fernando Coronil negotiates between these two positions and suggests that when

> applied to ex-colonial nations that occupy a subordinate position in the international system, postcoloniality appears as something of a euphemism, one that at once reveals and disguises contemporary forms of imperialism. ... But as a term associated with poststructuralism, postcoloniality conjures up a body of theory which may help overcome teleological narratives and illuminate the workings of power in social and cultural spaces reorganized by the circulation of ideas, peoples, and goods throughout an increasingly interconnected globe.

See his 'Can Postcoloniality be Decolonized? Imperial Banality and Postcolonial Power', *Public Culture* 5.1 (Fall 1992), p. 102.

4 Russell Jacoby, 'Marginal Returns: The Trouble With Post-Colonial Theory', *Lingua Franca* (September/October 1995), p. 30.

5 Arif Dirlik, 'The Postcolonial Aura: Third World Criticism in the Age of Global Capitalism', *Critical Inquiry* 20 (Winter 1994), p. 329. (Also in this volume, p. 294.)

6 Lorna Goodison in discussion during the ALA Women's Caucus Luncheon, African Literature Association Conference, 19 April 1993. Quoted in Carole Boyce Davies, *Black Women, Writing and Identity* (London: Routledge, 1994), p. 95.

7 Hazel Carby, *Reconstructing Womanhood: The Emergence of the Afro-American Woman Novelist* (New York: Oxford University Press, 1987), p. 15.

8 There has been some discussion of whether the term postcolonial should or should not be hyphenated. While there is by no means consensus on this issue, when used with the hyphen the term usually marks a temporal shift from the moment when colonialism officially ended to the period that comes after. Without the hyphen, the term refers to a form of critical practice that includes, but is not restricted to, poststructuralist analyses of colonialism and its legacies. See for instance, Barker *et al.*'s introduction to *Colonial Discourse/Postcolonial Theory* (Manchester: Manchester University Press, 1994), p. 4 as well as Vijay Mishra and Bob Hodge's 'What is Post(-)colonialism?' *Textual Practice* 5.3 (1991), p. 407.

9 Edward Said, *Orientalism* (New York: Vintage, 1979), p. 3. (Also in this volume, p. 21–2.)

10 Said, *Orientalism*, p. 3. (Also in this volume, p. 22.)

11 Francis Barker *et al.*, eds., *Europe and its Others: Proceedings of the Essex Conference*, 2 vols. (Colchester: University of Essex Press, 1985).

12 Centre for Contemporary Cutural Studies, *The Empire Strikes Back: Race and Racism in 70's Britain* (London: Hutchinson, 1982).

13 Ranajit Guha and Gayatri Chakravorty Spivak, eds., *Selected Subaltern Studies* (New Delhi: Oxford University Press, 1988), p. 35.

14 Henry Louis Gates, ed., *'Race,' Writing, and Difference*, special issue of *Critical Inquiry* 12.1 (Autumn 1985).

15 Benedict Anderson, *Imagined Communities: Reflections on the Origin and Spread of Nationalism* (London: Verso, 1983).

16 Anthony Appiah, 'Is the Post- in Postmodernism the Post- in Postcolonial?' *Critical Inquiry* 17 (Winter 1991), p. 353. (Also in this volume, p. 66.)

17 Robert Young, *White Mythologies: Writing History and the West* (London: Routledge, 1991), p. 2.

18 Some of the limitations of approaching these notions as fixed and stable are amply demonstrated by the work on gender in postcolonial studies. See for instance Rajeswari Sunder Rajan, *Real and Imagined Women* (London: Routledge, 1993), Deborah Gordon, ed., *Feminism and the Critique of Colonial Discourse, Inscriptions* 3/4 (1988), and much of Gayatri Chakravorty Spivak's work.

19 Gyan Prakash, 'Subaltern Studies as Postcolonial Criticism', *American Historical Review* 99.5 (December 1994), p. 1475 n. 1. In Dipesh Chakrabarty's argument reproduced here, Europe remains the sovereign subject of history with all others in a subordinate position to it.

20 The term 'subaltern' is drawn from Antonio Gramsci's writings and refers to a subordinate position in terms of class, gender, race and culture.

21 Prakash defines a foundational view as one which assumes 'that history is ultimately founded in and representable through some identity – individual, class, or structure – which resists further decomposition into heterogeneity'. See his 'Writing Post-Orientalist Histories of the Third World: Perspectives from Indian Historiography', *Comparative Studies in Society and History* 32.2 (1990), p. 397.

22 Prakash, 'Subaltern Studies as Postcolonial Criticism', p. 1475.

23 Gayatri Chakravorty Spivak, 'Poststructuralism, Marginality, Postcoloniality and Value', in Peter Collier and Helga Geyer-Ryan, eds., *Literary Theory Today* (Ithaca: Cornell University Press, 1990), p. 228. (Also in this volume, p. 206.)

24 See, for instance, Carole Boyce Davies, *Black Women*, pp. 81–2.

25 Bill Ashcroft, Gareth Griffiths and Helen Tiffin, *The Empire Writes Back: Theory and Practice in Post-colonial Literatures* (London: Routledge, 1989), p. 2.

26 Ashcroft, Griffiths and Tiffin, *The Empire Writes Back*, p. 2.

27 In fact, as a result of such formulations, postcolonial theory has repeatedly been brought to task for its so-called imperialist intentions whereby it consumes all local specificity. It is worth remarking that this text serves as the paradigmatic example of the sort of excess postcolonial theory has made possible in critiques as wide-ranging as McClintock's, Mukherjee's, Mishra's and Hodge's, Ahmad's, Dirlik's, etc.

28 Aijaz Ahmad, 'The Politics of Literary Postcoloniality', *Race and Class* 36.3 (1995), p. 9. (Also in this volume, p. 283.)

29 Anne McClintock points out that even as postcolonial theory 'promises a decentering of history in hybridity, syncreticism, multi-dimensional time, and so forth, the *singularity* of the term effects a re-centering of global history around the single rubric of European time'. See her 'The Angel of Progress: Pitfalls of the Term "Post-colonialism" ', *Social Text* 31/32 (1992), p. 86. See also Ella Shohat's essay in this volume for a critique of the 'ambiguous spatio-temporality' of the term postcolonial (p. 323).

30 Pico Iyer, 'The Empire Writes Back', *Time*, (8 February 1993), p. 52.

31 Ania Loomba and Suvir Kaul, 'Introduction: Location, Culture, Post-Coloniality', *Oxford Literary Review* 16.1/2 (1994), p. 13.

32 Benita Parry, 'Current Problems in the Study of Colonial Discourse', *Oxford Literary Review* 9.1/2 (1987), p. 40.

33 Parry, 'Current Problems in the Study of Colonial Discourse', p. 15.

34 Ahmad, 'The Politics of Literary Postcoloniality', p. 13. (Also in this volume, p. 286–7.)

35 Parry, 'Current Problems in the Study of Colonial Discourse', p. 34.

36 Parry, 'Current Problems in the Study of Colonial Discourse', p. 39.

37 Parry, 'Current Problems in the Study of Colonial Discourse', p. 35.

38 See for instance Neil Lazarus, 'National Consciousness and the Specificity of (Post) Colonial Intellectualism', in Francis Barker *et al.*, eds., *Colonial Discourse/Postcolonial Theory*, pp. 197–220; Anne Maxwell, 'The Debate on Current Theories of Colonial Discourse', *Kunapipi* 13.3 (1991), pp. 70–84; and Ania Loomba, 'Overworlding the Third World', *Oxford Literary Review* 13 (1991), pp. 164–91.

39 Spivak, 'Poststructuralism', p. 225. (Also in this volume, p. 204.)

40 Ahmad, 'The Politics of Literary Postcoloniality', p. 8. (Also in this volume, p. 282.)

41 Said, *Orientalism*, p. 12. (Also in this volume, p. 29.)

42 Gayatri Chakravorty Spivak, *Outside in the Teaching Machine* (New York: Routledge, 1993), p. 55.

43 Spivak, *Outside in the Teaching Machine*, p. 56.

44 Appiah, 'Is the Post- in Postmodernism', p. 348. (Also in this volume, p. 62.)

45 Arun Mukherjee, 'Whose Post-colonialism and Whose Postmodernism', *World Literature Written in English* 30.2 (1990), pp. 1–9. See also Aijaz Ahmad's 'Jameson's Rhetoric of Otherness and the "National Allegory" ', *Social Text* 17 (1989), pp. 3–25.

46 Robert Young, *White Mythologies*, p. 178.

47 For an essay exploring some of the 'Fanons' deployed by postcolonial critics, see Henry Louis Gates, 'Critical Fanonism', *Critical Inquiry* 17 (Spring 1991), pp. 457–70.

48 While postcolonial theory does interrogate Marxism, and particularly its traditional and orthodox varieties that explain all phenomena by recourse to Marx's analysis of the operation of modes of production, this interrogation by no means constitutes a rejection of Marxism *per se*. For several postcolonial theorists, including Gyan Prakash, Marxism is a most productive and often indispensable tool. See his *Bonded Histories: Genealogies of Labor Servitude in Colonial India* (Cambridge: Cambridge University Press, 1990).

PART ONE

SHIFTING TERRAINS

1

Edward Said

From *Orientalism* *

I

On a visit to Beirut during the terrible civil war of 1975–1976 a French journalist wrote regretfully of the gutted downtown area that 'it had once seemed to belong to . . . the Orient of Chateaubriand and Nerval.'[1] He was right about the place, of course, especially so far as a European was concerned. The Orient was almost a European invention, and had been since antiquity a place of romance, exotic beings, haunting memories and landscapes, remarkable experiences. Now it was disappearing; in a sense it had happened, its time was over. Perhaps it seemed irrelevant that Orientals themselves had something at stake in the process, that even in the time of Chateaubriand and Nerval Orientals had lived there, and that now it was they who were suffering; the main thing for the European visitor was a European representation of the Orient and its contemporary fate, both of which had a privileged communal significance for the journalist and his French readers.

Americans will not feel quite the same about the Orient, which for them is much more likely to be associated very differently with the Far East (China and Japan, mainly). Unlike the Americans, the French and the British – less so the Germans, Russians, Spanish, Portuguese, Italians, and Swiss – have had a long tradition of what I shall be calling *Orientalism*, a way of coming to terms with the Orient that is based on the Orient's special place in European Western experience. The Orient is not only adjacent to Europe; it is also the place of Europe's greatest and richest and oldest colonies, the source of its civilizations and languages, its cultural contestant, and one of its deepest and most recurring images of the Other. In addition, the Orient has helped to define Europe (or the West) as its contrasting image, idea, personality, experience. Yet none of this Orient is merely imaginative. The Orient is an integral part of European *material* civilization and culture. Orientalism expresses and represents that part culturally and even ideologically as a mode of discourse with supporting institutions, vocabulary, scholarship, imagery, doctrines, even colonial bureaucracies and colonial styles. In contrast, the American understanding of the Orient will seem considerably less dense, although our recent Japanese, Korean, and Indochinese adventures ought now to be creating a more sober, more realistic 'Oriental' awareness. Moreover, the vastly expanded American

* Edward Said, *Orientalism* (Vintage, 1978), pp. 1–15; 20–3; 205–8.

political and economic role in the Near East (the Middle East) makes great claims on our understanding of that Orient.

It will be clear to the reader (and will become clearer still throughout the many pages that follow) that by Orientalism I mean several things, all of them, in my opinion, interdependent. The most readily accepted designation for Orientalism is an academic one, and indeed the label still serves in a number of academic institutions. Anyone who teaches, writes about, or researches the Orient – and this applies whether the person is an anthropologist, sociologist, historian, or philologist – either in its specific or its general aspects, is an Orientalist, and what he or she does is Orientalism. Compared with *Oriental studies* or *area studies*, it is true that the term *Orientalism* is less preferred by specialists today, both because it is too vague and general and because it connotes the high-handed executive attitude of nineteenth-century and early-twentieth-century European colonialism. Nevertheless books are written and congresses held with 'the Orient' as their main focus, with the Orientalist in his new or old guise as their main authority. The point is that even if it does not survive as it once did, Orientalism lives on academically through its doctrines and theses about the Orient and the Oriental.

Related to this academic tradition, whose fortunes, transmigrations, specializations, and transmissions are in part the subject of this study, is a more general meaning for Orientalism. Orientalism is a style of thought based upon an ontological and epistemological distinction made between 'the Orient' and (most of the time) 'the Occident.' Thus a very large mass of writers, among whom are poets, novelists, philosophers, political theorists, economists, and imperial administrators, have accepted the basic distinction between East and West as the starting point for elaborate theories, epics, novels, social descriptions, and political accounts concerning the Orient, its people, customs, 'mind,' destiny, and so on. *This* Orientalism can accommodate Aeschylus, say, and Victor Hugo, Dante and Karl Marx. A little later in this introduction I shall deal with the methodological problems one encounters in so broadly construed a 'field' as this.

The interchange between the academic and the more or less imaginative meanings of Orientalism is a constant one, and since the late eighteenth century there has been a considerable, quite disciplined – perhaps even regulated – traffic between the two. Here I come to the third meaning of Orientalism, which is something more historically and materially defined than either of the other two. Taking the late eighteenth century as a very roughly defined starting point Orientalism can be discussed and analyzed as the corporate institution for dealing with the Orient – dealing with it by making statements about it, authorizing views of it, describing it, by teaching it, settling it, ruling over it: in short, Orientalism, as a Western style for dominating, restructuring, and having authority over the Orient. I have found it useful here to employ Michel Foucault's notion of a discourse, as described by him in *The Archaeology of Knowledge* and in *Discipline and Punish*, to identify Orientalism. My contention is that without examining Orientalism as a discourse one cannot possibly understand the enormously systematic discipline by which European culture was able to manage – and even produce – the Orient politically, sociologically, militarily, ideologically, scientifically, and imaginatively during the post-Enlightenment period. Moreover, so authoritative a position did Orientalism have that I believe no one writing, thinking, or acting on the Orient could do so without taking account of the limitations on thought and action imposed by Orientalism. In brief, because of Orientalism the Orient was not (and is not) a free subject of thought or action. This is not to say that Orientalism unilaterally determines what can be said about the Orient, but that it is the whole network of interests inevitably brought to bear on (and therefore always involved in) any occasion when that peculiar entity 'the Orient' is in question. How this happens is what this book tries to demonstrate. It also tries to show that European culture gained in strength and identity by setting itself off against the Orient as a sort of surrogate and even underground self.

Historically and culturally there is a quantitative as well as a qualitative difference between the Franco-British involvement in the Orient and – until the period of American ascendancy after World War II – the involvement of every other European and Atlantic power. To speak of Orientalism therefore is to speak mainly, although not exclusively, of a British and French cultural enterprise, a project whose dimensions take in such disparate realms as the imagination itself, the whole of India and the Levant, the Biblical texts and the Biblical lands, the spice trade, colonial armies and a long tradition of colonial administrators, a formidable scholarly corpus, innumerable Oriental 'experts' and 'hands,' an Oriental professorate, a complex array of 'Oriental' ideas (Oriental despotism, Oriental splendor, cruelty, sensuality), many Eastern sects, philosophies, and wisdoms domesticated for local European use – the list can be extended more or less indefinitely. My point is that Orientalism derives from a particular closeness experienced between Britain and France and the Orient, which until the early nineteenth century had really meant only India and the Bible lands. From the beginning of the nineteenth century until the end of World War II France and Britain dominated the Orient and Orientalism; since World War II America has dominated the Orient, and approaches it as France and Britain once did. Out of that closeness, whose dynamic is enormously productive even if it always demonstrates the comparatively greater strength of the Occident (British, French, or American), comes the large body of texts I call Orientalist.

It should be said at once that even with the generous number of books and authors that I examine, there is a much larger number that I simply have had to leave out. My argument, however, depends neither upon an exhaustive catalogue of texts dealing with the Orient nor upon a clearly delimited set of texts, authors, and ideas that together make up the Orientalist canon. I have depended instead upon a different methodological alternative – whose backbone in a sense is the set of historical generalizations I have so far been making in this Introduction – and it is these I want now to discuss in more analytical detail.

II

I have begun with the assumption that the Orient is not an inert fact of
It is not merely *there*, just as the Occident itself is not just *there* either. W
take seriously Vico's great observation that men make their own history
what they can know is what they have made, and extend it to geography: as
both geographical and cultural entities – to say nothing of historical entities –
such locales, regions, geographical sectors as 'Orient' and 'Occident' are man-
made. Therefore as much as the West itself, the Orient is an idea that has a
history and a tradition of thought, imagery, and vocabulary that have given it
reality and presence in and for the West. The two geographical entities thus
support and to an extent reflect each other.

Having said that, one must go on to state a number of reasonable qualifications. In the first place, it would be wrong to conclude that the Orient was
essentially an idea, or a creation with no corresponding reality. When Disraeli
said in his novel *Tancred* that the East was a career, he meant that to be
interested in the East was something bright young Westerners would find to be
an all-consuming passion; he should not be interpreted as saying that the East
was *only* a career for Westerners. There were – and are – cultures and nations
whose location is in the East, and their lives, histories, and customs have a
brute reality obviously greater than anything that could be said about them in
the West. About that fact this study of Orientalism has very little to contribute,
except to acknowledge it tacitly. But the phenomenon of Orientalism as I study
it here deals principally, not with a correspondence between Orientalism and
Orient, but with the internal consistency of Orientalism and its ideas about the
Orient (the East as career) despite or beyond any correspondence, or lack
thereof, with a 'real' Orient. My point is that Disraeli's statement about the
East refers mainly to that created consistency, that regular constellation of
ideas as the pre-eminent thing about the Orient, and not to its mere being, as
Wallace Stevens's phrase has it.

A second qualification is that ideas, cultures, and histories cannot seriously
be understood or studied without their force, or more precisely their configurations of power, also being studied. To believe that the Orient was created – or,
as I call it, 'Orientalized' – and to believe that such things happen simply as a
necessity of the imagination, is to be disingenuous. The relationship between
Occident and Orient is a relationship of power, of domination, of varying
degrees of a complex hegemony, and is quite accurately indicated in the title of
K. M. Panikkar's classic *Asia and Western Dominance*.[2] The Orient was
Orientalized not only because it was discovered to be 'Oriental' in all those
ways considered commonplace by an average nineteenth-century European,
but also because it *could be* – that is, submitted to being – *made* Oriental. There
is very little consent to be found, for example, in the fact that Flaubert's
encounter with an Egyptian courtesan produced a widely influential model of
the Oriental woman; she never spoke of herself, she never represented her
emotions, presence, or history. *He* spoke for and represented her. He was

foreign, comparatively wealthy, male, and these were historical facts of domination that allowed him not only to possess Kuchuk Hanem physically but to speak for her and tell his readers in what way she was 'typically Oriental.' My argument is that Flaubert's situation of strength in relation to Kuchuk Hanem was not an isolated instance. It fairly stands for the pattern of relative strength between East and West, and the discourse about the Orient that it enabled.

This brings us to a third qualification. One ought never to assume that the structure of Orientalism is nothing more than a structure of lies or of myths which, were the truth about them to be told, would simply blow away. I myself believe that Orientalism is more particularly valuable as a sign of European-Atlantic power over the Orient than it is as a veridic discourse about the Orient (which is what, in its academic or scholarly form, it claims to be). Nevertheless, what we must respect and try to grasp is the sheer knitted-together strength of Orientalist discourse, its very close ties to the enabling socio-economic and political institutions, and its redoubtable durability. After all, any system of ideas that can remain unchanged as teachable wisdom (in academies, books, congresses, universities, foreign-service institutes) from the period of Ernest Renan in the late 1840s until the present in the United States must be something more formidable than a mere collection of lies. Orientalism, therefore, is not an airy European fantasy about the Orient, but a created body of theory and practice in which, for many generations, there has been a considerable material investment. Continued investment made Orientalism, as a system of knowledge about the Orient, an accepted grid for filtering through the Orient into Western consciousness, just as that same investment multiplied – indeed, made truly productive – the statements proliferating out from Orientalism into the general culture.

Gramsci has made the useful analytic distinction between civil and political society in which the former is made up of voluntary (or at least rational and noncoercive) affiliations like schools, families, and unions, the latter of state institutions (the army, the police, the central bureaucracy) whose role in the polity is direct domination. Culture, of course, is to be found operating within civil society, where the influence of ideas, of institutions, and of other persons works not through domination but by what Gramsci calls consent. In any society not totalitarian, then, certain cultural forms predominate over others, just as certain ideas are more influential than others; the form of this cultural leadership is what Gramsci has identified as *hegemony*, an indispensable concept for any understanding of cultural life in the industrial West. It is hegemony, or rather the result of cultural hegemony at work, that gives Orientalism the durability and the strength I have been speaking about so far. Orientalism is never far from what Denys Hay has called the idea of Europe,[3] a collective notion identifying 'us' Europeans as against all 'those' non-Europeans, and indeed it can be argued that the major component in European culture is precisely what made that culture hegemonic both in and outside Europe: the idea of European identity as a superior one in comparison with all the non-European peoples and cultures. There is in addition the hegemony of European ideas about the Orient, themselves reiterating European superiority over Oriental backwardness, usually overriding the possibility that a more independent, or more skeptical, thinker might have had different views on the matter.

In a quite constant way, Orientalism depends for its strategy on this flexible *positional* superiority, which puts the Westerner in a whole series of possible relationships with the Orient without ever losing him the relative upper hand. And why should it have been otherwise, especially during the period of extraordinary European ascendancy from the late Renaissance to the present? The scientist, the scholar, the missionary, the trader, or the soldier was in, or thought about, the Orient because he *could be there*, or could think about it, with very little resistance on the Orient's part. Under the general heading of knowledge of the Orient, and within the umbrella of Western hegemony over the Orient during the period from the end of the eighteenth century, there emerged a complex Orient suitable for study in the academy, for display in the museum, for reconstruction in the colonial office, for theoretical illustration in anthropological, biological, linguistic, racial, and historical theses about man-kind and the universe, for instances of economic and sociological theories of development, revolution, cultural personality, national or religious character. Additionally, the imaginative examination of things Oriental was based more or less exclusively upon a sovereign Western consciousness out of whose unchallenged centrality an Oriental world emerged, first according to general ideas about who or what was an Oriental, then according to a detailed logic governed not simply by empirical reality but by a battery of desires, repres-sions, investments, and projections. If we can point to great Orientalist works of genuine scholarship like Silvestre de Sacy's *Chrestomathie arabe* or Edward William Lane's *Account of the Manners and Customs of the Modern Egyptians*, we need also to note that Renan's and Gobineau's racial ideas came out of the same impulse, as did a great many Victorian pornographic novels (see the analysis by Steven Marcus of 'The Lustful Turk'[4]).

And yet, one must repeatedly ask oneself whether what matters in Orien-talism is the general group of ideas overriding the mass of material – about which who could deny that they were shot through with doctrines of European superiority, various kinds of racism, imperialism, and the like, dogmatic views of 'the Oriental' as a kind of ideal and unchanging abstraction? – or the much more varied work produced by almost uncountable individual writers, whom one would take up as individual instances of authors dealing with the Orient. In a sense the two alternatives, general and particular, are really two perspectives on the same material: in both instances one would have to deal with pioneers in the field like William Jones, with great artists like Nerval or Flaubert. And why would it not be possible to employ both perspectives together, or one after the other? Isn't there an obvious danger of distortion (of precisely the kind that academic Orientalism has always been prone to) if either too general or too specific a level of description is maintained systematically?

My two fears are distortion and inaccuracy, or rather the kind of inaccuracy produced by too dogmatic a generality and too positivistic a localized focus. In trying to deal with these problems I have tried to deal with three main aspects of my own contemporary reality that seem to me to point the way out of the methodological or perspectival difficulties I have been discussing, difficulties that might force one, in the first instance, into writing a coarse polemic on so unacceptably general a level of description as not to be worth the effort, or in the second instance, into writing so detailed and atomistic a series of analyses as to lose all track of the general lines of force informing the field, giving it its special cogency. How then to recognize individuality and to reconcile it with its intelligent, and by no means passive or merely dictatorial, general and hegemonic context?

III

I mentioned three aspects of my contemporary reality [the third of these is not reproduced here]: I must explain and briefly discuss them now, so that it can be seen how I was led to a particular course of research and writing.

1. *The distinction between pure and political knowledge.* It is very easy to argue that knowledge about Shakespeare or Wordsworth is not political whereas knowledge about contemporary China or the Soviet Union is. My own formal and professional designation is that of 'humanist,' a title which indicates the humanities as my field and therefore the unlikely eventuality that there might be anything political about what I do in that field. Of course, all these labels and terms are quite unnuanced as I use them here, but the general truth of what I am pointing to is, I think, widely held. One reason for saying that a humanist who writes about Wordsworth, or an editor whose specialty is Keats, is not involved in anything political is that what he does seems to have no direct political effect upon reality in the everyday sense. A scholar whose field is Soviet economics works in a highly charged area where there is much government interest, and what he might produce in the way of studies or proposals will be taken up by policymakers, government officials, institutional economists, intelligence experts. The distinction between 'humanists' and persons whose work has policy implications, or political significance, can be broadened further by saying that the former's ideological color is a matter of incidental importance to politics (although possibly of great moment to his colleagues in the field, who may object to his Stalinism or fascism or too easy liberalism), whereas the ideology of the latter is woven directly into his material – indeed, economics, politics, and sociology in the modern academy are ideological sciences – and therefore taken for granted as being 'political.'

Nevertheless the determining impingement on most knowledge produced in the contemporary West (and here I speak mainly about the United States) is that it be nonpolitical, that is, scholarly, academic, impartial, above partisan or small-minded doctrinal belief. One can have no quarrel with such an ambition in theory, perhaps, but in practice the reality is much more problematic. No one has ever devised a method for detaching the scholar from the circumstances of life, from the fact of his involvement (conscious or unconscious) with a class, a set of beliefs, a social position, or from the mere activity of being a member of a society. These continue to bear on what he does professionally, even though naturally enough his research and its fruits do attempt to reach a level of relative freedom from the inhibitions and the restrictions of brute, everyday reality. For there is such a thing as knowledge that is less, rather than more, partial than the individual (with his entangling and distracting life circumstances) who produces it. Yet this knowledge is not therefore automatically nonpolitical.

Whether discussions of literature or of classical philology are fraught with – or have unmediated – political significance is a very large question that I have tried to treat in some detail elsewhere.[5] What I am interested in doing now is suggesting how the general liberal consensus that 'true' knowledge is fundamentally nonpolitical (and conversely, that overtly political knowledge is not 'true' knowledge) obscures the highly if obscurely organized political circumstances obtaining when knowledge is produced. No one is helped in understanding this today when the adjective 'political' is used as a label to discredit any work for daring to violate the protocol of pretended suprapolitical objectivity. We may say, first, that civil society recognizes a gradation of political importance in the various fields of knowledge. To some extent the political importance given a field comes from the possibility of its direct translation into economic terms; but to a greater extent political importance comes from the closeness of a field to ascertainable sources of power in political society. Thus an economic study of long-term Soviet energy potential and its effect on military capability is likely to be commissioned by the Defense Department, and thereafter to acquire a kind of political status impossible for a study of Tolstoi's early fiction financed in part by a foundation. Yet both works belong in what civil society acknowledges to be a similar field, Russian studies, even though one work may be done by a very conservative economist, the other by a radical literary historian. My point here is that 'Russia' as a general subject matter has political priority over nicer distinctions such as 'economics' and 'literary history,' because political society in Gramsci's sense reaches into such realms of civil society as the academy and saturates them with significance of direct concern to it.

I do not want to press all this any further on general theoretical grounds: it seems to me that the value and credibility of my case can be demonstrated by being much more specific, in the way, for example, Noam Chomsky has studied the instrumental connection between the Vietnam War and the notion of objective scholarship as it was applied to cover state-sponsored military research.[6] Now because Britain, France, and recently the United States are imperial powers, their political societies impart to their civil societies a sense of urgency, a direct political infusion as it were, where and whenever matters pertaining to their imperial interests abroad are concerned. I doubt that it is controversial, for example, to say that an Englishman in India or Egypt in the later nineteenth century took an interest in those countries that was never far from their status in his mind as British colonies. To say this may seem quite different from saying that all academic knowledge about India and Egypt is somehow tinged and impressed with, violated by, the gross political fact – and yet *that is what I am saying* in this study of Orientalism. For if it is true that no production of knowledge in the human sciences can ever ignore or disclaim its author's involvement as a human subject in his own circumstances, then it must also be true that for a European or American studying the Orient there can be no disclaiming the main circumstances of his actuality: that he comes up against the Orient as a European or American first, as an individual second. And to be a European or an American in such a situation is by no means an inert fact. It meant and means being aware, however dimly, that one belongs to a power with definite interests in the Orient, and more important that one belongs to a part of the earth with a definite history of involvement in the Orient almost since the time of Homer.

Put in this way, these political actualities are still too undefined and general to be really interesting. Anyone would agree to them without necessarily agreeing also that they mattered very much, for instance, to Flaubert as he wrote *Salammbô*, or to H. A. R. Gibb as he wrote *Modern Trends in Islam*. The trouble is that there is too great a distance between the big dominating fact, as I have described it, and the details of everyday life that govern the minute discipline of a novel or a scholarly text as each is being written. Yet if we eliminate from the start any notion that 'big' facts like imperial domination can be applied mechanically and deterministically to such complex matters as culture and ideas, then we will begin to approach an interesting kind of study. My idea is that European and then American interest in the Orient was political according to some of the obvious historical accounts of it that I have given here, but that it was the culture that created that interest, that acted dynamically along with brute political, economic, and military rationales to make the Orient the varied and complicated place that it obviously was in the field I call Orientalism.

Therefore, Orientalism is not a mere political subject matter or field that is reflected passively by culture, scholarship, or institutions; nor is it a large and diffuse collection of texts about the Orient; nor is it representative and expressive of some nefarious 'Western' imperialist plot to hold down the 'Oriental' world. It is rather a *distribution* of geopolitical awareness into aesthetic, scholarly, economic, sociological, historical, and philological texts; it is an *elaboration* not only of a basic geographical distinction (the world is made up of two unequal halves, Orient and Occident) but also of a whole series of 'interests' which, by such means as scholarly discovery, philological reconstruction, psychological analysis, landscape and sociological description, it not only creates but also maintains; it *is*, rather than expresses, a certain *will* or *intention* to understand, in some cases to control, manipulate, even to incorporate, what is a manifestly different (or alternative and novel) world; it is, above all, a discourse that is by no means in direct, corresponding relationship with political power in the raw, but rather is produced and exists in an uneven exchange with various kinds of power, shaped to a degree by the exchange with power political (as with a colonial or imperial establishment), power in- tellectual (as with reigning sciences like comparative linguistics or anatomy, or any of the modern policy sciences), power cultural (as with orthodoxies and canons of taste, texts, values), power moral (as with ideas about what 'we' do and what 'they' cannot do or understand as 'we' do). Indeed, my real argument is that Orientalism is – and does not simply represent – a considerable dimension of modern political-intellectual culture, and as such has less to do with the Orient than it does with 'our' world.

Because Orientalism is a cultural and a political fact, then, it does not exist in some archival vacuum; quite the contrary, I think it can be shown that what is thought, said, or even done about the Orient follows (perhaps occurs within) certain distinct and intellectually knowable lines. Here too a considerable degree of nuance and elaboration can be seen working as between the broad superstructural pressures and the details of composition, the facts of textuality. Most humanistic scholars are, I think, perfectly happy with the notion that texts exist in contexts, that there is such a thing as intertextuality, that the pressures of conventions, predecessors, and rhetorical styles limit what Walter Benjamin once called the 'overtaxing of the productive person in the name of ... the principle of "creativity,"' in which the poet is believed on his own, and out of his pure mind, to have brought forth his work.[7] Yet there is a reluctance to allow that political, institutional, and ideological constraints act in the same manner on the individual author. A humanist will believe it to be an interesting fact to any interpreter of Balzac that he was influenced in the *Comédie humaine* by the conflict between Geoffroy Saint-Hilaire and Cuvier, but the same sort of pressure on Balzac of deeply reactionary monarchism is felt in some vague way to demean his literary 'genius' and therefore to be less worth serious study. Similarly – as Harry Bracken has been tirelessly showing – philosophers will conduct their discussions of Locke, Hume, and empiricism without ever taking into account that there is an explicit connection in these classic writers between their 'philosophic' doctrines and racial theory, justifications of slavery, or arguments for colonial exploitation.[8] These are common enough ways by which contemporary scholarship keeps itself pure.

Perhaps it is true that most attempts to rub culture's nose in the mud of politics have been crudely iconoclastic; perhaps also the social interpretation of literature in my own field has simply not kept up with the enormous technical advances in detailed textual analysis. But there is no getting away from the fact that literary studies in general, and American Marxist theorists in particular, have avoided the effort of seriously bridging the gap between the superstructural and the base levels in textual, historical scholarship; on another occasion I have gone so far as to say that the literary-cultural establishment as a whole has declared the serious study of imperialism and culture off limits.[9] For Orientalism brings one up directly against that question – that is, to realizing that political imperialism governs an entire field of study, imagination, and scholarly institutions – in such a way as to make its avoidance an intellectual and historical impossibility. Yet there will always remain the perennial escape mechanism of saying that a literary scholar and a philosopher, for example, are trained in literature and philosophy respectively, not in politics or ideological analysis. In other words, the specialist argument can work quite effectively to block the larger and, in my opinion, the more intellectually serious perspective.

Here it seems to me there is a simple two-part answer to be given, at least so far as the study of imperialism and culture (or Orientalism) is concerned. In the first place, nearly every nineteenth-century writer (and the same is true enough of writers in earlier periods) was extraordinarily well aware of the fact of empire: this is a subject not very well studied, but it will not take a modern Victorian specialist long to admit that liberal cultural heroes like John Stuart Mill, Arnold, Carlyle, Newman, Macaulay, Ruskin, George Eliot, and even Dickens had definite views on race and imperialism, which are quite easily to be found at work in their writing. So even a specialist must deal with the knowledge that Mill, for example, made it clear in *On Liberty* and *Representative Government* that his views there could not be applied to India (he was an India Office functionary for a good deal of his life, after all) because the Indians were civilizationally, if not racially, inferior. The same kind of paradox is to be found in Marx, as I try to show in this book. In the second place, to believe that politics in the form of imperialism bears upon the production of literature, scholarship, social theory, and history writing is by no means equivalent to saying that culture is therefore a demeaned or denigrated thing. Quite the contrary: my whole point is to say that we can better understand the persistence and the durability of saturating hegemonic systems like culture when we realize that their internal constraints upon writers and thinkers were *productive*, not unilaterally inhibiting. It is this idea that Gramsci, certainly, and Foucault and Raymond Williams in their very different ways have been trying to illustrate. Even one or two pages by Williams on 'the uses of the Empire' in *The Long Revolution* tell us more about nineteenth-century cultural richness than many volumes of hermetic textual analyses.[10]

Therefore I study Orientalism as a dynamic exchange between individual authors and the large political concerns shaped by the three great empires – British, French, American – in whose intellectual and imaginative territory the writing was produced. What interests me most as a scholar is not the gross political verity but the detail, as indeed what interests us in someone like Lane or Flaubert or Renan is not the (to him) indisputable truth that Occidentals are superior to Orientals, but the profoundly worked over and modulated evidence of his detailed work within the very wide space opened up by that truth. One need only remember that Lane's *Manners and Customs of the Modern Egyptians* is a classic of historical and anthropological observation because of its style, its enormously intelligent and brilliant details, not because of its simple reflection of racial superiority, to understand what I am saying here.

The kind of political questions raised by Orientalism, then, are as follows: What other sorts of intellectual, aesthetic, scholarly, and cultural energies went into the making of an imperialist tradition like the Orientalist one? How did philology, lexicography, history, biology, political and economic theory, novel-writing, and lyric poetry come to the service of Orientalism's broadly imperialist view of the world? What changes, modulations, refinements, even revolutions take place within Orientalism? What is the meaning of originality, of continuity, of individuality, in this context? How does Orientalism transmit or reproduce itself from one epoch to another? In fine, how can we treat the cultural, historical phenomenon of Orientalism as a kind of *willed human work* – not of mere unconditioned ratiocination – in all its historical complexity, detail, and worth without at the same time losing sight of the alliance between cultural work, political tendencies, the state, and the specific realities of domination? Governed by such concerns a humanistic study can responsibly address itself to politics *and* culture. But this is not to say that such a study establishes a hard-and-fast rule about the relationship between knowledge and politics. My argument is that each humanistic investigation must formulate the nature of that connection in the specific context of the study, the subject matter, and its historical circumstances.

2. *The methodological question.* . . . My principal methodological devices for studying authority here are what can be called *strategic location*, which is a way of describing the author's position in a text with regard to the Oriental material he writes about, and *strategic formation*, which is a way of analyzing the relationship between texts and the way in which groups of texts, types of texts, even textual genres, acquire mass, density, and referential power among themselves and thereafter in the culture at large. I use the notion of strategy simply to identify the problem every writer on the Orient has faced: how to get hold of it, how to approach it, how not to be defeated or overwhelmed by its sublimity, its scope, its awful dimensions. Everyone who writes about the Orient must locate himself vis-à-vis the Orient; translated into his text, this location includes the kind of narrative voice he adopts, the type of structure he builds, the kinds of images, themes, motifs that circulate in his text – all of which add up to deliberate ways of addressing the reader, containing the Orient, and finally, representing it or speaking in its behalf. None of this takes place in the abstract, however. Every writer on the Orient (and this is true even of Homer) assumes some Oriental precedent, some previous knowledge of the Orient, to which he refers and on which he relies. Additionally, each work on the Orient *affiliates* itself with other works, with audiences, with institutions, with the Orient itself. The ensemble of relationships between works, audiences, and some particular aspects of the Orient therefore constitutes an analyzable formation – for example, that of philological studies, of anthologies of extracts from Oriental literature, of travel books, of Oriental fantasies – whose presence in time, in discourse, in institutions (schools, libraries, foreign services) gives it strength and authority.

It is clear, I hope, that my concern with authority does not entail analysis of what lies hidden in the Orientalist text, but analysis rather of the text's surface, its exteriority to what it describes. I do not think that this idea can be overemphasized. Orientalism is premised upon exteriority, that is, on the fact that the Orientalist, poet or scholar, makes the Orient speak, describes the Orient, renders its mysteries plain for and to the West. He is never concerned with the Orient except as the first cause of what he says. What he says and writes, by virtue of the fact that it is said or written, is meant to indicate that the Orientalist is outside the Orient, both as an existential and as a moral fact. The principal product of this exteriority is of course representation: as early as Aeschylus's play *The Persians* the Orient is transformed from a very far distant and often threatening Otherness into figures that are relatively familiar (in Aeschylus's case, grieving Asiatic women). The dramatic immediacy of representation in *The Persians* obscures the fact that the audience is watching a highly artificial enactment of what a non-Oriental has made into a symbol for the whole Orient. My analysis of the Orientalist text therefore places emphasis on the evidence, which is by no means invisible, for such representations *as representations*, not as 'natural' depictions of the Orient. This evidence is found just as prominently in the so-called truthful text (histories, philological analyses, political treatises) as in the avowedly artistic (i.e., openly imaginative) text. The things to look at are style, figures of speech, setting, narrative devices, historical and social circumstances, *not* the correctness of the representation, nor its fidelity to some great original. The exteriority of the representation is always governed by some version of the truism that if the Orient could represent itself, it would; since it cannot, the representation does the job, for the West, and *faute de mieux*, for the poor Orient. 'Sie können sich nicht vertreten, sie müssen vertreten werden,' as Marx wrote in *The Eighteenth Brumaire of Louis Bonaparte.*

Another reason for insisting upon exteriority is that I believe it needs to be made clear about cultural discourse and exchange within a culture that what is commonly circulated by it is not 'truth' but representations. It hardly needs to be demonstrated again that language itself is a highly organized and encoded system, which employs many devices to express, indicate, exchange messages and information, represent, and so forth. In any instance of at least written language, there is no such thing as a delivered presence, but a *re-presence*, or a representation. The value, efficacy, strength, apparent veracity of a written statement about the Orient therefore relies very little, and cannot instrumentally depend, on the Orient as such. On the contrary, the written statement is a presence to the reader by virtue of its having excluded, displaced, made supererogatory any such *real thing* as 'the Orient.' Thus all of Orientalism stands forth and away from the Orient: that Orientalism makes sense at all depends more on the West than on the Orient, and this sense is directly indebted to various Western techniques of representation that make the Orient visible, clear, 'there' in discourse about it. And these representations rely upon institutions, traditions, conventions, agreed-upon codes of understanding for their effects, not upon a distant and amorphous Orient.

The difference between representations of the Orient before the last third of the eighteenth century and those after it (that is, those belonging to what I call modern Orientalism) is that the range of representation expanded enormously in the later period. It is true that after William Jones and Anquetil-Duperron, and after Napoleon's Egyptian expedition, Europe came to know the Orient more scientifically, to live in it with greater authority and discipline than ever before. But what mattered to Europe was the expanded scope and the much greater refinement given its techniques for receiving the Orient. When around the turn of the eighteenth century the Orient definitively revealed the age of its languages – thus outdating Hebrew's divine pedigree – it was a group of Europeans who made the discovery, passed it on to other scholars, and preserved the discovery in the new science of Indo-European philology. A new powerful science for viewing the linguistic Orient was born, and with it, as Foucault has shown in *The Other of Things*, a whole web of related scientific interests. Similarly William Beckford, Byron, Goethe, and Hugo restructured the Orient by their art and made its colors, lights, and people visible through their images, rhythms, and motifs. At most, the 'real' Orient provoked a writer to his vision; it very rarely guided it.

Orientalism responded more to the culture that produced it than to its putative object, which was also produced by the West. Thus the history of Orientalism has both an internal consistency and a highly articulated set of relationships to the dominant culture surrounding it. My analyses consequently try to show the field's shape and internal organization, its pioneers, patriarchal authorities, canonical texts, doxological ideas, exemplary figures, its followers, elaborators, and new authorities; I try also to explain how Orientalism borrowed and was frequently informed by 'strong' ideas, doctrines, and trends ruling the culture. Thus there was (and is) a linguistic Orient, a Freudian Orient, a Spenglerian Orient, a Darwinian Orient, a racist Orient – and so on. Yet never has there been such a thing as a pure, or unconditional, Orient; similarly, never has there been a nonmaterial form of Orientalism, much less something so innocent as an 'idea' of the Orient. In this underlying conviction and in its ensuing methodological consequences do I differ from scholars who study the history of ideas. For the emphases and the executive form, above all the material effectiveness, of statements made by Orientalist discourse are possible in ways that any hermetic history of ideas tends completely to scant. Without those emphases and that material effectiveness Orientalism would be just another idea, whereas it is and was much more than that. Therefore I set out to examine not only scholarly works but also works of literature, political tracts, journalistic texts, travel books, religious and philological studies. In other words, my hybrid perspective is broadly historical and 'anthropological,' given that I believe all texts to be worldly and circumstantial in (of course) ways that vary from genre to genre, and from historical period to historical period.

... On several occasions I have alluded to the connections between Orientalism as a body of ideas, beliefs, clichés, or learning about the East, and other schools of thought at large in the culture. Now one of the important developments in nineteenth-century Orientalism was the distillation of essential ideas about the Orient – its sensuality, its tendency to despotism, its aberrant mentality, its habits of inaccuracy, its backwardness – into a separate and unchallenged coherence; thus for a writer to use the word *Oriental* was a reference for the reader sufficient to identify a specific body of information

about the Orient. This information seemed to be morally neutral and objectively valid; it seemed to have an epistemological status equal to that of
historical chronology or geographical location. In its most basic form, then,
Oriental material could not really be violated by anyone's discoveries, nor did
it seem ever to be revaluated completely. Instead, the work of various
nineteenth-century scholars and of imaginative writers made this essential
body of knowledge more clear, more detailed, more substantial – and more
distinct from 'Occidentalism.' Yet Orientalist ideas could enter into alliance
with general philosophical theories (such as those about the history of man-
kind and civilization) and diffuse world-hypotheses, as philosophers sometimes call them; and in many ways the professional contributors to Oriental
knowledge were anxious to couch their formulations and ideas, their scholarly
work, their considered contemporary observations, in language and terminology whose cultural validity derived from other sciences and systems of
thought.

The distinction I am making is really between an almost unconscious (and
certainly an untouchable) positivity, which I shall call *latent* Orientalism, and
the various stated views about Oriental society, languages, literatures, history,
sociology, and so forth, which I shall call *manifest* Orientalism. Whatever
change occurs in knowledge of the Orient is found almost exclusively in
manifest Orientalism; the unanimity, stability, and durability of latent Orientalism are more or less constant. In the nineteenth-century writers I analyzed in
Chapter Two, the differences in their ideas about the Orient can be characterized as exclusively manifest differences, differences in form and personal
style, rarely in basic content. Every one of them kept intact the separateness of
the Orient, its eccentricity, its backwardness, its silent indifference, its feminine
penetrability, its supine malleability; this is why every writer on the Orient,
from Renan to Marx (ideologically speaking), or from the most rigorous
scholars (Lane and Sacy) to the most powerful imaginations (Flaubert and
Nerval), saw the Orient as a locale requiring Western attention, reconstruction, even redemption. The Orient existed as a place isolated from the
mainstream of European progress in the sciences, arts, and commerce. Thus
whatever good or bad values were imputed to the Orient appeared to be
functions of some highly specialized Western interest in the Orient. This was
the situation from about the 1870s on through the early part of the twentieth
century – but let me give some examples that illustrate what I mean.

Theses of Oriental backwardness, degeneracy, and inequality with the West
most easily associated themselves early in the nineteenth century with ideas
about the biological bases of racial inequality. Thus the racial classifications
found in Cuvier's *Le Règne animal*, Gobineau's *Essai sur l'inégalité des races
humaines*, and Robert Knox's *The Races of Man* found a willing partner in
latent Orientalism. To these ideas was added second-order Darwinism, which
seemed to accentuate the 'scientific' validity of the division of races into
advanced and backward, or European-Aryan and Oriental-African. Thus the
whole question of imperialism, as it was debated in the late nineteenth century
by pro-imperialists and anti-imperialists alike, carried forward the binary

typology of advanced and backward (or subject) races, cultures, and societies. John Westlake's *Chapters on the Principles of International Law* (1894) argues, for example, that regions of the earth designated as 'uncivilized' (a word carrying the freight of Orientalist assumptions, among others) ought to be annexed or occupied by advanced powers. Similarly, the ideas of such writers as Carl Peters, Leopold de Saussure, and Charles Temple draw on the advanced/backward binarism[11] so centrally advocated in late-nineteenth-century Orientalism.

Along with all other peoples variously designated as backward, degenerate, uncivilized, and retarded, the Orientals were viewed in a framework constructed out of biological determinism and moral-political admonishment. The Oriental was linked thus to elements in Western society (delinquents, the insane, women, the poor) having in common an identity best described as lamentably alien. Orientals were rarely seen or looked at; they were seen through, analyzed not as citizens, or even people, but as problems to be solved or confined or – as the colonial powers openly coveted their territory – taken over. The point is that the very designation of something as Oriental involved an already pronounced evaluative judgment, and in the case of the peoples inhabiting the decayed Ottoman Empire, an implicit program of action. Since the Oriental was a member of a subject race, he had to be subjected: it was that simple. The *locus classicus* for such judgment and action is to be found in Gustave Le Bon's *Les Lois psychologiques de l'évolution des peuples* (1894).

But there were other uses for latent Orientalism. If that group of ideas allowed one to separate Orientals from advanced, civilizing powers, and if the 'classical' Orient served to justify both the Orientalist and his disregard of modern Orientals, latent Orientalism also encouraged a peculiarly (not to say invidiously) male conception of the world. I have already referred to this in passing during my discussion of Renan. The Oriental male was considered in isolation from the total community in which he lived and which many Orientalists, following Lane, have viewed with something resembling contempt and fear. Orientalism itself, furthermore, was an exclusively male province; like so many professional guilds during the modern period, it viewed itself and its subject matter with sexist blinders. This is especially evident in the writing of travelers and novelists: women are usually the creatures of a male power-fantasy. They express unlimited sensuality, they are more or less stupid, and above all they are willing. Flaubert's Kuchuk Hanem is the prototype of such caricatures, which were common enough in pornographic novels (e.g., Pierre Louÿs's *Aphrodite*) whose novelty draws on the Orient for their interest. Moreover the male conception of the world, in its effect upon the practicing Orientalist, tends to be static, frozen, fixed eternally. The very possibility of development, transformation, human movement – in the deepest sense of the word – is denied the Orient and the Oriental. As a known and ultimately an immobilized or unproductive quality, they come to be identified with a bad sort of eternality: hence, when the Orient is being approved, such phrases as 'the wisdom of the East.'

Notes

1 Thierry Desjardins, *Le Martyre du Liban* (Paris: Plon, 1976), p. 14.
2 K. M. Panikkar, *Asia and Western Dominance* (London: George Allen & Unwin, 1959).
3 Denys Hay, *Europe: The Emergence of an Idea*, 2nd edn (Edinburgh: Edinburgh University Press, 1968).
4 Steven Marcus, *The Other Victorians: A Study of Sexuality and Pornography in Mid-Nineteenth Century England* (1966; reprint edn, New York: Bantam Books, 1967), pp. 200–19.
5 See my *Criticism Between Culture and System* (Cambridge, MA: Harvard University Press, forthcoming).
6 Principally in his *American Power and the New Mandarins: Historical and Political Essays* (New York: Pantheon Books, 1969) and *For Reasons of State* (New York: Pantheon Books, 1973).
7 Walter Benjamin, *Charles Baudelaire: A Lyric Poet in the Era of High Capitalism*, trans. Harry Zohn (London: New Left Books, 1973), p. 71.
8 Harry Bracken, 'Essence, Accident and Race,' *Hermathena* 116 (Winter 1973), pp. 81–96.
9 In an interview published in *Diacritics* 6, no. 3 (Fall 1976), p. 38.
10 Raymond Williams, *The Long Revolution* (London: Chatto & Windus, 1961), pp. 66–7.
11 See Philip D. Curtin, ed., *Imperialism: The Documentary History of Western Civilization* (New York: Walker & Co., 1972), pp. 73–105.

2

Homi Bhabha

The Other Question *

> To concern oneself with the founding concepts of the entire history of philoso-
> phy, to deconstitute them, is not to undertake the work of the philologist or of the
> classic historian of philosophy. Despite appearances, it is probably the most
> daring way of making the beginnings of a step outside of philosophy.
>
> Jacques Derrida: *Structure, Sign and Play*

An important feature of colonial discourse is its dependence on the concept of 'fixity' in the ideological construction of otherness.[1] Fixity, as the sign of cultural/historical/racial difference in the discourse of colonialism, is a paradoxical mode of representation: it connotes rigidity and an unchanging order as well as disorder, degeneracy and daemonic repetition. Likewise the stereotype, which is its major discursive strategy, is a form of knowledge and identification that vacillates between what is always 'in place', already known, and something that must be anxiously repeated ... as if the essential duplicity of the Asiatic or the bestial sexual licence of the African that needs no proof, can never really, in discourse, be proved. It is this process of *ambivalence*, central to the stereotype, that my essay explores as it constructs a theory of colonial discourse. For it is the force of ambivalence that gives the colonial stereotype its currency: ensures its repeatability in changing historical and discursive conjunctures; informs its strategies of individuation and marginalisation; produces that effect of probabilistic truth and predictability which, for the stereotype, must always be in *excess* of what can be empirically proved or logically construed. Yet, the function of ambivalence as one of the most significant discursive and psychical strategies of discriminatory power – whether racist or sexist, peripheral or metropolitan – remains to be charted.

The absence of such a perspective has its own history of political expediency. To recognise the stereotype as an ambivalent mode of knowledge and power demands a theoretical and political response that challenges deterministic or functionalist modes of conceiving of the relationship between discourse and politics, and questions dogmatic and moralistic positions on the meaning of oppression and discrimination. My reading of colonial discourse suggests that the point of intervention should shift from the *identification* of images as positive or negative, to an understanding of the *processes of subjectification* made possible (and plausible) through stereotypical discourse. To judge the

* From *Screen* 24.6 (1983), pp. 18–36.

stereotyped image on the basis of a prior political normativity is to dismiss it, not to displace it, which is only possible by engaging with its *effectivity*; with the repertoire of positions of power and resistance, domination and dependence that constructs the colonial subject (both coloniser and colonised). I do not intend to deconstruct the colonial discourse to reveal its ideological misconceptions or repressions, to exult in its self-reflexivity, or to indulge its liberatory 'excess'. In order to understand the productivity of colonial power it is crucial to construct its regime of 'truth', not to subject its representations to a normalising judgement. Only then does it become possible to understand the *productive* ambivalence of the object of colonial discourse – that 'otherness' which is at once an object of desire and derision, an articulation of difference contained within the fantasy of origin and identity. What such a reading reveals are the boundaries of colonial discourse and it enables a transgression of these limits from the space of that otherness.

The construction of the colonial subject in discourse, and the exercise of colonial power through discourse, demands an articulation of forms of difference – racial and sexual. Such an articulation becomes crucial if it is held that the body is always simultaneously inscribed in both the economy of pleasure and desire and the economy of discourse, domination and power. I do not wish to conflate, unproblematically, two forms of the marking – and splitting – of the subject nor to globalise two forms of representation. I want to suggest, however, that there is a theoretical space and a political place for such an *articulation* – in the sense in which that word itself denies an 'original' identity or a 'singularity' to objects of difference – sexual or racial. If such a view is taken, as Feuchtwang[2] argues in a different context, it follows that the epithets racial or sexual come to be seen as modes of differentiation, realised as multiple, cross-cutting determinations, polymorphous and perverse, always demanding a specific and strategic calculation of their effects. Such is, I believe, the moment of colonial discourse. It is the most theoretically underdeveloped form of discourse, but crucial to the binding of a range of differences and discriminations that inform the discursive and political practices of racial and cultural hierarchisation.

Before turning to the construction of colonial discourse, I want to discuss briefly the process by which forms of racial/cultural/historical otherness have been marginalised in theoretical texts committed to the articulation of 'difference', '*significance*', 'contradiction', in order, it is claimed, to reveal the limits of Western representationalist discourse. In facilitating the passage 'from work to text' and stressing the arbitrary, differential and systemic construction of social and cultural signs, these critical strategies unsettle the idealist quest for meanings that are, most often, intentionalist and nationalist. So much is not in question. What does need to be questioned, however, is the *mode of representation of otherness*.

Where better to raise the question of the subject of racial and cultural difference than in Stephen Heath's masterly analysis of the chiaroscuro world of Welles' classic *A Touch of Evil?* I refer to an area of its analysis which has generated the least comment, that is, Heath's attention to the structuration of the border Mexico/USA that circulates through the text affirming and exchanging some notion of 'limited being'. Heath's work departs from the traditional analysis of racial and cultural differences, which identify stereotype and image, and elaborate them in a moralistic or nationalistic discourse that affirms the *origin* and *unity* of national identity. Heath's attentiveness to the contradictory and diverse sites within the textual system, which *construct* national/cultural differences in their deployment of the semes of 'foreignness', 'mixedness', 'impurity', as transgressive and corrupting, is extremely relevant. His attention to the turnings of this much neglected subject as sign (not symbol or stereotype) disseminated in the codes (as 'partition', 'exchange', 'naming', 'character', etc.), gives us a useful sense of the circulation and proliferation of racial and cultural otherness. Despite the awareness of the multiple or crosscutting determinations in the construction of modes of sexual and racial differentiation there is a sense in which Heath's analysis marginalises otherness. Although I shall argue that the problem of the border Mexico/USA is read too singularly, too exclusively under the sign of sexuality, it is not that I am not aware of the many proper and relevant reasons for that 'feminist' focus. The 'entertainment' operated by the realist Hollywood film of the '50s was always also a containment of the subject in a narrative economy of voyeurism and fetishism. Moreover, the displacement that organises any textual system, within which the display of difference circulates, demands that the play of 'nationalities' should participate in the sexual positioning, troubling the Law and desire. There is, nevertheless, a singularity and reductiveness in concluding that:

> Vargas is the position of desire, its admission and its prohibition. Not surprisingly he has two names: the name of desire is Mexican, Miguel ... that of the Law American – Mike. ... The film uses the border, the play between American and Mexican ... at the same time it seeks to hold that play finally in the opposition of purity and mixture which in turn is a version of Law and desire.[3]

However liberatory it is from one position to see the logic of the text traced ceaselessly between the Ideal Father and the Phallic Mother, in another sense, in seeing only one possible articulation of the differential complex 'race-sex' – it half colludes with the proffered images of marginality. For if the naming of Vargas is crucially mixed and split in the economy of desire, then there are other mixed economies which make naming and positioning equally problematic 'across the border'. To identify the 'play' on the border as purity and mixture and to see it as an allegory of Law and desire reduces the articulation of racial and sexual difference to what is dangerously close to becoming a circle rather than a spiral of *différance*. On that basis, it is not possible to construct the polymorphous and perverse collusion between racism and sexism as a *mixed economy*–for instance, the discourses of American cultural colonialism and Mexican dependency, the fear/desire of miscegenation, the American border as cultural signifier of a pioneering, male 'American' spirit always under threat from races and cultures beyond the border. If the death of the Father is the interruption on which the narrative is initiated, it is through that death that miscegenation is both possible and deferred; if, again, it is the purpose of the narrative to restore Susan as 'good object', it also becomes its project to deliver Vargas from his racial 'mixedness'. It is all there in Heath's splendid scrutiny of the text, revealed as he brushes against its grain. What is missing is the taking up of these positions as also the *object(ives)* of his analysis.

These objectives have been pursued in the January/February 1983 issue of *Screen* (volume 24, number 2), which addresses the problems of 'Racism, Colonialism and Cinema'. This is a timely and welcome intervention in the debate on realist narrative and its conditions of existence and representability – a debate which has hitherto engaged mainly with the 'subject' of gender and class within the social and textual formations of western bourgeois society. It would be inappropriate to review this issue of *Screen* here, but I would like to draw attention to Julianne Burton's 'The Politics of Aesthetic Distance: The Presentation of Representation in "São Bernardo"'. Burton produces an interesting reading of Hirzman's *São Bernardo* as a specific Third World riposte of dualistic metropolitan debates around realism and the possibilities of rupture. Although she doesn't use Barthes, it would be accurate to say that she locates the film as the 'limit-text' of both its own totalitarian social context *as well as* contemporary theoretical debates on representation.

Again, anti-colonialist objectives are admirably taken up by Robert Stam and Louise Spence in 'Colonialism, Racism and Representation', with a useful Brechtian emphasis on the politicisation of the *means* of representation, specifically point-of-view and suture. But despite the shift in political objectives and critical methods, there remains in their essay a limiting and traditional reliance on the stereotype as offering, *at any one time, a secure* point of identification. This is not compensated for (nor contradicted by) their view that, *at other times and places*, the same stereotype may be read in a contradictory way or, indeed, be misread. What is, therefore, a simplification in the process of stereotypical representation has a knock-on effect on their central point about the politics of point-of-view. They operate a passive and unitary notion of suture which simplifies the politics and 'aesthetics' of spectator-positioning by ignoring the ambivalent, psychical process of identification which is crucial to the argument. In contrast I suggest, in a very preliminary way, that the colonial stereotype is a complex, ambivalent, contradictory mode of representation, as anxious as it is assertive, and demands not only that we extend our critical and political objectives but that we change the object of analysis itself.

The difference of other cultures is other than the excess of signification or the trajectory of desire. These are theoretical strategies that are necessary to combat 'ethnocentricism' but they cannot, of themselves, unreconstructed, represent that otherness. There can be no inevitable sliding from the semiotic activity to the unproblematic reading of other cultural and discursive systems.[4] There is in such readings a will to power and knowledge that, in failing to specify the limits of their own field of enunciation and effectivity, proceeds to individualise otherness as the discovery of their own assumptions.

II

The difference of colonial discourse as an apparatus of power[5] will emerge more fully as the paper develops. At this stage, however, I shall provide what I take to be the minimum conditions and specifications of such a discourse. It is an apparatus that turns on the recognition and disavowal of racial/cultural/historical differences. Its predominant strategic function is the creation of a space for a 'subject peoples' through the production of knowledges in terms of which surveillance is exercised and a complex form of pleasure/unpleasure is incited. It seeks authorisation for its strategies by the production of knowledges of coloniser and colonised which are stereotypical but antithetically evaluated. The objective of colonial discourse is to construe the colonised as a population of degenerate types on the basis of racial origin, in order to justify conquest and to establish systems of administration and instruction. Despite the play of power within colonial discourse and the shifting positionalities of its subjects (e.g. effects of class, gender, ideology, different social formations, varied systems of colonisation, etc), I am referring to a form of governmentality that in marking out a 'subject nation', appropriates, directs and dominates its various spheres of activity. Therefore, despite the 'play' in the colonial system which is crucial to its exercise of power, colonial discourse produces the colonised as a fixed reality which is at once an 'other' and yet entirely knowable and visible. It resembles a form of narrative whereby the productivity and circulation of subjects and signs are bound in a reformed and recognisable totality. It employs a system of representation, a regime of truth, that is structurally similar to Realism. And it is in order to intervene within that system of representation that Edward Said proposes a semiotic of 'Orientalist' power, examining the varied European discourses which constitute 'the Orient' as an unified racial, geographical, political and cultural zone of the world. Said's analysis is revealing of, and relevant to, colonial discourse:

> Philosophically, then, the kind of language, thought, and vision that I have been calling orientalism very generally is a form of *radical realism*; anyone employing orientalism, which is the habit for dealing with questions, objects, qualities and regions deemed Oriental, will designate, name, point to, fix what he is talking or thinking about with a word or phrase, which then is considered either to have acquired, or more simply to be, reality. ... The tense they employ is the timeless eternal; they convey an impression of repetition and strength. ... For all these functions it is frequently enough to use the simple copula *is* (my emphasis).[6]

For Said, the *copula* seems to be the point at which Western Rationalism preserves the boundaries of sense for itself. Of this, too, Said is aware when he hints continually at a polarity or division at the very centre of Orientalism.[7] It is, on the one hand, a topic of learning, discovery, practice; on the other, it is the site of dreams, images, fantasies, myths, obsessions and requirements. It is a static system of 'synchronic essentialism', a knowledge of 'signifiers of stability' such as the lexicographic and the encyclopaedic. However, this site is continually under threat from diachronic forms of history and narrative, signs of instability. And, finally, this line of thinking is given a shape analogical to the dream-work, when Said refers explicitly to a distinction between 'an unconscious positivity' which he terms *latent* Orientalism, and the stated knowledges and views about the Orient which he calls *manifest* Orientalism.

Where the originality of this pioneering theory loses its inventiveness, and for me its usefulness, is with Said's reluctance to engage with the alterity and ambivalence in the articulation of these two economies which threaten to split the very object of Orientalist discourse as a knowledge and the subject positioned therein. He contains this threat by introducing a binarism within the argument which, in initially setting up in opposition these two discursive scenes, finally allows them to be correlated as a congruent system of representation that is unified through a political-ideological *intention* which, in his words, enables Europe to advance securely and *unmetaphorically* upon the Orient. Said identifies the *content* of Orientalism as the unconscious repository of fantasy, imaginative writings and essential ideas; and the *form* of manifest Orientalism as the historically and discursively determined, diachronic aspect. This division/correlation structure of manifest and latent Orientalism leads to the effectivity of the concept of discourse being undermined by what could be called the polarities of intentionality.

This produces a problem with Said's use of Foucault's concepts of power and discourse. The productivity of Foucault's concept of power/knowledge lies in its refusal of an epistemology which opposes essence/appearance, ideology/science. '*Pouvoir/Savoir*' places subjects in a relation of power and recognition that is not part of a symmetrical or dialectical relation – self/other, Master/Slave – which can then be subverted by being inverted. Subjects are always disproportionately placed in opposition or domination through the symbolic decentering of multiple power-relations which play the role of support as well as target or adversary. It becomes difficult, then, to conceive of the *historical* enunciations of colonial discourse without them being either functionally overdetermined or strategically elaborated or displaced by the *unconscious* scene of latent Orientalism. Equally, it is difficult to conceive of the process of subjectification as a placing *within* Orientalist or colonial discourse for the dominated subject without the dominant being strategically placed within it too. There is always, in Said, the suggestion that colonial power and discourse is possessed entirely by the coloniser, which is a historical and theoretical simplification. The terms in which Said's Orientalism is unified – the intentionality and unidirectionality of colonial power – also unify the subject of colonial enunciation.

This is a result of Said's inadequate attention to representation as a concept that articulates the historical and fantasy (as the scene of desire) in the production of the 'political' effects of discourse. He rightly rejects a notion of orientalism as the misrepresentation of an Oriental essence. However, having introduced the concept of 'discourse' he does not face up to the problems it makes for the instrumentalist notion of power/knowledge that he seems to require. This problem is summed up by his ready acceptance of the view that,

Representations are formations, or as Roland Barthes has said of all the operations of language, they are deformations.[8]

This brings me to my second point – that the closure and coherence attributed to the unconscious pole of colonial discourse and the unproblematised notion of the subject, restricts the effectivity of both power and knowledge. It is not possible to see how power functions productively as incitement and interdiction. Nor would it be possible, without the attribution of ambivalence to relations of power/knowledge, to calculate the traumatic impact of the return of the oppressed – those terrifying stereotypes of savagery, cannibalism, lust and anarchy which are the signal points of identification and alienation, scenes of fear and desire, in colonial texts. It is precisely this function of the stereotype as phobia and fetish that, according to Fanon, threatens the closure of the racial/epidermal schema for the colonial subject and opens the royal road to colonial fantasy.

Despite Said's limitations, or perhaps because of them, there is a forgotten, underdeveloped passage which, in cutting across the body of the text, articulates the question of power and desire that I now want to take up. It is this:

> Altogether an internally structured archive is built up from the literature that belongs to these experiences. Out of this comes a restricted number of typical encapsulations: the journey, the history, the fable, the stereotype, the polemical confrontation. These are the lenses through which the Orient is experienced, and they shape the language, perception, and form of the encounter between East and West. What gives the immense number of encounters some unity, however, is the vacillation I was speaking about earlier. Something patently foreign and distant acquires, for one reason or another, a status more rather than less familiar. One tends to stop judging things either as completely novel or as completely well-known; a new median category emerges, a category that allows one to see new things, things seen for the first time, as versions of a previously known thing. In essence such a category is not so much a way of receiving new information as it is a method of controlling what seems to be a threat to some established view of things. ... The threat is muted, familiar values impose themselves, and in the end the mind reduces the pressure upon it by accommodating things to itself as either 'original' or 'repetitious'. ... The orient at large, therefore, vacillates between the West's contempt for what is familiar and its shivers of delight in – or fear of – novelty.[9]

What is this other scene of colonial discourse played out around the 'median category'? What is this theory of encapsulation or fixation which moves between the recognition of cultural and racial difference and its disavowal, by affixing the unfamiliar to something established, in a form that is repetitious and vacillates between delight and fear? Is it not analogous to the Freudian fable of fetishism (and disavowal) that circulates within the discourse of colonial power, requiring the articulation of modes of differentiation – sexual and racial – as well as different modes of discourse – psychoanalytic and historical?

The strategic articulation of 'coordinates of knowledge' – racial and sexual – and their inscription in the play of colonial power as modes of differentiation, defence, fixation, hierarchisation, is a way of specifying colonial discourse which would be illuminated by reference to Foucault's post-structuralist concept of the *dispositif* or apparatus. Foucault stresses that the relations of knowledge and power within the apparatus are always a strategic response to *an urgent need* at a given historical moment – much as I suggested at the outset, that the force of colonial discourse as a theoretical and political intervention, was the *need*, in our contemporary moment, to contest singularities of difference and to articulate modes of differentiation. Foucault writes:

> ... the apparatus is essentially of a strategic nature, which means assuming that it is a matter of a certain manipulation of relations of forces, either developing them in a particular direction, blocking them, stabilising them, utilising them, etc. The apparatus is thus always inscribed in a play of power, but it is also always linked to certain coordinates of knowledge which issue from it but, to an equal degree, condition it. This is what the apparatus consists in: strategies of relations of forces supporting and supported by, types of knowledge.[10]

In this spirit I argue for the reading of the stereotype in terms of fetishism. The myth of historical origination – racial purity, cultural priority – produced in relation to the colonial stereotype functions to 'normalise' the multiple beliefs and split subjects that constitute colonial discourse as a consequence of its process of disavowal. The scene of fetishism functions similarly as, at once, a reactivation of the material of original fantasy – the anxiety of castration and sexual difference – as well as a normalisation of that difference and disturbance in terms of the fetish object as the substitute for the mother's penis. Within the apparatus of colonial power, the discourses of sexuality and race relate in a process of *functional overdetermination*, 'because each effect ... enters into resonance or contradiction with the others and thereby calls for a readjustment or a re-working of the heterogeneous elements that surface at various points.'[11]

There is both a structural and functional justification for reading the racial stereotype of colonial discourse in terms of fetishism.[12] My re-reading of Said establishes the *structural* link. Fetishism, as the disavowal of difference, is that repetitious scene around the problem of castration. The recognition of sexual difference – as the pre-condition for the circulation of the chain of absence and presence in the realm of the Symbolic – is disavowed by the fixation on an object that masks that difference and restores an original presence. The *functional* link between the fixation of the fetish and the stereotype (or the stereotype as fetish) is even more relevant. For fetishism is always a 'play' or vacillation between the archaic affirmation of wholeness/similarity – in Freud's terms: 'All men have penises'; in ours 'All men have the same skin/race/ culture' – and the anxiety associated with lack and difference – again, for Freud 'Some do not have penises'; for us 'Some do not have the same skin/race/ culture'. Within discourse, the fetish represents the simultaneous play between metaphor as substitution (masking absence and difference) and metonymy (which contiguously registers the perceived lack). The fetish or stereotype gives access to an 'identity' which is predicated as much on mastery and pleasure as it is on anxiety and defence, for it is a form of multiple and contradictory belief in its recognition of difference and disavowal of it. This conflict of pleasure/unpleasure, mastery/defence, knowledge/disavowal, absence/presence, has a fundamental significance for colonial discourse. For the scene of fetishism is also the scene of the reactivation and repetition of primal fantasy – the subject's desire for a pure origin that is always threatened by its division, for the subject must be gendered to be engendered, to be spoken.

The stereotype, then, as the primary point of subjectification in colonial discourse, for both coloniser and colonised, is the scene of a similar fantasy and defence – the desire for an originality which is again threatened by the differences of race, colour and culture. My contention is splendidly caught in Fanon's title *Black Skin White Masks* where the disavowal of difference turns the colonial subject into a misfit – a grotesque mimicry or 'doubling' that threatens to split the soul and whole, undifferentiated skin of the ego. The stereotype is not a simplification because it is a false representation of a given reality. It is a simplification because it is an arrested, fixated form of representation that, in denying the play of difference (that the negation through the Other permits), constitutes a problem for the *representation* of the subject in significations of psychic and social relations.

When Fanon talks of the positioning of the subject in the stereotyped discourse of colonialism, he gives further credence to my point. The legends, stories, histories and anecdotes of a colonial culture offer the subject a primordial Either/Or.[13] *Either* he is fixed in a consciousness of the body as a solely negating activity *or* as a new kind of man, a new genus. What is denied the colonial subject, both as coloniser and colonised is that form of negation which gives access to the recognition of difference in the Symbolic. It is that possibility of difference and circulation which would liberate the signifier of *skin/culture* from the signifieds of racial typology, the analytics of blood, ideologies of racial and cultural dominance or degeneration. 'Wherever he goes', Fanon despairs, 'The Negro remains a Negro' – his race becomes the ineradicable sign of *negative difference* in colonial discourses. For the stereotype impedes the circulation and articulation of the signifier of 'race' as anything other than its *fixity* as racism. We always already know that blacks are licentious, Asiatics duplicitous. . . .

III

There are two 'primal scenes' in Fanon's *Black Skin, White Masks*: two myths of the origin of the marking of the subject within the racist practices and discourses of a colonial culture. On one occasion a white girl fixes Fanon in a look and word as she turns to identify with her mother. It is a scene which echoes endlessly through his essay *The Fact of Blackness: 'Look*, a Negro . . . Mamma, *see* the Negro! I'm frightened. Frightened. Frightened'. 'What else could it be for me', Fanon concludes, 'but an amputation, an excision, a haemorrhage that spattered my whole body with black blood'.[14] Equally, he stresses the primal moment when the child encounters racial and cultural stereotypes in children's fictions, where white heroes and black demons are proffered as points of ideological and psychical identification. Such dramas are enacted *every day* in colonial societies, says Fanon, employing a theatrical metaphor – the scene – which emphasises the visible – the seen. I want to play on both these senses which refer at once to the site of fantasy and desire and to the sight of subjectification and power.

The drama underlying these dramatic 'everyday' colonial scenes is not difficult to discern. In each of them the subject turns around the pivot of the 'stereotype' to return to a point of total identification. The girl's gaze returns to her mother in the recognition and disavowal of the Negroid type; the black child turns away from himself, his race, in his total identification with the positivity of whiteness which is at once colour and no colour. In the act of disavowal and fixation the colonial subject is returned to the narcissism of the Imaginary and its identification of an ideal ego that is white and whole. For what these primal scenes illustrate is that looking/hearing/reading as sites of subjectification in colonial discourse are evidence of the importance of the visual and auditory imaginary for the *histories* of societies.[15]

It is in this context that I want to allude briefly to the problematic of seeing/ being seen. I suggest that in order to conceive of the colonial subject as the effect of power that is productive – disciplinary and 'pleasurable' – one has to see the *surveillance* of colonial power as functioning in relation to the regime of the *scopic drive*. That is, the drive that represents the pleasure in 'seeing', which has the look as its object of desire, is related both to the myth of origins, the primal scene, and the problematic of fetishism and locates the surveyed object within the 'imaginary' relation. Like voyeurism, surveillance must depend for its effectivity on 'the *active consent* which is its real or mythical correlate (but always real as myth) and establishes in the scopic space the illusion of the object relation'.[16] The ambivalence of this form of 'consent' in objectification – real as mythical – is the *ambivalence* on which the stereotype turns and illustrates that crucial bind of pleasure and power that Foucault asserts but, in my view, fails to explain.

My anatomy of colonial discourse remains incomplete until I locate the stereotype, as an arrested, fetishistic mode of representation within its field of identification, which I have identified in my description of Fanon's primal scenes, as the Lacanian schema of the Imaginary. The Imaginary[17] is the transformation that takes place in the subject at the formative mirror phase, when it assumes a *discrete* image which allows it to postulate a series of equivalences, samenesses, identities, between the objects of the surrounding world. However, this positioning is itself *problematic*, for the subject finds or recognises itself through an image which is simultaneously alienating and hence potentially confrontational. This is the basis of the close relation between the two forms of identification complicit with the Imaginary – narcissism and aggressivity. It is precisely these two forms of 'identification' that constitute the dominant strategy of colonial power exercised in relation to the stereotype which, as a form of multiple and contradictory belief, gives knowledge of difference and simultaneously disavows or masks it. Like the mirror phase 'the fullness' of the stereotype – its image *as* identity – is always threatened by 'lack'.

The construction of colonial discourse is then a complex articulation of the tropes of fetishism – metaphor and metonymy – and the forms of narcissistic and aggressive identification available to the Imaginary. Stereotypical racial discourse is a four-term strategy. There is a tie-up between the metaphoric or masking function of the fetish and the narcissistic object-choice and an opposing alliance between the metonymic figuring of lack and the aggressive phase of the Imaginary. A repertoire of conflictual positions constitute the subject in colonial discourse. The taking up of any one position, within a specific discursive form, in a particular historical conjuncture, is thus always problematic – the site of both fixity and fantasy. It provides a colonial 'identity' that is played out – like all fantasies of originality and origination – in the face and space of the disruption and threat from the heterogeneity of other positions. As a form of splitting and multiple belief, the 'stereotype' requires, for its successful signification, a continual and repetitive chain of other stereotypes. The process by which the metaphoric 'masking' is inscribed on a lack which must then be concealed gives the stereotype both its fixity and its phantasmatic quality – the *same old* stories of the Negro's animality, the Coolie's inscrutability or the stupidity of the Irish *must* be told (compulsively) again and afresh, and are differently gratifying and terrifying each time.

In any specific colonial discourse the metaphoric/narcissistic and the metonymic/aggressive positions will function simultaneously, but always strategically poised in relation to each other; similar to the moment of alienation which stands as a threat to Imaginary plentitude, and 'multiple belief' which threatens fetishistic disavowal. Caught in the Imaginary as they are, these shifting positionalities will never seriously threaten the dominant power relations, for they exist to exercise them pleasurably and productively. They will always pose the problem of difference as that between the pre-constituted, 'natural' poles of Black and White with all its historical and ideological ramifications. The *knowledge of the construction* of that 'opposition' will be denied the colonial subject. He is constructed within an apparatus of power which *contains*, in both senses of the word, an 'other' knowledge – a knowledge that is arrested and fetishistic and circulates through colonial discourse as that limited form of otherness, that fixed form of difference, that I have called the stereotype. Fanon poignantly describes the effects of this process for a colonised culture:

a continued agony rather than a total disappearance of the pre-existing culture. The culture once living and open to the future, becomes closed, fixed in the colonial status, caught in the yolk of oppression. Both present and mummified, it testifies against its members. ... The cultural mummification leads to a mummification of individual thinking. ... As though it were possible for a man to evolve otherwise than within the framework of a culture that recognises him and that he decides to assume.[18]

My four-term strategy of the stereotype tries tentatively to provide a structure and a process for the 'subject' of a colonial discourse. I now want to take up the problem of discrimination as the political effect of such a discourse and relate it to the question of 'race' and 'skin'. To that end it is important to remember that the multiple belief that accompanies fetishism does not only have disavowal value; it also has 'knowledge value' and it is this that I shall now pursue. In calculating this knowledge value it is crucial to consider what Fanon means when he says that:

> There is a quest for the Negro, the Negro is a demand, one cannot get along without him, he is needed, but only if he is made palatable in a certain way. Unfortunately the Negro knocks down the system and breaks the treaties.[19]

To understand this demand and how the native or Negro is made 'palatable' we must acknowledge some significant differences between the general theory of fetishism and its specific uses for an understanding of racist discourse. First, the fetish of colonial discourse – what Fanon calls the epidermal schema – is not, like the sexual fetish, a secret. Skin, as the key signifier of cultural and racial difference in the stereotype, is the most visible of fetishes, recognised as 'common knowledge' in a range of cultural, political, historical discourses, and plays a public part in the racial drama that is enacted every day in colonial societies. Secondly, it may be said that sexual fetish is closely linked to the 'good object'; it is the prop that makes the whole object desirable and lovable, facilitates sexual relations and can even promote a form of happiness. The stereotype can also be seen as that particular 'fixated' form of the colonial subject which *facilitates* colonial relations, and sets up a discursive form of racial and cultural opposition in terms of which colonial power is exercised. If it is claimed that the colonised are most often objects of hate, then we can reply with Freud that

> affection and hostility in the treatment of the fetish – which run parallel with the disavowal and acknowledgement of castration – are mixed in unequal proportions in different cases, so that the one or the other is more clearly recognisable.[20]

What this statement recognises is the wide *range* of the stereotype, from the loyal servant to Satan, from the loved to the hated; a shifting of subject positions in the circulation of colonial power which I tried to account for through the motility of the metaphoric/narcissistic and metonymic/aggressive system of colonial discourse. What remains to be examined, however, is the construction of the signifier of 'skin/race' in those regimes of visibility and discursivity – fetishistic, scopic, imaginary – within which I have located the stereotypes. It is only on that basis that we can construct its 'knowledge – value' which will, I hope, enable us to see the place of fantasy in the exercise of colonial power.

My argument relies upon a particular reading of the problematic of representation which, Fanon suggests, is specific to the colonial situation. He writes:

> the originality of the colonial context is that the economic substructure is also a superstructure ... you are rich because you are white, you are white because you are

rich. This is why Marxist analysis should always be slightly stretched every time we have to do with the colonial problem.[21]

Fanon could either be seen to be adhering to a simple reflectionist or determinist notion of cultural/social signification or, more interestingly, he could be read as taking an 'anti-repressionist' position (attacking the notion that ideology as miscognition, or misrepresentation, is the repression of the real). For our purposes I tend towards the latter reading which then provides a 'visibility' to the exercise of power; gives force to the argument that skin, as a signifier of discrimination, must be produced or processed as visible. As Abbot says, in a very different context,

> whereas repression banishes its object into the unconscious, forgets and attempts to forget the forgetting, discrimination must constantly invite its representations into consciousness, re-inforcing the crucial recognition of difference which they embody and revitalising them for the perception on which its effectivity depends. . . . It must sustain itself on the presence of the very difference which is also its object.[22]

What 'authorises' discrimination, Abbot continues, is the occlusion of the preconstruction or working-up of difference:

> this repression of production entails that the recognition of difference is procured in an innocence, as a 'nature'; recognition is contrived as primary cognition, spontaneous effect of the 'evidence of the visible'.[23]

This is precisely the kind of recognition, as spontaneous and visible, that is attributed to the stereotype. The difference of the object of discrimination is at once visible and natural – colour as the cultural/political *sign* of inferiority or degeneracy, skin as its natural '*identity*'. However, Abbot's account stops at the point of 'identification' and strangely colludes with the *success* of discriminatory practices by suggesting that their representations require the repression of the working-up of difference; to argue otherwise, according to him, would be to put the subject in

> an impossible awareness, since it would run into consciousness the heterogeneity of the subject as a place of articulation.[24]

Despite his awareness of the crucial recognition of difference for discrimination and its problematisation of repression, Abbot is trapped in his unitary place of articulation. He comes close to suggesting that it is possible, however momentarily and illusorily, for the *perpetrator* of the discriminatory discourse to be in a position that is *unmarked by the discourse* to the extent to which the *object* of discrimination is deemed natural and visible. What Abbot neglects is the facilitating role of contradiction and heterogeneity in the construction of authoritarian practices and their strategic, discursive fixations.

Although the 'authority' of colonial discourse depends crucially on its location in narcissism and the Imaginary, my concept of stereotype-as-suture is a recognition of the *ambivalence* of that authority and those orders of identification. The role of fetishistic identification, in the construction of discriminatory knowledges that depend on the 'presence of difference', is to provide a process of splitting and multiple/contradictory belief at the point of enunciation and subjectification. It is this crucial splitting of the ego which is represented in Fanon's description of the construction of the colonial subject as effect of stereotypical discourse: the subject primordially fixed and yet triply split between the incongruent knowledges of body, race, ancestors. Assailed by the stereotype,

> the corporeal schema crumbled, its place taken by a racial epidermal scheme. . . . It was no longer a question of being aware of my body in the third person but a triple person. . . . I was not given one, but two, three places.[25]

This process is best understood in terms of the articulation of multiple belief that Freud proposes in the essay on fetishism. It is a non-repressive form of knowledge that allows for the possibility of simultaneously embracing two contradictory beliefs, one official and one secret, one archaic and one progressive, one that allows the myth of origins, the other that articulates difference and division. Its knowledge 'value' lies in its orientation as a defence towards external reality, and provides, in Metz's words,

> the lasting matrix, the effective prototype of all those splittings of belief which man will henceforth be capable of in the most varied domains, of all the infinitely complex unconscious and occasionally conscious interactions which he will allow himself between believing and not-believing. . . .[26]

It is through this notion of splitting and multiple belief that, I believe, it becomes easier to see the bind of knowledge and fantasy, power and pleasure, that informs the particular regime of visibility deployed in colonial discourse. The visibility of the racial/colonial other is at once a point of identity ('Look, a Negro') and at the same time a *problem* for the attempted closure within discourse. For the recognition of difference as 'imaginary' points of identity and origin – such as Black and White – is disturbed by the representation of splitting in the discourse. What I called the play between the metaphoric-narcissistic and metonymic-aggressive moments in colonial discourse – that four-part strategy of the stereotype – crucially recognises the prefiguring of desire as a potentially conflictual, disturbing force in all those regimes of 'originality' that I have brought together. In the objectification of the scopic drive there is always the threatened return of the look; in the identification of the Imaginary relation there is always the alienating other (or mirror) which crucially returns its image to the subject; and in that form of substitution and fixation that is fetishism there is always the trace of loss, absence. To put it succinctly, the recognition and disavowal of 'difference' is always disturbed by the question of its representation or construction. The stereotype is in fact an 'impossible' object. For that very reason, the exertions of the 'official knowledges' of colonialism – pseudo-scientific, typological, legal-administrative, eugenicist – are imbricated at the point of their production of meaning and power with the fantasy that dramatises the impossible desire for a pure, undifferentiated origin. Not itself the object of desire but its setting, not an ascription of prior identities but their production in the syntax of the scenario of racist discourse, colonial fantasy plays a crucial part in those everyday scenes of subjectification in a colonial society which Fanon refers to repeatedly. Like fantasies of the origins of sexuality, the productions of 'colonial desire' mark the discourse as

> a favoured spot for the most primitive defensive reactions such as turning against oneself, into an opposite, projection, negation ... [27]

The problem of origin as the problematic of racist, stereotypical knowledge is a complex one and what I have said about its construction will come clear in this illustration from Fanon. Stereotyping is not the setting up of a false image which becomes the scapegoat of discriminatory practices. It is a much more ambivalent text of projection and introjection, metaphoric and metonymic strategies, displacement, overdetermination, guilt, aggressivity; the masking and splitting of 'official' and phantasmatic knowledges to construct the positionalities and oppositionalities of racist discourse:

> My body was given back to me sprawled out, distorted, recoloured, clad in mourning in that white winter day. The Negro is an animal, the Negro is bad, the Negro is mean, the Negro is ugly; look, a nigger, it's cold, the nigger is shivering, the nigger is shivering because he is cold, the little boy is trembling because he is afraid of the nigger, the nigger is shivering with cold, that cold that goes through your bones, the handsome little boy is trembling because he thinks that the nigger is quivering with rage, the little white boy throws himself into his mother's arms: Mama, the nigger's going to eat me up. [28]

It is the scenario of colonial fantasy which, in staging the ambivalence of desire, articulates the demand for the Negro which the Negro disrupts. For the stereotype is at once a substitute and a shadow. By acceding to the wildest fantasies (in the popular sense) of the coloniser, the stereotyped other reveals something of the 'fantasy' (as desire, defence) of that position of mastery. For if 'skin' in racist discourse is the visibility of darkness, and a prime signifier of the body and its social and cultural correlates, then we are bound to remember what Karl Abrahams[29] says in his seminal work on the scopic drive. The pleasure-value of darkness is a withdrawal in order to know nothing of the external world. Its symbolic meaning, however, is thoroughly ambivalent. Darkness signifies at once both birth and death; it is in all cases a desire to return to the fullness of the mother, a desire for an unbroken and undifferentiated line of vision and origin.

But surely there is another scene of colonial discourse in which the native or Negro meets the demand of colonial discourse; where the subverting 'split' is recuperable within a strategy of social and political control. It is recognisably true that the chain of stereotypical signification is curiously mixed and split, polymorphous and perverse, an articulation of multiple belief. The black is both savage (cannibal) and yet the most obedient and dignified of servants (the bearer of food); he is the embodiment of rampant sexuality and yet innocent as a child; he is mystical, primitive, simple-minded and yet the most worldly and accomplished liar, and manipulator of social forces. In each case what is being dramatised is a separation – *between* races, cultures, histories, *within* histories – a separation between *before* and *after* that repeats obsessively the mythical moment of disjunction. Despite the structural similarities with the play of need and desire in primal fantasies, the colonial fantasy does not try to cover up that moment of separation. It is more ambivalent. On the one hand, it proposes a teleology – under certain conditions of colonial domination and control the native is progressively reformable. On the other, however, it effectively displays the 'separation', makes it more visible. It is the visibility of this separation which, in denying the colonised the capacities of self-government, independence, western modes of civility, lends authority to the official version and mission of colonial power. Colonial fantasy is the continual dramatisation of emergence – of difference, freedom – as the beginning of a history which is repetitively denied. Such a denial is the clearly voiced demand of colonial discourse as the legitimation of a form of rule that is facilitated by the racist fetish. In concluding, I would like to develop a little further my working definition of colonial discourse given at the start of this article.

Racist stereotypical discourse, in its colonial moment, inscribes a form of governmentality that is informed by a productive splitting in its constitution of knowledge and exercise of power. Some of its practices recognise the difference of race, culture, history as elaborated by stereotypical knowledges, racial theories, administrative colonial experience, and on that basis institutionalise a range of political and cultural ideologies that are prejudicial, discriminatory, vestigial, archaic, 'mythical', and, crucially, are recognised as being so. By 'knowing' the native population in these terms, discriminatory and authoritarian forms of political control are considered appropriate. The colonised population is then deemed to be both the cause and effect of the system, imprisoned in the circle of interpretation. What is visible is the *necessity* of such rule which is justified by those moralistic and normative ideologies of amelioration recognised as the Civilising Mission or the White Man's Burden. However, there co-exist within the same apparatus of colonial power, modern systems and sciences of government, progressive 'Western' forms of social and economic organisation which provide the manifest justification for the project of colonialism – an argument which, in part, impressed Karl Marx. It is on the site of this co-existence that strategies of hierarchisation and marginalisation are employed in the management of colonial societies. And if my deduction from Fanon about the peculiar visibility of colonial power is acceptable to you, then I would extend that to say that it is a form of governmentality in which the 'ideological' space functions in more openly collaborative ways with political and economic exigencies. The barracks stand by the church which stands by the schoolroom; the cantonment stands hard by the 'civil lines'. Such visibility of the institutions and apparatuses of power is possible because the exercise of colonial power makes their *relationship* obscure, produces them as fetishes, spectacles of a 'natural'/racial pre-eminence. Only the seat of government is always elsewhere – alien and separate by that distance upon which surveillance depends for its strategies of objectification, normalisation and discipline.

The last word belongs to Fanon:

> ... this behaviour [of the coloniser] betrays a determination to objectify, to confine, to imprison, to harden. Phrases such as 'I know them', 'that's the way they are', show

this maximum objectification successfully achieved. ... There is on the one hand a culture in which qualities of dynamism, of growth, of depth can be recognised. As against this, [in colonial cultures] we find characteristics, curiosities, things, never a structure.[30]

Notes

1 There are two major problems with this account which emphasise the tentative and introductory nature of the essay. First, despite the subject's problematic accession to sexual difference which is crucial to my argument, the body in this text is male. Realising that the question of woman's relation to castration and access to the symbolic requires a very specific form of attention and articulation, I chose to be cautious till I had worked out its implications for colonial discourse. Secondly, the representation of class difference in the construction of the colonial subject is not specified adequately. Wanting to avoid any form of class determinism 'in the last instance' it becomes difficult, if crucial, to calculate its effectivity. I hope to face both these issues more fully in the book that I am working on at present: *Power and Spectacle: Colonial Discourse and the English Novel*, to be published by Methuen.

2 Stephan Feuchtwang, 'Socialist, Feminist and Anti-racist Struggles', *m/f* 4 (1980), p. 41.

3 Stephen Heath, 'Film and System, Terms of Analysis', Part II, *Screen* 16.2 (Summer 1975), p. 93.

4 For instance, having decentred the sign, Barthes finds Japan immediately insightful and visible and extends the empire of empty signs universally. Japan can only be the Anti-West: 'in the ideal Japanese house, devoid or nearly so of furniture, there is no place which in any way designates property; no seat, no bed, no table provides a point from which the body may constitute itself as subject (or master) of a space. The very concept of centre is rejected (burning frustration for Western man everywhere provided with his armchair and his bed, the owner of a domestic position).' Roland Barthes, *L'Empire des Signes*, translated by Noël Burch, *To the Distant Observer* (London: Scolar Press, 1979), pp. 13–14. For a reading of Kristeva relevant to my argument, see Gayatri Spivak, 'French Feminism in an International Frame', *Yale French Studies* 62 (1981), pp. 154–84.

5 This concept is discussed below.

6 Edward Said, *Orientalism* (London: Routledge & Kegan Paul, 1978), p. 72.

7 Said, *Orientalism*, p. 206.

8 Said, *Orientalism*, p. 273.

9 Said, *Orientalism*, pp. 58–9.

10 Michel Foucault, 'The Confession of the Flesh', in *Power/Knowledge*, (London: Harvester, 1980), p. 196.

11 Foucault, 'The Confession of the Flesh', p. 195.

12 See Sigmund Freud, 'Fetishism' [1927] in *On Sexuality*, vol. 7 (Harmondsworth: Pelican Freud Library, 1981), p. 345 ff; Christian Metz, *Psychoanalysis and Cinema: the Imaginary Signifier* (London: Macmillan, 1982), pp. 67–78. See also Steve Neale, 'The Same Old Story: Stereotypes and Differences', *Screen Education* 32/33 (Autumn/Winter 1979/80), pp. 33–7.

13 Frantz Fanon, *Black Skin, White Masks* (London: Paladin, 1970), see pp. 78–82.

14 Fanon, *Black Skin, White Masks*, p. 79.

15 Christian Metz, *Psychoanalysis*, pp. 59–60.

16 Metz, *Psychoanalysis*, pp. 62–3.

17 For the best account of Lacan's concept of the Imaginary see Jacqueline Rose, 'The Imaginary' in Colin MacCabe, ed., *The Talking Cure* (London: Macmillan, 1981).
18 Frantz Fanon, 'Racism and Culture', *Toward the African Revolution* (London: Pelican, 1970), p. 44.
19 Frantz Fanon, *Black Skin, White Masks*, p. 114.
20 Sigmund Freud, 'Fetishism', p. 357.
21 Frantz Fanon, *The Wretched of the Earth* (London: Penguin, 1969).
22 Paul Abbott, 'Authority', *Screen* 20.2 (Summer 1979), pp. 15–16.
23 Abbott, 'Authority', p. 16.
24 Abbott, 'Authority', p. 16.
25 Frantz Fanon, *Black Skin, White Masks*, p. 79.
26 Christian Metz, *Psychoanalysis*, p. 70.
27 J. Laplanche and J. B. Pontalis, 'Phantasy (or Fantasy)', *The Language of Psychoanalysis* (London: Hogarth, 1980), p. 318.
28 Frantz Fanon, *Black Skins, White Masks*, p. 80.
29 See Karl Abraham, 'Transformations of Scopophilia', *Selected Papers* (London: Hogarth, 1978).
30 Frantz Fanon, 'Racism and Culture', p. 44.

This article is a revision of a paper given at the Sociology of Literature Conference, Essex University, 1982 and published in Francis Barker, ed., *The Politics of Theory* (Colchester, 1983). I would like to thank Dr Stephan Feuchtwang of the City University for providing the critical and companionable context in which it was written, and Terry Eagleton for inviting me to speak on the subject at Oxford University and for his comments afterwards.

3

Kwame Anthony Appiah

Is the Post- in Postmodernism the Post- in Postcolonial? *

Tu t'appelais Bimbircokak
Et tout était bien ainsi
Tu es devenu Victor-Emile-Louis-Henri-Joseph
Ce qui
Autant qu'il m'en souvienne
Ne rappelle point ta parenté avec
Roqueffelère
            YAMBO OUOLOGUEM, 'A Mon Mari'

In 1987, the Center for African Art in New York organized a show entitled 'Perspectives: Angles on African Art.' The curator, Susan Vogel, had worked with a number of 'cocurators,' whom I list in order of their appearance in the table of contents of the exhibition catalogue: Ekpo Eyo, quondam director of the department of antiquities of the National Museum of Nigeria; William Rubin, director of the department of painting and sculpture at the Museum of Modern Art and organizer of its controversial exhibit, 'Primitivism and Twentieth-Century Art'; Romare Bearden, African-American painter; Ivan Karp, curator of African ethnology at the Smithsonian; Nancy Graves, European-American painter, sculptor, and filmmaker; James Baldwin, who surely needs no qualifying glosses; David Rockefeller, art collector and friend of the mighty; Lela Kouakou, Baule artist and diviner from the Ivory Coast (this a delicious juxtaposition, richest and poorest, side by side); Iba N'Diaye, Senegalese sculptor; and Robert Farris Thompson, Yale professor and African and African-American art historian.[1] In her introductory essay, Vogel describes the process of selection used to pick artworks for the show. The one woman and nine men were each offered a hundred-odd photographs of 'African art as varied in type and origin, and as high in quality, as we could manage' and asked to select ten for the show. Or, I should say more exactly, this is what was offered to eight of the men. For Vogel adds that 'in the case of the Baule artist, a man familiar only with the art of his own people, only Baule objects were placed in the pool of photographs' (*P*, p. 11). At this point we are directed to a footnote to the essay, which reads:

* From *Critical Inquiry* 17 (Winter 1991), pp. 336–57.

Showing him the same assortment of photos the others saw would have been interesting, but confusing in terms of the reactions we sought here. Field aesthetics studies, my own and others, have shown that African informants will criticize sculptures from other ethnic groups in terms of their own traditional criteria, often assuming that such works are simply inept carvings of their own aesthetic tradition (*P*, p. 17 n. 2).

I shall return to this irresistible footnote in a moment. But let me pause to quote further, this time from the words of David Rockefeller, who would surely never 'criticize sculptures from other ethnic groups in terms of [his] own traditional criteria,' discussing what the catalogue calls a 'Fanti female figure':

I own somewhat similar things to this, and I have always liked them. This is a rather more sophisticated version than the ones that I've seen, and I thought it was quite beautiful. . . . the total composition has a very contemporary, very Western look to it. It's the kind of thing, I think, that goes very well with . . . contemporary Western things. It would look very good in a modern apartment or house (*P*, p. 138).

We may suppose that Rockefeller was delighted to discover that his final judgment was consistent with the intentions of the sculpture's creators. For a footnote to the earlier checklist – the list of artworks ultimately chosen for the show – reveals that the Baltimore Museum of Art desires to 'make public the fact that the authenticity of the Fante figure in its collection has been challenged.' Indeed, work by Doran Ross suggests this object is almost certainly a modern piece produced in my hometown of Kumasi by the workshop of a certain Francis Akwasi, which 'specializes in carvings for the international market in the style of traditional sculpture. Many of its works are now in museums throughout the West, and were published as authentic by Cole and Ross' (yes, the same Doran Ross) in their classic catalogue, *The Arts of Ghana* (*P*, p. 29).

But then it is hard to be *sure* what would please a man who gives as his reason for picking another piece, this time a Senufo helmet mask, 'I have to say that I picked this because I own it. It was given to me by President Houphouet Boigny of the Ivory Coast' (*P*, p. 143); or who remarks 'concerning the market in African art':

the best pieces are going for very high prices. Generally speaking, the less good pieces in terms of quality are not going up in price. And that's a fine reason for picking the good ones rather than the bad. They have a way of becoming more valuable.

I look at African art as objects I find would be appealing to use in a home or an office. . . . I don't think it goes with everything, necessarily – although the very best perhaps does. But I think it goes well with contemporary architecture (*P*, p. 131).

There is something breathtakingly unpretentious in Rockefeller's easy movement between considerations of finance, aesthetics, and decor. In these responses, we have surely a microcosm of the site of the African in contemporary – which is, then, surely to say, postmodern – America.

I have quoted so much from Rockefeller not to emphasize the familiar fact that questions of what we call 'aesthetic' value are crucially bound up with market value, nor even to draw attention to the fact that this is known by those who play the art market. Rather I want to keep clearly before us the fact that David Rockefeller is permitted to say *anything at all* about the arts of Africa because he is a *buyer* and because he is at the *center*, while Lela Kouakou, who merely makes art and who dwells at the margins, is a poor African whose words count only as parts of the commodification[2] – both for those of us who constitute the museum public and for collectors, like Rockefeller – of Baule art.[3] I want to remind you, in short, of how important it is that African art is a *commodity*.

But the cocurator whose choice will set us on our way is James Baldwin, the only cocurator who picked a piece that was not in the mold of the Africa of 'Primitivism.' The sculpture that will be my touchstone is a Yoruba piece that carries the museum label, *Man with a Bicycle*. Here is some of what Baldwin said about it:

> This is something. This has got to be contemporary. He's really going to town! It's very jaunty, very authoritative. His errand might prove to be impossible. ... He is challenging something – or something has challenged him. He's grounded in immediate reality by the bicycle.... He's apparently a very proud and silent man. He's dressed sort of polyglot. Nothing looks like it fits him too well (*P*, p. 125).

Baldwin's reading of this piece is, of course and inevitably, 'in terms of [his] own ... criteria,' a reaction contextualized only by the knowledge that bicycles are new in Africa and that this piece, anyway, does not look anything like the works he recalls seeing from his earliest childhood at the Schomburg Museum in Harlem. His response torpedoes Vogel's argument for her notion that the only 'authentically traditional' African – the only one whose responses, as she says, could have been found a century ago – must be refused a choice among Africa's art cultures because he – unlike the rest of the cocurators, who are Americans and the European-educated Africans – will use his 'own ... criteria.' The message is that this Baule diviner, this authentically African villager, does not know what *we*, authentic postmodernists, now know: that the first and last mistake is to judge the Other on one's own terms. And so, in the name of this relativist insight, we impose our judgment: that Lela Kouakou may not judge sculpture from beyond the Baule culture zone, because he, like all the other African 'informants' we have met in the field, will read them as if they were meant to meet those Baule standards.

Worse than this, it is nonsense to explain Kouakou's responses as deriving from an ignorance of other traditions – if indeed he is, as he no doubt is supposed to be, like most 'traditional' artists today, if he is, for example, like Francis Akwasi of Kumasi. Kouakou may judge other artists by his own standards (what on earth else could he, could anyone, do save make no judgment at all?), but to suppose that he is unaware that there are other standards within Africa (let alone without) is to ignore a piece of absolutely basic cultural knowledge, common to most precolonial as well as to most colonial and postcolonial cultures on the continent: the piece of cultural knowledge that explains why the people we now call 'Baule' exist at all. To be Baule, for example, is, for a Baule, not to be a white person, not to be Senufo, not to be French.[4]

But Baldwin's *Man with a Bicycle* does more than give the lie to Vogel's strange footnote; it provides us with an image that can serve as a point of entry to my theme, a piece of contemporary African art that will allow us to explore the articulation of the postcolonial and the postmodern. *Man with a Bicycle* is described as follows in the exhibition catalogue:

> Man with a Bicycle
> Yoruba, Nigeria 20th century
> Wood and paint H. 35 ¾ in.
> The Newark Museum
>
> The influence of the Western world is revealed in the clothes and bicycle of this neo-traditional Yoruba sculpture which probably represents a merchant en route to market (*P*, p. 23).

It is this word *neotraditional* – a word that is almost right – that provides, I think, the fundamental clue.

But I do not know how to explain this clue without first saying how I keep my bearings in the shark-infested waters around the semantic island of the postmodern. The task of chasing the word *postmodernism* through the pages of Jean-François Lyotard and Fredric Jameson and Jürgen Habermas, in and out of the *Village Voice* and the *TLS* and even the *New York Times Book Review* is certainly exhausting. Yet there *is*, I think, a story to tell about all these stories – or, of course, I should say, there are many, but this, for the moment, is mine – and, as I tell it, the Yoruba bicyclist will eventually come back into view.

I do not (this will come as no surprise) have a definition of the postmodern to put in the place of Jameson's or Lyotard's, but there is now a rough consensus about the structure of the modern/postmodern dichotomy in the many domains – from architecture to poetry to philosophy to rock music to the movies – in which it has been invoked. In each of these domains there is an antecedent practice that laid claim to a certain exclusivity of insight, and in each of them 'postmodernism' is a name for the rejection of that claim to exclusivity, a rejection that is almost always more playful, though not necessarily less serious, than the practice it aims to replace. That this will not do as a *definition* of postmodernism follows from the fact that in each domain this rejection of exclusivity assumes a particular shape, one that reflects the specificities of its setting. To understand the various postmodernisms this way is to leave open the question of how their theories of contemporary social, cultural, and economic life relate to the actual practices that constitute that life – to leave open, then, the relations between postmodern*ism* and postmodern*ity*.[5]

It is an important question *why* this distancing of the ancestors should have become so central a feature of our cultural lives. The answer surely has to do with the sense in which art is increasingly commodified. To sell oneself and one's products as art in the marketplace, one must, above all, clear a space in which one is distinguished from other producers and products – and one does this by the construction and the marking of differences. To create a market for bottled waters, for example, it was necessary, first, to establish that subtle (even untastable) differences in mineral content and source of carbonation were essential modes of distinction.

It is this need for distinctions in the market that accounts for a certain intensification of the long-standing individualism of post-Renaissance art production: in the age of mechanical reproduction, aesthetic individualism, the characterization of the artwork as belonging to the oeuvre of an individual, and the absorption of the artist's life into the conception of the work can be seen precisely as modes of identifying objects for the market. The sculptor of the man with a bicycle, by contrast, will not be known by those who buy this object; his individual life will make no difference to the future history of his sculpture. (Indeed, he surely knows this, in the sense in which one knows anything whose negation one has never even considered.) Nevertheless, there is *some*thing about the object that serves to establish it for the market: the availability of Yoruba culture and of stories about Yoruba culture to surround the object and distinguish it from 'folk art' from elsewhere.

Postmodern culture is the culture in which all postmodernisms operate, sometimes in synergy, sometimes in competition; and because contemporary culture is, in a certain sense to which I shall return, transnational, postmodern culture is global – though that emphatically does not mean that it is the culture of every person in the world.

If postmodernism is the project of transcending some species of modernism, which is to say some relatively self-conscious, self-privileging project of a privileged modernity, our *neotraditional* sculptor of *Man with a Bicycle* is presumably to be understood, by contrast, as premodern, that is, traditional. (I am supposing, then, that being neotraditional is a way of being traditional; what work the *neo-* does is matter for a later moment.) And the sociological and anthropological narratives of tradition through which he or she came to be so theorized is dominated, of course, by Max Weber.

Weber's characterization of traditional (and charismatic) authority *in opposition* to rational authority is in keeping with his general characterization of modernity as the rationalization of the world; and he insisted on the significance of this characteristically Western process for the rest of humankind:

> A product of modern European civilization, studying any problem of universal history, is bound to ask himself to what combination of circumstances the fact should be attributed that in Western civilization, and in Western civilization only, cultural phenomena have appeared which (as we like to think) lie in a line of development having *universal* significance and value.[6]

Now there is certainly no doubt that Western modernity now has a universal *geographical* significance. The Yoruba bicyclist – like Sting and his Amerindian chieftains of the Amazon rain forest or Paul Simon and the Mbaqanga musicians of *Graceland* – is testimony to that. But, if I may borrow someone else's borrowing, the fact is that the Empire of Signs strikes back. Weber's 'as we like to think' reflects his doubts about whether the Western *imperium* over the world was as clearly of universal *value* as it was certainly of universal *significance*; and postmodernism fully endorses his resistance to this claim. The man with a bicycle enters our museums to be valued by us (Rockefeller tells us *how* it is to be valued), but just as the *presence* of the object reminds us of this fact, its *content* reminds us that the trade is two-way.

I want to argue that to understand our – our human – modernity, we must first understand why the rationalization of the world can no longer be seen as the tendency either of the West or of history, why, simply put, the modernist characterization of modernity must be challenged. To understand our world is to reject Weber's claim for the rationality of what he called rationalization and his projection of its inevitability; it is, then, to have a radically post-Weberian conception of modernity.

T. S. Eliot abhors the soullessness and the secularization of modern society, the reach of Enlightenment rationalism into the whole world. He shares Weber's account of modernity and more straightforwardly deplores it. Le Corbusier favors rationalization – a house is a 'machine for living in' – but he, too, shares Weber's vision of modernity. And, of course, the great rationalists – the believers in a transhistorical reason triumphing in the world – from Kant on, are the source of Weber's Kantian vision. Modernism in literature, architecture, and philosophy – the account of modernity that, on my model, *post* modernism in these domains seeks to subvert – may be for reason or against it, but in each domain rationalization, the pervasion of reason, is seen as the distinctive dynamic of contemporary history.

But the beginning of postmodern wisdom is to ask whether Weberian rationalization is in fact what has occurred historically. For Weber, charismatic authority – the authority of Stalin, Hitler, Mao, Che Guevara, Kwame Nkrumah – is antirational, yet modernity has been dominated by just such charisma. Secularization hardly seems to be proceeding: religions grow in all parts of the world; more than ninety per cent of North Americans still avow some sort of theism; what we call 'fundamentalism' is as alive in the West as it is in Africa and the Middle and Far Easts; Jimmy Swaggart and Billy Graham have business in Louisiana and California as well as in Costa Rica and Ghana.

What we can see in all these cases, I think, is not the triumph of Enlightenment Reason – which would have entailed exactly the end of charisma and the universalization of the secular – not even the penetration of a narrower instrumental reason into all spheres of life, but what Weber mistook for that: namely, the incorporation of all areas of the world and all areas of even formerly 'private' life into the money economy. Even in domains like religion where instrumental reason would recognize that the market has at best an ambiguous place, modernity has turned every element of the real into a sign, and the sign reads 'for sale.'

If Weberian talk of the triumph of instrumental reason can now be seen to be a mistake, the disenchantment of the world, that is, the penetration of a scientific vision of things, describes at most the tiny – and in the United States quite marginal – world of the higher academy and a few islands of its influence. What we have seen in recent times in the United States is not secularization – the end of religions – but their commodification; and with that commodification religions have reached further and grown – their markets have expanded – rather than died.

Postmodernism can be seen, then, as a retheorization of the proliferation of distinctions that reflects the underlying dynamic of cultural modernity, the need to clear oneself a space. Modernism saw the economization of the world as the triumph of reason; postmodernism rejects that claim, allowing in the realm of theory the same proliferation of distinctions that modernity had begun.

That, then, is how I believe the issue looks from here. But how does it look from the postcolonial spaces inhabited by *Man with a Bicycle*?

I shall speak about Africa, with confidence both that some of what I have to say will work elsewhere in the so-called Third World and that it will not work at all in some places. And I shall speak first about the producers of these so-called neotraditional artworks and then about the case of the African novel, because I believe that to focus exclusively on the novel (as theorists of contemporary African cultures have been inclined to do) is to distort the cultural situation and the significance of postcoloniality within it.

I do not know when *Man with a Bicycle* was made or by whom; African art has, until recently, been collected as the property of 'ethnic' groups, not of individuals and workshops, so it is not unusual that not one of the pieces in the 'Perspectives' show was identified in the checklist by the name of an individual artist, even though many of them are twentieth-century works. (And no one will be surprised, by contrast, that most of them *are* kindly labeled with the names of the people who own the largely private collections where they now live.) As a result I cannot say if the piece is literally postcolonial, produced after Nigerian independence in 1960. But the piece belongs to a genre that has certainly been produced since then: the genre that is here called *neotraditional*. Simply put, what is distinctive about this genre is that it is produced for the West.

I should qualify. Of course, many of the buyers of first instance live in Africa; many of them are juridically citizens of African states. But African bourgeois consumers of neotraditional art are educated in the Western style, and, if they want African art, they would often rather have a 'genuinely' traditional piece, by which I mean a piece that they believe to be made precolonially, or at least in a style and by methods that were already established precolonially. These buyers are a minority. Most of this art – *traditional* because it uses actual or supposed precolonial techniques but *neo-* (this, for what it is worth, is the explanation I promised earlier) because it has elements that are recognizably colonial or postcolonial in reference – has been made for Western tourists and other collectors.

The incorporation of these works in the West's museum culture and its art market has almost nothing, of course, to do with postmodernism. By and large, the ideology through which they are incorporated is modernist: it is the ideology that brought something called 'Bali' to Antonin Artaud, something called 'Africa' to Pablo Picasso, and something called 'Japan' to Roland Barthes. (This incorporation as an official Other was criticized, of course, from its beginnings: hence Oscar Wilde's observation that 'the whole of Japan is a pure invention. There is no such country, there are no such people.'[7]) What *is* postmodernist is Vogel's muddled conviction that African art should not be judged 'in terms of [someone else's] traditional criteria.' For modernism, primitive art was to be judged by putatively *universal* aesthetic criteria, and by these standards it was finally found possible to value it. The sculptors and painters who found it possible were largely seeking an Archimedean point outside their own cultures for a critique of a Weberian modernity. For *post*modernisms, by contrast, these works, however they are to be understood, cannot be seen as legitimated by culture- and history-transcending standards.

The *neotraditional* object is useful as a model, despite its marginality in most African lives, because its incorporation in the museum world (as opposed to the many objects made by the same hands that live peacefully in nonbourgeois homes: stools, for example) reminds one that in Africa, by contrast, the distinction between high culture and mass culture, in so far as if it makes sense at all, corresponds, by and large, to the distinction between those with and those without Western-style formal education as cultural consumers.

The fact that the distinction is to be made this way – in most of sub-Saharan Africa, excluding the Republic of South Africa – means that the opposition between high culture and mass culture is available only in domains where there is a significant body of Western formal training. This excludes (in most places) the plastic arts and music. There are distinctions of genre and audience in African music, and for various cultural purposes there is something we call 'traditional' music that we still practice and value; but village and urban dwellers alike, bourgeois and nonbourgeois, listen, through discs and, more important, on the radio, to reggae, to Michael Jackson, and to King Sonny Adé.

And this means that, by and large, the domain in which such a distinction makes the most sense is the one domain where that distinction is powerful and pervasive: namely, in African writing in Western languages. So that it is here that we find, I think, a place for consideration of the question of the *post*coloniality of contemporary African culture.

Postcoloniality is the condition of what we might ungenerously call a *comprador* intelligentsia: a relatively small, Western-style, Western-trained group of writers and thinkers, who mediate the trade in cultural commodities of world capitalism at the periphery. In the West they are known through the Africa they offer; their compatriots know them both through the West they present to Africa and through an Africa they have invented for the world, for each other, and for Africa.

All aspects of contemporary African cultural life – including music and some sculpture and painting, even some writings with which the West is largely not familiar – have been influenced, often powerfully, by the transition of African societies *through* colonialism, but they are not all in the relevant sense *post*colonial. For the *post-* in postcolonial, like the *post-* in postmodern, is the *post-* of the space-clearing gesture I characterized earlier, and many areas of contemporary African cultural life – what has come to be theorized as popular culture, in particular – are not in this way concerned with transcending, with going beyond, coloniality. Indeed, it might be said to be a mark of popular culture that its borrowings from international cultural forms are remarkably insensitive to, not so much dismissive of as blind to, the issue of neocolonialism or 'cultural imperialism.' This does not mean that theories of postmodernism are irrelevant to these forms of culture, for the internationalization of the market and the commodification of artworks are both central to them. But it *does* mean that these artworks are not understood by their producers or their consumers in terms of a postmodern*ism*: there is no antecedent practice whose claim to exclusivity of vision is rejected through these artworks. What is called 'syncretism' here is a consequence of the international exchange of commodities, but not of a space-clearing gesture.

Postcolonial intellectuals in Africa, by contrast, are almost entirely dependent for their support on two institutions: the African university, an institution whose intellectual life is overwhelmingly constituted as Western, and the Euro-American publisher and reader. Even when these writers seek to escape the West – as Ngugi wa Thiong'o did in attempting to construct a Kikuyu peasant drama – their theories of their situation are irreducibly informed by their Euro-American formation. Ngugi's conception of the writer's potential in politics is essentially that of the avant-garde, of left modernism.

Now this double dependence on the university and the European publisher means that the first generation of modern African novels – the generation of Chinua Achebe's *Things Fall Apart* and Camara Laye's *L'Enfant noir* – were written in the context of notions of politics and culture dominant in the French and British university and publishing worlds in the 1950s and 1960s. This does not mean that they were like novels written in Western Europe at that time, for part of what was held to be obvious both by these writers and by the high culture of Europe of the day was that new literatures in new nations should be anticolonial and nationalist. In one respect, these early novels seem to belong to the world of eighteenth- and nineteenth-century literary nationalism; they are theorized as the imaginative recreation of a common cultural past that is crafted into a shared tradition by the writer. They are in the tradition of Sir Walter Scott, whose *Minstrelsy of the Scottish Border* was intended, as he said in the introduction, to 'contribute somewhat to the history of my native country; the peculiar features of whose manners and character are daily melting and dissolving into those of her sister and ally.'[8] The novels of this first stage are thus realist legitimations of nationalism: they authorize a 'return to traditions' while at the same time recognizing the demands of a Weberian rationalized modernity.

From the later sixties on, such celebratory novels become rare.[9] For example, Achebe moves from the creation of a usable past in *Things Fall Apart* to a cynical indictment of politics in the modern sphere in *A Man of the People*. But I would like to focus on a francophone novel of the later sixties, a novel that thematizes in an extremely powerful way many of the questions I have been asking about art and modernity: I mean, of course, Yambo Ouologuem's *Le Devoir de violence*. This novel, like many of the second stage of which it is a part, represents a challenge to the novels of the first stage: it identifies the realist novel as part of the tactic of nationalist legitimation and so it is – if I may begin a catalogue of its ways-of-being-*post*-this-and-that – *postrealist*.

Now postmodernism is, of course, postrealist also. But Ouologuem's post-realism is motivated quite differently from that of such postmodern writers as, say, Thomas Pynchon. Realism naturalizes: the originary 'African novel,' such as Achebe's *Things Fall Apart* and Laye's *L'Enfant noir*, is 'realist.' Therefore, Ouologuem is against it; he rejects, indeed assaults, the conventions of realism. He seeks to delegitimate the forms of the realist African novel, in part, surely, because what it sought to naturalize was a nationalism that, by 1968, had plainly failed. The national bourgeoisie that took the baton of rationalization, industrialization, and bureaucratization in the name of nationalism, turned out to be a kleptocracy. Their enthusiasm for nativism was a rationalization of their urge to keep the national bourgeoisies of other nations, and particularly the powerful industrialized nations, out of their way. As Jonathan Ngate has observed, the world of *Le Devoir de violence* is one 'in which *the efficacy* of the call to the Ancestors as well as the Ancestors themselves is seriously called into question.'[10] That the novel is in this way postrealist allows its author to borrow, when he needs them, the techniques of modernism, which, as we learned from Jameson, are often also the techniques of postmodernism. It is helpful to remember at this point how Ouologuem is described on the back of the Éditions du Seuil first edition:

> Né en 1940 au Mali. Admissible à l'École normale supérieure. Licencié ès Lettres. Licencié en Philosophie. Diplômé d'Études supérieures d'Anglais. Prépare une thèse de doctorat de Sociologie.[11]

Borrowing from European modernism is hardly going to be difficult for someone so qualified. To be a Normalien is indeed, in Christopher Miller's charming formulation, 'roughly equivalent to being baptized by Bossuet.'[12]

Miller's discussion of *Le Devoir de violence* in *Blank Darkness* focuses usefully on theoretical questions of intertextuality raised by the novel's persistent massaging of one text after another into the surface of its own body. Ouologuem's book contains, for example, a translation of a passage from Graham Greene's 1934 novel *It's a Battlefield* (translated and improved, according to some readers!) and borrowings from Guy de Maupassant's *Boule de Suif* (hardly an unfamiliar work to francophone readers; if this latter is a theft, it is the adventurous theft of the kleptomaniac, who dares us to catch him at it). The book's first sentence artfully establishes the oral mode, by then an inevitable convention of African narration, with words that Ngate rightly describes as having the 'concision and the striking beauty and power of a proverb' (*FAF*, p. 64), and mocks us in this moment because the sentence echoes the beginning of André Schwarz-Bart's decidedly un-African 1959 Holocaust novel, *Le Dernier des justes*, an echo that more substantial later borrowings confirm.[13]

> *Nos yeux* boivent l'éclat du soleil, et, vaincus, s'étonnent de pleurer. *Maschallah! oua bismillah!* ... Un récit de l'aventure sanglante de la négraille – honte aux hommes de rien! – *tiendrait aisément dans* la première moitié de ce *siècle; mais la véritable histoire* des Nègres commence beaucoup, beaucoup plus *tôt*, avec les Saïfs, en l'an 1202 de notre ère, dans l'Empire africain de Nakem (*D*, p. 9).
>
> *Nos yeux* reçoivent la lumière d'étoiles mortes. Une biographie de mon ami Ernie *tiendrait aisément dans* le deuxième quart du XXe siècle; mais la véritable histoire d'Ernie Lévy commence très *tôt*, ... dans la vieille cité anglicane de York. Plus précisément: le 11 mars 1185.[14]

The reader who is properly prepared will expect an African holocaust. These echoes are surely meant to render ironic the status of the rulers of Nakem as descendants of Abraham El Héït, 'le Juif noir' (*D*, p. 12).

The book begins, then, with a sick joke against nativism at the unwary reader's expense. And the assault on realism is – here is my second signpost – postnativist; this book is a murderous antidote to a nostalgia for *Roots*. As Wole Soyinka has said in a justly well-respected reading, 'the Bible, the Koran, the historic solemnity of the griot are reduced to the histrionics of wanton boys masquerading as humans.'[15] It is tempting to read the attack on history here as a repudiation not of roots but of Islam, as Soyinka does when he goes on to say:

> A culture which has claimed indigenous antiquity in such parts of Africa as have submitted to its undeniable attractions is confidently proven to be imperialist; worse, it is demonstrated to be essentially hostile and negative to the indigenous culture.... Ouologuem pronounces the Moslem incursion into black Africa to be corrupt, vicious, decadent, elitist and insensitive. At the least such a work functions as a wide swab in the deck-clearing operation for the commencement of racial retrieval.[16]

But it seems to me much clearer to read the repudiation as a repudiation of national history, to see the text as postcolonially postnationalist as well as anti- (and thus, of course, post-) nativist. Indeed, Soyinka's reading here seems to be driven by his own equally representative tendency to read Africa as race and place into everything.[17]

Raymond Spartacus Kassoumi – who is, if anyone is, the hero of this novel – is, after all, a son of the soil, but his political prospects by the end of the narrative are less than uplifting. More than this, the novel explicitly thematizes, in the anthropologist Shrobenius (an obvious echo of the name of the German Africanist Leo Frobenius, whose work is cited by Léopold Senghor) the

mechanism by which the new elite has come to invent its traditions through the
'science' of ethnography:

> Saïf fabula et l'interprète traduisit, Madoubo répéta en français, raffinant les
> subtilités qui faisaient le bonheur de Shrobénius écrevisse humaine frappée de la
> manie tâtonnante de vouloir ressusciter, sous couleur d'autonomie culturelle, un
> univers africain qui ne correspondait à plus rien de vivant; ... il voulait trouver un
> sens métaphysique à tout. ... Il considérait que la vie africaine était art pur (*D*, p.
> 102).

> Saïf made up stories and the interpreter translated, Madoubo repeated in French,
> refining on the subtleties to the delight of Shrobenius, that human crayfish afflicted
> with a groping mania for resuscitating an African universe – cultural autonomy, he
> called it – which had lost all living reality; ... he was determined to find metaphysical
> meaning in everything. ... African life, he held, was pure art.[18]

At the start we had been told that 'there are few written accounts, and the
versions of the elders diverge from those of the griots, which differ in turn from
those of the chroniclers' (*BV*, p. 6). Now we are warned off the supposedly
scientific discourse of the ethnographers.[19]

Because *Le Devoir de violence* is a novel that seeks to delegitimate not only
the form of realism but the content of nationalism, it will to that extent seem to
us, misleadingly, postmodern: misleadingly, because what we have here is not
postmodern*ism* but postmoderniz*ation*; not an aesthetics but a politics, in the
most literal sense of the term. After colonialism, the modernizers said, comes
rationality; that is the possibility the novel rules out. Ouologuem's novel is
typical of novels of this second stage in that it is not written by someone who is
comfortable with and accepted by the new elite, the national bourgeoisie. Far
from being a celebration of the nation, then, the novels of the second,
postcolonial, stage are novels of delegitimation: they reject not only the
Western *imperium* but also the nationalist project of the postcolonial national
bourgeoisie. And, so it seems to me, the basis for that project of delegitimation
cannot be the postmodernist one: rather, it is grounded in an appeal to an
ethical universal. Indeed it is based, as intellectual responses to oppression in
Africa largely are based, in an appeal to a certain simple respect for human
suffering, a fundamental revolt against the endless misery of the last thirty
years. Ouologuem is hardly likely to make common cause with a relativism that
might allow that the horrifying new-old Africa of exploitation is to be understood, legitimated, in its own local terms.

Africa's postcolonial novelists, novelists anxious to escape neocolonialism,
are no longer committed to the nation; in this they will seem, as I have
suggested, misleadingly postmodern. But what they have chosen instead of the
nation is not an older traditionalism but Africa – the continent and its people.
This is clear enough, I think, in *Le Devoir de violence*. At the end of the novel
Ouologuem writes:

> Souvent il est vrai, l'âme veut rêver l'écho sans passé du bonheur. Mais, jeté dans
> le monde, l'on peut s'empêcher de songer que Saïf, pleuré trois millions de fois,

renaît sans cesse à l'Histoire, sous les cendres chaudes de plus de trente Républiques africaines (*D*, p. 207).

Often, it is true, the soul desires to dream the echo of happiness, an echo that has no past. But projected into the world, one cannot help recalling that Saïf, mourned three million times, is forever reborn to history beneath the hot ashes of more than thirty African republics (*BV*, pp. 181–2).

If we are to identify with anyone, it is with the 'la négraille,' the niggertrash, who have no nationality. For them one republic is as good (which is to say as bad) as any other. Postcoloniality has become, I think, a condition of pessimism.

Postrealist writing, postnativist politics, a *transnational* rather than a *national* solidarity – and pessimism: a kind of *post*optimism to balance the earlier enthusiasm for Ahmadou Kourouma's *Suns of Independence*. Postcoloniality is *after* all this: and its *post-*, like that of postmodernism, is also a *post-* that challenges earlier legitimating narratives. And it challenges them in the name of the suffering victims of 'more than thirty African republics.'

If there is a lesson in the broad shape of this circulation of cultures, it is surely that we are all already contaminated by each other, that there is no longer a fully autochthonous *echt-*African culture awaiting salvage by our artists (just as there is, of course, no American culture without African roots). And there is a clear sense in some postcolonial writing that the postulation of a unitary Africa over against a monolithic West – the binarism of Self and Other – is the last of the shibboleths of the modernizers that we must learn to live without.

In *Le Devoir de violence*, in Ouologuem's withering critique of 'Shrobéniusologie,' there were already the beginnings of this postcolonial critique of what we might call 'alteritism,' the construction and celebration of oneself as Other: 'voilà l'art nègre baptisé "esthétique" et marchandé – oye! – dans l'univers imaginaire des "échanges vivifiants"!' (*D*, p. 110) ['henceforth Negro art was baptized "aesthetic" and hawked in the imaginary universe of "vitalizing exchanges"' (*BV*, p. 94)]. After describing the fantasmatic elaboration of some interpretative mumbo jumbo 'invented by Saïf,' Ouologuem then announces that 'l'art nègre se forgeait ses lettres de noblesse au folklore de la spiritualité mercantiliste, oye oye oye' (*D*, p. 110) ['Negro art found its patent of nobility in the folklore of mercantile intellectualism, *oye, oye, oye*' (*BV*, p. 94)]. Shrobenius, the anthropologist, as apologist for 'his' people; a European audience that laps up this exoticized Other; African traders and producers of African art, who understand the necessity to maintain the 'mysteries' that construct their product as 'exotic'; traditional and contemporary elites, who require a sentimentalized past to authorize their present power: all are exposed in their complex and multiple mutual complicities.

'témoin: la splendeur de son art –, la grandeur des empires du Moyen Age constituait le visage vrai de l'Afrique, sage, belle, riche, ordonnée, non violente et puissante tout autant qu'humaniste – berceau même de la civilisation égyptienne.'

Salivant ainsi, Shrobénius, de retour au bercail, en tira un double profit: d'une part, il mystifia son pays, qui, enchanté, le jucha sur une haute chair sorbonicale, et, d'autre part, il exploita la sentimentalité négrillarde – par trop heureuse de s'entendre dire par un Blanc que 'l'Afrique était ventre du monde et berceau de civilisation'.

La négraille offrit par tonnes, conséquemment et gratis, masques et trésors artistiques aux acolytes de la 'shrobéniusologie' (*D*, p. 111).

'witness the splendor of its art – the true face of Africa is the grandiose empires of the Middle Ages, a society marked by wisdom, beauty, prosperity, order, nonviolence, and humanism, and it is here that we must seek the true cradle of Egyptian civilization.'

Thus drooling, Shrobenius derived a twofold benefit on his return home: on the one hand, he mystified the people of his own country who in their enthusiasm raised him to a lofty Sorbonnical chair, while on the other hand he exploited the sentimentality of the coons, only too pleased to hear from the mouth of a white man that Africa was 'the womb of the world and the cradle of civilization.'

In consequence the niggertrash donated masks and art treasures by the ton to the acolytes of 'Shrobeniusology' (*BV*, pp. 94–5).

A little later, Ouologuem articulates more precisely the interconnections of Africanist mystifications with tourism and the production, packaging, and marketing of African artworks.

Une école africaniste ainsi accrochée aux nues du symbolisme magico-religieux, cosmologique et mythique, était née: tant et si bien que durant trois ans, des hommes – et quels hommes!: des fantoches, des aventuriers, des apprentis banquiers, des politiciens, des voyageurs, des conspirateurs, des chercheurs – 'scientifiques', dit-on, en vérité sentinelles asservies, montant la garde devant le monument 'shrobéniusologique' du pseudo-symbolisme nègre, accoururent au Nakem.

Déjà, l'acquisition des masques anciens était devenue problématique depuis que Shrobénius et les missionnaires connurent le bonheur d'en acquérir en quantité. Saïf donc – et la pratique est courante de nos jours encore – fit enterrer des quintaux de masques hâtivement executés à la ressemblance des originaux, les engloutissant dans des mares, marais, étangs, marécages, lacs, limons – quitte à les exhumer quelque temps après, les vendant aux curieux et profanes à prix d'or. Ils étaient, ces masques, vieux de trois ans, *chargés*, disait-on, *du poids de quatre siècles de civilisation* (*D*, p. 112).

An Africanist school harnessed to the vapors of magico-religious, cosmological, and mythical symbolism had been born: with the result that for three years men flocked to Nakem – and what men! – middlemen, adventurers, apprentice bankers, politicians, salesmen, conspirators – supposedly 'scientists,' but in reality enslaved sentries mounting guard before the 'Shrobeniusological' monument of Negro pseudosymbolism.

Already it had become more than difficult to procure old masks, for Shrobenius and the missionaries had had the good fortune to snap them all up. And so Saif – and the practice is still current – had slapdash copies buried by the hundredweight, or sunk into ponds, lakes, marshes, and mud holes, to be exhumed later on and sold at exorbitant prices to unsuspecting curio hunters. These three-year-old masks were said to be *charged with the weight of four centuries of civilization* (*BV*, pp. 95–6).

Ouologuem here forcefully exposes the connections we saw earlier in some of Rockefeller's insights into the international system of art exchange, the international art world; we see the way in which an ideology of disinterested aesthetic value – the 'baptism' of 'Negro art' as 'aesthetic' – meshes with the international commodification of African expressive culture, a commodification that requires, by the logic of the space-clearing gesture, the manufacture of Otherness. (It is a significant bonus that it also harmonizes with the interior decor of contemporary apartments.) Shrobenius, 'ce marchand-confectionneur d'idéologie,' the ethnographer allied with Saif – image of the 'traditional' African ruling caste – has invented an Africa that is a body over against Europe, the juridical institution; and Ouologuem is urging us vigorously to refuse to be thus Other.

Sara Suleri has written recently, in *Meatless Days*, of being treated as an 'otherness machine' – and of being heartily sick of it.[20] Perhaps the predicament of the postcolonial intellectual is simply that *as* intellectuals – a category instituted in black Africa by colonialism – we are, indeed, always at the risk of becoming otherness machines, with the manufacture of alterity as our principal role. Our only distinction in the world of texts to which we are latecomers is that we can mediate it to our fellows. This is especially true when postcolonial meets postmodern; for what the postmodern reader seems to demand of Africa is all too close to what modernism – in the form of the postimpressionists – demanded of it. The rôle that Africa, like the rest of the Third World, plays for Euro-American postmodernism – like its better-documented significance for modernist art – must be distinguished from the rôle postmodernism might play in the Third World; what that might be it is, I think, too early to tell. What happens will happen not because we pronounce on the matter in theory, but will happen out of the changing everyday practices of African cultural life.

For all the while, in Africa's cultures, there are those who will not see themselves as Other. Despite the overwhelming reality of economic decline; despite unimaginable poverty; despite wars, malnutrition, disease, and political instability, African cultural productivity grows apace: popular literatures, oral narrative and poetry, dance, drama, music, and visual art all thrive. The contemporary cultural production of many African societies, and the many traditions whose evidences so vigorously remain, is an antidote to the dark vision of the postcolonial novelist.

And I am grateful to James Baldwin for his introduction to the *Man with a Bicycle*, a figure who is, as Baldwin so rightly saw, polyglot – speaking Yoruba and English, probably some Hausa and a little French for his trips to Cotonou or Cameroon, someone whose 'clothes do not fit him too well.' He and the other men and women among whom he mostly lives suggest to me that the place to look for hope is not just to the postcolonial novel, which has struggled to achieve the insights of Ouologuem or Mudimbe, but to the all-consuming vision of this less-anxious creativity. It matters little whom the work was made *for*; what we should learn from is the imagination that produced it. *Man with a Bicycle* is produced by someone who does not care that the bicycle is the white man's invention: it is not there to be Other to the Yoruba Self; it is there because someone cared for its solidity; it is there because it will take us further than our feet will take us; it is there because machines are now as African as novelists ... and as fabricated as the kingdom of Nakem.[21]

Notes

1 *Perspectives: Angles on African Art* (exhibition catalogue, Center for African Art, New York, 1987), p. 9; hereafter abbreviated *P*.

2 I should insist now, the first time that I use this word, that I do not share the widespread negative evaluation of commodification; its merits, I believe, must be assessed case by case. Certainly critics such as Kobena Mercer (for example, in his 'Black Hair/Style Politics,' *New Formations* 3 [Winter 1987]: pp. 33–54) have persuasively criticized any reflexive rejection of the commodity form, which so often reinstates the hoary humanist opposition between the 'authentic' and the 'commercial.' Mercer explores the avenues by which marginalized groups have manipulated commodified artifacts in culturally novel and expressive ways.

3 Once Vogel has thus refused Kouakou a voice, it is less surprising that his comments turn out to be composite also. On closer inspection, it turns out that there is no single Lela Kouakou who was interviewed like the other cocurators. Kouakou is, in the end, quite exactly an invention, thus literalizing the sense in which 'we,' and more particularly 'our' artists, are individuals while 'they,' and 'theirs,' are ethnic types.

4 It is absolutely crucial that Vogel does not draw her line according to racial or national categories: the Nigerian, the Senegalese, and the African-American cocurators are each allowed to be on 'our' side of the great divide. The issue here is something less obvious than racism.

5 Where the practice is theory – literary or philosophical – postmodernism as a *theory* of postmodernity can be adequate only if it reflects to some extent the realities of that practice, because the practice itself is fully theoretical. But when a postmodernism addresses, say, advertising or poetry, it may be adequate as an account of them even if it conflicts with their own narratives, their theories of themselves. For, unlike philosophy and literary theory, advertising and poetry are not largely *constituted* by their articulated theories of themselves.

6 Max Weber, *The Protestant Ethic and the Spirit of Capitalism*, trans. Talcott Parsons (London, 1930), p. 13.

7 Oscar Wilde, 'The Decay of Lying: An Observation,' *Intentions* (London, 1909), p. 45.

8 Walter Scott, *Minstrelsy of the Scottish Border: Consisting of Historical and Romantic Ballads* (London, 1883), pp. 51–2.

9 Somewhat along these lines, Neil Lazarus's *Resistance in Postcolonial African Fiction* (New Haven, Conn., 1990), pp. 1–26, offers a useful periodization of African fiction in relation to the 'great expectations' of the independence era and the 'mourning after.'

10 Jonathan Ngate, *Francophone African Fiction: Reading a Literary Tradition* (Trenton, N. J., 1988), p. 59; hereafter abbreviated *FAF*.

11 Yambo Ouologuem, *Le Devoir de Violence* (Paris, 1968), back cover; hereafter abbreviated *D*.

12 Christopher Miller, *Blank Darkness: Africanist Discourse in French* (Chicago, 1985), p. 218.

13 Ngate's focus on this initial sentence follows Aliko Songolo, 'The Writer, the Audience and the Critic's Responsibility: The Case of *Bound to Violence*,' in *Artist and Audience: African Literature as a Shared Experience* Richard O. Priebe and Thomas Hale, eds., (Washington, D. C., 1979); cited in *FAF*, p. 64.

14 For this comparison I have made my own translations, which are as literal as possible:

Our eyes drink the flash of the sun, and, conquered, surprise themselves by weeping. Maschallah! oua bismillah! ... An account of the bloody adventure of the nigger-trash – dishonor to the men of nothing – *could easily begin in the* first half of this *century; but true history of* the Blacks begins very much *earlier*, with the Saifs, in the year 1202 of our era, in the African kingdom of Nakem (*D*, p.9; my emphasis).

Our eyes receive the light of dead stars. A biography of my friend Ernie *could easily begin in the* second quarter of the 20th *century; but the true history* of Ernie Lévy begins much *earlier*, ... in the old Anglican city of York. More precisely: on the 11 March 1185 [André Schwarz-Bart, *Le Dernier des justes* (Paris, 1959), p. 11; my emphasis].

15 Wole Soyinka, *Myth, Literature and the African World* (Cambridge, 1976), p. 100.
16 Soyinka, *Myth, Literature and the African World*, p. 105.
17 I have discussed this matter in 'Soyinka and the Philosophy of Culture,' in P. O. Bodunrin, ed., *Philosophy in Africa: Trends and Perspectives* (Ile-Ife, Nigeria, 1985), pp. 250–63.
18 Ouologuem, *Bound to Violence*, trans. Ralph Manheim (London, 1968), p. 87; hereafter abbreviated *BV*.
19 Here we have the literary thematization of the Foucauldian theory proposed by V. Y. Mudimbe in his important recent intervention, *The Invention of Africa: Gnosis, Philosophy, and the Order of Knowledge* (Bloomington, Ind., 1988).
20 Sara Suleri, *Meatless Days* (Chicago, 1989), p. 105.
21 I learned a good deal from trying out earlier versions of these ideas at an NEH Summer Institute on 'The Future of the Avant-Garde in Postmodern Culture,' under the direction of Susan Suleiman and Alice Jardine at Harvard in July 1989; at the African Studies Association (under the sponsorship of the Society for African Philosophy in North America) in November 1989, where Jonathan Ngate's response was particularly helpful; and, as the guest of Ali Mazrui, at the Braudel Center at SUNY-Binghamton in May 1990. As usual, I wish I knew how to incorporate more of the ideas of the discussants on those occasions.

4

Stephen Slemon

Unsettling the Empire: Resistance Theory for the Second World *

My argument here comprises part of what I hope will become a larger meditation on the practice of 'post-colonial criticism,' and the problem it addresses is a phenomenon which twenty-five years ago would have seemed an embarrassment of riches. The sign of the 'post-colonial' has become an especially valent one in academic life (there are even careers to be made out of it), and like feminist theory or women's studies programs a decade ago, the area is witnessing an enormous convergence within it of diverse critical practices and cultural forces. We are now undergoing an important process of sorting through those forces and tendencies, investigating where affiliations lie and where they cross, examining the political and pedagogical goals of the area, and re-negotiating basic issues such as where our primary 'material' of study and of intervention lies. What I want to do in this paper is take a position within this process of questioning – but because this *is* a process, I want also to advance this position as provisional and temporary, a statement in search of that clarifying energy which emerges at the best of times out of friendly discussion and collegial exchange.

In specific terms, what I want to do in this paper is address two separate debates in critical theory, and then attempt to yoke them together into an argument for maintaining within a discourse of post-colonialism certain textual and critical practices which inhabit ex-colonial settler cultures and their literatures. The textual gestures I want to preserve for post-colonial theory and practice are various and dispersed, but the territory I want to reclaim for post-colonial pedagogy and research – and reclaim *not* as a unified and indivisible area but rather as a groundwork for certain modes of anti-colonial work – is that neither/nor territory of white settler-colonial writing which Alan Lawson has called the 'Second World.'

The first debate concerns the *field* of the 'post-colonial.' Is the 'post-colonial' a synonym for what Wallersteinian world-systems theory calls the periphery in economic relations? Is it another way of naming what other discourses would call the Third and Fourth Worlds? Is it a name for a discursive and representational set of practices which are grounded in a politics of anti-colonialism? Or is the term post-colonial simply another name for the old Commonwealth of

* From *World Literature Written in English* 30.2 (1990), pp. 30–41.

literary activity – a synonym for such unfortunate neologisms as 'the new literatures in English,' or what Joseph Jones in a fleeting moment of unitary hopefulness wanted to call 'Terranglia,' or what the Modern Languages Association of America in its continuing moment of exclusionary and yet proprietorial backyardism still wants to call 'English Literatures Other than British and American'?

The second debate I want to address concerns the nature of literary *resistance* itself. Is literary resistance something that simply issues forth, through narrative, against a clearly definable set of power relations? Is it something actually *there* in the text, or is it produced and reproduced in and through communities of readers and through the mediating structures of their own culturally specific histories? Do literary resistances escape the constitutive purchase of genre, and trope, and figure, and mode, which operate elsewhere as a contract between text and reader and thus a set of centralizing codes, or are literary resistances in fact necessarily *embedded* in the representational technologies of those literary and social 'texts' whose structures and whose referential codes they seek to oppose?

These questions sound like definitional problems, but I think in fact they are crucial ones for a critical industry which at the moment seems to find these two central terms – 'post-colonial' and 'resistance' – positively shimmering as objects of desire and self-privilege, and so easily appropriated to competing, and in fact hostile, modes of critical and literary practice. Arun Mukherjee makes this point with great eloquence when she asks what specificity, what residual grounding, remains with the term 'post-colonial' when it is applied indiscriminately to both Second- and Third-World literary texts.[1] The term 'resistance' recently found itself at the centre of a similar controversy, when it was discovered how very thoroughly a *failure* in resistance characterized some of the earlier political writing of the great theorist of *textual* resistance, Paul de Man. Both terms thus find themselves at the centre of a quarrel over the kinds of critical taxonomies that will be seen to perform legitimate work in articulating the relation between literary texts and the political world; and to say this is to recognize that critical taxonomies, like literary canons, issue forth from cultural institutions which continue to police what voices will be heard, which *kinds* of (textual) intervention will be made recognizable and/or classifiable, and what *authentic* forms of post-colonial textual resistance are going to look like. These debates are thus institutional: grounded in university curricula, and *about* pedagogical strategies. They are also about the question of authenticity itself: how a text emerges from a cultural grounding and speaks to a reading community, and how textual ambiguity or ambivalence proves pedagogically awkward when an apparatus called 'English studies' recuperates various writing practices holistically as 'literatures,' and then deploys them wholesale towards a discourse of inclusivity and coverage.

The first debate – the question of the 'post-colonial' – is grounded in the overlapping of three competing research or critical fields, each of which carries a specific cultural location and history. In the first of these fields, the term 'post-colonial' is an outgrowth of what formerly were 'Commonwealth' literary studies – a study which came into being *after* 'English' studies had been liberalized to include 'American' and then an immediate national or regional literature (Australian, Canadian, West Indian), and as a way of mobilizing the concept of national or geographical *difference* within what remains a unitary idea of 'English.' The second of these critical fields, in contrast, employs the term 'post-colonial' in considering the valency of subjectivity specifically within Third- and Fourth-World cultures, and within black, and ethnic, and First-Nation constituencies dispersed within First-World terrain. The institutionalizing of these two critical fields has made possible the emergence of a third field of study, however, where nation-based examinations of a variable literary Commonwealth, or a variable literary Third World, give way to specific analyses of the discourse of colonialism (and neo-colonialism), and where studies in cultural representativeness and literary mimeticism give way to the project of identifying the kinds of anti-colonialist resistance that can take place in literary writing.

The past few years have therefore witnessed an extraordinary burgeoning of 'post-colonial' criticism and theory, largely because the second and third of these pedagogical fields have at last gained hold within the First-World academy. 'Post-colonial' studies in 'English' now finds itself at a shifting moment, where three very different critical projects collide with one another on the space of a single signifier – and what will probably be a single course offering within an English studies program. Not surprisingly, this situation has produced some remarkable confusions, and they underpin the present debate over the specificity of the 'post-colonial' in the areas of literary and critical practice.

The confusion which concerns me here is the way in which the *project* of the third 'post-colonial' critical field – that is, of identifying the scope and nature of anti-colonialist resistance in writing – has been mistaken for the project of the second critical field, which concerns itself with articulating the literary nature of Third- and Fourth-World cultural groups. For whereas the first and second of these post-colonial critical fields work with whole nations or cultures as their basic units, and tend to seek out the defining characteristics under which *all* writing in that field can be subsumed, the third critical field is concerned with identifying a social force, colonialism, and with the attempt to understand the resistances to that force, *wherever* they lie. Colonialism, obviously, is an enormously problematical category: it is by definition transhistorical and unspecific, and it is used in relation to very different kinds of cultural oppression and economic control. But like the term 'patriarchy,' which shares similar problems in definition, the concept of colonialism, to this third critical field, remains crucial to a critique of past and present power relations in world affairs, and thus to a specifically *post*-colonial critical practice which attempts to understand the relation of literary writing to power and its contestations.

This mistaking of a pro-active, anti-colonialist critical project with nation-based studies in Third- and Fourth-World literary writing comes about for good reason – for it has been, and always will be, the case that the most important forms of resistance to any form of social power will be produced from within the communities that are most immediately and visibly sub-ordinated by that power structure. But when the idea of anti-colonial resistance becomes *synonymous* with Third- and Fourth-World literary writing, two forms of displacement happen. First, *all* literary writing which emerges from these cultural locations will be understood as carrying a radical and con-testatory content – and this gives away the rather important point that subjected peoples are sometimes capable of producing reactionary literary documents. And secondly, the idea will be discarded that important anti-colonialist literary writing can take place *outside* the ambit of Third- and Fourth-World literary writing – and this in effect excises the study of anti-colonialist Second-World literary activity from the larger study of anti-colonialist literary practice.

In practical terms, this excision springs in part from a desire to foreclose upon a *specific* form of 'Commonwealth' literary criticism. For a small number of old-school 'Commonwealth' critics, comparative studies across English literatures did indeed promise the renewal through 'art' of that lost cross-cultural unity which a capricious twentieth-century history had somehow denied for Britain and the empire. And so this excision provides an effective way of figuring one important objective of post-colonial criticism: and that is the rejection of neo-colonialist, Eurocentrist, and late capitalist purchase in the practice of post-colonial literary analysis.

This excision also springs from a rather healthy recognition that – as Linda Hutcheon has recently put it – the experience of colonialism, and therefore of post-colonialism, is simply *not* the same in, say, Canada as it is in the West Indies or in Africa or in India.[2] As Fourth-World literary writing continually insists, Second- and Third-World cultures do not inhabit the same political, discursive, and literary terrains in relation to colonialism. The excision of Second-World literary writing from the field of the 'post-colonial' therefore figures the importance of cultural *difference* within post-colonial criticism and theory – even if that difference is conscripted to the service of what remains at heart an extended nation-based critical practice founded on a unitary model and on the assumption of equivalent (as opposed to, say, 'shared') cultural and literary experience within a positivist and essentialist 'post-colonial' sphere.

Nevertheless, I want to argue, this conflating of the projects of the second and third post-colonial critical fields, and the consequent jettisoning of Second-World literary writing from the domain of the post-colonial, remains – in the Bloomian sense – a 'misreading,' and one which seems to be setting in train a concept of the 'post-colonial' which is remarkably purist and absolutist in tenor. Tim Brennan, one of the most interesting of the newly emerging US-based, First-World critics in the post-colonial field, has been an enormously forceful proponent for this conflation of the second and third post-colonial critical projects – for the refiguration of the post-colonial literary terrain as 'the literature not of the "colonies" but of the "colonized" '[3] – and he puts the argument for this position as follows:

[Writers such as] Nadine Gordimer or John Coetzee of South Africa, along with others from the white Commonwealth countries, while clearly playing [a] mediating role [between colonizer and colonized], are probably better placed in some category of the European novel of Empire because of their compromised positions of segregated privilege within colonial settler states. They are too much like the fictional 'us' of the so-called mainstream, on the inside looking out.[4]

Brennan's argument is actually more complex than this quotation suggests, for it hangs upon an extremely suggestive category called 'the novel of Empire,' which in another discussion would need to be unpacked. But for my purposes here, his argument is useful because it makes visible the fact that the foundational principle for this particular approach to the field of post-colonial criticism is at heart a simple binarism: the binarism of Europe and its Others, of colonizer and colonized, of the West and the Rest, of the vocal and the silent. It is also a centre/periphery model with roots in world-systems theory – and as so often happens with simple binary systems, this concept of the post-colonial has a marked tendency to blur when it tries to focus upon ambiguously placed or ambivalent material. In what seems to be emerging as the dominant focus of post-colonial literary criticism now – especially for literary criticism coming out of universities in the United States – this blurring is everywhere in evidence in relation to what world systems theory calls the field of 'semi-periphery,' and what follows behind it is a radical foreclosing by post-colonial criticism on settler/colonial writing: the radical ambivalence of colonialism's middle ground.

This foreclosing most commonly takes the rather simple form of stark forgetfulness, of overlooking the Second World entirely as though its literature and its critical traditions didn't even exist. An example of this forgetfulness is provided by Laura Donaldson in her otherwise scrupulously researched article in *diacritics* entitled 'The Miranda Complex.' Here Donaldson argues that while the trope of Prospero and Caliban has been done to death in anti-colonialist criticism (and here she relies upon an article by Houston Baker published in *Critical Inquiry* as her authority), the trope of Miranda and Caliban – the trope of the Anglo-European daughter in the multiple interpellations of both colonialism and patriarchy – has been 'virtually ignored'[5] by literary criticism. From a Second-World perspective, however, what *really* remains 'virtually ignored' – in a gesture so common as to be symptomatic of much of the US-based, First-World 'post-colonial' critical practice – is that body of critical works, published in Second-World critical journals by scholars such as Diana Brydon and Chantal Zabus, which discusses the Miranda-Caliban trope precisely in the terms Donaldson's article calls for.[6] In cases like this, where *diacritics* cites *Critical Inquiry*, Donaldson cites Baker, the academic star-system of First-World criticism inscribes itself wholesale into post-colonial studies, and a large and important body of astute anti-colonial literary critical work ends up simply getting lost in the move.

A more important form of this foreclosing process, however, is underscored by a much more substantive critical concern: and that is to preserve the concept of cultural *difference* in the critical articulation of literary post-colonialism.

Arun Mukherjee's 'Whose Post-Colonialism and Whose Postmodernism?' for example, advances in exemplary form the argument that 'post-colonial' studies in literary resistance inherently totalize dissimilar cultures when they consider the resistances to colonialism of both imperialism's 'white cousins' and its black, colonized subjects. Specifically, Mukherjee argues, this critical practice dangerously overlooks 'realist' writing from the Third and Fourth World, and ends up privileging the kind of post-colonial writing which takes resistance to colonialism as its primary objective. The argument for a post-colonial critical practice here, of course, has nothing to do with the kind of wilful forgetfulness which characterizes Donaldson's misreading; but it does promulgate a misreading of its own, I would argue, in mistaking the *project* of anti-colonialist criticism with the kind of nation-based descriptive criticism which characterizes the first post-colonial critical field I have been discussing. Here, I suspect, the conflation between the second and third post-colonial critical fields has become so naturalized that the *specific* project of the third post-colonial field seems no longer recognizable: the project of articulating the forms – and modes, and tropes, and figures – of anti-colonialist textual resistance, *wherever* they occur, and in *all* of their guises. A more damaging critique of the kind of critical practice Mukherjee objects to, I think, lies in the propensity of anti-colonialist critics (like myself) to overlook the range of anti-colonialist gestures which inhabit First-World, or imperial, writing itself.

At any rate, the new binaristic absolutism which seems to come in the wake of First-World accommodation to the fact of post-colonial literary and cultural criticism seems to be working in several ways to drive that trans-national region of ex-colonial settler cultures away from the field of post-colonial literary representation. The Second World of writing within the ambit of colonialism is in danger of disappearing: because it is not sufficiently pure in its anti-colonialism, because it does not offer up an experiential grounding in a common 'Third World' aesthetics, because its modalities of *post*-coloniality are too ambivalent, too occasional and uncommon, for inclusion within the field. This debate over the scope and nature of the 'post-colonial,' I now want to argue, has enormous investments in the second debate I want to discuss in this paper, for in fact the idea of both literary and political *resistance* to colonialist power is the hidden term, the foundational concept, upon which *all* these distinctions in the modality of the 'post-colonial' actually rest.

The debate over literary resistance is in fact a very complicated one, and criticism offers a seemingly endless set of configurations for the kinds of reading and writing practices which a theory of resistance might possibly comprise. In order to simplify this debate, however, I want to suggest that in rudimentary form the idea of literary resistance collapses into two general movements or concepts, each of which contains important distinctions that I won't address here.

The first concept of resistance is most clearly put forward by Selwyn Cudjoe in his *Resistance and Caribbean Literature* and by Barbara Harlow in her book, *Resistance Literature*.[7] For Cudjoe and Harlow, resistance is an act, or a set of acts, that is designed to rid a people of its oppressors, and it so thoroughly infuses the experience of living under oppression that it becomes an almost autonomous aesthetic principle. *Literary* resistance, under these conditions, can be seen as a form of contractual understanding between text and reader, one which is embedded in an experiential dimension and buttressed by a political and cultural aesthetic at work in the culture. And 'resistance literature,' in this definition, can thus be seen as that category of literary writing which emerges as an integral part of an organized struggle or resistance for national liberation.

This argument for literary 'resistance' is an important one to hold on to – but it is also a strangely untheorized position, for it fails to address three major areas of critical concern. The first is a political concern: namely, that centre/periphery notions of resistance can actually work to *reinscribe* centre/periphery relations and can 'serve an institutional function of securing the dominant narratives'.[8] The second problem with this argument is that it assumes that literary resistance is simply somehow *there* in the literary text as a structure of intentionality, and *there* in the social text as a communicative gesture of pure availability. Post-Lacanian and post-Althusserian theories of the *constructedness* of subjectivity, however, would contest such easy access to representational purity, and would argue instead that resistance is grounded in the *multiple* and *contradictory* structures of ideological interpellation or subject-formation – which would call down the notion that resistance can *ever* be 'purely' intended or 'purely' expressed in representational or communicative models. The third problem with this argument is that it has to set aside the very persuasive theory of power which Foucault puts forward in his *The Archaeology of Knowledge*: the theory that power *itself* inscribes its resistances and so, in the process, seeks to contain them.[9] It is this third objection, especially, which has energized the post-structuralist project of theorizing literary resistance – and in order to clarify what is going on in that theatre of critical activity I want to focus especially on Jenny Sharpe's wonderful article in *Modern Fiction Studies* entitled 'Figures of Colonial Resistance.'

Sharpe's article involves a reconsideration of the work of theorists such as Gayatri Spivak, Homi Bhabha, Abdul JanMohamed, and Benita Parry, each of whom has worked to correct the critical 'tendency to presume the transparency' of literary resistance in colonial and post-colonial writing,[10] and who collectively have worked to examine the ways in which resistance in writing must go beyond the mere 'questioning' of colonialist authority. There are important differences in how all of these theorists define literary resistance, but the two key points Sharpe draws out are, first, that you can never *easily* locate the sites of anti-colonial resistance – since resistance itself is always in some measure an '*effect* of the contradictory representation of colonial authority'[11] and never simply a 'reversal' of power – and secondly, that resistance itself is therefore never *purely* resistance, never *simply* there in the text or the interpretive community, but is always *necessarily* complicit in the apparatus it seeks to transgress. As Sharpe puts it: 'the colonial subject who can answer the colonizers back is the product of the same vast ideological machinery that silences the subaltern;'[12] and what she is saying here, basically, is that a *theory* of literary resistance *must* recognize the inescapable partiality, the incompleteness, the untranscendable *ambiguity* of literary or indeed *any* contra/dictory or contestatory act which employs a First-World medium for the figuration of a Third-World resistance, and which predicates a semiotics of *refusal* on a gestural mechanism whose first act must always be an acknowledgement and a *recognition* of the reach of colonialist power.

Sharpe's argument, that is, underscores the way in which literary resistance is necessarily in a place of ambivalence: between systems, between discursive worlds, implicit and complicit in both of them. And from this recognition comes the very startling but inevitable claim – made most spectacularly by Tim Brennan in his book on *Salman Rushdie and the Third World* – that the Third-World resistance writer, the Third-World resistance text, is necessarily self-produced as a doubly-emplaced and *mediated* figure – Brennan's term is 'Third-World Cosmopolitan' – between the First and the Third Worlds, and *within* the ambit of a First-World politics.

This brings me at last to the central thesis of my paper, which begins with the observation that there is a contradiction within the dominant trajectory of First-World post-colonial critical theory here – for that same theory which argues persuasively for the necessary *ambivalence* of post-colonial literary resistance, and which works to emplace that resistance squarely *between* First- and Third-World structures of representation, *also* wants to assign 'Second-World' or ex-colonial settler literatures unproblematically to the category of the literature of empire, the literature of the First World, precisely *because* of its ambivalent position within the First-World/Third-World, colonizer/colonized binary. Logically, however, it would seem that the argument being made by Spivak, Bhabha, Sharpe and others about the ambivalence of literary and other resistances – the argument that resistance texts are necessarily double, necessarily mediated, in their social location – is in fact nothing less than an argument *for* the emplacement of 'Second-World' literary texts within the field of the 'post-colonial': for if there *is* only a space for a *pure* Third- and Fourth-World resistance outside the First-World hegemony, then *either* you have to return to the baldly untheorized notion which informs the first position in the debate over literary resistance, *or* you have to admit that at least as far as writing is concerned, the 'field' of the genuinely *post*-colonial can never *actually* exist.

It is for this reason, I think, and not because of some vestigial nostalgia for an empire upon which the sun will never set, that many critics and theorists have argued long and hard for the preservation of white Australian, New Zealander, southern African, and Canadian literatures within the field of comparative 'post-colonial' literary studies. At bottom, the argument here is the one which Alan Lawson made at the Badlands Conference in Calgary in 1986: namely, that in order to avoid essentialism and to escape theoretical absolutism, we might profitably think of the category of the settler cultures of Australia, Canada, southern Africa, and New Zealand as inhabiting a 'Second World' of discursive polemics – of inhabiting, that is, the space of dynamic *relation* between those 'apparently antagonistic, static, aggressive, [and] disjunctive' binaries which colonialism 'settles' upon a landscape: binaries such as colonizer and colonized, foreign and native, settler and indigene, home and away.[13] Lawson is careful to note that such a doubleness or ambivalence in emplacement is by no means an exclusive domain or prerogative for 'Second-World' writing, and by no means an essentialist category governing *all* activity going on within the settler literatures. Rather, the 'Second World' – like the third of the three 'post-colonial' critical fields I have been discussing – is at root a *reading position*, and one which is and often has been taken up in settler and ex-colonial literature and criticism. The 'Second World,' that is, like 'postcolonial criticism' itself, is a critical manoeuvre, a reading and writing action; and embedded within it is a theory of communicative action akin in some ways to Clifford Geertz's thesis about 'intermediary knowledge,' or Gadamer's theory of an interpretive 'fusion of horizons.' 'The inherent awareness of both "there" and "here," and the cultural ambiguity of these terms,' writes Lawson, 'are not so much the boundaries of its cultural matrix, nor tensions to be resolved, but a space *within* which [the Second-World, post-colonial] literary text may move *while* speaking.' Lawson's definition of literary representation in the discursive 'Second World' thus articulates a figure for what many First-World critical theorists would correctly define as the limits and the condition of *post-colonial* forms of literary resistance. The irony is that many of those same First-World critics would define that 'post-colonial' as exclusively the domain of the Third and Fourth Worlds.

But what perhaps marks a *genuine* difference in the contestatory activity of Second- and Third-World post-colonial writing, I now want to argue, is that the *illusion* of a stable self/other, here/there binary division has *never* been available to Second-World writers, and that as a result the sites of figural contestation between oppressor and oppressed, colonizer and colonized, have been taken *inward* and *internalized* in Second-World post-colonial textual practice. By this I mean that the *ambivalence* of literary resistance itself is the 'always already' condition of Second-World settler and post-colonial literary writing, for in the white literatures of Australia, or New Zealand, or Canada, or southern Africa, anti-colonialist resistance has *never* been directed at an object or a discursive structure which can be seen as purely external to the self. The Second-World writer, the Second-World text, that is, have always been complicit in colonialism's territorial appropriation of land, and voice, and agency, and this has been their inescapable condition even at those moments when they have promulgated their most strident and most spectacular figures of postcolonial resistance. In the Second World, anti-colonialist resistances in literature must necessarily *cut across the individual subject*, and as they do so they also, necessarily, contribute towards that theoretically rigorous understanding of textual resistance which post-colonial *critical* theory is only now learning how to recognize. This ambivalence of emplacement is the *condition* of their possibility; it has been since the beginning; and it is therefore scarcely surprising that the ambivalent, the mediated, the conditional, and the radically *compromised* literatures of this undefinable Second World have an enormous amount yet to tell to 'theory' about the nature of literary resistance.

This *internalization* of the object of resistance in Second-World literatures, this internalization of the self/other binary of colonialist relations, explains why it is that it has always been Second-World *literary* writing rather than Second-World *critical* writing which has occupied the vanguard of a Second-World post-colonial literary or critical *theory*. Literary writing is *about* internalized conflict, whereas critical writing – for most practitioners – is still grounded in the ideology of unitariness, and coherence, and specific argumentative drive. For this reason, Second-World *critical* writing – with some spectacularly transgressive exceptions – has tended to miss out on the rigours of what, I would argue, comprises a necessarily ambivalent, necessarily contra/dictory or incoherent, anti-colonialist *theory* of resistance. In literary documents such as De Mille's *Strange Manuscript* or Furphy's *Such Is Life*, to name two nineteenth-century examples, or in the 're-historical' fictions of writers such as Fiona Kidman, Ian Wedde, Thea Astley, Peter Carey, Kate Grenville, Barbara Hanrahan, Daphne Marlatt, Susan Swan, and Rudy Wiebe – to name only a *few* from the contemporary period – this necessary *entanglement* of anti-colonial resistances within the colonialist machineries they seek to displace has been consistently thematized, consistently worked *through*, in ways that the unitary and logical demands of critical argumentation, at least in its traditional genres, have simply not allowed.

A fully adequate version of the argument I am making here would attempt to show in detail how at least one of these Second-World fictional texts manages to articulate a post-colonial or anti-colonial reading for resistance. For the purposes of the larger debate I am attempting to address, however, it may prove more useful to close with two subsidiary arguments about post-colonial critical practice, and then to open the floor – if one can do that in writing – to the kinds of critical cross-questioning which the field of post-colonial research and teaching at present needs to engage with.

The first point concerns a loss that I think we sustain if we hold too nostalgically to an expanded but at heart nation-based model of post-colonial criticism – whether that model applies to a 'Commonwealth' or to a 'Third- and Fourth-World' constituency. If 'post-colonial literature' becomes a term for designating an essential unitariness in the lived experience of different and dispersed peoples, all of the critical problems which accrue around nationalist models of critical definition – the hegemonic force of the concept of 'nation,' for example, and the necessary blindness that the concept settles upon the internally marginalized – will simply be carried forward into a new object of study, and we will be constrained to replay in our field all of the debates that have troubled each one of the positivist categories of period and place that comprise traditional English studies. Our object of attention will be differentiated from that of other areas by the usual categories, but our field, in essence, will remain an add-on discipline, a marker of the infinite ability of traditional English studies to accommodate national and historical difference within its inherently liberal embrace. We have a chance, however, to employ our field more radically: we can use it to raise questions about the kinds of work literary documents perform in culture, and we can use it to question the discourses of inclusivity and 'coverage' which have so often been deployed within English studies to depoliticize literary writing and to obscure the struggle for power which takes place within textual representation.

The second and final point I want to make concerns the way in which our interest in multiple, racially mixed, gendered and engendered, national and trans-national post-colonial literatures not only carries us inescapably into the theatre of colonialist and neo-colonialist power relations, but also carries us into the figurative domains of other modes of power as they appear in and are contested through the field of literary writing. Post-colonial texts are *also* concerned with the problem of privilege through racism and patriarchy, also at work contesting the kinds of hierarchical exclusion which operate through homophobia, and nationalism, and adultism; and in part this means that the debate over the post-colonial field and over the question of anti-colonialist literary resistance will never tell us everything about the struggles for power that actually take place under colonialism's baleful gaze. Rather, this debate tells us that all of our negotiations for change – in literature and criticism, in pedagogy, in immediate political engagement – are marked by provisionality and partiality, and are bounded by an historical specificity that does not simply translate itself into other theatres of social contestation. But more encouragingly, it also hints to us of the presence of figural activity for agency and resistance going on in cultural places we have somehow been taught to ignore. We need to specify our resistances to power, but we need also to recognize the ubiquity of resistances and to understand their incompleteness, their strengths, their losses and their gains. 'There is another world but it is in this one,' quotes Lawson. There is also a *second* world of post-colonial literary resistance, but it inhabits a place – a place of radical ambivalence – where too much post-colonial criticism in the First World has so far forgotten to look.

Notes

1 Arun Mukherjee, 'Whose Post-Colonialism and Whose Postmodernism?' *World Literature Written in English* 30.2 (1990), pp. 1–9.
2 Linda Hutcheon, ' "Circling the Downspout of Empire": Post-Colonialism and Postmodernism,' *Ariel* 20.4 (1989), pp. 149–75.
3 Timothy Brennan, *Salman Rushdie and the Third World: Myths of the Nation* (London: Macmillan, 1989), p. 5.
4 Brennan, *Salman Rushdie and the Third World*, pp. 35–6.
5 Laura Donaldson, 'The Miranda Complex: Colonialism and the Question of Feminist Reading,' *Diacritics* (Fall 1988), p. 68.
6 See Diana Brydon, 'Re-writing The Tempest,' *WLWE* 23.1 (1984), p. 75–88, and Chantal Zabus, 'A Calibanic Tempest in Anglophone and Francophone New World Writing,' *Canadian Literature* 104 (1985), pp. 35–50.
7 Selwyn R. Cudjoe, *Resistance in Caribbean Literature* (Athens, Ohio: Ohio University Press, 1980), and Barbara Harlow, *Resistance Literature* (New York and London: Methuen, 1987).

8 Jenny Sharpe, 'Figures of Colonial Resistance,' *Modern Fiction Studies* 35.1 (1989), p. 139.
9 Michel Foucault, *The Archaeology of Knowledge*, trans. A. M. Sheridan Smith (New York: Random House, 1973).
10 Sharpe, 'Figures,' p. 138.
11 Sharpe, 'Figures,' p. 145.
12 Sharpe, 'Figures,' p. 143.
13 Alan Lawson, ' "There Is Another World but It Is in This One": A Cultural Paradigm for the Second World,' Paper given at the Badlands Conference on Australian and Canadian literatures, Calgary, Alberta, 1986.

5

Benita Parry

Resistance Theory/Theorising Resistance or Two Cheers for Nativism *

it is not the literal past, the 'facts' of history, that shape us, but images of the past embodied in language ... we must never cease renewing those images, because once we do, we fossilise.

Brian Friel, *Translations*[1]

I

That the colonised were never successfully pacified is well known to the postcolonial study of colonialism and the long and discontinuous process of decolonisation.[2] But proposals on how resistance is to be theorised display fault-lines within the discussion that rehearse questions about subjectivity, identity, agency and the status of the reverse-discourse as an oppositional practice, posing problems about the appropriate models for contemporary counter-hegemonic work. An agenda which disdains the objective of restoring the colonised as subject of its own history does so on the grounds that a simple inversion perpetuates the coloniser/colonised opposition within the terms defined by colonial discourse, remaining complicit with its assumptions by retaining undifferentiated identity categories, and failing to contest the conventions of that system of knowledge it supposedly challenges. Instead the project of a postcolonial critique is designated as deconstructing and displacing the Eurocentric premises of a discursive apparatus which constructed the Third World not only for the west but also for the cultures so represented.[3]

The performance of such procedures does display Richard Terdiman's contention that 'no discourse is ever a monologue; nor could it ever be analyzed intrinsically ... everything that constitutes it always presupposes a horizon of competing, contrary utterances against which it asserts its own energies'.[4] However, the statements of the theoretical paradigms, where it can appear that the efficacy of colonialism's apparatus of social control in effecting strategies of disempowerment is totalised, are liable to be (mis)read as producing the colonised as a stable category fixed in a position of subjugation, hence

---

* From Francis Barker *et al.* eds., *Colonial Discourse/Postcolonial Theory* (Manchester University Press, 1994), pp. 172–93.

foreclosing on the possibility of theorising resistance. Even if this is a crass misrepresentation of the project, the colonised's refusals of their assigned positions as subjected and disarticulated are not – and within its terms cannot be – accorded centre stage.

The premise to modes of criticism within the postcolonial critique which are attentive to those moments and processes when the colonised clandestinely or overtly took up countervailing stances is that no system of coercion or hegemony is ever able wholly to determine the range of subject positions. For although the colonial is a product of colonialism's ideological machinery, the formation of its differentiated and incommensurable subjectivities is the effect of many determinants, numerous interpellations and various social practices.[5] A postcolonial rewriting of past contestation, dependent as it is on a notion of a multiply (dis)located native whose positions are provisional, and therefore capable of annulment and transgression, does not restore the foundational, fixed and autonomous individual; what it does resort to is the discourse of the subject inscribed in histories of insubordination produced by anti-colonial movements, deciphered from cryptic cultural forms and redevised from vestiges perpetuated through constant transmutation in popular memory and oral traditions.

There is of course abundant evidence of native disaffection and dissent under colonial rule, of contestation and struggle against diverse forms of institutional and ideological domination. Inscriptions and signs of resistance are discernible in official archives and informal texts, and can be located in narrativised instances of insurrection and organised political opposition. Traces of popular disobedience can also be recuperated from unwritten symbolic and symptomatic practices in which a rejection or violation of the subject positions assigned by colonialism is registered. Here the modes of refusal are not readily accommodated in the anticolonialist discourses written by the elites of the nationalist and liberation movements. Since they were not calculated to achieve predetermined political ends or to advance the cause of nation-building, the anarchic and nihilistic energies of defiance and identity-assertion, which were sometimes nurtured by dreams, omens and divination, and could take the form of theatre, violated notions of rational protest.[6]

If we look at the work of contemporary critics recuperating figures of colonial resistance, not from the rhetorical strategies of the dominant discourses but by revisiting dispersed and connotative informal sources, these projects do not appear as preoccupied with victimage, or as enacting a regressive search for an aboriginal and intact condition/tradition from which a proper sense of historicity is occluded – charges which have been made against such undertakings. As an instance of a resistant mode available to the colonial Caribbean, Wilson Harris cites limbo dancing, a practice stemming from Africa and reinterpreted on the slave ships of the Middle Passage, and which although indebted to the past – as is voodoo – is not an imitation of that past but rather 'a crucial inner re-creative response to the violations of slavery and indenture and conquest'.[7] Such a strategy is not the total recall of an African past since that African past in terms of tribal sovereignty or sovereignties was modified or traumatically eclipsed with the Middle Passage and with generations of change that followed. Limbo was rather the renascence of a new corpus of sensibility that could translate and accommodate African and other legacies within a new architecture of cultures.[8]

Does revisiting the repositories of memory and cultural survivals in the cause of postcolonial refashioning have a fixed retrograde valency? Such censure is surely dependent on who is doing the remembering and why: certainly as Rashmi Bhatnagar suggests, in some situations the mythologising of beginnings can be suspect 'in that it can unwittingly serve the reactionary forces of revivalism. Nowhere is this danger greater than in the Indian context, where the search for the source of Hindu identity in Vedic times has almost invariably led to a loss of commitment to our contemporary plural/secular identity'.[9] A very different impulse towards recuperating a very different history marked by discontinuities and erasures is attested by Edouard Glissant whose repeated references to the Acoma tree intimates that the need to renew or activate memories is distinct from the uncritical attempt to conserve tradition: 'One of the trees that has disappeared from the Martinican forest. We should not get too attached to the tree, we might then forget the forest. But we should remember it'.[10] In his aphoristic and fragmentary critical writings Glissant urges a postcolonial construction of the past that, far from being a desire to discover a remote paternity, is an imaginative reworking of the process of *métissage* or an infinite wandering across cultures including those of Africa. Because the slave trade snatched African-Caribbeans from their original matrix, erasing memory and precluding the ability to map a sequence, Glissant contends that it is the function of a contemporary counter-poetics to engender that tormented chronology:

> For history is not only absence for us. It is vertigo. The time that was never ours we must now possess. We do not see it stretch into our past and calmly take us into tomorrow, but it explodes in us as a compact mass, pushing through a dimension of emptiness where we must with difficulty and pain put it all back together.[11]

Since these are definitions of a discursively produced resurgent subjectivity that is volatile, polyglot and unconcerned with discovering the persistence of an original state, it would seem that critics who continue to valorise the identity struggle, and to reclaim forms of situated agency asserted in the struggle over representation, do so without returning to the notion of an ahistorical essential and unified self. In this vein Stuart Hall has braved the reprobation directed against ethnic identitarianism, to make a carefully modulated case for decoupling ethnicity from its equivalence with nationalism, imperialism, racism and the state as it functions in the dominant discourse, and appropriating it for a different usage in the current postcolonial discussion: 'The term ethnicity acknowledges the place of history, language and culture in the construction of subjectivity and identity, as well as the fact that all discourse is placed, positioned, situated, and all knowledge is contextual'.[12] Now although Hall is wary of postmodernism's 'absolutist discourse', since he considers that 'the politics of absolute dispersal is the politics of no action at all', he defines subjectivity as 'a narrative, a story, a history. Something constructed, told, spoken, not simply found',[13] and identity as an invention 'which is never complete, always in process, and always constituted within ... representation'.[14]

Hall is quite aware of the colonial subject as the product of multiple constitutions, of the contradictions and overdeterminations of postcolonial ideological positions – having written of these as always negotiated and negotiable – and of ethnic and cultural difference as sites of articulation. He has all the same directed attention to the indispensable role played in all colonial struggles by a conception of ' "cultural identity" in terms of one shared culture, a sort of collective "one true self" ... which people with a shared history and ancestry hold in common'. This, he adds, 'continues to be a very powerful and creative force in emergent forms of representation amongst hitherto marginalized peoples ... We should not ... underestimate or neglect ... the importance of the act of imaginative rediscovery which this conception of a rediscovered essential identity entails'.[15] And before we pillory Hall for reviving the myth of an organic communality, we should note that he emphasises the impossibility of its indivisible, homogeneous meaning, recognising this to be an 'imaginary reunification', imposing an 'imaginary coherence' on the experience of dispersal and fragmentation, and acknowledging that its other side is rupture and discontinuity.

Because in another register Henry Louis Gates Jr has reclaimed the *ethnos* from vilification as false consciousness,[16] it could appear that there is a move to restore affect to the fiction of identity, and rather than the toleration extended to its expedient use in political mobilisation, we see it embraced as a pleasure, and one that is all the greater because identity is now perceived as multi-located and polysemic – a situation that characterises postcoloniality and is at its most evident in the diasporic condition. An uninhibited statement of the gratification of inhabiting many cultures and identifying with all oppressions and persecutions, while electing to be affiliated to one's natal community, comes from the artist R. B. Kitaj, in whose paintings Rosa Luxembourg and Walter Benjamin are emblematic figures of that particular and permanent condition of diaspora in which he is at home:

> The compelling destiny of dispersion ... describes and explains my parable pictures, their dissolutions, repressions, associations, referrals, their text obsessions, their play of difference ... People are always saying that the meanings in my pictures refuse to be fixed, to be settled, to be stable: that's Diasporism ... Diasporist art is contradictory at its heart, being both internationalist and particularist ... The Diasporist's pursuit of a homeless logic of *ethnie* may be the radical core of a newer art than we can yet imagine ... the Jews do not own Diaspora, they are not the only Diasporists ... They are merely mine.[17]

There are moreover critics who testify to the possibility that the identity struggle of one community can serve as a model for other resistant discourses, since the self-definition articulated by, say, the black or the Jew in defiance of received representations can be communicated to different situations of contest against the authority of the dominant by marginals, exiles and subjugated populations.[18]

II

When we consider the narratives of decolonisation, we encounter rhetorics in which 'nativism' in one form or another is evident. Instead of disciplining these, theoretical whip in hand, as a catalogue of epistemological error, of essentialist mystifications, as a masculinist appropriation of dissent, as no more than an anti-racist racism, etc., I want to consider what is to be gained by an unsententious interrogation of such articulations which, if often driven by negative passion, cannot be reduced to a mere inveighing against iniquities or a repetition of the canonical terms of imperialism's conceptual framework. This of course means affirming the power of the reverse-discourse[19] by arguing that anticolonialist writings did challenge, subvert and undermine the ruling ideologies, and nowhere more so than in overthrowing the hierarchy of coloniser/colonised, the speech and stance of the colonised refusing a position of subjugation and dispensing with the terms of the coloniser's definitions.

The weak and strong forms of oppositional discursive practices have been designated as counter-identification and disidentification,[20] and re/citation and de/citation.[21] For Pêcheux a 'discourse-against' is that in which the subject of enunciation takes up a position of separation 'with respect to what "the universal subject" gives him to think ... (distantiation, doubt, interrogation, challenge, revolt) ... a struggle against ideological evidentness on the terrain of that evidentness, an evidentness with a negative sign, reversed on its own terrain'. Disidentification however 'constitutes a *working* (transformation-displacement) of the *subject-form* and not just its abolition'.[22] In Terdiman's terms, the technique of re/citation seeks 'to surround the[ir] antagonist and neutralize or explode it'; whereas de/citation, a total withdrawal from the orbit of the dominant, strives 'to exclude it totally, to expunge it'.[23] Neither writes off the force of the counter-discursive, and Terdiman, who concedes that reverse-discourses are always interlocked with and parasitic on the dominant they contest – working as opposition without effacing the antagonist, inhabiting and struggling with the dominant which inhabits them – maintains that they function to survey the limits and weaknesses of the dominant by mapping the internal incoherences: 'From this dialectic of discursive struggle, truths about the social formation – its characteristic modes of reproduction and its previously hidden vulnerabilities – inevitably emerge'.[24]

A recent discussion of nativism condenses many of the current censures of cultural nationalism for its complicity with the terms of colonialism's discourse, with its claims to ancestral purity and inscriptions of monolithic notions of identity cited as evidence of the failure to divest itself of the specific institutional determinations of the west. Although allowing the profound political significance of the decolonised writing themselves as subjects of a literature of their own, Anthony Appiah's critique, which is principally directed against its current forms, extends to older (all?) articulations. In exposing the operation of a 'nativist topology' – inside/outside, indigene/alien, western/traditional – it installs a topology of its own, where the coloniser is dynamic donor and the colonised is docile recipient, where the west initiates and the native imitates. Thus while the reciprocity of the colonial relationship is stressed, all power remains with western discourse. For example: 'the overdetermined course of cultural nationalism in Africa has been to make real the imaginary identities to which Europe has subjected us';[25] the rhetoric of 'intact indigenous traditions' and the very conception of an African personality and an African past are European inventions; the Third World intellectual is Europhone, immersed in the language and literature of the colonial countries. These statements could be modulated without underplaying or obscuring a necessary registration of western discursive power: Europe's fabrications of 'Africa' were deflected and subverted by African, Caribbean and African-American literary discourses; 'African identity' is the product of refusing Europe's gaze and returning its own anti-colonialist look; Europhone colonials transgress their immersion in European languages and literatures, seizing and diverting vocabularies, metaphors and literary traditions.

The occasion for Appiah's case against nativism is *Toward the decolonization of African literature* – whose authors, Chinweizu, Jemie and Madubuike, invite censure for taking an unqalified position on cultural autonomy – but its object is a critique of cultural nationalism's entrapment in a reverse-discourse:

> Railing against the cultural hegemony of the West, the nativists are of its party without knowing it. Indeed the very arguments, the rhetoric of defiance, that our nationalists muster are ... canonical, time tested ... In their ideological inscription, the cultural nationalists remain in a position of counteridentification ... which is to continue to participate in an institutional configuration – to be subjected to cultural identities they ostensibly decry ... Time and time again, cultural nationalism has followed the route of alternate genealogizing. We end up always in the same place; the achievement is to have invented a different past for it.[26]

The effect of this argument is to homogenise the varieties of nationalisms and to deny both originality and effectivity to its reverse-discourses. Such a contention is disputed by Partha Chatterjee's study which, despite a subtitle (*A derivative discourse*) encouraging selective citation in the interest of relegating nationalist thought as mimetic and while recognising the inherent contradiction of its reasoning within a framework of knowledge serving a structure of power it seeks to repudiate, is concerned to establish its *difference*: 'Its politics impel it to open up that framework of knowledge that presumes to dominate it, to displace that framework, to subvert its authority, to challenge its morality'.[27]

Some of the implications of arguments according a totalising power to colonialist discourses emerges in Rosalind O'Hanlon's discussion of current research concerned to emphasise the British 'invention' of nineteenth-century caste as a challenge to 'the notion of an ageless caste-bound social order', but which maximises the effectivity of 'colonial conjuring', and by occluding the 'complex and contradictory engagements with colonialist categories ... often produces a picture of Indian actors who are helpless to do anything but reproduce the structures of their own subordination'.[28] In this connection Ranajit Guha's eloquent inventory establishing the presence of an 'Indian idiom of politics' discernible in the many languages of the subcontinent, demonstrates that the modes of subaltern colonial resistance, far from being determined by forms and vocabularies borrowed from the dominant culture, were rearticulations of pre-colonial traditions of protest.[29]

Mindful of Robert Young's caution that the search for a 'nativist alternative' may simply represent 'the narcissistic desire to find an other that will reflect Western assumptions of selfhood',[30] I will argue that something quite different animates those modes of postcolonial critique concerned to reconstruct a story from tales, legends and idioms which are themselves transcriptions and improvisations of dissent that was never formally narrativised, and to produce an uncensorious but critical interrogation of colonial resistances when they were. It will be evident that the interest of such readings is to retain in the discussion that realm of imaginary freedom which these histories prefigured or configured, as well as to register decolonising struggles as an emancipatory project despite the egregious failures these brought in their wake. Although the assumption here is that the discourses or discursive retracings of past dissidence come to us already encoded with the elements of a counter-narrative (which diminishes the critics' claim to be performing the insurgent act), it is we who by appropriating it to our theoretical purposes alter the material, in the process making visible its erasures, suppressions and marginalisations, evident for example in the foregrounding of male figures of praxis and authority.

Elleke Boehmer's discussion of narratives of nationalist recuperation, identity reconstruction and nation formation shows how images of the female body were used to embody ideals of the wholeness of subjectivity, history and the state. Thus, while reversing colonialist iconography figuring penetration, pillage and dismemberment – 'repression upon the objectified, enslaved, colonised body' – such invocations of the female body 'rest[s] upon the assumption of predominantly masculine authority and historical agency', nationalism's core concepts nesting in the metaphor of the maternal body. Because, Boehmer argues, postcolonial discourses of self-determination 'have a considerable investment in nationalist concepts of "selving" and of retrieving history, the gender specifics of nationalist iconography are accepted, or borne with, or overlooked', the deconstructions of such configurations only now being effected in postcolonial literatures.[31] In a related register, Ella Shohat writes that 'Anticolonial intellectuals, though not particularly-preoccupied with gender issues, have ... used gender tropes to discuss colonialism', Césaire and Fanon implicitly subverting representations of rape by violent dark men and cultures, and fantasies of rescuing virginal white and at times dark women, 'while at the same time using gendered discourse to articulate oppositional struggle'.[32]

Such modulated attention to the retention of patriarchal positions in anticolonialist discourses points up the inadvisibility of using the sources to write an optimistic narrative of liberation struggles as 'ideologically correct'. But in order to do justice to their histories – to borrow a phrase from Jonathan Dollimore[33] – it is surely necessary to refrain from a sanctimonious reproof of modes of writing resistance which do not conform to contemporary theoretical rules about discursive radicalism. Instead I would argue that the task is to address the empowering effects of constructing a coherent identity or of cherishing and defending against calumniation altered and mutable indigenous forms, which is not the same as the hopeless attempt to locate and revive pristine pre-colonial cultures.[34] It is an unwillingness to abstract resistance from its moment of performance that informs my discussion of Césaire and Fanon as authors of liberation theories which today could stand accused of an essentialist politics. For, as I read them, both affirmed the invention of an insurgent, unified black self, acknowledged the revolutionary energies released by valorising the cultures denigrated by colonialism and, rather than construing the colonialist relationship in terms of negotiations with the structures of imperialism, privileged coercion over hegemony to project it as a struggle between implacably opposed forces – an irony made all too obvious in enunciations inflected, indeed made possible, by these very negotiations.

III

These remarks are a prelude to my considering whether those articulations of cultural nationalism I examine can be disposed of as a reverse ethnocentrism which simply reproduces existing categories, performing an identical function and producing the same effects as the system it contests. My route will be to Fanon via Négritude, an unsafe road since, despite its heterogeneous languages and its interrogations of western thought, this body of writing is routinely disparaged as the most exorbitant manifestation of a mystified ethnic essentialism, as an undifferentiated and retrograde discourse installing notions of a foundational and fixed native self and demagogically asserting the recovery of an immutable past. Perhaps this would account for the current tendency to ignore Fanon's voyage into and then around Négritude or to dismiss it as a detour not mapped onto his theories. However, as the path of his project passed through the thickets of uncertain affiliation and irresolute withholding before emerging as unequivocal denunciation, this suggests that the appointment of Fanon as exemplar of anticolonialist theory liberated from identitarian thinking should perhaps be qualified.

In his unsententious critique of decolonising discourses Edward Said suggests a progression from nativist through nationalist to liberation theory. While acknowledging the transgressive energies of the former in deranging the discourses of domination ranged against the colonised, and recognising the achievement of nationalist movements in winning statutory independence for the occupied territories, it is liberation writing which is credited with producing a politics of secular illumination, articulating a transformation of social consciousness beyond ethnicity and reconceiving the possibilities of human experience in non-imperialist terms.[35] Not only are the stages less disjunct than the periodisation suggests – messianic movements and Pan-Africanism were utopian in their goals, Nkrumah's nationalism was not exclusively Africanist, acknowledging as it did the recombinant qualities of a culture which had developed through assimilating Arabic and western features, and so on – but the liberation theory of Fanon and Césaire was more impure than is here indicated, nativism remaining audible despite the strenuous endorsements of a post-European, transnational humanism as the ultimate goal.

Négritude's moment of articulation and reception – before the nationalist movements in Africa and the Caribbean had gained momentum, but after Marxist critiques of colonialism had been developed within the Indian independence struggle – may testify to both its originality as a cultural-political position and its limitations as an ideology. Many of the contemporary objections to Négritude came from those who had welcomed its inception, and were delivered from a Marxist standpoint. These can be arranged into the following categories: systemised mystification construing 'black being' as irrational and 'black culture' as genetically determined, unified and transnational, thus fostering the universalising myth of a unified black identity in the face of its multiplicity and diversity; political error in failing to represent the anti-colonial struggle as the national liberation of all classes, or to acknowledge the specificities of each national culture in the colonised world and, in the case of the Caribbean, in driving a wedge between African and other oppressed communities; theoretical error in distorting African world-views and overlooking that the synthesising of indigenous with foreign elements in the colonised world had issued in complex and particularised modes of *mestizaje* or creolisation[36] – sometimes, though rarely, this fusing being differently represented as the reconciliation of the African with the western, or even complete cultural acclimatisation to the west.[37]

What is notable is that many critics of Négritude were prepared either to concede its liberating effects in fostering new modes of consciousness[38] or to offer alternative means of constituting reconceived identities. To counter the mystifications of Négritude, the Haitian writer Jacques Stéphen Alexis in the 1950s proposed 'marvellous realism' as a literary practice appropriate to producing the fantastic reality of the Caribbean's broken histories, different temporalities and creolised cultural identities.[39] In another register, René Depestre, who dissociated himself from Négritude's indifference to the diverse material conditions of cultural constitution and national character, emphasised the 'syncretic elaboration of cultural elements taken from Africa and Europe', offering an alternative and not dissimilar programme of ideological *'cimarronaje'* as the means for Caribbeans to resist depersonalisation: 'This cultural escape is an original form of rebellion which has manifested itself in religion, in folklore, in art and singularly in Caribbean literatures', the people in search of their identity becoming aware 'of the validity of their African heritage latent in our society'.[40]

The sustained attack on Négritude as an irrational ideology which perpetuated western stereotypes came during the 1960s from a new generation of African philosophers and intellectuals concerned to expose the errors in notions of Africanism and the African personality. Scholars such as Stanislas Adotevi, Marcien Towa and Paulin Hountondji attacked notions of the African as an intuitive being, of a fixed black essence and a static African culture, and dismissed 'ethnophilosophy' for failing to distinguish between cultural anthropology and philosophy's critical activity when attempting to demonstrate the existence of a distinctive African mode of philosophical thinking.[41] According to Irele, Hountondji refuses to concede 'any positive significance to the effort to rehabilitate African culture', asserting that the relationship between Négritude and the ideology it intends to combat revealed 'a peculiar ambiguity, a pathetic correspondence between the terms of African affirmation and the opposite system of ideas or representations proposed by the colonial ideology in its image of Africa'.[42] The revolutionary socialist Towa, however, despite his repudiation of a cultural nationalism that seeks to resuscitate a heritage of past values irrelevant to the modernising preoccupations and goals of contemporary Africa and his hostility to the state Négritude of Senegal and the Cameroons, acknowledges the inspiration of Césaire and has referred to him as the prophet of the revolution of black people: 'he announced the freedom of the Black [*Nègre*], he prophesied with his great voice the "Beautiful City", a world in which the Black could be himself, master of his destiny'.[43]

The presence of absolutist denunciations of Négritude makes it necessary to recall its historical juncture and to differentiate between the articulations subsumed under its rubric. As a structure of feeling and a seizure of the means of self-representation by a rebellious elite, Négritude was anticipated by the Haitian literary movement of the nineteenth century and in the United States by the Back to Africa Movements and later by Dubois's Pan-Negroism and Pan-Africanism.[44] The definitive articulations of Négritude are however usually attributed to the activities of students, writers and intellectuals from the French colonies, who were closely associated with African-American expatriates in Paris during the early 1930s, the prime movers being Senghor from Senegal, Césaire from Martinique and Léon Damas from French Guiana. (The subsequent dissemination of the movement was promoted by Alioune Diop's *Présence Africaine* which began publication in 1947.) Irele[45] has characterised Négritude as the francophone equivalent of Pan-Africanism and a distinct current in African national consciousness and cultural nationalism. All the same, the extent to which Négritude was embraced by the African-Caribbean diaspora is significant both to the willed construction of Africa as a country of the mind, rather than a representation of a geohistorical place, to the notion of 'Africa' as the homeland of dispersed populations in search of solidarity, and to the construing of black identity as creolised and dislocated. Here it could be noted that if there were exponents prone to definitions of an intrinsic black nature and a unified black culture centred on an eternal Africa, others deployed 'black' as a multi-inflected signifier of oppression and resistance, energising a discursive stance from which colonialism's most eloquent creatures interrogated the essentialising definitions foisted on peoples of African origins. In this mode, exemplified by Césaire's poetry, Négritude is not a recovery of a pre-existent state, but a textually invented history, an identity effected through figurative operations, and a tropological construction of blackness as a sign of the colonised condition and its refusal.

Commentators on Négritude tend to distinguish between Senghor's biologically determined notion of blackness as a distinctive mode of being and a collective identity in which emotion and intuition are located as the essential attributes of the race (though Senghor did insist on the actuality and desirability of cross-cultural fertilisation), and Césaire's historical/cultural concept. Arnold,[46] however, suggests that at the outset their views approximated, both having been influenced by the obscurantist ethnological notions of the subsequently discredited Frobenius, and by anti-rational philosophers such as Spengler and Bergson. But by the 1940s Césaire, at the time a member of the Communist Party, with which he broke in 1958,[47] was concerned, in his analysis of colonialism as economic exploitation and cultural aggression, to establish a theoretical rather than a metaphysical basis to Négritude, hence rejecting the attempt to essentialise an African world-view or to define it as a closed system. The perspective in his *Discourse on colonialism* is resolutely transnational and, while honouring an ante-European past, looks to a post-European future, the dossier on the west's sham humanism anticipating Fanon's execration in *The wretched of the earth*:

> The Indians massacred, the Moslem world drained of itself, the Chinese world defiled and perverted for a good century; the Negro world disqualified; mighty voices stilled forever; all this wreckage, all this waste, humanity reduced to a monologue, and you think that all this does not have its price? The truth is that this policy *cannot but bring about the ruin of Europe itself*, and that Europe, if it is not careful, will perish from the void it has created around itself ... what else has bourgeois Europe done? It has undermined civilizations, destroyed countries, ruined nationalities, extirpated 'the root of diversity'.[48]

Where Césaire is sure to be faulted by those who deplore nativist nostalgia is in his lament for what colonialism has destroyed:

> the wonderful Indian civilizations – and neither Deterding nor Royal Dutch nor Standard Oil will ever console me for the Aztecs and the Incas ... [for] extraordinary *possibilities* wiped out ... For my part I make a systematic defense of the non-European civilizations ... They were communal societies, never societies of the many for the few. They were societies that were not only ante-capitalist ... but also anti-capitalist ... I systematically defend our old Negro civilizations; they were courteous civilizations.[49]

An explicit reconstruction of Négritude's beginnings can be found in Césaire's 1967 interview with the Haitian writer and political activist René Depestre, where he speaks of the programme as a collective creation of Africans, North Americans, Antilleans, Guianans and Haitians who came together in Paris during the 1930s to give expression to their struggle against alienation and the politics of assimilation:

> We adopted the word *nègre* as a term of defiance ... We found a violent affirmation in the words *nègre* and *négritude* ... it is a concrete rather than an abstract coming to

consciousness ... We lived in an atmosphere of rejection, and we developed an inferiority complex ... I have always thought that the black man was searching for his identity. And ... if what we want is to establish this identity, then we must have a concrete consciousness of what we are – that is of the first fact of our lives: that we are black; that we were black and have a history.... [that] there have been beautiful and important black civilizations ... that its values were values that could still make an important contribution to the world.[50]

This concrete coming to consciousness was realized by Césaire as a poet; and because many of the writings of Négritude are open to some or all of the charges made against it as an ideological tendency, any argument that as a literary practice it performed a textual struggle for self-representation in which the indeterminacy of language ruptured fixed configurations, invented a multivalent blackness, and wrenched 'Africa' out of its time-bound naming and into new significations, is most readily made by referring to his over-determined and polysemic poetry. Although made possible, as he concedes, by surrealism, this exceeded the influence of European modes and violated its forms in what Arnold calls a 'sophisticated hybridization, corrosion and parody' of western traditions.[51]

In an essay on Césaire, James Clifford argues for uncoupling his coinage of Négritude from the 'elaboration of a broad black identity' and attaching it to 'very specific affirmations and negations', citing the passage in *Notebook* beginning 'my negritude is not ... '.[52] However Clifford's selective citation of 'The verb "marronner" / for René Depestre, Haitian poet' suggests that the trajectory of his case is directed at dissociating Césaire from Négritude. The poem, written in 1955 and subsequently published in numerous revised versions, was Césaire's response to Depestre's ready compliance with the Communist Party's decree against surrealism and for accessible and committed verse. Clifford's reading is appropriately concerned with how 'Césaire makes rebellion and the remaking of culture – the historical maroon experience – into a ... necessary new verb [that] names the New World poetics of continuous transgression and cooperative cultural activity'.[53] But what is occluded is, as Arnold argues, that the poem appeals to Depestre not to abandon his Négritude – 'Courageous tom-tom rider / is it true that you mistrust the native forest ... is it possible / that the rains of exile / have slackened the drum skin of your voice?' – entreating him to 'escape the shackles of European prosody' (Arnold) just as in the past slaves had escaped from bondage, to this end coining the neologism 'marronner': 'shall we escape like slaves Depestre, like slaves' (in an earlier version this read: 'Let's escape them Depestre let's escape them / As in the past we escaped our whip-wielding masters').[54]

It is possible to disregard Césaire's account of his intentions when he speaks of his poetry as a way to break the stranglehold of accepted French form in order to create a new language, 'an Antillean French, a black French ... one capable of communicating the African heritage'.[55] However, we cannot overlook that poetry which adapted the structure of some African languages, and drew on African folklores and cosmologies, does effect an identification with Africa – 'from brooding too long on the Congo / I have become a Congo resounding with forests and rivers'[56] – and does construct an imaginary Africa as signifier of the legacy shared by Africans of the continent and the diaspora. The 'Guinea' of his 'Ode to Guinea', written before the name was adopted by a post-independence territory, is the mythic land of the Caribbean creole languages – the 'Africa' or 'Guinea' that is the heaven of black peoples – and the 'Ethiopia' of 'Ethiopia ... / for Alioune Diop' embodies what Eshleman and Smith call 'the dignity lost to other African peoples', a location occupying a special place 'in the personal mythology of Négritude writers'.[57] By rewriting the stories of Africa's long oppressions – see 'All the way from Akkad, from Elam, from Sumer' and 'Africa' – Césaire derives an ethos common to all blacks, out of which an anti-colonial and ultimately an anti-capitalist identity can be constituted, as in 'A salute to the Third World / for Léopold Sedar Senghor' where connections between the Caribbean dispersal and the African motherland are forged before gesturing towards a larger and more inclusive solidarity.

Arnold's attention to the shifting values produced by images of blackness in *Notebook of a return to a native land* convinces that this is indeed 'The epic of Négritude' and a classic in the literature of decolonisation. What Arnold traces is how through the creation of a new style, the transformation of black consciousness and the self-construction of an African – Caribbean identity is enacted, the neologism 'Négritude' occurring both to hail past glories in Haiti and to signify abjection before its 'third and decisive statement of negritude' as reconciled to itself:[58] 'my negritude is not a / stone, its deafness hurled against the clamour of the day ... / my negritude is neither tower nor cathedral / it takes root in the red flesh of the soil / it takes root in the ardent flesh of the sky'.[59] As an instance of what Ella Shohat calls the use of gendered discourse in articulating anti-colonialist struggles, she cites Césaire's remark about adventurers violating Africa 'to make the stripping of her easier'.[60] Yet although his poetry does invoke Africa as inscribed on the woman's body (see 'Ode to Guinea', 'Hail to Guinea', 'Africa', 'Ethiopia' and 'A salute to the Third World'), and while the authoritative voice is masculine, the figure of suffering and endurance is not invariably the woman, and in *Notebook* the trope of Négritude is doubly gendered: 'all our blood aroused by the male heart of the sun / those who know about the feminity of the moon's oily body / the reconciled exultation of antelope and star / those whose survival travels in the germination of grass! / Eia perfect circle of the world, enclosed concordance'.[61]

The multivalencies of Césaire's Négritude pre-empts both closure and fixity, making it available to rearticulations covering other modes of oppression. It has since been reinvoked by national liberation movements and continues to be renewed in unforeseen ways within the postcolonial critique – as when James Snead, while acknowledging the necessity of preserving the specificity of historical experience, commends a 'broad-based, even militant usage of the term black as a unifying metaphor', and an object of cultural identification and ideological bonding;[62] or when Kobena Mercer looks back to the redefinition of black identity in Britain during the early 1980s as 'an empowering signifier of Afro-Asian alliances'.[63] What was it then in Négritude that caused Fanon to recognise it as liberating and resist it as mystifying before launching a concerted attack which was at pains to signal that its hold on his thinking had been relinquished?

IV

The somewhat schematic summary which Mudimbe,[64] in an otherwise modulated account of the movement, gives of Fanon's relationship to Négritude – namely that an initial affiliation gave way to a position based on situating African ideologies of otherness as the antithesis to colonialist constitution, the synthesis to be realised in political liberation – tends to smooth over the persistent instabilities in Fanon's writings where proclamations of a future beyond ethnicity continue to be intercepted by affirmations of the immediate need to construct an insurgent black subjectivity. In another register, what Abiola Irele neglects when he claims that Césaire's poetry provided 'the essential ground-plan for Fanon's phenomenological reflection on black existence' in *Black skin, white masks*[65] is that, despite its many salutations to Césaire's liberating influences and its moments of unstable identification, the study effects the problematization of Négritude. Fanon may well have perceived his mode of thinking as dialectical; however, the language of his flamboyant writing (he wrote a number of plays which he chose not to publish) is witness to the conflicting predications remaining disjunct. Although such incommensurability is especially marked in *Black skin, white masks*, where Marxism co-exists with existentialism and psychoanalysis, scholarly citation is juxtaposed to anecdote, and the torsions of self-analysis are precariously balanced against the poised interpretation of a historical condition, none of his writings – with the exception of the last section of *The wretched of the earth* – is without the discord of incompatible testimony. Hence I will argue that Fanon's writings function at a point of tension between cultural nationalism and transnationality, without 'resolving' the contradiction and without yielding an attachment to the one or the aspiration to the other.

It is this 'historical Fanon' who never quite abandoned 'all fixity of identity', an ironic figure who resists recuperation as the paradigmatic figure of liberation theory that is recognised by Henry Louis Gates Jr.[66] Thus when Fanon moved from the many different first-person-singular voices deployed in the psycho-autobiography of an assimilated and insulted Martinican tempted by Négritude to the 'we' of Algerians and unspecified African communities in polemical writings proclaiming a new international community, he continued to concede the importance of valorising pre-colonial histories and cultures that had been systematically disfigured and devalued by colonialism:

> it was with the greatest delight that they discovered that there was nothing to be ashamed of in the past, but rather dignity, glory and solemnity. The claim to a national culture in the past does not only rehabilitate that nation and serve as a justification for the hope of a future national culture. In the sphere of psycho-affective equilibrium it is responsible for an important change in the native.[67]

As I read it, both an intellectual apprehension of blackness as a construct ('what is often called the black soul is a white man's artifact')[68] and a visceral attachment to the powerful fiction of black identity are always evident in *Black skin, white masks*, the language of criticism repeatedly interrupted by articulations of empathy with the impulse. What I will try to trace is how the precise statements of intention as laid down in the Introduction – i.e. a clinical study of the attitudes of the modern Antillean Negro and a psychopathological explanation of the state of being an Antillean Negro – mutate into the multivocal enunciations of the essays that follow, and where the stated brief is exceeded when specified Negroes are displaced by 'the Negro' in the white world. (All existing translations of Fanon use this term for the black person of African descent.) At the start, which appears to have been written first and does not attempt to elide the ensuing contradictions, Fanon outlines his project as the attempt to effect the disalienation of the depersonalised Negro by offering a psychological analysis of the massive psychoexistential complex produced through the juxtasposition of the white and black races. Although a passage from Césaire's *Discourse on colonialism* serves as the epigraph, and the importance of social and economic realities is acknowledged, no further reference is made to colonialism as the specific situation of the pathological juxtaposition. What is given space in an address directed at white and black brothers is the perspective of transcending the present and an insistence that if the existing structure is to be eliminated and the Negro extricated from his universe, then unilateral liberation is insufficient.

So here we find the vision of a condition beyond ethnicity already in place – 'I believe that the individual should tend to take on the universality inherent in the human condition' – while the attempt of blacks 'to prove to white men, at all costs, the richness of their thought, the equal value of their intellect' (p. 12) is designated as a symptom of that vicious circle where whites are sealed in their whiteness and blacks in their blackness. To break out of this entrapment, fervour is eschewed, and digging into one's flesh to find meaning is scorned, the narrative voice in 'The fact of blackness' distancing itself from its portrayal of the desperate struggle of the educated Negro, 'slave of the spontaneous and cosmic Negro myth ... driven to discover the meaning of black identity', who 'with rage in his mouth and abandon in his heart ... buries himself in the vast black abyss' (p. 16).

The incommensurable enunciations of *Black skin, white masks* produce a dissonance that is something other than ambivalence, for the adoption of heuristic procedures in order to establish Négritude as a pathology involves the speaking subject voicing opposing stances with an equally passionate intensity – the process of discovering a black identity and history registering intimacy with that impulse simultaneously with recoil from the extravagance of its rhetoric and its recourse to the paralogical.[69] The graph of this learning process – if this is what it is – continues when the speaker adopts the stance of one who turns to antiquity in order to establish black creativity and achievement. Up to and including this moment, and let us suppose always in forensic mode, the strategies of affirming blackness, embracing unreason and reclaiming the past had been explored and found wanting, every move having been determined and countermanded by the white world's demands and reactions: 'Every hand was a losing hand for me' (p. 132). But how are we to read the protest against Sartre which is delivered in a register of unalloyed identification when the speaker takes up the position of that black person who had determined 'on the level of ideas and intellectual activity to reclaim my négritude', only to find that 'it was snatched away from me . . . Proof was presented that my effort was only a term in the dialectic . . . I felt I had been robbed of my last chance' (pp. 132, 133).

This is a reference to Sartre's *Black Orpheus*, which appeared in 1948 as the preface to Senghor's *Anthology of new Negro and Malagasy poetry*, and which Fanon designates as 'a date in the intellectualization of the *experience* of being black' when challenging its mistake not only in seeking 'the source of the source' but in blocking that source (p. 134).[70] Sartre's essay applauded the act whereby the oppressed seized a word hurled at them as an insult and turned it into a means of vindication, while at the same time relegating the movement as 'the weak stage of a dialectical progression'. In his schema, the theory and practice of white supremacy is the thesis, and Négritude the moment of negativity and thus dedicated to its own destruction: 'it is passage and not objective, means and not ultimate goal' (p. 60), this being the passing into the objective, positive, exact notion of the proletariat. Despite which Sartre commended the fashioning of a black subjectivity and the invention of an 'Africa beyond reach, *imaginary* continent' (p. 19), grasping as others since have not always done the revolutionary project carried out by poets of Négritude who, in 'degallicising' the oppressor's language, shattered its customary associations.

Is Fanon wearing one of the many masks he dons for exegetical purposes when he accuses Sartre of attributing Négritude to the forces of history? 'And so it is not I who make a meaning for myself, but it is the meaning that was already there, preexisting, waiting for me' (p. 134). This anger appears to be sustained when he censures the born Hegelian for forgetting that to attain consciousness of self, to grasp one own's being, 'consciousness has to lose itself in the night of the absolute' (p. 133). In destroying black zeal, what Sartre had failed to understand was that 'I needed to lose myself completely in Negritude . . . in terms of consciousness, black consciousness is immanent in its own eyes. I am not a potentiality of something, I am wholly what I am. I do not have to look for the universal . . . My Negro consciousness does not hold itself out as a lack. It is its own follower' (p. 135).[71]

If this could appear to be a vindication of Négritude's project, then in the last chapters, specified in the Introduction as an attempt at 'a psychopathological and philosophical explanation of the state of *being* a Negro' (p. 15), Fanon again disavows not only the Antillean Negroes' attempt to be white but the effort to maintain their alterity – 'Alterity of rupture, of conflict, of battle' (p. 222). By the time of the Conclusion, the impulse to discover a black past is unequivocally repudiated: 'In no way should I dedicate myself to the revival of an unjustly unrecognized Negro civilization' (p. 226), the denunciations moving towards a lofty detachment – 'I do not have the right to allow myself to be mired in what the past has determined. I am not the slave of the Slavery that dehumanized my ancestors ... The body of history does not determine a single one of my actions. I am my own foundation' (pp. 230–1) – before rising/ collapsing into the utopianism of his ultimate desire: 'That it may be possible for me to discover and to love man, wherever he may be. The Negro is not. Any more than the white man' (p. 231).

The 'drama of consciousness' performed in *Black skin, white masks* can be read as Fanon directing a scenario in which the players are alienated Antillean blacks learning or being weaned from the errors of both assimilation and Négritude, and hence as charting the move from the reactional, in which there is always resentment, to the actional (p. 222). But perhaps it traces the path of the author effecting his own cure within the space of its pages – Négritude marking the transgressive moment of emergence from the colonised condition, and the transition from Négritude to universal solidarity signalling disalienation and the transcendence of ethnicity. The problem here is that subsequent writings replay the dilemma of fashioning/disavowing black identity. Some years later in 'West Indians and Africans' Fanon continued to affirm Césaire's positive influence in valorising what West Indians had rejected, teaching them to look in the direction of Africa, and instead of identifying with and mimicking the white world, recognising themselves as transplanted children of black slaves. But now, writing in the third person about the West Indian, Fanon detaches himself from what he had proclaimed in the first person as a transformation of consciousness, by denying the existence of a Negro people, deriding the Africa of the West Indian imagination – 'Africa the hard and the beautiful, Africa exploding with anger, tumultuous bustle, splash, Africa land of truth'[72] – and pronouncing that 'It thus seems that the West Indian, after the great white error, is now living in the great black mirage'.[73]

The retreat from a wavering empathy with Négritude becomes an ambiguous critique in Fanon's address to the First Congress of Negro Writers and Artists in Paris in 1956. In his disobliging account of the meeting, where he intimates that the agenda was incoherent and the platform much given to demagogy, James Baldwin[74] observes that what Césaire left out of his eloquent speech reviling the colonial experience was precisely that it had produced men like himself. Since this is now something of a platitude, it is notable that Fanon did not dwell on his own colonialist formation, concentrating instead on colonialism as expropriation and spoliation matched by 'the sacking of cultural patterns', the natives having been induced by the overwhelming power and authority of the oppressor to repudiate their original forms of existence.[75] Having earlier protested at Sartre's relegation of Négritude to a minor term, Fanon now essentially follows his model, and while like Sartre he commends black affirmations in the face of white insult, the negative/positive evaluations of cultural revaluations interrupt each other in a double-voiced critique of the native intellectual's abrupt movement from ardent assimilation to the swooning before tradition:

This culture, abandoned, sloughed off, neglected, despised, becomes for the in-feriorized an object of passionate attachment ... The culture put into capsules, which has vegetated since the foreign domination, is revalorized. It is not reconceived, grasped anew, dynamized from within ... The past, becoming henceforth a constella-tion of values, becomes identified with the Truth.[76]

But at the moment when a reader could assume that this predicates a total rejection of Négritude's project, the perspective again shifts when cultural affirmation is marked as a necessary moment in the realisation of a combative position:

This rediscovery, this absolute valorization almost in defiance of reality, objectively indefensible, assumes an incomparable and subjective importance ... the plunge into the chasm of the past is the condition and source of freedom.[77]

Fanon's argument characterises native culture under colonialism as inert, stultified, lethargic, rigid, uncreative, with the natives reduced to despising their indigenous modes of existence – assertions for which much countervailing evidence can be adduced. However, for Fanon it was only when the movement for decolonisation was set in motion that there occurred a qualitative leap from stagnation to modernity, from passivity to insurgency. It is this 'zone of occult instability where the people dwell ... that fluctuating movement which they are just giving a shape to'[78] that remains unknown to those native writers and artists who, lagging behind the people and going against the current of history by seeking to revive abandoned traditions, forget 'that the forms of thought and what it feeds on, together with modern techniques of information, lan-guage and dress have dialectically reorganized the peoples' intelligences' (p. 181). Hence his eloquent defence of the natives' discovery of the past as a means of rehabilitation is countermanded when, and as it were in the same breath, disdain is directed at the recovery of old legends that will be 'in-terpreted in the light of a borrowed aestheticism and of a conception of the world which was discovered under other skies ... the poetic tom-tom rhythms breaking through the poetry of revolt' (pp. 179–81). In Fanon's argument the condition of possibility for producing a literature of combat is that writers take up arms on the side of the people, since only such writings will mould the national consciousness 'giving it form and contours and flinging open before it new and boundless horizons' (p. 193). That he could be formulaic in his appreciation of the arts is apparent in his comments on the blues as the black slave's lament, 'offered up for the admiration of the oppressor', and his prophecies that the 'end of racism would sound the knell of great Negro music',[79] or that as soon as the Negro comes to an understanding of himself, the jazz howl that whites perceived as an expression of nigger-hood will be replaced by 'his trumpet sound[ing] more clearly and his voice less hoarsely.[80]

Fanon's writings on National Culture can be read as a response to Césaire's Address to the First Congress in 1956 where, in countering Senghor's meta-physical version of Négritude, he had argued that whereas a culture must be national, a civilisation can be supranational, and that whereas specific African cultures had been decimated by enforced dispersal and colonial aggression, important elements of an African civilisation had persisted.[81] By this time Fanon's disenchantment with the official cultural nationalism of the newly independent African states had been exacerbated by the apostasy to the cause of the national liberation struggles of its most eloquent exponents – Senghor had underwritten De Gaulle's proposed Franco-African community and withheld Senegal's support for the Algerian liberation struggle; Césaire had backed the constitutional referendum on the Fifth Republic whereby Martinique would become as an overseas department of France, and Jacques Rabemananjara of Malagasy had voted against the Algerian people in the General Assembly of the United Nations (I will evade any questions of whether a theorist's public acts can be held to invalidate the theories he or she espouses). Fanon now took the position that any notion of a continental African culture, of 'Negroism', was a blind alley, stressing instead the heterogeneity of Negro and African – Negro cultures and the different concrete problems confronting specific black populations, and insisting that solidarity was forged not in declamations of a common culture but in political struggle. In his statement to the Second Congress of Black Artists and Writers in Rome in 1959,[82] Fanon declared that culture is necessarily the expression of the nation, just as the nation is the condition of culture, once again pointing to the error of the native intellectual's ways, whether assimilationist or 'Negroist'. Distinguishing between national consciousness and nationalism, Fanon maintained that the former was the most elaborate form of culture, and declared that the national period was the necessary space for the growth of an international dimension and of universalising values.[83]

    To the end there are signs of Fanon's links with the Négritude movement – the title of his last essays taken from *The Internationale* had previously been adapted by Jacques Roumain in a poem calling for a black revolt against the bourgeois white world, and he remained in touch with the editors of *Présence Africaine*.[84] Yet his repudiation of Négritude in his 1959 Address to the Congress is unqualified: like Trotsky, who scorned the notion of a proletarian culture since the proletariat would be abolished on the attainment of classless society, so Fanon now rejected black culture as an abstract populism: 'To believe that it is possible to create a black culture is to forget that niggers are disappearing, just as those people who brought them into being are seeing the break-up of their economic and cultural supremacy.[85] This optimism of the intellect is what Albert Memmi addresses when he remarks that for Fanon 'the day oppression ceases, the new man is supposed to appear before our eyes immediately',[86] although it should be noted that Fanon predicated this leap into the future, this instant emancipation on the transformative powers of a principled decolonising struggle: 'After the conflict there is not only the disappearance of the colonized man ... This new humanity cannot do otherwise than define a new humanism for itself and others. It is prefigured in the objectives and methods of the conflict'.[87]

The verso of these epiphanies to a future transcending ethnicity and nationalism is a measured demystification of Europe's 'spiritual adventure' undertaken at the expense of the rest of the world, and a call that the oppressed should slough off enslavement to its values by recognising the failure of its claims: 'Let us try to create the whole man, whom Europe has been incapable of bringing to triumphant birth'.[88] Here Fanon's writings appear as prematurely postcolonialist and are reminiscent of what Anthony Appiah, in discussing Ouologuem's 'post-realist' novels, describes as writings of delegitimation that inscribe a post-nativist politics and a transnational rather than a national solidarity: 'they reject not only the Western *imperium* but also the nationalist project of the postcolonial national bourgeoisie ... the basis for that project of delegitimation cannot be the postmodernist one: rather it is grounded in an appeal to an ethical universal'.[89] In turning away from Europe as a source and model of meanings and aspirations, Fanon's last writings look not to the fulfilment of the Enlightenment's ideals within the existing order but to decolonisation as the agency of a transfigured social condition; hence holding in place that vision of the anti-colonial struggle as a global emancipatory project and projecting the radical hope of an oppositional humanism. What is less certain is whether the time for transnational politics had come when Fanon was writing, whether it has now, and whether the prospect of his post-nativist 'whole man' is one that wholly delights.

Notes

1 Brian Friel, *Translations* (London, 1981), p. 66.
2 For Fanon, the colonised prior to modern movements for national independence were passive, stultified, unproductive. Presumably this characterisation applied only to the Caribbean and sub-Saharan Africa, since Algeria is credited with sustained military and cultural resistance against the French occupiers. See Frantz Fanon, *Toward the African revolution*, trans. Haakon Chevalier (New York, 1967), p. 65.
3 This position is elucidated and underwritten by Robert Young, *White mythologies: writing, history and the west* (London, 1990).
4 Richard Terdiman, *Discourse/counter discourse: the theory and practice of symbolic resistance in nineteenth-century France* (Ithaca, 1985), p. 36.
5 These issues are addressed by, amongst others, Paul Smith, *Discerning the subject* (Minneapolis, 1988), Diana Fuss, *Essentially speaking: feminism, nature and difference* (London, 1989), and, in a colonial context, Rosalind O'Hanlon, 'Recovering the subject: *Subaltern Studies* and histories of resistance in colonial South Asia', *Modern Asian Studies* 22.1 (1988), pp. 184–224 (see especially pp. 204–5). The framing of the agon of structure and agency has been questioned by Anthony Appiah in 'Tolerable falsehoods: agency and the interests of theory', in Jonathan Arac and Barbara Johnson, eds., *Some consequences of theory* (Baltimore, 1991), pp. 63–90.
6 Instances are the upsurge during the late nineteenth century of messianic movements and Ethiopian or Zionist Churches in sub-Saharan Africa which Thomas Hodgkin, in *Nationalism in colonial Africa* (London, 1956), has described as precipitating a clash between colonial and prophetic power; maroonage or the flight of slaves from the plantation and post-plantation systems of the Americas to an

outlaw life in the mountains and forests or to other territories; the concealment of meaning from master and overseer in creole and carnival; the parodic inversions of the coloniser's images in song and dance; non-cooperation with projects of 'social improvement'; adherence to traditions the occupiers sought to reform; idleness and malingering to circumvent and undermine the demands of enforced and indentured labour regulations; and – if one is tempted to adapt the schema of silent majorities devised by Jean Baudrillard in *In the shadow of the silent majorities*, trans. Paul Foss, Paul Patton and John Johnston (New York, 1983), to specify inertia as opposition to a contemporary condition saturated by information technology – silence as a weapon against political authority. The problem here is that silence can be read either as a sign of resignation to subjugation – being reduced to silence, as marking the refusal to speak or be heard within the oppressor's system of meanings, or as a form of nonspeaking subjectivity; it can also register an exclusion operated by the text – the hole in the narrative. Some of the modes listed above have been problematised by David Theo Goldberg, who maintains that 'The discourses promoting resistance to racism must not prompt identification with and in terms of categories fundamental to the discourse of oppression'. As examples of the failure to make this distinction, he cites the black separatist movement and the tactics of resistance used by plantation slaves: 'slow work and malingering undermined the plantation economy but reinforced the stereotype of laziness; self-mutilation increased labour costs but steeled the stereotype of barbarism'. See 'The social formation of racist discourse', in David Theo Goldberg, ed., *Anatomy of racism* (Minneapolis, 1990), pp. 313 and 318 n. 58. The terms of this strong reservation impinge on the argument for the effectivity of a reverse discourse pursued in this essay.

7 Wilson Harris, *History, fable and myth in the Caribbean and Guianas* (Georgetown, Guyana, 1974), p. 14.

8 Harris, *History, Fable and Myth in the Caribbean and Guianas*, p. 10.

9 Rashmi Bhatnagar, 'Uses and limits of Foucault: a study of the theme of origins in Edward Said's *Orientalism*', *Social Scientist* (Trivandrum) 158 (1986), p. 5. Ranajit Guha however has maintained that 'the appropriation of a past by conquest carried with it the risk of rebounding on its conquerors. It can end up by sacralizing the past for the subject people and encouraging it to use it in their effort to define and affirm their own identity'. See 'Dominance without hegemony and its historiography', in Ranajit Guha, ed., *Subaltern studies VI: Writings on South Asian history and society* (Delhi, 1989), p. 212.

10 Edouard Glissant, *Caribbean discourse: selected essays*, trans. Michael Dash (Virginia, 1989), p. 260.

11 Glissant, *Caribbean discourse: selected essays*, pp. 161–2.

12 Stuart Hall, 'New ethnicities', in *Black film British cinema*, ICA documents 7 London (1988), p. 29.

13 Stuart Hall, 'Minimal selves', in *The real me: postmodernism and the question of identity*, ICA documents 6 London (1987), p. 45.

14 Stuart Hall, 'Cultural identity and diaspora', in J. Rutherford, ed., *Identity, community, culture, difference* (London, 1990), p. 222.

15 Hall, 'Cultural identity and diaspora', pp. 223, 224.

16 Henry Louis Gates, Jr., 'Afterword: critical remarks', in Goldberg, *Anatomy of racism*, pp. 319–32.

17 R. B. Kitaj, *First diaspora manifesto* (London, 1989), pp. 35, 37, 39, 21.

18 See Manthia Diawara, 'Englishness and blackness: cricket as discourse on colonialism', *Callaloo* 13.4 (1991), pp. 830–44, and Elizabeth Grosz, 'Judaism and exile: the ethics of otherness', *New Formations* 12 (1990), pp. 77–88.

19 A case for the power of the reverse-discourse which uses the same categories and vocabulary as the texts of social control it contests is made by Jonathan Dollimore, citing Foucault's argument in *History of sexuality*, vol. 1: 'Deviancy returns from abjection by deploying just those terms which relegated it to that state in the first place – including "nature" and "essence" ... A complex and revealing dialectic between the dominant and the deviant emerges from histories of homosexual representation, especially from the homosexual (later gay) appropriations of nature and essence'. See Jonathan Dollimore, *Sexual dissidence: literatures, histories, theories* (Oxford, 1991), pp. 95–6.

20 Michel Pêcheux, *Language, semantics and ideology*, trans. Harbans Nagpal (London, 1982).

21 Terdiman, *Discourse/counter discourse*.

22 Pêcheux, *Language*, pp. 157, 159.

23 Terdiman, *Discourse/counter discourse*, pp. 68, 70.

24 Terdiman, *Discourse/counter discourse*, pp. 66.

25 K. A. Appiah, 'Out of Africa: topologies of nativism', *Yale Journal of Criticism* 1.2 (1988), p. 164.

26 Appiah, 'Out of Africa: topologies of nativism', pp. 162, 170.

27 Partha Chatterjee, *Nationalist thought and the colonial world: a derivative discourse?* (Delhi, 1986), p. 42.

28 Rosalind O'Hanlon, 'Cultures of rule, communities of resistance: gender, discourse and tradition in recent South Asian historiography', *Social Analysis* 25 (1989), pp. 98, 104, 100.

29 See Guha, 'Dominance without hegemony': 'peasant uprisings variously called *hool, dhing, bidroha, hangama, fituri*, etc; ... *hizrat* or desertion *en masse* of peasants or other labouring people ... ; ... *dharma* or protest by sitting down in the offender's presence with the pledge not to move until the redress of grievance; ... *hartal* or the general suspension of public activity; ... *dharmaghat* or withdrawal of labour; ... *jat mara*, or measures to destroy the offender's caste by refusal to render such specialist services as are required to insure him and his kin against pollution; ... *danga* or sectarian, ethnic, caste and class violence involving large bodies of the subaltern population' (p. 267).

30 Young, *White mythologies*, p. 165.

31 Elleke Boehmer, 'Transfiguring body into narrative in post-colonial writing', unpublished paper, 1991.

32 Ella Shohat, 'Imaging terra incognita: the disciplinary gaze of empire', *Public Culture* 3.2 (1991), pp. 56, 57. Where Shohat seems to be overstating her case is in suggesting that stories of sexual violence against Third World women are 'relatively privileged' over those of violence toward Third World men.

33 See Dollimore, *Sexual dissidence*, who argues for avoiding a 'theoreticist' writing-off of the histories of 'essentialist politics' (pp. 44–5).

34 But nor should the cost of the 'hybridity' effected by colonialism's invasions be uncounted: glossing Edward Brathwaite's definition of creolisation 'as one's adaptation to a new environment through the loss of parts of oneself and the gain of parts of the Other', Manthia Diawara adds that 'one must be aware of the fact that in fusing Whiteness with the seductiveness of hybridization, one is also sacrificing not only a part of Blackness, but, certain Black people'. See Manthia Diawara, 'The

nature of mother in *Dreaming rivers'*, *Third Text* 13 (1990–1), p. 82. These 'certain Black people', inhabiting extant although neither static or intact autochthonous cultures, emerge in Caroline Rooney's reading of a story by Ama Ata Aidoo where she draws attention to a narration which legitimates 'a culture that predates and is not erased by colonial founding fathers, who are not then an originating point of reference', and criticises the amnesia of those who, having embraced the metropolitan culture, renounce their natal communities. See her 'Are we in the company of feminists?; a preface for Bessie Head and Ama Ata Aidoo', in Harriet Devine Jump, ed., *Diverse voices* (Hemel Hempstead, 1991), p. 222.

35 See, for example, Edward Said, *Yeats and decolonization* (Derry, 1988), and *Culture and imperialism* (London, 1993).

36 In the late 1940s African writers and political activists close to the Communist Party – Gabriel d'Arboussier, Albert Franklin and Abdoulaye Ly – attacked Négritude for failing to give expression to the anti-imperalist revolution as a national liberation struggle fought by all classes, dismissing it as a mystification which placed the accent on the irrational aspects of African life and claimed the existence of a unique Negro culture – charges of which Césaire was exonerated. See Jacques Louis Hyams, *Leopold Sedar Senghor: an intellectual biography* (Edinburgh, 1971). Cf. Wole Soyinka, *Myth, literature and the African world* (Cambridge, 1976), who faults Négritude for negative and contradictory definitions, distortions of the African world-view and reinstalling blasphemies about the African as a non-analytic being.

37 During the 1950s and 1960s black writers who were the step-children of an Anglophone oppression tended to emphasise their western formation – see, for example, James Baldwin, 'Princes and powers', in his *Nobody knows my name* (New York, 1961), pp. 24–54, and Ezekiel Mphahlele, 'Remarks on negritude', in Hyams, *Leopold Sedar Senghor*, appendix VI – or to stress the fusion of African strains with other lines in the making of African American identity, see Ralph Ellison, 'Some questions and some answers' [1958], in his *Shadow and act* (London, 1967), pp. 261–72.

38 Mphahlele (in Hyams, *Leopold Sedar Senghor*) allowed the historical fact of Négritude as both a protest and a positive assertion of African cultural values, and Soyinka conceded that 'it had provided a life-line along which the dissociated individual could be pulled back to the source of his material essence and offered a prospect for the coming into being of new black social entities' (Soyinka, *Myth*, p. 64).

39 Michael Dash, 'Marvellous realism: the way out of negritude', *Caribbean Studies* 13.4 (1973), pp. 57–70.

40 René Depestre, 'Problems of identity for the black man in the Caribbean', in John Hearne, ed., *Carifesta forum* (Jamaica, 1976), pp. 62, 63. Depestre was subsequently to put a greater distance between his stance and that of Négritude, attributing its 'original sin ... and the adventures that destroyed its initial project' to 'the spirit that made it possible: anthropology', a criticism which Mudimbe reads as referring to techniques of ideological manipulation (cited by V. Y. Mudimbe, *The invention of Africa: gnosis, philosophy and the order of knowledge* [London, 1988], p. 187).

41 Abiola Irele, 'Contemporary thought in French speaking Africa', in Isaac James Mowoe and Richard Bjornson, eds., *The legacies of empire* (New York, 1986), pp. 121–58, and Mudimbe, *The invention of Africa*.

42 Irele, 'Contemporary thought', p. 147.

43 Cited in A. James Arnold, *Modernism and negritude: the poetry and poetics of Aimé Césaire* (Cambridge, Mass., 1981), p. 172. Towa's article 'Aimé Césaire, prophète de la révolution des peuples noirs' was published in *Abbia* (Cameroon) 21 (1969); on *Abbia* – founded in 1962 by William Eteki whose influential policies/politics attempted to reconcile Négritude with scientific knowledge in constructing a new African philosophy – see Richard Bjornson, *The African quest for freedom and identity: Cameroonian writing and the national experience* (Indiana, 1991), pp. 173–4.

44 There was apparently some continuity in Haiti where during the 1920s the journal *Revue indigène* was established, while in the 1930s a group of intellectuals and writers calling themselves Les Griots (a name borrowed from an African term for the profession of poet – historian – musician) coined the word *nigrité* to signal a rejection of assimilation and the reconstruction of an African identity. Similarly there were moves by literary coteries in Puerto Rico, Cuba and Brazil to locate the black communities of the territories within an African continuum and effect a bond of solidarity with other products of the African dispersal – as there were in the Harlem Renaissance.

45 Abiola Irele, 'The theory of negritude', in *Proceedings of the seminar on political theory and ideology in African society* (Edinburgh, 1970), pp. 162–90.

46 Arnold, *Modernism and negritude*.

47 Césaire's *Letter to Maurice Thorez* (1956) criticised the Communist Party's position on the Caribbean dependencies, questioned the applicability of orthodox Marxist analysis to Martinican conditions, rejected the thesis that the urban proletariat, which scarcely existed in Martinique, was necessarily the vanguard of revolution, and reiterated his adherence to Négritude (cited by Arnold, *Modernism and negritude*, p. 172). Two years later Césaire, apparently at the behest of André Malraux, supported De Gaulle's constitutional referendum whereby Martinique became an overseas department of the Fifth Republic.

48 Aimé Césaire, *Discourse on colonialism*, trans. Joan Pinkham (New York, 1972), pp. 57, 59.

49 Césaire, *Discourse on colonialism*, pp. 20, 22, 23, 31.

50 Césaire, *Discourse on colonialism*, pp. 74, 76.

51 So novel are language, syntax and trope that commentators have in glossing his poetry been moved to their own displays of stylistic pyrotechnics: 'A poem of Césaire ... bursts and turns on itself as a fuse, as bursting suns which turn and explode in new suns, in a perpetual surpassing. It is not a question of meeting in a calm unity of opposites but rather a forced coupling into a single sex, of black in its opposition to white'. See Jean-Paul Sartre, *Black Orpheus* [1948], trans. S. W. Allen (Paris, 1976), p. 36.

52 James Clifford, *The predicament of culture: twentieth-century ethnography, literature and art* (Cambridge, Mass. and London, 1988), p. 185.

53 Clifford, *The predicament of culture*, p. 181.

54 Aimé Césaire, *Collected poetry*, trans. with an introduction by Clayton Eshleman and Annette Smith (Berkeley, 1983), pp. 369–71.

55 Césaire, *Discourse on colonialism*, pp. 66 and 67.

56 Césaire, *Collected poetry*, p. 51.

57 See Eshleman and Smith, Introduction to Césaire, *Collected poetry*, p. 11, and Arnold, *Modernism and negritude*, p. 218.

58 Cf. Irele, 'Contemporary thought', p. 137: 'Césaire's poetry ... becomes quite literally an affect; a drama of consciousness, a sloughing off of processes by which

the complex of negative associations through which the black subject has been forced to perceive himself is overturned and transformed into a mode of mental liberation and ultimately of self-acceptance'. In their introduction to Césaire's poetry, Eshleman and Smith refer to French usages of words to designate things or persons belonging to the black race: the euphemistic 'Noir', the derogatory 'negro', and the more neutral 'nègre': 'it is in this light that one must read Césaire's use of the word "nègre" and its derivatives "négritude", "négrillon" and "négraille": he was making up a family of words based on what he considered the most insulting way to refer to black. The paradox, of course, was that this implicit reckoning with the blacks' ignominy, this process of self-irony and self-denigration, was the necessary step on the path to a new self-image and spiritual rebirth' (Césaire, *Collected poetry*, p. 27).

59 Césaire, *Collected poetry*, pp. 67, 69.

60 Shohat, 'Imagining terra incognita', p. 57.

61 Césaire, *Collected poetry*, p. 69.

62 James Snead, 'Black independent film', in *Black film British cinema*, ICA documents 7 London (1988), p. 48.

63 Kobena Mercer, 'Black art and the burden of representation', *Third Text* 10 (1990), p. 77.

64 Mudimbe, *The invention of Africa*.

65 Irele, 'Contemporary thought', p. 138.

66 Henry Louis Gates, Jr., 'Critical Fanonism', *Critical Inquiry* 17.3 (1991), pp. 457–70.

67 Frantz Fanon, *The wretched of the earth*, trans. Constance Farrington (New York, 1968), p. 170.

68 Frantz Fanon, *Black skin, white masks*, trans. Charles Lam Markman, intro. Homi Bhabha (London, 1986), p. 16. Further references included in the text.

69 See especially *Black skin, white masks*, pp. 113, 115, 122, 123–7.

70 For Mudimbe and Irele, Sartre's contribution was to have shifted Négritude from an ethnic to an historical concept and a revolutionary project, Mudimbe crediting Sartre with transforming it into a major political event and a philosophical critique of colonialism, while at the same time subjugating 'the militant's generosity of mind and heart to the fervour of a political philosophy' (Mudimbe, *The invention of Africa*, p. 84).

71 The movement of Fanon's argument resembles the tropological production of blackness's different registers in *Notebook of a return to the nativeland*.

72 Fanon, *Toward the African revolution*, p. 26.

73 Fanon, *Toward the African revolution*, p. 27.

74 Baldwin, 'Princes and powers'.

75 Fanon, *Toward the African revolution*, p. 33.

76 Fanon, *Toward the African revolution*, p. 41, 43.

77 Fanon, *Toward the African revolution*, p. 43.

78 Fanon, *The wretched of the earth*, p. 182. Further references are included in the text.

79 Fanon, *Toward the African revolution*, p. 37.

80 Fanon, *The wretched of the earth*, p. 195. The cultural agenda proposed by Fanon, in which an 'upward springing trend' is required in writing, dancing and singing, iterates the desiderata heard before and since in the programmes for the arts drawn up by radical political movements, bringing to mind Césaire's ironic reprimand to Depestre for supporting the then party line on poetry: 'Comrade Depestre / It is

undoubtedly a very serious problem / the relation between poetry and Revolution / the content determines the form / and what about keeping in mind as well the dialectical / backlash by which the form taking its revenge / chokes the poem like an accursed fig tree' (Césaire, *Collected poetry*, p. 371).

81 'Culture and colonization', cited in Arnold, *Modernism and negritude*, pp. 185–7.

82 In *The wretched of the earth*.

83 Writing on cultural resistance, Amilcar Cabral looked forward to the emergence of a *'universal culture'*, while calling for 'a spiritual reconversion of mentalities, a re-Africanization that will aim at the development of a people's culture and of all aboriginal positive cultural values'. See Amilcar Cabral, *Unity and struggle: speeches and writings*, trans. Michael Wolfers (London, 1980), p. 153. In his Memorial Lecture for Eduardo Modliane, 'National liberation and culture', in *Transition* 45 (1974), pp. 15–16, Cabral, who calls national liberation 'an act of culture', steers a course between concessions to and rejections of Négritude, advocating that a people freeing themselves from foreign rule must 'recapture the commanding heights of its own culture' and reject 'any kind of subjection to foreign culture', while repudiating the 'rather byzantine discussion of which African cultural values are specific or non-specific to Africa'. All the same he writes of the armed war of liberation as an 'expression of our culture and our African-ness. It must be expressed when it comes, in a ferment signifying above all the culture of the people which has freed itself' (p. 17). In the editorial, Cabral is cited as denouncing a notion, held even by the left, 'that imperialism made us enter history, at the moment when it began its adventures in our countries', substituting instead 'We consider that when imperialism arrived in Guiné, it made us leave history – our history'.

84 Peter Worsley, in 'Frantz Fanon and the "lumpenproletariat" ', in J. Savile and R. Miliband, eds., *The socialist register* (London, 1972), p. 197, suggests that 'It is more than possible that Roumain's poem rather than the Internationale, was the source of Fanon's title. It is a poem that saw the revolt of colour and the revolt of class as overlapping ... Roumain, after a "furious embittered rhapsody on the sufferings of the Negro", stops himself short with a POURTANT in capital letters – "And yet / I only want to belong to your race / workers and peasants of all countries" '.

85 Fanon, *The wretched of the earth*, pp. 188–9.

86 Albert Memmi, *Dominated man: notes toward a portrait* (New York, 1969), p. 88.

87 Fanon, *The wretched of the earth*, p. 197.

88 Fanon, *The wretched of the earth*, p. 253.

89 Appiah, 'Tolerable falsehoods', p. 353.

6

Stuart Hall

Cultural Identity and Diaspora *

A new cinema of the Caribbean is emerging, joining the company of the other 'Third Cinemas'. It is related to, but different from the vibrant film and other forms of visual representation of the Afro-Caribbean (and Asian) 'blacks' of the diasporas of the West – the new post-colonial subjects. All these cultural practices and forms of representation have the black subject at their centre, putting the issue of cultural identity in question. Who is this emergent, new subject of the cinema? From where does he/she speak? Practices of representation always implicate the positions from which we speak or write – the positions of *enunciation*. What recent theories of enunciation suggest is that, though we speak, so to say 'in our own name', of ourselves and from our own experience, nevertheless who speaks, and the subject who is spoken of, are never identical, never exactly in the same place. Identity is not as transparent or unproblematic as we think. Perhaps instead of thinking of identity as an already accomplished fact, which the new cultural practices then represent, we should think, instead, of identity as a 'production', which is never complete, always in process, and always constituted within, not outside, representation. This view problematises the very authority and authenticity to which the term, 'cultural identity', lays claim.

We seek, here, to open a dialogue, an investigation, on the subject of cultural identity and representation. Of course, the 'I' who writes here must also be thought of as, itself, 'enunciated'. We all write and speak from a particular place and time, from a history and a culture which is specific. What we say is always 'in context', *positioned*. I was born into and spent my childhood and adolescence in a lower-middle-class family in Jamaica. I have lived all my adult life in England, in the shadow of the black diaspora – 'in the belly of the beast'. I write against the background of a lifetime's work in cultural studies. If the paper seems preoccupied with the diaspora experience and its narratives of displacement, it is worth remembering that all discourse is 'placed', and the heart has its reasons.

There are at least two different ways of thinking about 'cultural identity'. The first position defines 'cultural identity' in terms of one shared culture, a sort of collective 'one true self', hiding inside the many other, more superficial

* From Jonathan Rutherford, ed., *Identity: Community, Culture, Difference* (Lawrence & Wishart, 1990), pp. 222–37.

or artificially imposed 'selves', which people with a shared history and ancestry hold in common. Within the terms of this definition, our cultural identities reflect the common historical experiences and shared cultural codes which provide us, as 'one people', with stable, unchanging and continuous frames of reference and meaning, beneath the shifting divisions and vicissitudes of our actual history. This 'oneness', underlying all the other, more superficial differences, is the truth, the essence, of 'Caribbeanness', of the black experience. It is this identity which a Caribbean or black diaspora must discover, excavate, bring to light and express through cinematic representation.

Such a conception of cultural identity played a critical role in all the post-colonial struggles which have so profoundly reshaped our world. It lay at the centre of the vision of the poets of 'Negritude', like Aimé Césaire and Leopold Senghor, and of the Pan-African political project, earlier in the century. It continues to be a very powerful and creative force in emergent forms of representation amongst hitherto marginalised peoples. In post-colonial societies, the rediscovery of this identity is often the object of what Frantz Fanon once called a

> passionate research ... directed by the secret hope of discovering beyond the misery of today, beyond self-contempt, resignation and abjuration, some very beautiful and splendid era whose existence rehabilitates us both in regard to ourselves and in regard to others.

New forms of cultural practice in these societies address themselves to this project for the very good reason that, as Fanon puts it, in the recent past,

> Colonisation is not satisfied merely with holding a people in its grip and emptying the native's brain of all form and content. By a kind of perverted logic, it turns to the past of oppressed people, and distorts, disfigures and destroys it.[1]

The question which Fanon's observation poses is, what is the nature of this 'profound research' which drives the new forms of visual and cinematic representation? Is it only a matter of unearthing that which the colonial experience buried and overlaid, bringing to light the hidden continuities it suppressed? Or is a quite different practice entailed – not the rediscovery but the *production* of identity. Not an identity grounded in the archaeology, but in the *re-telling* of the past?

We should not, for a moment, underestimate or neglect the importance of the act of imaginative rediscovery which this conception of a rediscovered, essential identity entails. 'Hidden histories' have played a critical role in the emergence of many of the most important social movements of our time – feminist, anti-colonial and anti-racist. The photographic work of a generation of Jamaican and Rastafarian artists, or of a visual artist like Armet Francis (a Jamaican-born photographer who has lived in Britain since the age of eight) is a testimony to the continuing creative power of this conception of identity within the emerging practices of representation. Francis's photographs of the peoples of The Black Triangle, taken in Africa, the Caribbean, the USA and the UK, attempt to reconstruct in visual terms 'the underlying unity of the black people whom colonisation and slavery distributed across the African diaspora'. His text is an act of imaginary reunification.

Crucially, such images offer a way of imposing an imaginary coherence on the experience of dispersal and fragmentation, which is the history of all enforced diasporas. They do this by representing or 'figuring' Africa as the mother of these different civilisations. This Triangle is, after all, 'centred' in Africa. Africa is the name of the missing term, the great aporia, which lies at the centre of our cultural identity and gives it a meaning which, until recently, it lacked. No one who looks at these textural images now, in the light of the history of transportation, slavery and migration, can fail to understand how the rift of separation, the 'loss of identity', which has been integral to the Caribbean experience only begins to be healed when these forgotten connections are once more set in place. Such texts restore an imaginary fullness or plentitude, to set against the broken rubric of our past. They are resources of resistance and identity, with which to confront the fragmented and pathological ways in which that experience has been reconstructed within the dominant regimes of cinematic and visual representation of the West.

There is, however, a second, related but different view of cultural identity. This second position recognises that, as well as the many points of similarity, there are also critical points of deep and significant *difference* which constitute 'what we really are'; or rather – since history has intervened – 'what we have become'. We cannot speak for very long, with any exactness, about 'one experience, one identity', without acknowledging its other side – the ruptures and discontinuities which constitute, precisely, the Caribbean's 'uniqueness'. Cultural identity, in this second sense, is a matter of 'becoming' as well as of 'being'. It belongs to the future as much as to the past. It is not something which already exists, transcending place, time, history and culture. Cultural identities come from somewhere, have histories. But, like everything which is historical, they undergo constant transformation. Far from being eternally fixed in some essentialised past, they are subject to the continuous 'play' of history, culture and power. Far from being grounded in a mere 'recovery' of the past, which is waiting to be found, and which, when found, will secure our sense of ourselves into eternity, identities are the names we give to the different ways we are positioned by, and position ourselves within, the narratives of the past.

It is only from this second position that we can properly understand the traumatic character of 'the colonial experience'. The ways in which black people, black experiences, were positioned and subject-ed in the dominant regimes of representation were the effects of a critical exercise of cultural power and normalisation. Not only, in Said's 'Orientalist' sense, were we constructed as different and other within the categories of knowledge of the West by those regimes. They had the power to make us see and experience ourselves as 'Other'. Every regime of representation is a regime of power formed, as Foucault reminds us, by the fatal couplet, 'power/knowledge'. But this kind of knowledge is internal, not external. It is one thing to position a subject or set of peoples as the Other of a dominant discourse. It is quite another thing to subject them to that 'knowledge', not only as a matter of imposed will and domination, by the power of inner compulsion and subjective con-formation to the norm. That is the lesson – the sombre majesty – of Fanon's insight into the colonising experience in *Black Skin, White Masks*.

This inner expropriation of cultural identity cripples and deforms. If its silences are not resisted, they produce, in Fanon's vivid phrase, 'individuals without an anchor, without horizon, colourless, stateless, rootless – a race of angels'.[2] Nevertheless, this idea of otherness as an inner compulsion changes our conception of 'cultural identity'. In this perspective, cultural identity is not a fixed essence at all, lying unchanged outside history and culture. It is not some universal and transcendental spirit inside us on which history has made no fundamental mark. It is not once-and-for-all. It is not a fixed origin to which we can make some final and absolute Return. Of course, it is not a mere phantasm either. It is *something* – not a mere trick of the imagination. It has its histories – and histories have their real, material and symbolic effects. The past continues to speak to us. But it no longer addresses us as a simple, factual 'past', since our relation to it, like the child's relation to the mother, is always-already 'after the break'. It is always constructed through memory, fantasy, narrative and myth. Cultural identities are the points of identification, the unstable points of identification or suture, which are made, within the discourses of history and culture. Not an essence but a *positioning*. Hence, there is always a politics of identity, a politics of position, which has no absolute guarantee in an unproblematic, transcendental 'law of origin'.

This second view of cultural identity is much less familiar, and more unsettling. If identity does not proceed, in a straight, unbroken line, from some fixed origin, how are we to understand its formation? We might think of black Caribbean identities as 'framed' by two axes or vectors, simultaneously operative: the vector of similarity and continuity; and the vector of difference and rupture. Caribbean identities always have to be thought of in terms of the dialogic relationship between these two axes. The one gives us some grounding in, some continuity with, the past. The second reminds us that what we share is precisely the experience of a profound discontinuity: the peoples dragged into slavery, transportation, colonisation, migration, came predominantly from Africa – and when that supply ended, it was temporarily refreshed by indentured labour from the Asian subcontinent. (This neglected fact explains why, when you visit Guyana or Trinidad, you see, symbolically inscribed in the faces of their peoples, the paradoxical 'truth' of Christopher Columbus's mistake: you *can* find 'Asia' by sailing west, if you know where to look!) In the history of the modern world, there are few more traumatic ruptures to match these enforced separations from Africa – already figured, in the European imaginary, as 'the Dark Continent'. But the slaves were also from different countries, tribal communities, villages, languages and gods. African religion, which has been so profoundly formative in Caribbean spiritual life, is precisely *different* from Christian monotheism in believing that God is so powerful that he can only be known through a proliferation of spiritual manifestations, present everywhere in the natural and social world. These gods live on, in an underground existence, in the hybridised religious universe of Haitian voodoo, pocomania, Native pentacostalism, Black baptism, Rastafarianism and the black Saints Latin American Catholicism. The paradox is that it was the uprooting of slavery and transportation and the insertion into the plantation economy (as well as the symbolic economy) of the Western world that 'unified' these peoples across their differences, in the same moment as it cut them off from direct access to their past.

Difference, therefore, persists – in and alongside continuity. To return to the Caribbean after any long absence is to experience again the shock of the 'doubleness' of similarity and difference. Visiting the French Caribbean for the first time, I also saw at once how different Martinique is from, say, Jamaica: and this is no mere difference of topography or climate. It is a profound difference of culture and history. And the difference *matters*. It positions Martiniquains and Jamaicans as *both* the same *and* different. Moreover, the boundaries of difference are continually repositioned in relation to different points of reference. Vis-à-vis the developed West, we are very much 'the same'. We belong to the marginal, the underdeveloped, the periphery, the 'Other'. We are at the outer edge, the 'rim', of the metropolitan world – always 'South' to someone else's *El Norte.*

At the same time, we do not stand in the same relation of the 'otherness' to the metropolitan centres. Each has negotiated its economic, political and cultural dependency differently. And this 'difference', whether we like it or not, is already inscribed in our cultural identities. In turn, it is this negotiation of identity which makes us, vis-à-vis other Latin American people, with a very similar history, different – Caribbeans, *les Antilliennes* ('islanders' to their mainland). And yet, vis-à-vis one another, Jamaican, Haitian, Cuban, Guadeloupean, Barbadian, etc . . .

How, then, to describe this play of 'difference' within identity? The common history – transportation, slavery, colonisation – has been profoundly formative. For all these societies, unifying us across our differences. But it does not constitute a common *origin*, since it was, metaphorically as well as literally, a translation. The inscription of difference is also specific and critical. I use the word 'play' because the double meaning of the metaphor is important. It suggests, on the one hand, the instability, the permanent unsettlement, the lack of any final resolution. On the other hand, it reminds us that the place where this 'doubleness' is most powerfully to be heard is 'playing' within the varieties of Caribbean musics. This cultural 'play' could not therefore be represented, cinematically, as a simple, binary opposition – 'past/present', 'them/us'. Its complexity exceeds this binary structure of representation. At different places, times, in relation to different questions, the boundaries are re-sited. They become, not only what they have, at times, certainly been – mutually excluding categories, but also what they sometimes are – differential points along a sliding scale.

One trivial example is the way Martinique both *is* and *is not* 'French'. It is, of course, a *département* of France, and this is reflected in its standard and style of life, Fort de France is a much richer, more 'fashionable' place than Kingston – which is not only visibly poorer, but itself at a point of transition between being 'in fashion' in an Anglo-African and Afro-American way – for those who can afford to be in any sort of fashion at all. Yet, what is distinctively 'Martiniquais' can only be described in terms of that special and peculiar supplement which the black and mulatto skin adds to the 'refinement' and sophistication of a Parisian-derived *haute couture*: that is, a sophistication which, because it is black, is always transgressive.

To capture this sense of difference which is not pure 'otherness', we need to deploy the play on words of a theorist like Jacques Derrida. Derrida uses the anomalous 'a' in his way of writing 'difference' – *differance* – as a marker which sets up a disturbance in our settled understanding or translation of the word/ concept. It sets the word in motion to new meanings without erasing the *trace* of its other meanings. His sense of *differance*, as Christopher Norris puts it, thus

> remains suspended between the two French verbs 'to differ' and 'to defer' (post-pone), both of which contribute to its textual force but neither of which can fully capture its meaning. Language depends on difference, as Saussure showed ... the structure of distinctive propositions which make up its basic economy. Where Derrida breaks new ground ... is in the extent to which 'differ' shades into 'defer' ... the idea that meaning is always deferred, perhaps to this point of an endless supplementarity, by the play of signification.[3]

This second sense of difference challenges the fixed binaries which stabilise meaning and representation and show how meaning is never finished or completed, but keeps on moving to encompass other, additional or supplementary meanings, which, as Norris puts it elsewhere,[4] 'disturb the classical economy of language and representation'. Without relations of difference, no representation could occur. But what is then constituted within representation is always open to being deferred, staggered, serialised.

Where, then, does identity come in to this infinite postponement of meaning? Derrida does not help us as much as he might here though the notion of the 'trace' goes some way towards it. This is where it sometimes seems as if Derrida has permitted his profound theoretical insights to be reappropriated by his disciples into a celebration of formal 'playfulness', which evacuates them of their political meaning. For if signification depends upon the endless repositioning of its differential terms, meaning, in any specific instance, de-pends on the contingent and arbitrary stop – the necessary and temporary 'break' in the infinite semiosis of language. This does not detract from the original insight. It only threatens to do so if we mistake this 'cut' of identity – this *positioning*, which makes meaning possible – as a natural and permanent, rather than an arbitrary and contingent 'ending' – whereas I understand every such position as 'strategic' and arbitrary, in the sense that there is no perma-nent equivalence between the particular sentence we close, and its true meaning, as such. Meaning continues to unfold, so to speak, beyond the arbitrary closure which makes it, at any moment, possible. It is always either over- or under-determined, either an excess or a supplement. There is always something 'left over'.

It is possible, with this conception of 'difference', to rethink the positionings and repositionings of Caribbean cultural identities in relation to at least three 'presences', to borrow Aimée Cesaire's and Leopold Senghor's metaphor: *Présence Africaine*, *Présence Européenne*, and the third, most ambiguous, presence of all – the sliding term, *Présence Americaine*. Of course, I am collapsing, for the moment, the many other cultural 'presences' which constitute the complexity of Caribbean identity (Indian, Chinese, Lebanese, etc). I mean America, here, not in its 'first-world' sense – the big cousin to the North whose 'rim' we occupy, but in the second, broader sense: America, the 'New World', *Terra Incognita*.

Présence Africaine is the site of the repressed. Apparently silenced beyond memory by the power of the experience of slavery, Africa was, in fact present everywhere: in the everyday life and customs of the slave quarters, in the languages and patois of the plantations, in names and words, often disconnected from their taxonomies, in the secret syntactical structures through which other languages were spoken, in the stories and tales told to children, in religious practices and beliefs, in the spiritual life, the arts, crafts, musics and rhythms of slave and post-emancipation society. Africa, the signified which could not be represented directly in slavery, remained and remains the unspoken, unspeakable 'presence' in Caribbean culture. It is 'hiding' behind every verbal inflection, every narrative twist of Caribbean cultural life. It is the secret code with which every Western text was 're-read'. It is the ground-bass of every rhythm and bodily movement. *This* was – is – the 'Africa' that 'is alive and well in the diaspora'.[5]

When I was growing up in the 1940s and 1950s as a child in Kingston, I was surrounded by the signs, music and rhythms of this Africa of the diaspora, which only existed as a result of a long and discontinuous series of transformations. But, although almost everyone around me was some shade of brown or black (Africa 'speaks'!), I never once heard a single person refer to themselves or to others as, in some way, or as having been at some time in the past, 'African'. It was only in the 1970s that this Afro-Caribbean identity became historically available to the great majority of Jamaican people, at home and abroad. In this historic moment, Jamaicans discovered themselves to be 'black' – just as, in the same moment, they discovered themselves to be the sons and daughters of 'slavery'.

This profound cultural discovery, however, was not, and could not be, made directly, without 'mediation'. It could only be made *through* the impact on popular life of the post-colonial revolution, the civil rights struggles, the culture of Rastafarianism and the music of reggae – the metaphors, the figures or signifiers of a new construction of 'Jamaican-ness'. These signified a 'new' Africa of the New World, grounded in an 'old' Africa: – a spiritual journey of discovery that led, in the Caribbean, to an indigenous cultural revolution; this is Africa, as we might say, necessarily 'deferred' – as a spiritual, cultural and political metaphor.

It is the presence/absence of Africa, in this form, which has made it the privileged signifier of new conceptions of Caribbean identity. Everyone in the

Caribbean, of whatever ethnic background, must sooner or later come to terms with this African presence. Black, brown, mulatto, white – all must look *Présence Africaine* in the face, speak its name. But whether it is, in this sense, an *origin* of our identities, unchanged by four hundred years of displacement, dismemberment, transportation, to which we could in any final or literal sense return, is more open to doubt. The original 'Africa' is no longer there. It too has been transformed. History is, in that sense, irreversible. We must not collude with the West which, precisely, normalises and appropriates Africa by freezing it into some timeless zone of the primitive, unchanging past. Africa must at last be reckoned with by Caribbean people, but it cannot in any simple sense by merely recovered.

It belongs irrevocably, for us, to what Edward Said once called an 'imaginative geography and history', which helps 'the mind to intensify its own sense of itself by dramatising the difference between what is close to it and what is far away'.[6] It 'has acquired an imaginative or figurative value we can name and feel'.[7] Our belongingness to it constitutes what Benedict Anderson calls 'an imagined community'.[8] To *this* 'Africa', which is a necessary part of the Caribbean imaginary, we can't literally go home again.

The character of this displaced 'homeward' journey – its length and complexity – comes across vividly, in a variety of texts. Tony Sewell's documentary archival photographs, Garvey's Children: the Legacy of Marcus Garvey, tells the story of a 'return' to an African identity which went, necessarily, by the long route through London and the United States. It 'ends', not in Ethiopia but with Garvey's statue in front of the St Ann Parish Library in Jamaica: not with a traditional tribal chant but with the music of Burning Spear and Bob Marley's Redemption Song. This is our 'long journey' home. Derek Bishton's courageous visual and written text, *Black Heart Man* – the story of the journey of a *white* photographer 'on the trail of the promised land' – starts in England, and goes, through Shashemene, the place in Ethiopia to which many Jamaican people have found their way on their search for the Promised Land, and slavery; but it ends in Pinnacle, Jamaica, where the first Rastafarian settlements was established, and 'beyond' – among the dispossessed of 20th-century Kingston and the streets of Handsworth, where Bishton's voyage of discovery first began. These symbolic journeys are necessary for us all – and necessarily circular. This is the Africa we must return to – but 'by another route': what Africa has *become* in the New World, what we have made of 'Africa': 'Africa' – as we re-tell it through politics, memory and desire.

What of the second, troubling, term in the identity equation – the European presence? For many of us, this is a matter not of too little but of too much. Where Africa was a case of the unspoken, Europe was a case of that which is endlessly speaking – and endlessly speaking *us*. The European presence interrupts the innocence of the whole discourse of 'difference' in the Caribbean by introducing the question of power. 'Europe' belongs irrevocably to the 'play' of power, to the lines of force and consent, to the role of the *dominant*, in Caribbean culture. In terms of colonialism, underdevelopment, poverty and the racism of colour, the European presence is that which, in visual representation, has positioned the black subject within its dominant regimes of representation: the colonial discourse, the literatures of adventure and exploration, the romance of the exotic, the ethnographic and travelling eye, the tropical languages of tourism, travel brochure and Hollywood and the violent, pornographic languages of *ganja* and urban violence.

Because *Présence Européenne* is about exclusion, imposition and expropriation, we are often tempted to locate that power as wholly external to us – an extrinsic force, whose influence can be thrown off like the serpent sheds its skin. What Frantz Fanon reminds us, in *Black Skin, White Masks*, is how this power has become a constitutive element in our own identities.

> The movements, the attitudes, the glances of the other fixed me there, in the sense in which a chemical solution is fixed by a dye. I was indignant; I demanded an explanation. Nothing happened. I burst apart. Now the fragments have been put together again by another self.[9]

This 'look', from – so to speak – the place of the Other, fixes us, not only in its violence, hostility and aggression, but in the ambivalence of its desire. This brings us face to face, not simply with the dominating European presence as the site or 'scene' of integration where those other presences which it had actively disaggregated were recomposed – re-framed, put together in a new way; but as the site of a profound splitting and doubling – what Homi Bhabha has called 'the ambivalent identifications of the racist world . . . the "otherness" of the self inscribed in the perverse palimpsest of colonial identity'.[10]

The dialogue of power and resistance, of refusal and recognition, with and against *Présence Européenne* is almost as complex as the 'dialogue' with Africa. In terms of popular cultural life, it is nowhere to be found in its pure, pristine state. It is always-already fused, syncretised, with other cultural elements. It is always-already creolised – not lost beyond the Middle Passage, but ever-present: from the harmonics in our musics to the ground-bass of Africa, traversing and intersecting our lives at every point. How can we stage this dialogue so that, finally, we can place it, without terror or violence, rather than being forever placed by it? Can we ever recognise its irreversible influence, whilst resisting its imperialising eye? The engima is impossible, so far, to resolve. It requires the most complex of cultural strategies. Think, for example, of the dialogue of every Caribbean filmmaker or writer, one way or another, with the dominant cinemas and literature of the West – the complex relationship of young black British filmmakers with the 'avant-gardes' of European and American filmmaking. Who could describe this tense and tortured dialogue as a 'one way trip'?

The Third, 'New World' presence, is not so much power, as ground, place, territory. It is the juncture-point where the many cultural tributaries meet, the 'empty' land (the European colonisers emptied it) where strangers from every other part of the globe collided. None of the people who now occupy the islands – black, brown, white, African, European, American, Spanish, French, East Indian, Chinese, Portugese, Jew, Dutch – originally 'belonged' there. It is the space where the creolisations and assimilations and syncretisms were negotiated. The New World is the third term – the primal scene – where the fateful/fatal encounter was staged between Africa and the West. It also has to be understood as the place of many, continuous displacements: of the original pre-Columbian inhabitants, the Arawaks, Caribs and Amerindians, permanently displaced from their homelands and decimated; of other peoples displaced in different ways from Africa, Asia and Europe; the displacements of slavery, colonisation and conquest. It stands for the endless ways in which Caribbean people have been destined to 'migrate'; it is the signifier of migration itself – of travelling, voyaging and return as fate, as destiny; of the Antillean as the prototype of the modern or postmodern New World nomad, continually moving between centre and periphery. This preoccupation with movement and migration Caribbean cinema shares with many other 'Third Cinemas', but it is one of our defining themes, and it is destined to cross the narrative of every film script or cinematic image.

Présence Americaine continues to have its silences, its suppressions. Peter Hulme, in his essay on 'Islands of Enchantment'[11] reminds us that the word 'Jamaica' is the Hispanic form of the indigenous Arawak name – 'land of wood and water' – which Columbus's re-naming ('Santiago') never replaced. The Arawak presence remains today a ghostly one, visible in the islands mainly in museums and archeological sites, part of the barely knowable or usable 'past'. Hulme notes that it is not represented in the emblem of the Jamaican National Heritage Trust, for example, which chose instead the figure of Diego Pimienta, 'an African who fought for his Spanish masters against the English invasion of the island in 1655' – a deferred, metonymic, sly and sliding representation of Jamaican identity if ever there was one! He recounts the story of how Prime Minister Edward Seaga tried to alter the Jamaican coat-of-arms, which consists of two Arawak figures holding a shield with five pineapples, surmounted by an alligator. 'Can the crushed and extinct Arawaks represent the dauntless character of Jamaicans? Does the low-slung, near extinct crocodile, a cold-blooded reptile, symbolise the warm, soaring spirit of Jamaicans?' Prime Minister Seaga asked rhetorically.[12] There can be few political statements which so eloquently testify to the complexities entailed in the process of trying to represent a diverse people with a diverse history through a single, hegemonic 'identity'. Fortunately, Mr Seaga's invitation to the Jamaican people, who are overwhelmingly of African descent, to start their 'remembering' by first 'forgetting' something else, got the comeuppance it so richly deserved.

The 'New World' presence – America, *Terra Incognita* – is therefore itself the beginning of diaspora, of diversity, of hybridity and difference, what makes Afro-Caribbean people already people of a diaspora. I use this term here metaphorically, not literally: diaspora does not refer us to those scattered tribes whose identity can only be secured in relation to some sacred homeland to which they must at all costs return, even if it means pushing other people into the sea. This is the old, the imperialising, the hegemonising, form of 'ethnicity'. We have seen the fate of the people of Palestine at the hands of this backward-looking conception of diaspora – and the complicity of the West with it. The diaspora experience as I intend it here is defined, not by essence or purity, but by the recognition of a necessary heterogeneity and diversity; by a conception of 'identity' which lives with and through, not despite, difference; by *hybridity*. Diaspora identities are those which are constantly producing and reproducing themselves anew, through transformation and difference. One can only think here of what is uniquely – 'essentially' – Caribbean: precisely the mixes of colour, pigmentation, physiognomic type; the 'blends' of tastes that is Caribbean cuisine; the aesthetics of the 'cross-overs', of 'cut-and-mix', to borrow Dick Hebdige's telling phrase, which is the heart and soul of black music. Young black cultural practitioners and critics in Britain are increasingly coming to acknowledge and explore in their work this 'diaspora aesthetic' and its formations in the post-colonial experience:

> Across a whole range of cultural forms there is a 'syncretic' dynamic which critically appropriates elements from the master-codes of the dominant culture and 'creolises' them, disarticulating given signs and re-articulating their symbolic meaning. The subversive force of this hybridising tendency is most apparent at the level of language itself where creoles, patois and black English decentre, destabilise and carnivalise the linguistic domination of 'English' – the nation-language of master-discourse – through strategic inflections, re-accentuations and other performative moves in semantic, syntactic and lexical codes.[13]

It is because this New World is constituted for us as place, a narrative of displacement, that it gives rise so profoundly to a certain imaginary plenitude, recreating the endless desire to return to 'lost origins', to be one again with the mother, to go back to the beginning. Who can ever forget, when once seen rising up out of that blue-green Caribbean, those islands of enchantment? Who has not known, at this moment, the surge of an overwhelming nostalgia for lost origins, for 'times past'? And yet, this 'return to the beginning' is like the imaginary in Lacan – it can neither be fulfilled nor requited, and hence is the beginning of the symbolic, of representation, the infinitely renewable source of desire, memory, myth, search, discovery – in short, the reservoir of our cinematic narratives.

We have been trying, in a series of metaphors, to put in play a different sense of our relationship to the past, and thus a different way of thinking about cultural identity, which might constitute new points of recognition in the discourses of the emerging Caribbean cinema and black British cinemas. We have been trying to theorise identity as constituted, not outside but within representation; and hence of cinema, not as a second-order mirror held up to reflect what already exists, but as that form of representation which is able to constitute us as new kinds of subjects, and thereby enable us to discover places from which to speak. Communities, Benedict Anderson argues in *Imagined Communities* are to be distinguished, not by their falsity/genuineness, but by the style in which they are imagined.[14] This is the vocation of modern black cinemas: by allowing us to see and recognise the different parts and histories of ourselves, to construct those points of identification, those positionalities we call in retrospect our 'cultural identities'.

We must not therefore be content with delving into the past of a people in order to find coherent elements which will counteract colonialism's attempts to falsify and harm ... A national culture is not a folk-lore, nor an abstract populism that believes it can discover a people's true nature. A national culture is the whole body of efforts made by a people in the sphere of thought to describe, justify and praise the action through which that people has created itself and keeps itself in existence.[15]

Notes

1 Frantz Fanon, 'On National Culture', in *The Wretched of the Earth* (London 1963), p. 170.
2 Fanon, *On National Culture*, p. 176.
3 Christopher Norris, *Deconstruction: Theory and Practice* (London 1982), p. 32.
4 Christopher Norris, *Jacques Derrida* (London 1987), p. 15.
5 Stuart Hall, *Resistance Through Rituals* (London 1976).
6 Edward Said, *Orientalism* (London 1985), p. 55.
7 Said, *Orientalism*, p. 55.
8 Benedict Anderson, *Imagined Communities: Reflections on the Origin and Spread of Nationalism* (London 1982).
9 Frantz Fanon, *Black Skin, White Masks* (London 1986), p. 109.
10 Homi Bhabha, 'Foreword' to Fanon, *Black Skin*, p. xv.
11 In *New Formations*, no. 3 (Winter 1987).
12 *Jamaica Hansard*, vol. 9, 1983–4, p. 363. Quoted in Hulme, *New Formations*.
13 Kobena Mercer, 'Diaspora Culture and the Dialogic Imagination', in M. Cham and C. Watkins, eds., *Blackframes: Critical Perspectives on Black Independent Cinema* (1988), p. 57.
14 Anderson, *Imagined Communities*, p. 15.
15 Fanon, 'On National Culture', p. 188.

7

Rey Chow

*Where Have All the Natives Gone?**

The inauthentic native

A couple of years ago, I was serving on a faculty search committee at the University of Minnesota. The search was for a specialist in Chinese language and literature. A candidate from the People's Republic of China gave a talk that discussed why we still enjoy reading the eighteenth-century classic, *The Dream of the Red Chamber*. The talk was a theoretical demonstration of how no particular interpretation of this book could exhaust the possibilities of reading. During the search committee's discussion of the various candidates afterwards, one faculty member, an American Marxist, voiced his disparaging view of this particular candidate in the following way: 'The talk was not about why we still enjoy reading *The Dream of the Red Chamber*. It was about why she enjoys reading it. She does because she likes capitalism!'

This colleague of mine stunned me with a kind of discrimination that has yet to be given its proper name. The closest designation we currently have for his attitude is racism, that is, a reduction of someone from a particular group to the stereotypes, negative *or* positive, we have of that group. But what is at stake here is not really 'race' as much as it is the assumption that a 'native' of communist China ought to be faithful to her nation's official political ideology. Instead of 'racial' characteristics, communist beliefs became the stereotype with which my colleague was reading this candidate. The fact that she did not speak from such beliefs but instead from an understanding of the text's irreducible plurality (an understanding he equated with 'capitalism') greatly disturbed him; his lament was that this candidate had betrayed our expectation of what communist 'ethnic specimens' ought to be.

My colleague's disturbance takes us to the familiarly ironic scenarios of anthropology, in which Western anthropologists are uneasy at seeing 'natives' who have gone 'civilized' or who, like the anthropologists themselves, have taken up the active task of shaping their own culture. Margaret Mead, for instance, found the interest of certain Arapesh Indians (in Highland New Guinea) in cultural influences other than their own 'annoying' since, as James Clifford puts it, '*Their* culture collecting complicated hers.'[1] Similarly, Claude Lévi-Strauss, doing his 'fieldwork' in New York on American ethnology, was

* From Angelika Bammer, ed., *Displacements: Cultural Identities in Question* (Indiana University Press, 1994), pp. 125–51.

troubled by the sight, in the New York Public Library reading room where he was doing research for his *Elementary Structures of Kinship*, of a feathered Indian with a Parker pen. As Clifford comments:

> For Lévi-Strauss the Indian is primarily associated with the past, the 'extinct' societies recorded in the precious Bureau of American Ethnology *Annual Reports*. The anthropologist feels himself 'going back in time.' ... In modern New York an Indian can appear only as a survival or a kind of incongruous parody.[2]

My colleague shares the predicament of Mead and Lévi-Strauss in so far as the stereotypical 'native' is receding from view. What confronts the Western scholar is the discomforting fact that the natives are no longer staying in their frames. In the case of the faculty search at Minnesota, what I heard was not the usual desire to *archaize* the modern Chinese person,[3] but rather a valorizing, on the part of the Western critic, of the official political and cultural difference of the People's Republic of China as the designator of the candidate's supposed 'authenticity.' If a native from the People's Republic of China espouses capitalism, then she has already been corrupted. An ethnic specimen that was not pure was not of use to him.

The native as image

In the politics of identifying 'authentic' natives, several strands of the word 'identification' are at stake: How do we identify the native? How do we identify with her? How do we construct the native's 'identity'? What processes of identification are involved? We cannot approach this politics without being critical of a particular relation to *images* that is in question.

In his volume of essays exploring film culture, Fredric Jameson writes that 'The visual is *essentially* pornographic. ... Pornographic films are ... only the potentiation of films in general, which ask us to stare at the world as though it were a naked body.'[4] This straightforward definition of the visual image sums up many of the problems we encounter in cultural criticism today, whether or not the topic in question is film. The activity of watching is linked by projection to physical nakedness. Watching is theoretically defined as the primary agency of violence, an act that pierces the other, who inhabits the place of the passive victim on display. The image, then, is an aggressive sight that reveals itself in the other; it is the site of the aggressed. Moreover, the image is what has been devastated, left bare, and left behind by aggression – hence Jameson's view that it is naked and pornographic.

For many, the image is also the site of possible change. In many critical discourses, the image is implicitly the place where battles are fought and strategies of resistance negotiated. Such discourses try to inhabit this image-site by providing alternative sights, alternative ways of watching *that would change the image*. Thus one of the most important enterprises nowadays is that of investigating the 'subjectivity' of the other-as-oppressed-victim. 'Subjectivity' becomes a way to change the defiled image, the stripped image, the image-reduced-to-nakedness, by showing the truth behind/beneath/around it. The problem with the reinvention of subjectivity as such is that it tries to combat the politics of the image, a politics that is conducted on surfaces, by a politics of depths, hidden truths, and inner voices. The most important aspect of the image – its power precisely as image and nothing else – is thus bypassed and left untouched.[5] It is in this problematic of *the image as the bad thing to be replaced* that I lodge the following arguments about the 'native.'

The question in which I am primarily interested is: Is there a way of 'finding' the native without simply ignoring the image, or substituting a 'correct' image of the ethnic specimen for an 'incorrect' one, or giving the native a 'true' voice 'behind' her 'false' image? How could we deal with the native in an age when there is no possibility of avoiding the reduction/abstraction of the native as image? How can we write about the native by not ignoring the defiled, degraded image that is an inerasable part of her status – that is, by not resorting to the idealist belief that everything would be all right if the inner truth of the native were restored because the inner truth would lead to the 'correct' image? I want to highlight the native – nowadays often a synonym for the oppressed, the marginalized, the wronged – because I think that the space occupied by the native in postcolonial discourses is also the space of error, illusion, deception, and filth. How would we write this space in such a way as to refuse the facile turn of sanctifying the defiled image with pieties and thus enriching ourselves precisely with what can be called the surplus value of the oppressed, a surplus value that results from *exchanging* the defiled image for something more noble?

The native as silent object

The production of the native is in part the production of our postcolonial modernity. Before elaborating on the relation between 'native' and 'modernity,' however, I want to examine how current theoretical discussions of the native problematize the space of the native in the form of a symptom of the white man. Following Lacan, I use 'symptom' not in the derogatory sense of a dispensable shadow but in the sense of something that gives the subject its ontological consistency and its fundamental structure. Slavoj Žižek explains the non-pejorative sense of 'symptom' this way:

> If, however, we conceive the symptom as Lacan did in his last writings and seminars, namely as a particular signifying formation which confers on the subject its very ontological consistency, enabling it to structure its basic, constitutive relationship towards enjoyment (*jouissance*), then the entire relationship [between subject and symptom] is reversed, for if the symptom is dissolved, the subject itself disintegrates. In this sense, 'Woman is a symptom of man' means that man himself exists only through woman qua his symptom: his very ontological consistency depends on, is 'externalized' in, his symptom.[6]

As the white man's symptom, as that which is externalized in relation to the white-man-as-subject, the space occupied by the native is essentially objective, the space of the object.

Because of the symptomatic way non-white peoples are constructed in postcoloniality, and because 'symptom' is conventionally regarded in a secondary, derivative sense, many critics of colonialism attempt to write about these peoples in such a way as to wrest them away from their status as symptom or object. The result is a certain inevitable subjectivizing, and here the anti-imperialist project runs a parallel course with the type of feminist project that seeks to restore the truth to women's distorted and violated identities by theorizing female subjectivity. We see this in Frantz Fanon's formulation of the native. Like Freud's construction of woman (which, though criticized, is repeated by many feminists), Fanon's construction of the native is Oedipal. Freud's question was 'What does woman want?' Fanon, elaborating on the necessity of violence in the native's formation, asks, 'What does the black man want?'[7] The native (the black man) is thus imagined to be an angry son who wants to displace the white man, the father. While Freud would go on to represent woman as lack, Fanon's argument is that the native is someone from whom something has been stolen. The native, then, is also lack.

This Oedipal structure of thinking – a structure of thinking that theorizes subjectivity as compensation for a presumed lack – characterizes discourses on the non-West in a pervasive manner, including, occasionally, the discourse of those who are otherwise critical of its patriarchal overtones. In her reading of Julia Kristeva's *About Chinese Women*, for instance, Gayatri Spivak criticizes Kristeva's ethnocentric sense of 'alienation' at the sight of some Chinese women in Huxian Square. Kristeva's passage goes as follows:

> An enormous crowd is sitting in the sun: they wait for us wordlessly, perfectly still. Calm eyes, not even curious, but slightly amused or anxious: in any case, piercing, and certain of belonging to a community with which we will never have anything to do.[8]

Citing this passage, which is followed a few pages later by the question, 'Who is speaking, then, before the stare of the peasants at Huxian?,'[9] Spivak charges Kristeva for being primarily interested in her own identity rather than in these other women's. While I agree with this observation, I find Spivak's formulation of these other women's identity in terms of 'envy' troubling:

> Who is speaking here? An effort to answer that question might have revealed more about the mute women of Huxian Square, *looking with qualified envy* at the 'incursion of the West' (my emphasis).[10]

Doesn't the word 'envy' here remind us of that condition ascribed to women by Freud, against which feminists revolt – namely, 'penis envy'? 'Envy' is the other side of the 'violence' of which Fanon speaks as the fundamental part of the native's formation. But both affects – the one of wanting to *have* what the other has; the other, of destroying the other so that one can *be* in his place – are affects produced by a patriarchal ideology that assumes that the other at the low side of the hierarchy of self/other is 'lacking' (in the pejorative, undesirable sense). Such an ideology, while acknowledging that a lack cannot be filled, also concentrates on how it might be filled (by the same thing), even if imperfectly. The fate of the native is then like that of Freud's woman: Even though she will never have a penis, she will for the rest of her life be trapped within the longing for it and its substitutes.

What we see in the accounts by Kristeva and Spivak is a battle for demonstrating the *unspeaking* truth of the native. While Spivak shows how the articulation of the Western critic is itself already a sign of her privileged identity, for Kristeva it is the limits of Western articulation and articulation itself that have to be recognized in the presence of the silent Chinese women. Throughout Kristeva's encounter with these women, therefore, we find descriptions of the others' looking – their 'calm eyes,' their 'indefinable stare,'[11] and so on – that try to capture their undisturbed presence. If these others have been turned into objects, it is because these objects' gaze makes the Western 'subject' feel alienated from her own familiar (familial) humanity:

> They don't distinguish among us man or woman, blonde or brunette, this or that feature of face or body. As though they were discovering some weird and peculiar animals, harmless but insane.[12]

> I don't feel like a foreigner, the way I do in Baghdad or New York. I feel like an ape, a martian, an *other*.[13]

Between a critical desire to subjectivize them with envy and a 'humble' gesture to revere them as silent objects, is there any alternative for these 'natives'?

Kristeva's way of 'giving in' to the strangeness of the other is a philosophical and semiotic gesture that characterizes many European intellectuals, whose discourse becomes self-accusatory and, *pace* Rousseau, confessional when confronted by the other.[14] When that other is Asia and the 'Far East,' it always seems as if the European intellectual must speak in absolute terms, making this other an utterly incomprehensible, terrifying, and fascinating spectacle. For example, after visiting Japan, Alexandre Kojève, who had asserted that history had come to an end (he was convinced of this in the United States, where he thought he found the 'classless society' predicted by Marx as the goal of human history), wrote a long footnote to the effect that his experience with the Japanese had radically changed his opinion about history. For Kojève in 1959, like Roland Barthes about a decade later, the formalized rituals of Japanese society suggested that the Japanese had arrived at the end of history three centuries earlier. As Barthes would say, semiologically, that Japanese culture is made up of empty signs, Kojève writes:

> all Japanese without exception are currently in a position to live according to totally *formalized* values – that is, values completely empty of all 'human' content in the 'historical' sense. Thus, in the extreme, every Japanese is in principle capable of committing, from pure snobbery, a perfectly 'gratuitous' *suicide*. ... [15]

Michel Serres, on the other hand, also finds 'the end of history' when he goes east, but it is in agricultural China that he finds the absolute totality of the other. Confronted with the Chinese who have to make use of every bit of land for cultivation, Serres comments with statements like the following in an essay called 'China Loam':

> Farming has covered over everything like a tidal wave.
> It is the totality.
> This positiveness is so complete, so compact, that it can only be expressed negatively. There is no margin, no gap, no passes, no omission, no waste, no vestiges. The fringe, the fuzzy area, the refuse, the wasteland, the open-space have all disappeared: no surplus, no vacuum, no history, no time.[16]

> Here the utmost limit of what we call history had already been reached a thousand years ago.[17]

To the extent that it is our own limit that we encounter when we encounter another, all these intellectuals can do is to render the other as the negative of what they are and what they do. As Serres puts it, the spectacle of China's total rationality is so 'positive, so rational, so well-adapted that one can only speak of it in negative terms.'[18] As such, the 'native' is turned into an absolute entity in the form of an image (the 'empty' Japanese ritual or 'China loam'), whose silence becomes the occasion for *our* speech.[19] The gaze of the Western scholar is 'pornographic' and the native becomes a mere 'naked body' in the sense described by Jameson. Whether positive or negative, the construction of the native remains at the level of image-identification, a process in which 'our' own identity is measured in terms of the degrees to which we resemble her and to which she resembles us. Is there a way of conceiving of the native beyond imagistic resemblance?

This question is what prompts Spivak's bold and provocative statement, 'The subaltern cannot speak.'[20] Because it seems to cast the native permanently in the form of a silent object, Spivak's statement foreseeably gives rise to pious defenses of the native as a voiced subject and leads many to jump on the band-wagon of declaring solidarity with 'subalterns' of different kinds. Speaking sincerely of the multiple voices of the native woman thus, Benita Parry criticizes Spivak for assigning an absolute power to the imperialist discourse:

> Since the native woman is constructed within multiple social relationships and positioned as the product of different class, caste and cultural specificities, it should be possible to locate traces and testimony of women's voice on those sites where women inscribed themselves as healers, ascetics, singers of sacred songs, artisans and artists, and by this to modify Spivak's model of the silent subaltern.[21]

In contrast to Spivak, Parry supports Homi Bhabha's argument that since a discursive system is inevitably split in enunciation, the colonist's text itself already contains a native voice – ambivalently. The colonial text's 'hybridity,' to use Bhabha's word, means that the subaltern has spoken.[22] But what kind of an argument is it to say that the subaltern's 'voice' can be found in the *ambivalence* of the imperialist's speech? It is an argument which ultimately makes it unnecessary to come to terms with the subaltern since she has already 'spoken,' as it were, in the system's gaps. All we would need to do would be to continue to study – to deconstruct – the rich and ambivalent language of the imperialist! What Bhabha's word 'hybridity' revives, in the masquerade of deconstruction, anti-imperialism, and 'difficult' theory, is an old functionalist notion of what a dominant culture permits in the interest of maintaining its own equilibrium. Such functionalism informs the investigatory methods of classical anthropology and sociology as much as it does the colonial policies of the British Empire. The kind of subject constitution it allows, a subject constitution firmly inscribed in Anglo-American liberal humanism, is the other side of the process of image-identification, in which we try to make the native more like us by giving her a 'voice.'

The charge of Spivak's essay, on the other hand, is a protest against the *two* sides of image-identification, the *two* types of freedom the subaltern has been allowed – object formation and subject constitution – which would result either in the subaltern's protection (as object) from her own kind or her achievement as a voice assimilable to the project of imperialism. That is why Spivak concludes by challenging precisely the optimistic view that the subaltern has already spoken: 'The subaltern cannot speak. There is no virtue in global laundry lists with "woman" as a pious item.'[23]

Instead, a radical alternative can be conceived only when we recognize the essential *untranslatability* from the subaltern discourse to imperialist discourse. Using Jean-François Lyotard's notion of the *différend*, which Spivak explains as 'the inaccessibility of, or untranslatability from, one mode of discourse in a dispute to another,'[24] she argues the impossibility of the subaltern's constitution *in life*.[25] The subaltern cannot speak, not because there are not activities in which we can locate a subaltern mode of life/culture/subjectivity, but because, as is indicated by the critique of thought and articulation given to us by Western intellectuals such as Lacan, Foucault, Barthes, Kristeva, and Derrida (Spivak's most important reference), 'speaking' itself belongs to an already well-defined structure and history of domination. As Spivak says in an interview: 'If the subaltern can speak then, thank God, the subaltern is not a subaltern any more.'[26]

It is only when we acknowledge the fact that the subaltern cannot speak that we can begin to plot a different kind of process of identification for the native. It follows that, within Spivak's argument, it is a *silent* gesture on the part of a young Hindu woman, Bhuvaneswari Bhaduri, who committed suicide during her menstruation so that the suicide could not be interpreted as a case of illicit pregnancy, that becomes a telling instance of subaltern writing, a writing whose message is only understood retrospectively.[27] As such, the 'identity' of the native is inimitable, beyond the resemblance of the image. The type of identification offered by her silent space is what may be called symbolic identification. In the words of Slavoj Žižek:

> in imaginary identification we imitate the other at the level of resemblance – we identify ourselves with the image of the other inasmuch as we are 'like him,' while in symbolic identification we identify ourselves with the other precisely at a point at which he is inimitable, at the point which eludes resemblance.[28]

Local resurrections, new histories

As an issue of postcoloniality, the problem of the native is also the problem of modernity and modernity's relation to 'endangered authenticities.'[29] The question to ask is not whether we can return the native to her authentic origin, but what our fascination with the native means in terms of the irreversibility of modernity.

There are many commendable accounts of how the native in the non-Western world has been used by the West as a means to promote and develop its own intellectual contours.[30] According to these accounts, modernism, especially the modernism that we associate with the art of Modigliani, Picasso, Gauguin, the novels of Gustave Flaubert, Marcel Proust, D. H. Lawrence, James Joyce, Henry Miller, and so forth, was possible only because these 'first world' artists with famous names incorporated into their 'creativity' the culture and art work of the peoples of the non-West. But while Western artists continue to receive attention specifically categorized in time, place, and name, the treatment of the works of non-Western peoples continues to partake of systemic patterns of exploitation and distortion.

Apart from the general attribution of 'anonymity' to native artists, 'native works' have been bifurcated either as timeless (in which case they would go into art museums) or as historical (in which case they would go into ethnographic museums). While most cultural critics today are alert to the pitfalls of the 'timeless art' argument, many are still mired in efforts to invoke 'history,' 'contexts,' and 'specificities' as ways to resurrect the native. In doing so, are they restoring to the native what has been stolen from her? Or are they in fact avoiding the genuine problem of the native's status as object by providing *something* that is more manageable and comforting – namely, a phantom history in which natives appear as our equals and our images, in our shapes and our forms? Nancy Armstrong summarizes our predicament this way:

> The new wave of culture criticism still assumes that we must either be a subject who partakes in the power of gazing or else be an object that is by implication the object of a pornographic gaze. The strategy of identifying people according to 'subject positions' in a vast and intricate differential system of interests and needs is perhaps the most effective way we now have of avoiding the problem incurred whenever we classify political interests by means of bodies inscribed with signs of race, class, and gender. But even the 'subject' of the critical term 'subject position' tends to dissolve too readily back into a popular and sentimental version of the bourgeois self. By definition, this self grants priority to an embodied subject over the body as an object. To insist on being 'subjects' as opposed to 'objects' is to assume that we must have certain powers of observation, classification, and definition in order to exist; these powers make 'us' human. According to the logic governing such thinking as it was formulated in the nineteenth century, only certain kinds of subjects are really subjects; to be human, anyone must be one of 'us.'[31]

As we challenge a dominant discourse by 'resurrecting' the victimized voice/self of the native with our readings – and such is the impulse behind many 'new historical' accounts – we step, far too quickly, into the otherwise silent and invisible place of the native and turn ourselves into living agents/witnesses for her. This process, in which *we* become visible, also neutralizes the untranslatability of the native's experience and the history of that untranslatability. The hasty supply of original 'contexts' and 'specificities' easily becomes complicitous with the dominant discourse, which achieves hegemony precisely by its capacity to convert, recode, make transparent, and thus represent even those experiences that resist it with a stubborn opacity. The danger of historical contextualization turning into cultural corporations is what leads Clifford to say:

> I do not argue, as some critics have, that non-Western objects are properly understood only with reference to their original milieux. Ethnographic contextualizations are as problematic as aesthetic ones, as susceptible to purified, ahistorical treatment.[32]

The problem of modernity, then, is not simply an 'amalgamating' of 'disparate experience'[33] but rather the confrontation between what are now called the 'first' and 'third' worlds in the form of the *différend*, that is, the untranslatability of 'third world' experiences into the 'first world.' This is because, in order for her experience to become translatable, the 'native' cannot simply 'speak' but must also provide the justice/justification for her speech, a justice/justification that has been destroyed in the encounter with the imperialist.[34] The native's victimization consists in the fact that the active evidence – the original witness – of her victimization may no longer exist in any intelligible, coherent shape. Rather than saying that the native has already spoken because the dominant hegemonic discourse is split/hybrid/different from itself, and rather than restoring her to her 'authentic' context, we should argue that it is the native's silence which is the most important clue to her displacement. That silence is at once the *evidence* of imperialist oppression (the naked body, the defiled image) and what, in the absence of the original witness to that oppression, must act in its place by *performing* or *feigning* as the pre-imperialist gaze.

A brown man's eye for a white man's eye

As part of my argument, I read an anti-imperialist text whose intentions are both anti-pornographic (anti-the-bad-'image'-thing) and restorative. Despite such intentions, this text is, I believe, an example of how cultural criticism can further engender exploitation of the native, who is crossed out not once (by the imperialist forces of domination), nor twice (by the cultural processes of subjection), but three times – the third time by the anti-imperialist critic himself.

In his book, *The Colonial Harem*, Malek Alloula focuses on picture postcards of Algerian women produced and sent home by the French during the early decades of the twentieth century. Alloula's point is a simple one, namely, that these native women have been used as a means to represent a European phantasm of the Oriental female. The mundane postcard therefore supports, through its pornographic gaze at the female native, the larger French colonial project in Algeria. Alloula describes his own undertaking as an attempt 'to return this immense postcard to its sender.'[35]

There is no return to any origin which is not already a construction and therefore a kind of writing. Here Alloula writes by explicitly identifying with the naked or half-naked women: 'What I read on these cards does not leave me indifferent. It demonstrates to me, were that still necessary, the desolate poverty of *a gaze that I myself*, as an Algerian, *must have been the object of* at some moment in my personal history' (my emphasis).[36] This claim of identification with the women as image and as object notwithstanding, the male critic remains invisible himself. If the picture postcards are the kind of *evidence-and-witness* of the oppression of the native that I have been talking about, then what happens in Alloula's text is an attempt to fill in the space left open by the silent women by a self-appointed gesture of witnessing, which turns into a second gaze at the 'images' of French colonialism. The Algerian women are exhibited as objects not only by the French but also by Alloula's discourse. Even though the male critic sympathizes with the natives, his status as invisible writing subject is essentially *different from*, not identical with, the status of the pictures in front of us.

The anti-imperialist charge of Alloula's discourse would have us believe that the French gaze at these women is pornographic while his is not. This is so because he distinguishes between erotism and pornography, calling the picture postcards a 'suberotism' (which is the book title in French and the title of the last chapter). In her introduction to the book, Barbara Harlow supports the point of Alloula's project by citing Spivak's statement, 'brown women saved by white men from brown men'.[37] In effect, however, because Alloula is intent on captivating the essence of the colonizer's discourse as a way to retaliate against his enemy, his own discourse coincides much more closely with the enemy's than with the women's. What emerges finally is not an identification between the critic and the images of the women as he wishes, but an identification between the critic and the gaze of the colonialist-photographer *over the images of the women*, which become bearers of multiple exploitations. Because Alloula's identification is with the gaze of the colonialist-photographer, the women remain frozen in their poses.[38] The real question raised by Alloula's text is therefore not, Can brown women be saved from brown men by white men, but, Can brown women be saved from white men by brown men?

Alloula writes: 'A reading of the sort that I propose to undertake would be entirely superfluous if there existed photographic traces of the gaze of the colonized upon the colonizer.'[39] The problem of a statement like this lies in the way it hierarchizes the possibilities of native discourse: had there been photographs that reciprocate in a symmetrical fashion the exploitative gaze of the colonizer, he says, he would not have to write his book. His book is second best. The desire for revenge – to do to the enemy *exactly* what the enemy did to him, so that colonizer and colonized would meet eye to eye – is the fantasy of envy and violence that has been running throughout masculinist anti-imperialist discourse since Fanon. This fantasy, as I have already suggested, is Oedipal in structure.

To make his project what he intended it to be – a *symbolic* identification, as defined by Žižek, with the native women not only as images but also as oppressed victims with their own stories – Alloula would need to follow either one of two alternatives. The first of these would require, in a manner character-istic of the poststructuralist distrust of anything that seems 'spontaneous' or 'self-evident,' a careful reading of the materiality of the images.[40] Such a reading would show that what is assumed to be pornographic is not necessarily so, but is more often a projection, onto the images, of the photographer's (or viewer's) own repression.[41] As it stands, however, Alloula's 'reading' only understands the images in terms of *content* rather than as a signifying process which bears alternative clues of reading that may well undo its supposed messages. Alloula bases his reading on very traditional assumptions of the visual as the naked, by equating photography with a 'scopic desire' to unveil what is 'inside' the women's clothes, etc. Thus he not only confirms Jameson's notion that 'the visual is essentially pornographic,' but unwittingly provides a demonstration of how this is so in his own anti-pornographic writing.

On the other hand, if the problem with poststructuralist analysis is that it too happily dissolves the pornographic obviousness of the images and thus misses their abusive structuration, then a second alternative would have been for Alloula to exclude images from his book. Alloula's entire message could have been delivered verbally. Instead, the images of the Algerian women are exposed a second time and made to stand as a transparent medium, a homo-erotic link connecting the brown man to the white man, connecting 'third world' nationalism to 'first world' imperialism. What results is neither a dissembling of the pornographic apparatus of imperialist domination nor a restoration of the native to her 'authentic' history, but a perfect symmetry between the imperialist and anti-imperialist gazes, which cross over the images of native women as silent objects.

The native in the age of discursive reproduction

Modernity is ambivalent in its very origin. In trying to become 'new' and 'novel' – a kind of primary moment – it must incessantly deal with its connection with what *precedes* it – what was primary to it – in the form of a destruction. As Paul de Man writes, 'modernity exists in the form of a desire to wipe out whatever came earlier, in the hope of reaching at last a point that could be called a true present, a point of origin that marks a new departure.'[42] If the impetus of modernity is a criticism of the past, then much of our cultural criticism is still modernist.

Many accounts of modernity view the world retrospectively, in sadness. The world is thought of as a vast collection, a museum of lives which has been more or less stabilized for/by our gaze. To an anthropologist like Lévi-Strauss in the 1940s, a city like New York 'anticipates humanity's entropic future and gathers up its diverse pasts in decontextualized, collectible forms.'[43] The cosmopolita-nizing of humanity also signals the vanishing of human diversity, an event the modern anthropologist laments. Isn't there much similarity between the nostalgic culture-collecting of a Lévi-Strauss and what is being undertaken in the name of 'new historicism,' which always argues for preserving the 'specifics' of particular cultures? Despite the liberalist political outlook of many of its practitioners, the new historical enterprise often strikes one as being in agreement with Francis Fukuyama's pronouncement about 'the end of history':

> In the post-historical period there will be neither art nor philosophy, just the perpetual caretaking of the museum of human history. I can feel in myself, and see in others around me, a powerful nostalgia for the time when history existed.[44]

Why are we so fascinated with 'history' and with the 'native' in 'modern' times? What do we gain from our labor on these 'endangered authenticities' which are presumed to be from a different time and a different place? What can be said about the juxtaposition of 'us' (our discourse) and 'them'? What kind of *surplus value* is derived from this juxtaposition?

These questions are also questions about the irreversibility of modernity. In the absence of that original witness of the native's destruction, and in the untranslatability of the native's discourse into imperialist discourse, natives, like commodities, become knowable only through routes that diverge from their original 'homes.' Judging from the interest invested by contemporary cultural studies in the 'displaced native,' we may say that the native is precisely caught up in the twin process of what Arjun Appadurai calls 'commoditization by diversion' and 'the aesthetics of decontextualization,' a process in which

> value ... is accelerated or enhanced by placing objects and things in unlikely contexts. ... Such diversion is ... an instrument ... of the (potential) intensification of commoditization by the enhancement of value attendant upon its diversion. This enhancement of value through the diversion of commodities from their customary circuits underlies the plunder of enemy valuables in warfare, the purchase and display of 'primitive' utilitarian objects, the framing of 'found' objects, the making of collections of any sort. In all these examples, diversions of things combine the aesthetic impulse, the entrepreneurial link, and the touch of the morally shocking.[45]

Appadurai, whose intention is to argue that 'commodities, like persons, have social lives,'[46] refrains from including human beings in his account of commodities. By centering the politics of commoditization on *things* in exchange, he anthropomorphizes things but avoids blurring the line between things and people, and thus preserves the safe boundaries of an old, respectable humanism. However, the most critical implication of his theory begins precisely where he stops. Where Appadurai would not go on, we must, and say that *persons, like things, have commodified lives*: The commoditization of 'ethnic specimens' is *already* part of the conceptualization of 'the social life of things' indicated in the title of his volume. The forces of commoditization, as part and parcel of the 'process' of modernity, do not distinguish between things and people.

To elaborate this, let us turn for a moment to the texts of that great modernist, Walter Benjamin. I have in mind 'Eduard Fuchs: Collector and

Historian,' 'The Work of Art in the Age of Mechanical Reproduction,' and 'Theses on the Philosophy of History.' Together these texts offer a writing of the native that has yet to be fully recognized.[47]

Benjamin was himself a passionate collector of books, art, and other objects.[48] As an allegorist, Benjamin's writing is often remarkable for the way it juxtaposes dissimilar things, allowing them to illuminate one another suddenly and unexpectedly. Such is the way he reads the 'modernity' of the collector and the making of literature by a poet like Baudelaire. Like the process of 'commoditization by diversion' described by Appadurai, Baudelaire's poetry specializes in wresting things from their original contexts. Following Benjamin's allegorical method, I juxtapose his description of Baudelaire with anthropologist Sally Price's description of modernist art collecting:

> Tearing things out of the context of their usual interrelations – which is quite normal where commodities are being exhibited – is a procedure very characteristic of Baudelaire.[49]

> Once rescued from their homes among the termites and the elements, the objects come into the protective custody of Western owners, something like orphans from a Third-World war, where they are kept cool, dry, and dusted, and where they are loved and appreciated.[50]

Such a juxtaposition makes way for a reading of Benjamin's theses of *history* against the background of primitive art in civilized places (to allude to the title of Price's book). What emerges in this reading is not so much the violence of Benjamin's messianism as the affinity and comparableness between that violence and the violence of modernist collecting. Think, for instance, of the notion of 'a fight for the history of the oppressed.' If we refuse, for the time being, the common moralistic reading of this notion (a reading which emphasizes the salvational aspect of Benjamin's writings and which dominates Benjamin scholarship) and instead insert 'the oppressed' into the collection of things that fascinate Benjamin, we see that 'the oppressed' shares a similar status with a host of other cultural objects – books, antiques, art, toys, and prostitutes. The language of fighting, plundering, stealing, and abducting is uniformly the language of 'wresting objects from native settings.'[51] The violent concept that is often quoted by Benjamin lovers as a way to read against 'progress' – the concept of blasting open the continuum of history[52] – is as much a precise description of imperialism's relentless destruction of local cultures as it is a 'politically correct' metaphor for redeeming the history of 'the oppressed.'

By underlining the mutual implication of Benjamin's discourse and the discourse of imperialism, my aim is not that of attacking the 'ambiguous' or 'problematic' moral stance of Benjamin the writer. Rather, it is to point out the ever-changing but ever-present complicity between our critical articulation and the political environment at which that articulation is directed. Because of this, whenever the oppressed, the native, the subaltern, and so forth are used to represent the point of 'authenticity' for our critical discourse, they become at the same time the place of myth-making and an escape from the impure nature of political realities. In the same way that 'native imprints' suggest 'primitivism' in modernist art, we turn, increasingly with fascination, to the oppressed to locate a 'genuine' critical origin.

Consider now Benjamin's argument in the essay with which we are all familiar, 'The Work of Art in the Age of Mechanical Reproduction.' The usual understanding of this essay is that Benjamin is describing a process in which the technology of mechanical reproduction has accelerated to such a degree that it is no longer relevant to think of the 'original' of any art work. The age of mechanical reproduction is an age in which the aura of art – its ties to a particular place, culture, or ritual – is in decline. Benjamin is at once nostalgic about the aura and enchanted by its loss. While the aura represents art's close relation with the community that generates it, the loss of the aura is the sign of art's emancipation into mass culture, a new collective culture of 'collectibles.'

For our present purposes, we can rethink the aura of an art object as that 'historical specificity' which makes it unique to a particular place at a particular time. The vast machines of modernist production and reproduction now make this 'historical specificity' a thing of the past and a concept in demise. Instead of the authentic, mysterious work with its irreproducible aura, we have technologically reproduced 'copies' which need not have the original as a referent in the market of mass culture. The original, marked by some unique difference that sets it apart from the mass-produced copies, becomes now a special prize of collectors with exquisite but old-fashioned 'taste.'

Benjamin's notion of the aura and its decline partakes of the contradictions inherent to modernist processes of displacement and identification. The displaced object is both a sign of violence and of 'progress.' Purloined aggressively from its original place, this displaced object becomes infinitely reproducible in the cosmopolitan space. Displacement constitutes identity, but as such it is the identity of the ever-shifting. Benjamin shows how the new reproductive technology such as film brings the object within close proximity to the viewer and at the same time allows the viewer to experiment with different viewing positions. From the perspective of the 1990s, the irony of Benjamin's 1936 essay is that while he associated the new perceptive possibilities brought by mechanical reproduction with communist cultural production, he was actually describing the modes of receptivity that have become standard fare for audiences in the capitalist world.[53]

Such contradictions help in some way to explain the double-edged process in which we find ourselves whenever we try to resuscitate the 'ethnic specimen' or 'native cultures.' Once again, we need to extend Benjamin's conceptualization, a conceptualization that is ostensibly only about objects – works of art and their mechanical reproduction – to human beings. Once we do that, we see that in our fascination with the 'authentic native,' we are actually engaged in a search for the equivalent of the aura even while our search processes themselves take us farther and farther away from that 'original' point of identification. Although we act like good communists who dream of finding and serving the 'real people,' we actually live and work like dirty capitalists accustomed to switching channels constantly. As we keep switching channels and browsing through different 'local' cultures, we produce an infinite number of 'natives,' all with predictably automaton-like features that do not so much de-universalize Western hegemony as they confirm its protean capacity for infinite displacement. The 'authentic' native, like the aura in a kind of *mise en abîme*, keeps receding from our grasp. Meanwhile our machinery churns out inauthentic and imperfect natives who are always already copies. The most radical message offered to us by Benjamin's texts is that the commodified aspects of mass reproduction, often described with existentialist angst as alienated labor, are actually a displacement *structural* to the modernist hand-ling of history, in which the problematic of the authentic native now returns with a vengeance. We could rewrite the title of Benjamin's essay as 'The Native in the Age of Discursive Reproduction.'

In his lecture at the Annual Conference of the Semiotic Society of America in the fall of 1990, J. Hillis Miller returns to Benjamin's remarkable essay as part of a discussion about cultural studies in the age of digital reproduction.[54] One of the scandalous points Miller makes is that Benjamin's formulation of communism and fascism in terms of the 'politicization of art' and the 'aestheti-cization of politics' is actually a reversible one.[55] Therein lies its danger. What Miller means is that what begins as a mobilization for political change based on an interest in/respect for the cultural difference of our others (the politicization of art) can easily grow into its ugly opposite. That is to say, the promotion of a type of politics that is based on the need to distinguish between 'differences' may consequently lead, as in the case of the Nazis, to an oppression that springs from the transformation of 'difference' into 'superiority'. Any pride that 'we' are stronger, healthier, and more beautiful can become, in effect, the aestheti-cization of politics.

Accordingly, it is ironic that in much of the work we do in cultural studies today, we resort to cultural/ethnic/local 'difference' not as an open-ended process but as a preordained fact. The irony is that such a valorization of cultural difference occurs at a time when difference-as-aura-of-the-original has long been problematized by the very availability – and increasing indispensa-bility – of our reproductive apparatuses. Following the drift of Benjamin's argument, Miller writes:

> this celebration of cultural specificity has occurred at a time when that specificity is being drastically altered by technological and other changes that are leading to internationalization of art and of culture generally. The work of cultural studies inevitably participates in that uprooting. ... [A]rchival work ... is another form of the digital reproduction that puts everything on the same plane of instant avail-ability. ... By a paradox familiar to anthropologists, the effort of understanding, preservation, and celebration participates in the drastic alteration of the cultures it would preserve. The more cultural studies try to save and empower local cultures the more they may endanger them.[56]

For Miller, to hang onto the 'local' as the absolutely different – that is, absolutely identical with itself – means to attempt to hang onto a rigid stratification of the world in the age of digital reproduction:

if the politicizing of art is only the specular image of the aestheticizing of politics, can the former as exemplified in cultural studies be exempt from the terrible possibilities of the aestheticizing of politics? ... [T]he more cultural studies works for the celebration, preservation, and empowerment of subordinated cultures the more it may aid in the replication of just those political orders it would contest. ... Are not cultural studies caught in a form of the penchant of all national aestheticisms and aesthetic nationalisms toward war?[57]

The native as other and Other

So far my argument has demonstrated a few things. I present the place of the native as that of the image and the silent object, which is often equated with a kind of 'lack' in a pejorative sense. After Fanon, we tend to fill this lack with a type of discourse that posits envy and violence as the necessary structure of the native's subjectivity. Corresponding to this is the wave of 'new history' which wants to resurrect the native by restoring her to her original context. But new historicism, as a modernist collecting of culture specimens, inevitably comes up against its own aporia, namely, that the possibility of *gathering* 'endangered authenticities' is also the possibility of dispensing with the authentic altogether. This is indicated by the collage of Benjamin's critical items – history, collecting, and the mechanical reproduction of art – in which the aura is experienced only in ruin. We are left with the question of how cultural difference can be imagined without being collapsed into the neutrality of a globalist technocracy (as the possibilities of mechanical reproduction imply) and without being frozen into the lifeless 'image' of the other that we encounter in Alloula's book.

Alloula's book is disturbing because its use of the image, albeit a problematic one, none the less confronts us with the reality of a *relation* which is neither innocuous nor avoidable. This is the relation between technological reproduction and cultural displacement. If technological reproduction is inevitable, is not cultural displacement also? If cultural displacement is conceived derogatorily, must technological reproduction be condemned moralistically then? Does the necessity of the first make the second a necessary virtue, or does the problematic nature of the second render the first equally problematic? This nexus of questions becomes most poignant when the representation of the 'native' is not only in the form of a visual other, but explicitly in the form of a pornographic image produced by the technology of photography. Should the criticism of this kind of image lead to 1) the criticism of the visual image itself (if, as Jameson says, the visual is essentially pornographic); 2) an alternative form of conceiving of 'otherness' that is completely free of the image; and 3) a subsequent construction of the 'native' as 'truth' rather than 'falsehood'?

While we have no simple answer to these questions, we know that 'false' images are going to remain with us whether or not we like it. That is not simply because they are willfully planted there by individuals desiring to corrupt the world; rather it is because the image itself is traditionally always regarded with suspicion, as a site of duplicity if not of direct degeneration. Is there a way in which we can re-imagine our relation to the 'pornographic' image of the native?

Ever since Jean-Jacques Rousseau, the native has been imagined as a kind of total other – a utopian image whose imaginary self-sufficiency is used as a stage for the incomplete (or 'antagonistic')[58] nature of human society. Rousseau's savage is 'self-sufficient' because he possesses *nothing* and is in that sense indifferent and independent. The true difference between the savage and civil man is that man is completable only through others; that is, his identity is always obtained through otherness:

> the savage lives within himself; social man lives always outside himself; he knows how to live only in the opinion of others, it is, so to speak, from their judgment alone that he derives the sense of his own experience.[59]

Rousseau's formulation of the native is interesting not simply because of its idealism. To be sure, this idealism continues to be picked up by other intellectuals such as Kristeva, Barthes, Serres, and others, who (mis)apply it to *specific other cultures*. In doing so, they limit and thus demolish the most important aspect of Rousseau's text, which is that the idealized native is, literally, topographically *nowhere*. No cruise ship ever takes us to see a self-sufficient 'native,' nor are the remains of any such person to be found at any archeological site.

Rousseau's savage is, then, not simply a cultural 'other,' but, in Lacanian language, the Other (big Other) that exists before 'separation,' before the emergence of the *objet petit a*, the name for those subjectivized, privatized, and missing parts of the whole.[60] Why is this important? Because it enables us to imagine the native in a way that has been foreclosed by the Manichaean aesthetics[61] in which she is always already cast – as the white man's other, as the degraded and falsified image, as the subject constituted solely by her envy and violence, *and* as the 'identity' that can never free itself of any of this 'pornography.' My invocation of the big Other is hence not an attempt to depoliticize the realities of displaced identities in the postimperialist world; rather, it is an attempt to broaden that politics to include more *general* questions of exploitation, resistance, and survival by using the historical experience of the 'native' as its shifting ground.

A moment in Homi Bhabha's reading of Fanon suggests a similar attempt at a more extended politics when he points out how Fanon, writing in times of political urgency, has limited it to the colonial situation:

> At times Fanon attempts too close a correspondence between the *mise-en-scène* of unconscious fantasy and the phantoms of racist fear and hate that stalk the colonial scene; he turns too hastily from the ambivalences of identification to the antagonistic identities of political alienation and cultural discrimination; he is too quick to name the Other, to personalize its presence in the language of colonial racism – 'the real Other for the white man is and will continue to be the black man. And conversely.' These attempts, in Fanon's words, to restore the dream to its proper political time and cultural space can, at times, blunt the edge of Fanon's brilliant illustrations of the complexity of psychic projections in the pathological colonial relation.[62]

While not giving up the politically urgent sense in which Fanon wrote, Bhabha indicates that the criticism of the history of colonialism via the problematic of the native's (the black man's) identification can in fact lead to an understanding of the larger problems of otherness that do not necessarily emerge exclusively in anticolonial discourse. This openness, which is not as expediently committed to a particular 'position' as most self-declared political discourses are, is to be differentiated from the kind of idealization of another *culture* in the form of a totality that is absolutely different (and indifferent) to our own. This openness is not an attempt to recuperate an originary, primordial space before the sign. Rather, it is a total sign, the Other, the *entire* function of which is to contest the limits of the conventional (arbitrary) sign itself.[63] We may call this big Other the big Difference.

How does the big Other work? It works by combating the construction of the native as the straightforward or direct 'other' of the colonizer. Instead, it adds to this 'image' of the native the ability to look, so that the native is 'gaze' as well. But this is not the gaze of the native-as-subject, nor the gaze of the anti-imperialist critic like Alloula; rather it is a simulation of the gaze that witnessed the native's oppression prior to her becoming image. (For instance, it is the video camera that records policemen beating their black victim, Rodney King, with clubs in Los Angeles, as he 'resists arrest' by pleading for his life.) The big Other thus functions to supplement the identification of the native-as-image in the form of *evidence-cum-witness* that I have been talking about.[64]

In other words, the agency of the native cannot simply be imagined in terms of a resistance against the image – that is, *after* the image has been formed – nor in terms of a subjectivity that existed *before*, beneath, inside, or outside the image. It needs to be rethought as that which bears witness to its own demolition – in a form that is at once image and gaze, but a gaze that exceeds the moment of colonization.

What I am suggesting is a mode of understanding the native in which the native's existence – that is, an existence before becoming 'native' – precedes the arrival of the colonizer. Contrary to the model of Western hegemony in which the colonizer is seen as a primary, active 'gaze' subjugating the native as passive 'object,' I want to argue that it is actually the colonizer who feels looked at by the native's gaze. This gaze, which is neither a threat nor a retaliation, makes the colonizer 'conscious' of himself, leading to his need to turn this gaze around and look at himself, henceforth 'reflected' in the native-object. It is the self-reflection of the colonizer that produces the colonizer as subject (potent gaze, source of meaning and action) and the native as his image, with all the pejorative meanings of 'lack' attached to the word 'image.' Hegel's story of human 'self-consciousness' is then not what he supposed it to be – a story about Western Man's highest achievement – but a story about the disturbing effect of Western Man's encounter with those others that Hegel considered primitive. Western Man henceforth became 'self-conscious,' that is, uneasy and uncomfortable, in his 'own' environment.

Because this 'originary' *witnessing* is, temporally speaking, lost forever, the native's defiled image must *act* both as 'image' (history of her degradation) and as that witnessing gaze. In the silence of the native-as-object – a silence not immediately distinguishable from her ascribed silence/passivity – the indifference of the 'originary' witness appears again – in simulation. Like the silent picture postcards reproduced by Alloula, this simulated gaze is *between* the image and the gaze of the colonizer. Where the colonizer undresses her, the native's nakedness stares back at him both as the defiled image of his creation *and* as the indifferent gaze that says, there was nothing – no secret – to be unveiled underneath my clothes. That secret is your fantasm.

The native is not the non-duped

I conclude by returning to the issue with which I began, the issue of authenticity. As anthropologist Brian Spooner writes:

> In seeking authenticity people are able to use commodities to express themselves and fix points of security and order in an amorphous modern society. But the evolving relationship between the search for personal authenticity inside and the search for authenticity in carefully selected things outside has received relatively little attention.[65]

My argument *for* the native's status as an indifferent defiled image is really an attempt to get at the root of the problem of the image, in which our cultural studies is deeply involved whenever it deals with 'the other.' Because the image, in which the other is often cast, is always distrusted as illusion, deception, and falsehood, attempts to salvage the other often turn into attempts to uphold the other as the non-duped – the site of authenticity and true knowledge. Critics who do this can also imply that, having absorbed the primal wisdoms, they are the non-duped themselves.

In a recent essay, 'How the Non-Duped Err,' Žižek describes the paradox of deception. Žižek, as Jonathan Elmer writes, 'concurs with Lacan that *"les non-dupes errent,"* that those who think they are undeceived are the fools.'[66] In his work, Žižek often refers to the classic topos in Lacan, the topos that only human beings can 'deceive by feigning to deceive,' or deceive by telling the truth.[67] That this can happen depends on the fact that we all assume that there is always something else under the mask. One deep-rooted example is that under the mask of civilization we are 'savages': the savage/primitive/native is then the 'truth' that is outside/under the symbolic order. The cultural critic who holds on to such a notion of the native is, by analogy, a psychotic subject:

> the psychotic subject's distrust of the big Other, his *idée fixe* that the big Other (embodied in his intersubjective community) is trying to deceive him, is always and necessarily supported by an unshakable belief in a consistent Other, an Other without gaps, an 'Other of the Other' ... a non-deceived agent holding the reins. His mistake does not consist in his radical disbelief, in his conviction that there is a universal deception – here he is quite right, the symbolic order is ultimately the order of a fundamental deception – his mistake lies on the contrary in his being too easy of belief and supposing the existence of a hidden agency manipulating this deception, trying to dupe him. ...[68]

For us working in anti-imperialist discourse, this 'hidden agency manipulating ... deception' would be precisely 'imperialism,' 'colonialism,' 'capitalism,' and so forth. According to Žižek, our identification with the native in the form of a radical *disbelief* in the defiled images produced by these symbolic orders would not be wrong. What is problematic is our attempt to point to them as if they were one consistent manipulator that is trying to fool us consistently. Our fascination with the native, the oppressed, the savage, and all such figures is therefore a desire to hold onto an unchanging certainty somewhere outside our own 'fake' experience. It is a desire for being 'non-duped,' which is a not-too-innocent desire to seize control.

To insist on the native as an indifferent, defiled image is then to return to the native a capacity for distrusting and resisting the symbolic orders that 'fool' her, while not letting go of the 'illusion' that has structured her survival. To imagine the coexistence of defilement and indifference *in* the native-object is not to neutralize the massive destructions committed under such orders as imperialism and capitalism. Rather, it is to invent a dimension beyond the deadlock between native and colonizer in which the native can only be the colonizer's defiled image and the anti-imperialist critic can only be psychotic. My argument is: Yes, 'natives' are represented as defiled images – that is the fact of our history. But must we represent them a second time by turning history 'upside down,' this time giving them the sanctified status of the 'non-duped'? Defilement and sanctification belong to the same symbolic order.

So where have all the 'natives' gone? They have gone ... between the defiled image and the indifferent gaze. The native is not the defiled image and not not the defiled image. And she stares indifferently, mocking our imprisonment within imagistic resemblance and our self-deception as the non-duped.

Notes

1 James Clifford, *The Predicament of Culture: Twentieth-Century Ethnography, Literature, and Art* (Cambridge, MA: Harvard University Press, 1988), p. 232.

2 Clifford, *The Predicament of Culture*, p. 245.

3 I discuss this in the first chapter of my *Woman and Chinese Modernity: The Politics of Reading Between West and East* (Minneapolis: University of Minnesota Press, 1991). One criticism that Sinologists deeply invested in the culture of ancient China often make about contemporary Chinese people is that they are too 'Westernized.'

4 Fredric Jameson, *Signatures of the Visible* (New York: Routledge, 1990), p. 1. Jameson's notion of pornography owes its origins, in part at least, to fictional explorations of the relations between sexual images and technology such as J. G. Ballard's *Crash* (first published by Farrar, Straus & Giroux, Inc. in 1973), described by its author as 'the first pornographic novel based on technology.' See Ballard, 'Introduction to the French Edition' (first published in French in 1974 and in English in 1975), *Crash* (first Vintage Books edition, 1985), p. 6. I am grateful to Chris Andre of Duke University for pointing this out to me.

5 Jean Baudrillard's theory of 'seduction' offers a strong critique of modern theory's tendency to go toward depths, thus ignoring the subversive potential of the superficial. See his *Seduction*, trans. Brian Singer (New York: St. Martin's, 1990).

6 Slavoj Žižek, 'Rossellini: Woman As Symptom of Man,' *October* 54 (1990), p. 21.

7 See Homi Bhabha, ' "What Does the Black Man Want?" ' *New Formations* 1 (1987) pp. 118–24. Bhabha's argument is that 'the black man wants the objectifying confrontation with otherness' (p. 120). This essay is based on Bhabha's introduction to Frantz Fanon's *Black Skin, White Masks* (London: Pluto, 1986).

8 Julia Kristeva, *About Chinese Women*, trans. Anita Barrows (New York: Marion Boyars, 1977, 1986), p. 11.

9 Kristeva, *About Chinese Women*, p. 15.

10 Gayatri Chakravorty Spivak, 'French Feminism in an International Frame,' in *Other Worlds: Essays in Cultural Politics* (London: Methuen, 1987), p. 141.

11 Kristeva, *About Chinese Women*, p. 13.

12 Kristeva, *About Chinese Women*, p. 11.

13 Kristeva, *About Chinese Women*, p. 12.

14 As Jacques Derrida writes of Lévi-Strauss: 'the critique of ethnocentrism, a theme so dear to the author of *Tristes Tropiques*, has most often the sole function of constituting the other as a model of original and natural goodness, of accusing and humiliating oneself, of exhibiting its being-unacceptable in an anti-ethnocentric mirror.' See Jacques Derrida, *Of Grammatology*, trans. Gayatri Chakravorty Spivak (Baltimore: Johns Hopkins University Press, 1976), p. 114.

15 Alexandre Kojève, *Introduction to the Reading of Hegel: Lectures on the Phenomenology of Spirit*, assembled by Raymond Queneau, Allan Bloom, ed. and trans. James H. Nichols, Jr. (Ithaca: Cornell University Press, 1989), p. 162. Barthes's reading of Japan is found in his *Empire of Signs*, trans. Richard Howard (New York: Hill, 1982). For a discussion of Kojève's conception of Japan's 'post-historic' condition, see Miyoshi and Harootunian, Introduction, 'Postmodernism and Japan,' *The South Atlantic Quarterly* 87.3 (1988), pp. 392–94, rpt. as Masao Miyoshi and H. D. Harootunian, eds., *Postmodernism and Japan* (Durham NC: Duke University Press, 1989). In his *Suicidal Narrative in Modern Japan: The Case of Dazai Osamu* (Princeton: Princeton University Press, 1990), Alan Wolfe offers an astute reading of Kojève's problematic pronouncement and its Orientalist assumptions against the complex background of modern Japanese literature and culture. See especially pp. 216–17 and pp. 220–2 of Wolfe's book.

16 Michel Serres, *Detachment*, trans. Genevieve James and Raymond Federman (Athens, OH: Ohio University Press, 1989), p. 5.

17 Serres, *Detachment*, p. 6.

18 Serres, *Detachment*, p. 5.

19 'However impeccably the content of an "other" culture may be known, however anti-ethnocentrically it is represented, it is its location as the "closure" of grand theories, the demand that, in analytic terms, it be always the "good" object of knowledge, the docile body of difference, that reproduces a relation of domination and is the most serious indictment of the institutional powers of critical theory'. (Homi Bhabha, 'The Commitment to Theory,' in Jim Pines and Paul Willemen, eds., *Questions of Third Cinema* [London: British Film Inst., 1989], p. 124).

20 See 'Can the Subaltern Speak?' in Cary Nelson and Lawrence Grossberg, eds., *Marxism and the Interpretation of Culture* (Urbana: University of Illinois Press, 1988), p. 308. The Spivak of this essay is very different from the one who speaks of 'envy' on behalf of the silent Chinese women in 'French Feminism in an International Frame,' precisely because she does not read the subaltern in Oedipalized terms.

21 Benita Parry, 'Problems in Current Theories of Colonial Discourse,' *Oxford Literary Review* 9.1–2 (1987), p. 35.

22 Parry, 'Problems in Current Theories of Colonial Discourse,' pp. 39–43. Bhabha's view is expressed in many of his essays; see, for instance, 'The Other Question – the Stereotype and Colonial Discourse,' *Screen* 24.6 (1983), pp. 18–36; 'Of Mimicry and Man: The Ambivalence of Colonial Discourse,' *October* 28 (1984), pp. 125–33; 'Signs Taken for Wonders: Questions of Ambivalence and Authority under a Tree Outside Delhi, May 1817,' *Critical Inquiry* 12.1 (1985), pp. 144–65. Rpr. in Henry Louis Gates, Jr., ed., *'Race,' Writing, and Difference* (Chicago: University of Chicago Press, 1985), pp. 163–84. See also 'DissemiNation: Time, Narrative, and the Margins of the Modern Nation,' in Homi K. Bhabha, ed., *Nation and Narration* (London: Routledge, 1990), pp. 291–322.

23 Spivak, 'Subaltern,' p. 308.

24 Spivak, 'Subaltern,' p. 300.

25 Jean-François Lyotard, *The Differend: Phrases in Dispute*, trans. Georges Van Den Abbeele (Minneapolis: University of Minnesota Press, 1988):

> I would like to call a *differend* [*différend*] the case where the plaintiff is divested of the means to argue and becomes for that reason a victim. ... A case of differend between two parties takes place when the 'regulation' of the conflict that opposes them is done in the idiom of one of the parties while the wrong suffered by the other is not signified in that idiom (p. 9).

26 Gayatri Chakravorty Spivak, 'The New Historicism: Political Commitment and the Postmodern Critic,' in Sarah Harasym, ed., *The Post-Colonial Critic: Interviews, Strategies, Dialogues* (London: Routledge, 1990), p. 158.

27 Spivak, 'Subaltern,' pp. 307–8.

28 Slavoj Žižek, *The Sublime Object of Ideology* (New York: Verso, 1989), p. 109.

29 Clifford *Predicament*, p. 5.

30 See, for instance, Sally Price, *Primitive Art in Civilized Places* (Chicago: University of Chicago Press, 1989); Marianna Torgovnick, *Gone Primitive: Savage Intellects, Modern Lives* (Chicago: University of Chicago Press, 1990); the many essays in James Clifford and George Marcus, eds., *Writing Culture: The Poetics and Politics of Ethnography* (Berkeley: University of California Press, 1986); and George Marcus and Michael M. J. Fischer, eds., *Anthropology as Cultural Critique: An Experimental Moment in the Human Sciences* (Chicago: University of Chicago Press, 1986).

31 Nancy Armstrong, 'The Occidental Alice,' *differences* 2.2 (1990), p. 33.

32 Clifford, *Predicament*, p. 12.

33 This is T. S. Eliot's view of the poet's mind when it is 'perfectly equipped for its work.' See 'The Metaphysical Poets,' in Frank Kermode ed., *Selected Prose of T. S. Eliot* (New York: Harcourt; Farrar, 1975), p. 64. This well-known discussion of the metaphysical poets' relevance to modernity was in part a criticism of Samuel Johnson's remark of them that 'the most heterogeneous ideas are yoked by violence together' (Eliot, 'Metaphysical,' p. 60).

34 See Lyotard's definition of the *différend*, cited in note 25.

35 Malek Alloula, *The Colonial Harem*, trans. Myrna Godzich and Wlad Godzich (Minneapolis: University of Minnesota Press, 1986), p. 5.

36 Allovla, *The Colonial Harem*, p. 5.

37 Barbara Harlow, 'Introduction,' op. cit., p. xviii. Spivak's statement, 'White men are saving brown women from brown men,' is found in 'Subaltern,' pp. 296–7. She is describing the British intervention in *sati* (widow sacrifice) in British India, whereby

the colonizer attempted to coopt native women under the pretext of freeing them from oppression by their own men.

38 See a similar criticism made by Winifred Woodhull, 'Unveiling Algeria,' *Genders* 10 (1991), pp. 121–6. Because Alloula never really addresses the question of women's interests, Woodhull argues, he ultimately 'repeats the gesture of the colonizer by making of the veiled woman the screen on which he projects *his* fantasy ... of an Algerian nation untroubled by questions of women's oppression' (p. 126). See also Mieke Bal, 'The Politics of Citation,' *Diacritics* 21.1 (1991), pp. 25–45, for an argument about the complicity between the critic of colonial visual practice and colonial exploitation itself. Alloula's book is one of several Bal shows as lacking in a careful critique of the critic's own sexist and colonizing position.

39 Woodhull, 'Unveiling Algeria,' p. 5.

40 Deconstructionist anti-colonial critics such as Bhabha have, for instance, elaborated on the 'ambivalence' of the image in the following terms:

> the image – as point of identification – marks the site of an ambivalence. Its representation is always spatially split – it makes *present* something that is *absent* – and temporally deferred – it is the representation of a time that is always elsewhere, a repetition. The image is only ever an *appurtenance* to authority and identity; it must never be read mimetically as the 'appearance' of a 'reality.' The access to the image of identity is only ever possible in the *negation* of any sense of originality of plenitude, through the principle of displacement and differentiation (absence/presence; representation/repetition) that always renders it a liminal reality. (Bhabha, ' "What Does the Black Man Want?" ' p. 120.)

41 For an example of a poststructuralist analysist of how pornography is in the eye of the beholder, see Judith Butler, 'The Force of Fantasy: Feminism, Mapplethorpe, and Discursive Excess,' *differences* 2.2 (1990), pp. 105–25.

42 Paul de Man, *Blindness and Insight: Essays in the Rhetoric of Contemporary Criticism* (Minneapolis: University of Minnesota Press, 1983), p. 148.

43 Clifford, *Predicament*, p. 244.

44 Francis Fukuyama, 'The End of History?' *The National Interest* 16 (1989), p. 18.

45 Arjun Appadurai, 'Introduction: Commodities and the Politics of Value,' in Arjun Appadurai, ed., *The Social Life of Things: Commodities in Cultural Perspective* (Cambridge: Cambridge University Press, 1986), p. 28.

46 Appadurai, *The Social Life of Things*, p. 3.

47 Walter Benjamin, 'Edward Fuchs: Collector and Historian,' trans. Knut Tarnowski, in Andrew Arato and Eike Gebhardt, eds., *The Essential Frankfurt School Reader* (New York, Urizen, 1978), pp. 225–53; 'The Work of Art in the Age of Mechanical Production,' in Walter Benjamin, *Illuminations*, ed. Hannah Arendt, trans, Harry Zohn (New York: Schocken, 1969), pp. 217–51; and 'Theses on the Philosophy of History,' *Illuminations*, pp. 253–64.

48 In the brief introduction to 'Edward Fuchs,' the editors of *The Essential Frankfurt School Reader* write: 'the presentation of Fuchs, the collector and often crude materialist, must also be read as one of Benjamin's self-presentations, and even as an *apologia pro vita sua* in the face of criticism' (p. 225).

49 Walter Benjamin, 'Central Park,' trans. Lloyd Spencer (with the help of Mark Harrington), *New German Critique* 34 (1985), p. 41.

50 Price, *Primitive Art*, p. 76.

51 Price, *Primitive Art*, p. 74.

52 'History is the subject of a structure whose site is not homogeneous, empty time, but time filled by the presence of the now [*Jetztzeit*]. Thus, to Robespierre ancient Rome was a past charged with the time of the now which he blasted out of the continuum of history.' 'The awareness that they are about to make the continuum of history explode is characteristic of the revolutionary classes at the moment of their action' (Benjamin, 'Theses,' p. 261).

53 See also Benjamin's similar argument in 'The Author as Producer,' trans. Edmund Jephcott, in *The Essential Frankfurt School Reader*, pp. 254–69.

54 Miller's reading of 'aura' is poststructuralist.

> The fact that the modern work of art is reproducible casts its shadow back not just to remove the aura from traditional works but to reveal that aura was always an ideological formation. That is what Benjamin means by saying film in itself, as a means of mechanical reproduction, is revolutionary criticism of traditional concepts of art. As the technological changes Benjamin describes have proceeded apace, the opposition between traditional man or woman and the masses disappears and with it the pertinence of the idea of a people with a specific culture. We are all to some degree members of what Benjamin invidiously calls the 'masses.' We are members of a transnational, multilinguistic, worldwide technological culture that makes the pieties of nationalism seem more and more outdated, nostalgic, perhaps even dangerously reactionary. ('The Work of Cultural Criticism in the Age of Digital Reproduction,' Annual Conference of the Semictic Society of America, manuscript, 1990, p. 10.)

> A substantially modified version of Miller's essay is found in his book *Illustrations* (Cambridge, MA: Harvard University Press, 1992), many of the views of which I do not share. My present discussion, however, is based entirely on the earlier lecture.

55 'The problem with all Benjamin's symmetrical oppositions is that they tend to dissolve through the effort of thinking they facilitate,' Miller, 'The Work of Cultural Criticism', p. 10.

56 Miller, 'The Work of Cultural Criticism,' p. 18.

57 Miller, 'The Work of Cultural Criticism,' pp. 19–20.

58 The notion of a radical 'antagonism' that structures sociality by making it incapable of self-identification or closure is argued by Ernesto Laclau and Chantal Mouffe in *Hegemony and Socialist Strategy: Towards a Radical Democratic Politics*, trans. Winston Moore and Paul Cammack (London: Verso, 1985). See especially chapter three, 'Beyond the Positivity of the Social: Antagonisms and Hegemony.'

59 Jean-Jacques Rousseau, *A Discourse on Inequality*, trans. Maurice Cranston (London: Penguin, 1984).

60 Gilles Deleuze and Félix Guattari make a comparable point when they, criticizing Freudian psychoanalysis as an anthropomorphic representation of sex, equate Lacan's 'big Other' with what they call 'nonhuman sex.' See Gilles Deleuze and Félix Guattari, *Anti-Oedipus: Capitalism and Schizophrenia*, preface Michel Foucault, trans. Robert Hurley, Mark Seem, and Helen R. Lane (Minneapolis: University of Minnesota Press, 1983), pp. 295; 308–10. Deleuze and Guattari's notion of 'part objects' or 'partial objects' is, of course, very different. They are not 'part' of any 'whole,' but molecular machinic flows and breaks.

61 I take this phrase from Abdul R. JanMohamed, *Manichean Aesthetics: The Politics of Literature in Colonial Africa* (Amherst: University of Massachusetts Press, 1983).

62 Bhabha, ' "What Does the Black Man Want?" ' p. 121.

63 In Saussure, the linguistic sign (made up of a relationship between signifier and signified) is arbitrary because it is conventional – in the sense that it works only within a coherent system of differences. See Ferdinand de Saussure, *Course in General Linguistics*, Charles Bally *et al.*, eds., trans. Wade Baskin (Glasgow: Fontana/Collins, 1974).

64 This essay was completed in mid-1991. The subsequent verdict on the King beating in 1992 demonstrated once again the dominant culture's ability to manipulate images to its own advantage by sabotaging the witnessing function crucial to any evidence of abuse. Once it succeeds in divorcing the act of witnessing from the image, the dominant culture can appoint itself as the 'true' witness whose observation and interpretation of the image is held as the most accurate one. The Rodney King video and the racial riots that followed the verdict thus became 'evidence' not for the historical white discrimination against blacks, but for how necessary that discrimination is!

65 Brian Spooner, 'Weavers and Dealers: The Authenticity of an Oriental Carpet,' in Appadurai *Social Life*, p. 226.

66 Jonathan Elmer, review of Slavoj Žižek's *The Sublime Object of Ideology*, *Qui Parle* 4.1 (1990), p. 122.

67 Slavoj Žižek, 'How the Non-Duped Err,' *Qui Parle* 4.1 (1990), p. 3. Žižek quotes the Freudian joke about Polish Jews often mentioned by Lacan: 'one of them asks the other in an offended tone: "Why are you telling me that you are going to Lemberg, when you are really going to Lemberg?" ' p. 3. See also *Sublime Object*, p. 197.

68 Žižek, 'How the Non-Duped Err,' p. 12.

PART TWO

DISCIPLINING KNOWLEDGE

8

Barbara Christian

*The Race for Theory**

I have seized this occasion to break the silence among those of us, critics, as we are now called, who have been intimidated, devalued by what I call the race for theory. I have become convinced that there has been a takeover in the literary world by Western philosophers from the old literary élite, the neutral humanists. Philosophers have been able to effect such a takeover because so much of the literature of the West has become pallid, laden with despair, self-indulgent, and disconnected. The New Philosophers, eager to understand a world that is today fast escaping their political control, have redefined literature so that the distinctions implied by that term, that is, the distinctions between everything written and those things written to evoke feeling as well as to express thought, have been blurred. They have changed literary critical language to suit their own purposes as philosophers, and they have reinvented the meaning of theory.

My first response to this realization was to ignore it. Perhaps, in spite of the egocentrism of this trend, some good might come of it. I had, I felt, more pressing and interesting things to do, such as reading and studying the history and literature of black women, a history that had been totally ignored, a contemporary literature bursting with originality, passion, insight, and beauty. But unfortunately it is difficult to ignore this new takeover, since theory has become a commodity which helps determine whether we are hired or promoted in academic institutions – worse, whether we are heard at all. Due to this new orientation, works (a word which evokes labor) have become texts. Critics are no longer concerned with literature, but with other critics' texts, for the critic yearning for attention has displaced the writer and has conceived of himself as the center. Interestingly in the first part of this century, at least in England and America, the critic was usually also a writer of poetry, plays, or novels. But today, as a new generation of professionals develops, he or she is increasingly an academic. Activities such as teaching or writing one's response to specific works of literature have, among this group, become subordinated to one primary thrust, that moment when one creates a theory, thus fixing a constellation of ideas for a time at least, a fixing which no doubt will be replaced in another month or so by somebody else's competing theory as the

* From Abdul R. JanMohamed and David Lloyd, eds., *The Nature and Context of Minority Discourse* (Oxford University Press, 1990), pp. 37–49.

race accelerates. Perhaps because those who have effected the takeover have the power (although they deny it) first of all to be published, and thereby to determine the ideas which are deemed valuable, some of our most daring and potentially radical critics (and by *our* I mean black, women, third world) have been influenced, even coopted, into speaking a language and defining their discussion in terms alien to and opposed to our needs and orientation. At least so far, the creative writers I study have resisted this language.

For people of color have always theorized – but in forms quite different from the Western form of abstract logic. And I am inclined to say that our theorizing (and I intentionally use the verb rather than the noun) is often in narrative forms, in the stories we create, in riddles and proverbs, in the play with language, since dynamic rather than fixed ideas seem more to our liking. How else have we managed to survive with such spiritedness the assault on our bodies, social institutions, countries, our very humanity? And women, at least the women I grew up around, continuously speculated about the nature of life through pithy language that unmasked the power relations of their world. It is this language, and the grace and pleasure with which they played with it, that I find celebrated, refined, critiqued in the works of writers like Morrison and Walker. My folk, in other words, have always been a race for theory – though more in the form of the hieroglyph, a written figure which is both sensual and abstract, both beautiful and communicative. In my own work I try to illuminate and explain these hieroglyphs, which is, I think, an activity quite different from the creating of the hieroglyphs themselves. As the Buddhists would say, the finger pointing at the moon is not the moon.

In this discussion, however, I am more concerned with the issue raised by my first use of the term, *the race for theory*, in relation to its academic hegemony, and possibly of its inappropriateness to the energetic emerging literatures in the world today. The pervasiveness of this academic hegemony is an issue continually spoken about – but usually in hidden groups, lest we, who are disturbed by it, appear ignorant to the reigning academic élite. Among the folk who speak in muted tones are people of color, feminists, radical critics, creative writers, who have struggled for much longer than a decade to make their voices, their various voices, heard, and for whom literature is not an occasion for discourse among critics but is necessary nourishment for their people and one way by which they come to understand their lives better. Clichéd though this may be, it bears, I think, repeating here.

The race for theory, with its linguistic jargon, its emphasis on quoting its prophets, its tendency towards 'Biblical' exegesis, its refusal even to mention specific works of creative writers, far less contemporary ones, its preoccupations with mechanical analyses of language, graphs, algebraic equations, its gross generalizations about culture, has silenced many of us to the extent that some of us feel we can no longer discuss our own literature, while others have developed intense writing blocks and are puzzled by the incomprehensibility of the language set adrift in literary circles. There have been, in the last year, any number of occasions on which I had to convince literary critics who have pioneered entire new areas of critical inquiry that they did have something to say. Some of us are continually harassed to invent wholesale theories regardless of the complexity of the literature we study. I, for one, am tired of being asked to produce a black feminist literary theory as if I were a mechanical man. For I believe such theory is prescriptive – it ought to have some relationship to practice. Since I can count on one hand the number of people attempting to be black feminist literary critics in the world today, I consider it presumptuous of me to invent a theory of how we *ought* to read. Instead, I think we need to read the works of our writers in our various ways and remain open to the intricacies of the intersection of language, class, race, and gender in the literature. And it would help if we share our process, that is, our practice, as much as possible since, finally, our work *is* a collective endeavor.

The insidious quality of this race for theory is symbolized for me by the very name of this special issue – Minority Discourse – a label which is borrowed from the reigning theory of the day and is untrue to the literatures being produced by our writers, for many of our literatures (certainly Afro-American literature) are central, not minor, and by the titles of many of the articles, which illuminate language as an assault on the other, rather than as possible communication, and play with, or even affirmation of another. I have used the passive voice in my last sentence construction, contrary to the rules of Black English, which like all languages has a particular value system, since I have not placed responsibility on any particular person or group. But that is precisely because this new ideology has become so prevalent among us that it behaves like so many of the other ideologies with which we have had to contend. It appears to have neither head nor center. At the least, though, we can say that the terms 'minority' and 'discourse' are located firmly in a Western dualistic or 'binary' frame which sees the rest of the world as minor, and tries to convince the rest of the world that it *is* major, usually through force and then through language, even as it claims many of the ideas that we, its 'historical' other, have known and spoken about for so long. For many of us have never conceived of ourselves only as somebody's *other*.

Let me not give the impression that by objecting to the race for theory I ally myself with or agree with the neutral humanists who see literature as pure expression and will not admit to the obvious control of its production, value, and distribution by those who have power, who deny, in other words, that literature is, of necessity, political. I am studying an entire body of literature that has been denigrated for centuries by such terms as *political*. For an entire century Afro-American writers, from Charles Chestnutt in the nineteenth century through Richard Wright in the 1930s, Imamu Baraka in the 1960s, Alice Walker in the 1970s, have protested the literary hierarchy of dominance which declares when literature is literature, when literature is great, depending on what it thinks is to its advantage. The Black Arts Movement of the 1960s, out of which Black Studies, the Feminist Literary Movement of the 1970s, and Women's Studies grew, articulated precisely those issues, which came *not* from the declarations of the New Western philosophers but from these groups' reflections on their own lives. That Western scholars have long believed their ideas to be universal has been strongly opposed by many such groups. Some of my colleagues do not see black critical writers of previous decades as eloquent enough. Clearly they have not read Wright's 'Blueprint for Negro Writing,' Ellison's *Shadow and Act*, Chesnutt's resignation from being a writer, or Alice Walker's 'Search for Zora Neale Hurston.' There are two reasons for this general ignorance of what our writer-critics have said. One is that black writing has been generally ignored in this country. Since we, as Toni Morrison has put it, are seen as a discredited people, it is no surprise, then, that our creations are also discredited, but this is also due to the fact that until recently dominant critics in the Western World have also been creative writers who have had access to the upper middle class institutions of education and until recently our writers have decidedly been excluded from these institutions and in fact have often been opposed to them. Because of the academic world's general ignorance about the literature of black people and of women, whose work too has been discredited, it is not surprising that so many of our critics think that the position arguing that literature is political begins with these New Philosophers. Unfortunately, many of our young critics do not investigate the reasons *why* that statement – literature is political – is now acceptable when before it was not; nor do we look to our own antecedents for the sophisticated arguments upon which we can build in order to change the tendency of any established Western idea to become hegemonic.

For I feel that the new emphasis on literary critical theory is as hegemonic as the world which it attacks. I see the language it creates as one which mystifies rather than clarifies our condition, making it possible for a few people who know that particular language to control the critical scene – that language surfaced, interestingly enough, just when the literature of peoples of color, of black women, of Latin Americans, of Africans began to move to 'the center.' Such words as *center* and *periphery* are themselves instructive. *Discourse, canon, texts*, words as latinate as the tradition from which they come, are quite familiar to me. Because I went to a Catholic Mission school in the West Indies, I must confess that I cannot hear the word 'canon' without smelling incense, that the word 'text' immediately brings back agonizing memories of Biblical exegesis, that 'discourse' reeks for me of metaphysics forced down my throat in those courses that traced *world* philosophy from Aristotle through Thomas Aquinas to Heidegger. 'Periphery' too is a word I heard throughout my childhood, for if anything was seen as being at the periphery, it was those small Caribbean islands which had neither land mass nor military power. Still I noted how intensely important this periphery was, for U.S. troops were continually invading one island or another if any change in political control even seemed to be occurring. As I lived among folk for whom language was an absolutely necessary way of validating our existence, I was told that the minds of the world lived only in the small continent of Europe. The metaphysical language of the New Philosophy, then, I must admit, is repulsive to me and is one reason why I raced from philosophy to literature, since the latter seemed to me to have the possibilities of rendering the world as large and as complicated as I experienced it, as sensual as I knew it was. In literature I sensed the possibility of the integration of feeling/knowledge, rather than the split between the abstract and the emotional in which Western philosophy inevitably indulged.

Now I am being told that philosophers are the ones who write literature, that authors are dead, irrelevant, mere vessels through which their narratives ooze, that they do not work nor have they the faintest idea what they are doing; rather they produce texts as disembodied as the angels. I am frankly astonished that scholars who call themselves Marxists or post-Marxists could seriously use such metaphysical language even as they attempt to deconstruct the philosophical tradition from which their language comes. And as a student of literature, I am appalled by the sheer ugliness of the language, its lack of clarity, its unnecessarily complicated sentence constructions, its lack of pleasurableness, its alienating quality. It is the kind of writing for which composition teachers would give a freshman a resounding F.

Because I am a curious person, however, I postponed readings of black women writers I was working on and read some of the prophets of this new literary orientation. These writers did announce their disatisfaction with some of the cornerstone ideas of their own tradition, a dissatisfaction with which I was born. But in their attempt to change the orientation of Western scholarship, they, as usual, concentrated on themselves and were not in the slightest interested in the worlds they had ignored or controlled. Again I was supposed to know *them*, while they were not at all interested in knowing *me*. Instead they sought to 'deconstruct' the tradition to which they belonged even as they used the same forms, style, language of that tradition, forms which necessarily embody its values. And increasingly as I read them and saw their substitution of their philosophical writings for literary ones, I began to have the uneasy feeling that their folk were not producing any literature worth mentioning. For they always harkened back to the masterpieces of the past, again reifying the very texts they said they were deconstructing. Increasingly, as *their* way, *their* terms, *their* approaches remained central and became the means by which one defined literary critics, many of my own peers who had previously been concentrating on dealing with the other side of the equation, the reclamation and discussion of past and *present* third world literatures, were diverted into continually discussing the new literary theory.

From my point of view as a critic of contemporary Afro-American women's writing, this orientation is extremely problematic. In attempting to find the deep structures in the literary tradition, a major preoccupation of the new New Criticism, many of us have become obsessed with the nature of reading itself to the extent that we have stopped writing about literature being written today. Since I am slightly paranoid, it has begun to occur to me that the literature being produced *is* precisely one of the reasons why this new philosophical-literary-critical theory of relativity is so prominent. In other words, the literature of blacks, women of South America and Africa, etc., as overtly 'political' literature was being preempted by a new Western concept which proclaimed that reality does not exist, that everything is relative, and that every text is silent about something – which indeed it must necessarily be.

There is, of course, much to be learned from exploring how we know what we know, how we read what we read, an exploration which, of necessity, can have no end. But there also has to be a 'what,' and that 'what,' when it is even mentioned by the new philosophers, are texts of the past, primarily Western male texts, whose norms are again being transferred onto third world, female texts as theories of reading proliferate. Inevitably a hierarchy has now developed between what is called theoretical criticism and practical criticism, as mind is deemed superior to matter. I have no quarrel with those who wish to philosophize about how we know what we know. But I do resent the fact that this particular orientation is so privileged and has diverted so many of us from doing the first readings of the literature being written today as well as of past works about which nothing has been written. I note, for example, that there is little work done on Gloria Naylor, that most of Alice Walker's works have not been commented on – despite the rage around *The Color Purple* – that there has yet to be an in-depth study of Frances Harper, the nineteenth-century abolitionist poet and novelist. If our emphasis on theoretical criticism continues, critics of the future may have to reclaim the writers we are now ignoring, that is, if they are even aware these artists exist.

I am particularly perturbed by the movement to exalt theory, as well, because of my own adult history. I was an active member of the Black Arts Movement of the sixties and know how dangerous theory can become. Many today may not be aware of this, but the Black Arts Movement tried to create Black Literary Theory and in doing so became prescriptive. My fear is that when Theory is not rooted in practice, it becomes prescriptive, exclusive, élitish.

An example of this prescriptiveness is the approach the Black Arts Movement took towards language. For it, blackness resided in the use of black talk which they defined as hip urban language. So that when Nikki Giovanni reviewed Paule Marshall's *Chosen Place, Timeless People*, she criticized the novel on the grounds that it was not black, for the language was too elegant, too white. Blacks, she said, did not speak that way. Having come from the West Indies where we do, some of the time, speak that way, I was amazed by the narrowness of her vision. The emphasis on *one way* to be black resulted in the works of Southern writers being seen as non-black since the black talk of Georgia does not sound like the black talk of Philadelphia. Because the ideologues, like Baraka, come from the urban centers they tended to privilege their way of speaking, thinking, writing, and to condemn other kinds of writing as not being black enough. Whole areas of the canon were assessed according to the dictum of the Black Arts Nationalist point of view, as in Addison Gayle's *The Way of the New World*, while other works were ignored because they did not fit the scheme of cultural nationalism. Older writers like Ellison and Baldwin were condemned because they saw that the intersection of Western and African influences resulted in a new Afro-American culture, a position with which many of the Black Nationalist idealogues disagreed. Writers were told that writing love poems was not being black. Further examples abound.

It is true that the Black Arts Movements resulted in a necessary and important critique both of previous Afro-American literature and of the white-established literary world. But in attempting to take over power, it, as Ishmael Reed satirizes so well in *Mumbo Jumbo*, became much like its opponent, monolithic and downright repressive.

It is this tendency towards the monolithic, monotheistic, etc., which worries me about the race for theory. Constructs like the *center* and the *periphery* reveal that tendency to want to make the world less complex by organizing it according to one principle, to fix it through an idea which is really an ideal. Many of us are particularly sensitive to monolithism since one major element of ideologies of dominance, such as sexism and racism, is to dehumanize people by stereotyping them, by denying them their variousness and complexity. Inevitably, monolithism becomes a metasystem, in which there is a controlling ideal, especially in relation to pleasure. Language as one form of pleasure is immediately restricted, and becomes heavy, abstract, prescriptive, monotonous.

Variety, multiplicity, eroticism are difficult to control. And it may very well be that these are the reasons why writers are often seen as *persona non grata* by political states, whatever form they take, since writers/artists have a tendency to refuse to give up their way of seeing the world and of playing with possibilities; in fact, their very expression relies on that insistence. Perhaps that is why creative literature, even when written by politically reactionary people, can be so freeing, for in having to embody ideas and recreate the world, writers cannot merely produce 'one way.'

The characteristics of the Black Arts Movement are, I am afraid, being repeated again today, certainly in the other area to which I am especially tuned. In the race for theory, feminists, eager to enter the halls of power, have attempted their own prescriptions. So often I have read books on feminist literary theory that restrict the definition of what *feminist* means and overgeneralize about so much of the world that most women as well as men are excluded. Nor seldom do feminist theorists take into account the complexity of life – that women are of many races and ethnic backgrounds with different histories and cultures and that as a rule women belong to different classes that have different concerns. Seldom do they note these distinctions, because if they did they could not articulate a theory. Often as a way of clearing themselves they do acknowledge that women of color, for example, do exist, then go on to do what they were going to do anyway, which is to invent a theory that has little relevance for us.

That tendency towards monolithism is precisely how I see the French feminist theorists. They concentrate on the female body as the means to creating a female language, since language, they say, is male and necessarily conceives of woman as other. Clearly many of them have been irritated by the theories of Lacan for whom language is phallic. But suppose there are peoples in the world whose language was invented primarily in relation to women, who after all are the ones who relate to children and teach language. Some Native American languages, for example, use female pronouns when speaking about nongender specific activity. Who knows who, according to gender, created languages. Further, by positing the body as the source of everything French feminists return to the old myth that biology determines everything and ignore the fact that gender is a social rather than a biological construct.

I could go on critiquing the positions of French feminists who are themselves more various in their points of view than the label which is used to describe them, but that is not my point. What I am concerned about is the authority this school now has in feminist scholarship – the way it has become *authoritative discourse*, monologic, which occurs precisely because it does have access to the means of promulgating its ideas. The Black Arts Movement was able to do this for a time because of the political movements of the 1960s – so too with the French feminists who could not be inventing 'theory' if a space had not been created by the Women's Movement. In both cases, both groups posited a theory that excluded many of the people who made that space possible. Hence one of the reasons for the surge of Afro-American women's writing during the 1970s and its emphasis on sexism in the black community is precisely that when the ideologues of the 1960s said *black*, they meant *black male*.

I and many of my sisters do not see the world as being so simple. And perhaps that is why we have not rushed to create abstract theories. For we know there are countless women of color, both in America and in the rest of the world to whom our singular ideas would be applied. There is, therefore, a caution we feel about pronouncing black feminist theory that might be seen as a decisive statement about Third World women. This is not to say we are not theorizing. Certainly our literature is an indication of the ways in which our theorizing, of necessity, is based on our multiplicity of experiences.

There is at least one other lesson I learned from the Black Arts Movement. One reason for its monolithic approach had to do with its desire to destroy the power which controlled black people, but it was a power which many of its ideologues wished to achieve. The nature of our context today is such that an approach which desires power singlemindedly must of necessity become like that which it wishes to destroy. Rather than wanting to change the whole model, many of us want to be at the center. It is this point of view that writers like June Jordan and Audre Lorde continually critique even as they call for empowerment, as they emphasize the fear of difference among us and our need for leaders rather than a reliance on ourselves.

For one must distinguish the desire for power from the need to become empowered – that is, seeing oneself as capable of and having the right to determine one's life. Such empowerment is partially derived from a knowledge of history. The Black Arts Movement did result in the creation of Afro-American Studies as a concept, thus giving it a place in the university where one might engage in the reclamation of Afro-American history and culture and pass it on to others. I am particularly concerned that institutions such as Black Studies and Women's Studies, fought for with such vigor and at some sacrifice, are not often seen as important by many of our black or women scholars precisely because the old hierarchy of traditional departments is seen as superior to these 'marginal' groups. Yet, it is in this context that many others of us are discovering the extent of our complexity, the interrelationships of different areas of knowledge in relation to a distinctly Afro-American or female experience. Rather than having to view our world as subordinate to others, or rather than having to work as if we were hybrids, we can pursue ourselves as subjects.

My major objection to the race for theory, as some readers have probably guessed by now, really hinges on the question, 'for whom are we doing what we are doing when we do literary criticism?' It is, I think, the central question today especially for the few of us who have infiltrated the academy enough to be wooed by it. The answer to that question determines what orientation we take in our work, the language we use, the purposes for which it is intended.

I can only speak for myself. But what I write and how I write is done in order to save my own life. And I mean that literally. For me literature is a way of knowing that I am not hallucinating, that whatever I feel/know *is*. It is an affirmation that sensuality is intelligence, that sensual language is language that makes sense. My response, then, is directed to those who write what I read and to those who read what I read – put concretely – to Toni Morrison and to people who read Toni Morrison (among whom I would count few academics). That number is increasing, as is the readership of Walker and Marshall. But in no way is the literature Morrison, Marshall, or Walker create supported by the academic world. Nor given the political context of our society, do I expect that to change soon. For there is no reason, given who controls these institutions, for them to be anything other than threatened by these writers.

My readings do presuppose a need, a desire among folk who like me also want to save their own lives. My concern, then, is a passionate one, for the literature of people who are not in power has always been in danger of extinction or of cooptation, not because we do not theorize, but because what we can even imagine, far less who we can reach, is constantly limited by societal structures. For me, literary criticism is promotion as well as understanding, a response to the writer to whom there is often no response, to folk who need the writing as much as they need anything. I know, from literary history, that writing disappears unless there is a response to it. Because I write about writers who are now writing, I hope to help ensure that their tradition has continuity and survives.

So my 'method,' to use a new 'lit. crit.' word, is not fixed but relates to what I read and to the historical context of the writers I read *and* to the many critical activities in which I am engaged, which may or may not involve writing. It is a learning from the language of creative writers, which is one of surprise, so that I might discover what language I might use. For my language is very much based on what I read and how it affects me, that is, on the surprise that comes from reading something that compels you to read differently, as I believe literature does. I, therefore, have no set method, another prerequisite of the new theory, since for me every work suggests a new approach. As risky as that might seem, it is, I believe, what intelligence means – a tuned sensitivity to that which is alive and therefore cannot be known until it is known. Audre Lorde puts it in a far more succinct and sensual way in her essay 'Poetry is not a Luxury':

> As they become known to and accepted by us, our feelings and the honest exploration of them become sanctuaries and spawning grounds for the most radical and daring of ideas. They become a safe-house for that difference so necessary to change and the conceptualization of any meaningful action. Right now, I could name at least ten ideas I would have found intolerable or incomprehensible and frightening, except as they came after dreams and poems. This is not idle fantasy, but a disciplined attention to the true meaning of 'it feels right to me.' We can train ourselves to respect our feelings and to transpose them into a language so they can be shared. And where that language does not yet exist, it is our poetry which helps to fashion it. Poetry is not only dream and vision; it is the skeleton architecture of our lives. It lays the foundations for a future of change, a bridge across our fears of what has never been before.[1]

Notes

1 Audre Lorde, *Sister Outsider* (Trumansburg, NY: The Crossing Press, 1984), p. 37.

Biodun Jeyifo

The Nature of Things: Arrested Decolonization and Critical Theory*

Olofi created the earth and all the things in it. He created beautiful things and ugly things. He created Truth and he created Falsehood. He made Truth big and powerful, but he made Falsehood skinny and weak. And he made them enemies. He gave Falsehood a cutlass, unbeknownst to Truth. One day, the two met and started fighting. Truth, being so big and powerful felt confident, and also very complacent since he didn't know that Falsehood had a cutlass. So Falsehood cunningly cut off Truth's head. This jolted and enraged Truth and he started scrambling around for his head. He stumbled on Falsehood and, knocking him down, Truth felt the head of Falsehood which he took to be his own. His strength being truly awesome, a mere pull from Truth yanked off the head of Falsehood and this Truth placed on his own neck. And from that day what we have had is this grotesque and confusing mismatch: the body of Truth; the head of Falsehood.

An Afro-Cuban myth

The messenger pointed in his direction and the other man followed with his eye and saw Ezeulu. But he only nodded and continued to write in his big book. When he finished what he was writing he opened a connecting door and disappeared into another room. He did not stay long there; when he came out again he beckoned at Ezeulu, and showed him into the white man's presence. He too was writing, but with his left hand. The first thought that came to Ezeulu on seeing him was to wonder whether any black could ever achieve the same mastery over book as to write it with the left hand.

Chinua Achebe, Arrow of God

The nature of things

There can hardly be a greater affirmation for literary criticism than the view offered by Frank Kermode in his book, *Forms of Attention*, to the effect that critical discourse (which Kermode blithely calls 'conversations') is the primary medium in which literature survives.[1] What Kermode calls 'perpetual modernity' is achieved by a literary work, or a writer, only to the extent that they continue not only to be read but also to be talked and written about. His contention might of course seem like saying the obvious in a more fanciful, sophisticated critical idiom, Shakespeare being always a ready instantiation of

* From *Research in African Literatures* 21 (1990), pp. 33–47.

his point. But part of the fascination of Kermode's ruminations in this monograph – as canonically orthodox as his arguments are – is that he concedes that 'mere' opinion often weighs as much, if not even more, than solid 'knowledge' in securing lasting reputation or 'perpetual modernity' for a work or an author. As we shall see, the vexed distinction between 'opinion' and 'knowledge' is a crucial factor in the instability of critical discourse as the medium in which literature survives, merely subsists, or suffers total oblivion. But first, a few qualifications on Kermode's conception of critical discourse are necessary in approaching the subject of this essay: scholarly critical discourse and the fate of African literature[s].[2]

First of all, critical discourse not only assures the survival of literature, it also determines the condition in which it survives and the uses to which it will be put. For it to play such a role, it must accede to a position of power relative to other discourses, both within and beyond the domains of literature and the Humanities, a point central to much of contemporary post-modern critical theory.[3] Some of these parallel or competing discourses are either incorporated into the 'dominant' discourse or neutralized, marginalized. At this level where one discourse achieves relative dominance over other discourses, we are beyond the power of individual scholars, critics or theorists to serve as arbiters of opinion, knowledge, or value, no matter how gifted or influential they might be. What gives a particular critical discourse its decisive effectivity under these circumstances is the combination of historical, institutional and ideological factors that make the discourse a 'master' discourse which translates the avowed will-to-truth of all discourse into a comsummated, if secret, will-to-power. In other words, this 'master' discourse becomes the discourse of the 'master,' in its effects and consequences at least, if not in its conscious intentions. Once we recognize this discourse and the privileged subject position(s) out of which it speaks, once we identify the 'natural' magisterial register of its accents, we can recognize how its avowed will-to-truth masks the will-to-power which pervades all discourse, especially when we recognize discourse as epistemic behaviour. Such observations imply that, at a fundamental level, all discourse is agonistic particularly when, as in the present case, we are in a social and historical context which is massively overdetermined.

The foregoing discussion is especially relevant to current debates over the pertinence of theory to African literature where 'theory' almost always implies 'their' theory in relation to 'our' literature, Western or 'eurocentric' evaluative norms and criteria in relation to non-Western traditions of writing.[4] If these objections are valid, the traditions of critical discourse on African literature that we have 'inherited' – traditions whose premises, frames of intelligibility, and conditions of possibility have been yoked to foreign, historically imperialist perspectives and institutions of discursive power – raise serious problems with regard to the survival and vitality of its object, African literature. Thus, the question of an African critical discourse which is self-constituted and self-constituting in line with the forces acting on the production of African literature is intimately connected with the fate of that literature.

But what exactly is a self-constituted and self-constituting African critical discourse? Does it exist? If it does not (yet) exist, is there a need for its existence, or an aspiration for its constitution? What established positions have emerged in the debates that have taken place during the last two decades on these questions? Since these are large questions which we cannot hope to adequately explore in one essay, I would like to focus on one single, but crucial aspect of these debates: the emergence of African literature as an academic discipline. As I hope to demonstrate, this is one area of critical discourse on African literature in which 'theory' can play a decisive role in clearing up the confusion and sterile acrimony that have characterized many attempts to define a role for the scholar of African literature and to stake a claim of validity and legitimacy for the 'discipline' of African literary studies. With few exceptions, these debates have been under-theorized or characterized by the assumption that it is an untheorizable discursive space ontologically charged with the mysteries that supposedly lie at the heart of the nature of things.

Nothing better reveals the troubled state of critical discourse on African literature than the problematic accession of the literature to the status of an object of study in Africa and, perhaps more crucially, in Europe and North America. The historical emergence of this phenomenon, if not its historicity, has been the subject of many international conferences and seminars, many essays and books.[5] The diverse expressions of this phenomenon need not concern us here, especially the early exchanges on the definition of African literature or the delimitation of its constitutive elements. What stands at the center of these debates and what concerns us in this essay, is the clearly emergent subsumption of *all* criticism and scholarship on African literature into two basic, supposedly distinct, polarized camps: first, the foreign, white, European or North American critic or scholar and second, the native, black African 'counterpart.' It is impossible to underestimate the hypostasis that presides over the representations which govern debates over this presumed dichotomy.[6] Clearly what is called for is, first, the careful identification of this hypostasis and, second, its demythologization by a theoretical critique that presents it with its secret, repressed conditions of possibility – the structured conditions and relationships of its being-in-the-world, to use the Heideggerian formulation.

Two early observations of Soyinka and Achebe draw attention to the exceptionally problematic nature of the conventional dichotomy between 'foreign' and 'local,' external and homegrown in the constituted publics of modern African literature. In 'And After the Narcissist?', an early essay which perhaps marks Soyinka's emergence as a 'strong' presence in the then newly emergent field of African literature, he makes the following observation:

> In any culture, the cycle of rediscovery – Negritude or Renaissance enlightment or pre-Raphaelite – must, before the wonder palls, breed its own body of the literature of self-worship. African writing has suffered from an additional infliction: apart from

his own discovery the African writer has experienced rediscovery by the external eye. It is doubtful if the effect of this has any parallel in European literature.[7]

As elaborated in this essay, the 'effect' without parallel in European literary history is the inculcation and promotion in African writing of themes and attitudes deleterious to the health and vitality of the nascent literary tradition by an exoticizing, paternalistic foreign commentary. Soyinka's indictments are specific: 'quaintness mongers,' 'exoticists,' and 'primitivists' are the designations he applies to these foreign critics. The following sentence captures the tone of Soyinka's umbrage at the promotion by the 'external eye' of themes, trends, and a particular *type* of African writer: 'The average published writer in the first few years of the post-colonial era was the most celebrated skin of incompetence to obscure the true flesh of the African dilemma.'[8] This questioning of a dislocated foreign commentary on African literature is given a slightly different inflection by Achebe in 'The Novelist as Teacher,' an essay which has come to be regarded as his manifesto:

> I am assuming, of course, that our writer and his society live in the same place. I realize that a lot has been made of the allegation that African writers have to write for European and American readers because African readers, where they exist at all, are only interested in reading text-books. I don't know if African writers will always have a foreign audience in mind. What I do know is that they don't have to.[9]

The point of these two observations is that both writers perceive an abnormal mutation, in what is normally regarded as the rather normal existence (or co-existence) of local and foreign readerships for *any* literature. Although neither author goes deeply into the historical and ideological roots of the epistemological consequences of the situation, their objections are not based on the mere fact that such scholars and critics are 'foreign,' 'non-African,' 'alien' rather than being 'native,' 'African,' an 'indigene.' Both Soyinka and Achebe argue in a rational way and refuse to base their contentions on the 'nature of things.'

We are in an entirely different order of critical discourse when we engage a vast array of African critics and scholars for whom African literature is 'our own literature' and non-African critics and scholars for whom the literature is 'theirs.' For them, it 'belongs' to Africans, even when they themselves defend the usefulness and relevance of *their* participation in the criticism of African literature. This view concerns the staking and conceding of 'natural' proprietary rights in the criticism of African literature, and it is one of the few consensual positions between virtually all critics and scholars of African literature. Such a phenomenon is neither surprising not particularly problematic: who would deny that Chinese literature 'belongs' to the Chinese, Japanese literature to the Japanese, and Russian literature to the Russians? What is anomalous, and problematic is that this point, which in most other cases is taken for granted and silently passed over in the criticism of specific works or authors, becomes, in this instance, a grounding, foundational critical rubric, a norm of evaluation and commentary. Pushed to the limits of its expression, it becomes a veritable *ontologization* of the critical enterprise: only Africans must criticize or evaluate African literature, or slightly rephrased, only Africans can give a 'true' evaluation of African literary works. Of course nobody expresses this ontologization and racialization of this 'truth' quite so blatantly, but the tone, the inflections, the nuances are often not too far from it. Among the most clamorous advocates of this viewpoint, Chinweizu is exemplary in his constant deployment of the collective, proprietary pronoun 'we,' which he invariably uses in a supremely untroubled fashion as if he were absolutely certain of its axiomatic representativeness:

> Of course, Americans or Europeans or Chinese may choose to study African literature and interpret it for American, Russian audiences. There we Africans have no say. It is their business entirely what they do with it, or tell their people about it; we cannot tell them what to say. . . . We don't say that others should not do what they want with African literature. But we do say that, if what they say has consequences in Africa, either through their journals and books which we read in Africa, or through the students whom we send them to educate, then they should be conscious of the fact that they are no longer interpreting African literature for British or Americans exclusively, but are doing so for Africans too.[10]

Being 'African' as a criterion of participating in the critical discourse is always, of course, refracted through other somewhat less hypostatized mediations. There is, first, the refraction through *culturalism*, which either implies sharing ethnic identity with an author, or speaking the same 'native' language, or *living* the culture and thus being rooted in its customs, mores and codes. There is also the refraction of the 'Africanness' of the critic through the appeal to 'experience,' which excludes all those alien to an ethnic-communal or racial-continental experience. In the famous controversy between Ernest Emenyonu and Bernth Lindfors over Cyprian Ekwensi, Emenyonu's espousal of his priviledged 'Africanness' in correcting Lindfors' 'alien' evaluation of Ekwensi embraces all these expressions: ontology, culturalism, and facile experiential empiricism.[11] Lindfors' rebuttals of Emenyonu from the standpoint of an *Africanist* critical fortress is not without its occlusions of crucial epistemological and ideological issues in the politics of interpretation; moreover, his halting, carping tone in this debate is fairly representative of the discomfiture most *foreign* Africanist critics and scholars experience when confronted with the full charge of the proprietorial espousals of the 'native' critic:

> The native critic, it has been argued, is better equipped than anyone else to appreciate the creative genius of his own culture. He is able to achieve this . . . partly because his upbringing has endowed him with superior insights into the workings of his society, the ground upon which this truth stands. Yet it would seem that . . . if all interpretation were left to native critics, truth might be sought principally on a local level, its universal dimensions all but forgotten. Common sense just does not allow a single tribe of critics to claim a monopoly of clear vision. Every individual will have his blind spots, and some critics – native as well as foreign – will be much blinder than others.[12]

Negritude writers have of course been the most prominent advocates of the nativist position. Its influence went beyond its immediate historical context, transcending its institutional and practical consolidation in *Présence Africaine*.

However, by pushing the ontological rubric too far, by hypostatizing an hypostasis and reifying a reification, Negritude effectively argued itself out of relevance in the debate over who has proprietory rights to the turf of African critical discourse. Who could stake a claim to serious critical, *evaluative* rights on the basis of Senghor's famous slogan: Emotion is Negro as Reason is Greek? Even to 'native' critics eager to assert 'natural' territorial rights to a virgin field, some of Senghor's Negritudist excesses could not but be a great embarrassment. Criticism is, after all, an eminently *rational* activity, whereas 'emotion,' 'feeling,' 'intuition,' 'rhythm,' and some of the other 'keywords' of Negritude are characteristically relegated to the margin of the critical enterprise. As shocking as the following passage from Senghor may be to Reason, innumerable others can easily be culled from Senghor's theoretical musings on the supposed ontology of black African aesthetics:

> The African is as it were shut up inside his black skin. He lives in primordial night. He does not begin by distinguishing himself from the object, the tree or stone, the man or animal or social event. He does not keep it at a distance. He does not analyze it. Once he has come under its influence, he takes it like a blind man, still living, into his hands. He does not fix it or kill it. He turns it over and over in his supple hands, he fingers it, he feels it. The African is one of the worms created on the Third Day . . . a pure sensory field. Subjectively, at the end of his antennae, like an insect, he discovers the other. He is moved to his bowels, going out in a centrifugal movement from the subject to the object on the waves sent out from the Other.[13]

Behind the claims and counter-claims the 'foreign' scholar-critics and 'native' claimants of 'natural' proprietory rights to critical insights lies a vastly displaced play of unequal power relations between the two camps. The fact of this displacement accounts for some of the bizarre self-representations and the occlusions of the social production of meaning by individual scholars and critics from either camp. Unfortunately few critics or scholars have paid close, scrupulous, critical attention to this issue. Only rarely, as in the following observations by Steven Arnold, does the Africanist scholar acknowledge the vastly unequal relations of power and privilege between African and non-African scholars and critics of African literature:

> If expatriates have won the right to take part in African literature unmolested – unless their work merits abuse – their role in assisting to broaden the margin of freedom of African literature, as part of a larger struggle, has not been acknowledged. International consciousness and pressure have been a definite fertilizing factor in the growth of our discipline and the object it studies. Nevertheless a very serious imbalance exists in the funding of research on African literatures. Non-Africans can get money to do what Africans often could do better, yet the Africans must sit and watch it get done. Justice, as well as intellectual probity in our discipline, demands that bodies such as UNESCO be pressured to back more basic research in the humanities so that the patronage and political pressure of state and bilateral government sponsorship of research can be minimized.[14]

Although such observations admit a privileged access to research funding by European or American scholars relative to their African counterparts, Arnold remains silent about the possibility that this situation may involve impersonal structural power relationships on an international, global scale. Most non-African scholars of African literature would strenuously repudiate the suggestion that they exercise power over their African colleagues. For isn't the business of criticism and scholarship a matter of the individual scholar's conscience, integrity, and competence? To confront the evasions behind such assumptions, which are not by themselves invalid, we must confront the historical dialectic of the professionalization of African literary study and the attendant crystallization of scholars and critics into the Nationalist and Africanist schools.[15] By doing so we can engage the great paradox, surrounding the study of African literature today: historic de-colonization having initially enabled the curricular legitimation of African literary study in African universities and schools, the equally historic arrest of de-colonization has swung the center of gravity of African literary study away from Africa to Europe and America.

One could hardly find better exemplifications of the basic tensions in the Africanist school of African literary discourse than in two essays of Albert Gérard, 'The Study of African Literature: Birth and Early Growth of a New Learning' and 'Is Anything Wrong with African Literary Studies?'[16] Beyond the zealous wish expressed in both essays for the attainment of a rigorous scientificity in African literary studies, a deep tension marks the spirit that animates both essays.

The earlier essay, 'The Study of African Literature,' is an authoritative, learned, and informative historical account of the study of African literature. Many in the discipline would be surprised to learn from this essay how far back the study of African literatures goes; moreover, the humbling realization that the present generation of scholars did not initiate the discipline but have much to learn from hitherto unrecognized precursors cannot but be salutary. All told, Gérard's essay makes a powerful case for the collaborative comparatist nature of what needs to be done in shoring up the scholarly foundations of the discipline.

The latter essay, 'Is Anything Wrong with African Literary Studies?' has a more limited purview; its purpose is more ideologically inspired, its tone marked by deep anxiety, the anxiety that the discipline has not yet attained the standards required by the leading professional associations and journals in the developed, industrialized countries. Nothing reveals how this anxiety generates tension than Gérard's vascilliations in his views about the complementary but distinct roles of Africans and non-Africans in the new, fledgeling discipline of African literary studies. We can perceive how this tension emerges in the juxtaposition of two passages, one from each essay, on the adequacy of the 'scientific' training of the 'native' literary scholar:

> In francophone and lusophone countries, both colonial and post-colonial authorities have hitherto managed effectively to prevent any significant development of vernacular writing. The situation is different in the former British empire, even though very little official help or even encouragement has been forthcoming from the post-colonial leadership. All the more reason for literary scholars to do what they can

within the limits of their competence. Clearly, only native speakers of the languages involved are truly competent. *The problem is that they have seldom been properly initiated into the mysteries of modern literary scholarship* (my emphasis).[17]

This thaumatological representation of the 'scientificity' of literary scholarship is hardly different from the famous passage from Achebe's *Arrow of God*. It is cited as the second epigraph to this essay, and in it Ezeulu observes the 'white man's' 'mastery over book as to write it with the left hand.' Does that gap still exist? Does the 'native' scholar come into 'modern literary scholarship' through such mystified encrustations, or does she come to 'it' through the adequacy of the institutional apparatus of literary study and its socio-economic environment? Gérard's views in the *earlier* essay is a remarkable departure from the mystagogy of literary scholarship that the latter essay, the essay of 'anxiety of (professional) rejection' purveys:

> The enormous rise in the quality as well as quantity of contributions by African scholars was of two fold significance: not only did it testify to the seriousness of the training dispensed in the increasingly numerous universities of black Africa but also to the scholars' growing awareness of the social environment at a time – the late sixties – when creative artists were becoming more and more vocally critical of the newly 'established' societies.[18]

I have focussed on Gérard's essays for two reasons. First, Gérard is probably the most prolific Africanist in the discipline today, followed closely by Bernth Lindfors. Second, and more importantly, these two essays, and others like them, establish the two main planks on which Africanist literary scholarship rests: the claim of historical depth and the demand for a rigorous, conscientious scientificity. Although linked, these criteria are clearly separate. The historical priority of 'Africanist' literary scholarship over the 'Nationalist' variety consists of the fact that, according to Gérard, European Africanist interest in the continent's languages and literatures dates from the Enlightenment,[19] whereas 'Nationalist' literary scholarship emerged only after, and *because* of political decolonization in the late twentieth century. Only a European with a rigorous philological education could thus have been an Africanist in the early days of the profession. The single-minded collection of documents, materials, artifacts, and archives on Africa had begun and it was often not even necessary for Africanists to have actually been to Africa.

Anthropology was the central intellectual model in early Africanist studies, and a concern once expressed by Evans-Pritchard with regard to the study of Amerindians is also applicable to Africa: 'with the exception of Morgan's study of the Iroquois (1851),' he acknowledged, 'not a single anthropologist conducted field studies till the end of the nineteenth century.'[20] This approach to the study of African literature can be found as recent as 1974 when Graham-White boasted about the circumstances under which he wrote his book, *The Drama of Black Africa*: 'How did an Englishman living in the United States, who has never visited Africa, come to write a book on African drama?'[21] A special mode of the production of knowledge is involved here – a mode that privileges the axiological exteriority and distance of a sovereign cognitive subject from the object of that knowledge. In this case, the object of this knowledge is Africa, its cultural production, its human sciences, its historical encounter with itself and other peoples, other societies and cultures. 'Science' both demands and validates that exteriority and distance, that positivist 'science' which, as Foucault has shown, had its roots in the Enlightenment separation of Reason and Madness. The historic divisions which constitute positivist science are thus regarded as forming the basis of *any* discipline that aspires to professionalism and 'scientificity.' These are the divisions that separate truth from error, knowledge from opinion, rigor from shoddiness, expertise from dilletantism, objectivity from bias, application from laziness. In strict compliance with these distinctions, Lindfors and Gérard *magisterially* castigate the simplifications, prolixities, triteness, over-generalizations, and bombast that, according to them, suffuse much of African critical discourse. The frames of intelligibility (which, for instance, permits Graham-White to declare that 'tragedy' does not exist in pre-colonial African performance traditions, even though he had never set foot on the continent),[22] and the techniques of evaluation which approximate most closely this regime of 'truth' derive from varieties of formalist, New Critical and aestheticist approaches to the analysis and evaluation of African literary works. Among African Africanist literary scholars, Solomon Iyasere, Eldred Jones and Daniel Izebaye have been crusading spirits for this broad paradigm. Their eternal despair is that the discipline has not been won away, and *cannot* perhaps be won away, from nonliterary, extra-literary, or 'impure' critical concerns.

These 'extra-literary' and 'non-literary' concerns are precisely what the advocates of a Nationalist literary scholarship emphasize. One of the founding texts of this school is the famous passage from Fanon's *The Wretched of the Earth* where Fanon delineates three phases in the emergence of modern African literature: an 'apprentice' stage of derivativeness and imitativeness of European traditions; a phase of protest, romanticism, and idyllic nostalgia; and a revolutionary phase of 'a fighting literature.'[23] This brilliant, heuristic schema of Fanon's has inspired applications, misapplications and counter-positions in African literary criticism.[24] I would also draw attention to the 'Report of the Commission on Literature' of the Second Congress of Negro Writers and Artists in Rome, 1959 as another major document of this school.[25] Agostinho Neto's little-known 'On Literature and National Culture,' a conflation of several short addresses given by the late poet and statesman to the Angolan Writers' Union between 1977 and 1978 also qualifies as an important document of Nationalist literary discourse in the way it connects freedom of artistic expression, experimentation, and innovation with commitment to the tasks of constructing a socialist democracy in the conditions of underdevelopment.[26]

But strictly in terms of laying the principles and foundations of a *curricular* and *disciplinary* consolidation for the use of African literature in the schools and universities of independent Africa, the document produced by Ngugi wa Thiong'o and his colleagues at the University of Nairobi in 1968 is incontrovertibly the most important document of all.[27] Apart from its specific views and positions, this document put a definitive stamp on a historic fact that has all but receded into a zone of amnesia in accounts of the intellectual and cultural history of postcolonial Africa – the fact that the constitution of African literary study as a legitimate academic discipline with certified degrees and professional specialization began in Africa, not in Europe or America. The Nairobi document boldly took the nationalist logic of the tentative deliberations at earlier conferences on the topic (Kampala, Dakar and Freetown) to its logical conclusion. However, the vague impulse of these earlier conferences to 'indigenize' some aspects of the literature curriculum became in this document a manifest nationalist programme only by abandoning the 'Africanist' scruples of Eldred Jones and others, who espoused an 'objective' literary scholarship based on truly 'aesthetic,' formal criteria of evaluation. In this way, the Nationalist scholarly and critical rubric instituted its own occlusion, which is repeated by Ngugi who proclaimed the necessity for the scholar to be committed to the truth and then moved on to a list of ideological and political factors which *always* condition the scholar's commitment to truth. In the process, Ngugi makes it clear that *his* ideal scholar would place 'truth' in the service of national liberation and the construction of a social order that favors the mass of urban workers and rural producers at the base of the socioeconomic pyramid in neo-colonial Africa. Such a regime of 'truth' and 'knowledge' involves an underspecification of those scholarly criteria emphasized by Africanists: 'objectivity,' 'rigour,' formalism, 'literary' norms of evaluation, the structure of the 'text' and the economy of its effects on readers. Conversely, there is an overspecification of the extra-literary criteria decried by Africanists: the literary scholar's ideological commitment to the cause of the oppressed and against Africa's continued dependency, tyrannical misrule, and what Ngugi has termed the 'culture of silence.' This dual movement of under-specification of *intrinsic*, formalist criteria and overspecification of *extrinsic*, 'political' criteria affords us a means of overcoming the seemingly unbridgeable breach between the two camps.

Two considerations patently reduce the seeming breach between the narrowly professional scholar-critics of African literature and their ideologically motivated adversaries. First, the dichotomy does not hold true for most scholars in either camp; most non-African Africanists tend to be politically liberal, while their African fellow travellers tend to be politically conservative, although not openly or militantly anti-nationalist. In light of these factors, a rather vague, but sincere, well-meaning liberalism informs most 'Africanist' literary criticism, although sometimes the naivete about the structure and direction of global politics and its impingement on African literature and critical discourse is truly awesome. Second, 'Nationalist' scholars and critics are not always indifferent to questions of form, artistic design, or intrinsic criteria of evaluation: some of Ngugi's critical essays, some of Abiola Irele's articles and monographs, and Ngara's book on the African novel evince sensitive, informed explorations of these 'intrinsic' questions.[28]

The real danger in a dichotomization of the two camps is located elsewhere: in recent times, 'Africanists' have come to hold sway over the discipline in an especially problematic manner, and their narrowly formulated agenda increasingly dominates perceptions of 'what is to be done' at the present time in the field. This agenda consists primarily of winning respectability and legitimacy for the discipline of African literary study *in the developed countries*. Bernth Lindfors, whose influence has been felt during his long and able tenure as editor of *Research in African Literature*, perhaps the dominant scholarly journal in the field, has even written a statement entitled 'On Disciplining Students in a Nondiscipline,' essentially a manifesto for such an agenda.[29] On account of this agenda and its uncritical acceptance by a large segment of the profession, the extensive, ground-breaking syntheses in contemporary Western literary theory (on knowledge and power relations, on the politics of interpretation, on the always agonistic, always *constructed* nature of representation and signification) has washed over the 'Africanist' critical establishment without leaving significant traces. In the deafening silence on the connection between demands for critical fidelity or rigorous analytical techniques and the positions of entrenched power and privilege (or lack of them) from which any scholar or critic evaluates or theorizes, only feminist critics, and to a lesser extent, Marxists, have systematically drawn attention to the political grounding or *situatedness* of critical discourse.

The 'Africanist' fetishization of professionalism and the 'Nationalist' occlusion of technical, formalistic concerns, in the abstract, idealist constructions of these schools, could be corrected by drawing upon the work of literary scholars in other societies, other periods, other discursive spaces, scholars who have brilliantly synthesized attributes separated in the false binarism that keeps the best features of 'Africanist' and 'Nationalist' schools apart – scholars like Samuel Johnson, Matthew Arnold, Eric Auerbach, Ernst Fischer, Walter Benjamin, Raymond Williams. The very fact that we *need* to insist on this reminder, this re-memory of a powerful motive force in all intellectual history, including the history of Western literary criticism, is itself the product of a willed *lacuna* with regard to the understanding of our present historic context: arrested de-colonization world-wide and the fluid, uncertain conjuncture initiated by Gorbachev's call for 'de-ideologization' of international relations between states. This 'historic space' defines and consecrates the shift away from the African continent, away from African universities where the center of gravity of serious, engaged study and teaching of African literature was initially located. However in apprehending this phenomenon, we enter into a seemingly endless chain of determinations and effects, for this shift itself results from a combination of other factors impacting on all African countries today: heavy external debt burdens, economic stagnation conjoined with rampant inflation (what some radical economists have given the arresting neologism of 'stagflation'), drastic scarcity of books and journals, the lack of spending power to purchase them even when they are available, the material impoverishment of the educational infrastructure, the massive demoralization of teachers, etc., etc. From this perspective we can see that African literary study today is truly 'over-determined' in the full Althusserian sense of the term.

This over-determination defines the relevance of the first epigraph to this essay, the Afro-Cuban myth that gives powerful figural articulation to the aporia under which we all, singly or collectively, work today. Whatever genuine 'truths' our studies and readings generate, there is always the uncomfortable, compromising 'falsehood' of its massive displacement from its true center of gravity on the African continent, there is always the harrowing 'falsehood' involved in the production and reproduction of Africa's marginalization from the centers of economic and discursive power in an inequitable capitalist world system.

Notes

1 Frank Kermode, *Forms of Attention* (Chicago and London: The University of Chicago Press, 1985).
2 I am bracketing the pluralization of African literature here because, while most scholars now accept the diverse currents and traditions of written and oral literatures in Africa, I shall be using the collective unpluralized designation in this essay. This is based on my belief that my observations in the essay are pertinent to critical discourse on any of the currents and traditions of African Literature.
3 Diane Macdowell, *Theories of Discourse* (New York: Basil Blackwell, 1986). I am using the term 'post-modern critical theory' loosely here to both indicate the broad range of contemporary theoretical schools and approaches which have problematized the conventional certitudes about the nature, content and methodologies of literary study and artistic representation, and the more focussed theoretical work on the nature of critical discourse and power – work which has drawn substantially on the publications of Althusser, Foucault, and others. See Michel Foucault, *Madness and Civilization: A History of Insanity in the Age of Reason* (New York: Vintage Books, 1973).
4 See Henry Louis Gates, 'Authority (White), Power, and the (Black) Critic; or it's all Greek to me,' and Elaine Showalter, 'A Criticism of Our Own: Autonomy and Assimilation on Afro-American and Feminist Literary Theory,' both in Ralph Cohen, ed., *The Future of Literary Theory* (New York and London: Routledge, 1989).
5 Gerald Moore, ed., *African Literature and the University* (Ibaden: Ibaden University Press, 1965); Christopher Heywood, ed., *Perspectives on African Literature: Selections from the Proceedings* (New York: African Publishing Corp., 1971); Thomas Hale and Richard Priebe, eds., *The Teaching of African Literature: Selected Working Papers from the African Literature Association* (Austin, Texas: University of Texas Press, 1977); Bernth Lindfors, ed., *Research Priorities in African Literatures* (New York: Hans Zell Publishers, 1984); *Littératures africaines et enseignement: actes du colloque de Bordeaux* (Talence: Presses Universitaires de Bordeaux, 1985); Stephen Arnold, ed., *African Literature Studies: The Present State/L'Etat Présent* (Washington, D.C.: Three Continents Press, 1985).
6 The 'classic' Marxist text on *hypostasis* is of course Marx's 'The German Ideology,' where, using the image of inversion ('camera obscura'), Marx analyzes hypostasis as a form of ideological self-mystification and as a false consciousness of the 'real' conditions of social relations of production. I have retained this conception here but infused some aspects of the Althusserian notion of ideology as a structured, produced, and necessary 'imaginary' of the real.

7 Wole Soyinka, 'And After the Narcissist?' *African Forum* 1.4 (1966), p. 56.

8 Wole Soyinka, 'The Writer in a Modern African State,' in *Art, Dialogue, and Outrage: Essays on Literature and Culture* (Ibadan: New Horn Press, 1988), p. 17.

9 Chinua Achebe, 'The Novelist as Teacher,' in *Morning Yet on Creation Day* (Garden City, N.Y.: Anchor Press, 1975), p. 42.

10 Chinweizu, 'The Responsibilities of Scholars of African Literature,' in Lindfors, *Research Priorities*, pp. 16–17.

11 Ernest Emenyonu, 'African Literature: What does it Take to be its Critic?' *African Literature Today* 5 (1971), pp. 1–11, and Bernth Lindfors, 'The Blind Men and the Elephant,' *African Literature Today* 7 (1975), pp. 53–64.

12 Lindfors, 'Blind Men,' pp. 53–4.

13 John Reed and Clive Wake, eds., *Prose and Poetry: Leopold Sedar Senghor* (London: Heinemann, 1976).

14 Stephen Arnold, 'African Literary Studies: The Emergence of a New Discipline,' in Arnold, *African Literature*, p. 60.

15 It is necessary to emphasize that by these terms I intend a typology which has a *polemical*, rather than a theoretically rigorous or 'scientific' status of validity. Thus the 'Africanist' rubric implies professional specialism rendered as a sort of Weberian ideal type, and the 'Nationalist' rubric connotes a heuristic-polemical rendering of critical positions which span a spectrum involving, among others, cultural-nationalist, Marxist or 'Fanonist,' feminist and even 'nativist' views and discourses on African literature. I hope the elaboration of this particular deployment of 'Nationalism' in the essay makes it clear that the conflation of so many diverse views and positions is sufficiently self-aware and non-essentialist. For recent important discussions of African and Third-World literatures and nationalism as a political, ideological, and discursive formation, see Frederic Jameson, 'Third-World Literature in the Era of Multinational Capital,' *Social Text* 15 (1986), pp. 65–88, and Aijaz Ahmad, 'Jamesons's Rhetoric of Otherness and the "National" Allegory,' *Social Text* 17 (1987), pp. 3–12.

16 Albert Gérard, 'The Study of African Literature: Birth and Early Growth of a New Branch of Learning,' *Canadian Review of Comparative Literature*, (Winter 1980), pp. 67–98, and 'Is Anything Wrong with African Literary Studies?' in Arnold, *African Literature*, pp. 17–26.

17 Gérard, 'Is Anything Wrong,' pp. 22–3.

18 Gérard, 'The Study of African Literature,' pp. 75–6.

19 Gérard, 'The Study of African Literature'.

20 Johannes Fabian, *Time and the Other: How Anthropology Makes its Object* (New York: Columbia University Press, 1983), p. 175.

21 Anthony Graham-White, *The Drama of Black Africa* (New York: Samuel French, 1974), p. viii.

22 Biodun Jeyifo, 'The Reinvention of Theatrical Traditions: Critical Discourses on Interculturalism in the African Theatre,' in *Proceedings of an International Conference on Interculturalism in World Theatre*, Bad Homburg, West Germany (forthcoming).

23 Frantz Fanon, *The Wretched of the Earth* (New York: Grove Press, 1963), pp. 178–9.

24 James Booth, *Writers and Politics in Nigeria* (New York: Africana Publishers, 1980), and Janheinz Jahn, *A History of Neo-African Literature*, trans. Oliver Coburn and Ursula Lehbruger (London: Faber, 1968), pp. 277–83.

25 Second Congress of Negro Writers and Artists, 'Resolution on Literature,' *Présence Africaine*, Feb–May 24–25 (1959), pp. 423–8.

26 *Ufahamu*, 11.2 (Fall 1981–Winter 1982), pp. 7–18.

27 Ngugi wa Thiong'o, *Homecoming: Essays on African and Caribbean Literature, Culture and Politics* (New York: Heinemann, 1972), pp. 145–50.

28 Abiola Irele, *The African Experience in Literature and Ideology* (London: Heinemann, 1981), and Emmanuel Ngara, *Art and Ideology in the African Novel* (London: Heinemann, 1985).

29 Lindfors in Hale and Priebe, *The Teaching of African Literature*, pp. 41–7.

10

Chandra Talpade Mohanty

Under Western Eyes: Feminist Scholarship and Colonial Discourses*

Any discussion of the intellectual and political construction of 'third world feminisms' must address itself to two simultaneous projects: the internal critique of hegemonic 'Western' feminisms, and the formulation of autonomous, geographically, historically, and culturally grounded feminist concerns and strategies. The first project is one of deconstructing and dismantling; the second, one of building and constructing. While these projects appear to be contradictory, the one working negatively and the other positively, unless these two tasks are addressed simultaneously, 'third world' feminisms run the risk of marginalization or ghettoization from both mainstream (right and left) and Western feminist discourses.

It is to the first project that I address myself. What I wish to analyze is specifically the production of the 'third world woman' as a singular monolithic subject in some recent (Western) feminist texts. The definition of colonization I wish to invoke here is a predominantly *discursive* one, focusing on a certain mode of appropriation and codification of 'scholarship' and 'knowledge' about women in the third world by particular analytic categories employed in specific writings on the subject which take as their referent feminist interests as they have been articulated in the U.S. and Western Europe. If one of the tasks of formulating and understanding the locus of 'third world feminisms' is delineating the way in which it resists and *works against* what I am referring to as 'Western feminist discourse,' an analysis of the discursive construction of 'third world women' in Western feminism is an important first step.

Clearly Western feminist discourse and political practice is neither singular nor homogeneous in its goals, interests, or analyses. However, it is possible to trace a coherence of *effects* resulting from the implicit assumption of 'the West' (in all its complexities and contradictions) as the primary referent in theory and praxis. My reference to 'Western feminism' is by no means intended to imply that it is a monolith. Rather I am attempting to draw attention to the similar effects of various textual strategies used by writers which codify Others

* From Chandra Mohanty *et al.* eds., *Third World Women and the Politics of Feminism* (Indiana University Press, 1991), pp. 51–80. This is an updated and modified version of an essay published in *Boundary 2* 12.3, 13.1 (Spring/Fall 1984), and reprinted in *Feminist Review* 30 (Autumn 1988).

as non-Western and hence themselves as (implicitly) Western. It is in this sense that I use the term *Western feminist*. Similar arguments can be made in terms of middle-class urban African or Asian scholars producing scholarship on or about their rural or working-class sisters which assumes their own middle-class cultures as the norm, and codifies working-class histories and cultures as Other. Thus, while this essay focuses specifically on what I refer to as 'Western feminist' discourse on women in the third world, the critiques I offer also pertain to third world scholars writing about their own cultures, which employ identical analytic strategies.

It ought to be of some political significance, at least, that the term *colonization* has come to denote a variety of phenomena in recent feminist and left writings in general. From its analytic value as a category of exploitative economic exchange in both traditional and contemporary Marxisms[1] to its use by feminist women of color in the U.S. to describe the appropriation of their experiences and struggles by hegemonic white women's movements,[2] colonization has been used to characterize everything from the most evident economic and political hierarchies to the production of a particular cultural discourse about what is called the 'third world.'[3] However sophisticated or problematical its use as an explanatory construct, colonization almost invariably implies a relation of structural domination, and a suppression – often violent – of the heterogeneity of the subject(s) in question.

My concern about such writings derives from my own implication and investment in contemporary debates in feminist theory, and the urgent political necessity (especially in the age of Reagan/Bush) of forming strategic coalitions across class, race, and national boundaries. The analytic principles discussed below serve to distort Western feminist political practices, and limit the possibility of coalitions among (usually white) Western feminists and working-class feminists and feminists of color around the world. These limitations are evident in the construction of the (implicitly consensual) priority of issues around which apparently *all* women are expected to organize. The necessary and integral connection between feminist scholarship and feminist political practice and organizing determines the significance and status of Western feminist writings on women in the third world, for feminist scholarship, like most other kinds of scholarship, is not the mere production of knowledge about a certain subject. It is a directly political and discursive *practice* in that it is purposeful and ideological. It is best seen as a mode of intervention into particular hegemonic discourses (for example, traditional anthropology, sociology, literary criticism, etc.); it is a political praxis which counters and resists the totalizing imperative of age-old 'legitimate' and 'scientific' bodies of knowledge. Thus, feminist scholarly practices (whether reading, writing, critical, or textual) are inscribed in relations of power – relations which they counter, resist, or even perhaps implicitly support. There can, of course, be no apolitical scholarship.

The relationship between 'Woman' – a cultural and ideological composite Other constructed through diverse representational discourses (scientific, literary, juridical, linguistic, cinematic, etc.) – and 'women' – real, material subjects of their collective histories – is one of the central questions the practice of feminist scholarship seeks to address. This connection between women as historical subjects and the re-presentation of Woman produced by hegemonic discourses is not a relation of direct identity, or a relation of correspondence or simple implication.[4] It is an arbitrary relation set up by particular cultures. I would like to suggest that the feminist writings I analyze here discursively colonize the material and historical heterogeneities of the lives of women in the third world, thereby producing/re-presenting a composite, singular 'third world woman' – an image which appears arbitrarily constructed, but nevertheless carries with it the authorizing signature of Western humanist discourse.[5]

I argue that assumptions of privilege and ethnocentric universality, on the one hand, and inadequate self-consciousness about the effect of Western scholarship on the 'third world' in the context of a world system dominated by the West, on the other, characterize a sizable extent of Western feminist work on women in the third world. An analysis of 'sexual difference' in the form of a cross-culturally singular, monolithic notion of patriarchy or male dominance leads to the construction of a similarly reductive and homogeneous notion of what I call the 'third world difference' – that stable, ahistorical something that apparently oppresses most if not all the women in these countries. And it is in the production of this 'third world difference' that Western feminisms appropriate and 'colonize' the constitutive complexities which characterize the lives of women in these countries. It is in this process of discursive homogenization and systematization of the oppression of women in the third world that power is exercised in much of recent Western feminist discourse, and this power needs to be defined and named.

In the context of the West's hegemonic position today, of what Anouar Abdel-Malek calls a struggle for 'control over the orientation, regulation and decision of the process of world development on the basis of the advanced sector's monopoly of scientific knowledge and ideal creativity,' Western feminist scholarship on the third world must be seen and examined precisely in terms of its inscription in these particular relations of power and struggle. There is, it should be evident, no universal patriarchal framework which this scholarship attempts to counter and resist – unless one posits an international male conspiracy or a monolithic, ahistorical power structure. There is, however, a particular world balance of power within which any analysis of culture, ideology, and socioeconomic conditions necessarily has to be situated. Abdel-Malek is useful here, again, in reminding us about the inherence of politics in the discourses of 'culture':

> Contemporary imperialism is, in a real sense, a hegemonic imperialism, exercising to a maximum degree a rationalized violence taken to a higher level than ever before – through fire and sword, but also through the attempt to control hearts and minds. For its content is defined by the combined action of the military-industrial complex and the hegemonic cultural centers of the West, all of them founded on the advanced levels of development attained by monopoly and finance capital, and supported by

the benefits of both the scientific and technological revolution and the second industrial revolution itself.[6]

Western feminist scholarship cannot avoid the challenge of situating itself and examining its role in such a global economic and political framework. To do any less would be to ignore the complex interconnections between first and third world economies and the profound effect of this on the lives of women in all countries. I do not question the descriptive and informative value of most Western feminist writings on women in the third world. I also do not question the existence of excellent work which does not fall into the analytic traps with which I am concerned. In fact I deal with an example of such work later on. In the context of an overwhelming silence about the experiences of women in these countries, as well as the need to forge international links between women's political struggles, such work is both pathbreaking and absolutely essential. However, it is both to the *explanatory potential* of particular analytic strategies employed by such writing, and to their *political effect* in the context of the hegemony of Western scholarship that I want to draw attention here. While feminist writing in the U.S. is still marginalized (except from the point of view of women of color addressing privileged white women), Western feminist writing on women in the third world must be considered in the context of the global hegemony of Western scholarship – i.e., the production, publication, distribution, and consumption of information and ideas. Marginal or not, this writing has political effects and implications beyond the immediate feminist or disciplinary audience. One such significant effect of the dominant 'representations' of Western feminism is its conflation with imperialism in the eyes of particular third world women.[7] Hence the urgent need to examine the *political* implications of our *analytic* strategies and principles.

My critique is directed at three basic analytic principles which are present in (Western) feminist discourse on women in the third world. Since I focus primarily on the Zed Press Women in the Third World series, my comments on Western feminist discourse are circumscribed by my analysis of the texts in this series.[8] This is a way of focusing my critique. However, even though I am dealing with feminists who identify themselves as culturally or geographically from the 'West,' as mentioned earlier, what I say about these presuppositions or implicit principles holds for anyone who uses these methods, whether third world women in the West, or third world women in the third world writing on these issues and publishing in the West. Thus, I am not making a culturalist argument about ethnocentrism; rather, I am trying to uncover how ethnocentric universalism is produced in certain analyses. As a matter of fact, my argument holds for any discourse that sets up its own authorial subjects as the implicit referent, i.e., the yardstick by which to encode and represent cultural Others. It is in this move that power is exercised in discourse.

The first analytic presupposition I focus on is involved in the strategic location of the category 'women' vis-à-vis the context of analysis. The assumption of women as an already constituted, coherent group with identical interests and desires, regardless of class, ethnic or racial location, or contradictions, implies a notion of gender or sexual difference or even patriarchy which can be applied universally and cross-culturally. (The context of analysis can be anything from kinship structures and the organization of labor to media representations.) The second analytical presupposition is evident on the methodological level, in the uncritical way 'proof' of universality and cross-cultural validity are provided. The third is a more specifically political presupposition underlying the methodologies and the analytic strategies, i.e., the model of power and struggle they imply and suggest. I argue that as a result of the two modes – or, rather, frames – of analysis described above, a homogeneous notion of the oppression of women as a group is assumed, which, in turn, produces the image of an 'average third world woman.' This average third world woman leads an essentially truncated life based on her feminine gender (read: sexually constrained) and her being 'third world' (read: ignorant, poor, uneducated, tradition-bound, domestic, family-oriented, victimized, etc.). This, I suggest, is in contrast to the (implicit) self-representation of Western women as educated, as modern, as having control over their own bodies and sexualities, and the freedom to make their own decisions.

The distinction between Western feminist re-presentation of women in the third world and Western feminist self-presentation is a distinction of the same order as that made by some Marxists between the 'maintenance' function of the housewife and the real 'productive' role of wage labor, or the characterization by developmentalists of the third world as being engaged in the lesser production of 'raw materials' in contrast to the 'real' productive activity of the first world. These distinctions are made on the basis of the privileging of a particular group as the norm or referent. Men involved in wage labor, first world producers, and, I suggest, Western feminists who sometimes cast third world women in terms of 'ourselves undressed' (Michelle Rosaldo's term),[9] all construct themselves as the normative referent in such a binary analytic.

'Women' as category of analysis, or: we are all sisters in struggle

By women as a category of analysis, I am referring to the crucial assumption that all of us of the same gender, across classes and cultures, are somehow socially constituted as a homogeneous group identified prior to the process of analysis. This is an assumption which characterizes much feminist discourse. The homogeneity of women as a group is produced not on the basis of biological essentials but rather on the basis of secondary sociological and anthropological universals. Thus, for instance, in any given piece of feminist analysis, women are characterized as a singular group on the basis of a shared oppression. What binds women together is a sociological notion of the 'sameness' of their oppression. It is at this point that an elision takes place between 'women' as a discursively constructed group and 'women' as material subjects of their own history.[10] Thus, the discursively consensual homogeneity of 'women' as a group is mistaken for the historically specific material reality of groups of women. This results in an assumption of women as an always already constituted group, one which has been labeled 'powerless,' 'exploited,' 'sexually harassed,' etc., by feminist scientific, economic, legal, and sociological discourses. (Notice that this is quite similar to sexist discourse labeling women weak, emotional, having math anxiety, etc.) This focus is not on uncovering the material and ideological specificities that constitute a particular group of women as 'powerless' in a particular context. It is, rather, on finding a variety of cases of 'powerless' groups of women to prove the general point that women as a group are powerless.

In this section I focus on five specific ways in which 'women' as a category of analysis is used in Western feminist discourse on women in the third world. Each of these examples illustrates the construction of 'third world women' as a homogeneous 'powerless' group often located as implicit *victims* of particular socioeconomic systems. I have chosen to deal with a variety of writers – from Fran Hosken, who writes primarily about female genital mutilation, to writers from the Women in International Development school, who write about the effect of development policies on third world women for both Western and third world audiences. The similarity of assumptions about 'third world women' in all these texts forms the basis of my discussion. This is not to equate all the texts that I analyze, nor is it to equalize their strengths and weaknesses. The authors I deal with write with varying degrees of care and complexity; however, the *effect* of their representation of third world women is a coherent one. In these texts women are defined as victims of male violence (Fran Hosken); victims of the colonial process (Maria Cutrufelli); victims of the Arab familial system (Juliette Minces); victims of the economic development process (Beverley Lindsay and the [liberal] WID School); and finally, victims of *the* Islamic code (Patricia Jeffery). This mode of defining women primarily in terms of their *object status* (the way in which they are affected or not affected by certain institutions and systems) is what characterizes this particular form of the use of 'women' as a category of analysis. In the context of Western women writing/studying women in the third world, such objectification (however benevolently motivated) needs to be both named and challenged. As Valerie Amos and Pratibha Parmar argue quite eloquently, 'Feminist theories which examine our cultural practices as "feudal residues" or label us "traditional", also portray us as politically immature women who need to be versed and schooled in the ethos of Western feminism. They need to be continually challenged ....'[11]

Women as victims of male violence

Fran Hosken, in writing about the relationship between human rights and female genital mutilation in Africa and the Middle East, bases her whole discussion/condemnation of genital mutilation on one privileged premise: that the goal of this practice is 'to mutilate the sexual pleasure and satisfaction of woman.'[12] This, in turn, leads her to claim that woman's sexuality is controlled, as is her reproductive potential. According to Hosken, 'male sexual politics' in Africa and around the world 'share the same political goal: to assure female dependence and subservience by any and all means.' Physical violence against women (rape, sexual assault, excision, infibulation, etc.) is thus carried out 'with an astonishing consensus among men in the world.'[13] Here, women are defined consistently as the *victims* of male control – the 'sexually oppressed.'[14] Although it is true that the potential of male violence against women circumscribes and elucidates their social position to a certain extent, defining women as archetypal victims freezes them into 'objects-who-defend-themselves,' men into 'subjects-who-perpetrate-violence,' and (every) society into powerless (read: women) and powerful (read: men) groups of people. Male violence must be theorized and interpreted *within* specific societies, in order both to understand it better and to effectively organize to change it.[15] Sisterhood cannot be assumed on the basis of gender; it must be forged in concrete historical and political practice and analysis.

Women as universal dependents

Beverly Lindsay's conclusion to the book *Comparative Perspectives of Third World Women: The Impact of Race, Sex and Class* states: 'dependency relationships, based upon race, sex and class, are being perpetuated through social, educational, and economic institutions. These are the linkages among Third World Women.' Here, as in other places, Lindsay implies that third world women constitute an identifiable group purely on the basis of shared dependencies. If shared dependencies were all that was needed to bind us together as a group, third world women would always be seen as an apolitical group with no subject status. Instead, if anything, it is the *common context* of political struggle against class, race, gender, and imperialist hierarchies that may constitute third world women as a strategic group at this historical juncture. Lindsay also states that linguistic and cultural differences exist between Vietnamese and black American women, but 'both groups are victims of race, sex, and class.' Again black and Vietnamese women are characterized by their victim status.[16]

Similarly, examine statements such as 'My analysis will start by stating that all African women are politically and economically dependent,' ... 'Nevertheless, either overtly or covertly, prostitution is still the main if not the only source of work for African women.'[17] *All* African women are dependent. Prostitution is the only work option for African women as a *group*. Both statements are illustrative of generalizations sprinkled liberally through a recent Zed Press publication, *Women of Africa: Roots of Oppression*, by Maria Rosa Cutrufelli, who is described on the cover as an Italian writer, sociologist, Marxist, and feminist. In the 1980s, is it possible to imagine writing a book entitled *Women of Europe: Roots of Oppression*? I am not objecting to the use of universal groupings for descriptive purposes. Women from the continent of Africa can be descriptively characterized as 'women of Africa.' It is when 'women of Africa' becomes a homogeneous sociological grouping characterized by common dependencies or powerlessness (or even strengths) that problems arise – we say too little and too much at the same time.

This is because descriptive gender differences are transformed into the division between men and women. Women are constituted as a group via dependency relationships vis-à-vis men, who are implicitly held responsible for these relationships. When 'women of Africa' as a group (versus 'men of Africa' as a group?) are seen as a group precisely because they are generally dependent and oppressed, the analysis of specific historical differences becomes impossible, because reality is always apparently structured by division – two mutually exclusive and jointly exhaustive groups, the victims and the oppressors. Here the sociological is substituted for the biological, in order, however, to create the same – a unity of women. Thus, it is not the descriptive potential of gender difference but the privileged positioning and explanatory potential of gender difference as the *origin* of oppression that I question. In using 'women of Africa' (as an already constituted group of oppressed peoples) as a category of analysis, Cutrufelli denies any historical specificity to the location of women as subordinate, powerful, marginal, central, or otherwise, vis-à-vis particular social and power networks. Women are taken as a unified 'powerless' group prior to the analysis in question Thus, it is then merely a matter of specifying the context *after the fact*. 'Women' are now placed in the context of the family, or in the workplace, or within religious networks, almost as if these systems existed outside the relations of women with other women, and women with men.

The problem with this analytic strategy, let me repeat, is that it assumes men and women are already constituted as sexual-political subjects prior to their entry into the arena of social relations. Only if we subscribe to this assumption is it possible to undertake analysis which looks at the 'effects' of kinship structures, colonialism, organization of labor, etc., on women, who are defined in advance as a group. The crucial point that is forgotten is that women are produced through these very relations as well as being implicated in forming these relations. As Michelle Rosaldo argues, 'woman's place in human social life is not in any direct sense a product of the things she does (or even less, a function of what, biologically, she is) but the meaning her activities acquire through concrete social interactions.'[18] That women mother in a variety of societies is not as significant as the value attached to mothering in these societies. The distinction between the act of mothering and the status attached to it is a very important one – one that needs to be stated and analyzed contextually.

Married women as victims of the colonial process

In Lévi-Strauss's theory of kinship structure as a system of the exchange of women, what is significant is that exchange itself is not constitutive of the subordination of women; women are not subordinate because of the *fact* of exchange, but because of the *modes* of exchange instituted, and the values attached to these modes. However, in discussing the marriage ritual of the Bemba, a Zambian matrilocal, matrilineal people, Cutrufelli in *Women of Africa* focuses on the fact of the marital exchange of women before and after

Western colonization, rather than the value attached to this exchange in this particular context. This leads to her definition of Bemba women as a coherent group affected in a particular way by colonization. Here again, Bemba women are constituted rather unilaterally as victims of the effects of Western colonization.

Cutrufelli cites the marriage ritual of the Bemba as a multistage event 'whereby a young man becomes incorporated into his wife's family group as he takes up residence with them and gives his services in return for food and maintenance.'[19] This ritual extends over many years, and the sexual relationship varies according to the degree of the girl's physical maturity. It is only after she undergoes an initiation ceremony at puberty that intercourse is sanctioned, and the man acquires legal rights over her. This initiation ceremony is the more important act of the consecration of women's reproductive power, so that the abduction of an uninitiated girl is of no consequence, while heavy penalty is levied for the seduction of an initiated girl. Cutrufelli asserts that the effect of European colonization has changed the whole marriage system. Now the young man is entitled to take his wife away from her people in return for money. The implication is that Bemba women have now lost the protection of tribal laws. However, while it is possible to see how the structure of the traditional marriage contract (versus the postcolonial marriage contract) offered women a certain amount of control over their marital relations, only an analysis of the political significance of the actual practice which privileges an initiated girl over an uninitiated one, indicating a shift in female power relations as a result of this ceremony, can provide an accurate account of whether Bemba women were indeed protected by tribal laws *at all times*.

However, it is not possible to talk about Bemba women as a homogeneous group within the traditional marriage structure. Bemba women *before* the initiation are constituted within a different set of social relations compared to Bemba women *after* the initiation. To treat them as a unified group characterized by the fact of their 'exchange' between male kin is to deny the sociohistorical and cultural specificities of their existence, and the differential *value* attached to their exchange before and after their initiation. It is to treat the initiation ceremony as a ritual with no political implications or effects. It is also to assume that in merely describing the *structure* of the marriage contract, the situation of women is exposed. Women as a group are positioned within a given structure, but there is no attempt made to trace the effect of the marriage practice in constituting women within an obviously changing network of power relations. Thus, women are assumed to be sexual-political subjects prior to entry into kinship structures.

Women and familial systems

Elizabeth Cowie, in another context, points out the implications of this sort of analysis when she emphasizes the specifically political nature of kinship structures which must be analyzed as ideological practices which designate men and women as father, husband, wife, mother, sister, etc. Thus, Cowie suggests, women as women are not *located* within the family. Rather, it is *in* the family, as an effect of kinship structures, that women as women are *constructed*, defined within and by the group.[20] Thus, for instance, when Juliette Minces cites *the* patriarchal family as the basis for 'an almost identical vision of women' that Arab and Muslim societies have, she falls into this very trap.[21] Not only is it problematical to speak of a vision of women shared by Arab and Muslim societies (i.e., over twenty different countries) without addressing the particular historical, material, and ideological power structures that construct such images, but to speak of the patriarchal family or the tribal kinship structure as the origin of the socioeconomic status of women is to again assume that women are sexual-political subjects prior to their entry into the family. So while on the one hand women attain value or status within the family, the assumption of a singular patriarchal kinship system (common to all Arab and Muslim societies) is what apparently structures women as an oppressed group in these societies! This singular, coherent kinship system presumably influences another separate and given entity, 'women.' Thus, all women, regardless of class and cultural differences, are affected by this system. Not only are *all* Arab and Muslim women seen to constitute a homogeneous oppressed group, but there is no discussion of the specific *practices* within the family which constitute women as mothers, wives, sisters, etc. Arabs and Muslims, it appears, don't change at all. Their patriarchal family is carried over from the times of the prophet Mohammed. They exist, as it were, outside history.

Women and religious ideologies

A further example of the use of 'women' as a category of analysis is found in cross-cultural analyses which subscribe to a certain economic reductionism in describing the relationship between the economy and factors such as politics and ideology. Here, in reducing the level of comparison to the economic relations between 'developed and developing' countries, any specificity to the question of women is denied. Mina Modares, in a careful analysis of women and Shi'ism in Iran, focuses on this very problem when she criticizes feminist writings which treat Islam as an ideology separate from and outside social relations and practices, rather than a discourse which includes rules for economic, social, and power relations within society.[22] Patricia Jeffery's otherwise informative work on Pirzada women in purdah considers Islamic ideology a partial explanation for the status of women in that it provides a justification for the purdah.[23] Here, Islamic ideology is reduced to a set of ideas whose internalization by Pirzada women contributes to the stability of the system. However, the primary explanation for purdah is located in the control that Pirzada men have over economic resources, and the personal security purdah gives to Pirzada women.

By taking a specific version of Islam as *the* Islam, Jeffery attributes a singularity and coherence to it. Modares notes, ' "Islamic Theology" then becomes imposed on a separate and given entity called "women." A further unification is reached: Women (meaning *all women*), regardless of their differing positions within societies, come to be affected or not affected by Islam. These conceptions provide the right ingredients for an unproblematic possibility of a cross-cultural study of women.'[24] Marnia Lazreg makes a similar argument when she addresses the reductionism inherent in scholarship on women in the Middle East and North Africa:

> A ritual is established whereby the writer appeals to religion as *the* cause of gender inequality just as it is made the source of underdevelopment in much of moderniza-tion theory. In an uncanny way, feminist discourse on women from the Middle East and North Africa mirrors that of theologians' own interpretation of women in Islam. ...
>   The overall effect of this paradigm is to deprive women of self-presence, of being. Because women are subsumed under religion presented in fundamental terms, they are inevitably seen as evolving in nonhistorical time. They virtually have no history. Any analysis of change is therefore foreclosed.[25]

While Jeffery's analysis does not quite succumb to this kind of unitary notion of religion (Islam), it does collapse all ideological specificities into economic relations, and universalizes on the basis of this comparison.

Women and the development process

The best examples of universalization on the basis of economic reductionism can be found in the liberal 'Women in Development' literature. Proponents of this school seek to examine the effect of development on third world women, sometimes from self-designated feminist perspectives. At the very least, there is an evident interest in and commitment to improving the lives of women in 'developing' countries. Scholars such as Irene Tinker and Michelle Bo Bram-sen, Ester Boserup, and Perdita Huston[26] have all written about the effect of development policies on women in the third world.[27] All three women assume 'development' is synonymous with 'economic development' or 'economic progress.' As in the case of Minces's patriarchal family, Hosken's male sexual control, and Cutrufelli's Western colonization, development here becomes the all-time equalizer. Women are affected positively or negatively by economic development policies, and this is the basis for cross-cultural comparison.

For instance, Perdita Huston states that the purpose of her study is to describe the effect of the development process on the 'family unit and its individual members' in Egypt, Kenya, Sudan, Tunisia, Sri Lanka, and Mexico. She states that the 'problems' and 'needs' expressed by rural and urban women in these countries all center around education and training, work and wages, access to health and other services, political participation, and legal rights. Huston relates all these 'needs' to the lack of sensitive development policies which exclude women as a group or category. For her, the solution is simple: implement improved development policies which emphasize training for women fieldworkers, use women trainees, and women rural development officers, encourage women's cooperatives, etc. Here again, women are as-sumed to be a coherent group or category prior to their entry into 'the development process.' Huston assumes that all third world women have similar problems and needs. Thus, they must have similar interests and goals. However, the interests of urban, middle-class, educated Egyptian housewives, to take only one instance, could surely not be seen as being the same as those of their uneducated, poor maids. Development policies do not affect both groups of women in the same way. Practices which characterize women's status and roles vary according to class. Women are constituted as women through the complex interaction between class, culture, religion, and other ideological institutions and frameworks. They are not 'women' – a coherent group – solely on the basis of a particular economic system or policy. Such reductive cross-cultural comparisons result in the colonization of the specifics of daily existence and the complexities of political interests which women of different social classes and cultures represent and mobilize.

Thus, it is revealing that for Perdita Huston, women in the third world countries she writes about have 'needs' and 'problems,' but few if any have 'choices' or the freedom to act. This is an interesting representation of women in the third world, one which is significant in suggesting a latent self-presentation of Western women which bears looking at. She writes, 'What surprised and moved me most as I listened to women in such very different cultural settings was the striking commonality – whether they were educated or illiterate, urban or rural – of their most basic values: the importance they assign to family, dignity, and service to others.'[28] Would Huston consider such values unusual for women in the West?

What is problematical about this kind of use of 'women' as a group, as a stable category of analysis, is that it assumes an ahistorical, universal unity between women based on a generalized notion of their subordination. Instead of analytically *demonstrating* the production of women as socioeconomic political groups within particular local contexts, this analytical move limits the definition of the female subject to gender identity, completely bypassing social class and ethnic identities. What characterizes women as a group is their gender (sociologically, not necessarily biologically, defined) over and above everything else, indicating a monolithic notion of sexual difference. Because women are thus constituted as a coherent group, sexual difference becomes coterminous with female subordination, and power is automatically defined in binary terms: people who have it (read: men), and people who do not (read: women). Men exploit, women are exploited. Such simplistic formulations are historically reductive; they are also ineffectual in designing strategies to combat oppressions. All they do is reinforce binary divisions between men and women.

What would an analysis which did not do this look like? Maria Mies's work illustrates the strength of Western feminist work on women in the third world which does not fall into the traps discussed above. Mies's study of the lace makers of Narsapur, India, attempts to carefully analyze a substantial household industry in which 'housewives' produce lace doilies for consumption in the world market.[29] Through a detailed analysis of the structure of the lace industry, production and reproduction relations, the sexual division of labor, profits and exploitation, and the overall consequences of defining women as 'non-working housewives' and their work as 'leisure-time activity,' Mies demonstrates the levels of exploitation in this industry and the impact of this production system on the work and living conditions of the women involved in it. In addition, she is able to analyze the 'ideology of the housewife,' the notion of a woman sitting in the house, as providing the necessary subjective and sociocultural element for the creation and maintenance of a production system that contributes to the increasing pauperization of women, and keeps them totally atomized and disorganized as workers. Mies's analysis shows the effect of a certain historically and culturally specific mode of patriarchal organization, an organization constructed on the basis of the definition of the lace makers as 'non-working housewives' at familial, local, regional, statewide, and international levels. The intricacies and the effects of particular power networks not only are emphasized, but they form the basis of Mies's analysis of how this particular group of women is situated at the center of a hegemonic, exploitative world market.

This is a good example of what careful, politically focused, local analyses can accomplish. It illustrates how the category of women is constructed in a variety of political contexts that often exist simultaneously and overlaid on top of one another. There is no easy generalization in the direction of 'women' in India, or 'women in the third world'; nor is there a reduction of the political construction of the exploitation of the lace makers to cultural explanations about the passivity or obedience that might characterize these women and their situation. Finally, this mode of local, political analysis which generates theoretical categories from within the situation and context being analyzed, also suggests corresponding effective strategies for organizing against the exploitation faced by the lace makers. Narsapur women are not mere victims of the production process, because they resist, challenge, and subvert the process at various junctures. Here is one instance of how Mies delineates the connections between the housewife ideology, the self-consciousness of the lace makers, and their interrelationships as contributing to the latent resistances she perceives among the women:

> The persistence of the housewife ideology, the self-perception of the lace makers as petty commodity producers rather than as workers, is not only upheld by the structure of the industry as such but also by the deliberate propagation and reinforcement of reactionary patriarchal norms and institutions. Thus, most of the lace makers voiced the same opinion about the rules of *purdah* and seclusion in their communities which were also propagated by the lace exporters. In particular, the *Kapu* women said that they had never gone out of their houses, that women of their community could not do any other work than housework and lace work etc. but in spite of the fact that most of them still subscribed fully to the patriarchal norms of the *gosha* women, there were also contradictory elements in their consciousness. Thus, although they looked down with contempt upon women who were able to work outside the house – like the untouchable *Mala* and *Madiga* women or women of other lower castes, they could not ignore the fact that these women were earning more money precisely because they were *not* respectable housewives but workers.

At one discussion, they even admitted that it would be better if they could also go out and do coolie work. And when they were asked whether they would be ready to come out of their houses and work in one place in some sort of a factory, they said they would do that. This shows that the *purdah* and housewife ideology, although still fully internalized, already had some cracks, because it has been confronted with several contradictory realities.[30]

It is only by understanding the *contradictions* inherent in women's location within various structures that effective political action and challenges can be devised. Mies's study goes a long way toward offering such analysis. While there are now an increasing number of Western feminist writings in this tradition,[31] there is also, unfortunately, a large block of writing which succumbs to the cultural reductionism discussed earlier.

Methodological universalisms, or: women's oppression is a global phenomenon

Western feminist writings on women in the third world subscribe to a variety of methodologies to demonstrate the universal cross-cultural operation of male dominance and female exploitation. I summarize and critique three such methods below, moving from the simplest to the most complex.

First, proof of universalism is provided through the use of an arithmetic method. The argument goes like this: the greater the number of women who wear the veil, the more universal is the sexual segregation and control of women.[32] Similarly, a large number of different, fragmented examples from a variety of countries also apparently add up to a universal fact. For instance, Muslim women in Saudi Arabia, Iran, Pakistan, India, and Egypt all wear some sort of a veil. Hence, this indicates that the sexual control of women is a universal fact in those countries in which the women are veiled.[33] Fran Hosken writes, 'Rape, forced prostitution, polygamy, genital mutilation, pornography, the beating of girls and women, purdah (segregation of women) are all violations of basic human rights'.[34] By equating purdah with rape, domestic violence, and forced prostitution, Hosken asserts its 'sexual control' function as the primary explanation for purdah, whatever the context. Institutions of purdah are thus denied any cultural and historical specificity, and contradictions and potentially subversive aspects are totally ruled out.

In both these examples, the problem is not in asserting that the practice of wearing a veil is widespread. This assertion can be made on the basis of numbers. It is a descriptive generalization. However, it is the analytic leap from the practice of veiling to an assertion of its general significance in controlling women that must be questioned. While there may be a physical similarity in the veils worn by women in Saudi Arabia and Iran, the specific meaning attached to this practice varies according to the cultural and ideological context. In addition, the symbolic space occupied by the practice of purdah may be similar in certain contexts, but this does not automatically indicate that the practices themselves have identical significance in the social realm. For example, as is well known, Iranian middle-class women veiled themselves during the 1979 revolution to indicate solidarity with their veiled working-class sisters, while in contemporary Iran, mandatory Islamic laws dictate that all Iranian women wear veils. While in both these instances, similar reasons might be offered for the veil (opposition to the Shah and Western cultural colonization in the first case, and the true Islamicization of Iran in the second), the concrete *meanings* attached to Iranian women wearing the veil are clearly different in both historical contexts. In the first case, wearing the veil is both an oppositional and a revolutionary gesture on the part of Iranian middle-class women; in the second case, it is a coercive, institutional mandate.[35] It is on the basis of such context-specific differentiated analysis that effective political strategies can be generated. To assume that the mere practice of veiling women in a number of Muslim countries indicates the universal oppression of women through sexual segregation not only is analytically reductive, but also proves quite useless when it comes to the elaboration of oppositional political strategy.

Second, concepts such as reproduction, the sexual division of labor, the family, marriage, household, patriarchy, etc., are often used without their specification in local cultural and historical contexts. Feminists use these concepts in providing explanations for women's subordination, apparently assuming their universal applicability. For instance, how is it possible to refer to 'the' sexual division of labor when the *content* of this division changes radically from one environment to the next, and from one historical juncture to another? At its most abstract level, it is the fact of the differential assignation of tasks according to sex that is significant; however, this is quite different from the *meaning* or *value* that the content of this sexual division of labor assumes in different contexts. In most cases the assigning of tasks on the basis of sex has an ideological origin. There is no question that a claim such as 'women are concentrated in service-oriented occupations in a large number of countries around the world' is descriptively valid. Descriptively, then, perhaps the existence of a similar sexual division of labor (where women work in service occupations such as nursing, social work, etc., and men in other kinds of occupations) in a variety of different countries can be asserted. However, the concept of the 'sexual division of labor' is more than just a descriptive category. It indicates the differential *value* placed on 'men's work' versus 'women's work.'

Often the mere existence of a sexual division of labor is taken to be proof of the oppression of women in various societies. This results from a confusion between and collapsing together of the descriptive and explanatory potential of the concept of the sexual division of labor. Superficially similar situations may have radically different, historically specific explanations, and cannot be treated as identical. For instance, the rise of female-headed households in middle-class America might be construed as a sign of great independence and feminist progress, whereby women are considered to have *chosen* to be single parents, there are increasing numbers of lesbian mothers, etc. However, the recent increase in female-headed households in Latin America,[36] where women might be seen to have more decision-making power, is concentrated among the poorest strata, where life choices are the most constrained economically. A similar argument can be made for the rise of female-headed families among black and Chicana women in the U.S. The positive correlation between this and the level of poverty among women of color and white working-class women in the U.S. has now even acquired a name: the feminization of poverty. Thus, while it is possible to state that there is a rise in female-headed households in the U.S. and in Latin America, this rise cannot be discussed as a universal indicator of women's independence, nor can it be discussed as a universal indicator of women's impoverishment. The *meaning* of and *explanation* for the rise obviously vary according to the sociohistorical context.

Similarly, the existence of a sexual division of labor in most contexts cannot be sufficient explanation for the universal subjugation of women in the work force. That the sexual division of labor does indicate a devaluation of women's work must be shown through analysis of particular local contexts. In addition, devaluation of *women* must also be shown through careful analysis. In other words, the 'sexual division of labor' and 'women' are not commensurate analytical categories. Concepts such as the sexual division of labor can be useful only if they are generated through local, contextual analyses.[37] If such concepts are assumed to be universally applicable, the resultant homogenization of class, race, religious, and daily material practices of women in the third world can create a false sense of the commonality of oppressions, interests, and struggles between and among women globally. Beyond sisterhood there are still racism, colonialism, and imperialism!

Finally, some writers confuse the use of gender as a superordinate category of organizing analysis with the universalistic proof and instantiation of this category. In other words, empirical studies of gender differences are confused with the analytical organization of cross-cultural work. Beverly Brown's review of the book *Nature, Culture and Gender* best illustrates this point.[38] Brown suggests that nature:culture and female:male are superordinate categories which organize and locate lesser categories (such as wild/domestic and biology/technology) within their logic. These categories are universal in the sense that they organize the universe of a system of representations. This relation is totally independent of the universal substantiation of any particular category. Her critique hinges on the fact that rather than clarify the generalizability of nature:culture:: female:male as subordinate organization categories, *Nature, Culture and Gender* construes the universality of this equation to lie at the level of empirical truth, which can be investigated through fieldwork. Thus, the usefulness of the nature:culture:: female:male paradigm as a universal mode of the organization of representation within any particular sociohistorical system is lost. Here, methodological universalism is assumed on the basis of the reduction of the nature:culture :: female:male analytic categories to a demand for empirical proof of its existence in different cultures. Discourses of representation are confused with material realities, and the distinction made earlier between 'Woman' and 'women' is lost. Feminist work which blurs this distinction (which is, interestingly enough, often present in certain Western feminists' self-representation) eventually ends up constructing monolithic images of 'third world women' by ignoring the complex and mobile relationships between their historical materiality on the level of specific oppressions and political choices, on the one hand, and their general discursive representations, on the other.

To summarize: I have discussed three methodological moves identifiable in feminist (and other academic) cross-cultural work which seeks to uncover a universality in women's subordinate position in society. The next and final section pulls together the previous sections, attempting to outline the political effects of the analytical strategies in the context of Western feminist writing on women in the third world. These arguments are not against generalization as much as they are for careful, historically specific generalizations responsive to complex realities. Nor do these arguments deny the necessity of forming strategic political identities and affinities. Thus, while Indian women of different religions, castes, and classes might forge a political unity on the basis of organizing against police brutality toward women,[39] an *analysis* of police brutality must be contextual. Strategic coalitions which construct oppositional political identities for themselves are based on generalization and provisional unities, but the analysis of these group identities cannot be based on universalistic, ahistorical categories.

The subject(s) of power

This last section returns to an earlier point about the inherently political nature of feminist scholarship, and attempts to clarify my point about the possibility of detecting a colonialist move in the case of a hegemonic first–third world connection in scholarship. The nine texts in the Zed Press Women in the Third World series that I have discussed[40] focused on the following common areas in examining women's 'status' within various societies: religion, family/kinship structures, the legal system, the sexual division of labor, education, and finally, political resistance. A large number of Western feminist writings on women in the third world focus on these themes. Of course the Zed texts have varying emphases. For instance, two of the studies, *Women of Palestine* and *Indian Women in Struggle*, focus explicitly on female militance and political involvement, while *Women in Arab Society* deals with Arab women's legal, religious, and familial status. In addition, each text evidences a variety of methodologies and degrees of care in making generalizations. Interestingly enough, however, almost all the texts assume 'women' as a category of analysis in the manner designated above.

Clearly this is an analytical strategy which is neither limited to these Zed Press publications nor symptomatic of Zed Press publications in general. However, each of the particular texts in question assumes 'women' have a coherent group identity within the different cultures discussed, prior to their entry into social relations. Thus, Omvedt can talk about 'Indian women' while referring to a particular group of women in the State of Maharashtra, Cutrufelli about 'women of Africa,' and Minces about 'Arab women' as if these groups of women have some sort of obvious cultural coherence, distinct from men in these societies. The 'status' or 'position' of women is assumed to be self-evident, because women as an already constituted group are *placed* within religious, economic, familial, and legal structures. However, this focus whereby women are seen as a coherent group across contexts, regardless of class or ethnicity, structures the world in ultimately binary, dichotomous terms, where women are always seen in opposition to men, patriarchy is always necessarily male dominance, and the religious, legal, economic, and familial systems are implicitly assumed to be constructed by men. Thus, both men and women are always apparently constituted whole populations, and relations of dominance and exploitation are also posited in terms of whole peoples – wholes coming into exploitative relations. It is only when men and women are seen as different categories or groups possessing different *already constituted* categories of experience, cognition, and interests as *groups* that such a simplistic dichotomy is possible.

What does this imply about the structure and functioning of power relations? The setting up of the commonality of third world women's struggles across classes and cultures against a general notion of oppression (primarily the group in power – i.e., men) necessitates the assumption of what Michel Foucault calls the 'juridico-discursive' model of power, the principal features of which are 'a negative relation' (limit and lack), an 'insistence on the rule' (which forms a binary system), a 'cycle of prohibition,' the 'logic of censorship,' and a 'uniformity' of the apparatus functioning at different levels.[41] Feminist discourse on the third world which assumes a homogeneous category – or group – called women necessarily operates through the setting up of originary power divisions. Power relations are structured in terms of a unilateral and undifferentiated source of power and a cumulative reaction to power. Opposition is a generalized phenomenon created as a response to power – which, in turn, is possessed by certain groups of people.

The major problem with such a definition of power is that it locks all revolutionary struggles into binary structures – possessing power versus being powerless. Women are powerless, unified groups. If the struggle for a just society is seen in terms of the move from powerless to powerful for women as a *group*, and this is the implication in feminist discourse which structures sexual difference in terms of the division between the sexes, then the new society would be structurally identical to the existing organization of power relations, constituting itself as a simple *inversion* of what exists. If relations of domination and exploitation are defined in terms of binary divisions – groups which dominate and groups which are dominated – surely the implication is that the accession to power of women as a group is sufficient to dismantle the existing organization of relations? But women as a group are not in some sense essentially superior or infallible. The crux of the problem lies in that initial assumption of women as a homogeneous group or category ('the oppressed'), a familiar assumption in Western radical and liberal feminisms.[42]

What happens when this assumption of 'women as an oppressed group' is situated in the context of Western feminist writing about third world women?

It is here that I locate the colonialist move. By contrasting the representation of women in the third world with what I referred to earlier as Western feminisms' self-presentation in the same context, we see how Western feminists alone become the true 'subjects' of this counterhistory. Third world women, on the other hand, never rise above the debilitating generality of their 'object' status.

While radical and liberal feminist assumptions of women as a sex class might elucidate (however inadequately) the autonomy of particular women's struggles in the West, the application of the notion of women as a homogeneous category to women in the third world colonizes and appropriates the pluralities of the simultaneous location of different groups of women in social class and ethnic frameworks; in doing so it ultimately robs them of their historical and political *agency*. Similarly, many Zed Press authors who ground themselves in the basic analytic strategies of traditional Marxism also implicitly create a 'unity' of women by substituting 'women's activity' for 'labor' as the primary theoretical determinant of women's situation. Here again, women are constituted as a coherent group not on the basis of 'natural' qualities or needs but on the basic of the sociological 'unity' of their role in domestic production and wage labor.[43] In other words, Western feminist discourse, by assuming women as a coherent, already constituted group which is placed in kinship, legal, and other structures, defines third world women as subjects *outside* social relations, instead of looking at the way women are constituted *through* these very structures.

Legal, economic, religious, and familial structures are treated as phenomena to be judged by Western standards. It is here that ethnocentric universality comes into play. When these structures are defined as 'underdeveloped' or 'developing' and women are placed within them, an implicit image of the 'average third world woman' is produced. This is the transformation of the (implicitly Western) 'oppressed woman' into the 'oppressed third world woman.' While the category of 'oppressed woman' is generated through an exclusive focus on gender difference, 'the oppressed third world woman' category has an additional attribute – the 'third world difference!' The 'third world difference' includes a paternalistic attitude toward women in the third world.[44] Since discussions of the various themes I identified earlier (kinship, education, religion, etc.) are conducted in the context of the relative 'underdevelopment' of the third world (which is nothing less than unjustifiably confusing development with the separate path taken by the West in its development, as well as ignoring the directionality of the first–third world power relationship), third world women as a group or category are automatically and necessarily defined as religious (read 'not progressive'), family-oriented (read 'traditional'), legal minors (read 'they-are-still-not-conscious-of-their-rights'), illiterate (read 'ignorant'), domestic (read 'backward'), and sometimes revolutionary (read 'their-country-is-in-a-state-of-war; they-must-fight!'). This is how the 'third world difference' is produced.

When the category of 'sexually oppressed women' is located within particular systems in the third world which are defined on a scale which is normed through Eurocentric assumptions, not only are third world women defined in a particular way prior to their entry into social relations, but since no connections are made between first and third world power shifts, the assumption is reinforced that the third world just has not evolved to the extent that the West has. This mode of feminist analysis, by homogenizing and systematizing the experiences of different groups of women in these countries, erases all marginal and resistant modes and experiences.[45] It is significant that none of the texts I reviewed in the Zed Press series focuses on lesbian politics or the politics of ethnic and religious marginal organizations in third world women's groups. Resistance can thus be defined only as cumulatively reactive, not as something inherent in the operation of power. If power, as Michel Foucault has argued recently, can really be understood only in the context of resistance,[46] this misconceptualization is both analytically and strategically problematical. It limits theoretical analysis as well as reinforces Western cultural imperialism. For in the context of a first/third world balance of power, feminist analyses which perpetrate and sustain the hegemony of the idea of the superiority of the West produce a corresponding set of universal images of the 'third world woman,' images such as the veiled woman, the powerful mother, the chaste virgin, the obedient wife, etc. These images exist in universal, ahistorical splendor, setting in motion a colonialist discourse which exercises a very specific power in defining, coding, and maintaining existing first/third world connections.

To conclude, then, let me suggest some disconcerting similarities between the typically authorizing signature of such Western feminist writings on women in the third world, and the authorizing signature of the project of humanism in general – humanism as a Western ideological and political project which involves the necessary recuperation of the 'East' and 'Woman' as Others. Many contemporary thinkers, including Foucault, Derrida, Kristeva, Deleuze and Guattari, and Said,[47] have written at length about the underlying anthropomorphism and ethnocentrism which constitute a hegemonic humanistic problematic that repeatedly confirms and legitimates (Western) Man's centrality. Feminist theorists such as Luce Irigaray, Sarah Kofman, and Hélène Cixous[48] have also written about the recuperation and absence of woman/women within Western humanism. The focus of the work of all these thinkers can be stated simply as an uncovering of the political *interests* that underlie the binary logic of humanistic discourse and ideology whereby, as a valuable recent essay puts it, 'the first (majority) term (Identity, Universality, Culture, Disinterestedness, Truth, Sanity, Justice, etc.), which is, in fact, secondary and derivative (a construction), is privileged over and colonizes the second (minority) term (difference, temporality, anarchy, error, interestedness, insanity, deviance, etc.), which is in fact, primary and originative.'[49] In other words, it is only in so far as 'Woman/Women' and 'the East' are defined as *Others*, or as peripheral, that (Western) Man/Humanism can represent him/itself as the center. It is not the center that determines the periphery, but the periphery that, in its boundedness, determines the center. Just as feminists such as Kristeva and Cixous deconstruct the latent anthropomorphism in Western discourse, I have suggested a parallel strategy in this essay in uncovering a latent ethnocentrism in particular feminist writings on women in the third world.[50]

As discussed earlier, a comparison between Western feminist self-presentation and Western feminist re-presentation of women in the third world yields significant results. Universal images of 'the third world woman' (the veiled woman, chaste virgin, etc.), images constructed from adding the 'third world difference' to 'sexual difference,' are predicated upon (and hence obviously bring into sharper focus) assumptions about Western women as secular, liberated, and having control over their own lives. This is not to suggest that Western women *are* secular, liberated, and in control of their own lives. I am referring to a *discursive* self-presentation, not necessarily to material reality. If this were a material reality, there would be no need for political movements in the West. Similarly, only from the vantage point of the West is it possible to define the 'third world' as underdeveloped and economically dependent. Without the overdetermined discourse that creates the *third* world, there would be no (singular and privileged) first world. Without the 'third world woman,' the particular self-presentation of Western women mentioned above would be problematical. I am suggesting, then, that the one enables and sustains the other. This is not to say that the signature of Western feminist writings on the third world has the same authority as the project of Western humanism. However, in the context of the hegemony of the Western scholarly establishment in the production and dissemination of texts, and in the context of the legitimating imperative of humanistic and scientific discourse, the definition of 'the third world woman' as a monolith might well tie into the larger economic and ideological praxis of 'disinterested' scientific inquiry and pluralism which are the surface manifestations of a latent economic and cultural colonization of the 'non-Western' world. It is time to move beyond the Marx who found it possible to say: They cannot represent themselves; they must be represented.

Notes

1 Cf. particularly contemporary theorists such as Paul A. Baran, *The Political Economy of Growth* (New York: Monthly Review Press, 1962), Samir Amin, *Imperialism and Unequal Development* (New York: Monthly Review Press, 1977), and Andre Gunder-Frank, *Capitalism and Underdevelopment in Latin America* (New York: Monthly Review Press, 1967).

2 Cf. especially Cherríe Moraga and Gloria Anzaldúa, eds., *This Bridge Called My Back: Writings by Radical Women of Color* (New York: Kitchen Table Press, 1983), Barbara Smith, ed., *Home Girls: A Black Feminist Anthology* (New York: Kitchen Table Press, 1983), Gloria Joseph and Jill Lewis, *Common Differences: Conflicts in Black and White Feminist Perspectives* (Boston: Beacon Press, 1981), and Cherríe Moraga, *Loving in the War Years* (Boston: South End Press, 1984).

3 Terms such as *third* and *first world* are very problematical both in suggesting oversimplified similarities between and among countries labeled thus, and in implicitly reinforcing existing economic, cultural, and ideological hierarchies which are

conjured up in using such terminology. I use the term '*third world*' with full awareness of its problems, only because this is the terminology available to us at the moment. The use of quotation marks is meant to suggest a continuous questioning of the designation. Even when I do not use quotation marks, I mean to use the term critically.

4 I am indebted to Teresa de Lauretis for this particular formulation of the project of feminist theorizing. See especially her introduction in de Lauretis, *Alice Doesn't: Feminism, Semiotics, Cinema* (Bloomington: Indiana University Press, 1984); see also Sylvia Wynter, 'The Politics of Domination,' unpublished manuscript.

5 This argument is similar to Homi Bhabha's definition of colonial discourse as strategically creating a space for a subject people through the production of knowledges and the exercise of power. The full quote in Homi Bhabha, 'The Other Question – The Stereotype and Colonial Discourse,' *Screen* 24.6 (1983), p. 23, reads: '[colonial discourse is] an apparatus of power ... an apparatus that turns on the recognition and disavowal of racial/cultural/historical differences. Its predominant strategic function is the creation of a space for a subject people through the production of knowledges in terms of which surveillance is exercised and a complex form of pleasure/unpleasure is incited. It (i.e. colonial discourse) seeks authorization for its strategies by the production of knowledges by coloniser and colonised which are stereotypical but antithetically evaluated.'

6 Anouar Abdel-Malek, *Social Dialectics: Nation and Revolution* (Albany: State University of New York Press, 1981), pp. 145–6.

7 A number of documents and reports on the UN International Conferences on Women, Mexico City, 1975, and Copenhagen, 1980, as well as the 1976 Wellesley Conference on Women and Development, attest to this. Nawal el Saadawi, Fatima Mernissi, and Mallica Vajarathon, in 'A Critical Look at the Wellesley Conference,' *Quest* 4.2 (Winter 1978), pp. 101–7, characterize this conference as 'American-planned and organized,' situating third world participants as passive audiences. They focus especially on the lack of self-consciousness of Western women's implication in the effects of imperialism and racism in their assumption of an 'international sisterhood.' A recent essay by Valerie Amos and Pratibha Parmar, 'Challenging Imperial Feminism,' *Feminist Review* 17 (1984), pp. 3–19, characterizes as 'imperial' Euro-American feminism which seeks to establish itself as the only legitimate feminism.

8 The Zed Press Women in the Third World series is unique in its conception. I choose to focus on it because it is the only contemporary series I have found which assumes that 'women in the third world' are a legitimate and separate subject of study and research. Since 1985, when this essay was first written, numerous new titles have appeared in the Women in the Third World series. Thus, I suspect that Zed has come to occupy a rather privileged position in the dissemination and construction of discourses by and about third world women. A number of the books in this series are excellent, especially those which deal directly with women's resistance struggles. In addition, Zed Press consistently publishes progressive feminist, antiracist, and antiimperialist texts. However, a number of the texts written by feminist sociologists, anthropologists, and journalists are symptomatic of the kind of Western feminist work on women in the third world that concerns me. Thus, an analysis of a few of these particular works in this series can serve as a representative point of entry into the discourse I am attempting to locate and define. My focus on these texts is therefore an attempt at an internal critique: I simply expect and demand

more from this series. Needless to say, progressive publishing houses also carry their own authorizing signatures.

9 M. A. Rosaldo, 'The Use and Abuse of Anthropology: Reflections on Feminism and Cross-Cultural Understanding,' *Signs* 53 (1980), pp. 389–417.

10 Elsewhere I have discussed this particular point in detail in a critique of Robin Morgan's construction of 'women's herstory' in her introduction to Morgan, ed., *Sisterhood Is Global: The International Women's Movement Anthology* (New York: Anchor Press/Doubleday; Harmondsworth: Penguin, 1984). See my 'Feminist Encounters: Locating the Politics of Experience,' *Copyright* 1 (1987), 'Fin de Siecle 2000,' pp. 30–44, especially pp. 35–7.

11 Amos and Parmar, 'Challenging,' p. 7.

12 Fran Hosken, 'Female Genital Mutilation and Human Rights,' *Feminist Issues* 1.3 (1981), p. 11.

13 Hosken, 'Female Genital Mutilation and Human Rights,' p. 14.

14 Another example of this kind of analysis is Mary Daly's *Gyn/Ecology: The Metaethics of Radical Feminism* (Boston: Beacon Press, 1978). Daly's assumption in this text, that women as a group are sexually victimized, leads to her very problematic comparison between the attitudes toward women witches and healers in the West, Chinese footbinding, and the genital mutilation of women in Africa. According to Daly, women in Europe, China, and Africa constitute a homogeneous group as victims of male power. Not only does this label (sexual victims) eradicate the specific historical and material realities and contradictions which lead to and perpetuate practices such as witch hunting and genital mutilation, but it also obliterates the differences, complexities, and heterogeneities of the lives of, for example, women of different classes, religions, and nations in Africa. As Audre Lorde pointed out in 'An Open Letter to Mary Daly,' in Moraga and Anzaldúa, *This Bridge*, pp. 94–7, women in Africa share a long tradition of healers and goddesses that perhaps binds them together more appropriately than their victim status. However, both Daly and Lorde fall prey to universalistic assumptions about 'African women' (both negative and positive). What matters is the complex, historical range of power differences, commonalities, and resistances that exist among women in Africa which construct African women as 'subjects' of their own politics.

15 See Felicity Eldhom, Olivia Harris, and Kate Young, 'Conceptualising Women,' *Critique of Anthropology 'Women's Issue'* 3 (1977), for a good discussion of the necessity to theorize male violence within specific societal frameworks, rather than assume it as a universal fact.

16 Beverley Lindsay, ed., *Comparative Perspectives of Third World Women: The Impact of Race, Sex and Class* (New York: Praeger, 1983), pp. 298, 306.

17 Maria Rosa Cutrufelli, *Women of Africa: Roots of Oppression* (London: Zed Press, 1983), pp. 13, 33.

18 Rosaldo, 'Use and Abuse,' p. 400.

19 Cutrufelli, *Women of Africa*, p. 43.

20 Elizabeth Cowie, 'Woman as Sign,' *m/f* 1 (1978), pp. 49–63.

21 Juliette Minces, *The House of Obedience: Women in Arab Society* (London: Zed Press, 1980), especially p. 23.

22 Mina Modares, 'Women and Shi'ism in Iran,' *m/f* 5 and 6 (1981), pp. 61–82.

23 Patricia Jeffery, *Frogs in a Well: Indian Women in Purdah* (London: Zed Press, 1979).

24 Modares, 'Women and Shi'ism,' p. 63.

25 Marnia Lazreg, 'Feminism and Difference: The Perils of Writing as a Woman on Women in Algeria,' *Feminist Issues* 14.1 (Spring 1988), p. 87.

26 Irene Tinker and Michelle Bo Bramsen, eds., *Women and World Development* (Washington, D.C.: Overseas Development Council, 1972); Ester Boserup, *Women's Role in Economic Development* (New York: St. Martin's Press; London: Allen and Unwin, 1970); Perdita Huston, *Third World Women Speak Out* (New York: Praeger, 1979).

27 These views can also be found in differing degrees in collections such as Wellesley Editorial Committee, ed., *Women and National Development: The Complexities of Change* (Chicago: University of Chicago Press, 1977), and *Signs*, Special Issue, 'Development and the Sexual Division of Labor,' 7.2 (Winter 1981). For an excellent introduction of WID issues, see ISIS, *Women in Development: A Resource Guide for Organization and Action* (Philadelphia: New Society Publishers, 1984). For a politically focused discussion of feminism and development and the stakes for poor third world women, see Gita Sen and Caren Grown, *Development Crises and Alternative Visions: Third World Women's Perspectives* (New York: Monthly Review Press, 1987).

28 Huston, *Speak Out*, p. 115.

29 Maria Mies, *The Lace Makers of Narsapur: Indian Housewives Produce for the World Market* (London: Zed Press, 1982).

30 Mies, *The Lace Makers of Narsapur*, p. 157.

31 See essays by Vanessa Maher, Diane Elson and Ruth Pearson, and Maila Stevens in Kate Young, Carol Walkowitz, and Roslyn McCullagh, eds., *Of Marriage and the Market: Women's Subordination in International Perspective* (London: CSE Books, 1981); and essays by Vivian Mota and Michelle Mattelart in June Nash and Helen I. Safa, eds., *Sex and Class in Latin America: Women's Perspectives on Politics, Economics and the Family in the Third World* (South Hadley, Mass.: Bergin and Garvey, 1980). For examples of excellent, self-conscious work by feminists writing about women in their own historical and geographical locations, see Marnia Lazreg, 'Feminism and Difference,' on Algerian women, Gayatri Chakravorty Spivak's 'A Literary Representation of the Subaltern: A Woman's Text from the Third World,' in her *In Other Worlds: Essays in Cultural Politics* (New York: Methuen, 1987), pp. 241–68, and Lata Mani's essay 'Contentious Traditions: The Debate on SATI in Colonial India,' *Cultural Critique* 7 (Fall 1987), pp. 119–56.

32 Ann Deardon, ed., *Arab Women* (London: Minority Rights Group Report no. 27, 1975), pp. 4–5.

33 Deardon, *Arab Women*, pp. 7, 10.

34 Hosken, 'Female,' p. 15.

35 For detailed discussion, see Azar Tabari, 'The Enigma of the Veiled Iranian Women,' *Feminist Review* 5 (1980), pp. 19–32.

36 Olivia Harris, 'Latin American Women – An Overview,' in Olivia Harris, ed., *Latin American Women* (London: Minority Rights Group Report no. 57, 1983), pp. 4–7. Other MRG Reports include Ann Deardon, *Arab Women* and Rounaq Jahan, ed., *Women in Asia* (London: Minority Rights Group Report no. 45, 1980).

37 See Eldhom, Harris and Young, 'Conceptualising Women.'

38 Marilyn Strathern and Carol McCormack, eds., *Nature, Culture and Gender* (Cambridge: Cambridge University Press, 1980). Beverly Brown, 'Displacing the Difference – Review, *Nature, Culture and Gender*' *m/f* 8 (1983), pp. 79–89.

39 Madhu Kishwar and Ruth Vanita, *In Search of Answers: Indian Women's Voices from Manushi* (London: Zed Press, 1984).

40 List of Zed Press Publications: Patricia Jeffery, *Frogs in a Well: Indian Women in Purdah* (1979); Latin American and Caribbean Women's Collective, *Slaves of Slaves: The Challenge of Latin American Women* (1980); Gail Omvedt, *We Shall Smash This Prison: Indian Women in Struggle* (1980); Juliette Minces, *The House of Obedience: Women in Arab Society* (1980); Bobby Siu, *Women of China: Imperialism and Women's Resistance, 1900–1949* (1981); Ingela Bendt and James Downing, *We Shall Return: Women in Palestine* (1982); Maria Rosa Cutrufelli, *Women of Africa: Roots of Oppression* (1983); Maria Mies, *The Lace Makers of Narsapur: Indian Housewives Produce for the World Market* (1982); Miranda Davis, ed., *Third World/Second Sex: Women's Struggles and National Liberation* (1983).

41 Michel Foucault, *Power/Knowledge* (New York: Pantheon, 1980), pp. 135–45.

42 For succinct discussions of Western radical and liberal feminisms, see Hester Eisenstein, *Contemporary Feminist Thought* (Boston: G. K. Hall & Co., 1983), and Zillah Eisenstein, *The Radical Future of Liberal Feminism* (New York: Longman, 1981).

43 Donna Haraway, 'A Manifesto for Cyborgs: Science, Technology and Socialist Feminism in the 1980s,' *Socialist Review* 80 (March/April 1985), esp. p. 76.

44 Amos and Parmar describe the cultural stereotypes present in Euro-American feminist thought: 'The image is of the passive Asian woman subject to oppressive practices within the Asian family with an emphasis on wanting to "help" Asian women liberate themselves from their role. Or there is the strong, dominant Afro-Caribbean woman, who despite her "strength" is exploited by the "sexism" which is seen as being a strong feature in relationships between Afro-Caribbean men and women' ('Challenging,' p. 9). These images illustrate the extent to which paternalism is an essential element of feminist thinking which incorporates the above stereotypes, a paternalism which can lead to the definition of priorities for women of color by Euro-American feminists.

45 I discuss the question of theorizing experience in my 'Feminist Encounters' and in an essay coauthored with Biddy Martin, 'Feminist Politics: What's Home Got to Do with It?', in Teresa de Lauretis, ed., *Feminist Studies/Critical Studies* (Bloomington: Indiana University Press, 1986), pp. 191–212.

46 This is one of M. Foucault's central points in his reconceptualization of the strategies and workings of power networks in *Power/Knowledge* and in *History of Sexuality: Volume One* (New York: Random House, 1978).

47 See Foucault, *Power/Knowledge* and *History of Sexuality: Volume One*, Jacques Derrida, *Of Grammatology* (Baltimore: Johns Hopkins University Press, 1974), Julia Kristeva, *Desire in Language* (New York: Columbia University Press, 1980), Giles Deleuze and Felix Guattari, *Anti-Oedipus: Capitalism and Schizophrenia* (New York: Viking, 1977), and Edward Said, *Orientalism* (New York: Random House, 1978).

48 Luce Irigaray, 'This Sex Which Is Not One' and 'When the Goods Get Together,' in Elaine Marks and Isabel De Courtivron, eds., *New French Feminisms* (New York: Schocken Books, 1981); Sarah Kofman in Elizabeth Berg, 'The Third Woman,' *Diacritics* (Summer 1982), pp. 11–20, Helene Cixous, 'The Laugh of the Medusa,' in Marks and De Courtivron, *New French Feminisms*.

49 William V. Spanos, 'Boundary 2 and the Polity of Interest: Humanism, the "Center Elsewhere" and Power,' *Boundary 2* 12.3/13.1 (Spring/Fall 1984).

50 For an argument which demands a new conception of humanism in work on third world women, see Marnia Lazreg, 'Feminism and Difference.' While Lazreg's position might appear to be diametrically opposed to mine, I see it as a provocative

and potentially positive extension of some of the implications that follow from my arguments. In criticizing the feminist rejection of humanism in the name of 'essential Man,' Lazreg points to what she calls an 'essentialism of difference' within these very feminist projects. She asks: 'To what extent can Western feminism dispense with an ethics of responsibility when writing about different women? The point is neither to subsume other women under one's own experience nor to uphold a separate truth for them. Rather, it is to allow them to *be* while recognizing that what they are is just as meaningful, valid, and comprehensible as what we are.... Indeed, when feminists essentially deny other women the humanity they claim for themselves, they dispense with any ethical constraint. They engage in the act of splitting the social universe into us and them, subject and objects' (pp. 99–100).

This essay by Lazreg and an essay by S. P. Mohanty entitled 'Us and Them: On the Philosophical Bases of Political Criticism,' *Yale Journal of Criticism* 2 (March 1989), pp. 1–31, suggest positive directions for self-conscious cross-cultural analyses, analyses which move beyond the deconstructive to a fundamentally productive mode in designating overlapping areas for cross-cultural comparison. The latter essay calls not for a 'humanism' but for a reconsideration of the question of the 'human' in a posthumanist context. It argues that (1) there is no necessary 'incompatibility between the deconstruction of Western humanism' and such 'a positive elaboration' of the human, and moreover that (2) such an elaboration is essential if contemporary political–critical discourse is to avoid the incoherences and weaknesses of a relativist position.

This essay would not have been possible without S. P. Mohanty's challenging and careful reading. I would also like to thank Biddy Martin for our numerous discussions about feminist theory and politics. They both helped me think through some of the arguments herein.

11

Gayatri Chakravorty Spivak

*Poststructuralism, Marginality, Postcoloniality and Value**

This essay is not about the difference between Africa and Asia, between the United States and Britain. It is about the difference and the relationship between academic and 'revolutionary' practices in the interest of social change. The radical academic, *when she is in the academy*, might reckon that names like 'Asian' or 'African' (or indeed 'American' or 'British') have histories that are not anchored in identities but rather secure them. We cannot exchange as 'truth', in the currency of the university, what might be immediate needs for identitarian collectivities. This seems particularly necessary in literary criticism today, with its vigorous investments in cultural critique. If academic and 'revolutionary' practices do not bring each other to productive crisis, the power of the script has clearly passed elsewhere. There can be no universalist claims in the human sciences. This is most strikingly obvious in the case of establishing 'marginality' as a subject-position in literary and cultural critique. The reader must accustom herself to starting from a particular situation and then to the ground shifting under her feet.

I am speaking at a conference on Cultural Value at Birkbeck College, the University of London, on 16 July 1988. The speaker is obliged to think of her cultural identity in such a case. From what space is she speaking, in what space is the representative member of the audience placing her? What does the audience expect to hear today, here?

Presumed cultural identity often depends on a name. In Britain in July of 1988 a section of underclass 'Asians' was vigorously demanding to be recognized as different from underclass 'Blacks', basically because they felt that on account of their cultural attributes of mildness, thrift, domesticity and industriousness, they were, unlike the lazy and violent peoples of African origin, responsible and potentially upwardly mobile material.

* From Peter Collier and Helga Geyer-Ryan, eds., *Literary Theory Today* (Cornell University Press, 1990), pp. 219–44.

This essay is based on an address made at a conference on Cultural Value at Birbeck College, the University of London, on 16 July 1988. To situate it in a general argument which distinguishes postcoloniality from migrancy, see the version included as 'Marginality in the Teaching Machine', in Spivak, *Outside in the Teaching Machine* (New York: Routledge, 1993), pp. 53–76.

Distinguishing between Africa and Asia in terms of kinship to Europe is an old story. As a politically correct Asian, I find this story deplorable. Yet it can be said that a well-placed Asian academic can afford to find it deplorable. To a London audience, academics and cultural workers, eager to hear a speech on cultural value, it is important that the speaker's identity that afternoon was 'Asian', with underclass differentiations out of sight. Unless we continue to nurse the platitudinous conviction that the masses are necessarily identical with 'the revolutionary vanguard', or conversely that, stepping into the university, 'The truth has made us free', we must attend to the possibility of such dissension, and their imbrication with the history and burden of names. Identitarianism can be as dangerous as it is powerful, and the radical teacher in the university can hope to work, however indirectly, toward controlling the dangers by making them visible.[1]

In the United States, where the speaker lives and teaches, her cultural identity is not 'Asian', although it would be recognized as a geographically correct description by most people. In the United States, 'Asians' are of Chinese, Japanese and, of late, Vietnamese extraction. The complex and class-differentiated scenario of the absence or presence of their solidarity with African-Americans is yet another story. In the United States, she is 'Indian'. Subterfuges of nomenclature that are by now standard have almost (though not completely) obliterated the fact that that name lost some specificity in the first American genocide.

The feeling of cultural identity almost always presupposes a language. In that sense, I suppose I feel a Bengali. Yet in the London of July 1988, that name was negotiable as well. The places of 'Bengali' concentration are populated by disenfranchized immigrant Bangladeshis. This seems to me to have a real political logic, not unrelated to national languages, which probably escapes most metropolitan British users of the name. Yet, considering the two-hundred-year-old history of the British representation (in both senses) of Bengal and vice versa, my loss of that name in that place is not without a certain appropriate irony.[2]

To whom did they want to listen, then, this representative audience in London? Since, if they had been attending to the coding of proper names, the references were up for grabs.

The name 'Third World' is useful because, for any metropolitan audience, it can cover over much unease. For these listeners, the speaker's identity might well have been 'Third World'. (In the United States this would undoubtedly have been the case. It nicely marks the difference between Britain as the central ex-colonial, and the United States as a central neo-colonial power.)[3] Sociologists have been warning us against using this expression, contaminated at birth by the new economic programmes of neo-colonialism.[4] And, indeed, in the discipline of sociology, in the decade spanning *The New International Division of Labour* and *The End of the Third World*, the genealogy of a culturalist use of that term seems rather shabby.[5] What need does it satisfy? It gives a proper name to a generalized margin.

A word to name the margin. Perhaps that is what the audience wanted to hear: a voice from the margin. If there is a buzzword in cultural critique now, it is 'marginality'. Every academic knows that one cannot do without labels. To this particular label, however, Foucault's caution must be applied, and we must attend to its *Herkunft* or descent. When a cultural identity is thrust upon one because the centre wants an identifiable margin, claims for marginality assure validation from the centre. It should then be pointed out that what is being negotiated here is not even a 'race or a social type' (as in the passage below) but an economic principle of identification through separation.

> The analysis of *Herkunft* often involves a consideration of race or social type. But the traits it attempts to identify are not the exclusive generic characteristics of an individual, a sentiment, or an idea, which permit us to qualify them as 'Greek' or 'English' [or 'Third World']; rather, it seeks the subtle, singular, and subindividual marks that might possibly intersect in them to form a network that is difficult to unravel.[6]

The academy

In order to bypass that comparison, the speaker can now provisionally choose a name that will not keep her in (the representation of) a margin so thick with context. With all the perils attendant upon a declared choice, she 'chooses' the institutional appellation 'teacher'. It is, most often for such speakers and audiences, writers and readers, a university, and I am a university teacher. That context is in its own way no thinner, but at least speaker and audience share it most obviously.

When we begin to teach 'marginality', we start with the source books of the contemporary study of the cultural politics of colonialism and its aftermath: the great texts of the 'Arab World', most often Frantz Fanon, a Christian psycho-analyst from Martinique.[7] (I mention these details in anticipation of the fifth section below.)

It is also from this general context that we find the source book in our discipline: Edward Said's *Orientalism*.[8] (A word on *our* discipline: since the conference was held under the auspices of a Department of English with a small inter-disciplinary component in Culture Studies, I took it to be the collective professional identity of the majority, with all genealogy suspended; and this text is *Literary Theory Today*.)

Said's book was not a study of marginality, not even of marginalization. It was the study of the construction of an object, for investigation and control. The study of colonial discourse, directly released by work such as Said's, has, however, blossomed into a garden where the marginal can speak and be spoken, even spoken for. It is an important (and beleaguered) part of the discipline now.[9]

As this material begins to be absorbed into the discipline, the long-established but supple, heterogeneous and hierarchical power-lines of the institutional 'dissemination of knowledge' continue to determine and over-determine their condition of representability. It is at the moment of infiltration or insertion, sufficiently under threat by the custodians of a fantasmatic high Western culture, that the greatest caution must be exercised.[10] The price of success must not compromise the enterprise irreparably. In that spirit of caution, it might not be inappropriate to notice that, as teachers we are now involved in the construction of a new object of investigation – 'the third world', 'the marginal' – for institutional validation and certification. One has only to analyse carefully the proliferating but exclusivist 'third World-ist' job descriptions to see the packaging at work. It is as if, in a certain way, we are becoming complicitous in the perpetration of a 'new orientalism'. Foucault writes:

> No 'local centers', 'no pattern of transformation' could function if, through a series of successive linkages [*enchâinements successifs*], it were not eventually written into [*s'inscrivait*] an over-all strategy ... The [*disciplinary*] apparatus [*dispositif*], precisely to the extent that it [is] insular and heteromorphous with respect to the other great 'manoeuvres'...[11]

Let us attempt to read the possibility of our unwilling or unwitting perpetration of a 'new orientalism' as the inscription of an 'overall strategy'.

It is not only that lines separate ethnic, gender and class prejudice in the metropolitan countries from *indigenous* co-operation with neo-colonialism outside, in the Third World proper. It is also that arguments from culturalism, multi-culturalism and ethnicity, however insular and heteromorphous they might seem from the great narratives of the techniques of global financial control, can work to obscure such separations in the interests of the production of a neo-colonial discourse. Today the old ways, of imperial adjudication and open systemic intervention cannot sustain unquestioned legitimacy. Neo-colonialism is fabricating its allies by proposing a share of the centre in a seemingly new way (not a rupture but a displacement): disciplinary support for the conviction of authentic marginality by the (aspiring) elite.

If we keep the possibility of such inscriptions in mind, we might read differently the specific examples of the working of 'local forces', close to home. Here are three. The first two are more directly inscribed into the economic text as it rewards the construction of objects of investigation: funded proposals. What sells today? 'A pattern of transformation'. The third works through what one might call the text of metropolitan representation and self-representation. Here are examples:

1   Quotation from a grant proposal written by a brilliant young Marxist academic:

> Taking the 'magical realism' of Garcia Marquez as a paradigmatic case of Third World literary production, I will argue that science fiction ... may be considered, so to speak, the Third World fiction of the industrial nations.

How is the claim to marginality being negotiated here? The radicals of the industrial nations want to *be* the Third World. Why is 'magical realism' paradigmatic of Third World literary production? In a bit, and in the hands of the less gifted teacher, only that literary style will begin to count as ethnically authentic. There is, after all, a reason why Latin America qualifies as the norm of 'the Third World' for the United States, even as India used to be the authentic margin for the British. It is interesting that 'magical realism', a style of Latin American provenance, has been used to great effect by some expatriate or diasporic subcontinentals writing in English.[12] Yet as the Ariel–Caliban debates dramatize, Latin America has *not* participated in decolonization. Certainly this formal conduct of magical realism can be said to allegorize, in the strictest possible sense, a socius and a political configuration where 'decolonization' cannot be narrativized. What are the implications of pedagogic gestures that monumentalize *this* style as the right Third World style? In the greater part of the Third World, the problem is that the declared rupture of 'decolonization' boringly repeats the rhythms of colonization with the consolidation of recognizable styles.

2   A feminist who has done inspiring and meticulous work on the European discursive text of mothering, a friend and ally. (Again, the interest of this essay lies in a general auto-critique of our moment in criticism, not in the exposure of an imagined enemy. That indeed is why the speaker put aside the name 'Asian/Indian/Bengali/Third World' and took the microphone as 'literary/culturalist/academic'.)

My friend was looking for speakers to comment on postmodern styles in the context of the third world. She did not want her funded institute on the *avant-garde* to be 'Eurocentric'. I told her that I could only comment on a handful of writers in my native language. Her question: but do these writers show their awareness of being in a minority, being marginals? No, I said, and asked a counter-question: Isn't it 'Eurocentric' to choose only such writers who write in the consciousness of marginality and christen them 'Third World'? Answer: One must begin somewhere.

'One must begin somewhere' is a different sentiment when expressed by the unorganized oppressed and when expressed by the beneficiary of the consolidated disciplinary structure of a central neo-colonialist power. If we were studying this move in the perspective of nineteenth-century colonial discursive production, what would we say about the margin being constituted to suit the institutional convenience of the colonizer? If the 'somewhere' that one begins from is the most privileged site of a neo-colonial educational system, in an institute for the training of teachers, funded by the state, does that gesture of convenience not become the normative point of departure? Does not participation in such a privileged and authoritative apparatus require the greatest vigilance?

'If a genealogical analysis of a scholar were made ... his *Herkunft* would quickly divulge the official papers of the scribe and the pleading of the lawyer – their father – in their apparently disinterested attention ... ' (*LCP*, p. 147). Should we imagine ourselves free of this analysis? Should we not attempt also to 'write the history of the present?' Why, as we clear ourselves of the alibi of occupying the centre or seeking validation by/as the centre, should we think that we do not resemble 'the confused and anonymous European' of the nineteenth century, 'who no longer knows himself or what name he should adopt', to whom 'the historian offers ... the possibility of alternate identities, more individualized and substantial than his own?' (*LCP*, p. 160).

As a result of a decade of colonial discourse studies percolating into disciplinary pedagogy and its powerful adjuncts, and of the imbrication of techniques of knowledge with strategies of power, who claims marginality in the larger post-colonial field? What might this have to do with the old scenario of empowering a privileged group or a group susceptible to upward mobility as the authentic inhabitants of the margin? Should we not cast a genealogical eye over what we have spawned in literary criticism and the study of culture, since a study of the strategies of the margin must not be stopped?

> One must not suppose that there exists a certain sphere of 'marginality' that would be the legitimate concern of a free and disinterested scientific inquiry were it not the object of mechanisms of exclusion brought to bear by the economic or ideological requirements of power. If 'marginality' is being constituted as an area of investigation, this is only because relations of power have established it as a possible object; and conversely, if power is able to take it as a target, this is because techniques of knowledge [disciplinary regulations] were capable of switching it on [*investir*].[13] Between techniques of knowledge and strategies of power, there is no exteriority, even if they have specific roles *and are linked together on the basis of their difference* ... Not to look for who has the power in the order of marginality ... and who *is* deprived of it ... But to look rather for the pattern of the modifications which the relationships of force imply by the very nature of their process.
>
> (*HS*, p. 98–9, emphasis and contextual modification added.)

3   My third example comes from Benita Parry. Ms Parry is, once again, an ally, and she was kind enough to draw my attention to the fact that in a recent issue of the *Oxford Literary Review* on colonialism, she had charged Homi Bhabha, Abdul JanMohammed and Gayatri Spivak basically with not being able to listen to the voice of the native.[14]

Postcoloniality

It is in my response to her that the name 'postcolonial' comes fully into play, which, incidentally, makes the Latin-American as paradigmatic (stylistic) example tremble.

In a piece on J. M. Coetzee's novel *Foe*, I have approached Benita Parry's question by contrasting Defoe's Robinson Crusoe, the mercantile capitalist who trains Friday, represented as the willing proto-colonial subject, with Coetzee's Susan Barton, the anachronistic eighteenth-century Englishwoman who longs to give the muted racial other a voice.[15] Rather than repeat my argument, I will take the liberty of quoting myself, with contextual modifications:

> When Benita Parry takes us to task for not being able to listen to the natives, or to let the natives speak, she forgets that the three of us, post-colonials, are 'natives' too. We talk like Defoe's Friday, only much better. Three hundred years have passed, and territorial imperialism has changed to neo-colonialism. The resistant post-colonial has become a scandal.
>
> Why is the name 'post-colonial' specifically useful in our moment?

Those of us present in that room in Birkbeck College, or indeed the writers and readers of this collection, who are from formerly colonized countries, are able to communicate to each other, to exchange, to establish sociality, because we have had access to the culture of imperialism. Shall we then assign to that culture, to borrow Bernard Williams's phrase, a measure of 'moral luck?'[16] I think there can be no doubt that the answer is 'no'. This impossible 'no' to a structure, which one critiques, yet inhabits intimately, is the deconstructive philosophical position, and the everyday here and now named 'post-coloniality' is a case of it.[17]

Further, whatever the identitarian ethnicist claims of native or fundamental origin (implicit for example, in Benita Parry's exhortation to hear the voice of the native), the political claims that are most urgent in decolonized space are tacitly recognized as coded within the legacy of imperialism: nationhood, constitutionality, citizenship, democracy, even culturalism. Within the historical frame of exploration, colonization, decolonization – what is being effectively reclaimed is a series of regulative political concepts, the *supposedly* authoritative narrative of whose production was written elsewhere, in the social formations of Western Europe. They're being reclaimed, indeed claimed, as concept-metaphors for which no historically adequate referent may be advanced from postcolonial space, yet that does not make the claims less important. A concept-metaphor without an adequate referent is a catachresis. These claims for founding catachreses also make postcoloniality a deconstructive case.

> The centre, on the other hand, still longs for the object of conscientious traditional ethnography: 'where women inscribed themselves as healers, ascetics, singers of sacred songs, artisans and artists,' writes Benita Parry.
>
> I have no objection to conscientious ethnography, although I am a bit frightened by its relationship to the history of the discipline of anthropology. My especial word to Parry, however, is that her efforts as well as mine are judged by the exclusions practised through the intricate workings of the techniques of knowledge and the strategies of power, which have a history rather longer and broader than our individual benevolence and avowals.[18]

Value

The persistent critique of what one must inhabit, the persistent consolidation of claims to founding catachreses, involve an incessant re-coding of diversified fields of value. Let us attempt to imagine 'identity', so cherished a foothold, as flash-points in this re-coding of the circuitry.

Let us, then, for the moment at least, arrest the understandable need to fix and diagnose the identity of the most deserving marginal. Let us also suspend the mood of self-congratulation as saviours of marginality. Let us peer, however blindly, into the constantly shifting and tangling network of the techniques of knowledge and the strategies of power through the question of value. This is not an invitation to step into the sunlit arena where values are so broad that philosophers can wrangle about it with reference to imaginary societies: ethical universals and cultural particularity.[19]

In fact, Marx's use of the word 'value' may be seen as catachrestical to the philosophical usage. Which amounts to saying that the appropriate definitions of value might be versions of the re-coding of what Marx names 'value'.[20]

'Value' is the name of that 'contentless and simple [*inhaltslos und einfach*]' thing by way of which Marx rewrote not mediation, but the possibility of the mediation that makes possible in its turn all exchange, all communication, sociality itself.[21] Marx's especial concern is the appropriation of the human capacity to produce, not objects, nor anything tangible, but that simple contentless thing which is *not* pure form; the possibility of mediation (through coding) so that exchange and sociality can exist. Marx's point of entry is the economic coding of value, but the notion itself has a much more supple range. As Marx wrote, to Engels, 'the issue of the matter of value is too decisive for the whole book' (what subsequently became the three volumes of *Capital* and the *Theories of Surplus Value*).[22]

In the early 1970s, *Anti-Oedipus* attempted to extend the range of the Marxian argument from value by applying it to the production and appropriation of value in affective and social rather than merely economic coding. This was their appeal against Althusser, to read again the first chapter of *Capital*, where the talk is of value – the contentless originary thing of human production – *before* it gets fully coded into an economic system of equivalences and entailed social relations. Their suggestion was that, since capital decoded and deterritorialized the socius by releasing the abstract as such, capitalism must manage this crisis via many reterritorializations, among which the generalized, *psychoanalytic* mode of production of affective value operates by way of a generalized systemic institution of equivalence, however spectacular in its complexity and discontinuity.

The codings of value in the politico-cognitive sphere, through the discursive system of marginality, whether by way of psychoanalysis, culturalism, or economism, is still part of this crisis-management. In the discipline, to take the most familiar everyday examples: 'What is worth [the German word for "value"] studying, teaching, and talking about' appears as 'What can best be parcelled out into a fourteen- or ten-week format'; 'What are the best available textbooks' (where 'best' and the 'production of the best' are altogether coded); 'What are the most manageable paper topics' (produced by the techniques of knowledge in the United States primary and *secondary* education system); 'How best can it be proved that this can be integrated into the English curriculum without disturbing the distribution requirements'; 'What projects funded'; 'What books marketed'. Paradoxically, as these necessary practicalities – 'one must begin somewhere' become tacitly accepted working rules for the planners, the recipients (students, audiences) often think in terms of pedagogy as only consciousness transformation, conference speech as only agenda. I am not suggesting that there is a positive space of 'marginality' to be recovered on the other side of the incessant coding. 'Marginality', as it is becoming part of the disciplinary–cultural parlance, is in fact the name of a certain constantly changing set of representations that is the condition and effect of it. It is coded in the currency of the equivalencies of knowledge. That currency measures the magnitude of value in the sphere of knowledge.

We cannot grasp values as such; it is a possibility for grasping, without content. But if we position ourselves *as identities* in terms of links in the chain of a value-coding as if they were persons and things, and go on to ground our practice on that positioning, we become part of the problem in the ways I am describing.[23]

Work in gendering in principle sees the socius as an affectively coded site of exchange and surplus. The simple contentless moment of value as it is gender-coded has historically led to the appropriation of the sexual differential, subtracted from, but represented as, the theoretical fiction of sexual identity. (Economically codable value is the differential subtracted from the theoretical fiction of use-value in the identity of production and consumption.)[24] Gayle Rubin's 'The Traffic in Women: Notes on the "Political Economy" of Sex' was a pathbreaking essay in the analysis of gender-coding.[25] Kalpana Bardhan's writings on the status of Indian women is the only scholarly work in the frame of postcoloniality in the subaltern context that I have seen which shares the presupposition that gender determinacy is the coding of the value-differential allowing for the possibility of the exchange of affective value, negotiating 'sexuality' rather than sexual identity.[26]

The operation of value makes every commitment negotiable, however urgent it might seem or be. For the *long* haul emancipatory social intervention is not *primarily* a question of redressing victimage by the assertion of (class- or gender- or ethno-cultural) identity. It is a question of developing a vigilance for systemic appropriations of the social capacity to produce a *differential* that is one basis of exchange into the networks of cultural of class- or gender-identity.

In the field of ethno-cultural politics, the postcolonial teacher can help to develop this vigilance rather than continue pathetically to dramatize victimage or assert a spurious identity. She says 'no' to the 'moral luck' of the culture of imperialism while recognizing that she must inhabit it, indeed invest it, to criticize it.

(Indeed, the specificity of 'postcoloniality' understood in this way can help us to grasp that no historically (or philosophically) adequate claims can be produced in any space for the guiding words of political, military, economic, ideological emancipation and oppression. You take positions in terms not of the discovery of historical or philosophical grounds, but in terms of reversing, displacing, and seizing the apparatus of value-coding. This is what it means to say 'the agenda of onto-cultural commitments is negotiable'. In that sense 'postcoloniality', far from being marginal, can show the irreducible margin in the centre: we are always *after* the empire of reason, our claims to it always short of adequate. In the hands of identitarians, alas, this can lead to further claims of marginality. 'We are all postcolonials ... ')

Claiming catachreses from a space that one cannot not want to inhabit and yet must criticize is, then, the deconstructive predicament of the postcolonial.

It is my hope that this sense will put a particular constraint upon the metropolitan marginal or indigenous elite, in whose ranks I can belong, not to produce a merely 'antiquarian history' which seeks the continuities of soil, language and urban life in which our present is rooted and, 'by cultivating in a delicate manner that which existed for all time, ... tr[y] to conserve for posterity the conditions under which we were born' (*LCP*, p. 162).

It is in this spirit that I will view *Genesis*, a film by Mrinal Sen.

Let me spell it out here. Postcoloniality in general is not subsumable under the model of the revolutionary or resistant marginal in metropolitan space. If 'black Britain' or the 'rainbow coalition' in the United States are taken as paradigmatic of, say, India or the new African nations, the emphasis falls on Britain or the States as nation-states. It is in this sense that the aggressive use made by an earlier nationalism of the difference between culture and political power has now been reversed only in political *intent*. The main agenda there is still to explode the fantasmatic 'whiteness' of the metropolitan nation. In a powerful recent essay, Tim Mitchell has suggested that the typical Orientalist attitude was 'the world as exhibition'.[27] The 'new orientalism' views 'the world as immigrant'. It is meretricious to suggest that this reminder undervalues the struggle of the marginal in metropolitan space. It is to remember that that struggle cannot be made the unexamined referent for all postcoloniality without serious problems. No 'two-way dialogue' in 'the great currents of international cultural exchange' forgets this.[28]

Thus an art film out of India (*Genesis*), or out of Mali (Cisse Souleymane's *Yeelen*) cannot resemble *Thé au harem d'Archimède* (Mehdi Charef, French/ Algerian). The last sequence of Alain Tanner's new film *Une flamme dans le coeur*, placing Mercedes (the Arab woman in Paris) in Cairo, attempts to point at this problematic.

Genesis: a film by Mrinal Sen (1986)

Current postcolonial claims to the names that are the legacy of the European, enlightenment (sovereignty, constitutionality, self-determination, nationhood, citizenship, even culturalism) are catachrestical claims, their strategy a displacing and seizing of a coding of value.[29] It can show us the negotiable agenda of a cultural commitment to marginality, whereas ethnicist academic agendas make a fetish of identity. The project, as always, is the recoding of value as the differential possibility of exchange and the channelling of surplus. Postcoloniality as agency can make visible that the basis of *all* serious ontological commitment is catachrestical, because negotiable through the information that identity is, *in the larger sense*, a text.[30] It can show that the alternative to Europe's long story – generally translated as 'great narratives' – is not only short tales (*petits récits*) but tampering with the authority of storylines.[31] In *all* beginning, repetition, signature:

> In order for the tethering to the source to occur, what must be retained is the absolute singularity of a signature-event and a signature-form ... But ... a signature

must have a repeatable, iterable, imitable form; it must be able to be detached from the present and singular intention of its production.[32]

The first sequence of the film, repeating the formula, 'as always, yet once again', ends in a shot of recognizably north Indian men and women, peasantry or the urban poor dressed in their best, lining up to be perfunctorily interrogated and put their thumb prints on a long scroll. As the voice-over intones: 'As always, yet once again, they lost everything they had and became slaves again.' In the manner of didactic allegories, some signals are clear to some groups tied together by the various value-codings (systems of representation) the elements of which are being manipulated by Sen with a certain panache. Indigenous radicals sense the pervasiveness and ubiquity of bonded labour as a mode of production.[33] India fanciers perceive the famous Indian cyclical time. Slightly more knowledgeable Indians perhaps catch an ironic reference to Krishna's famous promise in the *Gita*: 'I take on existence from eon to eon, for the rescue of the good and the destruction of the evil, in order to reestablish the Law.'[34]

Some would notice an *in medias res* reference to the sequential narrative of the modes of production, a reminder of the young Marx's impatience with the question of origins, an impatience that was never given up: 'If you ask about the creation of nature and of man, then you are abstracting from nature and man. ... Do not think and do not ask me questions, for as soon as you think and ask questions, your *abstraction* from the existence of nature and man has no meaning.'[35]

In this articulation of history in terms of the mode of production of (economic) value, the 'worker' is represented as collectively caught in the primitive signature (at its most proximate the thumb print, the body's mark), the originary contract – the first codification/identification. Both of these things take on importance in the film's subsequent emphasis on the name of the father and its use of the radical counterfactual.

Banality and the desert

At any rate, it is only after this pre-originary scene of repetition that the title flashes on the screen: GENESIS. It looks a bit self-consciously solemn, in large letters by itself on the screen. The ethnographically savvy viewer would find it banal, the savvy diasporic would find it embarrassingly pre-postmodern, the metropolitan third worldist would perhaps suppress the embarrassment because it's a third-world allegory of the birth of a nation – 'genesis' does mean birth – which unfortunately misses the appropriate style of magical realism. The 'non-theoretical' metropolitan third-worldist would prefer something more de Sica style, like the recent *Salaam Bombay*, or Adoor Gopalakrishnan's *Face to Face* with its heavy contemporary cultural content, spelling out the fate of a Western theory in the context of the encroachment of industrial capitalism in rural India, or even Sen's earlier films, where the super-realistic technique achieved its obsessive brilliance by laying bare, for the most part, the workings of the urban lower middle class of West Bengal. The appropriate,

appropriate diagnosis is (historically and in the present) and then speak of it as one case, rather than as the self-identical authority.[42] This permits one not to be trapped by authority, to look at other codings, other constellations. Let us try out this coding on the space named 'Rajasthan'.

In *Kiss of the Spider Woman*, the use of early Hollywood technicolour at the end is carefully framed in diverse filmic idioms, so that we can adjust our look. In *Genesis*, the unframed yet noticeably regressive use of lyric space and the wide screen, unproblematic light, primary colours, can be seen as denoting 'Desert'. Yes, this *is* the desert area of North-West India, but we are, rather aggressively, not in veridical space. The stones of the ruins move, to denote insubstantiality, and the sound of an anachronistic aeroplane is the response of a god created out of a skull before the dawn of serious technology. North-West India pushes toward the desert of West Asia as the felicitous theatre of *Genesis*. No garden in the beginning, but a desert in the middle of history. (West Asia, the Middle East, itself reveals the catachrestical nature of absolute directional naming of parts of the globe. It can only exist as an absolute descriptive if Europe is presupposed as the centre.) This is no particular place, negotiable as the desert area of North-West India, pushing toward West Asia, but not quite West Asia; perhaps the very looseness of this reference questions the heavy, scholarly, period films, the benevolent anti-racist films (sometimes the benevolent racist films, one can hardly tell the difference) that have been made about the Bible story in its appropriate geographical context.

There is something of this loose-knit denotation of space in the language of the film as well. The film is made by an Indian whose native language is not Hindi, the national language. Do you see it now? To be in a new 'nation' (itself catachrestical to the appropriate development of nations), speak *for* it, in a national language that is not one's mother-tongue. But what is a mother-tongue?

A mother-tongue is a language with a history – in that sense it is 'instituted' – before our birth and after our death, where patterns that can be filled with anyone's motivation have laid themselves down. In this sense it is ' "unmotivated" but not capricious'.[43] We learn it in a 'natural' way and fill it once and for all with our own 'intentions' and thus make it 'our own' for the span of our life and then leave it without intent – as unmotivated and uncapricious as we found it (without intent) when it found us – for its other users: 'The "unmotivatedness" of the sign requires a synthesis in which the completely other is announced as such – without any simplicity, any identity, and resemblance or continuity – within what is not it.'[44]

Thus the seemingly absurd self-differential of a non-native speaker of a national language can be used to show that this *is* the name of the game, that this is only an instantiated representation of how one is 'at home' in a language. There is no effort in *Genesis* to produce the rich texture of 'authentic' Hindi, nor its Beckettized skeleton. This is just the spare Hindi of a man slightly exiled from his national language. And as such, one notices its careful focusing.

The extreme edge of Hindi as the 'national language' is a peculiar concoction with a heavily Sanskritized artificial idiom whose most notable confection is the speech of the flight attendants on Indian airplane flights. By contrast, Hindi as it is spoken and written is enriched by many Arabic and Persian loan-words ('loan-words' is itself – you guessed it, a catachrestical concept-metaphor: 'Those French words which we are so proud of pronouncing accurately are themselves only blunders made by the Gallic lips which mispronounced Latin or Saxon, our language being merely a defective pronunciation of several others' said Proust's Marcel).[45] And, in Sen's predictable stock Hindi, those are some of the words emphasized in an eerie light, adding, as it were, to that non-specific desert aura, the cradle of genesis, Arabia and Persia, somewhere off the Gulf, real enough today as the stage of imperialist inhumanity. These 'loan-words' move history out of the methodological necessity of a pre-supposed origin. You will see what I mean if I list the three most important: *zarurat* (necessity), *huq* (right), and the most interesting to me, *khud muqtar*.

The sub-title translates this last expression as 'self-reliant' or 'independent'. The trader keeps repeating this phrase with contempt to the weaver and the farmer, whom he exploits, as a kind of scornful reprimand: 'You went to the market yourself, to check up on the price of what you're producing for me. You want to represent yourself. You want to be *khud muqtar*.' 'Independent' gives the exchange too nationalist an aura. The actual phrase would be something more like pleading your own case, and would underscore an everyday fact: in spite of efforts at Sanskritization, much of the language of legal procedure in India comes, understandably, from court Persian.

The aura of a place which is the semi-Japhetic desert, a semi-Japhetic language arranged by a non-native speaker; the perfect staging for *Genesis*. In the beginning is an impossible language marked with a star. Progress is made by way of the imagined identity of an original caught between two translations.[46] This is neither Africa nor East Asia, nor yet the Americas. It is an old score being actively reshuffled, not the rather youthful debate about a third world identity.

The postcolonial teacher can renegotiate some of the deceptive 'banality' of the film to insert the 'Third World' into the text of value.

Woman and Engels

The film loosens the tight logic of progression of the mode of production narrative most movingly by taking a distance from the tough, outdated, comprehensive, ambitious reasonableness of the Engelsian account of the origin of the family.[47] Rumour has it that the intellectuals of the majority left party in Calcutta have said about this part of the film that Sen hadn't really understood his Engels. Again, the authority of the authoritative account, the appropriate reading, are invoked. We are caught in a much more over-determined web than you think – inappropriate use of Hindi, inappropriate use of Engels, India Tourist Board use of Rajasthan: and you think you're just watching an *Indian* film, even that you want just to listen to the voice of the native.

Woman in *Genesis* marks the place of the radical counterfactual: the road not taken of an alternative history which will not allow the verification of a possible world *by the actual one*.[48] The two moments that I would like to discuss are in that sense not 'true to history' but full of the possibility of pedagogic exactitude.

A work of art (I use this expression because I feel wary about our present tendency to avoid such old-fashioned phrases for no reason but to show that we are politically correct, although our presuppositions are in many ways un-altered) is a part of history and society, but its function is not to behave like 'history' and 'sociology' as disciplinary formations. My general argument, here as elsewhere, has been that, *in terms of this characteristic*, and as long as it does not itself become a totalizing masterword, art or the pedagogy of art can point at the ultimately catachrestical limits of being human in the will to truth, life, or power. But with the resistance to the menace of catachresis (use or mention, mention as use) comes a tendency to dismiss such arguments as 'nothing but' the aestheticization of the political (the assumption being, of course, that the veridical is *eo ipso* political).[49] I leave the suggestion aside, then, and look at the representation of the woman as the radical counterfactual in history.

Engels finds the origin of class exploitation in the sexual division of labour in the structure of support around the reproduction of society. Woman's labour-power, the power to produce children, was according to Engels, fetishized into a relationship of dependence and subordination. It is quite possible that this Engelsian script has written the woman as she suddenly appears on the screen in the *Genesis*, for she is shown *after* the monogamian family. The flood has killed her former husband and children. But, in *this* historical moment, in *this* text, in *this* 'self-mediated birth', she negotiates reproduction as agent of production, able to articulate a position *against* the perversion of her agency.

In this counterfactual account, it is the woman who points out the problem of the fetish-character of the commodity. It is in answer to her question ('does the weaver have the right [*huq*] to satisfy the need [*zarurat*] of the farmer for a new cloth?) that the distinction between productive consumption and individual consumption and the meaning of bondage as non-ownership of the means of production emerge in the false haven. The trader lets the weaver weave a new cloth for his friend the farmer. This is not producing a use-value, but merely including the cloth as part of their real subsistence wage. But Sen represents another change in this moment inaugurated by the questioning of the curious woman (remember 'Genesis?'). The trader gives the weaver money. The desert is being inserted into generalized commodity exchange.

Is this how it happened? Probably not. And certainly not according to most great narratives, anthropological or politico-economic. Yet why not? Women's story is not the substance of great narratives. But women are curious, they have a knack of asking the outsider's uncanny questions, even though they are not encouraged to *take* credit for what follows. Thus, here too, the two men will tell her 'you won't understand' when they go to a distant market with their money, although her curiosity produced the money.

The point is not to contradict Engels but rather to see the counterfactual presentation of the woman as the motor of 'effective' history. It is no disrespect to Engels to suggest, *in this way*, that his text too is held by a certain value-coding where women's victimage rather than agency is foregrounded. And is this sequence in the film also a fragmentary transvaluation of Eve's much maligned responsibility for the inauguration of knowledge?

It is perhaps not surprising that it is within the most touristic footage in the film that Sen fabricates the emergence of the autonomous aesthetic moment. No knowledge of Indic aesthetics or ethnics is required to flesh out the bold strokes, which I list below:

1   The possibility of autonomous representation as one of the gifts of generalized commodity exchange: in order to dream, all you need is money.
2   The framing of the aesthetic as such so that its production can be hidden. The two men willingly hide themselves until the woman, decorated with silver anklets, appears as an aesthetic object.
3   True to the autonomy of the aesthetic in this allegorical context, the aesthetic object is endowed with a hermetically represented subjectship. The woman sings, without sub-titles. GENESIS in the beginning, in English (?) in the 'original', marks postcolonial accessibility. Here, framed in the film, is a parody of culturalist art, inaccessible except to the authentic native; the audience of postcoloniality has no access to the authentic text. The song is in a Rajasthani dialect, ironically the only verbal marker that this is 'Rajasthan'. It is, however, the most stunningly double-edged moment in the film. For it is also a negotiation of a banality belonging to the internationally accessible idiom of a general 'Indian' mass culture of long standing – the Bombay film industry: the woman breaking into a folk song. Unlike the rest of the film which creates interesting collages of musical idioms, this lilting singing voice is autonomous and unaccompanied. There is also an interesting manipulation of gazes here.
4   As the sequence cuts to a scene at the well, the wordless tune infects the noise of the pulley. Labour is aestheticized.

Aesthetic objectification and commodity exchange bring out the supplement of sexual possessiveness that was implicit in the text. The two men are individualized by jealousy. If we must quote Engels, the here and now of the film, preceded by all those cycles of disaster, is clearly post-lapsarian:

> Monogamy does not by any means make its appearance in history as the reconciliation of man and woman, still less as the highest form of such reconciliation. On the contrary, it appears as the subjection of one sex by the other, as the proclamation of a conflict between the sexes entirely unknown hitherto in prehistoric times. ... The first class-antagonism which appears in history coincides with the development of the antagonism between man and woman in monogamian marriage, and the first class-oppression with that of the female sex by the male.[50]

The film is not an origin story, but a story of once again, once again. What we are watching here is not the 'first class-oppression', but the discontinuity between developed class oppression and gender oppression. The woman had shared class oppression with the weaver and the farmer. The men join the merchant, their master, in the role of gender oppressor. Neither truth to Engels, nor truth to Rajasthani kinship patterns is needed here, although both help in creating the aura of fields of meaning. Again, postcoloniality is a mode of existence whose importance and fragility would be destroyed by techniques of specialist knowledge as they work with strategies of power. To get a grasp on how the agency of the postcolonial is being obliterated in order to inscribe him and her as marginals, culture studies must use, but actively frame and resist specialisms. It must, at all costs, retain its skill as a strategy that works on cases with shifting identities. 'The overthrow of mother right was the *world-historic defeat of the female sex.* ... In order to guarantee the fidelity of the wife, that is, the paternity of the children, the woman is placed in the man's absolute power.'[51]

The woman in the film is finally pregnant. The men are obsessed by the question of paternity. In the spare dialogue, a point is made that does not apply only to the 'third world' or 'the marginals'; the point that the real issue in the overthrow of mother right is not merely ownership but control. The woman is the subject of knowledge; she *knows* the name of the father in the most literal way. This scandalous power is modified and shifted into 'a strange reversal': power is consolidated *in* the name of the father and the woman is reduced to the figure who cannot know. Again counterfactually, the woman is given the right to answer the question of the name of the father and of mother right:

SHE:	*I* am the one to tell you?
HE (THE FARMER):	Then who else can?
HE (THE WEAVER):	It's my child, isn't it?
SHE:	Why are you asking me?
HE:	Who else shall I ask?
SHE:	Ask yourself. Ask your friend.

When the question of right (*huq*) is posed, she answers in terms of the men's need (*zarurat*). In the simple language of affective exchange she speaks mother right. This, too, is counterfactual, for it has little in common with the heavily coded exchange-system of matriarchal societies.

SHE:	What difference will it make who the father is?
HE:	Who has the right over it?
SHE:	I don't know who has the right over it. I accepted you both. In three we were one. Now you talk of rights, you want to be master. The enemy is not outside, but in. This child is mine.

This moment does not belong in the accounting of history, and the men do not get her point. 'Our first sin was to call her a whore', they mutter. The admission has, strictly speaking, no counterfactual consequence. The eruption of jealousy, the enmity between comrades, the defeat of the female sex seem to mark a moment of rupture. The tempo speeds up. This disaster is neither drought nor flood, but a quick succession of colonial wars – on camels, with bombs; succeeded by neo-colonialism, 'development' – a bulldozer.

In a completely unexpected final freeze-frame, what comes up from below is a Caterpillar bulldozer. You see the word CATERPILLAR on its nose and, again, it's not a subtitle; like GENESIS, it's a word that the postcolonial understands. The innumerable links between capitalism and patriarchy are not spelled out. The film ends with the immediately recognizable banality of the phallus – the angle of the shot focuses attention on the erect pipe so that you don't even quite know that it's a bulldozer. The sub-title becomes part of the text again, and the catachresis is brutally shifted into the literality of the present struggle.

Let us imagine a contrast between this bulldozer and the bulldozer in *Sammy and Rosie Get Laid*, so textualized that it can work as a rich symbol. In Sen the lexicon is resolutely and precariously 'outside'. Pedagogy here must try to retrench from that outside the presence of a banal globality, which must not be retranslated into the autonomy of the art object or its status as ethnic evidence, the particular voice of the marginal. Our agency must not be re-inscribed through the benevolence of the discipline.

Postscript

Not all 'postcolonial' texts have to look like *Genesis*. In fact, I do not know what the paradigmatic postcolonial stylistic production would be. At any rate, this essay is as much about a postcolonial style of pedagogy as about the look of a postcolonial text.[52]

We must, however, attend to taxonomic talk of paradigms and such, for 'no "local centre," no "pattern of transformation" could function if, through a series of sequences, it did not eventually enter into an over-all strategy' (*HS*, p. 99). But this attention cannot be our goal and norm. We must arrest the emergence of disciplinary currency by keeping our eye on the double (multiple and irregular) movement of the local *and* the over-all.

In chapter 1 of *Capital* Marx speaks of four forms of value: the simple; the total or expanded; the general; and money.

The 'simple' form of value (20 yards of linen = one coat) is heuristic or accidental. The 'general', where all value is economically expressed in terms of *one* commodity, is on its way to the money form. The second form – 'the total or expanded' – is where 'z commodity A = u commodity B or v commodity C or = w Commodity D or = x commodity E or = etc.'.[53]

In the Western European mid-nineteenth century Marx felt that the most appropriate object of investigation for an emancipatory critique was capital. In the analysis of capital (traffic in economic value-coding), which releases the abstract as such, it is necessary for both capitalist and critical activist to use the most logical form of value (general and then money) as his tool. This is a lesson that we cannot ignore. But in the analysis of contemporary capital*ism* in the broadest sense, taking patriarchy (traffic in affective value-coding) and neo-colonialism (traffic in epistemic–cognitive–political–institutional value-coding) into account, it is 'the total or Expanded Form of Value', where 'the series of [the] representations [of value] never comes to an end', which 'is a motley mosaic of disparate and unconnected expressions', where the endless series of expressions are all different from each other, and where 'the totality has no single, unified form of appearance', that Foucault, or Deleuze, or indeed, implicitly, Gayle Rubin choose as their analytical field.[54] 'We must conceive discourse as a series of discontinuous segments whose tactical function is neither uniform nor stable' (*HS*, p. 100).

Rubin, Deleuze and Guattari seem to know their relationship to Marx. Kalpana Bardhan, like Sen, although necessarily in a different form, gives us the ingredients for an expanded analysis from within the generalist position (adhering to the importance of the general or money form). Rubin's work is in some ways most exciting, because she comes to the threshold of the total expanded form (which she calls, somewhat metaphorically, 'political economy') from a staunchly humanist–structuralist position.

As for Marx's and Foucault's apparently opposed claims for their methodological choices, the only *useful* way to read them is as being dependent upon their objects of investigation.[55] Thus, *in the economic sphere*, 'the total or expanded form' is 'defective' as a form of analysis (Marx). And *in the cognitive–political sphere* 'it is a question of orienting ourselves to a conception of power which *replaces* the privilege of the law with the viewpoint of the stake [*enjeu*]' (Foucault, *HS*, p. 102; emphasis added).[56] I have tried to flesh out their relationship by reading the production of 'marginality' as a taxonomic diagnosis in our trade; and suggesting that, here and now, 'postcoloniality' may serve as the name of a strategy that repeatedly undoes the seeming opposition.

Notes

1 It is my conviction of the power of collectivities that will not allow me to ignore that the realization of the 'potential' is an incessantly betrayed struggle undermined by the longing for upward class mobility in those among the non-revolutionary underclass who feel they might have the possibility of a foothold in the ladder. In the rest of this first section I try to argue that radical teachers at universities – an important apparatus of upward class mobility – should attend to the nature of the institution that is their contractual space – and not ignore their obligation by claiming a spurious marginality, and declare the desire for the revolution as its accomplishment. I believe the teacher, *while operating within the institution*, can foster the emergence of a committed collectivity by not making her institutional commitment invisible.

2 See Ranajit Guha, *A Rule of Property for Bengal: An Essay on the Idea of Permanent Settlement* (New Delhi: Orient Longman, 1981); and Victor Kiernan, *Marxism and Imperialism* (London: Edward Arnold, 1974), pp. 206f. I hope the reader will not consider this mention of the name 'Bengali' a proof of 'high flying Bengali cultural revanchism'. There seems no way around the fact that the speaker's native language is Bengali.

3 In 'Representing the Colonized: Anthropology's Interlocutors', Edward Said is quite correct in reminding us that 'We should first take scrupulous note of how ... the United States has replaced the great earlier empires as *the* dominant outside

force' (*Critical Inquiry* 15 [Winter 1989], p. 215). It seems to me that the displacements entailed by this shift in conjuncture must also be kept in mind. 'The West' is not monolithic.

4 See Carl Pletsch, 'The Three Worlds, or the Division of Social Scientific Labor, circa 1950–1975', *Comparative Studies in Society and History* 23. 4 (October, 1981).

5 Folker Froebel, Jurgen Heinrichs and Otto Kreve, *The New International Division of Labour: Structural Unemployment in Industrialized Countries and Industrialization in Developing Countries*, trans. Pete Burgess (Cambridge: Cambridge University Press, 1980); Nigel Harris, *The End of the Third World: Newly Industrializing Countries and the Decline of an Ideology* (London: Penguin, 1986).

6 Michel Foucault, *Language, Counter-Memory, Practice: Selected Essays and Interviews*, trans. Donald F. Bouchard and Sherry Simon (Ithaca: Cornell University Press, 1977), p. 145. Hereafter cited in text as *LCP*.

7 Experts in the mainstream are not charitable to this impulse: 'Many acts of revenge have been and are still taken against citizens of the former colonial powers, whose sole personal crime is that of belonging to the nation in question ... That Europe should in her turn be colonized by the peoples of Africa, of Asia, or of Latin America (we are far from this, I know) would be a "sweet revenge," but cannot be considered my ideal ... This extraordinary success [that the colonized peoples have adopted our customs and have put on clothes] is chiefly due to one specific feature of Western civilization which for a long time was regarded as a feature of man himself, its development and prosperity among Europeans thereby becoming proof of their superiority: it is, paradoxically, Europeans' capacity to understand the other' (Tzvetan Todorov, *The Conquest of America: the Question of the Other*, trans. Richard Howard [New York: Harper and Row, 1984], pp. 256, 258). Or to give only two examples, this comment on 'Sartre's creative use of terrorism. The true precursor of Sartre was not so much Marx as Sorel, whose belief in the efficacy of violence as a purgative anticipated his own. Curiously Sartre's apologia for "terrorism-fraternity" found its real home not on French soil, but in the underdeveloped countries of the third world, where terror was recommended, as a cure-all for colonial-induced psychopathologies' (Steven B. Smith, *Reading Althusser: An Essay on Structural Marxism* [Ithaca: Cornell University Press, 1984], p. 67).

8 Said, *Orientalism* (New York: Pantheon Books, 1978).

9 For a more detailed consideration of the attendant pedagogical situation, see Spivak, 'The Making of Americans, the Teaching of English, and the Future of Culture Studies,' *New Literary History* 21 (1990), pp. 781–98. For a brief checklist of required reading, see Chinua Achebe, 'Colonialist Criticism', *Morning Yet On Creation Day: Essays* (Garden City, Anchor Press, 1975); Ngugi Wa Thiong'o, *Writers in Politics* (London: Heinemann, 1981); Ashis Nandy, *The Intimate Enemy: Loss and Recovery of Self Under Colonialism* (New York: Oxford University Press, 1983); Ranajit Guha and Gayatri Spivak, eds., *Selected Subaltern Studies* (New York: Oxford University Press, 1988); Stuart Hall and James Donald, *Politics and Ideology* (London: Open University Press, 1985); Hazel Carby, *Reconstructing Womanhood: the Emergence of Afro-American Women Novelists* (New York: Oxford University Press, 1987); Sneja Gunew (with Uyen Loewald), 'The Mother Tongue and Migration', *Australian Feminist Studies*, 1 (Summer, 1985); Trinh T. Minh-ha and Jean-Paul Bourdier, *African Spaces: Designs for Living in Upper Volta* (New York, Africana Press, 1985); Paulin J. Hountondji, *African Philosophy: Myth and Reality*, trans. Henri Evans (Bloomington: Indiana University Press, 1983); Henry Louis Gates, Jr., *Figures in Black: Worlds, Signs and the 'Racial' Self* (New

York: Oxford University Press, 1986); Lata Mani, 'Contentious Traditions: The Debate on SATI in Colonial India', *Cultural Critique* 7 (Autumn, 1987); Mick Taussig, *Shamanism, Colonialism and the Wild Man: A Study in Terror and Healing*, (Chicago: University of Chicago Press, 1987); Mary Louise Pratt, 'Scratches on the Face of the Country; or What Mr Barrow Saw in the Land of the Bushmen', *Critical Inquiry* 12. 1 (Autumn 1985). Of the numerous journals coming out in the field, one might name *Cultural Critique, New Formations, Criticism, Heresy, and Interpretation, Inscriptions, Third Text.*

10 For a superb analysis of this fantasm in the context of the United States, see Barbara Herrnstein Smith, 'Cult-Lit: Hirsch, Literacy, and "The National Culture" ', *South Atlantic Quarterly* (Winter, 1990).

11 Michel Foucault, *The History of Sexuality, Vol. 1: An Introduction*, trans. Robert Hurley (New York: Vintage Books, 1980), p. 99. Hereafter cited in text as *HS*.

12 Fredric Jameson, 'On Magic Realism in Film', *Critical Inquiry* 12. 2 (Winter, 1986). Most noticeable texts are, of course, V. S. Naipaul *Guerrillas* (New York: Alfred A. Knopf, 1975) and Salman Rushdie, *Midnight's Children* (New York: Alfred A. Knopf, 1981).

13 The Freudian term *'Besetzung'*, translated as 'cathexis' in the standard edition, is translated *'investissement'* [lit. investment] in French. The Freudian term means, roughly, 'to occupy with desire'. Since Foucault did not use Freudian terms in their strict sense, 'cathecting' or 'occupying with desire' might be inadvisable here. On the other hand 'invest' has *only* an economic meaning in English and the psychoanalytic usage is never far below the surface in poststructuralist French writers. I decided on the somewhat odd 'switch it on'.

14 Benita Parry, 'Problems in Current Theories of Colonial Discourse', *Oxford Literary Review* 9. 1/2 (1987).

15 Coetzee, *Foe* (New York: Viking Penguin, 1987).

16 For interesting speculations on 'moral luck', see Bernard Williams, *Moral Luck: Philosophical Papers 1973–1980* (Cambridge: Cambridge University Press, 1981), pp. 20–39. But moral luck is an after-the-fact assignment. 'The justification, if there is to be one, will be essentially retrospective' (p. 24). The impossible and intimate 'no' might thus involve our consideration of the historical production of our cultural exchangeability. Why does it involve the long haul toward a future? I attempt to answer this in the text. (I am also aware that the delicacy of Williams's concern with the individual moral agent is travestied when transferred to something like 'the culture of imperialism'. It would be interesting to 'apply' Williams's brilliantly inconclusive speculations to individual imperialist reformists.)

17 Spivak, 'Theory in the Margin: Coetzee's *Foe* reading Defoe's *Crusoe/Roxana*', in Jonathan Arac and Barbara Johnson (eds.), *Consequences of Theory* (Baltimore: Johns Hopkins University Press, 1991).

18 Spivak, 'Theory in the Margin'.

19 Most thoughtfully for example, in Richard Rorty, 'Solidarity and Objectivity?' in John Rajchman and Cornel West, eds., *Post-Analytic Philosophy* (New York: Columbia University Press, 1985).

20 Whenever someone attempts to put together a 'theory of practice' where the intending subject as absolute ground is put into question, catachrestical master-words become necessary, because language can never fully bypass the pre-supposition of such a ground. The particular word is, in such a case, the best that will serve, but also, and necessarily, a misfit. (There can, of course, be no doubt that the Marxian theory of ideology put into question the intending subject as absolute

ground.) The choice of these master-words obliges the taking on of the burden of the history of the meanings of the word in the language (paleonymy). Thus 'value' (as 'writing' in Derrida or 'power' in Foucault) must necessarily *also* mean its 'ordinary' language meanings: material worth as well as idealist values, and create the productive confusion that can, alone, give rise to practice. It must be said, however, that these master-words are misfits only if the ordinary use of language is presupposed to have fully fitting cases. Thus 'to fit' is itself a catachresis and points to a general theory of language as catachrestical that must be actively marginalized in all its uses. For a development of 'active marginalization' see Spivak, 'Theory in the Margins'.

21 Karl Marx, *Capital: A Critique of Political Economy*, trans. Ben Fowkes (New York: Vintage Books, 1977), vol. 1, p. 90.

22 Karl Marx, *Selected Correspondence* (Moscow: Progress Publishers, 1975), p. 228.

23 Williams uses 'currency' in this sense in *Moral Luck*, p. 35. Yet because he can only see value-coding as singular and rational, rather than heterogeneous and coherent, he dismisses it as impossible in the moral sphere, and indeed is sceptical about the possibility of a moral *philosophy* on related grounds. I am in basic sympathy with his position though I cannot accept his presuppositions and conclusions about 'currency'. Here perhaps attending to the metaphoricity of a concept would help. For the metaphoricity of the concept of currency, as for concepts and metaphors in general, see Derrida, 'White Mythology: Metaphor in the Text of Philosophy', in *Margins of Philosophy*, trans. Alan Bass (Chicago: University of Chicago Press, 1982), pp. 207–71.

24 I have discussed this in 'Scattered Speculations on the Question of Value', in Spivak, *In Other Worlds: Essays in Cultural Politics* (New York: Methuen, 1987).

25 Gayle Rubin, 'The Traffic in Women: Notes on the "Political Economy" of Sex', in Rayna R. Reiter, ed., *Toward an Anthropology of Women* (New York: Monthly Review Press, 1975), pp. 157–210.

26 See, for example, Kalpana Bardhan, 'Women: Work, Welfare and Status. Forces of Tradition and Change in India', *South Asia Bulletin* 6. 1 (Spring, 1986). Because of the heavy weight of positivist empiricism in her discipline (development economics), she has to be read somewhat against the grain.

27 Tim Mitchell, 'The World as Exhibition', *Comparative Studies in Society and History* 31. 2 (April, 1989).

28 The *intellectual* kinship between Africa and African-Americans is an example of such international cultural exchange. This is rather different from the issue of the heterogeneity of the metropolitan underclass. I should of course also mention the cultural and political solidarity between Arab-Americans and the Palestine Liberation struggle as an example of two-way exchange. My general point about academic practice in defining marginality and postcoloniality remains generally unaffected by this.

29 The *OED* defines 'catachresis' as 'abuse or perversion of a trope or metaphor'. We appropriate this to indicate the originary 'abuse' constitutive of language-production, where both concept and metaphor are 'wrested from their proper meaning'. Thus, in the narrow sense, a word for which there is no *adequate* referent to be found.

30 Some of us have been intoning this larger sense, with not too much effect against what Geoff Bennington calls 'the beginner's error of conflating "text" in Derrida's sense with "discourse" ' ('L'arroseur arrosé(e)', *New Formations* 7 [Spring 1989], p. 36). See also Spivak, 'Speculation on Reading Marx: After Reading Derrida', in

Derek Attridge *et al.*, eds., *Post-structuralism and the Question of History* (Cambridge: Cambridge University Press, 1987), p. 30.

31 Jean-François Lyotard, *The Postmodern Condition: A Report on Knowledge*, trans. Geoff Bennington and Brian Massumi (Minneapolis: University of Minnesota Press, 1984).

32 Derrida, 'Signature Event Context', in *Glyph* 1, p. 194.

33 For an extraordinary staging of this pervasiveness and ubiquity, and indeed a reinscription of 'India' from that perspective, see Mahasweta Devi, 'Douloti the Bountiful', in Spivak, trans. *Imaginary Maps* (New York: Routledge, 1994).

34 J. B. van Bruitenen (trans.), *The Bhagawadgita in the Mahabharata* (Chicago, 1981), p. 87.

35 Karl Marx, 'Economic and Philosophical Manuscripts', in Rodney Livingstone and Gregor Benton (trans.), *Early Writings* (Harmondsworth: Penguin, 1975), p. 20.

36 Antonio Gramsci, 'The Study of Philosophy', in *Selections from the Prison Notebooks*, trans. Quintin Hoare and Geoffrey Nowell Smith (New York: International Publishers, 1971), p. 324.

37 I take this distinction from Foucault, *The Archaeology of Knowledge*, trans. A. M. Sheridan Smith (New York: Pantheon Books, 1972), pp. 88–105.

38 The *OED* defines 'parabasis' as 'going aside', 'address to the audience in the poet's name, unconnected with the action of the drama'. We appropriate this as a transaction between postcolonial subject positions, persistently going aside from typical allegorical continuity.

39 For a treatment of the Armenian case from the point of view of catachrestical claims to nationhood, see David Kasanjian and Anahid Kassabian, 'Naming the Armenian Genocide', *New Formations* 8 (Summer 1989), pp. 81–98. Boris Kagarlitsky, *The Thinking Reed: Intellectuals and the Soviet State: 1917 to the Present*, trans. Brian Pearce (London: Verso, 1988), fast becoming the text on the new USSR, does not yet take into account the breaking open of the available value-coding of ethnicity and nationalism.

40 'Cultural and Political Power of Cinematic Language', paper delivered at conference on 'Problems of Cultural Representation in Global Cinema' (Boston Film/ Video Institute, 26–30 April 1989).

41 Umberto Melotti unwittingly exposes this in *Marx and the Third World*, trans. Pat Ransford (London: Macmillan, 1977), pp. 28–9.

42 For 'truth' as one case of a general iterability, see Derrida, *Limited Inc. abc ...*, trans. Samuel Weber (Baltimore: Johns Hopkins University Press, 1977).

43 Derrida, *Of Grammatology*, trans. Spivak (Baltimore: Johns Hopkins University Press, 1976), p. 46.

44 Derrida, *Of Grammatology*, p. 47. I am naturalizing Derrida's general description. Derrida's next sentence makes clear that his concern is more sub-individual than language-acquisition.

45 Marcel Proust, *Cities of the Plains*, trans. C. K. Scott Moncrieff (New York: Vintage Books, 1970), p. 99. Professor Jessie Hornsby's extraordinary knowledge of Proust helped me locate a merely remembered passage.

46 Star: 'This *Ursprache* as German scholars termed it ... which we might term Proto-Indo-European ... could be reconstructed ... The asterisk being used by convention to indicate reconstructed parent words which were not directly attested by any language known ... ' (Colin Renfrew, *Archaeology and Language: The Puzzle of Indo-European Origins* [New York: Cambridge University Press, 1987], p. 14). Caught between two translations: 'Indeed it was not until 1947 that a good bilingual

inscription was found at the site of Karatepe, written in Phoenician (a well-known Semitic language) as well as in hieroglyphic Hittite, so that real progress could be made with it' (Renfrew, *Archaeology and Language*, p. 51). Japhetic: 'the story in the book of Genesis of the three sons of Noah, Ham, Shem and Japheth was taken as a perfectly acceptable explanation of the divergence of early languages. The languages of Africa were thus termed Hamitic, those of the Levant Semitic, and those to the land of the north Japhetic' (Renfrew, *Archaeology and Language*, p. 13). Since 'Semitic' is still in use, I am using 'Japhetic' within the allegorical frame of the authority still given to the Biblical myth in certain situations of global politics. See Volosinov's underscoring of a differentiated origin for 'Japhetic' languages in his discussion of N. Ja Marr in *Marxism and the Philosophy of Language*, trans. Ladislav Mateika and I. R. Titunik (New York: Seminar Press, 1973), pp. 72, 76, 101.

47 Frederick Engels, *The Origin of the Family, Private Property and the State* (New York: Pathfinder Press, 1972). Gayle Rubin's sympathetic critique of Engels in 'Traffic' is exemplary.

48 This is in striking contrast to the story's 'source', Samaresh Basu's 'Uratiya', a poignant semi-fantastic staging of patriarchal conflict. Another case of the narrativization of an alternative history that will not allow the verification of a possible world by the actual world is brilliantly telescoped in the tribal half-caste woman's utterance in Mahasweta Devi's 'The Hunt': 'If my mother had killed her white daughter at birth ... I would not have been' ('The Hunt', in *Imaginary Maps*).

49 For my statement of the argument, see Spivak, *In Other Worlds*, pp. 241–7; for a dismissal where concept and rhetoric are resolutely identified with the disciplines of 'philosophy' and 'literary criticism' (aesthetics), see Jürgen Habermas, *The Philosophical Discourse of Modernity*, trans. Fredrick Lawrence (Cambridge: MIT Press, 1987), pp. 161–210.

50 Engels, *Origin*, pp. 74–5.

51 Engels, *Origin*, pp. 68–9.

52 For a taxonomy of possible diversity here, see for example the articles in *Cultural Critique*, 6 and 7 (Spring and Autumn, 1987).

53 Marx, *Capital*, vol. 1, p. 156.

54 Marx, *Capital*, vol. 1, pp. 156, 157.

55 For a detailed study of Marx and Foucault, see Barry Smart, *Foucault, Marxism and Critique* (London: Routledge, 1983).

56 Marx, *Capital*, vol. 1, p. 156.

12

Dipesh Chakrabarty

Postcoloniality and the Artifice of History: Who Speaks for 'Indian' Pasts?*

Push thought to extremes.
Louis Althusser

I

It has recently been said in praise of the postcolonial project of *Subaltern Studies* that it demonstrates, 'perhaps for the first time since colonization,' that 'Indians are showing sustained signs of reappropriating the capacity to represent themselves [within the discipline of history].'[1] As a historian who is a member of the *Subaltern Studies* collective, I find the congratulation contained in this remark gratifying but premature. The purpose of this article is to problematize the idea of 'Indians' 'representing themselves in history.' Let us put aside for the moment the messy problems of identity inherent in a transnational enterprise such as *Subaltern Studies*, where passports and commitments blur the distinctions of ethnicity in a manner that some would regard as characteristically postmodern. I have a more perverse proposition to argue. It is that in so far as the academic discourse of history – that is, 'history' as a discourse produced at the institutional site of the university – is concerned, 'Europe' remains the sovereign, theoretical subject of all histories, including the ones we call 'Indian,' 'Chinese,' 'Kenyan,' and so on. There is a peculiar way in which all these other histories tend to become variations on a master narrative that could be called 'the history of Europe.' In this sense, 'Indian' history itself is in a position of subalternity; one can only articulate subaltern subject positions in the name of this history.

While the rest of this article will elaborate on this proposition, let me enter a few qualifications. 'Europe' and 'India' are treated here as hyperreal terms in that they refer to certain figures of imagination whose geographical referents remain somewhat indeterminate.[2] As figures of the imaginary they are, of course, subject to contestation, but for the moment I shall treat them as though they were given, reified categories, opposites paired in a structure of domina-

* From *Representations* 37 (Winter, 1992), pp. 1–26.

tion and subordination. I realize that in treating them thus I leave myself open to the charge of nativism, nationalism, or worse, the sin of sins, nostalgia. Liberal-minded scholars would immediately protest that any idea of a homogeneous, uncontested 'Europe' dissolves under analysis. True, but just as the phenomenon of orientalism does not disappear simply because some of us have now attained a critical awareness of it, similarly a certain version of 'Europe,' reified and celebrated in the phenomenal world of everyday relationships of power as the scene of the birth of the modern, continues to dominate the discourse of history. Analysis does not make it go away.

That Europe works as a silent referent in historical knowledge itself becomes obvious in a highly ordinary way. There are at least two everyday symptoms of the subalternity of non-Western, third-world histories. Third-world historians feel a need to refer to works in European history; historians of Europe do not feel any need to reciprocate. Whether it is an Edward Thompson, a Le Roy Ladurie, a George Duby, a Carlo Ginzburg, a Lawrence Stone, a Robert Darnton, or a Natalie Davis – to take but a few names at random from our contemporary world – the 'greats' and the models of the historian's enterprise are always at least culturally 'European.' 'They' produce their work in relative ignorance of non-Western histories, and this does not seem to affect the quality of their work. This is a gesture, however, that 'we' cannot return. We cannot even afford an equality or symmetry of ignorance at this level without taking the risk of appearing 'old-fashioned' or 'outdated.'

The problem, I may add in parenthesis, is not particular to historians. An unselfconscious but nevertheless blatant example of this 'inequality of ignorance' in literary studies, for example, is the following sentence on Salman Rushdie from a recent text on postmodernism: 'Though Saleem Sinai [of *Midnight's Children*] narrates in English ... his intertexts for both writing history and writing fiction are doubled: they are, on the one hand, from Indian legends, films, and literature and, on the other, from the West – *The Tin Drum, Tristram Shandy, One Hundred Years of Solitude*, and so on.'[3] It is interesting to note how this sentence teases out only those references that are from 'the West.' The author is under no obligation here to be able to name with any authority and specificity the 'Indian' allusions that make Rushdie's intertexuality 'doubled.' This ignorance, shared and unstated, is part of the assumed compact that makes it 'easy' to include Rushdie in English department offerings on postcolonialism.

This problem of asymmetric ignorance is not simply a matter of 'cultural cringe' (to let my Australian self speak) on our part or of cultural arrogance on the part of the European historian. These problems exist but can be relatively easily addressed. Nor do I mean to take anything away from the achievements of the historians I mentioned. Our footnotes bear rich testimony to the insights we have derived from their knowledge and creativity. The dominance of 'Europe' as the subject of all histories is a part of a much more profound theoretical condition under which historical knowledge is produced in the third world. This condition ordinarily expresses itself in a paradoxical manner. It is this paradox that I shall describe as the second everyday symptom of our subalternity, and it refers to the very nature of social science pronouncements themselves.

For generations now, philosophers and thinkers shaping the nature of social science have produced theories embracing the entirety of humanity. As we well know, these statements have been produced in relative, and sometimes absolute, ignorance of the majority of humankind – i.e., those living in non-Western cultures. This in itself is not paradoxical, for the more self-conscious of European philosophers have always sought theoretically to justify this stance. The everyday paradox of third-world social science is that *we* find these theories, in spite of their inherent ignorance of 'us,' eminently useful in understanding our societies. What allowed the modern European sages to develop such clairvoyance with regard to societies of which they were empirically ignorant? Why cannot we, once again, return the gaze?

There is an answer to this question in the writings of philosophers who have read into European history an entelechy of universal reason, if we regard such philosophy as the self-consciousness of social science. Only 'Europe,' the argument would appear to be, is *theoretically* (i.e., at the level of the fundamental categories that shape historical thinking) knowable; all other histories are matters of empirical research that fleshes out a theoretical skeleton which is substantially 'Europe.' There is one version of this argument in Edmund Husserl's Vienna lecture of 1935, where he proposed that the fundamental difference between 'oriental philosophies' (more specifically, Indian and Chinese) and 'Greek-European science' (or as he added, 'universally speaking: philosophy') was the capacity of the latter to produce 'absolute theoretical insights,' that is *'theoria'* (universal science), while the former retained a 'practical-universal,' and hence 'mythical-religious,' character. This 'practical-universal' philosophy was directed to the world in a 'naive' and 'straightforward' manner, while the world presented itself as a 'thematic' to *theoria*, making possible a praxis 'whose aim is to elevate mankind through universal scientific reason.'[4]

A rather similar epistemological proposition underlies Marx's use of categories like 'bourgeois' and 'prebourgeois' or 'capital' and 'precapital.' The prefix *pre* here signifies a relationship that is both chronological and theoretical. The coming of the bourgeois or capitalist society, Marx argues in the *Grundrisse* and elsewhere, gives rise for the first time to a history that can be apprehended through a philosophical and universal category, 'capital.' History becomes, for the first time, *theoretically* knowable. All past histories are now to be known (theoretically, that is) from the vantage point of this category, that is in terms of their differences from it. Things reveal their categorical essence only when they reach their fullest development, or as Marx put it in that famous aphorism of the *Grundrisse*: 'Human anatomy contains the key to the anatomy of the ape.'[5] The category 'capital,' as I have discussed elsewhere, contains within itself the legal subject of Enlightenment thought.[6] Not surprisingly, Marx said in that very Hegelian first chapter of *Capital*, vol. 1, that the secret of 'capital,' the category, 'cannot be deciphered until the notion of human equality has acquired the fixity of a popular prejudice.'[7] To continue with Marx's words:

> Even the most abstract categories, despite their validity – precisely because of their abstractness – for all epochs, are nevertheless ... themselves ... a product of historical relations. Bourgeois society is the most developed and the most complex historic organization of production. The categories which express its relations, the comprehension of its structure, thereby also allow insights into the structure and the relations of production of all the vanished social formations out of whose ruins and elements it built itself up, whose partly still unconquered remnants are carried along within it, whose mere nuances have developed explicit significance within it, etc. ... The intimations of higher development among the subordinate animal species ... can be understood only after the higher development is already known. The bourgeois economy thus supplies the key to the ancient.[8]

For 'capital' or 'bourgeois,' I submit, read 'Europe.'

II

Neither Marx nor Husserl spoke – not at least in the words quoted above – in a historicist spirit. In parenthesis, we should also recall here that Marx's vision of emancipation entailed a journey beyond the rule of capital, in fact beyond the notion of juridical equality that liberalism holds so sacred. The maxim 'From each according to his ability to each according to his need' runs quite contrary to the principle of 'Equal pay for equal work,' and this is why Marx remains – the Berlin Wall notwithstanding (or not standing!) – a relevant and fundamental critic of both capitalism and liberalism and thus central to any postcolonial, postmodern project of writing history. Yet Marx's methodological/epistemological statements have not always successfully resisted historicist readings. There has always remained enough ambiguity in these statements to make possible the emergence of 'Marxist' historical narratives. These narratives turn around the theme of 'historical transition.' Most modern third-world histories are written within problematics posed by this transition narrative, of which the overriding (if often implicit) themes are those of development, modernization, capitalism.

This tendency can be located in our own work in the _Subaltern Studies_ project. My book on working-class history struggles with the problem.[9] Sumit Sarkar's (another colleague in the _Subaltern Studies_ project) _Modern India_, justifiably regarded as one of the best textbooks on Indian history written primarily for Indian universities, opens with the following sentences:

> The sixty years or so that lie between the foundation of the Indian National Congress in 1885 and the achievement of independence in August 1947 witnessed perhaps the greatest transition in our country's long history. A transition, however, which in many ways remains grievously incomplete, and it is with this central ambiguity that it seems most convenient to begin our survey.[10]

What kind of a transition was it that remained 'grievously incomplete'? Sarkar hints at the possibility of there having been several by naming three:

So many of the aspirations aroused in the course of the national struggle remained unfulfilled – the Gandhian dream of the peasant coming into his own in *Ram-rajya* [the rule of the legendary and the ideal god-king Ram], as much as the left ideals of social revolution. And as the history of independent India and Pakistan (and Bangladesh) was repeatedly to reveal, even the problems of a complete bourgeois transformation and successful capitalist development were not fully solved by the transfer of power of 1947 (p. 4).

Neither the peasant's dream of a mythical and just kingdom, nor the Left's ideal of a social[ist] revolution, nor a 'complete bourgeois transformation' – it is within these three absences, these 'grievously incomplete' scenarios that Sarkar locates the story of modern India.

It is also with a similar reference to 'absences' – the 'failure' of a history to keep an appointment with its destiny (once again an instance of the 'lazy native', shall we say?) – that we announced our project of *Subaltern Studies*:

> It is the study of this *historic failure of the nation to come to its own*, a failure due to the *inadequacy* [emphasis added] of the bourgeoisie as well as of the working class to lead it into a decisive victory over colonialism and a bourgeois-democratic revolution of the classic nineteenth-century type ... or [of the] 'new democracy' [type] – *it is the study of this failure which constitutes the central problematic of the historiography of colonial India.*[11]

The tendency to read Indian history in terms of a lack, an absence, or an incompleteness that translates into 'inadequacy' is obvious in these excerpts. As a trope, however, it is an ancient one, going back to the hoary beginnings of colonial rule in India. The British conquered and represented the diversity of 'Indian' pasts through a homogenizing narrative of transition from a 'medieval' period to 'modernity.' The terms have changed with time. The 'medieval' was once called 'despotic' and the 'modern,' 'the rule of law.' 'Feudal/capitalist' has been a later variant.

When it was first formulated in colonial histories of India, this transition narrative was an unashamed celebration of the imperialist's capacity for violence and conquest. To give only one example among the many available, Alexander Dow's *History of Hindostan*, first published in three volumes between 1770 and 1772, was dedicated to the king with a candor characteristic of the eighteenth century when one did not need a Michel Foucault to uncover the connection between violence and knowledge: 'The success of Your Majesty's arms,' said Dow, 'has laid open the East to the researches of the curious.'[12] Underscoring this connection between violence and modernity, Dow added:

> The British nation have become the conquerors of Bengal and they ought to extend some part of their fundamental jurisprudence to secure their conquest. ... The sword is our tenure. It is an absolute conquest, and it is so considered by the world (vol. 1, p. cxxxviii).

This 'fundamental jurisprudence' was the 'rule of law' that contrasted, in Dow's narrative, with a past rule that was 'arbitrary' and 'despotic.' In a further gloss Dow explained that 'despotism' did not refer to a 'government of mere caprice and whim,' for he knew enough history to know that that was not true of India. Despotism was the opposite of English constitutional government; it was a system where 'the legislative, the judicial and the executive power [were] vested in the prince.' This was the past of unfreedom. With the establishment of British power, the Indian was to be made a legal subject, ruled by a government open to the pressures of private property ('the foundation of public prosperity,' said Dow) and public opinion, and supervised by a judiciary where 'the distributers of justice ought to be independent of everything but law [as] otherwise the officer [the judge] becomes a tool of oppression in the hands of despotism' (vol. 1, pp. xcv, cl, cxl–cxli).

In the nineteenth and twentieth centuries, generations of elite Indian nationalists found their subject positions, as nationalists, within this transition narrative that, at various times and depending on one's ideology, hung the tapestry of 'Indian history' between the two poles of the homologous sets of oppositions, despotic/constitutional, medieval/modern, feudal/capitalist. Within this narrative shared between imperialist and nationalist imaginations, the 'Indian' was always a figure of lack. There was always, in other words, room in this story for characters who embodied, on behalf of the native, the theme of 'inadequacy' or 'failure.' Dow's recommendation of a 'rule of law' for Bengal/India came with the paradoxical assurance (to the British) that there was no danger of such a rule 'infusing' in the natives 'a spirit of freedom':

> To make the natives of the fertile soil of Bengal free, is beyond the power of political arrangement. ... Their religion, their institutions, their manners, the very disposition of their minds, form them for passive obedience. To give them property would only bind them with stronger ties to our interests, and make them our subjects; or if the British nation prefers the name – more our slaves (vol. 1, pp. cxl–cxli).

We do not need to be reminded that this would remain the cornerstone of imperial ideology for many years to come – subjecthood but not citizenship, as the native was never adequate to the latter – and would eventually become a strand of liberal theory itself.[13] This was of course where nationalists differed. For Rammohun Roy as for Bankimchandra Chattopadhyay, two of India's most prominent nationalist intellectuals of the nineteenth century, British rule was a necessary period of tutelage that Indians had to undergo in order to prepare precisely for what the British denied but extolled as the end of all history: citizenship and the nation state. Years later, in 1951, an 'unknown' Indian who successfully sold his 'obscurity' dedicated the story of his life thus:

> To the memory of the
> British Empire in India
> Which conferred subjecthood on us
> But withheld citizenship;
> To which yet
> Everyone of us threw out the challenge
> 'Civis Britannicus Sum'
> Because
> All that was good and living
> Within us

Was made, shaped, and quickened
By the same British Rule.[14]

In nationalist versions of this narrative, as Partha Chatterjee has shown, it was the peasants and the workers, the subaltern classes, who were given to bear the cross of 'inadequacy,' for, according to this version, it was they who needed to be educated out of their ignorance, parochialism, or, depending on your preference, false consciousness.[15] Even today the Anglo-Indian word *communalism* refers to those who allegedly fail to measure up to the 'secular' ideals of citizenship.

That British rule put in place the practices, institutions, and discourse of bourgeois individualism in the Indian soil is undeniable. Early expressions – that is, before the beginnings of nationalism – of this desire to be a 'legal subject' make it clear that to Indians in the 1830s and 1840s to be a 'modern individual' was to become a 'European.' *The Literary Gleaner*, a magazine in colonial Calcutta, ran the following poem in 1842, written in English by a Bengali schoolboy eighteen years of age. The poem apparently was inspired by the sight of ships leaving the coast of Bengal 'for the glorious shores of England':

Oft like a sad bird I sigh
To leave this land, though mine own land it be;
Its green robed meads, – gay flowers and cloudless sky
Though passing fair, have but few charms for me.
For I have dreamed of climes more bright and free
Where virtue dwells and heaven-born liberty
Makes even the lowest happy; – where the eye
Doth sicken not to see man bend the knee
To sordid interest: – climes where science thrives,
And genius doth receive her guerdon meet;
Where man in all his truest glory lives,
And nature's face is exquisitely sweet:
For those fair climes I heave the impatient sigh,
There let me live and there let me die.[16]

In its echoes of Milton and seventeenth-century English radicalism, this is obviously a piece of colonial pastiche.[17] Michael Madhusudan Dutt, the young Bengali author of this poem, eventually realized the impossibility of being 'European' and returned to Bengali literature to become one of our finest poets. Later Indian nationalists, however, abandoned such abject desire to be 'Europeans' themselves. Nationalist thought was premised precisely on the assumed universality of the project of becoming individuals, on the assumption that 'individual rights' and abstract 'equality' were universals that could find home anywhere in the world, that one could be both an 'Indian' and a 'citizen' at the same time. We shall soon explore some of the contradictions of this project.

Many of the public and private rituals of modern individualism became visible in India in the nineteenth century. One sees this, for instance, in the sudden flourishing in this period of the four basic genres that help express the modern self: the novel, the biography, the autobiography, and history.[18] Along with these came modern industry, technology, medicine, a quasibourgeois (though colonial) legal system supported by a state that nationalism was to take over and make its own. The transition narrative that I have been discussing underwrote, and was in turn underpinned by, these institutions. To think this narrative was to think these institutions at the apex of which sat the modern state,[19] and to think the modern or the nation state was to think a history whose theoretical subject was Europe. Gandhi realized this as early as 1909. Referring to the Indian nationalists' demands for more railways, modern medicine, and bourgeois law, he cannily remarked in his book *Hind Swaraj* that this was to 'make India English' or, as he put it, to have 'English rule without the Englishman.'[20] This 'Europe,' as Michael Madhusudan Dutt's youthful and naive poetry shows, was of course nothing but a piece of fiction told to the colonized by the colonizer in the very process of fabricating colonial domination.[21] Gandhi's critique of this 'Europe' is compromised on many points by his nationalism, and I do not intend to fetishize his text. But I find his gesture useful in developing the problematic of nonmetropolitan histories.

III

I shall now return to the themes of 'failure,' 'lack,' and 'inadequacy' that so ubiquitously characterize the speaking subject of 'Indian' history. As in the practice of the insurgent peasants of colonial India, the first step in a critical effort must arise from a gesture of inversion.[22] Let us begin from where the transition narrative ends and read 'plenitude' and 'creativity' where this narrative has made us read 'lack' and 'inadequacy.'

According to the fable of their constitution, Indians today are all 'citizens.' The constitution embraces almost a classically liberal definition of citizenship. If the modern state and the modern individual, the citizen, are but the two inseparable sides of the same phenomenon, as William Connolly argues in *Political Theory and Modernity*, it would appear that the end of history is in sight for us in India.[23] This modern individual, however, whose political/public life is lived in citizenship, is also supposed to have an interiorized 'private' self that pours out incessantly in diaries, letters, autobiographies, novels, and, of course, in what we say to our analysts. The bourgeois individual is not born until one discovers the pleasures of privacy. But this is a very special kind of 'private' – it is, in fact, a deferred 'public,' for this bourgeois private, as Jürgen Habermas has reminded us, is 'always already oriented to an audience [*Publikum*].'[24]

Indian public life may mimic on paper the bourgeois legal fiction of citizenship – the fiction is usually performed as a farce in India – but what about the bourgeois private and its history? Anyone who has tried to write 'French' social history with Indian material would know how impossibly difficult the task is.[25] It is not that the form of the bourgeois private did not come with European rule. There have been, since the middle of the nineteenth century, Indian novels, diaries, letters, and autobiographies, but they seldom yield pictures of an endlessly interiorized subject. Our autobiographies are remarkably 'public' (with constructions of public life that are not necessarily modern) when written by men, and they tell the story of the extended family when written by women.[26] In any case, autobiographies in the confessional mode are notable for their absence. The single paragraph (out of 963 pages) that Nirad Chaudhuri spends on describing the experience of his wedding night in the second volume of his celebrated and prize-winning autobiography is as good an example as any other and is worth quoting at some length. I should explain that this was an arranged marriage (Bengal, 1932), and Chaudhuri was anxious lest his wife should not appreciate his newly acquired but unaffordably expensive hobby of buying records of Western classical music. Our reading of Chaudhuri is handicapped in part by our lack of knowledge of the intertextuality of his prose – there may have been at work, for instance, an imbibed puritanical revulsion against revealing 'too much.' Yet the passage remains a telling exercise in the construction of memory, for it is about what Chaudhuri 'remembers' and 'forgets' of his 'first night's experience.' He screens off intimacy with expressions like 'I do not remember' or 'I do not know how' (not to mention the very Freudian 'making a clean breast of'), and this self-constructed veil is no doubt a part of the self that speaks:

> I was terribly uneasy at the prospect of meeting as wife a girl who was a complete stranger to me, and when she was brought in ... and left standing before me I had nothing to say. I saw only a very shy smile on her face, and timidly she came and sat by my side on the edge of the bed. I do not know how after that both of us drifted to the pillows, to lie down side by side. [Chaudhuri adds in a footnote: 'Of course, fully dressed. We Hindus ... consider both extremes – fully clad and fully nude – to be modest, and everything inbetween as grossly immodest. No decent man wants his wife to be an *allumeuse*.'] Then the first words were exchanged. She took up one of my arms, felt it and said: 'You are so thin. I shall take good care of you.' I did not thank her, and I do not remember that beyond noting the words I even felt touched. The horrible suspense about European music had reawakened in my mind, and I decided to make a clean breast of it at once and look the sacrifice, if it was called for, straight in the face and begin romance on such terms as were offered to me. I asked her timidly after a while: 'Have you listened to any European music?' She shook her head to say 'No.' Nonetheless, I took another chance and this time asked: 'Have you heard the name of a man called Beethoven?' She nodded and signified 'Yes.' I was reassured, but not wholly satisfied. So I asked yet again: 'Can you spell the name?' She said slowly: 'B, E, E, T, H, O, V, E, N.' I felt very encouraged ... and [we] dozed off.[27]

The desire to be 'modern' screams out of every sentence in the two volumes of Chaudhuri's autobiography. His legendary name now stands for the cultural history of Indo-British encounter. Yet in the 1500-odd pages that he has written in English about his life, this is the only passage where the narrative of Chaudhuri's participation in public life and literary circles is interrupted to make room for something approaching the intimate. How do we read this text, this self-making of an Indian male who was second to no one in his ardor for the public life of the citizen, yet who seldom, if ever, reproduced in writing the other side of the modern citizen, the interiorized private self unceasingly reaching out for an audience? Public without private? Yet another instance of the 'incompleteness' of bourgeois transformation in India?

These questions are themselves prompted by the transition narrative that in turn situates the modern individual at the very end of history. I do not wish to confer on Chaudhuri's autobiography a representativeness it may not have. Women's writings, as I have already said, are different, and scholars have just begun to explore the world of autobiographies in Indian history. But if one result of European imperialism in India was to introduce the modern state and the idea of the nation with their attendant discourse of 'citizenship,' which, by the very idea of 'the citizen's rights' (i.e., 'the rule of law'), splits the figure of the modern individual into 'public' and 'private' parts of the self (as the young Marx once pointed out in his *On the Jewish Question*), these themes have existed – in contestation, alliance, and miscegenation – with other narratives of the self and community that do not look to the state/citizen bind as the ultimate construction of sociality.[28] This as such will not be disputed, but my point goes further. It is that these other constructions of self and community, while documentable in themselves, will never enjoy the privilege of providing the metanarratives or teleologies (assuming that there cannot be a narrative without at least an implicit teleology) of our histories. This is so partly because these narratives often themselves bespeak an antihistorical consciousness; that is, they entail subject positions and configurations of memory that challenge and undermine the subject that speaks in the name of history. 'History' is precisely the site where the struggle goes on to appropriate, on behalf of the modern (my hyperreal Europe), these other collocations of memory.

To illustrate these propositions, I will now discuss a fragment of this contested history in which the modern private and the modern individual were embroiled in colonial India.[29]

IV

What I present here are the outlines, so to speak, of a chapter in the history of bourgeois domesticity in colonial Bengal. The material – in the main texts produced in Bengali between 1850 and 1920 for teaching women that very Victorian subject, 'domestic science' – relates to the Bengali Hindu middle class, the *bhadralok* or 'respectable people.' British rule instituted into Indian life the trichotomous ideational division on which modern political structures rest, e.g., the state, civil society, and the (bourgeois) family. It was therefore not surprising that ideas relating to bourgeois domesticity, privacy, and individuality should come to India via British rule. What I want to highlight here, however, through the example of the *bhadralok*, are certain cultural operations by which the 'Indians' challenged and modified these received ideas in such a way as to put in question two fundamental tenets underlying the idea of 'modernity' – the nuclear family based on companionate marriage and the secular, historical construction of time.

As Meredith Borthwick, Ghulam Murshid, and other scholars have shown, the eighteenth-century European idea of 'civilization' culminated, in early nineteenth-century India, in a full-blown imperialist critique of Indian/Hindu domestic life, which was now held to be inferior to what became mid-Victorian ideals of bourgeois domesticity.[30] The 'condition of women' question in nineteenth-century India was part of that critique, as were the ideas of the 'modern' individual, 'freedom,' 'equality,' and 'rights.' In passages remarkable for their combination of egalitarianism and orientalism, James Mill's *The History of British India* (1817) joined together the thematic of the family/nation and a teleology of 'freedom':

> The condition of women is one of the most remarkable circumstances in the manners of nations. ... The history of uncultivated nations uniformly represents the women as in a state of abject slavery, from which they slowly emerge as civilisation advances. ... As society refines upon its enjoyments ... the condition of the weaker sex is gradually improved, till they associate on equal terms with the men, and occupy the place of voluntary and useful coadjutors. A state of dependence more strict and humiliating than that which is ordained for the weaker sex among the Hindus cannot be easily conceived.[31]

As is well known, the Indian middle classes generally felt answerable to this charge. From the early nineteenth century onward a movement developed in Bengal (and other regions) to reform 'women's conditions' and to give them formal education. Much of this discourse on women's education was emancipationist in that it spoke the language of 'freedom,' 'equality,' and 'awakening,' and was strongly influenced by Ruskinian ideals and idealization of bourgeois domesticity.[32] If one looks on this history as part of the history of the modern individual in India, an interesting feature emerges. It is that in this literature on women's education certain terms, after all, were much more vigorously debated than others. There was, for example, a degree of consensus over the desirability of domestic 'discipline' and 'hygiene' as practices reflective of a state of modernity, but the word *freedom*, yet another important term in the rhetoric of the modern, hardly ever acted as the register of such a social consensus. It was a passionately disputed word, and we would be wrong to assume that the passions reflected a simple and straightforward battle of the sexes. The word was assimilated to the nationalist need to construct cultural boundaries that supposedly separated the 'European' from the 'Indian.' The dispute over this word was thus central to the discursive strategies through which a subject position was created enabling the 'Indian' to speak. It is this subject position that I want to discuss here in some detail.

What the Bengali literature on women's education played out was a battle between a nationalist construction of a cultural norm of the patriarchal, patrilocal, patrilineal, extended family and the ideal of the patriarchal, bourgeois nuclear family that was implicit in the European/imperialist/universalist discourse on the 'freedoms' of individualism, citizenship, and civil society.[33] The themes of 'discipline' and 'order' were critical in shaping nationalist imaginings of aesthetics and power. 'Discipline' was seen as the key to the power of the colonial (i.e., modern) state, but it required certain procedures for redefining the self. The British were powerful, it was argued, because they were disciplined, orderly, and punctual in every detail of their lives, and this was made possible by the education of 'their' women who brought the virtues of discipline into the home. The 'Indian' home, a colonial construct, now fared badly in nationalist writings on modern domesticity. To quote a Bengali text on women's education from 1877:

> The house of any civilised European is like the abode of gods. Every household object is clean, set in its proper place and decorated; nothing seems unclean or smells foul. ... It is as if [the goddess of] order [*srinkhala*, 'order, discipline'; *srinkhal*, 'chains'] had become manifest to please the [human] eye. In the middle of the room would be a covered table with a bouquet of flowers on it, while around it would be [a few] chairs nicely arranged [with] everything sparkling clean. But enter a house in our country and you would feel as if you had been transported there by your destiny to make you atone for all the sins of your life. [A mass of] cowdung torturing the senses ... dust in the air, a growing heap of ashes, flies buzzing around ... a little boy urinating into the ground and putting the mess back into his mouth. ... The whole place is dominated by a stench that seems to be running free. ... There is no order anywhere, the household objects are so unclean that they only evoke disgust.[34]

This self-division of the colonial subject, the double movement of recognition by which it both knows its 'present' as the site of disorder and yet moves away from this space in desiring a discipline that can only exist in an imagined but 'historical' future, is a rehearsal, in the context of the discussion of the bourgeois domestic in colonial India, of the transition narrative we have encountered before. A historical construction of temporality (medieval/modern, separated by historical time), in other words, is precisely the axis along which the colonial subject splits itself. Or to put it differently, this split *is* what is history; writing history is performing this split over and over again.

The desire for order and discipline in the domestic sphere thus may be seen as having been a correlate of the nationalist, modernizing desire for a similar discipline in the public sphere, that is for a rule of law enforced by the state. It is beyond the scope of this paper to pursue this point further, but the connection between personal discipline and discipline in public life was to reveal itself in what the nationalists wrote about domestic hygiene and public health. The connection is recognizably modernist, and it is what the Indian modern shared with the European modern.[35] What I want to attend to, however, are the differences between the two. And this is where I turn to the other important aspect of the European modern, the rhetoric of 'freedom' and 'equality.'

The argument about 'freedom' – in the texts under discussion – was waged around the question of the Victorian ideals of the companionate marriage, that is, over the question as to whether or not the wife should also be a friend to the husband. Nothing threatened the ideal of the Bengali/Indian extended family (or the exalted position of the mother-in-law within that structure) more than this idea, wrapped up in notions of bourgeois privacy, that the wife was also to be a friend or, to put it differently, that the woman was now to be a modern individual. I must mention here that the modern individual, who asserts his/her individuality over the claims of the joint or extended family, almost always appears in nineteenth- and early twentieth-century Bengali literature as an embattled figure, often the subject of ridicule and scorn in the same Bengali fiction and essays that otherwise extolled the virtues of discipline and scientific rationality in personal and public lives. This irony had many expressions. The most well-known Bengali fictional character who represents this moral censure of modern individuality is Nimchand Datta in Dinabandhu Mitra's play *Sadhabar ekadashi* (1866). Nimchand, who is English-educated, quotes Shakespeare, Milton, or Locke at the slightest opportunity and uses this education arrogantly to ignore his duties toward his extended family, finds his nemeses in alcohol and debauchery. This metonymic relationship between the love of 'modern'/English education (which stood for the romantic individual in nineteenth-century Bengal) and the slippery path of alcohol is suggested in the play by a conversation between Nimchand and a Bengali official of the colonial bureaucracy, a Deputy Magistrate. Nimchand's supercilious braggadocio about his command of the English language quickly and inevitably runs to the subject of drinks (synonymous, in middle-class Bengali culture of the period, with absolute decadence):

> I read English, write English, speechify in English, think in English, dream in English – mind you, it's no child's play – now tell me, my good fellow, what would you like to drink? – Claret for ladies, sherry for men and brandy for heroes.[36]

A similar connection between the modern, 'free' individual and selfishness was made in the literature on women's education. The construction was undisguisedly nationalist (and patriarchal). *Freedom* was used to mark a difference between what was 'Indian' and what was 'European/English.' The ultra-free woman acted like a *memsahib* (European woman), selfish and shameless. As Kundamala Devi, a woman writing for a women's magazine *Bamabodhini patrika*, said in 1870: 'Oh dear ones! If you have acquired real knowledge, then give no place in your heart to *memsahib*-like behaviour. This is not becoming in a Bengali housewife.'[37] The idea of 'true modesty' was mobilized to build up this picture of the 'really' Bengali woman.[38] Writing in 1920, Indira Devi dedicated her *Narir ukti* [A Woman Speaks] – interestingly enough, a defense of modern Bengali womanhood against criticisms by (predominantly) male writers – to generations of ideal Bengali women whom she thus described: 'Unaffected by nature, of pleasant speech, untiring in their service [to others], oblivious of their own pleasures, [while] moved easily by the suffering of others, and capable of being content with very little.'[39]

This model of the 'modern' Bengali/Indian woman – educated enough to appreciate the modern regulations of the body and the state but yet 'modest' enough to be unselfassertive and unselfish – was tied to the debates on 'freedom.' 'Freedom' in the West, several authors argued, meant *jathechhachar*, to do as one pleased, the right to self-indulgence. In India, it was said, *freedom* meant freedom from the ego, the capacity to serve and obey voluntarily. Notice how the terms *freedom* and *slavery* have changed positions in the following quote:

To be able to subordinate oneself to others and to *dharma* [duty/moral order/proper acton] ... to free the soul from the slavery of the senses, are the first tasks of human freedom. ... That is why in Indian families boys and girls are subordinate to the parents, wife to the husband and to the parents-in-law, the disciple to the guru, the student to the teacher ... the king to *dharma* ... the people to the king, [and one's] dignity and prestige to [that of] the community [*samaj*].[40]

There was an ironical twist to this theorizing that needs to be noted. Quite clearly, this theory of 'freedom-in-obedience' did not apply to the domestic servants who were sometimes mentioned in this literature as examples of the 'truly' unfree, the nationalist point being that (European) observers commenting on the unfree status of Indian women often missed (so some nationalists argued) this crucial distinction between the housewife and the domestic. Obviously, the servants were not yet included in the India of the nationalist imagination.

Thus went the Bengali discourse on modern domesticity in a colonial period when the rise of a civil society and a quasimodern state had already inserted the modern questions of 'public' and 'private' into middle-class Bengali lives. The received bourgeois ideas about domesticity and connections between the domestic and the national were modified here in two significant ways. One strategy, as I have sought to demonstrate, was to contrapose the cultural norm of the patriarchal extended family to the bourgeois patriarchal ideals of the companionate marriage, to oppose the new patriarchy with a redefined version of the old one(s). Thus was fought the idea of the modern private. The other strategy, equally significant, was to mobilize, on behalf of the extended family, forms and figurations of collective memory that challenged, albeit ambiguously, the seemingly absolute separation of 'sacred' and 'secular' time on which the very modern ('European') idea of history was/is based.[41] The figure of the 'truly educated,' 'truly modest,' and 'truly Indian' woman is invested, in this discussion of women's education, with a sacred authority by subordinating the question of domestic life to religious ideas of female auspiciousness that joined the heavenly with the mundane in a conceptualization of time that could be only antihistorical. The truly modern housewife, it was said, would be so auspicious as to mark the eternal return of the cosmic principle embodied in the goddess Lakshmi, the goddess of domestic well-being by whose grace the extended family (and clan, and hence, by extending the sentiment, the nation, *Bharatlakshmi*) lived and prospered. Thus we read in a contemporary pamphlet: 'Women are the Lakshmis of the community. If they undertake to improve themselves in the sphere of *dharma* and knowledge ... there will be an automatic improvement in [the quality of] social life.'[42] Lakshmi, regarded as the Hindu god Vishnu's wife by about A.D. 400, has for long been held up in popular Hinduism, and in the everyday pantheism of Hindu families, as the model of the Hindu wife, united in complete harmony with her husband (and his family) through willful submission, loyalty, devotion, and chastity.[43] When women did not follow her ideals, it was said, the (extended) family and the family line were destroyed by the spirit of Alakshmi (not-Lakshmi), the dark and malevolent reverse of the Lakshmi principle. While women's education and the idea of discipline as such were seldom opposed in this discourse regarding the modern individual in colonial Bengal, the line was drawn at the point where modernity and the demand for bourgeois privacy threatened the power and the pleasures of the extended family.

There is no question that the speaking subject here is nationalist and patriarchal, employing the clichéd orientalist categories, 'the East' and 'the West.'[44] However, of importance to us are the two denials on which this particular moment of subjectivity rests: the denial, or at least contestation, of the bourgeois private and, equally important, the denial of historical time by making the family a site where the sacred and the secular blended in a perpetual reenactment of a principle that was heavenly and divine.

The cultural space the antihistorical invoked was by no means harmonious or nonconflictual, though nationalist thought of necessity tried to portray it to be so. The antihistorical norms of the patriarchal extended family, for example, could only have had a contested existence, contested both by women's struggles and by those of the subaltern classes. But these struggles did not necessarily follow any lines that would allow us to construct emancipatory narratives by putting the 'patriarchals' clearly on one side and the 'liberals' on the other. The history of modern 'Indian' individuality is caught up in too many contradictions to lend itself to such a treatment.

I do not have the space here to develop the point, so I will make do with one example. It comes from the autobiography of Ramabai Ranade, the wife of the famous nineteenth-century social reformer from the Bombay Presidency, M. G. Ranade. Ramabai Ranade's struggle for self-respect was in part against the 'old' patriarchal order of the extended family and for the 'new' patriarchy of companionate marriage, which her reform-minded husband saw as the most civilized form of the conjugal bond. In pursuit of this ideal, Ramabai began to share her husband's commitment to public life and would often take part (in the 1880s) in public gatherings and deliberations of male and female social reformers. As she herself says: 'It was at these meetings that I learnt what a meeting was and how one should conduct oneself at one.'[45] Interestingly, however, one of the chief sources of opposition to Ramabai's efforts were (apart from men) the other women in the family. There is of course no doubt that they, her mother-in-law and her husband's sisters, spoke for the old patriarchal extended family. But it is quite instructive to listen to their voices (as they come across through Ramabai's text, for they also spoke for their own sense of self-respect and their own forms of struggle against men:

> You should not really go to these meetings [they said to Ramabai]. ... Even if the men want you to do these things, you should ignore them. You need not say no: but after all, you need not do it. They will then give up, out of sheer boredom. ... You are outdoing even the European women.

Or this:

> It is she [Ramabai] herself who loves this frivolousness of going to meetings. Dada [Mr. Ranade] is not at all so keen about it. But should she not have some sense of proportion of how much the women should actually do? If men tell you to do a

hundred things, women should take up ten at the most. After all men do not understand these practical things! ... The good woman [in the past] never turned frivolous like this. ... That is why this large family ... could live together in a respectable way. ... But now it is all so different! If Dada suggests one thing, this woman is prepared to do three. How can we live with any sense of self-respect then and how can we endure all this? (pp. 84–5)

These voices, combining the contradictory themes of nationalism, of patriarchal clan-based ideology, of women's struggles against men, and opposed at the same time to friendship between husbands and wives, remind us of the deep ambivalences that marked the trajectory of the modern private and bourgeois individuality in colonial India. Yet historians manage, by maneuvers reminiscent of the old 'dialectical' card trick called 'negation of negation,' to deny a subject position to this voice of ambivalence. The evidence of what I have called 'the denial of the bourgeois private and of the historical subject' is acknowledged but subordinated in their accounts to the supposedly higher purpose of making Indian history look like yet another episode in the universal and (in their view, the ultimately victorious) march of citizenship, of the nation state, of themes of human emancipation spelled out in the course of the European Enlightenment and after. It is the figure of the citizen that speaks through these histories. And so long as that happens, my hyperreal Europe will continually return to dominate the stories we tell. 'The modern' will then continue to be understood, as Meaghan Morris has so aptly put it in discussing her own Australian context, 'as a *known history*, something which has *already happened elsewhere*, and which is to be reproduced, mechanically or otherwise, with a local content.' This can only leave us with a task of reproducing what Morris calls 'the project of positive unoriginality.'[46]

V

Yet the 'originality' – I concede that this is a bad term – of the idioms through which struggles have been conducted in the Indian subcontinent has often been in the sphere of the nonmodern. One does not have to subscribe to the ideology of clannish patriarchy, for instance, to acknowledge that the metaphor of the sanctified and patriarchal extended family was one of the most important elements in the cultural politics of Indian nationalism. In the struggle against British rule, it was frequently the use of this idiom – in songs, poetry, and other forms of nationalist mobilization – that allowed 'Indians' to fabricate a sense of community and to retrieve for themselves a subject position from which to address the British. I will illustrate this with an example from the life of Gandhi, 'the father of the nation,' to highlight the political importance of this cultural move on the part of the 'Indian.'

My example refers to the year 1946. There had been ghastly riots between the Hindus and the Muslims in Calcutta over the impending partition of the country into India and Pakistan. Gandhi was in the city, fasting in protest over the behavior of his own people. And here is how an Indian intellectual recalls the experience:

Men would come back from their offices in the evening and find food prepared by the family [meaning the womenfolk] ready for them; but soon it would be revealed that the women of the home had not eaten the whole day. They [apparently] had not felt hungry. Pressed further, the wife or the mother would admit that they could not understand how they could go on [eating] when Gandhiji was dying for their own crimes. Restaurants and amusement centres did little business; some of them were voluntarily closed by the proprietors. ... The nerve of feeling had been restored; the pain began to be felt. ... Gandhiji knew when to start the redemptive process.[47]

We do not have to take this description literally, but the nature of the community imagined in these lines is clear. It blends, in Gayatri Spivak's words, 'the feeling of community that belongs to national links and political organizations' with 'that other feeling of community whose structural model is the [clan or the extended] family.'[48] Colonial Indian history is replete with instances where Indians arrogated subjecthood to themselves precisely by mobilizing, within the context of 'modern' institutions and sometimes on behalf of the modernizing project of nationalism, devices of collective memory that were both antihistorical and antimodern.[49] This is not to deny the capacity of 'Indians' to act as subjects endowed with what we in the universities would recognize as 'a sense of history' (what Peter Burke calls 'the renaissance of the past') but to insist at the same time that there were also contrary trends, that in the multifarious struggles that took place in colonial India, antihistorical constructions of the past often provided very powerful forms of collective memory.[50]

There is then this double bind through which the subject of 'Indian' history articulates itself. On the one hand, it is both the subject and the object of modernity, because it stands for an assumed unity called the 'Indian people' that is always split into two – a modernizing elite and a yet-to-be-modernized peasantry. As such a split subject, however, it speaks from within a meta-narrative that celebrates the nation state; and of this metanarrative the theoretical subject can only be a hyperreal 'Europe,' a 'Europe' constructed by the tales that both imperialism and nationalism have told the colonized. The mode of self-representation that the 'Indian' can adopt here is what Homi Bhabha has justly called 'mimetic.'[51] Indian history, even in the most dedicated socialist or nationalist hands, remains a mimicry of a certain 'modern' subject of 'European' history and is bound to represent a sad figure of lack and failure. The transition narrative will always remain 'grievously incomplete.'

On the other hand, maneuvers are made within the space of the mimetic – all therefore within the project called 'Indian' history – to represent the 'difference' and the 'originality' of the 'Indian,' and it is in this cause that the antihistorical devices of memory and the antihistorical 'histories' of the subaltern classes are appropriated. Thus peasant/worker constructions of 'mythical' kingdoms and 'mythical' pasts/futures find a place in texts designated 'Indian' history precisely through a procedure that subordinates these narratives to the rules of evidence and to the secular, linear calendar that the writing of 'history' must follow. The antihistorical, antimodern subject, therefore, cannot speak itself as 'theory' within the knowledge procedures of the university even when these knowledge procedures acknowledge and 'document' its existence. Much like Spivak's 'subaltern' (or the anthropologist's peasant who can only have a quoted existence in a larger statement that belongs to the anthropologist alone), this subject can only be spoken for and spoken of by the transition narrative that will always ultimately privilege the modern (i.e., 'Europe').[52]

So long as one operates within the discourse of 'history' produced at the institutional site of the university, it is not possible simply to walk out of the deep collusion between 'history' and the modernizing narrative(s) of citizenship, bourgeois public and private, and the nation state. 'History' as a knowledge system is firmly embedded in institutional practices that invoke the nation state at every step – witness the organization and politics of teaching, recruitment, promotions, and publication in history departments, politics that survive the occasional brave and heroic attempts by individual historians to liberate 'history' from the metanarrative of the nation state. One only has to ask, for instance: Why is history a compulsory part of education of the modern person in all countries today including those that did quite comfortably without it until as late as the eighteenth century? Why should children all over the world today have to come to terms with a subject called 'history' when we know that this compulsion is neither natural nor ancient?[53] It does not take much imagination to see that the reason for this lies in what European imperialism and third-world nationalisms have achieved together: the universalization of the nation state as the most desirable form of political community. Nation states have the capacity to enforce their truth games, and universities, their critical distance notwithstanding, are part of the battery of institutions complicit in this process. 'Economics' and 'history' are the knowledge forms that correspond to the two major institutions that the rise (and later universalization) of the bourgeois order has given to the world – the capitalist mode of production and the nation state ('history' speaking to the figure of citizen).[54] A critical historian has no choice but to negotiate this knowledge. She or he therefore needs to understand the state on its own terms, i.e., in terms of its self-justificatory narratives of citizenship and modernity. Since these themes will always take us back to the universalist propositions of 'modern' (European political philosophy – even the 'practical' science of economics that now seems 'natural' to our constructions of world systems is (theoretically) rooted in the ideas of ethics in eighteenth-century Europe[55] – a third-world historian is condemned to knowing 'Europe' as the original home of the 'modern,' whereas the 'European' historian does not share a comparable predicament with regard in the pasts of the majority of humankind. Thus follows the everyday subalternity of non-Western histories with which I began this paper.

Yet the understanding that 'we' all do 'European' history with our different and often non-European archives opens up the possibility of a politics and project of alliance between the dominant metropolitan histories and the subaltern peripheral pasts. Let us call this the project of provincializing 'Europe,' the 'Europe' that modern imperialism and (third-world) nationalism have, by their collaborative venture and violence, made universal. Philosophically, this project must ground itself in a radical critique and transcendence of liberalism (i.e., of the bureaucratic constructions of citizenship, modern state, and bourgeois privacy that classical political philosophy has produced), a ground that late Marx shares with certain moments in both poststructuralist thought and feminist philosophy. In particular, I am emboldened by Carole Pateman's courageous declaration – in her remarkable book *The Sexual Contract* – that the very conception of the modern individual belongs to patriarchal categories of thought.[56]

VI

The project of provincializing 'Europe' refers to a history that does not yet exist; I can therefore only speak of it in a programmatic manner. To forestall misunderstanding, however, I must spell out what it is *not* while outlining what it could be.

To begin with, it does not call for a simplistic, out-of-hand rejection of modernity, liberal values, universals, science, reason, grand narratives, totalizing explanations, and so on. Fredric Jameson has recently reminded us that the easy equation often made between 'a philosophical conception of totality' and 'a political practice of totalitarianism' is 'baleful.'[57] What intervenes between the two is history – contradictory, plural, and heterogeneous struggles whose outcomes are never predictable, even retrospectively, in accordance with schemas that seek to naturalize and domesticate this heterogeneity. These struggles include coercion (both on behalf of and against modernity) – physical, institutional, and symbolic violence, often dispensed with dreamy-eyed idealism – and it is this violence that plays a decisive role in the establishment of meaning, in the creation of truth regimes, in deciding, as it were, whose and which 'universal' wins. As intellectuals operating in academia, we are not neutral to these struggles and cannot pretend to situate ourselves outside of the knowledge procedures of our institutions.

The project of provincializing 'Europe' therefore cannot be a project of 'cultural relativism.' It cannot originate from the stance that the reason/ science/universals which help define Europe as the modern are simply 'culture-specific' and therefore only belong to the European cultures. For the point is not that Enlightenment rationalism is always unreasonable in itself but rather a matter of documenting how – through what historical process – its 'reason,' which was not always self-evident to everyone, has been made to look 'obvious' far beyond the ground where it originated. If a language, as has been said, is but a dialect backed up by an army, the same could be said of the narratives of 'modernity' that, almost universally today, point to a certain 'Europe' as the primary habitus of the modern.

This Europe, like 'the West,' is demonstrably an imaginary entity, but the demonstration as such does not lessen its appeal or power. The project of provincializing 'Europe' has to include certain other additional moves: 1) the recognition that Europe's acquisition of the adjective *modern* for itself is a piece of global history of which an integral part is the story of European imperialism; and 2) the understanding that this equating of a certain version of Europe with 'modernity' is not the work of Europeans alone; third-world nationalisms, as modernizing ideologies *par excellence*, have been equal part-ners in the process. I do not mean to overlook the anti-imperial moments in the careers of these nationalisms; I only underscore the point that the project of provincializing 'Europe' cannot be a nationalist, nativist, or atavistic project. In unraveling the necessary entanglement of history – a disciplined and institu-tionally regulated form of collective memory – with the grand narratives of 'rights,' 'citizenship,' the nation state, 'public' and 'private' spheres, one cannot but problematize 'India' at the same time as one dismantles 'Europe.'

The idea is to write into the history of modernity the ambivalences, contra-dictions, the use of force, and the tragedies and the ironies that attend it. That the rhetoric and the claims of (bourgeois) equality, of citizens' rights, of self-determination through a sovereign nation state have in many circumstances empowered marginal social groups in their struggles is undeniable – this recognition is indispensable to the project of *Subaltern Studies*. What effec-tively is played down, however, in histories that either implicitly or explicitly celebrate the advent of the modern state and the idea of citizenship is the repression and violence that are as instrumental in the victory of the modern as is the persuasive power of its rhetorical strategies. Nowhere is this irony – the undemocratic foundations of 'democracy' – more visible than in the history of modern medicine, public health, and personal hygiene, the discourses of which have been central in locating the body of the modern at the intersection of the public and the private (as defined by, and subject to negotiations with, the state). The triumph of this discourse, however, has always been dependent on the mobilization, on its behalf, of effective means of physical coercion. I say 'always' because this coercion is both originary/foundational (i.e., historic) as well as pandemic and quotidian. Of foundational violence, David Arnold gives a good example in a recent essay on the history of the prison in India. The coercion of the colonial prison, Arnold shows, was integral to some of the earliest and pioneering research on the medical, dietary, and demographic statistics of India, for the prison was where Indian bodies were accessible to modernizing investigators.[58] Of the coercion that continues in the names of the nation and modernity, a recent example comes from the Indian campaign to eradicate smallpox in the 1970s. Two American doctors (one of them pre-sumably of 'Indian' origin) who participated in the process thus describe their operations in a village of the Ho tribe in the Indian state of Bihar:

> In the middle of gentle Indian night, an intruder burst through the bamboo door of the simple adobe hut. He was a government vaccinator, under orders to break resistance against smallpox vaccination. Lakshmi Singh awoke screaming and scrambled to hide herself. Her husband leaped out of bed, grabbed an axe, and chased the intruder into the courtyard. Outside a squad of doctors and policemen quickly overpowered Mohan Singh. The instant he was pinned to the ground, a second vaccinator jabbed smallpox vaccine into his arm. Mohan Singh, a wiry 40-year-old leader of the Ho tribe, squirmed away from the needle, causing the

vaccination site to bleed. The government team held him until they had injected enough vaccine. ... While the two policemen rebuffed him, the rest of the team overpowered the entire family and vaccinated each in turn. Lakshmi Singh bit deep into one doctor's hand, but to no avail.[59]

There is no escaping the idealism that accompanies this violence. The subtitle of the article in question unselfconsciously reproduces both the military and the do-gooding instincts of the enterprise. It reads: 'How an army of samaritans drove smallpox from the earth.'

Histories that aim to displace a hyperreal Europe from the center toward which all historical imagination currently gravitates will have to seek out relentlessly this connection between violence and idealism that lies at the heart of the process by which the narratives of citizenship and modernity come to find a natural home in 'history.' I register a fundamental disagreement here with a position taken by Richard Rorty in an exchange with Jürgen Habermas. Rorty criticizes Habermas for the latter's conviction 'that the story of modern philosophy is an important part of the story of the democratic societies' attempts at self-reassurance.'[60] Rorty's statement follows the practice of many Europeanists who speak of the histories of these 'democratic societies' as if these were self-contained histories complete in themselves, as if the self-fashioning of the West were something that occurred only within its self-assigned geographical boundaries. At the very least Rorty ignores the role that the 'colonial theater' (both external and internal) – where the theme of 'freedom' as defined by modern political philosophy was constantly invoked in aid of the ideas of 'civilization,' 'progress,' and latterly 'development' – played in the process of engendering this 'reassurance.' The task, as I see it, will be to wrestle ideas that legitimize the modern state and its attendant institutions, in order to return to political philosophy – in the same way as suspect coins returned to their owners in an Indian bazaar – its categories whose global currency can no longer be taken for granted.[61]

And, finally – since 'Europe' cannot after all be provincialized within the institutional site of the university whose knowledge protocols will always take us back to the terrain where all contours follow that of my hyperreal Europe – the project of provincializing Europe must realize within itself its own impossibility. It therefore looks to a history that embodies this politics of despair. It will have been clear by now that this is not a call for cultural relativism or for atavistic, nativist histories. Nor is this a program for a simple rejection of modernity, which would be, in many situations, politically suicidal. I ask for a history that deliberately makes visible, within the very structure of its narrative forms, its own repressive strategies and practices, the part it plays in collusion with the narratives of citizenships in assimilating to the projects of the modern state all other possibilities of human solidarity. The politics of despair will require of such history that it lays bare to its readers the reasons why such a predicament is necessarily inescapable. This is a history that will attempt the impossible: to look toward its own death by tracing that which resists and escapes the best human effort at translation across cultural and other semiotic systems, so that the world may once again be imagined as radically heterogeneous. This, as I have said, is impossible within the knowledge protocols of academic history, for the globality of academia is not independent of the globality that the European modern has created. To attempt to provincialize this 'Europe' is to see the modern as inevitably contested, to write over the given and privileged narratives of citizenship other narratives of human connections that draw sustenance from dreamed-up pasts and futures where collectivities are defined neither by the rituals of citizenship nor by the nightmare of 'tradition' that 'modernity' creates. There are of course no (infra)structural sites where such dreams could lodge themselves. Yet they will recur so long as the themes of citizenship and the nation state dominate our narratives of historical transition, for these dreams are what the modern represses in order to be.

Notes

1 Ranajit Guha and Gayatri Chakravorty Spivak, eds., *Selected Subaltern Studies* (New York, 1988); Ronald Inden, 'Orientalist Constructions of India,' *Modern Asian Studies* 20. 3 (1986), p. 445.

2 I am indebted to Jean Baudrillard for the term *hyperreal* (see his *Simulations* [New York, 1983]), but my use differs from his.

3 Linda Hutcheon, *The Politics of Postmodernism* (London, 1989), p. 65.

4 Edmund Husserl, *The Crisis of European Sciences and Transcendental Philosophy*, trans. David Carr (Evanston, Ill., 1970), pp. 281–85. See also Wilhelm Halbfass, *India and Europe: An Essay in Understanding* (New York, 1988), pp. 167–8.

5 See the discussion in Karl Marx, *Grundrisse: Foundations of the Critique of Political Economy*, trans. Martin Nicholas (Harmondsworth, 1973), pp. 469–512; and in Marx, *Capital: A Critique of Political Economy*, 3 vols. (Moscow, 1971), vol. 3, pp. 593–613.

6 See Dipesh Chakrabarty, *Rethinking Working-Class History: Bengal, 1890–1940* (Princeton, N.J., 1989), chap. 7.

7 Marx, *Capital*, vol. 1, p. 60.

8 Marx, *Grundrisse*, p. 105.

9 See Chakrabarty, *Rethinking Working-Class History*, chap. 7, in particular.

10 Sumit Sarkar, *Modern India, 1885–1947* (Delhi, 1985), p. 1.

11 Guha and Spivak, *Selected Subaltern Studies*, p. 43. The words quoted here are Guha's. But I think they represent a sense of historiographical responsibility that is shared by all the members of the Subaltern Studies collective.

12 Alexander Dow, *History of Hindostan*, 3 vols. (London, 1812–16), dedication, vol. 1.

13 See L. T. Hobhouse, *Liberalism* (New York, 1964), pp. 26–7.

14 Nirad C. Chaudhuri, *The Autobiography of an Unknown Indian* (New York, 1989), dedication page.

15 Partha Chatterjee, *Nationalist Thought and the Colonial World: A Derivative Discourse?* (London, 1986).

16 *Mudhusudan rachanabali* [Bengali] (Calcutta, 1965), p. 449. See also Jogindranath Basu, *Michael Madhusudan Datter jibancharit* [Bengali] (Calcutta, 1978), p. 86.

17 My understanding of this poem has been enriched by discussions with Marjorie Levinson and David Bennett.

18 I am not making the claim that all of these genres necessarily emerge with bourgeois individualism. See Natalie Zemon Davis, 'Fame and Secrecy: Leon Modena's *Life as an Early Modern Autobiography*,' *History and Theory* 27 (1988), pp. 103–18; and Davis, 'Boundaries and Sense of Self in Sixteenth-Century France,' in Thomas C. Heller *et al.*, eds., *Reconstructing Individualism: Autonomy, Individuality, and the Self in Western Thought* (Stanford, Calif., 1986), pp. 53–63. See also Philippe Lejeune, *On Autobiography*, trans. Katherine Leary (Minneapolis, 1989), pp. 163–84.

19 See the chapter on Nehru in Chatterjee, *Nationalist Thought*.

20 M. K. Gandhi, *Hind Swaraj* (1909), in *Collected Works of Mahatma Gandhi*, vol. 10 (Ahmedabad, 1963), p. 15.

21 See the discussion in Gauri Viswanathan, *Masks of Conquest: Literary Studies and British Rule in India* (London, 1989), pp. 128–41, passim.

22 Ranajit Guha, *Elementary Aspects of Peasant Insurgency in Colonial India* (New Delhi, 1983), chap. 2.

23 William E. Connolly, *Political Theory and Modernity* (Oxford, 1989). See also David Bennett, 'Postmodernism and Vision: Ways of Seeing (at) the End of History,' (forthcoming).

24 Jürgen Habermas, *The Structural Transformation of the Public Sphere: An Inquiry into a Category of Bourgeois Society* (Cambridge, Mass., 1989), p. 49.

25 See Sumit Sarkar, 'Social History: Predicament and Possibilities,' in Iqbal Khan, ed., *Fresh Perspective on India and Pakistan: Essays on Economics, Politics, and Culture* (Oxford, 1985), pp. 256–74.

26 For reasons of space, I shall leave this claim here unsubstantiated, though I hope to have an opportunity to discuss it in detail elsewhere. I should qualify the statement by mentioning that in the main it refers to autobiographies published between 1850 and 1910. Once women join the public sphere in the twentieth century, their self-fashioning takes on different dimensions.

27 Nirad C. Chaudhuri, *Thy Hand, Great Anarch!: India, 1921–1952* (London, 1987), pp. 350–51.

28 See Karl Marx, *On the Jewish Question*, in *Early Writings* (Harmondsworth, 1975), pp. 215–22.

29 For a more detailed treatment of what follows, see my paper 'Colonial Rule and the Domestic Order,' to be published in David Arnold and David Hardiman, eds., *Subaltern Studies*, vol. 8.

30 Meredith Borthwick, *The Changing Role of Women in Bengal, 1849–1905* (Princeton, N. J., 1984); Ghulam Murshid, *Reluctant Debutante: Response of Bengali Women to Modernisation, 1849–1905* (Rajshahi, 1983). On the history of the word *civilization*, see Lucien Febvre, '*Civilisation*: Evolution of a Word and a Group of Ideas,' in Peter Burke, ed., *A New Kind of History: From the Writings of Febvre*, trans. K. Folca (London, 1973), pp. 219–57. I owe this reference to Peter Sahlins.

31 James Mill, *The History of British India*, vol. 1, ed., H. H. Wilson (London, 1840), pp. 309–10.

32 Borthwick, *Changing Role*.

33 The classic text where this assumption has been worked up into philosophy is of course *Hegel's Philosophy of Right*, trans. T. M. Knox (Oxford, 1967), pp. 110–22. See also Joanna Hodge, 'Women and the Hegelian State,' in Ellen Kennedy and Susan Mendus, eds., *Women in Western Philosophy* (Brighton, 1987), pp. 127–58; Simon During, 'Rousseau's Heirs: Primitivism, Romance, and Other Relations Between the Modern and the Nonmodern' (forthcoming); Joan B. Landes, *Women*

and the Public Sphere in the Age of the French Revolution (Ithaca, N. Y., 1988); Mary Ryan, *Women in Public: Between Banners and Ballots, 1825–1880* (Baltimore, 1990).

34 Anon., *Streesiksha*, vol. 1 (Calcutta, 1877), pp. 28–9.

35 I develop this argument further in Dipesh Chakrabarty, 'Open Space/Public Place: Garbage, Modernity, and India,' *South Asia* (forthcoming).

36 *Dinabandhu racanabali*, ed., Kshetra Gupta (Calcutta, 1981), p. 138.

37 Borthwick, *Changing Role*, p. 105.

38 I discuss this in more detail in Chakrabarty, 'Colonial Rule.'

39 Indira Devi, *Narir ukti* (Calcutta, 1920), dedication page.

40 Deenanath Bandyopadhyaya, *Nanabishayak prabandha* (Calcutta, 1887), pp. 30–1. For a genealogy of the terms *slavery* and *freedom* as used in the colonial discourse of British India, see Gyan Prakash, *Bonded Histories: Genealogies of Labor Servitude in Colonial India* (Cambridge, 1990).

41 Peter Burke, *The Renaissance Sense of the Past* (London, 1970).

42 Bikshuk [Chandrasekhar Sen], *Ki holo!* (Calcutta, 1876), p. 77.

43 David Kinsley, *Hindu Goddesses: Visions of the Divine Feminine in the Hindu Religious Tradition* (Berkeley, 1988), pp. 19–31; Manomohan Basu, *Hindu acar byabahar* (Calcutta, 1873), p. 60; H. D. Bhattacharya, 'Minor Religious Sects,' in R. C. Majumdar, ed., *The History and Culture of the Indian People: The Age of Imperial Unity*, vol. 2 (Bombay, 1951), pp. 469–71; Upendranath Dhal, *Goddess Lakshmi: Origin and Development* (Delhi, 1978). The expression *everyday pantheism* was suggested to me by Gayatri Chakravorty Spivak (personal communication).

44 See the chapter on Bankim in Chatterjee, *Nationalist Thought*.

45 *Ranade: His Wife's Reminiscences*, trans. Kusumavati Deshpande (Delhi, 1963), p. 77.

46 Meaghan Morris, 'Metamorphoses at Sydney Tower,' *New Formations* 11 (Summer 1990), p. 10.

47 Amiya Chakravarty, quoted in Bhikhu Parekh, *Gandhi's Political Discourse* (London, 1989), p. 163.

48 Gayatri Chakravorty Spivak, 'Can the Subaltern Speak?,' in Cary Nelson and Lawrence Grossberg, eds., *Marxism and the Interpretation of Culture* (Urbana, Ill., 1988), p. 277.

49 See *Subaltern Studies*, vols. 1–7 (Delhi, 1982–91); and Ashis Nandy, *The Intimate Enemy: Loss and Recovery of Self Under Colonialism* (Delhi, 1983).

50 *Subaltern Studies*, vols. 1–7, and Guha, *Elementary Aspects*.

51 Homi Bhabha, 'Of Mimicry and Man: The Ambivalence of Colonial Discourse,' in Annette Michelson *et al.*, eds., *October: The First Decade, 1976–1986* (Cambridge, Mass., 1987), pp. 317–26; also Bhabha, ed., *Nation and Narration* (London, 1990).

52 Spivak, 'Can the Subaltern Speak?' Also see Spivak's interview published in *Socialist Review* 20. 3 (July–September 1990), pp. 81–98.

53 On the close connection between imperialist ideologies and the teaching of history in colonial India, see Ranajit Guha, *An Indian Historiography of India: A Nineteenth-Century Agenda and Its Implications* (Calcutta, 1988).

54 Without in any way implicating them in the entirely of this argument, I may mention that there are parallels here between my statement and what Gyan Prakash and Nicholas Dirks have argued elsewhere. See Gyan Prakash, 'Writing Post-Orientalist Histories of the Third World: Perspectives from Indian Historiography,' *Comparative Studies in Society and History* 32. 2 (April 1990), pp. 383–408; Nicholas

B. Dirks, 'History as a Sign of the Modern,' *Public Culture* 2. 2 (Spring 1990), pp. 25–33.

55 See Amartya Kumar Sen, *Of Ethics and Economics* (Oxford, 1987). Tessa Morris-Suzuki's *A History of Japanese Economic Thought* (London, 1989) makes interesting reading in this regard. I am grateful to Gavan McCormack for bringing this book to my attention.

56 Carole Pateman, *The Sexual Contract* (Stanford, Calif., 1988), p. 184.

57 Fredric Jameson, 'Cognitive Mapping,' in Nelson and Grossberg, *Marxism and the Interpretation of Culture*, p. 354.

58 David Arnold, 'The Colonial Prison: Power, Knowledge, and Penology in Nineteenth-Century India,' in Arnold and Hardiman, *Subaltern Studies*, vol. 8. I have discussed some of these issues in a Bengali article: Dipesh Chakrabarty, 'Sarir, samaj, o rashtra: Oupanibeshik bharate mahamari o janasangskriti,' *Anustup*, 1988.

59 Lawrence Brilliant with Girija Brilliant, 'Death for a Killer Disease,' *Quest*, May/June 1978, p. 3. I owe this reference to Paul Greenough.

60 Richard Rorty, 'Habermas and Lyotard on Postmodernity,' in Richard J. Bernstein, ed., *Habermas and Modernity* (Cambridge, Mass., 1986), p. 169.

61 For an interesting and revisionist reading of Hegel in this regard, see the exchange between Charles Taylor and Partha Chatterjee in *Public Culture* 3. 1 (1990). My book *Rethinking Working-Class History* attempts a small beginning in this direction.

Many different audiences in the United States and Australia have responded to versions of this paper and helped me with their criticisms. My benefactors are too numerous to mention individually but the following have been particularly helpful: the editorial board of *Representations* for criticisms conveyed through Thomas Laqueur; Benedict Anderson, Arjun Appadurai, David Arnold, Marjorie Beale, Partha Chatterjee, Natalie Davis, Nicholas Dirks, Simon During, John Foster, Ranajit Guha, Jeanette Hoorn, Martin Jay, Jenny Lee, David Lloyd, Fiona Nicoll, Gyanendra Pandey, Craig Reynolds, Joan Scott, and Gayatri Spivak. And very special thanks to Christopher Healy for sharing both the intellectual and the physical labor that went into this paper.

13

Paul Gilroy

'The Whisper Wakes, the Shudder Plays': 'Race', Nation and Ethnic Absolutism *

The Queen Mother swayed in a gentle dance when one of three steel bands began playing a lilting reggae tune. Five yards away, swaying with her, were a group of Rastafarians wearing the red, yellow and green tea cosy hats which are the badge of their pot-smoking set.

Daily Mail, 21 April, 1983

The nation has been and is still being, eroded and hollowed out from within by implantation of unassimilated and unassimilable populations ... alien wedges in the heartland of the state.

Enoch Powell, 9 April, 1976

Methinks I see in my mind a noble and puissant Nation rousing herself like a strong man after sleep, and shaking her invincible locks.

Milton

Racism has been described above [in the first chapter] as a discontinuous and unevenly developed process. It exists in plural form, and I have suggested that it can change, assuming different shapes and articulating different political relations. Racist ideologies and practices have distinct meanings bounded by historical circumstances and determined in struggle. This chapter moves away from general argument to focus on the distinctive characteristics of the racism which currently runs through life in Britain.

This particular form, which Martin Barker and others[1] have labelled 'the new racism', will be examined below with a view to focusing on the nature of its newness – the job it does in rendering our national crisis intelligible. It will be argued that its novelty lies in the capacity to link discourses of patriotism, nationalism, xenophobia, Englishness, Britishness, militarism and gender difference into a complex system which gives 'race' its contemporary meaning. These themes combine to provide a definition of 'race' in terms of culture and identity. What new right philosopher John Casey has called 'The whole life of

* From *There Ain't No Black in the Union Jack* (Routledge, 1991), pp. 43–57; 59–71.

the people'.[2] 'Race' differences are displayed in culture which is reproduced in educational institutions and, above all, in family life. Families are therefore not only the nation in microcosm, its key components, but act as the means to turn social processes into natural, instinctive ones.

These ideas have hosted an extraordinary convergence between left and right, between liberals and conservatives and between racists and some avowed anti-racists. These politically opposed groups have come together around an agreed definition of what 'race' adds up to. Their agreement can itself be understood as marking the newness of a new racism which confounds the traditional distinctions between left and right. Conservative thinkers, whether or not they follow the *Salisbury Review* in arguing that 'the conscious-ness of nationhood is the highest form of political consciousness',[3] are forced by the nature of their beliefs to be open about their philosophies of race and national belonging. The British left, caught between a formal declaration of internationalism and the lure of a pragmatic, popular patriotism[4], is less explicit and has been confounded by the shifting relationship between national sentiment, 'race' and class politics.[5] This difficulty is encountered in acute form by English socialist writers but it can be traced back into the writings of Marx and Engels.[6]

'Race', nation and the rhetoric of order

In his thoughtful study of nationalism, *Imagined Communities*, Benedict Anderson seeks to clarify the relationship between racism and nationalism by challenging Tom Nairn's[7] argument that these two forms of ideology are fundamentally related in that the former derives from the latter. Anderson's conclusion is worth stating at length:

> The fact of the matter is that nationalism thinks in terms of historical destinies, while racism dreams of eternal contaminations transmitted from the origins of time through an endless sequence of loathsome copulations. ... The dreams of racism actually have their origins in the ideologies of class, rather than those of nation: above all in claims to divinity among rulers and to blue or white blood and breeding among aristocracies. No surprise then that ... on the whole, racism and anti-semitism manifest themselves, not across national boundaries but within them. In other words they justify not so much foreign wars as domestic repression and domination.[8]

In support of this point, Anderson cites the fact that regardless of its internal 'race' politics, South Africa continues to enjoy amicable diplomatic relations with prominent black politicians from various African states. This is a curious example because the formulation of the apartheid system, in particular the homelands policy, can be read as an attempt to externalize those 'internal' 'race' problems by representing them as the interaction of separate states which rest on distinct cultural and historical identities.[9]

Anderson's theory claims that racism is essentially antithetical to nationalism because nations are made possible in and through print languages rather than notions of biological difference and kinship. Thus, he argues that anyone can in theory learn the language of the nation they seek to join and through the process of naturalization become a citizen enjoying formal equality under its laws. Whatever objections can be made to Anderson's general argument, his privileging of the written word over the spoken word for example, it simply does not apply in the English/British case. The politics of 'race' in this country is fired by conceptions of national belonging and homogeneity which not only blur the distinction between 'race' and nation, but rely on that very ambiguity for their effect. Phrases like 'the Island Race' and 'the Bulldog Breed' vividly convey the manner in which this nation is represented in terms which are simultaneously biological and cultural. It is important to recognize that the legal concept of patriality, introduced by the Immigration Act of 1968, codified this cultural biology of 'race' into statute law as part of a strategy for the exclusion of black settlers.[10] This act specified that immigration controls would not apply to any would-be settler who could claim national membership on the basis that one of their grandparents had been born in the UK. The Nationality Act of 1981 rationalized the legal vocabulary involved so that patrials are now known as British citizens.

A further objection to Anderson's position emerges from consideration of how the process of black settlement has been continually described in military metaphors which offer war and conquest as the central analogies for immigration. The enemy within, the unarmed invasion, alien encampments, alien territory and new commonwealth occupation have all been used to describe the black presence in this way. Enoch Powell, whose careful choice of symbols and metaphors suggests precise calculation, typifies this ideological strand:

> It is ... truly when he looks into the eyes of Asia that the Englishman comes face to face with those who would dispute with him the possession of his native land.[11]

This language of war and invasion is the clearest illustration of the way in which the discourses which together constitute 'race' direct attention to national boundaries, focusing attention on the entry and exit of blacks. The new racism is primarily concerned with mechanisms of inclusion and exclusion. It specifies who may legitimately belong to the national community and simultaneously advances reasons for the segregation or banishment of those whose 'origin, sentiment or citizenship' assigns them elsewhere. The excluded are not always conceived as a cohesive rival nation. West Indians, for example, are seen as a bastard people occupying an indeterminate space between the Britishness which is their colonial legacy and an amorphous, ahistorical relationship with the dark continent and those parts of the new world where they have been able to reconstitute it. Asians on the other hand, as the Powell quote above suggests, are understood to be bound by cultural and biological ties which merit the status of a fully formed, alternative national identity. They pose a threat to the British way of life by virtue of their strength and cohesion. For different reasons, both groups are judged to be incompatible with authentic forms of Englishness.[12] The obviousness of the differences they manifest in their cultural lives underlines the need to maintain strong and effective controls on who may enter Britain. The process of national decline is presented as coinciding with the dilution of once homogeneous and continuous national stock by alien strains. Alien cultures come to embody a threat which, in turn, invites the conclusion that national decline and weakness have been precipitated by the arrival of blacks. The operation of banishing blacks, repatriating them to the places which are congruent with their ethnicity and culture, becomes doubly desirable. It assists in the process of making Britain great again and restores an ethnic symmetry to a world distorted by imperial adventure and migration.

What must be explained, then, is how the limits of 'race' have come to coincide so precisely with national frontiers. This is a central achievement of the new racism. 'Race' is bounded on all sides by the sea. The effect of this ideological operation is visible in the way that the word 'immigrant' became synonymous with the word 'black' during the 1970s. It is still felt today as black settlers and their British-born children are denied authentic national membership on the basis of their 'race' and, at the same time, prevented from aligning themselves within the 'British race' on the grounds that their national allegiance inevitably lies elsewhere. This racist logic has pinpointed obstacles to genuine belonging in the culture and identity of the alien interlopers. Both are central to the theories of 'race' and nation which have emerged from the political and philosophical work of writers associated with Britain's 'new right'.[13]

As part of their lament that the national heart no longer beats as one, Peregrine Worsthorne has pointed out that 'though Britain is a multi-racial society, it is still a long way from being a multi-racial nation'.[14] This is an important distinction which was also made fourteen years earlier by Enoch Powell. He drew attention to the difference between the merely formal membership of the national community provided by its laws, and the more substantive membership which derives from the historic ties of language, custom and 'race'. Parliament, suggested Powell, can change the law, but national sentiment transcends such narrow considerations: 'the West Indian does not by being born in England, become an Englishman. In law, he becomes a United Kingdom citizen by birth; in fact he is a West Indian or an Asian still'.[15]

It has been revealed that, at the suggestion of Churchill, a Conservative cabinet discussed the possibility of using 'Keep Britain White' as an electoral slogan as early as 1955.[16] Yet it is in the period between Powell's and Worsthorne's statements above that a truly popular politics of 'race' and nation flowered in Britain. Its growth, emanating mainly though not exclusively from the right[17] marks the divergence of what can loosely be called the patrician and populist orientations in the modern Conservative Party.

The 'metaphysics of Britishness'[18] which links patriotism, xenophobia, militarism, and nationalism into a series of statements on 'race' was a key element in the challenge to the old leadership between 1964 and 1970 and in the reconstitution of the party under Thatcher. These themes have been fundamental to the popularity of the party and conservative intellectuals have not concealed their instrumental use. The language of one nation provides a link between the populist effect of 'race' and a more general project which has attempted to align the British People with an anti-statism and in particular with Conservative criticism of the 'guilty public schoolboys' of the liberal intelligentsia who have wrecked the country with their consensual approach to politics. They are the men who imposed mass immigration on a reluctant populace.

'Race' is also identified as a means by which the mass of the population may be directly addressed. As Maurice Cowling puts it,

> Mr Powell attaches the highest value to working class opinion. It is one of his special audiences and one, moreover, that he thinks deserves a better diet than the awful pieties with which Mr Jenkins and his allies had hoped to lead it into a liberal future.[19]

The themes of national culture and identity have long histories inside the Conservative political tradition.[20] Yet the populist[21] form in which they emerge as Powellism breaks decisively with its predecessors even if its object, the conception of a 'unity of national sentiment transcending classes'[22] remains the same. The reconstitution of Powellism as Thatcherism[23] points to the consolidation of a new political language which has became progressively more dominant within the representation of the present crisis and which, more specifically, has solved a profound political problem for the right. The 'one nation' message has been a means to escape from the shadows of paternalism which were the undoing of Alec Douglas Home. The national symbols of Powellism/Thatcherism are significant not only because a populist orientation is their primary characteristic. Conservative intellectuals have been candid about the role these ideas have played in the rebirth of their party which, in the period after Wilson, lacked a language adequate to its social and political vision. This problem was described vividly in an editorial which looked at the 1970s in the first issue of the new right journal *Salisbury Review*: 'never before had it seemed so hard to recreate the verbal symbols, the images and axioms, through which the concept of authority could be renewed'. The solution to it involved making 'race' and nation the framework for a rhetoric of order through which modern conservatism could voice populist protest against Britain's post-imperial plight and marshal its historic bloc. Enoch Powell's superficially simple question 'what kind of people are we?' summoned those very images and axioms and answered itself powerfully in the negative. 'We' were not muggers, 'we' were not illegal immigrants, 'we' were not criminals, Rastafarians, aliens or purveyors of arranged marriages. 'We' were the lonely old lady taunted by 'wide-grinning piccaninnies'. 'We' were the only white child in a class full of blacks. 'We' were the white man, frightened that in fifteen to twenty years, 'the black man would have the whip hand over us'. The black presence is thus constructed as a problem or threat against which a homogeneous, white, national 'we' could be unified. To put this operation into perspective, it must be emphasized that these were not the only images and definitions of nationhood which were mobilized during this period. Other voices from the left and from the black communities themselves were to be heard. Even within the right there were alternative conceptualizations of the relationship between 'race' and nation which were more in keeping with a patrician reading of imperial history. On behalf of the populist new right, Powell has had to challenge these as well as the 'madness' of the liberal integrationists. His attack on the Queen's Christmas message of 1983 and by implication on the 'multi-racialist' stance of other members of the royal household is particularly revealing. It crystalizes some of the competing definitions of the nation which are even now in play.

Powell attacked the Queen's attachment to the Commonwealth and re-buked her advisers for not encouraging her to speak more as a 'British monarch to the British Nation'. She was, said Powell, 'more concerned for the susceptibilities and prejudices of a vociferous minority of newcomers than for the great mass of her subjects'. The racial message in this last sentence characteristically derives its full power from the absence of any overt reference to the black presence. The *Sun* picked up the inferred racial message and splashed the headlines 'Enoch Raps Queen. She must speak up more for whites' across its front page.[24] Powell censured the Queen further, for mouth-ing speeches which 'suggest that she has the interests and affairs of other countries, in other continents, as much or more at heart than those of her own people'. The *Sun* acknowledged the use of political 'code words' in Mr Powell's outburst and provided a summary of his 'basic message' in plain English. 'The Queen has allowed herself to be used as a mouthpiece for racial minorities, and ought to spend more time speaking out for the white majority.'

Powell's speech ended with a warning to those who were responsible for misleading the Crown and thereby disrupting the constitutional balance between monarch and people. It is a cogent if cryptic statement of his populism: 'The place of the crown in the affections of the people would be threatened if they began to sense that the crown was not in unique and exclusive sympathy with the people of the United Kingdom which their mutual dependance ought to imply.' The message in this last point is a little obscure but is similar to that which emerges from Powell's earlier comments on the relationship between formal (legal) citizenship and the substantive cultural identity which defines genuine membership of the British nation. Monarchs come and go, but the historic continuity which constructs the British people has a longer life span than any individual sovereign and, in Powell's view, a political privilege.

I have already introduced the idea that the new racism's newness can be gauged by its capacity to operate across the broad range of political opinion. This claim can be pursued further. The distinction which Powell and Wors-thorne make between authentic and inauthentic types of national belonging, appears in an almost identical form in the work of Raymond Williams.[25] It provides a striking example of the way in which the cultural dimensions of the new racism confound the left/right distinction.

Williams combines a discussion of 'race' with comments on patriotism and nationalism. However, his understanding of 'race' is restricted to the social and cultural tensions surrounding the arrival of 'new peoples'. For him, as with the right, 'race' problems begin with immigration. Resentment of 'unfamiliar neighbours' is seen as the beginning of a process which ends in ideological specifications of 'race' and 'superiority'. Williams, working his way towards a 'new and substantial kind of socialism', draws precisely the same picture of the relationship between 'race', national identity and citizenship as Powell:

> ... it is a serious misunderstanding ... to suppose that the problems of social identity are resolved by formal (merely legal) definitions. For unevenly and at times precariously, but always through long experience substantially, an effective awareness of social identity depends on actual and sustained social relationships. To reduce social identity to formal legal definitions, at the level of the state, is to collude in the alienated superficialities of 'the nation' which are limited functional terms of the modern ruling class.[26]

These remarks are part of Williams's response to anti-racists who would answer the denial that blacks can be British by saying 'They are as British as you are.' He dismisses this reply as 'the standard liberal' variety. His alternative conception stresses that social identity is a product of 'long experience'. But this prompts the question – how long is long enough to become a genuine Brit? His insistence that the origins of racial conflicts lie in the hostility between strangers in the city makes little sense given the effects of the 1971 Immigration Act in halting primary black settlement. More disturbingly, these arguments effectively deny that blacks can share a significant 'social identity' with their white neighbours who, in contrast to more recent arrivals, inhabit what Williams calls 'rooted settlements' articulated by 'lived and formed identities'. He describes the emergence of racial conflict where

> an English working man (English in the terms of sustained modern integration) protests at the arrival or presence of 'foreigners' or 'aliens' and now goes on to specify them as 'blacks'.

Williams does not appear to recognize black as anything other than the subordinate moment in an ideology of racial supremacy. His use of the term 'social identity' is both significant and misleading. It minimizes the specificities of nationalism and ideologies of national identity and diverts attention from analysis of the political processes by which national and social identities have been aligned. Several questions which are absolutely central to contemporary 'race' politics are thus obscured. Under what conditions is national identity able to displace or dominate the equally 'lived and formed' identities which are based on age, gender, region, neighbourhood or ethnicity? How has it come to be expressed in racially exclusive forms? What happens when 'social identities' become expressed in conflicting political organizations and movements and when they appeal to the authority of nature and biology to rationalize the relations of domination and subordination which exist between them? How these social identities relate to the conspicuous differences of language and culture is unclear except where Williams points out that the forms of identity fostered by the 'artificial order' of the nation state are incomplete and empty when compared to 'full social identities in their real diversity'. This does not, of course, make them any the less vicious. Where racism demands repatriation and pivots on the exclusion of certain groups from the imagined community of the nation, the contradictions around citizenship that Williams dismisses as 'alienated superficialities' remain important constituents of the political field. They provide an important point of entry into the nation's sense of itself. Where racial oppression is practised with the connivance of legal institutions – the police and the courts – national and legal subjectivity will also become the focus of political antagonism. Williams's discussion of 'race' and nation does not address these issues and is notable for its refusal to examine the concept of racism which has its own historic relationship with ideologies of Englishness, Britishness and national belonging.

Quite apart from Williams's apparent endorsement of the presuppositions of the new racism, the strategic silences in his work contribute directly to its strength and resiliance. The image Williams has chosen to convey his grasp of 'race' and nation, that of a resentful English working man, intimidated by the alterity of his alien neighbours is, as we shall see below, redolent of other aspects of modern Conservative racism and nationalism.

The national community in peace and war

The imagery of black settlement as an invasion and the close association between racism and nationalism make it impossible to discuss the contemporary politics of 'race' without reference to the war with Argentina during 1982. The war analogy of black settlement laid the discursive foundations on which connections could be made between conflict abroad and the subversive activities of the fifth column within. The supreme expression of this theme was Margaret Thatcher's speech at Cheltenham on 3 July 1982. This defined the 'Falklands Factor' so as to link the struggle against the 'Argies' with the battle against British workers: the NUR and ASLEF (the rail unions) whose industrial actions were to be undone by the fact that such activities did not 'match the spirit' of the reborn Britain.

> What has indeed happened is that now once again Britain is not prepared to be pushed around. We have ceased to be a nation in retreat. We have instead a new-found confidence – born in the economic battles at home and tested and found true 8,000 miles away. That confidence comes from the rediscovery of ourselves and grows with the recovery of our self respect.

This speech, like Powell's critique of the royal household, made no open references to the issue of 'race'. Other new right thinkers were less circumspect. Wars, it was argued, are key moments in the process of national self-realization – the willingness to lay down one's life being the definition of a true patriot. The great distance involved and the tenuous constitutional connection between Britain and Port Stanley led commentators to speculate about the nature of the ties which could bind our national destiny to the fate of our distant 'kith and kin' in the South Atlantic. Peregrine Worsthorne went straight to the point:

If the Falkland Islanders were British citizens with black or brown skins, spoke with strange accents or worshipped different Gods it is doubtful whether the Royal Navy and Marines would today be fighting for their liberation.[27]

The Falklands episode celebrated the cultural and spiritual continuity which could transcend 8,000 miles and call the nation to arms in defence of its own distant people. Images of the nation at war were also used to draw attention to problems inherent in 'multi-racialism' at home. There was a rich irony discovered in the contrast between the intimacy of the 'natural' if long-distance relationship with the Falklanders and the more difficult task of relating to alien intruders who persisted in disrupting life in Britain and were not seen to be laying down their lives for the greater good. Again Worsthorne was the first to point this out: 'Most Britons today identify more easily with those of the same stock 8,000 miles away ... than they do with West Indian or Asian immigrants living next door.'[28] His potent image draws directly on Powell and emphasizes the strength of the cultural ties which mark the boundaries of 'race' as well as the exclusion of blacks from the definitions of nationality which matter most. The article from which it comes was as important for its recognition of the interrelationship of black and white life in the urban context as for the invocation of a mystic nationhood which would only be revealed on the battlefield. In the heat of combat, the nation would discover, or rather remember, what truly 'turned it on'. The implicit need to recognize and devalue the quality of 'transracial' relationships between neighbours contains a tacit acknowledgement that such relationships do exist, even if the white Britons involved relinquish their membership of Worsthorne's nation at the point at which these friendships are conceived.

The popular power of patriotism revealed by the Falklands episode was not lost on commentators of the left. Their responses to it have significantly been characterized by a reluctance to challenge the model of national greatness and the metaphysical order of belonging on which it rests. In an influential piece which noted that the Falklands had 'stirred up an ugly nationalist sediment which would cloud our cultural and political life', E. P. Thompson argued that we would pay for the war 'for a long time in rapes and racism in our cities'.[29] Eric Hobsbawm, on the other hand, advanced a resolute polemic in favour of a 'left patriotism'. Patriotism, he wrote, would only spill over into undesirable xenophobia, racism and jingoism if the left allowed it to be 'falsely' separated from the sentiments and aspirations of the working class. It is dangerous, he continued 'to leave patriotism exclusively to the right' and, in language reminiscent of Thompson's own frequent invocations of the popular traditions of British radicalism, he made a plea for a political orientation which could demonstrate radical patriotism and class consciousness could be yoked together in front of the socialist cart:

> The dangers of ... patriotism always were and still are obvious, not least because it was and is enormously vulnerable to ruling-class jingoism, to anti-foreign nationalism and of course in our days to racism. ... The reason why nobody pays much attention to the, let's call it, jingoism of the chartists is that it was combined with and

masked by an enormous militant class consciousness. It's when the two are separated, that the dangers are particulary obvious. Conversely when the two go together in harness, they multiply not only the force of the working class but its capacity to place itself at the head of a broad coalition for social change and they even give it the possibility of wrestling hegemony from the class enemy.[30]

In a similar article, principally notable for its blank refusal to use the words 'race' or racism, Robert Gray of the Communist Party's 'Theory and Ideology Committee' attacked 'national nihilism in the name of abstract internationalism' and argued that what was required was a 'redefinition of the interests of the nation around the alternative leadership of the working class'. None of these contributions, even those which concede the unfortunate ambiguities in nationalist ideology, make any attempt to show how this valuable redefinition might be achieved. Apart from pointing out the conspicuous success of nationalist sentiment in renovating the Tory project, few arguments are made which justify the need to make the nation state a primary focus of radical political consciousness. It is as if the only problem with nationalism is that the Tories have secured a near exclusive monopoly of it.

The possibility of politically significant connections between nationalism and contemporary racism is either unseen or felt to be unworthy of detailed discussion. More importantly, the types of subjectivity which nationalisms bring into being and put to work pass unquestioned. The problem has become how socialists can (re)possess them from the right.

Two anachronistic images of Britain lurk behind these omissions. The first depicts the nation as a homogeneous and cohesive formation in which an even and consensual cultural field provides the context for hegemonic struggle. The second is attached to the idea that this country is, and must continue to be, a major world power. Patriotism, even in its combative proto-socialist form, is empty without a filling of national pride. British socialists have so far remained silent about how this misplaced pride can be detached from the vestigial desire for imperial greatness which has so disfigured recent political life.[31]

The frequency with which Labour's senior spokespeople invoke the national interest as a verbal bludgeon introduces another note of caution. What is this interest? How is it created? How can it be identified? And where does it reside? If appealing to it is nothing more than a rhetorical motif, why has it become necessary at this moment in time? What needs does it address in those who respond to it? Michael Ignatieff's discussion of the 1984–5 coal dispute illustrates some of these difficulties.[32] Throughout this article, the national interest is taken for granted as a meaningful analytic category. 'No one lives apart from the national community', writes Ignatieff. Governments which fail to uphold it lose their electoral support. The police and the courts are its own institutions.

Like many socialists in the post-Falklands period, Ignatieff argues that 'The left crucially overestimates Mrs Thatcher's electoral appeal if it believes that she has succeeded in monopolising the language of "one nation" '. He opts to ignore the regional conflicts which were also at the heart of the coal dispute and which, I would argue, call into question the viability and desirability of the appeal to national unity to which he aspires. There is no reason why a political language based on the invocation of national identity should be the most effective where people recognize and define themselves primarily in terms of *regional* or *local* tradition. No coherent argument is provided as to why, for example, socialists should answer the voices of Wales, Yorkshire or Tyneside – all places where regional traditions are a key axis of political organization – with a language of the British national interest. 'Geordie', 'Hinny', 'Brummie' or 'Scouse' may all be political identities which are more in harmony with the advancement of socialist politics in this country than those conjured into being by the phrase 'fellow Britons' or even by the word citizen, given the way in which citizenship is allocated and withheld on racial grounds. These regional or local subjectivities simply do not articulate with 'race' in quite the same way as their national equivalent.

Colin Mercer's discussion of nation[33] parallels Ignatieff's and arrives at a similar image of British socialism: held to ransom by its national culture. Mercer 'owns up' to a 'sneaking admiration for Enoch Powell's prose' and thus recognizes his complicity in 'certain pleasures of Englishness'. He describes himself and by extension his audience of left cultural politicians, as unable either to 'interrupt' or 'stand outside' the complex combination of discursive effects that provide pleasure at the very moment in which 'Englishness' is constituted. The possibility that this particular brand of 'Englishness' may also enjoy a class character is left unexplored.

When it comes to their patriotism, it would appear that England's left intellectuals become so many radical rabbits transfixed and immobile in the path of an onrushing populist nationalism. How does the language of public good they propose, a necessary addition to radical speech if ever there was one, become the language of a nation so cohesive that 'no one lives outside the national community'? Indeed, the suggestion that no one lives outside the national community is only plausible if the issue of racism is excluded. What is being described by these writers is a national community, not imagined in the way that Benedict Anderson has suggested, but actual. The construction of that community is overlooked. It is accepted a priori as the structure around which the struggle to gain hegemony must take place.

The work of other socialist thinkers can be used to show that the images of paralysis which emerge from the work of Mercer and Ignatieff are only mild cases of this patriotic English disease. Where these two are simply inert in the face of national identity and its pleasures, E. P. Thompson, for example, is positively enthusiastic. He begins his pamphlet analysing the 1983 election by declaring 'whatever doubts we have, we can all think of things in the British way of life which we like, and we would want to protect these from attack'.[34] Thompson laments the fact that 'a large part of our free press has been bought, over our heads by money (some of it foreign money)'. For him, the activities of the womens' peace movement are 'characteristically British', their mass action at the Greenham Common airbase on 12 December 1982 was 'a very untidy, low-key, British sort of do'. Thompson's version of Britishness locates the lingering greatness of the nation in the inheritance of popular resistance as well as in cultural achievements:

> This has not only been a nation of bullies. It has been a nation of poets and inventors, of thinkers and of scientists, held in some regard in the world. It has been, for a time, no less than ancient Greece before us, a place of innovation in human culture.[35]

It is tempting to dispute the special status which Thompson accords to British culture and in particular his suggestion that modern Britain and ancient Greece are the primary innovators in human culture. However, these claims are not the main issue. What is more important is the way in which the preferred elements of English/British culture and society are described as if their existence somehow invalidated the side of our national heritage from which socialists are inclined to disassociate themselves.

Nationhood is not an empty receptacle which can be simply and spontaneously filled with alternative concepts according to the dictates of political pragmatism. The ideological theme of national belonging may be malleable to some extent but its links with the discourses of classes and 'races' and the organizational realities of these groups are not arbitrary. They are confined by historical and political factors which limit the extent to which nationalism becomes socialist at the moment that its litany is repeated by socialists. The intention may be radical but the effects are unpredictable, particularly where culture is also conceived within discrete, separable, national units coterminous with the boundaries of the nation state.

Having said this, it is impossible to deny that the language of the nation offers British socialists a rare opportunity. Through it, they can, like Thompson, begin to say 'we' and 'our' rather than 'I' and 'my'. It encourages them to speak beyond the margins of sectional interest to which they are confined by party and ideology. But there is a problem in these plural forms: who do they include, or, more precisely for our purposes, do they help to reproduce blackness and Englishness as mutually exclusive categories? Why is the racial inflection in the language of nation continually overlooked? And why are contemporary appeals to 'the people' in danger of transmitting themselves as appeals to the white people?

An answer to these questions can only begin from recognition of the way that Britain's languages of 'race' and nation have been articulated together. The effect of their combination can be registered even where 'race' is not overtly referred to, or where it is discussed outside of crude notions of superiority and inferiority. The discourses of nation and people are saturated with racial connotations. Attempts to constitute the poor or the working class as a class across racial lines are thus disrupted. This problem will have to be acknowledged directly if socialists are to move beyond puzzling over why black Britons (who as a disproportionately underprivileged group, ought to be their stalwart supporters) remain suspicious and distant from the political institutions of the working-class movement.[36]

Labour's occasional attempts to address nationalist sentiment have, as Anthony Barnett has demonstrated[37], been a site of further difficulties. However, the concept of 'Churchillism' with which Barnett has tried to pin down the patriotic junction of Labourism and 'Thatcherism' is not adequate to all the permutations of Labour's failure. It plays down the specific attributes and appeal of socialist nationalism and suggests that the 'fatal dementia of national pride' has been injected into British socialism from the outside. However, left nationalism is a more organic, historic property of British socialism. Michael Foot's benign view of Enoch Powell's 'rivers of blood' intervention as a 'tragic irony' and 'pathos'[38] and Neil Kinnock's recent claim to working-class patriotism:

> ... a confident and generous patriotism of freedom and fairness, not one of prejudice, vanity, or the patriotism of the 'presidential puppet' ... a patriotism that is forgotten when the chequebook is waved ... a patriotism which holds that our values are not for sale to anyone at any price at any time,[39]

suggest a longer pedigree for 'Churchillism' than the association of 'Tory belligerents, Labour reformists, revolutionary anti-fascists, and the liberal intelligentsia' which Barnett[40] proposes as its genealogy. If the writings of left intellectuals are anything to go by, it is born from something altogether more cultural than political; something rooted, not in the end of empire, but in the imperial experience itself.[41] A more complex illustration of these problems can be found in Tony Benn's[42] attempt to define the British crisis in terms of a descent into colonial status. *New Socialist*, the Labour Party journal introduced his piece thus:

> ... the British establishment has opted for survival as the colonial administrators of a subject country. Tony Benn calls for the Labour movement to lead a national liberation struggle and restore to us our democratic rights.

Benn's description of the socialist struggle against the Thatcher government as a national liberation struggle was certainly imaginative. It was a clear attempt to harness for the left the yearning for a return to national greatness which has been used effectively by the right. It addressed the British inability to accept the end of empire and the national discomfort at the loss of world pre-eminence. It substitutes a stark image of reduced national status for the metaphysical yearning for greatness amplified by both Conservatives and the Alliance parties in their 1983 election manifestos.[43] Yet the bloodshed and ruthless mass violence characteristic of decolonization have not, other than in the six counties of Northern Ireland, been evident in recent British politics. The effect of Benn's words on black citizens for whom decolonization is a memory rather than a metaphor is hard to estimate. It is, however, difficult to resist the conclusion that his choice of imagery trivialized the bitter complexities of anti-colonial struggle.

I am not suggesting that the differences between Labour and Conservative languages of nation and patriotism are insignificant, but rather that these languages overlap significantly. In contemporary Britain, statements about nation are invariably also statements about 'race'. The Conservatives appear to recognize this and seek to play with the ambiguities which this situation creates. Their recent statements on the theme of Britishness betray a sophisticated grasp of the interface between 'race' and nation created in the post-'rivers of blood' era. During the coal dispute, for example, in a speech on the enduring power of the national constitution entitled 'Why Democracy Will Last', Mrs Thatcher invoked the memory of the Somerset case of 1772. Lord Mansfield's famous judgment in this case declared that British slaveholders could no longer compel their slaves to leave the country against their will.[44] It matters little that Mrs Thatcher quoted the case wrongly, suggesting that it brought slavery in this country to an end. With no trace of irony, her speech boldly articulates an apparently anti-racist position at the heart of a nationalist and authoritarian statement in which the mining communities were identified as 'enemies within'.[45]

The Conservatives' ethnic election poster of 1983 provides further insight into the right's grasp of these complexities. The poster was presumably intended to exploit ambiguities between 'race' and nation and to salve the sense of exclusion experienced by the blacks who were its target. The poster appeared in the ethnic minority press during May 1983 and was attacked by black spokespeople for suggesting that the categories black and British were mutually exclusive. It set an image of a young black man, smartly dressed in a suit with wide lapels and flared trousers, above the caption 'Labour says he's black. Tories say he's British'. The text which followed set out to reassure readers that 'with Conservatives there are no "blacks" or "whites", just people'. A variant on the one nation theme emerged, entwined with criticism of Labour for treating blacks 'as a "special case", as a group all on your own'. At one level, the poster states that the category of citizen and the formal belonging which it bestows on its black holders are essentially colourless, or at least colour-blind. Yet as the writings of Powell and Worsthorne above illustrate, populist racism does not recognize the legal membership of the national community conferred by its legislation as a substantive guarantee of Britishness. 'Race' is, therefore, despite the text, being defined beyond these legal definitions in the sphere of culture. There is more to Britishness than a passport. Nationhood, as Alfred Sherman pointed out in 1976,

> remains ... man's main focus of identity, his link with the wider world, with past and future, 'a partnership with those who are living, those who are dead and those who are to be born'. .... It includes national character reflected in the way of life ... a passport or residence permit does not automatically implant national values or patriotism.[46]

At this point the slightly too large suit worn by the young man, with its unfashionable cut and connotations of a job interview, becomes a key signifier. It conveys what is being asked of the black readers as the price of admission to the colour-blind form of citizenship promised by the text. Blacks are being invited to forsake all that marks them out as culturally distinct before real Britishness can be guaranteed. National culture is present in the young man's clothing. Isolated and shorn of the mugger's key icons – a tea-cosy hat and the dreadlocks of Rastafari – he is redeemed by his suit, the signifier of British civilization. The image of black youth as a problem is thus contained and rendered assimilable. The wolf is transformed by his sheep's clothing. The solitary maleness of the figure is also highly significant. It avoids the hidden threat of excessive fertility which is a constant presence in the representation of black women. This lone young man is incapable of swamping 'us'. He is alone because the logics of racist discourse militate against the possibility of making British blackness visible in a family or an inter-generational group.[47] The black family is presented as incomplete, deviant and ruptured.

Culture and identity in nations and families

The conception of nationness which emerges from the writings and speeches cited above involves a distinct theory of culture and identity which can be described as ethnic absolutism. Most clearly but by no means exclusively theorized in the work of the new right, it views nations as culturally homogeneous 'communities of sentiment' in which a sense of patriotic belonging can and should grow to become an important source of moral and political ideas.

The new racism which is articulated by these premises tends to deny that 'race' is a meaningful biological category. 'Race' is seen instead as a cultural issue. Enoch Powell has, for example, referred to skin colour as a 'uniform' for political conflict.[48] He has even attacked the policy of 'ethnic monitoring' because it involves a spurious attempt to categorize people by their non-existent biological 'race'.[49]

Mrs Lurline Champagne, a black nurse and delegate to the Conservative Party conference in 1985, was given an ovation 'much longer than most ministers' by her party after she declared 'I am a Conservative, black and British and proud of all three.' This was hardly the action of an organization which understands 'racial' differences as a matter of biological hierarchy. The superficial pluralism represented by her ovation masks new, cultural definitions of 'race' which are just as intractable. Mrs Champagne was, in her moment of glory, the exception that proved the rule. For contemporary Britain, the limits of nation coincide with the lines of 'race'.

The cultural definition of 'race' is sometimes conveyed in attempts to define the English as a 'race' separable from the Scots, Welsh, and Irish whose skin colour they share. Britishness, if it is discussed rather than simply extrapolated from Englishness, is seen to emerge as the sum of these cultures. Alien (i.e. black) cultures have been introduced into this country with disastrous effect: 'the indigenous population perceives its own predicament as that of physical pressure and attack'.[50] The increased competition for limited resources and the variety of disruptive behaviours introduced by the immigrant population create problems for the national community. The most profound difficulties are uncovered by trying to dilute our nationhood and national culture so that they can accommodate alien interlopers and their formally but not substantively British children. The most important recent example of this type of cultural conflict was the controversy around attempts to dismiss the Bradford headmaster Ray Honeyford.

Honeyford published a series of articles in *The Times Educational Supplement* and *Salisbury Review*[51] arguing, among other things, for a culturalist view of 'race' and racial conflict. From this perspective, he stressed the role of schools as agencies for socializing 'Afro-Asian settler children' into the mores which racially harmonious life in contemporary Britain required of them. He argued that the presence of these alien children in British schools was an impediment to the education of white children and sought to rescue educational theory from the clutches of the multi-culturalists who would

> teach all our pupils to denigrate the British Empire. . . . The multi-culturalists are a curious mixture: well-meaning liberals and clergymen suffering from a rapidly dating post-imperial guilt; teachers building a career by jumping onto the latest educational bandwaggon; a small but increasing group of professional Asian and West Indian intellectuals; and a hard core of left-wing political extremists often with a background of polytechnic sociology.[52]

Honeyford's antipathy towards anti-racism was second only to his patriotic reverence for the sanctity of British culture, jeopardized by the 'alien wedge'. His stand created demands that he should be sacked for violating the 'anti-racist policy' of the education authority who employed him to head a school in which the majority of pupils were black. The anti-racists, who were quick to brand him a racist, were less able to demonstrate why and how this was the case. His plight, beleaguered while black parents organized to withdraw their children from his school, became a populist rallying point for the new right,[53] illustrating the destructive consequences of local authority anti-racism in general. Honeyford was presented as a martyr in the popular press.[54] The detail of Honeyford's cultural racism is less important here than the fact that its very cultural qualities prevented it from being recognized as racism at all. Culture almost biologized by its proximity to 'race' becomes so potent a force that it can block and interrupt indefinitely what was once thought to be a 'natural' long-term process of assimilation in which schools played a crucial role.[55] The manifest cultural differences visible in public – at school – originate and are reproduced in private – in black families. They become the focus of resentment because they will not allow blacks to yield to Britishness. The attachment to non-British cultures which endures in black communities and from which much of their apparent strength and cohesion derives, is cited as the final proof that the entry of aliens into the national community is not only hazardous but practically impossible. Repatriation is therefore the only logical political solution to this problem and has the additional value of being a populist proposal.

The absolutist view of black and white cultures, as fixed, mutually impermeable expressions of racial and national identity, is a ubiquitous theme in racial 'common sense',[56] but it is far from secure. It is constantly under challenge from the activities of blacks who pass through the cultural and ideological net which is supposed to screen Englishness from them, and from the complex organic process which renders black Britons partially soluble in the national culture which their presence helps transform.

The Falklands war was not, therefore, the only moment at which the discourses of 'race' and nation erupted into popular politics and culture. They are always there, being struggled over. Racial differentiation, national belonging and the contradictory identities and ethnicities they map out are, for example, a continuous presence in press coverage of the royal family, in sports reporting, where the nation assumes its everyday shape, and in coverage of deportations under British immigration law. All are important sites on which the limits of the nation as well as its character are routinely established.

The emergence of black athletes, often very successful, in British colours has generated some interesting material bearing significant ideological contradictions. When the young black boxer Frank Bruno is hailed 'the Brawn of Britain' but tells the popular papers that 'if he wasn't Britain's hottest heavy weight prospect for years ... he would like to be Princess Di ... because she's got so much going for her'[57] his words are a window on these contradictions. Decathlete Daley Thompson's refusal to carry the Union Jack at the Commonwealth Games in September 1982 was an earlier example. His reluctance was interpreted by some commentators as evidence of his partial commitment to Britishness and Britain.[58] Thompson told the management of the English team that he did not want to carry the flag and refused to provide any further explanation. He was tracked down to his quarters but reporters could not speak to him because 'he was said to be asleep'. Phil Hubble, a white swimmer, was asked to take Thompson's place. He told *The Times* 'Naturally, I'm very proud and honoured.' Thompson's coarse banter with Princess Anne at the Olympic Games in Los Angeles may provide evidence of his rehabilitation, but the questioning of black commitment to national identity remains a sub-text of the sports pages.[59]

The problem appeared in somewhat different form during 1984 when the South African runner Zola Budd obtained British citizenship within ten days of her application.[60] Though her father claimed citizenship by descent, Ms Budd was not granted hers under the patriality rules which operate to exclude blacks. The Home Office admitted that her ancestry had been taken into account in their decision, but she was not naturalized; she did not need to be. The ties were there for all to see. Her grandfather's house in now decaying inner-city Hackney was discovered by the *Daily Mail*[61] and paraded as evidence of her historic British roots. Even when she spoke to reporters in Afrikaans, the possibility that her culture might erect obstacles to her being truly British was unmentioned. Unlike black settlers and their children, Zola was recognized as being of 'kith and kin' – an important category in the folk grammar of contemporary racism. The term is used to indicate the durability of national ties which do cross over into the territory of other states, and to establish the common identity of the sons and daughters of Britannia who have come to inhabit what is known as the old commonwealth: Canada, Australia, New Zealand, and now the Falklands. Zola's Englishness was felt to be so far beyond dispute that when young blacks demonstrated against her reluctance to denounce apartheid, reports of their protest branded them as alien traitors and unBritish racists. They were deprived of the right to belong to the national community and their action at South London's Crystal Palace stadium prompted the *Sun* to suggest that they 'return to their original homelands. There is no place for them in Britain.'[62] In Parliament, a Tory MP asked the Prime Minister if she agreed that the campaign against Budd was 'petty minded and despicable' and asked her further to condemn the demonstrators' 'ignorant abuse of South Africa'. Mrs Thatcher replied 'I agree with my honorable friend. I thought the treatment of a 17 year old girl was utterly appalling and a disgrace to those who meted it out to her.'[63]

Perhaps because it involves the public fragmentation of family units, the coverage of deportations has become a second important space in which the contradictions around 'race', culture and national belonging are aired. The image of isolated Asian women reluctantly climbing aboard the aircraft which will repatriate them and their children has become a particularly potent signifier of the victim status of the whole Asian community. It is proof that this group has been brought to grief by cultural values which burden them with overlarge families and refine the natural cunning that leads them to persistently strive to evade immigration laws.[64]

One case which throws the complex fusion of 'race' and nation into stark relief did not end in the deportation of the Asian family who had initially been told to quit Britain. The case of Rodney and Gail Pereira is interesting because it demonstrates how the absolutist conception of ethnicity and national membership can be disrupted by its own cultural definitions of who is and who isn't a true Brit. The Pereiras did not hail from an inner city. They were denizens of Bishop's Waltham in rural Hampshire. Their campaign to stay ended in success after a Home Office minister used his discretion under the act to allow them to remain in Britain legally. Their white neighbours had campaigned vociferously in their favour and publicly celebrated the victory which had been gained by bombarding the Home Office with a 'blizzard of petition forms'.[65] The *Daily Mail* also lent its support, yet it was not this campaign which swung official opinion in the Pereiras' favour. In a leader article in *The Times*, new right ideologue and associate editor of the newspaper, Ronald Butt, explained that the minister concerned had been impressed by the

... approach that Mr and Mrs Pereira had to living in Britain and the attitude towards them of their English neighbours ... they played an active part in village life ... they were popular ... in short, they showed a positive commitment to Britain and to the English way of life which gave their case an aspect beyond the simple convenience to themselves of living here.[66]

The *Daily Telegraph* told its readers that the Pereiras 'who are English speaking Roman Catholics ... feared that they would be discriminated against in India'.[67] The other papers provided myriad illustrations of the way that the couple and their 3-year-old daughter Keira had become integrated into life in their pastoral idyll. The *Guardian* revealed that despite the child's foreign name, she had 'played a mouse on her Sunday school's float of Noah's Ark at this year's May carnival'.[68] Among hundreds of offers of help received by the couple was an anonymous promise of £100,000! The process of transformation from alien to Briton is conveyed vividly in an accumulation of details like these.

Butt used his discussion of their case to attack the redefinition of racism which has meant that it is understood no longer as merely 'disliking individuals because of the colour of their skin'. In his opinion, the new definition wrongly criticized as racist the 'preference for accepting people with a strong inclination to be assimilated into the British community and who are in numbers which assist this process'. He described the anti-racists who operate this expanded definition of racism as being anxious only about people who, unlike the Pereiras, have 'little commitment to English life and culture'. His opposition to anti-racism then turned to attempts to develop multi-cultural educational curricula. He concluded:

> The case of the Pereiras has helped us to understand what the argument has always been really about – and that is much more identity and culture than colour.

This definition of 'race' in terms of identity and culture is not the exclusive property of the new right. It has also been articulated recently by some tendencies and groupings inside the black and anti-racist movements who, though opposed to Butt's conclusions, manage to duplicate in precise detail many of his underlying assumptions about the content and scope of racial difference. Nowhere has this been more clearly stated than in discussion of the issue of 'transracial' fostering and adoption.

This debate which flared in 1983[69] has centred on the issue of whether white families can provide adequately for the needs of the black foster-child or adoptee. This question has been central to the political organization of groups of black workers in social services and local authorities.

The Association of Black Social Workers and Allied Professionals (AB-SWAP) submitted evidence to the House of Commons Select Committee in March 1983 which dealt with the topic in detail.[70] Their submission provides an opportunity to gauge the understanding of 'race' which informs the demand that black children be placed exclusively with black families. If such families cannot be found, the evidence suggests that black children remain in local authority institutions where they can be nurtured to a 'positive black identity' by black staff. ABSWAP is centrally concerned with the issue of ethnic cultures and their role in establishing 'race'. The latter is understood almost exclusively in terms of the formation of an individual 'racial identity'. This process is placed in jeopardy by putting black children in white families. ABSWAP suggests that the essential ingredient in any substitute home for black children in care is its capacity to enhance the child's 'positive black identity'. This identity, which is understood to be wholly discontinuous with white identity regardless of age, gender, class or neighbourhood considerations, arises where the child's blackness is mirrored by those around it, where role models are to hand, and where the child is adequately protected from racial abuse. A more sophisticated version of the same theory is advanced elsewhere by John Small, President of the Association.[71] He argues that 'the issue of [racial] identity should be given priority above all other factors' and explains the existence of 'identity confusion' in black children adopted by whites as the result of the children's internalization of parental super-egos which contain a negative concept of black people.

ABSWAP defines 'transracial' placements as 'a microcosm of the oppression of black people in this society' because 'black children are being used to satisfy the needs of white families'. Their evidence continues:

> The most valuable resource of any ethnic group are its children. ... The black community cannot possibly maintain any dignity in this country ... if black children are taken away from their parents and reared exclusively [sic] by another race. ... Transracial placements poses [sic] the most dangerous threat to the harmonious society to which we aspire. ... It is in essence 'internal colonialism' and a new form of slave trade, but this time only black children are used.[72]

The organization states that the interests of the black child are paramount, but this rapidly becomes a tautology. These interests are simultaneously identified in a primary need for 'security and belonging' which can only be met 'within a family or community which is similar in cultural and racial characteristics'.

The definition of 'race' which informs these arguments elides the realms of culture and biology in the same way as the volkish new-right preoccupation with 'kith and kin'. Its political counterpart is a variety of black cultural nationalism which relies on mystical and essentialist ideas of a transcendental blackness.[73] Both ABSWAP and Small reject the term 'mixed race' not because they believe there is only one 'race' which therefore cannot be mixed, but because the term is said to imply 'the superior race quotient' (*sic*) and carry with it an implicit notion of domination and subordination. The effect of their theory is to further fragment the possibility of an expanded political definition of blackness which can encompass diverse 'racial' histories from Africa, Asia and the Caribbean. It also consigns children of what they call 'mixed parentage' to racial indeterminacy, particularly if they are brought up by a single white parent. These children could also have found space in a more politically focused definition of 'race'.

The tone of ABSWAP and Small's work suggests that anyone who concedes that a black child may be better off in a white household than in a local authority home, is advocating the kidnapping of young blacks and their compulsory rearing by whites. Theirs is the voice of a black nationalism which, though it may have political pertinence in other social formations, is sadly misplaced in this country where the black population is too small, too diverse and too fragmented to be conceptualized as a single cohesive nation. There are several other fundamental objections which can be registered to these arguments and the theory of 'race' and culture which they espouse. They reduce the complexity of self-image and personality formation in the black child to the single issue of 'race'/colour. The personality which expresses an ahistorical essence of blackness and which is judged by the black professionals to be the only identity which can match the needs of the black child (gender is again indeterminate), is guaranteed to emerge once the process of state-regulated, professionalized colour-matching is complete. This schema depends on a thoroughly idealized conception of black family life which does nothing more than simply invert the pathological assumptions which apparently characterize much of social work intervention in this area.[74] The juggling of children through ethnic categories and their shunting between adoptive and foster parents on the basis of 'race' and culture has been seized on by the new right as further proof of the disastrous consequences of local authority anti-racism.[75]

At this point it becomes important to ask why much needed criticism of the way that racism is institutionalized in social work practice gets subsumed by the rhetoric of black cultural nationalism. The beginnings of an answer to this question can be found by looking at the ideology of ethnic absolutism as part of the response of black professionals to the political contradictions they experience working inside local government bureaucracies. The attempt to view blacks as a culturally homogeneous national unit may be more significant for what it reveals about the internal politics of social services departments (SSDs) than for any light it sheds on the contemporary meaning of 'races'. Emphasizing ethnic particularity has become an important means to rationalize the practice of these departments. It organizes their clients into discrete groups with separate needs and problems which have been identified as expressive of the various cultures they inhabit. It is possible to see the invocation of racial identity and culture in the mystic forms of kinship and blood characteristic of cultural nationalism as the means with which black professionals in these institutions have sought to justify the special quality of their relationships with their black clients. These ideas provide a superficially coherent ideological reply to the contradictory position black professionals occupy. Their perch in the institutions of the local state is contradictory in both class and 'race' terms. Their membership of the professional and managerial class and the power relationships which their jobs give them relative to a largely poor and dispossessed clientele, call notions of simple racial solidarity into question. Yet, while these black social workers and allied professionals are local state servants with statutory obligations to other government agencies, their job and status do not completely insulate them from the 'race' politics of the client group which calls out to them across the boundaries of class division. This ideology of black cultural nationalism is their response. Barney Rooney[76] has pinpointed some of these problems:

> What really happens is that you recruit black people as social workers to relieve alienation, but you recruit only those who have nothing to do with the alienated sections, either in racial or cultural background, or indeed in the work which they undertake, but they attract members of their own communities ... to social services.

Paul Stubbs has suggested that an important part of SSDs' responses to increased work with black clients has been the introduction of black workers who are formally and informally allocated the work of dealing with black clients.[77] He argues that their ability to do this work in the manner which is expected by the SSDs hinges on the capacity to measure professional relationships and competences against the allegiance prompted by shared ethnic identity. This ability has become, he argues, the basis on which black staff are evaluated by superiors and colleagues. If this is so, the intensity with which black cultural nationalism emerges from the ABSWAP material can be interpreted. Its origins may lie in the management of potential conflicts between professionalism and 'racial' identification. The variety of ethnic absolutism which is produced, banishes, or at least salves, the pain which grows in the tension of trying to be black and professional at the same time. It has settled on the issue of 'transracial' fostering and adoption not only because of the obvious emotional charge attached to the central symbols involved – mother, child, family – but because of the need to articulate an answer, however confused, to the racist theory of black families as pathologically disorganized and deficient. The strength and durability of black families can be asserted in the face of this negative portrait only if the issue of why black children are taken into care in the first place is avoided. On a television discussion of these issues the chair of ABSWAP, David Divine, repeatedly claimed that the 'black community has been denied the right to look after its own'.[78] This position dovetails with the Thatcherite rolling back of social services and health care provision[79] and provides an important example of how the political strategy of black nationalism can intersect with the programme of the radical right.

Conclusion

This chapter has sought to identify the links between the discourses of 'race' and nation and to use their proximity as an argument against the pre-eminent place which the idea of nationhood continues to enjoy in the work of English socialists and the practice of black cultural nationalists. Apart from the overlap with the concerns and premises of the right, there are other reasons why the language of nation has become an inappropriate one for the black movement and the socialist movement in Britain. The uneven development of national crisis has, for example, exacerbated regional differences to the point that we can speak routinely of two nations – north and south. These nations, which sometimes appear to co-exist with difficulty, are more than simply competing metaphors of Englishness.[80] The difference between them is rooted in the mode of production and is expressed not least in the different relationships each enjoys to national decline and de-industrialization. The industrial geography of the present crisis and changes in the geographies of class hierarchy and gender patterns of employment have been identified by Doreen Massey[81] who has concluded that a new spatial division of labour is being created. This must be taken into account in discussions of the political language and concepts which radicals will require if they are to end the dominance of authoritarian populist nationalism.

Quite apart from 'racial' and gender considerations, the steady fragmentation of national unity and its recomposition along new economic and regional axes, militates against the language of patriotism and people retaining its wide popular appeal. Changes in Britain are matched by changes outside, in the character and composition of capital which has begun to organize itself into productive structures and operations which transcend the limits of the nation state and cannot therefore be combated by workers' organizations trapped and confused within national borders. The need to develop international dialogues and means of organization which can connect locality and immediacy across the international division of labour is perhaps more readily apparent to black populations who define themselves as part of a diaspora, and who have recent experience of migration as well as acute memories of slavery and international indenture.

I have not intended to suggest that the attempt to turn these insights into political practice necessitates the abandonment of any idea of Englishness or Britishness. We are all, no doubt, fond of things which appear unique to our national culture – queueing perhaps, or the sound of leather on willow. What must be sacrificed is the language of British nationalism which is stained with the memory of imperial greatness. What must be challenged is the way that these apparently unique customs and practices are understood as expressions of a pure and homogeneous nationality. British socialists often interpret the things they like or wish to encourage as repositories and emblems of national sentiment. Socialists from Orwell to Thompson have tried to find the answer to their marginalization in the creation of a popular patriotism, and described the oppression of the working class in nationalist images as diverse as 'the Norman yoke',[82] and Tony Benn's colonial analogy discussed above. Their output owes its nationalist dimensions to several sources. It has been forged not only in the peculiarities of the route which brought the English proletariat into being within national limits[83] marked by the early liquidation of the peasant class and the protracted dominance of the aristocracy, but also by the concepts and methods of historical materialism itself. These have been shown to play a role in the reproduction of a blind spot around nationalism as far as Marxists are concerned.[84] Marx and Engels' assertion that the workers have no fatherland sits uncomfortably beside their practice as German nationalists and its accompanying theory of historic and non-historic peoples which differentiated between 'the large viable European nations' and the 'ruins of peoples' (*Volkerabfalle*) which are found here and there and which are no longer capable of national existence.[85] Their dismissal of the nationalist movements which might arise from among 'historyless' peoples (*Geschitlossen Volker*) whose national communities did not conform to the precise equation of state and language which could guarantee them historical being, is one of the fundamental moments in which the Eurocentrism and statism of Marxism are brought into being. It illustrates the limitations that history has placed on the value of Marxian insights which may not be appropriate to the analysis of the relationship between 'race', nation and class in the post-industrial era. This legacy must be re-examined and dealt with if the hold of nationalism on today's socialists is to be broken. Its inversion in the form of black cultural nationalism simply replicates the problem.

Notes

1 Martin Barker, *The New Racism* (London: Junction Books, 1981). Barker's concept has been usefully developed by Mark Duffield, 'New Racism ... New Realism: Two Sides of the Same Coin', *Radical Philosophy* 37 (Summer 1984) and Errol Lawrence, 'In the Abundance of Water the Fool is Thirsty: Sociology and Black Pathology', in Centre for Contemporary Cultural Studies, eds., *The Empire Strikes Back* (London: Hutchinson, 1982).

2 John Casey, 'One Nation: The Politics of Race', *Salisbury Review* 1 (1982). See also Casey's 'Tradition and Authority', in M. Cowling, ed., *Conservative Essays* (London: Cassell, 1978).

3 Editorial, *Salisbury Review* 1 (1983).

4 J. Seabrook, 'The War against Jingoism', *Guardian* (31 March 1986). See also the reply by Dafydd Elis Thomas, 'In a Loveless State', *Guardian* (14 April 1986).

5 The works of Anthony Barnett and Patrick Wright are honourable and notable exceptions here. See A. Barnett, 'Iron Britannia', *New Left Review* 134 (July/August 1982); 'The Dangerous Dream', *New Statesman* 105. 2726 (17 June 1983); 'Getting it Wrong and Making it Right', *New Socialist* (Sept./Oct. 1983); 'Fortress Thatcher', in Ayrton, Englehart and Ware, eds., *World View 1985* (London: Pluto Press, 1984); and Patrick Wright, *On Living in an Old Country* (London: Verso, 1985). Wright, in particular, tries to break the deadlock between these tendencies in a bold and innovative manner. The success of his attempt is, however, qualified by the fact that it is secured on the terrain of history. Barnett has consistently pointed to the profound relationship between Labourism and nationalism as well as to the contemporary dangers inherent in a populist nationalism.

6 K. Marx and F. Engels, *The Revolutions of 1848* ed., D. Fernbach (Harmondsworth: Penguin, 1973).

7 Tom Nairn, *The Break Up of Britain* (London: New Left Books, 1977).

8 Benedict Anderson, *Imagined Communities: Reflections on the Origin and Spread of Nationalism* (London: Verso, 1983), p. 136.

9 H. Wolpe, 'Capitalism and Cheap Labour-power in South Africa: From Segregation to Apartheid', in H. Wolpe, ed., *The Articulation of Modes of Production* (London: Routledge & Kegan Paul, 1980).

10 WING, *Worlds Apart: Women Under Immigration and Nationality Law* (London: Pluto Press, 1985).

11 Speech at Southall (4 November 1971).

12 Lawrence, 'In the Abundance of Water'.

13 A. Gamble, *The Conservative Nation* (London: RKP, 1974) and R. Levitas, *The Ideology of the New Right* (Oxford: Polity Press, 1986).

14 *Sunday Telegraph* (27 June 1982).

15 Speech at Eastbourne (16 November 1968).

16 H. Macmillan, *At the End of the Day* (London: Macmillan, 1973).

17 J. Rex, 'The Race Relations Catastrophe', in T. Burgess, ed., *Matters of Principle: Labour's Last Chance* (Harmondsworth: Penguin, 1968); see also *Guardian* (30 September 1965).

18 A. Carter, 'Masochism for the Masses', *New Statesman* (3 June 1983).

19 Cowling, *Conservative Essays*. See also P. Foot, *The Rise of Enoch Powell* (Harmondsworth: Penguin, 1969).

20 G. Bennett, *The Concept of Empire from Burke to Attlee*, 2nd edn (London: Adam and Charles Black, 1962).

21 Jose Nun has produced a definitive discussion of this concept in his exchange with Ernesto Laclau in *Latin American Research Unit Studies* 3.2–3 (1980).

22 Cowling, *Conservative Essays*.

23 Barnett, 'Fortress Thatcher', and P. Worsthorne, *Sunday Telegraph* (12 June 1983).

24 *Sun* (21 January 1984).

25 Raymond Williams, *Towards 2000* (Harmondsworth: Pelican, 1983), and F. Mulhern, 'Towards 2000: News From You Know Where', *New Left Review* 148 (Nov./Dec. 1984).

26 Williams, *Towards 2000*, p. 195.

27 *Sunday Telegraph* (23 May 1982).

28 *Sunday Telegraph* (27 June 1982).

29 E. P. Thompson, *Zero Option* (London: Merlin, 1982).

30 *Guardian* (20 December 1982), reprinted from *Marxism Today*, January 1983.

31 Barnett, 'Getting it Wrong'; the *Sun* (25 May 1982).

32 *New Statesman* (14 December 1984).

33 *Formations* 1.1 (1983), p. 99.

34 E. P. Thompson, *The Defence of Britain* (London: END/CND, 1983).

35 Thompson, *The Defence of Britain*, p. 34.

36 See M. Fitzgerald, *Political Parties and Black People: Participation, Representation, and Exploitation*, (Runneymede/GLC, 1984), and D. Studlar, 'The Ethnic Vote: Problems of Analysis and Interpretation', *New Community* 11 (1983); 'Nonwhite Policy Preferences, Political Participation, and the Political Agenda in Britain', unpublished paper prepared for Conference on Race and Politics, St Hugh's College, Oxford, 28–30 September 1984; ' "Waiting for the Catastrophe": Race and the Political Agenda in Britain', *Patterns of Prejudice* 19.1 (1985).

37 Barnett, 'Iron Britannia'.

38 M. Foot, *Loyalists and Loners* (London: Collins, 1986). See also 'The Lives of Enoch', an extract from this book, *Guardian* (12 March 1986).

39 *Guardian* (8 March 1986); see also reply by Hugo Young, 'The Love that Dares to Speak its Name too Often', *Guardian* (11 March 1986).

40 Barnett, 'Iron Britannia'.

41 J. M. Mackenzie, *Propaganda and Empire* (Manchester: Manchester University Press, 1984), and *Imperialism and Popular Culture* (Manchester: Manchester University Press, 1986).

42 Tony Benn, 'Britain as a Colony', *New Socialist* 1 (Sept./Oct. 1981).

43 Barnett, 'Getting it Wrong'.

44 F. Shyllon, *Black Slaves in Britain* (Oxford: IRR/Oxford University Press, 1974), and *Black People in Britain* (Oxford: Oxford University Press, 1977).

45 Speech at the Carlton Club (26 November 1984).

46 *Sunday Telegraph* (8 September 1976).

47 The best example of this is the contrast between television situation comedies featuring blacks and whites. It is notable that none of the series featuring blacks seem able to portray inter-generational relations between black characters or show their experiences over time, in a diachronic dimension.

The BBC series 'Frontline' (1985) about the relationship between two black brothers, one a 'Rasta', the other a policeman, began significantly with the death of their mother. An equivalent programme centred on a fractured white family in which notions of locality and 'ethnicity' play a similar role – 'Only Fools and Horses' – builds its humour out of the tension between generations.

48 E. Powell, *A Nation or No Nation?* (London: Batsford, 1978).

49 *Guardian* (11 March 1985).

50 Speech to Stretford Young Conservatives (21 January 1977).

51 G. Seidel, 'The White Discursive Order: The British New Right's Discourse on Cultural Racism with Particular Reference to the *Salisbury Review*', unpublished paper presented to the University of Utrecht summer school of Critical Theory, June 1985.

52 R. Honeyford, 'Multi-Ethnic Intolerance', *Salisbury Review* (Summer 1983), p. 13.

53 R. Butt, 'Multi Cultural Consequences', *Times Educational Supplement* (24 May 1985).

54 A good selection of the many articles on Honeyford's case would include *Daily Mail* (17 and 18 December 1985); the *Sun* (12 April, 20 June, 30 November 1985); the *Spectator* (22 June 1985); and the Centre for Policy Studies pamphlet 'The Trials of Ray Honeyford: Problems in Multi-Cultural Education' (1985).

55 Hazel Carby, 'Schooling in Babylon', in CCCS, eds., *The Empire Strikes Back*.

56 Lawrence, 'In the Abundance of Water'.

57 *Mirror* (24 April 1986).

58 *The Times* and *Sun* (28 September 1982).

59 As far as 'race' and the Royals is concerned see Helen Chappell's 'The Wedding and The People', *New Society* (30 July 1981) and coverage of the discovery of a 'Little Black Sambo' book in Prince William's nursery, the *Sun* (26 September 1985). Away from the domestic scene, the Queen's 1985 tour of the Caribbean saw her confronted with a 'giant roasted rat' at a State Banquet in Belize. This meal, and the monarch's polite 'picking at it' neatly symbolized the cultural difference between us and them. The story featured on the front page of the *Mirror* (12 October 1985).

A good range of coverage from various sports about the contradictions between 'race' and nation can be gained from the following. Geoff Capes, an ex-police officer and currently Britain's strongest man, is something of a John Bull figure in the popular press. His relationship with an Asian woman for whom he abandoned his wife and children was the subject of a detailed article 'Why Do They Sneer At My Black Beauty?' in the *Sun* (27 November 1984).

There is plenty of cricket coverage which deals directly with 'race' politics, partly because of the South African connections of several England players, but mostly because the West Indies team has managed to inflict a series of humiliating defeats on England during the last few years. At the time of writing, England has not beaten the West Indies in a test for twelve years. Much of the more racist coverage centres on the question of whether the West Indian fast bowling violates either the letter or the spirit of cricket's laws. See E. M. Wellings, 'Government Without Backbone', in *Wisden Cricket Monthly* (March 1985), and coverage of Mike Gatting's nose injury on England's 1986 tour of the Caribbean, *Mirror* (20 February 1986). On the black spectators see the account of the West Indian victory at the Oval (15 August 1984). The *Sun*'s account, 'Mob Rule Triumphs', is the best illustration.

60 *Guardian* (27 April 1984).

61 *Daily Mail* (16 April 1984).

62 *Sun* (27 April 1984).

63 *Hansard* Commons debates (26 April 1984), col. 880.

64 P. Parmar, 'Hateful Contraries', *Ten 8* 16 (1984); A. Sherman, 'Britain is not Asia's Fiancée', *Daily Telegraph* (9 November 1979).

65 *Guardian* (23 May 1984).

66 *The Times* (31 May 1984).

67 *Daily Telegraph* (23 May 1984).
68 *Guardian* (23 May 1984).
69 See Jeremy Laurence in *New Society* (30 June 1983), and Ann Shearer, 'The Race Issue must be Faced' in the *Guardian* (26 January 1983). Also Jeannette Kupfermann, 'Love is more Important than your Parents' Colour', *Daily Mail* (14 February 1983).
70 ABSWAP, *Black Children in Care: Evidence to the House of Commons Social Services Committee* (1983).
71 John Small, 'The Crisis in Adoption', *International Journal of Social Psychiatry* 30.1–2 (Spring 1984).
72 ABSWAP, *Black Children in Care*.
73 M. Marable, *Blackwater Historical Studies in Race, Class Consciousness and Revolution* (Dayton: Black Praxis Press, 1981), and M. Marable, *Race, Reform and Rebellion: The Second Reconstruction in Black America, 1945–1982* (London: Macmillan, 1984).
74 P. Stubbs, 'The Employment of Black Social Workers: from "Ethnic Sensitivity" to "Anti-racism?" ', *Critical Social Policy* 12 (1985).
75 R. Kerridge, 'Fostering Apartheid', *The Spectator* (6 July 1985).
76 B. Rooney, 'Active Mistakes – A Grass Roots Report', *Multiracial Social Work* 1 (1980).
77 Stubbs, 'The Employment'.
78 *Black on Black*, Channel 4 (26 February 1985).
79 D. Bull and P. Wilding, *Thatcherism and the Poor*, Child Poverty Action Group Poverty Pamphlet, no. 59 (1983).
80 M. J. Weiner, *English Culture and the Decline of Industrial Spirit 1850–1980* (Cambridge: Cambridge University Press, 1981).
81 Doreen Massey, *Spatial Divisions of Labour* (London: Macmillan, 1984).
82 E. Hobsbawm, 'The Historians' Group of the Communist Party', in Cornforth, ed., *Rebels and Their Causes: Essays in Honour of A. L. Morton* (London: Lawrence & Wishart, 1978).
83 P. Linebaugh, 'All the Atlantic Mountains Shook', *Labour/Le Travail* 10 (Autumn 1982), and 'Reply to Sweeny', *Labour/Le Travail* 14 (Autumn 1984).
84 E. Gellner, *Nations and Nationalism* (Oxford: Basil Blackwell, 1983); G. Kitching, 'Nationalism: the Instrumental Passion', *Capital and Class* 25 (Spring 1985); E. Nimni, 'The Great Historical Failure: Marxist Theories of Nationalism', *Capital and Class* 25 (Spring 1985); Tom Naim, *The Break Up of Britain*.
85 C. Robinson, *Black Marxism* (London: Zed, 1982).

PART THREE

LOCATING PRACTICE

14

Aijaz Ahmad

*The Politics of Literary Postcoloniality**

Let me start by confessing that the current discussions of postcolonialism in the domain of *literary* theory produce in me a peculiar sense of *déjà vu*, even a degree of fatigue.[1] There had been in the 1970s, in the field of political theory, a fulsome debate on the issue of postcolonialism, but with specific reference to the type of postcolonial *states* that arose in Asia and Africa after postwar decolonisations. Indeed, I had myself published something of a postscript to that debate. Now, as this same term resurfaces in literary theory, without even a trace of memory of that earlier debate, I am reminded of something that the Cuban-American critic, Roman de la Campa, said to me in conversation, to the effect that 'postcoloniality' is postmodernism's wedge to colonise literatures outside Europe and its North American offshoots – which I take the liberty to understand as saying that what used to be known as 'Third World literature' gets rechristened as 'postcolonial literature' when the governing theoretical framework shifts from Third World nationalism to postmodernism.[2] The more substantial issues that are involved in the current expositions of what gets called 'postcolonial criticism' I shall take up presently, but it may be better to enter into the subject through an anecdote.

As I moved into a friend's flat for a week's residence in London this past June, I spotted a book on her shelf called *Colonial Discourse and Postcolonial Theory: a Reader*.[3] This interested me because I have believed for some time that the term 'postcoloniality' is a late-coming twin of that earlier term 'colonial discourse'. That some others would make so direct and so positive a connection between the two terms was intriguing. So, I looked at the table of contents, stopped at section 4, entitled 'Theorising post-coloniality'; then I looked up the page number for the first essay in that section, entitled 'What is post(-)colonialism?', with its bracketed hyphen. As I started reading, I soon came upon *this*, all in the space of a dozen lines:

> The condemnation of Rushdie by the Islamic postcolonial world raises the interesting questions about the category of the postcolonial itself ... For the Islamic postcolonial world the moral is clear and succinct: to write in the language of the coloniser is to write from within death itself ... postcolonial writers who write in the

* From *Race and Class* 36.3 (1995), pp. 1–20.

language of the Empire are marked off as traitors to the cause of a reconstructive postcolonialism ... postcolonial writers compose under the shadow of 'death'.[4]

This, I thought, was odd on several counts. The first to ban *Satanic Verses* was not a Muslim country but the Indian government, hardly Islamic even in pretension. In turn, English is virtually the official language of India; 40 per cent of all publishing in India is done in English; India publishes more English books than any other country except the US and UK; and more English-speakers are said to reside in India today than in Britain. We might also recall, for the sake of accuracy, that Khomeini's retrograde *fatwa* declared Rushdie as 'traitor' to *Islam*, not to some 'reconstructive postcolonialism'; otherwise, much Islamicist propaganda issues from Tehran in the English language. In Iran, Pakistan, Malaysia, the Arab world, millions of people write and generally conduct the business of life in English or French. No one gets killed, or otherwise punished, for doing so. The claim that 'postcolonial writers compose under the shadow of death' is simply preposterous, whatever the blanket term 'postcolonial writer' might mean.

More to the point, *when* was Iran colonial? In what sense can the regime of Irani clerics be called 'postcolonial'? Was the antecedent Pahlavi regime also 'postcolonial'? Would the Shah have issued a *fatwa* against Rushdie? What do we gain by suspending profound distinctions between a monarchical autocracy and clerical fascism, so as to denounce an undifferentiated 'postcolonial Islamic world', in the name of the generality of the newly marketed category of 'postcolonial writers'?

Four titles away from this book was another, entitled *Outside in the Teaching Machine*,[5] by Gayatri Spivak. Since none of the chapter headings had the word 'postcolonialism' in it, I fastened on the two with the word 'marginality' and the term 'culture studies' in them, because 'postcolonialism' was likely to crop up in both. I was glad to have been right, and what interested me in particular was a passage that she quoted on page 60 from an earlier essay of her own, and which again she rewrote for pages 280–1:

> Postcoloniality – the heritage of imperialism in the rest of the globe – is a deconstructive case. As follows: Those of us from formerly colonised countries are able to communicate with each other and with the metropolis, to exchange and to establish sociality and transnationality, because we have had access to the culture of imperialism. Shall we then assign to that culture, in the words of the ethical philosopher Bernard Williams, a measure of 'moral luck'? I think there can be no question that the answer is 'no'. This impossible 'no' to a structure which one critiques, yet inhabits intimately, is the deconstructive philosophical position, and the everyday here and now of 'postcoloniality' is a case of it. Further, the political claims that are most urgent in decolonised space are tacitly recognised as coded within the legacy of imperialism: nationhood, constitutionality, citizenship, democracy, socialism, even culturalism ... They are thus being reclaimed, indeed claimed as concept metaphors for which no *historically* adequate referent may be advanced from postcolonial space.[6]

What struck me first about this passage is how much at variance Spivak's position is from that of Edward Said. In Said's essay, 'Third World intellectuals and metropolitan culture',[7] the line of demarcation between the so-called 'colonial' and 'postcolonial' intellectuals was that the 'colonial' ones spoke from positions imbibed from metropolitan culture while 'postcolonial' ones spoke from *outside* those positions. That argument was unsustainable enough;[8] now, in Spivak's formulation, postcoloniality itself equals the 'heritage of imperialism' which the postcolonial critic inhabits deconstructively – or, as Bhabha would say, ambivalently.

The virtue of the passage, at any rate, is that Spivak does tell us directly what she means by 'postcoloniality'. It means, she says, 'the heritage of imperialism in the rest of the globe'. The word 'heritage' in this context is striking, as if 'imperialism' was a matter of the past. Equally striking is the phrase 'rest of the globe', which suggests that postcoloniality is a condition found outside the United States, Britain and France. This is curious, because my impression is that it is in these countries, plus Australia, that postcolonial intellectuals actually live and do their theorising. All this we can let pass. Because even more striking is that the 'legacy of imperialism' that Spivak identifies in this defining passage consists almost entirely of political concepts and practices – 'nationhood, constitutionality, citizenship, democracy, socialism' – for which, according to her, 'no *historically* adequate referent may be advanced from postcolonial space'.

This is a matter of political history, so I shall take it up directly; and, since I have little knowledge of a thing called 'postcolonial space', I shall refer only to India, about which I am able to make some minimal claims of knowledge. With that clarification, let me take up this so-called 'heritage of imperialism' word by word.

It is the claim of British colonial historiography that Britain bestowed nationhood on India through conquest and administration; for this colonialist outlook, Indian nationhood is certainly a 'legacy of imperialism'. The fact, however, is that, to the extent that India is a nation at all, it became so not through British administration but in the course of the anticolonial movement, which was internally far more democratic than the colonial state and which mobilised some 20 million peasant households in the struggle against colonialism; the main British contribution to this process was that, at the beginning of the second world war, and in response to the Quit India Movement, Britain made an irrevocable commitment to Jinnah and thereby contributed to the subsequent Partition of the country. The '*historically* adequate referent' for Indian nationhood exists in India in the shape of the history of the national movement itself. Similarly, Indian democracy has nothing to do with the 'heritage of imperialism'. As late as 1946, one year before Independence, franchise had been extended to only a small minority of the population. By contrast, the most important – virtually the only worthwhile – political achievement of the modern Indian state is that it became a secular, democratic republic immediately after Independence. The Indian state now gives us that secular democracy more in the breach than the observance, but it is still worth recalling that nowhere in Europe or North America was adult franchise implemented with such low levels of literacy and material well-being as in

India immediately after Independence; nowhere in Europe or North America did women get the vote in the founding moment of electoral democracy – in India they did.[9]

The same applies to citizenship, which exists only to the extent that the people in their collectivity are able to give laws unto themselves. No one can be a citizen of a colonial state, and citizenship itself cannot be a so-called 'heritage of imperialism'. The precise aim of the anticolonial movement in India was to institute citizenship and to put in place a constitutionality that was derived not from colonial authority but from a constituent assembly. None of it amounts to a 'heritage of imperialism'. Even so, not the least remarkable of Spivak's assertions is, of course, that there is no '*historically* adequate referent' for 'socialism' in India. It would surely be news to those many millions of Indians who have punctually voted for the communist tickets over almost half a century if they were to be told that they are mere progeny of Lord Mountbatten. The '*historically* adequate referent' for socialism in India, I should have thought, was the same as anywhere else, namely the development of capitalism and the consequent division of society into classes of the modern type.

The point could perhaps be made that in describing them as the 'heritage of imperialism' Professor Spivak is referring here simply to the European origin of these words, concepts and practices. This too would be strange. *Words* may have originated in Europe, but the historical adequacy of the *referent* can only be established through reference to practices undertaken within India by Indian political subjects. Even with regard to concepts, I did not know that mere *origins* – ('myth of origins'?) – mattered all that much in postmodern discourse, nor does it seem appropriate that everything that originates in Europe should be consigned so unilaterally to the 'heritage of imperialism', unless we subscribe to an essentialist notion of an undifferentiated 'Europe' where everything and everyone is imperialist. In stressing this matter of *origins*, and in declaring that there is no '*historically* adequate referent' for democracy and socialism in India, Spivak is treading on very dangerous ground, unwittingly repeating what the Indian right wing says all the time. There is a powerful political movement in India which says that Indian Muslims and Christians are not true Indians because they subscribe to religions that did not *originate* in India; that Indian socialists are not true Indians because Marxism *originated* in Europe; that the Indian state should not be a secular state because secularism is a western construct. There are influential social scientists who argue that parliamentary democracy does not suit Indian conditions, and that India should invent indigenous social sciences and indigenous political forms. In conceding that democracy, socialism and constitutionality are the 'heritage of imperialism', Spivak concedes, I think, far too much.

But why should the word 'postcoloniality' carry the burden of such meanings? With this question, I should like to turn away from Spivak's definitional passage and address the broader question of the very status of this term. What

I want to recall again is that the first major debate on the idea of post-colonialism took place not during the past few years but some years earlier, and that not in cultural theory but in political theory, with the object of inquiry at that time being not 'postcolonial literature' or the 'postcolonial intellectual' but the 'postcolonial state'. That debate was initiated with Hamza Alavi's article, and respondents included Sherry Girling, Malorie Pompermeyer, Immanuel Wallerstein, John Saul, Zeimann and Lanzendörfer – and even myself when I published an article in 1985. This was some thirteen years after Alavi's original piece but well before the term resurfaced in literary theory, without even the trace of that earlier debate but with the radically altered and deliberately obscured meaning of the term itself.[10] This is not the place to recapitulate that debate but I did refer to it obliquely in a recent book of mine, as follows:

> these terms, 'colonial' and 'postcolonial' ... are key analytic categories which are used for periodisation of history as regards the rule over peoples of particular countries by ruling classes of other countries; for the fundamental shifts that take place with decolonisation in forms of state and relations between different national formations, units of capital, classes, and economies; for the internal reorganisation of state personnel, modes of governance and appropriation as well as circulation of surpluses nationally and internationally, when sovereign regimes are constituted in former colonies. This analytic distinction rests upon the fundamental fact that the ruling class of a colony is located outside the colony and that the colonial state is the instrument of that externally-based ruling class; with decolonisation, this structural feature of the dominated formation no longer applies and the formation therefore ceases to be colonial, regardless of any other kind of dependence. In Marxist thought, these categories have a precise meaning because they refer not to the date of decolonisation but to identifiable structural shifts in state and society, and in the hierarchy of systemic determinations which structure the relations between the imperialist bourgeoisie and the direct producers of the imperialised but sovereign nation-state in the territory that was previously a colony.
>
> These categories have no analytic value, nor any theoretical status, when they are mobilised to homogenise very complex structures of intellectual productions or the trajectories and subjectivities of individual writers and critics or broad intellectual strata ... For particular intellectuals or clusters of them, colonial cultural ambience can last far beyond the moment of decolonisation; for others, rejection of cultural dominance of the colonising country can take place, and often does take place, well before the actual dissolution of the colonial state. Careers of historians and teachers like Susobhan Sarkar, sociologists like A. R. Desai, militants and intellectuals like E.M.S. Namboodripad, not to speak of D.D. Kosambi – mathematician, Sanskritist, anthropologist, historian of ancient India – span many years of both the colonial and the postcolonial periods ... and none of them can be categorised as either a 'colonial' or a 'postcolonial' intellectual, either in terms of chronology or in terms of their attitude towards European ideas.[11]

I might add that my disagreements with Hamza Alavi, whose work I otherwise greatly admire, had been argued on very specific and quite different grounds.[12] It is worth remarking, though, that in periodising our history in the triadic terms of precolonial, colonial and postcolonial, the conceptual apparatus of 'postcolonial criticism' privileges as primary the role of colonialism as the principle of structuration in that history, so that all that came before colonialism becomes its own prehistory and whatever comes after can only be lived as infinite aftermath. That may well be how it appears to those who look at that history from the outside – to those, in other words, who look at the former colonies in Asia and Africa from inside the advanced capitalist countries – but not to those who live inside that history. In India, for example, it is very difficult to treat the social and cultural consequences of colonialism as discrete and *sui generis*; in histories of gender and caste and class, the precolonial and the colonial – and now, some half a century later, the postcolonial – are too deeply intertwined for that sort of treatment. But, then, there have been other countries – such as Turkey which has *not* been colonised, or Iran and Egypt, whose occupation had not led to colonisation of the kind that India suffered where the onset of capitalist modernity and their incorporation in the world capitalist system brought about state apparatuses as well as social and cultural configurations that were, nevertheless, remarkably similar to the ones in India, which *was* fully colonised. In this context, we should speak not so much of colonialism or postcolonialism but of capitalist modernity, which takes the colonial form in particular places and at particular times. After all, the United States was also once a colony, or a cluster of colonies; so was Latin America to the south of the US, Canada in the north, not to speak of the Caribbean islands. But later history has taken in each case a very different turn. When applied too widely, powerful terms of this kind simply lose their analytic power, becoming mere jargon.

As the terms 'postcolonial' and 'postcolonia*lism*' resurfaced during the 1980s, this time in literary and cultural theories and in deconstructive forms of history-writing, and as these terms were then conjoined with a newly coined 'postcoloniali*ty*', this resurfacing included no memory of how the term had come into being in the first place. In some usages, the word 'postcolonial' still attempted a periodisation, so as to refer to that which came *after* colonialism – though this sense of periodisation was itself used differently by different critics. But this word 'postcolonial' was to be used increasingly not so much for periodisation as for designating some kinds of literary and literary-critical writings, and eventually some history-writing, as *generically* postcolonial, while other writings in those same domains of literature, literary criticism and history-writing presumably were not.

This aggrandised sense of the term, as connoting generic definitions of periods, authors and writings gathered force through a system of mutual citations and cross-referencing among a handful of influential writers and their associates. About Edward Said's sharp distinction between the so-called 'colonial' and 'postcolonial' intellectuals, I have written elsewhere at some length.[13] Robert Young, who had until a decade ago devoted himself almost entirely to propagating French poststructuralism in the British Isles, with hardly a thought to spare for the erstwhile colonies, suddenly emerged as a leading theorist of what got called 'postcolonial criticism': even though he hardly uses the term in his *White Mythologies*, the book signifies his first major

awakening to the fact of imperialism, but in a world already populated by
poststructuralist thought and punctuated by those three masters of postcoloniality – Said, Bhabha and Spivak – to whom he devoted the last three
chapters of the book.[14] In turn, Gyan Prakash would then invoke Young's
authority – and that of the Subalternist group in which Gayatri Spivak more or
less belongs – in his own squabbles with David Washbrook.[15] In another sort of
inflation, Homi Bhabha would cite Jameson's magnificent reading of *Lord Jim*
in *The Political Unconscious* to declare that Jameson himself was practising
'postcolonial criticism'[16] – which is probably news to Jameson himself, considering that Bhabha says on the previous page that 'the postcolonial perspective resists the attempt at holistic forms of social explanation'.[17] Also, so
far as I know, Jameson has never broken with concepts of history and progress,
or with the further concept of modes of production, whereas, according to
Gyan Prakash, the main virtue of 'postcolonial criticism' is precisely that it has
abandoned the nationalist ideas of history and reason as well as the modes-of-
production metanarratives of Marxism. Meanwhile, Bhabha's own book,
Location of Culture, comes to us with handsome praise from Edward Said and
Toni Morrison.

But within the field of literature, we also have, alongside 'postcolonial
criticism', the quite different category of 'postcolonial *writing*'. This quite
different, and in its own way quite common, usage refers simply to literary
compositions – plays, poems, fiction – of non-white minorities located in
Britain and North America – while efforts are now under way also to designate
the contemporary literatures of Asia and Africa as 'postcolonial' and thus to
make them available for being read according to the protocols that metropolitan criticism has developed for reading what it calls 'minority literatures'. It is
in this sense that some British universities seem to be institutionalising that
singular pedagogical object which is variously called 'new literatures', 'emergent literatures' and 'postcolonial literatures'. In some ways, this specific sense
of *postcolonial literature* converges partly with the category of 'multiculturalism' and 'minority literature', even 'Third World literature', as these categories
arose somewhat earlier; but, then, it also converges with the term 'Others' as it
was used in the phrase 'Europe and its Others'. In at least one of the many
nuances, 'postcolonial' is simply a polite way of saying not-white, not-Europe,
or perhaps not-Europe-but-inside-Europe.

Let me turn briefly, though, to the matter of the term's spatial and temporal
applications. In usages spawned by such influential books as *The Empire Writes
Back*, and especially in much writing emanating from Australia, the terms
'colonial' and 'postcolonial' are applied not just to what is generally called the
'Third World' but also to the United States, Canada, New Zealand, Australia
itself, so that what remains to be done, I suppose, is to see how this singular
thing, 'postcoloniality', functions in the United States and in Vietnam, both
colonies of Europe at one time or another.[18] This inclusion of countries like the
United States among the postcolonies, and the fixing of the beginning of
postcolonialism with the first moment of colonising itself, serves, of course, to

extend both the spatial and temporal scope of postcoloniality quite considerably. But I have seen articles in a great many places, including the special issue of *Social Text* on postcoloniality, which push the use of the term 'colonialism' *back* to such configurations as the Incas, the Ottomans and the Chinese, well before the European colonial empires began; and then bring the term *forward* to cover all kinds of national oppressions, as, for example, the savagery of the Indonesian government in East Timor.[19] 'Colonialism' thus becomes a transhistorical thing, always present and always in process of dissolution in one part of the world or another, so that everyone gets the privilege, sooner or later, at one time or another, of being coloniser, colonised and postcolonial – sometimes all at once, in the case of Australia, for example.

The fundamental effect of constructing this globalised transhistoricity of colonialism is one of evacuating the very meaning of the word and dispersing that meaning so wide that we can no longer speak of determinate histories of determinate structures such as that of the postcolonial state, the role of this state in reformulating the compact between the imperialist and the national capitals, the new but nationally differentiated labour regimes, legislations, cultural complexes, etc. Instead, we have a globalised *condition* of *postcoloniality* that can be *described* by the 'postcolonial critic' but never fixed as a determinate structure of power against which determinate forms of struggle may be possible outside the domains of discourse and pedagogy. Given this dispersal of meaning by the very authors who use the term, it would appear more fruitful to ignore their mutual differences and to concentrate on the problems that arise from such deployments.

First, the field of application: Arif Dirlik is, I think, quite correct in pointing out that the term begins immediately to break down because it designates far too many things, all at once.[20] It is said to refer, first, to conditions that are said to prevail in the former colonies, such as India. But the same term is also made to refer to a *global* condition of the relation between the West and the Rest, whether or not any one of the Rest was actually colonised – so that 'postcoloniality' becomes a 'post' not only of colonialism but also of an indeterminate larger thing. At the same time, the term 'postcolonial' also comes to us as the name of a *discourse* about the condition of 'postcoloniality', so that certain *kinds* of critics are 'postcolonial' and others not (Bhabha supremely so; myself mercifully no, as Dirlik carefully points out). Following on which is the attendant assertion that only those critics, who believe not only that colonialism has more or less ended but who also subscribe to the idea of the end of Marxism, nationalism, collective historical subjects and revolutionary possibility as such, are the *true* postcolonials, while the rest of us, who do not quite accept this apocalyptic anti-Marxism, are not postcolonial at all. In this formulation, then, that which is designated as postcolonial discourse presumes the prior consent to theoretical postmodernity. Between postcoloniality as it exists in a former colony like India, and postcoloniality as the condition of discourse practised by such critics as Homi Bhabha, there would appear to be a very considerable gap. *This* gap postcolonial theory seeks to fill by a remarkably circular logic: we live in the postcolonial *period*, hence in a postcolonial *world*, but neither all intellectuals nor all discourses of this *period* and this *world* are *postcolonial* because, in order to be a properly *postcolonial discourse*, the discourse must be *postmodern*, mainly of the deconstructive kind, so that only those intellectuals can be truly *postcolonial* who are also *postmodern*.

Several of these issues get focused quite sharply if we look at only three of the themes that are quite common among such critics: (a) the theme of 'hybridity', 'ambivalence' and 'contingency', as it surfaces especially in Bhabha's writing but also much beyond; (b) the theme of the collapse of the nation-state as a horizon of politics; and (c) the theme of globalised, postmodern electronic culture, which is seen at times as a form of global entrapment and at other times as yielding the very pleasures of global hybridity. Let me take up very briefly the latter two issues – decline of the nation-state; globalisation of the electronic media – before I offer more extended comments on the concepts of hybridity and contingency.

It is doubtless true that independence of the nation-state in the imperialised world is getting greatly circumscribed by the global offensives of capital, and that the imperial formations, especially in Western Europe, are marked by an increasing interpenetration of national capitals, so that transnationally integrated finance capital has achieved a far greater autonomy with regard to state controls exercised in individual countries. But that is only one side of the story. That south-eastern Europe and the territories of the erstwhile Soviet Union are marked today by the emergence – more or less catastrophic emergence – of more and more ethnically-based nation-states should lay to rest all the euphoria about the global decline of the nation-state. At the apex of the world system, on the other hand, the nation-state is alive and well in both the United States and Japan. In Western Europe itself, the Union rests on negotiations among nation-states, and the largest and most powerful of these nation-states, Germany, has just achieved an *expanded* national unification and is unlikely to surrender its national interests to the Union, as not only its negotiations within the Union and the unilateral exercise of financial power by its national bank but also its newly defined national interests in Eastern Europe amply demonstrate.

Within Asia and Africa, the past decades have witnessed not the decline of the nation-state form but its further consolidation, as a mechanism for regulating markets and revenues, as a site for the production of national bourgeoisies and as an agent in local and regional wars. Within regions, national economies are more differentiated today than they were on the morrow of independence, as the experience of South Asia testifies. Transnational projects such as that of Arab nationalism have collapsed as the national bourgeoisie of each state has developed its own particularist interests. Alongside this trajectory, surely, imperialism has penetrated far more deeply into national economies than was the case in earlier decades. More significantly, most national bourgeoisies have achieved a far greater level of capital accumulation and have therefore developed a contradictory attitude towards their own nation-state: they wish to more or less bypass the regulatory aspects of this state (through liberalisation, marketisation, etc.), and yet utilise it both for securing the domestic conditions of production favourable to capital (by guaranteeing domestic labour regimes, by ensuring infrastructural development, etc.) and for facilitating the articulation between domestic and foreign capitals. In other words, the new national bourgeoisies, like imperialist capital itself, want a weak nation-state in relation to capital and a strong one in relation to labour. The famous 'retreat of the state' is a retreat, mainly, from the realm of welfare and social entitlements, combined, however, with very aggressive interventions in favour of capital, as much in the so-called 'liberalisation' schemes of countries like India as in the monetarist policies of the Reaganite-Thatcherite Right in the West – not to speak of the dissolution of the communist regimes and the rise of conservative, market-friendly regimes in the erstwhile Comecon countries. It is in this framework that the nation-state remains, globally, the horizon for any form of politics that adopts the life-processes of the working classes as its point of departure, and which seeks to address the issue of the exploitation of *poorer* women, the destruction of the natural environment by national as well as transnational capitals, or the rightward drift of ideological superstructures, all of which are deeply connected with labour regimes, gender-related legislations and ideologies, and investment and extraction plans guaranteed by the nation-state.

The structural dialectic of imperialism *includes*, in other words, the deepening penetration of all available global spaces by the working of capital *and* intensification of the nation-state form simultaneously. This dialectic produces contradictory effects in realms of culture and ideology. The same Arab magnates and Irani mullahs who chase petrodollars across the globe – those same saffron yuppies who are opening up the Bombay Stock Exchange and the computer industry of Bangalore for foreign capital – organise their own lives around the fetishism of commodities bequeathed to them by advanced capital but are also the ones most vociferous in propagating the discourse of Authenticity and cultural differentialism in the name of Islam in one space, Hinduism in another, in order to forge protofascist nationalisms for the working masses of their own nations, so as to wean them away from the progressive projects of socialism and anti-imperialist nationalisms. Within this context, speaking with virtually mindless pleasure of transnational cultural hybridity, and of politics of contingency, amounts, in effect, to endorsing the cultural claims of transnational capital itself.

For it is the claim of IBM, CNN, etc., that they are indeed the harbingers of a culture of global productivities, knowledges, pleasures. Again, it is doubtless true that a global informational regime is being constructed. But is one to celebrate this process as a globalised hybridity or to conceptualise it as the penetration of far-flung, globally dispersed households by uniform structures of imperialist ideology that now have the technological means to bypass the national educational and informational grids, so that the national and metropolitan sections of capital can be integrated ideologically, via CNN, as much as they are integrated economically in, let us say, the Bombay Stock Exchange? The answer to that question would determine, in discussions of politics, whether one foregrounds the contingent moment of TV-induced hyperreality or the structural offensive of capital. Furthermore, this regime of electronic pleasures is being imposed at a time when the African continent is mired in a secular decline of its economic systems and infrastructural facilities, to the extent that some two-thirds of the population in sub-Saharan Africa is said to live below the living standards of the colonial period, with the increasing decay of roadworks, transport facilities, electrical grids, schools, textbook production and the social fabric in general, not to speak of nationwide epidemics and ethnic genocides. It is not at all clear how the celebration of a postcolonial, transnational, electronically produced cultural hybridity is to be squared with this systematic decay of countries and continents, and with decreasing chances for substantial proportions of the global population to obtain conditions of bare survival, let alone electronic literacy and gadgetry.

Such are, in short, the material coordinates. What is the internal logic of this theorising? The idea of hybridity – which presents itself as a critique of essentialism, partakes of a carnivalesque collapse and play of identities, and comes under a great many names – takes essentially two forms: cultural hybridity and what one might call philosophical and even political hybridity. The basic idea that informs the notion of cultural hybridity is in itself simple enough, namely that the traffic among modern cultures is now so brisk that one can hardly speak of discrete national cultures that are not fundamentally transformed by that traffic. In its generality this idea can only be treated as a truism, since a generalisation of that order cannot in any specific sense be *wrong*. The steps that follow this truism are more problematic, however. At two ends of this same argument, this condition of cultural hybridity is said to be (a) specific to the migrant, more pointedly the migrant *intellectual*, living and working in the western metropolis; and, at the same time (b) a generalised condition of postmodernity into which all contemporary cultures are now irretrievably ushered – so that the figure of the migrant, especially the migrant (postcolonial) intellectual residing in the metropolis, comes to signify a universal condition of hybridity and is said to be the Subject of a Truth that individuals living within their national cultures do not possess. Edward Said's term for such Truth-Subjects of postcoloniality is 'cultural amphibians'; Salman Rushdie's treatment of migrancy ('floating upward from history, from memory, from time', as he characterises it) is likewise invested in this idea of the migrant having a superior understanding of *both* cultures than what more sedentary individuals might understand of their own cultures.[21] By the time we get to Bhabha, the celebration of cultural hybridity, as it is available to the migrant intellectual in the metropolis, is accented even further:

> America leads to Africa; the nations of Europe and Asia meet in Australia; the margins of the nation displace the centre ... The great Whitmanesque sensorium of America is exchanged for a Warhol blowup, a Kruger installation, or Mapplethorpe's naked bodies.[22]

In Bhabha's writing, the postcolonial who has access to such monumental and global pleasures is remarkably free of gender, class, identifiable political location. In other words, this figure of the postcolonial intellectual has a taken-for-grantedness of a male, bourgeois onlooker, not only the lord of all he surveys but also enraptured by his own lordliness. Telling us that 'the truest eye may now belong to the migrant's double vision,'[23] we are given also the ideological location from which this 'truest eye' operates: 'I want to take my stand on the shifting margins of cultural displacement – that confounds any profound or "authentic" sense of a "national" culture or "organic" intellectual.'[24] Having thus dispensed with Antonio Gramsci – and more generally with the idea that a sense of place, of belonging, of some stable commitment to one's class or gender or nation may be useful for defining one's politics – Bhabha then spells out his own sense of politics:

> The language of critique is effective not because it keeps for ever separate the terms of the master and the slave, the mercantilist and the Marxist, but to the extent to which it overcomes the given grounds of opposition and opens up a space of 'translation': a place of hybridity ... This is a sign that history is *happening*, in the pages of theory.[25]

Cultural hybridity ('truest eye') of the migrant intellectual, which is posited as the negation of the 'organic intellectual' as Gramsci conceived of it, is thus conjoined with a philosophical hybridity (Bhabha's own 'language of critique') which likewise confounds the distinction between 'the mercantilist and the Marxist' so that 'history' does indeed become a mere 'happening' – 'in the pages of theory', for the most part. These hybridities, cultural and philosophical, lead then to a certain conception of politics which Bhabha outlines in his essay, 'The postcolonial and the postmodern: the question of agency', where we are again told that 'the individuation of the agent occurs in a moment of displacement',[26] because 'contemporary postcolonial discourses are rooted in specific histories of cultural displacement'.[27] This pairing of hybridity and agential displacement then calls forth a politics of 'contingency', while contingency is defined 'as the defining term of counter-hegemonic strategies'. This elaboration of hybrid, displaced, contingent forms of politics is accomplished with the aid of a great many writers, including Ranajit Guha ('Guha's elaborations of rebel consciousness as contradiction are strongly suggestive of agency as the activity of the contingent')[28] and Veena Das. The latter reference should detain us somewhat, since it comes with a direct quotation from Das, greatly approved by Bhabha, which denies that there may be such a thing as an enduring caste consciousness to which one might refer in order to understand any particular caste conflict of the kind that is so common in present-day India. I therefore quote both Bhabha and Das as she herself is quoted by Bhabha:

> In her excellent essay 'Subaltern as perspective' Das demands a historiography of the subaltern that displaces the paradigm of social action as defined by rational action. She seeks a form of discourse where affective and iterative writing develops its own language ... This is the historical movement of hybridity as camouflage, as a contesting, antagonistic agency functioning in the time lag of sign/symbol, which is a

space in-between the rules of engagement. It is this theoretical form of political agency I've tried to develop that Das beautifully fleshes out in a historical argument:

> It is the nature of the conflict in which a caste or tribe is locked which may provide the characteristics of the historical moment; to assume that we may know *a priori* the mentalities of castes and communities is to take an essentialist perspective which the evidence produced in the very volumes of *Subaltern Studies* would not support.[29]

Setting aside the matter of the '*a priori*' (no one has argued in favour of *a priori* knowledges), the striking feature of Das's perspective is its advocacy that, when it comes to caste conflicts, each historical moment must be treated as *sui generis* and as carrying within itself its own explanation – unless one is willing to be accused of that dirty thing, 'essentialism'. That any understanding of a particular conflict must *include* an understanding of its particularity is so obvious as to be not worth repeating. What Das is advocating here is not just that obvious point but that the understanding of each conflict be *confined* to the characteristics of that conflict. What she denies radically is that caste mentalities may indeed have historical depth and enduring features *prior* to their eruption in the form of a particular conflict. What is denied, in other words, is that caste is a structural and not merely a contingent feature in the distribution of powers and privileges in Indian society, and that members of particular castes are actual bearers of those earlier histories of power and dispossession, so that the conflicts in which castes get 'locked' (to use Das's own telling word) are inseparable from those histories, no matter how much a particular expression of that enduring conflict may be studied in its uniqueness. It is always convenient for the bourgeoisie that the worker forgets the history of how capital is accumulated and looks at the current capitalist simply as the provider of jobs, and it is always convenient for the upper-class Indian to deny that the caste conflicts of today are, generally speaking, conflicts between the beneficiaries and the victims of the caste structure. When the theorist, Bhabha or Das or any other, denies the structural endurance of histories and calls upon us to think only of the contingent moment, we are in effect being called upon to overlook the position of class and caste privileges from which such theories emanate and such invocations issue.

In terms of his own logic, though, Bhabha is right. Das's denial that there might be such a thing as a caste mentality and her assertion that all historical moments are *sui generis* is entirely consistent with Bhabha's own assertion that explanations for human action must be non-rational and that historical agents are constituted in displacement. Such premises preclude, I would argue, the very bases of political action. For the idea of a collective human agent (e.g., organised groups of the exploited castes fighting for their rights against upper-caste privilege) presumes both what Habermas calls communicative rationality as well as the possibility of rational action as such; it presumes, in other words, that agencies are constituted not in flux and displacement but in given historical locations.

History does not consist of perpetual migration, so that the universality of
'displacement' that Bhabha claims both as the general human condition and
the desirable philosophical position is tenable neither as description of the
world nor as generalised political possibility. He may wish to erase the
distinction between commerce and revolution, between 'the mercantile and
the Marxist', and he is welcome to his preferences; but that hardly amounts to
a 'theory' of something called postcoloniality. Most individuals are really not
free to fashion themselves anew with each passing day, nor do communities
arise out of and fade into the thin air of the infinitely contingent. Among the
migrants themselves, only the privileged can live a life of constant mobility and
surplus pleasure, between Whitman and Warhol as it were. Most migrants tend
to be poor and experience displacement not as cultural plenitude but as
torment; what they seek is not displacement but, precisely, a *place* from where
they may begin anew, with some sense of a stable future. Postcoloniality is also,
like most things, a matter of class.

I have argued that the contemporary dialectic of imperialist capital involves
both (a) more profound penetration of all available global spaces and (b)
greater proliferation of the nation-state form, with contradictory effects in the
fields of culture and ideology, in a situation where rapid realignments of
political hegemony on the global scale are producing among the professional
intelligentsia a characteristic loss of historical depth and perspective. The
tendency in cultural criticism is to waver constantly between the opposing
polarities of cultural differentialism and cultural hybridity. We have, on the
one hand, so extreme a rhetoric against Reason and Universality, and such
finalist ideas of cultural difference that each culture is said to be so discrete and
self-referential, so autonomous in its own authority, as to be unavailable for
cognition or criticism from a space outside itself, lest the outsider be seen as a
bearer of that Enlightenment rationality which is said to be colonising and
repressive *tout court*. The ideational logic of this cultural differentialism is to
privilege self-representation over all other kinds of representation and to treat
self-representation as a moment of absolute authenticity, as if between the self
and its representation there could be no moment of bad faith or false consciousness. In its softer form, the logic of this position is that of pure identity
politics; in the harder form, this same logic produces those many protofascisms
that are stalking the world, from Iran to the former Yugoslavia, and from
France to India.

At the other end of the spectrum, we have so vacuous a notion of cultural
hybridity as to replace all historicity with mere contingency; to lose all sense of
specificity in favour of the hyper-reality of an eternal and globalised present;
and to dispense with all structural persistence of the *longue durée* so remorse-
lessly that the present becomes both opaque and wholly self-referential.
Bhabha's own polemic against what he calls the 'long past' and 'organic nation'
is significant in this regard. It is doubtless true that modern electronics have
given to corporate capital unprecedented powers to penetrate spaces that had
hitherto remained relatively unreachable. It is also true that the contemporary

phase of capital involves unprecedented scales of movement not only of capital and commodities but also personnel. It is also the case, however, that the entire logic of the kind of cultural 'hybridity' that Bhabha celebrates presumes the intermingling of Europe and non-Europe in a context already determined by advanced capital, in the aftermath of colonialism. In this account, non-Europeans hardly ever encounter each other and never without a prior European modulation of the very field of that encounter. Nor do these celebrations of hybridity foreground the unequal relations of cultural power *today*; rather, intercultural hybridity is presented as a transaction of displaced equals which somehow transcends the profound inequalities engendered by colonialism itself. Into whose culture is one to be hybridised and on whose terms? The wilful relegation of this question to obscurity reveals nevertheless that the underlying logic of this celebratory mode is that of the limitless freedom of a globalised marketplace which pretends that all consumers are equally resourceful and in which all cultures are equally available for consumption, in any combination that the consumer desires. Only to the extent that all cultures are encountered in commodified forms does it become possible to claim that none commands more power than any other or that the consumer alone is the sovereign of all hybridisation. This playful 'hybridity' conceals the fact that commodified cultures are equal only to the extent of their commodification. At the deepest level, however, the stripping of all cultures of their historicity and density, reducing them to those lowest common denominators which then become interchangeable, produces not a universal equality of all cultures but the unified culture of a Late Imperial marketplace that subordinates cultures, consumers and critics alike to a form of untethering and moral loneliness that wallows in the depthlessness and whimsicality of postmodernism – the cultural logic of Late Capitalism, in Jameson's superb phrase – in a great many guises, including the guises of 'hybridity', 'contingency', etc.

Against this conception of 'hybridity', it would be erroneous to posit those claims of Authenticity that come to us from so many religious revivalisms and protofascist nationalisms of our time. However, *this* 'hybridity' must also be sharply distinguished from that very common life-process through which people move *within* national boundaries or encounter each other without mediation by colonialism and its aftermath. In one form or another, such cross-fertilisation of cultures has been endemic to all movements of people, from country to city, from city to city, from one site of labour to another at shorter or longer distances; and all such movements in history have involved the travel, contact, transmutation, hybridisation of ideas, values and behavioural norms. Thus it is that not only Hinduism, which is by its nature multiform, but also Islam, despite its scripturalist component, has led myriad different cultural lives, at different times and locations. Far from being specifically postmodern, physical mobilities and cultural cross-fertilisation are woven into the dynamics of historical time itself, in an unending dialectic of persistence and change, so that communities and individuals are neither mere repetitions of the past nor ever free to refashion themselves, *sui generis*, out of any clay that happens to be at hand. That one is free to invent oneself and one's community, over and over again, as one goes along, is usually an illusion induced by availability of surpluses – of money-capital or cultural capital, or both. That frenzied and constant refashioning of the Self, through which one merely consumes oneself under the illusion of consuming the world, is a specific mode of postmodern alienation which Bhabha mistakenly calls 'hybridity', 'contingency', 'post-coloniality'.

In the finalist notions of cultural differentialism, whereby no culture is or ought to be available for correction by another culture, historical time is simply denied as actually having happened. Instead, a mythic past is posited as the only true moment of cultural authenticity, hence the only measure of time, so that the vocation of history is to turn upon itself and recoup that mythic measure and rehabilitate that lost but ever-present Authenticity, always in pursuit of a past that never was.[30] On the other hand, the celebratory invocations of a uniquely postmodern hybridity, uniquely available to migrants residing in metropolitan cities and emanating from there to the rest of the globe, is, in a profound sense, simply the opposite of cultural differentialism, equally anti-historical, even though denying the actuality of historical depth in its own terms, as mere 'myth of origin', myths of 'deep nation' and the 'long past', etc. The striking thing, of course, is that strands in poststructuralist thought are equally available to both these anti-histories, the identitarian-particularist anti-history as well as the globalising-hybridist anti-history.

Notes

1 This essay is extracted from a much longer text which I began drafting as I lectured on different aspects of this theme in various colleges and universities. Versions of this particular extract have been presented at Birkbeck College, London; Flinders University, Adelaide; and the University of Hong Kong. A related extract, based on the lecture delivered at the State University of New York at Stony Brook, is to appear in Michael Sprinker and Roman de la Campa, eds., *Late Imperial Culture* (London: Verso, forthcoming). The full text on this subject – including a crucial section on the relation between this postmodern, culturalist theory of postcoloniality and the Fukuyamaist End-of-History narratives – will appear in a book I am now finishing.

2 I myself know little about how culturalist postcoloniality is taking charge of Latin American literature, but de la Campa's essay, 'Latin America and the Advent of Postcolonial Criticism', which he was kind enough to show me in manuscript, contains much useful reference and a great many insights.

3 Patrick Williams and Laura Chrisman, eds., *Colonial Discourse and Postcolonial Theory: a Reader* (London: Harvester Wheatsheaf, 1993).

4 Williams and Chrisman, *Colonial Discourse and Postcolonial Theory*, p. 277.

5 G. Spivak, *Outside in the Teaching Machine* (London: Routledge, 1993).

6 This same passage occurs in the book in three different versions. One presumes, therefore, that Professor Spivak attaches some considerable importance to it.

7 E. Said, 'Third World Intellectuals and Metropolitan Culture', *Raritan* (Winter 1990).

8 See my discussion of this essay in *In Theory: Classes, Nations, Literatures* (London: Verso, 1992), pp. 203–11.

9 As Spivak's colleagues in the Subaltern Studies group, notably Partha Chatterjee and Gyanendra Pandey, distance themselves from ideas of secularism as such, it is not clear where other members of this group stand on such issues. For a recent antisecular statement of this kind, see Partha Chatterjee, 'Secularism and Toleration', in *Economic and Political Weekly* (9 July 1994).

10 See, for the scope of the discussion, Hamza Alavi, 'The State in Postcolonial Societies: Pakistan and Bangladesh', in *New Left Review* 74 (July–August 1972), reprinted in Kathleen Gough and Hari P. Sharma, eds., *Imperialism and South Asia* (New York: Monthly Review Press, 1973); Sherry Girling, 'The State in Postcolonial Societies – Pakistan and Bangladesh: Comments on Hamza Alavi', in *Working Papers on the Capitalist State* (San José, 2/1973), pp. 49–51; Malorie Pompermeyer, 'The State and Dependent Development', and Immanuel Wallerstein, 'Comments on "The State and Dependent Development"' (San José, 1/73), pp. 25–7 and 27–8; John Saul, 'The State in Postcolonial Societies', in *Socialist Register 1974* (London: Merlin Press, 1974), reprinted in John Saul, *The State and Revolution in East Africa* (New York: Monthly Review Press, 1979); W. Zeimann and M. Lanzendörfer, 'The State in Peripheral Societies', *Socialist Register 1977* (London: Merlin Press, 1977); and Aijaz Ahmad, 'Class, Nation and State: Intermediate Classes in Peripheral Societies', in Dale Johnson, ed., *Middle Classes in Dependent Countries* (Beverly Hills: Sage, 1985).

11 *In Theory*, pp. 204–5.

12 For a review of that debate, and specifically of my own differences with Alavi's well-known essay, see my forthcoming essay, 'Postcolonialism: what's in a name?' in *Late Imperial Culture*.

13 *In Theory*, pp. 204–11.

14 Robert Young, *White Mythologies: Writing History and the West* (London and New York: Routledge, 1990).

15 Gyan Prakash, 'Postcolonial Criticism and Indian Historiography', *Social Text* 31/32 (1992); see also his 'Writing Post-Orientalist Histories of the Third World: Perspectives from Indian Historiography', *Comparative Studies in Society and History*. 32.2 (April 1990) In his essay, 'The Postcolonial Aura: Third World Criticism in the Age of Global Capitalism', *Critical Inquiry* 20 (Winter 1994), Arif Dirlik notes accurately, that unlike his more seasoned colleagues, Gyan Prakash, a new member of the Subaltern Studies group, has actually made the effort to define 'post colonialism' concretely and has therefore made the more obvious errors. (Dirlik himself is a historian of modern China and his undue praise for the rest of this group perhaps indicates both the uncertainty of his knowledge of Indian historiography and the probable fact that he has acquired that knowledge in the United States, where Subalternism has made its principal mark).

16 Homi Bhabha, *The Location of Culture* (London and New York: Routledge, 1994), p. 174.

17 Bhabha, *The Location of Culture*, p. 173.

18 See Bill Ashcroft, Gareth Griffiths and Helen Tiffin, *The Empire Writes Back: Theory and Practice in Postcolonial Literatures* (London and New York: Routledge, 1989), where, already on page 2, we read: 'We use the term "postcolonial", however, to cover all the cultures affected by the imperial process from the moment of colonisation to the present day. So the literatures of African countries, Australia, Bangladesh, Canada ... Malta, New Zealand ... South Pacific Island countries ...

are all postcolonial literatures. The literature of the USA should also be placed in this category'.

19 *Social Text* 31/32 (1992). See, in particular, Anne McClintock, 'The Angel of Progress: Pitfalls of the Term Postcolonialism', who enumerates some of the 'pitfalls' in her opening pages and then goes on to inflate the meaning of the term 'colonialism' so markedly that all territorial aggressions ever undertaken in human history come to fall under this singular dispensation, thus erasing, among other things, the specificity of that capitalist colonialism which the nation-states of Europe uniquely produced.

20 Arif Dirlik, 'The Postcolonial Aura'.

21 The quoted phrases here are from Said's essay in *Raritan*, and from Salman Rushdie, *Shame* (New York: Random Houe, 1984), p. 91.

22 Homi K. Bhabha, ed., *Nation and Narration* (London: Routledge, 1990), p. 6.

23 Homi Bhabha, *The Location of Culture*, p. 5.

24 Bhabha, *The Location of Culture*, p. 21.

25 Bhabha, *The Location of Culture*, p. 25.

26 Bhabha, *The Location of Culture*, p. 185.

27 Bhabha, *The Location of Culture*, p. 172.

28 Bhabha, *The Location of Culture*, p. 187.

29 Bhabha, *The Location of Culture*, pp. 192–3. Das is quoted from R. Guha, ed., *Subaltern Studies*, Vol. VI (Delhi: Oxford University Press, 1989).

30 For a brilliant treatment of this Authenticist anti-politics in the context of Islam, see Aziz Al-Azmeh, *Islams and Modernities* (London: Verso, 1993).

15

Arif Dirlik

The Postcolonial Aura: Third World Criticism in the Age of Global Capitalism*

'When exactly ... does the "post-colonial" begin?' queries Ella Shohat in a recent discussion of the subject.[1] Misreading the question deliberately, I will supply here an answer that is only partially facetious: When Third World intellectuals have arrived in First World academe.

My goal in the discussion below is twofold: to review the term *postcolonial*, and the various intellectual and cultural positions associated with it, in the context of contemporary transformations in global relationships, and to examine the reconsiderations of problems of domination and hegemony as well as of received critical practices that these transformations require. *Postcolonial* is the most recent entrant to achieve prominent visibility in the ranks of those 'post' marked words (seminal among them, *postmodernism*) that serve as signposts in(to) contemporary cultural criticism. Unlike other 'post' marked words, *postcolonial* claims as its special provenance the terrain that in an earlier day used to go by the name of Third World. It is intended, therefore, to achieve an authentic globalization of cultural discourses by the extension globally of the intellectual concerns and orientations originating at the central sites of Euro-American cultural criticism and by the introduction into the latter of voices and subjectivities from the margins of earlier political and ideological colonialism that now demand a hearing at those very sites at the center. The goal, indeed, is no less than to abolish all distinctions between center and periphery as well as all other 'binarisms' that are allegedly a legacy of colonial(ist) ways of thinking and to reveal societies globally in their complex heterogeneity and contingency. Although intellectuals who hail from one part of that terrain, India, have played a conspicuously prominent role in its formulation and dissemination, the appeals of postcoloniality seem to cut across national, regional, and even political boundaries, which on the surface at least seems to substantiate its claims to globalism.

My answer to Shohat's question is only partially facetious because the popularity that the term *postcolonial* has achieved in the last few years has less to do with its rigorousness as a concept or with the new vistas it has opened up

* From *Critical Inquiry* (Winter 1994), pp. 328–56.

for critical inquiry than it does with the increased visibility of academic intellectuals of Third World origin as pacesetters in cultural criticism. I want to suggest that most of the critical themes that postcolonial criticism claims as its fountainhead predated the appearance, or at least the popular currency, of *postcolonial*. Whether there was a postcolonial consciousness (before it was so termed) that might have played a part in the production of those themes is a question to which I will return below. As far as it is possible to tell from the literature, however, it was only from the mid-1980s that the label *postcolonial* was attached to those themes with increasing frequency, and that in conjunction with the use of the label to describe academic intellectuals of Third World origin. From this time, these so-called postcolonial intellectuals seemed to acquire an academic respectability that they did not have before.[2] A description of a diffuse group of intellectuals and their concerns and orientations was to turn by the end of the decade into a description of a global condition, in which sense it has acquired the status of a new orthodoxy both in cultural criticism and in academic programs. Shohat's question above refers to this global condition; yet, given the ambiguity imbedded in the term *postcolonial*, it seems justifiable to redirect her question to the emergence of postcolonial intellectuals in order to put the horse back in front of the cart. This redirection is also intended to underline the First World origins (and situation) of the term.

My answer is also facetious, however, because merely pointing to the ascendant role that intellectuals of Third World origin have played in propagating *postcolonial* as a critical orientation within First World academia begs the question as to why they and their intellectual concerns and orientations have been accorded the respectability that they have. The themes that are now claimed for postcolonial criticism, both in what they repudiate of the past and in what they affirm for the present, I suggest, resonate with concerns and orientations that have their origins in a new world situation that has also become part of consciousness globally over the last decade. I am referring here to that world situation created by transformations within the capitalist world economy, by the emergence of what has been described variously as global capitalism, flexible production, late capitalism, and so on, terms that have disorganized earlier conceptualizations of global relations, especially relations comprehended earlier by such binaries as colonizer/colonized, First World/ Third World, and the 'West and the Rest,' in all of which the nation-state was taken for granted as the global unit of political organization. It is no reflection on the abilities of postcolonial critics to suggest that they and the critical orientations that they represent have acquired a respectability dependent on the conceptual needs of the social, political, and cultural problems thrown up by this new world situation. It is, however, a reflection on the ideology of postcolonialism that, with rare exceptions (see *PCC*),[3] postcolonial critics have been silent on the relationship of the idea of postcolonialism to its context in contemporary capitalism; indeed, they have suppressed the necessity of considering such a possible relationship by repudiating a foundational role to capitalism in history.

To consider this relationship is my primary goal in the discussion below. I argue, first, that there is a parallel between the ascendancy in cultural criticism of the idea of postcoloniality and an emergent consciousness of global capitalism in the 1980s and, second, that the appeals of the critical themes in postcolonial criticism have much to do with their resonance with the conceptual needs presented by transformations in global relationships caused by changes within the capitalist world economy. This also explains, I think, why a concept that is intended to achieve a radical revision in our comprehension of the world should appear to be complicitous in 'the consecration of hegemony,' as Shohat has put it ('NP,' p. 110). If postcolonial as concept has not necessarily served as a fountainhead for the criticism of an earlier ideology of global relationships, it has nevertheless helped concentrate under one term what previously had been diffused among many. At the same time, however, postcolonial criticism has been silent about its own status as a possible ideological effect of a new world situation after colonialism. Postcolonial as a description of intellectuals of Third World origin needs to be distinguished, I suggest below, from postcolonial as a description of this world situation. In this latter usage, the term mystifies both politically and methodologically a situation that represents not the abolition but the reconfiguration of earlier forms of domination. The complicity of postcolonial in hegemony lies in postcolonialism's diversion of attention from contemporary problems of social, political, and cultural domination, and in its obfuscation of its own relationship to what is but a condition of its emergence, that is, to a global capitalism that, however fragmented in appearance, serves as the structuring principle of global relations.

Postcolonial intellectuals and postcolonial criticism

The term *postcolonial* in its various usages carries a multiplicity of meanings that need to be distinguished for analytical purposes. Three uses of the term seem to me to be especially prominent (and significant): (*a*) as a literal description of conditions in formerly colonial societies, in which case the term has concrete referents, as in postcolonial societies or postcolonial intellectuals; (*b*) as a description of a global condition after the period of colonialism, in which case the usage is somewhat more abstract and less concrete in reference, comparable in its vagueness to the earlier term *Third World*, for which it is intended as a substitute; and (*c*) as a description of a discourse on the above-named conditions that is informed by the epistemological and psychic orientations that are products of those conditions.

Even at its most concrete, the significance of *postcolonial* is not transparent because each of its meanings is overdetermined by the others. Postcolonial intellectuals are clearly the producers of a postcolonial discourse, but who exactly are the postcolonial intellectuals? Here the contrast between *postcolonial* and its predecessor term, *Third World*, may be revealing. The term *Third World*, postcolonial critics insist, was quite vague in encompassing within one uniform category vastly heterogeneous historical circumstances and in locking in fixed positions, structurally if not geographically, societies and populations that shifted with changing global relationships. Although this objection is quite valid, the fixing of societal locations, misleadingly or not, permitted the identification of, say, Third World intellectuals with the concreteness of places of origin. *Postcolonial* does not permit such identification. I wondered above whether there might have been a postcolonial consciousness, by which I mean the consciousness that postcolonial intellectuals claim as a hallmark of their intellectual endeavors, even before it was so labeled. Probably there was, although it was invisible because subsumed under the category Third World. Now that postcoloniality has been released from the fixity of Third World location, the identity of the postcolonial is no longer structural but discursive. Postcolonial in this perspective represents an attempt to regroup intellectuals of uncertain location under the banner of postcolonial discourse. Intellectuals in the flesh may produce the themes that constitute postcolonial discourse, but it is participation in the discourse that defines them as postcolonial intellectuals. Hence it is important to delineate the discourse so as to identify postcolonial intellectuals themselves.

Gyan Prakash frames concisely a question that, I think, provides the point of departure for postcolonial discourse: How does the Third World write 'its own history?'[4] Like other postcolonial critics, such as Gayatri Chakravorty Spivak, he finds the answer to his question in the model of historical writing provided by the work on Indian history of the *Subaltern Studies* group (see 'PH,' p. 399), which also provides, although it does not exhaust, the major themes in postcolonial discourse.[5]

These themes are enunciated cogently in a recent essay by Prakash, which, to my knowledge, offers the most condensed exposition of postcolonialism currently available. Prakash's introduction to his essay is worth quoting at some length:

One of the distinct effects of the recent emergence of postcolonial criticism has been to force a radical re-thinking and re-formulation of forms of knowledge and social identities authored and authorized by colonialism and western domination. For this reason, it has also created a ferment in the field of knowledge. This is not to say that colonialism and its legacies remained unquestioned until recently: nationalism and marxism come immediately to mind as powerful challenges to colonialism. But both of these operated with master-narratives that put Europe at its center. Thus, when nationalism, reversing Orientalist thought, attributed agency and history to the subjected nation, it also staked a claim to the order of Reason and Progress instituted by colonialism; and when marxists pilloried colonialism, their criticism was framed by a universalist mode-of-production narrative. Recent postcolonial criticism, on the other hand, seeks to undo the Eurocentrism produced by the institution of the west's trajectory, its appropriation of the other as History. It does so, however, with the acute realization that postcoloniality is not born and nurtured in a panoptic distance from history. The postcolonial exists as an aftermath, as an after – after being worked over by colonialism. Criticism formed in this process of the enunciation of discourses of domination occupies a space that is neither inside nor outside the history of western domination but in a tangential relation to it. This is what Homi Bhabha calls an in-between, hybrid position of practice and negotiation, or what

Gayatri Chakravorty Spivak terms catachresis; 'reversing, displacing, and seizing the apparatus of value-coding.'[6]

To elaborate on these themes, postcolonial criticism repudiates all master narratives, and since the most powerful current master narratives are the products of a post-Enlightenment European constitution of history and therefore Eurocentric, postcolonial criticism takes the critique of Eurocentrism as its central task. Foremost among these master narratives to be repudiated is the narrative of modernization, in both its bourgeois and its Marxist incarnations. Bourgeois modernization, or 'developmentalism,' represents the renovation and redeployment of 'colonial modernity . . . as economic development' ('PH,' p. 393). Marxism, while it rejects bourgeois modernization, nevertheless perpetuates the teleological assumptions of the latter by framing inquiry in a narrative of modes of production in which postcolonial history appears as a transition (or an aborted transition) to capitalism (see 'PH,' p. 395).[7] The repudiation of the narrative of modes of production, I should add, does not mean the repudiation of Marxism; postcolonial criticism acknowledges a strong Marxist inspiration (see 'PC,' pp. 14–15 and *PCC*).[8] Needless to say, Orientalism's constitution of the colony as Europe's Other, that is, as an essence without history, must be repudiated. But so must nationalism and its procedures of representation that, while challenging Orientalism, have perpetuated the essentialism of Orientalism by affirming a national essence in history (see 'PH,' pp. 390–1). If it is necessary to repudiate master narratives, it also is necessary to resist all spatial homogenization and temporal teleology. This requires the repudiation of foundational historical writing. According to Prakash, a foundational view is one that assumes 'that history is ultimately founded in and representable through some identity – individual, class, or structure – which resists further decomposition into heterogeneity ('PH,' p. 397). The most significant conclusion to follow from the repudiation of foundational historiography is the rejection of capitalism as a foundational category on the grounds that 'we cannot thematize Indian history in terms of the development of capitalism and simultaneously contest capitalism's homogenization of the contemporary world' ('PC,' p. 13). (Obviously, given the logic of the argument, any Third World country could be substituted here for India.) Postfoundational history, in its repudiation of essence and structure and simultaneous affirmation of heterogeneity, also repudiates any fixing of the Third World subject and, therefore, of the Third World as a category:

> The rejection of those modes of thinking which configure the third world in such irreducible essences as religiosity, underdevelopment, poverty, nationhood, [and] non-Westernness . . . unsettle[s] the calm presence that the essentialist categories – east and west, first world and third world – inhabit in our thought. This disruption makes it possible to treat the third world as a variety of shifting positions which have been discursively articulated in history. Viewed in this manner, the Orientalist, nationalist, Marxist, and other historiographies become visible as discursive attempts to constitute their objects of knowledge, that is, the third world. As a result, rather than appearing as a fixed and essential object, the third world emerges as a

series of historical positions, including those that enunciate essentialisms ('PH,' p. 384).

It is noteworthy here that with the repudiation of capitalism and structure as foundational categories there is no mention of a capitalist structuring of the world, however heterogeneous and discrepant the histories within it, as a constituting moment of history. Finally, postfoundational history approaches 'third-world identities as relational rather than essential' ('PH,' p. 399). Post-foundational history (which is also postcolonial history) shifts attention from national origin to subject-position. The consequence is the following:

> The formation of third-world positions suggests engagement rather than insularity. It is difficult to overlook the fact that all of the third-world voices identified in this essay, speak within and to discourses familiar to the 'West' instead of originating from some autonomous essence, which does not warrant the conclusion that the third-world historiography has always been enslaved, but that the careful main-tenance and policing of East–West boundaries has never succeeded in stopping the flows across and against boundaries and that the self–other opposition has never quite been able to order all differences into binary opposites. The third world, far from being confined to its assigned space, has penetrated the inner sanctum of the first world in the process of being 'third-worlded' – arousing, inciting, and affiliating with the subordinated others in the first world. It has reached across boundaries and barriers to connect with the minority voices in the first world: socialists, radicals, feminists, minorities ('PH,' p. 403).

This statement is representative of postcolonialism's stance on contemporary global relations (and of its claims to transcending earlier conceptualizations of the world). So, attention needs to be shifted from national origin to subject-position; hence a politics of location takes precedence over politics informed by fixed categories (in this case the nation, though obviously other categories such as Third World and class are also implied). Also, although First and Third World positions may not be interchangeable, they are nevertheless quite fluid, which implies a need to qualify if not to repudiate binary oppositions in the articulation of their relationship. Hence local interactions take priority over global structures in the shaping of these relationships, which implies that they are better comprehended historically in their heterogeneity than structurally in their fixity. These conclusions follow from the hybridness or 'in-betweenness' of the postcolonial subject that is not to be contained within fixed categories or binary oppositions. Since postcolonial criticism has focused on the postcolonial subject to the exclusion of an account of the world outside of the subject, the global condition implied by postcoloniality appears at best as a projection onto the world of postcolonial subjectivity and epistemology – a discursive constitu-tion of the world, in other words, in accordance with the constitution of the postcolonial subject, much as it had been constituted earlier by the epistemolo-gies that are the object of postcolonial criticism.

If postcolonial criticism as discourse is any guide to identifying postcolonial intellectuals, the literal sense of *postcolonial* is its least significant aspect, if it is not altogether misleading. Viewed in terms of the themes that I have outlined above, postcolonial, on the one hand, is broadly inclusive; as intellectual concerns these themes are by no means the monopoly of postcolonial criticism, and one does not have to be post*colonial* in any strict sense of the term to share in them, for which the most eloquent evidence is that they were already central to cultural discussions before they were so labeled. Crucial premises of postcolonial criticism, such as the repudiation of post-Enlightenment meta-narratives, were enunciated first in post-structuralist thinking and the various postmodernisms that it has informed.[9] Taking the term literally as post*colonial*, some practitioners of postcolonial criticism describe former settler colonies – such as the United States and Australia – as postcolonial, regardless of their status as First World societies and colonizers themselves of their indigenous populations.[10] (Though to be fair, the latter could also be said of many Third World societies.) At the same time, the themes of postcolonial criticism have been prominent in the cultural discourses of Third World societies that were never, strictly speaking, colonies, or that conducted successful revolutions against Euro-American domination, or, like China, both. Nor are there clear temporal boundaries to the use of the term because the themes it encompasses are as old as the history of colonialism. To use the example of China again, such themes as the status of native history vis-à-vis Euro-American conceptualizations of history, national identity and its contested nature, national historical trajectory in the context of global modernization, and even questions of subjectivity created by a sense of in-betweenness are as old as the history of the Chinese encounter with the Euro-American West.[11] One might go so far as to suggest that, if a crisis in historical consciousness, with all its implications for national and individual identity, is a basic theme of postcoloniality, then the First World itself is postcolonial. To the extent that the Euro-American self-image was shaped by the experience of colonizing the world (since the constitution of the Other is at once also the constitution of the Self), the end of colonialism presents the colonizer as much as the colonized with a problem of identity. The crisis created by the commemoration of the 500th anniversary of Columbus's adventure comes to mind immediately.

On the other hand, the term *postcolonial*, understood in terms of its discursive thematics, excludes from its scope most of those who inhabit or hail from post*colonial* societies. It does not account for the attractions of modernization and nationalism to vast numbers in Third World populations, let alone to those marginalized by national incorporation in the global economy. Prakash seems to acknowledge this when he observes that 'outside the first world, in India itself, the power of western discourses operates through its authorization and deployment by the nation-state – the ideologies of modernization and instrumentalist science are so deeply sedimented in the national body politic that they neither manifest themselves nor function exclusively as forms of imperial power' ('PC,' p. 10). It excludes the many ethnic groups in post*colonial* societies (among others) that, obviously unaware of their hybridity, go on massacring one another. It also excludes radical postcolonials. Intellectuals in India have asked Gayatri Spivak to explain 'questions that arise out of the way you perceive yourself ("The post-colonial diasporic Indian who seeks to decolonize the mind"), and the way you constitute us (for convenience, "native" intellectuals),' to which Spivak's answer is: 'your description of how I constitute you does not seem quite correct. I thought I constituted you, equally with the diasporic Indian, as the post-colonial intellectual!' The interrogators are not quite convinced: 'Perhaps the relationship of distance and proximity between you and us is that what we write and teach has political and other actual consequences for us that are in a sense different from the consequences, or lack of consequences, for you.' They express doubts in another sense as well: 'What are the theories or explanations, the narratives of affiliation and disaffiliation that you bring to the politically contaminated and ambivalent function of the non-resident Indian (NRI) who comes back to India, however temporarily, upon the wings of progress?' (*PCC*, pp. 67–8). As phrased by Prakash, it is not clear that even the work of the *Subaltern Studies* collective, which serves as the inspiration of so much of the thematics of postcoloniality, may be included under postcolonial. I have no wish to impose an unwarranted uniformity on *Subaltern Studies* writers, but it seems that their more radical ideas, chief among them the idea of class, are somewhat watered down in the course of their representation in the enunciation of postcolonial criticism.[12] It is also misleading in my opinion to classify as postcolonial critics intellectuals as widely different politically as Edward Said, Aijaz Ahmad, Homi Bhabha, Gyan Prakash, Gayatri Spivak, and Lata Mani. In a literal sense, they may all share in postcoloniality and some of its themes. Said's situation as a Palestinian intellectual does not permit him to cross the borders of Israel with the ease that his in-betweenness might suggest (which also raises the question for postcolonial critics of what borders are at issue). Ahmad, vehemently critical of the Three Worlds concept, nevertheless grounds his critique within the operations of capital, which is quite different from Prakash's denial of a foundational status to capitalism.[13] Spivak and Mani, though quite cognizant of the different roles in different contexts that in-betweenness imposes upon them, nevertheless ground their politics firmly in feminism (and, in the case of Spivak, Marxism).[14]

Finally, Kwame Anthony Appiah, examining the notion of postcoloniality in Africa, points to another pitfall in the literal use of post*colonial*, this time a temporal one. Appiah shares in the understanding of postcolonial as postmodernization, post-Third World, and postnationalist and points out that while the first generation of African writers after the end of colonialism were nationalists, the second generation has rejected nationalism.[15] In a recent discussion (a response to the controversy provoked by his criticism of postcolonial sub-Saharan Africa), Achille Mbembe suggests why this should be the case when he states that 'the younger generation of Africans have no direct or immediate experience' of colonization, whatever role it may have played as a foundational event in African history.[16] Postcolonial, in other words, is applicable not to all of the post*colonial* period but only to that period after colonialism when, among other things, a forgetting of its effects has begun to set in.

What then may be the value of a term that includes so much beyond and excludes so much of its own postulated premise, the colonial? What it leaves us with is what I have already hinted at: postcolonial, rather than a description of anything, is a discourse that seeks to constitute the world in the self-image of intellectuals who view themselves (or have come to view themselves) as postcolonial intellectuals. That is, to recall my initial statement concerning Third World intellectuals who have arrived in First World academe, post-colonial discourse is an expression not so much of agony over identity, as it often appears, but of newfound power. Two further questions need to be addressed before I elaborate further on this proposition: one concerns the role intellectuals from India have played in the enunciation of postcolonial discourse; the other concerns the language of this discourse.

Spivak comments (in passing) in an interview that, 'in India, people who can think of the three-worlds explanation are totally pissed off by not being recognized as the centre of the non-aligned nations, rather than a "Third-World" country' (*PCC*, p. 91). Indian intellectuals (and others in India) are not the only ones 'pissed off' at being categorized as just another Third World people; such can be found in any Third World country (my country of origin, Turkey, and the country I study, China, come to mind immediately), which speaks to the sorry state of Third World consciousness, if there is one. It is also impossible to say whether or not Indian intellectuals' anger at such categorization has anything to do with the themes that appear in postcolonial discourse, particularly with the repudiation of Third World as a category. Nevertheless, intellectuals from India, as I noted above, have been prominent in identifying themselves as postcolonial intellectuals as well as in enunciating postcolonial criticism. There is nothing wrong with this, of course, except a certain confusion has been introduced into the discourse. Specific problems in Indian historiography and general problems of a global condition described as post-colonial get confused with the projection globally of subjectivities that are (on the basis of the disagreements among Indian intellectuals to which I alluded above) representative of very few intellectuals in India. Most of the generalizations that appear in the discourse of postcolonial intellectuals from India may appear novel in the historiography of India but are not discoveries from broader perspectives. It is no reflection on the historical writing of *Subaltern Studies* historians that their qualifications of class in Indian history, their views on the nation as contested category, and their injunction that the history of capitalism be understood in terms of the fracturing consequences of local and national resistance to it as well as its triumphant, homogenizing effects, however well taken, do not represent earth-shattering conceptual innovations; as Said notes in his foreword to *Selected Sulbaltern Studies*, these approaches represent the application in Indian historiography of trends in historical writing that were quite widespread by the 1970s, under the impact of social historians such as E. P. Thompson, Eric Hobsbawm, and a whole host of others.[17] All this indicates is that historians of India were participants in the transformations in historical thinking in all areas, transformations in which Third World sensibilities were just one among a number of events that also included post-structuralism, new ways of thinking about Marxism, and the entry into history of feminism. To be sure, I think it very important that Third World sensibilities be brought into play repeatedly in order to counteract the tendency toward cultural imperialism of First World thinkers and historians who apply concepts of First World derivation globally without giving a second thought to the social differences that must qualify those concepts historically and contextually, but this is no reason to inflate a postcolonial sensibility, especially one that is itself bound by national and local experiences, indefinitely. And yet such a tendency (for which *Subaltern Studies* writers may themselves not be responsible at all) is plainly visible in the exposition of postcoloniality by someone like Prakash, who, writing of Indian historiography in one sentence, projects his observations globally in the very next one.

These observations are not intended to single out postcolonial intellectuals from India, which would be misleading not only about Indian intellectuals in general but also about postcolonial intellectuals in general. The appeals of postcoloniality are not restricted to intellectuals of any one national origin, and the problems to which I pointed above are problems of a general nature, born out of a contradiction between an insistence on heterogeneity, difference, and historicity and a tendency to generalize from the local to the global while denying that there are global forces at work that may condition the local in the first place. What my observations point to is a new assertiveness on the part of Third World intellectuals that makes this procedure possible. Another example may be found among Chinese intellectuals, in the so-called Confucian revival in recent years. These writers obviously do not describe themselves as postcolonial, for their point of departure is the newfound power of Chinese societies within global capitalism that, if anything, shows in their efforts to suppress memories of an earlier day when China, too, suffered from Euro-American hegemony (though not colonialism). In their case, the effort takes the form of articulating to the values of capitalism a Confucianism that in an earlier day was deemed to be inconsistent with capitalist modernization. Hence Confucianism has been rendered into a prime mover of capitalist development and has also found quite a sympathetic ear among First World ideologues who now look to a Confucian ethic to relieve the crisis of capitalism.[18] Although Confucianism in its urge to become part of a hegemonic ideology of capitalism differs from postcoloniality, it nevertheless shares with postcoloniality the counterhegemonic self-assertiveness of a group of formerly Third World intellectuals. And it may not be a coincidence that Chinese intellectuals in First World academia have played a major part in the enunciation of this Confucian revival, although it is by no means restricted to them.

The second question that needs to be considered concerns the language of postcolonial discourse, which is the language of First World post-structuralism, as postcolonial critics themselves readily concede, although they do not dwell too long on its implications. Prakash indicates this problem in his statement that 'all of the third-world voices identified in "Writing Post-Orientalist Histories" speak within and to discourses familiar to the "West," ' but he goes on to conceal its implications in his conclusion that this discursive fluency proves only that the 'maintenance and policing of East–West boundaries has never succeeded in stopping the flows across and against boundaries,' as if the flows in the two directions have been equal in their potency ('PH,' p. 403). More important, Prakash's obfuscation enables us to place temporally a postcoloniality that otherwise may stretch across the entire history of colonialism. Here, once again, a comparison with China may be instructive, this time over the issue of Marxism. Postcolonial critics insist that they are Marxists, but Marxists who reject the 'nineteenth-century heritage' of Marxism with its universalistic pretensions that ignored historical differences ('PC,' p. 15). Chinese Marxist revolutionaries in the 1930s faced and addressed the problem of articulating Marxism to Chinese conditions (and vice versa). Their answer was that Marxism must be translated into a Chinese vernacular not just in a national but, more importantly, in a local sense: the language of the peasantry. The result was what is commonly called the Sinification of Marxism, embodied in so-called Mao Zedong Thought.[19] The approach of postcolonial critics to a similar problem is not to translate Marxism into a national (which is rejected) or local (which is affirmed) vernacular but to rephrase it in the language of post-structuralism, in which Marxism is deconstructed, decentered, and so on. In other words, a critique that starts off with a repudiation of the universalistic pretensions of Marxist language ends up not with its dispersion into local vernaculars but with a return to another First World language with universalistic epistemological pretensions. It enables us, at least, to locate postcolonial criticism in the contemporary First World.

This is not a particularly telling point. Postcolonial critics recognize that the 'critical gaze' their studies 'direct at the archeology of knowledge enshrined in the west arises from the fact that most of them are being written in the first-world academy' ('PC,' p. 10). In drawing attention to the language of post-colonial discourse, I seek, however, to deconstruct postcolonial intellectuals' professions of hybridity and in-betweenness. The hybridity to which post-colonial criticism refers is uniformly between the post*colonial* and the First World, never, to my knowledge, between one post*colonial* intellectual and another. But hybridity and in-betweenness are not very revealing concepts in the former case either. Whereas postcolonial criticism quite validly points to the overdetermination of concepts and subjectivities (and I am quite sure that postcolonial subjectivity is overdetermined, while less sure that it is more so than any other), it conveniently ignores the part location in ideological and institutional structures plays in the resolution of contradictions presented by hybridity – and the consequences of location in generating vast differences in power.[20] If the language of postcolonial discourse is any guide to its ideological direction, in this case the contradictions presented by hybridity would seem to be given direction by the location of postcolonial intellectuals in the academic institutions of the First World. However much postcolonial intellectuals may insist on hybridity and the transposability of locations, not all positions are equal in power, as Spivak's interrogators in India seem to recognize in their reference to the 'wings of progress' that brought her to India. To insist on hybridity against one's own language, it seems to me, is to disguise not only ideological location but also the differences of power that go with different locations. Postcolonial intellectuals in their First World institutional location are ensconced in positions of power not only vis-à-vis the 'native' intellectuals back at home but also vis-à-vis their First World neighbors here. My neighbors in Farmville, Virginia, are no match in power for the highly paid, highly prestigious postcolonial intellectuals at Columbia, Princeton, or Duke; some of them might even be willing to swap positions and take the anguish that comes with hybridity so long as it brings with it the power and the prestige it seems to command.

'Postcoloniality,' Appiah writes, 'has become ... a condition of pessimism,'[21] and there is much to be pessimistic about the world situation of which postcoloniality is an expression. This is not the message of postcolonialism, however, as it acquires respectability and gains admission in United States academic institutions. Whereas this discourse shares in the same themes as postcolonial discourses everywhere, it rearranges these themes into a celebration of the end of colonialism, as if the only tasks left for the present were to abolish its ideological and cultural legacy. Although this approach may sound convincing, by fixing its gaze on the past it in fact avoids confronting the present. The current global condition appears in the discourse only as a projection of the subjectivities and epistemologies of First World intellectuals of Third World origin; the discourse constitutes the world in the self-image of these intellectuals, which makes it an expression not of powerlessness but of newfound power. Postcolonial intellectuals have arrived in the First World academy not only because they have broken new intellectual ground (although they have rephrased older themes) but also because intellectual orientations that earlier were regarded as marginal or subversive have acquired a new respectability. Postcoloniality, it has been noted, has found favor even among academic conservatives who prefer it to a less tractable vocabulary that insists on keeping in the foreground contemporary problems of political division and oppression.[22]

Postcoloniality already has been the subject of some telling criticism. Critics have noted that, in spite of its insistence on historicity and difference, postcoloniality mimics in its deployment the 'ahistorical and universalizing' tendencies in colonialist thinking ('NP,' p. 99). 'If the theory promises a decentering of history in hybridity, syncreticism, multidimensional time, and so forth,' Anne McClintock writes, 'the *singularity* of the term effects a re-centering of global history around the single rubric of European time. Colonialism returns at the moment of its disappearance.'[23] In a world situation in which severe inequalities persist in older colonial forms or in their neocolonial reconfigurations, moreover, 'the unified temporality of "postcoloniality" risks reproducing the colonial discourse of an allochronic other, living in another time, still lagging behind us, the genuine postcolonials' ('NP,' p. 104). The spatial homogenization that accompanies a 'unified temporality' not only fails to discriminate between vastly different social and political situations but also to the extent that it 'fails to discriminate between the diverse modalities of hybridity,' may end up in 'the consecration of hegemony' ('NP,' p. 110). Failing to make such discriminations and lacking a sense of totality, postcoloniality, as Rosalind O'Hanlon and David Washbrook observe, also ends up mimicking methodologically the colonialist epistemology that it sets out to repudiate:

> The solutions it offers – methodological individualism, the depoliticising insulation of social from material domains, a view of social relations that is in practice extremely voluntaristic, the refusal of any kind of programmatic politics – do not seem to us radical, subversive, or emancipatory. They are on the contrary conservative and implicitly authoritarian, as they were indeed when recommended more overtly in the heyday of Britain's own imperial power.[24]

Postcolonialism's repudiation of structure and totality in the name of history ironically ends up not in an affirmation of historicity but in a self-referential, universalizing historicism that reintroduces through the back door an un-examined totality; it projects globally what are but local experiences. The problem here may be the problem of all historicism without a sense of structure. Without a web of translocal relationships, it is impossible to determine what is different, heterogeneous, and local. In his critique of 'essentializing' procedures (of India, of the Third World), Prakash offers as a substitute an understanding of these categories in terms of 'relationships' but does not elaborate on what these relationships might be. The critique of an essentialist fixing of the Third World is not novel; Carl E. Pletsch's eloquent critique of three worlds theory (without the aid of postcoloniality), published a decade ago, enunciated clearly the problem of ideological essentializing in modernization theory.[25] Nor is Prakash's conceptual 'innovation' – relationships – truly new. Pletsch himself pointed to global relationships as part of the conceptual underpinnings of modernization theory as well as to their importance in understanding problems of development, and an understanding of modern global history in terms of relationships, needless to say, is the crucial thesis of world-system analysis.

The difference between world-system analysis and Prakash's postfoundational understanding of relationships is Prakash's rejection of foundational categories, chief among them, capitalism. What O'Hanlon and Washbrook say on this issue is worth quoting at some length:

> What [Prakash's] position leaves quite obscure is what status exactly this category of 'capitalist modernity' occupies for him. If our strategy should be to 'refuse' it in favour of marginal histories, of multiple and heterogeneous identities, this suggests that capitalist modernity is nothing more than a potentially disposable fiction, held in place simply by our acceptance of its cognitive categories and values. Indeed, Prakash is particularly disparaging of Marxist and social historians' concern with capitalism as a 'system' of political economy and coercive instrumentalities. Yet in other moments Prakash tells us that history's proper task is to challenge precisely this 'homogenization of the world by contemporary capitalism.' If this is so, and there is indeed a graspable logic to the way in which modern capitalism has spread itself globally, how are we to go about the central task of comprehending this logic in the terms that Prakash suggests? ('AO,' p. 147)

Prakash's answer to his critics simply evades the issues raised in this passage (while coming close to granting a central role to capitalism) because to recognize them would make his postfoundational history untenable (see 'PC,' pp. 13–14). Fernando Coronil outlines the political consequences of the postcolonialist repudiation of metanarratives in his observation that such opposition 'produces disjointed mininarratives which reinforce dominant worldviews; reacting against determinisms, it presents free-floating events; refusing to fix identity in structural categories, it essentializes identity through difference; resisting the location of power in structures or institutions, it diffuses it throughout society and ultimately dissolves it.'[26] It also relieves 'self-defined minority or subaltern critics,' O'Hanlon and Washbrook note, of the necessity of 'doing what they constantly demand of others, which is to histori-cise the conditions of their own emergence as authoritative voices – conditions which could hardly be described without reference of some kind to material and class relations' ('AO,' pp. 165–6).

Finally, the postcolonial repudiation of the Third World is intimately linked with the repudiation of capitalism's structuring of the modern world. Once again, essentialism serves as a straw man, diverting attention from radical conceptualizations of the Third World that are not essentialist but relational, as in world-system approaches. Rather than fixing it ahistorically, as Prakash would have it, the world-system approach comprehends the Third World as a structural position within a capitalist world order, a position that changes with changing structural relationships. To be sure, world-system analysis, like one based on modernization, locates the Third World discursively, but, as I have argued above, so does postcolonialist analysis. The question then becomes how well competing discourses account for historical changes in global relation-ships and the oppositional practices to which they point. I will say more on the former below. As for oppositional practices, postcoloniality by its very logic permits little beyond local struggles and, since it makes no reference to structure or totality, directionless ones at that. For all its contradictions, Shohat writes, ' "Third World" usefully evokes structural commonalities of struggles. The invocation of the "Third World" implies a belief that the shared history of neocolonialism and internal racism form sufficient common ground for alli-ances among … diverse peoples. If one does not believe or envision such commonalities, then indeed the term "Third World" should be discarded' ('NP,' p. 111).

The denial of capitalism's foundational status also reveals a culturalism in the postcolonialist argument that has important ideological consequences. This involves the issue of Eurocentrism. Without capitalism as the foundation for European power and the motive force of its globalization, Eurocentrism would have been just another ethnocentrism (comparable to any other ethno-centrism from the Chinese and the Indian to the most trivial tribal solipsism). An exclusive focus on Eurocentrism as a cultural or ideological problem that blurs the power relationships that dynamized it and endowed it with hege-monic persuasiveness fails to explain why, in contrast to regional or local ethnocentrisms, this particular ethnocentrism was able to define modern global history and itself as the universal aspiration and end of that history. By throwing the cover of culture over material relationships, as if the one had little to do with the other, such a focus diverts criticism of capitalism to the criticism of Eurocentric ideology, which not only helps postcolonialism disguise its own ideological limitation but also, ironically, provides an alibi for inequality, exploitation, and oppression in their modern guises under capitalist relationships. The postcolonialist argument projects upon the past the same mystification of the relationship between power and culture that is characteristic of the ideology of global capitalism of which it is a product.

These criticisms, however vehement on occasion, do not necessarily indicate that postcolonialism's critics deny it all value; indeed, critics such as Coronil, McClintock, and Shohat explicitly acknowledge some value to the issues raised by postcolonialism and postcolonial intellectuals. There is no denying that postcolonialism expresses not only a crisis in the ideology of linear progress but also a crisis in the modes of comprehending the world associated with such concepts as Third World and nation-state. Nor is it to be denied that as the global situation has become blurred with the disappearance of socialist states, with the emergence of important differences economically and politically among so-called Third World societies, and with the diasporic motions of populations across national and regional boundaries, fragmentation of the global into the local has emerged into the foreground of historical and political consciousness. Crossing national, cultural, class, gender, and ethnic boundaries, moreover, with its promise of a genuine cosmopolitanism, is appealing in its own right.

Within the institutional site of the First World academy, fragmentation of earlier metanarratives appears benign (except to hidebound conservatives) for its promise of more democratic, multicultural, and cosmopolitan epistemologies. In the world outside the academy, however, it shows in murderous ethnic conflict, continued inequalities among societies, classes, and genders, and the absence of oppositional possibilities that, always lacking in coherence, are rendered even more impotent than earlier by the fetishization of difference, fragmentation, and so on.

The confounding of ideological metanarratives with actualities of power renders the predicament more serious. To mistake fragmentation in one realm with fragmentation in the other ignores the possibility that ideological fragmentation may represent not the dissolution of power but its further concentration. It is necessary, to account for this possibility, to retain a sense of structure and totality in the confrontation of fragmentation and locality, the alternative to which may be complicity in the consolidation of hegemony in the very process of questioning it. Although postcoloniality represents an effort to adjust to a changing global situation, it appears for that very reason as an exemplary illustration of this predicament. Critics have hinted at its possible relationship to a new situation in the capitalist transformation of the world. Without examining this relationship at length, I would like to look at this relationship more closely.

Global capitalism and the condition of postcoloniality

David Harvey and Fredric Jameson, among others, perceive a relationship between postmodernism and a new phase in the development of capitalism that has been described variously as late capitalism, flexible production or accumulation, disorganized capitalism, and global capitalism.[27] As a child of postmodernism, postcolonialism too is expressive of the logic of this phase of capitalism, but on Third World terrain.

Fundamental to the structure of the new global capitalism (the term I prefer) is what Folker Fröbel and others have described as 'a new international division of labor,' that is, the transnationalization of production where, through subcontracting, the process of production (of even the same commodity) is globalized.[28] The international division of labor in production may not be entirely novel, but new technologies have increased spatial extension as well as speed of production to an unprecedented level. These same technologies have endowed capital and production with novel mobility; seeking maximum advantage for capital against labor as well as freedom from social and political interference, production seems to be constantly changing its location – hence flexible production. For these reasons, analysts perceive in global capitalism a qualitative difference from past, similar practices – indeed, a new phase of capitalism.

Also important to this new phase is the decentering of capitalism nationally. In other words, it is increasingly difficult to point to any nation or region as the center of global capitalism. More than one analyst (in a position of power) has found an analogue to the emerging organization of production in the northern European Hanseatic League of the early modern period (that is, the period before the emergence of nation-states); in other words, a network of urban formations, without a clearly definable center, whose links to one another are far stronger than their relationships to their immediate hinterlands.[29]

The medium linking the contemporary global capitalist network together is the transnational corporation, which has taken over from national markets as the locus of economic activity not as a passive medium for the transmission of capital, commodities, and production but as a determinant of that transmission and its direction. Whereas the analogy with the Hanseatic League suggests decentralization, production under global capitalism is in fact heavily concentrated in the corporation. With power lodged in transnational corporations, which by definition transcend nations in their organization and loyalties, the power of the nation-state to regulate the economy internally is constricted, while global regulation (and defense) of the economic order emerges as a major task. This is manifested not only in the proliferation of global organizations but also in efforts to organize extranational regional organizations to give coherence to the functioning of the economy.[30]

The transnationalization of production is the source at once of unprecedented global unity and of unprecedented fragmentation in the history of capitalism. The homogenization of the globe economically, socially, and culturally is such that Marx's predictions finally seem to be on the point of vindication. At the same time, however, there is a parallel process of fragmentation at work; globally, in the disappearance of a center to capitalism, locally, in the fragmentation of the production process into subnational regions and localities. As supranational regional organizations such as the European Economic Community, the Pacific Basin Economic Community, and the North American Free Trade Zone (to mention some that have been realized or are the objects of intense organizational activity) manifest this fragmentation at the global level, localities within a single nation competing with one another to place themselves in the pathways of transnational capital represent it at the most basic local level. Nations themselves, it is arguable, historically represented attempts to contain fragmentation, but under attack from the outside (transnational organization) and the inside (subnational economic regions and localities), it is not quite clear how this new fragmentation is to be contained.[31]

Yet perhaps the most important consequence of the transnationalization of capital is that, for the first time in the history of capitalism, the capitalist mode of production, divorced from its historically specific origins in Europe, appears as an authentically global abstraction. The narrative of capitalism is no longer a narrative of the history of Europe; non-European capitalist societies now make their own claims on the history of capitalism. Corresponding to economic fragmentation, in other words, is cultural fragmentation, or, to put it in its positive guise, multiculturalism. The most dramatic instance of this new cultural situation may be the effort over the last decade to reconcile capitalism with the so-called Confucian values of East Asian societies, which is a reversal of a long-standing conviction (in Europe and East Asia) that Confucianism was historically an obstacle to capitalism. I think it is arguable that the end of Eurocentrism is an illusion because capitalist culture as it has taken shape has Eurocentrism built into the very structure of its narrative, which may explain why, even as Europe and the United States lose their domination of the capitalist world economy, European and American cultural values retain their domination. It is noteworthy that what makes something like the East Asian Confucian revival plausible is not its offer of alternative values to those of Euro-American origin but its articulation of native culture into a capitalist narrative. Having said this, it is important to reiterate nevertheless that the question of world culture has become much more complex than in earlier phases of capitalism.

The fragmentation of space and its consequences for Eurocentrism also imply a fragmentation of the temporality of capitalism; the challenge to Eurocentrism, in other words, means that it is possible to conceive of the future in ways other than those of Euro-American political and social models. Here, once again, it is difficult to distinguish reality from illusion, but the complexity is undeniable.

Finally, the transnationalization of production calls into question earlier divisions of the world into First, Second, and Third Worlds. The Second World, the world of socialism, is for all practical purposes of the past. But the new global configuration also calls into question the distinctions between the First and Third Worlds. Parts of the earlier Third World are today on the pathways of transnational capital and belong in the 'developed' sector of the world economy. Likewise, parts of the First World marginalized in the new global economy are hardly distinguishable in way of life from what used to be viewed as the Third World. It may not be fortuitous that the North-South distinction has gradually taken over from the earlier division of the globe into three worlds, unless we remember that the references of North and South are not merely to concrete geographic locations but are also metaphorical. North connotes the pathways of transnational capital, and South, the marginalized populations of the world, regardless of their location – which is where post-coloniality comes in.

Ideologues of global capital have described this condition as 'global region-alism' or 'global localism,' adding quickly, however, that global localism is 80 per cent global and only 20 per cent local.[32] They have also appropriated for capital the radical ecological slogan, 'Think global, act local.'[33]

The situation created by global capitalism helps explain certain phenomena that have become apparent over the last two or three decades, but especially since the eighties: global motions of peoples (and, therefore, cultures), the weakening of boundaries (among societies, as well as among social categories), the replications in societies internally of inequalities and discrepancies once associated with colonial differences, simultaneous homogenization and frag-mentation within and across societies, the interpenetration of the global and the local, and the disorganization of a world conceived in terms of three worlds or nation-states. Some of these phenomena have also contributed to an appearance of equalization of differences within and across societies, as well as of democratization within and among societies. What is ironic is that the managers of this world situation themselves concede that they (or their organizations) now have the power to appropriate the local for the global, to admit different cultures into the realm of capital (only to break them down and remake them in accordance with the requirements of production and con-sumption), and even to reconstitute subjectivities across national boundaries to create producers and consumers more responsive to the operations of capital. Those who do not respond, or the 'basket cases' that are not essential to those operations – four-fifths of the global population by the managers' count – need not be colonized; they are simply marginalized. What the new flexible production has made possible is that it is no longer necessary to utilize explicit coercion against labor at home or in colonies abroad. Those peoples or places that are not responsive to the needs (or demands) of capital, or are too far gone to respond 'efficiently,' simply find themselves out of its pathways. And it is easier even than in the heyday of colonialism or modernization theory to say convincingly: It is their own fault.

If I may now return to Shohat's question with which I began this essay – 'When exactly ... does the "post-colonial" begin?' – and give it a less facetious answer consistent with her intention, the answer is, with the emergence of global capitalism, not in the sense of an exact coincidence in time but in the sense that the one is a condition for the other. There is little that is remarkable about this conclusion, which is but an extension to postcolonialism of the relationship that Harvey and Jameson have established between postmodernism and developments within capitalism. If postcolonialism is a progeny of postmodernism, then these developments within capitalism are also directly or indirectly pertinent to understanding postcolonialism. Postcolonial critics readily concede the debt they owe to postmodernist and post-structuralist thinking; indeed, their most original contribution would seem to lie in their rephrasing of older problems in the study of the Third World in the language of post-structuralism. What is truly remarkable, therefore, is that a consideration of the relationship between postcolonialism and global capitalism should be absent from the writings of postcolonial intellectuals, an absence all the more remarkable because this relationship, which pertains not only to cultural and epistemological but also to social and political formations, is arguably less abstract and more direct than any relationship between global capitalism and postmodernism.

Postcoloniality represents a response to a genuine need, the need to overcome a crisis of understanding produced by the inability of old categories to account for the world. The metanarrative of progress that underlies two centuries of thinking is in deep crisis. Not only have we lost faith in progress but also progress has had actual disintegrative effects. More important, over the last decade in particular our sense of a clear progression of time and events has been jumbled. During these years, conservatism has become revolutionary (the Reagan revolution); revolutionaries have turned first into conservatives and then into reactionaries (as in formerly socialist countries such as the Soviet Union and China); religious millenarianisms long thought to be castaways from Enlightenment have made a comeback into politics, sometimes, as in the United States, allied to high-tech revolutions; and fascism has been reborn out of the ashes of Communist regimes. The crisis of progress has brought in its wake a crisis of modernization, more in its Marxist than in its bourgeois guise, and called into question the structure of the globe as conceived by modernizationalists and radicals alike in the decades after World War II, that is, as three worlds. Whether they be fixed geographically or structurally, in bourgeois or in Marxist social theory, the three worlds are indeed no longer tenable. The globe has become as jumbled up spatially as the ideology of progress has temporally. Third Worlds have appeared in the First World and First Worlds in the Third. New diasporas have relocated the Self there and the Other here, and consequently borders and boundaries have been confounded. And the flow of culture has been at once homogenizing and heterogenizing; some groups share in a common global culture regardless of location even as they are alienated from the culture of their hinterlands while others are driven back into cultural legacies long thought to be residual to take refuge in cultural havens that are as far apart from one another as they were at the origins of modernity – even though they may be watching the same TV shows.

Politically speaking, the Second and Third Worlds have been the major casualties of this crisis. The Second World, the world of socialist states, is already, to put it bluntly, history. What has happened to the Third World (the immediate subject of postcoloniality) may be less apparent but no less significant. We may note here that the two major crises of the early nineties that are global in implication are the crises occasioned by Iraq's invasion of Kuwait and the current situation in Somalia. In the Gulf crisis, a Third World country appeared as the imperialist culprit against a socially and politically reactionary but economically powerful neighbor and had to be driven back by the combined armies of the First, Second, and Third Worlds, led by an imperial power now turned into a paradigm of righteousness. The 'invasion' – I borrow the word from a TV report – of Somalia, if anything, is more revealing. If in the case of the Gulf crisis one Third World country had to be saved from another, in Somalia we have a Third World country that has to be saved from itself. The Third World, viewed by radicals only two decades ago as a hope for the future, now has to be saved from itself. The crisis could not get much deeper.

Postcoloniality addresses this situation of crisis that eludes understanding in terms of older conceptualizations,[34] which may explain why it created immediate ferment in intellectual circles. But this still begs the question, why now? – and why has it taken the intellectual direction it has? After all, there is more than one conceptual way out of a crisis, and we must inquire why this particular way has acquired immediate popularity – in First World institutions. To put it bluntly, postcoloniality is designed to *avoid* making sense of the current crisis and, in the process, to cover up the origins of postcolonial intellectuals in a global capitalism of which they are not so much victims as beneficiaries.

Postcoloniality resonates with the problems thrown up by global capitalism. As the crisis of the Third World has become inescapably apparent during the decade of the eighties, so have the effects of global capitalism. The Reagan (and Thatcher) revolution was not so much a revolution heralding a new beginning as a revolution aimed at reorganizing the globe politically so as to give free reign to a global capitalism that strained against the harness of political restrictions. The overthrow of socialist states was one part of the program. Another was taming the Third World, if necessary by invasion, preferably by encirclement with economic sanctions or with Patriot missiles. But these are at best tactics of last resort. By far the best option is control from the inside through the creation of classes amenable to incorporation into or alliance with global capital.

I use the word *control* here advisedly; under conditions of global capitalism, control is not to be imposed, it has to be negotiated. Transnational capital is no longer just Euro-American, and neither is modernity. The complicated social and cultural composition of transnational capitalism makes it difficult to sustain a simple equation between capitalist modernity and Eurocentric (and patriarchal) cultural values and political forms. Others who have achieved success within the capitalist world system demand a voice for their values within the culture of transnational capital and the East Asian Confucian revival to which I referred above is exemplary of the phenomenon. Eurocentrism, as the very condition for the emergence of these alternative voices, retains its cultural hegemony; but it is more evident than ever before that, for this hegemony to be sustained, the boundaries must be rendered more porous in order to absorb alternative cultural possibilities that might otherwise serve as sources of destructive oppositions. (The mutual bashing between Japan and the United States in recent years, which revives racist and Orientalist vocabulary, attests to the dangers of conflict within the very ranks of transnational capital.) And who knows, in the end, what values are most functional to the needs of changing capital? Commentator after commentator has remarked in recent years that the communitarian values of Confucianism may be more suitable to a contemporary managerial capitalism than the individualistic values of the entrepreneurial capitalism of an earlier day. What is clear is that global capitalism is (and must be) much more fluid culturally than a Eurocentric capitalism.

This is also the condition of postcoloniality and the cultural moves associated with it. Knuckleheaded conservatives, anxious to explain away cultural problems by substituting worries about the machinations of subversives for systemic analysis, attribute the cultural problems that became apparent in the eighties (most recently, multiculturalism) to the invasion of academic institutions and politics in general by Marxists, feminists, ethnics, and so on. What they ignore is the possible relationship between the Reagan economic revolution and these cultural developments. That is, in their very globalism, the cultural requirements of transnational corporations can no longer afford the cultural parochialism of an earlier day. Focusing on liberal arts institutions, some conservative intellectuals overlook how much headway multiculturalism has made with business school administrators and the managers of transnational corporations, who are eager all of a sudden to learn the secrets of East Asian economic success in 'oriental' philosophies, who cannibalize cultures all over the world in order to better market their commodities, and who have suddenly become aware of a need to internationalize academic institutions (which often takes the form not of promoting scholarship in a conventional sense but of 'importing' and 'exporting' students and faculty). While in an earlier day it might have been Marxist and feminist radicals, with the aid of a few ethnics, who spearheaded multiculturalism, by now the initiative has passed into the hands of 'enlightened' administrators and trustees who are quite aware of the 'manpower' needs of the new economic situation. No longer so much a conflict between conservatives and radicals (although that dimension, too, is obviously there), the conflict shapes up now as a conflict between an older elite, comprised in part of a small business interest now threatened by domestic and foreign competition, and the elite vanguard of international business. Among the foremost and earliest of United States advocates of transnationalism and multiculturalism is the *Harvard Business Review*.

The Reaganites may have been misled by the visions, which have not materialized, of Dinesh D'Souza and his imitators. Their failure to grasp the social and political consequences of economic victory for the transnationalism that they engineered became apparent during the recent elections when, against the calls from right-wingers for a return to such traditional American values as Eurocentrism, patriarchalism, and racism, George Bush often looked befuddled, possibly because he grasped much better than men like Pat Buchanan the dilemmas presented by the victory of transnationalism over all its competitors in the Second and Third Worlds. The result has been the victory of high-tech yuppies, who are much better attuned to the new world situation and to the difficulties it presents. It is no coincidence that Robert Reich, frequent contributor to the *Harvard Business Review*, keen analyst of developments within the capitalist world economy, and an advocate of the borderless economy is a close confidant of President Clinton.

This is, I think, also the context for the emergence of postcoloniality and for its rapid success in academic institutions as a substitute for earlier conceptualizations of the world. Postcoloniality, in the particular direction it has taken as a discourse, also resonates with the problems of the contemporary world. It addresses issues that may have been present all along in global studies but are now rephrased to attune to issues in global capitalism: Eurocentrism and its relationship to capitalism; the kind of modernity that is relevant to a postmodern, postsocialist, post-Third World situation; the place of the nation in development; the relationship between the local and the global; the place of borders and boundaries in a world where capital, production, and peoples are in constant motion; the status of structures in a world that more than ever seems to be without recognizable structure; interpenetrations and reversals between the different worlds; borderlands subjectivities and epistemologies (hybridity); homogeneity versus heterogeneity; and so forth.

Postcoloniality, however, is also appealing because it disguises the power relations that shape a seemingly shapeless world and contributes to a conceptualization of that world that both consolidates and subverts possibilities of resistance. Postcolonial critics have engaged in valid criticism of past forms of ideological hegemony but have had little to say about its contemporary figurations. Indeed, in their simultaneous repudiation of structure and affirmation of the local in problems of oppression and liberation, they have mystified the ways in which totalizing structures persist in the midst of apparent disintegration and fluidity. They have rendered into problems of subjectivity and epistemology concrete and material problems of the everyday world. While capital in its motions continues to structure the world, refusing it foundational status renders impossible the cognitive mapping that must be the point of departure for any practice of resistance and leaves such mapping as there is in the domain of those who manage the capitalist world economy.[35] Indeed, in the projection of the current state of conceptual disorganization upon the colonial past, postcolonial critics have also deprived colonialism of any but local logic, so that the historical legacy of colonialism (in Iraq, or Somalia, or, for that matter, any Third World society) appears irrelevant to the present. Thus the burden of persistent problems is shifted onto the victims themselves.

'Postcoloniality,' Appiah writes, 'is the condition of what we might ungenerously call a *comprador* intelligentsia.'[36] I think this is missing the point because the world situation that justified the term *comprador* no longer exists. I would suggest instead that postcoloniality is the condition of the intelligentsia of global capitalism. The question, then, is not whether this global intelligentsia can (or should) return to national loyalties but whether, in recognition of its own class-position in global capitalism, it can generate a thoroughgoing criticism of its own ideology and formulate practices of resistance against the system of which it is a product.

Notes

1 Ella Shohat, 'Notes on the "Post-Colonial,"' *Social Text* 31/32 (1992), p. 103; hereafter abbreviated 'NP.'

2 In 1985, Gayatri Spivak insisted in an interview that she did not belong to the 'top level of the United States academy' because she taught in the South and the Southwest whereas the 'cultural elite in the United States inhabit the Northeastern seaboard or the West coast' (Gayatri Chakravorty Spivak, *The Post-Colonial Critic: Interviews, Strategies, Dialogues*, ed. Sarah Harasym [New York, 1990], p. 114); hereafter abbreviated *PCC*. Since then Spivak has moved to Columbia University.

3 See also Arjun Appadurai, 'Global Ethnoscapes: Notes and Queries for a Transnational Anthropology,' in *Recapturing Anthropology: Working in the Present*, ed. Richard G. Fox (Santa Fe, N. Mex, 1991), pp. 191–210. Aijaz Ahmad, whom I do not include among the postcolonial critics here, does an excellent job of relating the problems of postcoloniality to contemporary capitalism, if only in passing and somewhat differently from the way I do below. See Aijaz Ahmad, 'Jameson's Rhetoric of Otherness and the "National Allegory,"' *Social Text* 17 (Fall 1987), pp. 3–25 and *In Theory: Classes, Nations, Literatures* (London, 1992).

4 Gyan Prakash, 'Writing Post-Orientalist Histories of the Third World: Perspectives from Indian Historiography,' *Comparative Studies in Society and History* 32 (Apr. 1990), p. 383; hereafter abbreviated 'PH.'

5 See Spivak, 'Subaltern Studies: Deconstructing Historiography,' in *Selected Subaltern Studies*, ed. Ranajit Guha and Spivak (New York, 1988), pp. 3–32.

6 Prakash, 'Postcolonial Criticism and Indian Historiography,' *Social Text* 31/32 (1992), p. 8; hereafter abbreviated 'PC.' I use Prakash's discussions of postcoloniality as my point of departure here because he has made the most systematic attempts at accounting for the concept and also because his discussions bring to the fore the implications of the concept for historical understanding. As this statement reveals, Prakash himself draws heavily on the characteristics of postcolonial consciousness delineated by others, especially Homi K. Bhabha, who has been responsible for the prominence in discussions of postcoloniality of the vocabulary of hybridity and so on. Bhabha's work, however, is responsible for more than the vocabulary of postcolonialism, as he has proven himself to be something of a master of political mystification and theoretical obfuscation, of a reduction of social and political problems to psychological ones, and of the substitution of poststructuralist linguistic manipulation for historical and social explanation – all of which show up in much postcolonial writing, but rarely with the same virtuosity (and incomprehensibleness) that he brings to it. For some of his more influential writings, see Homi K. Bhabha, 'Of Mimicry and Man: The Ambivalence of Colonial Discourse,' *October* 28 (Spring 1984), pp. 125–33; 'The Commitment to Theory,' in *Questions of Third World Cinema*, ed. Jim Pines and Paul Willemen (London, 1989), pp. 111–32; 'The Other Question: Difference, Discrimination and the Discourse of Colonialism,' in *Literature, Politics and Theory*, ed. Francis Barker *et al.* (London, 1986), pp. 148–72; and 'Introduction: Narrating the Nation' and 'DissemiNation: Time, Narrative, and

the Margins of the Modern Nation,' in *Nation and Narration*, ed. Bhabha (London, 1990), pp. 1–7, 291–322. Bhabha is exemplary of the Third World intellectual who has been completely reworked by the language of First World cultural criticism.

7 See also Dipesh Chakrabarty, 'Postcoloniality and the Artifice of History: Who Speaks for "Indian" Pasts?' *Representations*, 37 (Winter 1992), p. 4.

8 As the term *subaltern* would indicate, Antonio Gramsci's inspiration is readily visible in the works of *Subaltern Studies* historians.

9 Indeed, Lyotard has defined *postmodern* as 'incredulity toward metanarratives' (Jean-François Lyotard, *The Postmodern Condition: A Report on Knowledge*, trans. Geoff Bennington and Brian Massumi [Minneapolis, 1984], p. xxiv).

10 See Bill Ashcroft, Gareth Griffiths, and Helen Tiffin eds.,*The Empire Writes Back: Theory and Practice in Post-Colonial Literatures*, (London, 1989), p. 2.

11 For discussions of similar problems in Chinese historiography, see Joseph R. Levenson, *Confucian China and Its Modern Fate: A Trilogy* (Berkeley, 1968); Rey Chow, *Woman and Chinese Modernity: The Politics of Reading between West and East* (Minneapolis, 1991); Arif Dirlik, *Revolution and History: The Origins of Marxist Historiography in China, 1919–1937* (Berkeley, 1978); and Dirlik, 'Marxism and Chinese History: The Globalization of Marxist Historical Discourse and the Problem of Hegemony in Marxism,' *Journal of Third World Studies* 4 (Spring, 1987), pp. 151–64.

12 This is at any rate a question that needs to be clarified. It seems to me that Prakash's denial of foundational status to class goes beyond what is but a *historicization* of class in the work of *Subaltern Studies* historians similar to that found in, say, E. P. Thompson's *The Making of the English Working Class* (London, 1963). For a note on the question of class, see Chakrabarty, 'Invitation to a Dialogue,' *Subaltern Studies: Writings on South Asian History and Society*, ed. Ranajit Guha, 5 vols. (Oxford, 1982–87), vol. 4, pp. 364–76. The procedure of generalization may also play a part in the deradicalization of *Subaltern Studies* ideas by removing them from their specific historiographical context where they *do* play an innovative, radical role. For instance, the qualification of the role of colonialism in Indian history is intended by these historians to bring to the fore the mystifications of the past in nationalist histories and hence is a radical act. Made into a general principle of postcolonialism, this qualification downplays the role of colonialism in history. For an acknowledgment of doubt concerning the success of *Subaltern Studies* historiography, see Chakrabarty, 'Postcoloniality and the Artifice of History.'

13 Note not just the ideas but the tone in the following statement by Ahmad:

> But one could start with a radically different premise, namely the proposition that we live not in three worlds but in one; that this world includes the experience of colonialism and imperialism on both sides of Jameson's global divide ...; that societies in formations of backward capitalism are as much constituted by the division of classes as are societies in the advanced capitalist countries; that socialism is not restricted to something called the second world but is simply the name of a resistance that saturates the globe today, as capitalism itself does; that the different parts of the capitalist system are to be known not in terms of binary opposition but as a contradictory unity, with differences, yes, but also with profound overlaps (Ahmad, 'Jameson's Rhetoric of Otherness and the "National Allegory," ' p. 9).

14 See Spivak, 'Can the Subaltern Speak?' in *Marxism and the Interpretation of Culture*, ed. Cary Nelson and Lawrence Grossberg (Urbana, Ill., 1988), pp. 271–313,

and Lata Mani, 'Multiple Mediations: Feminist Scholarship in the Age of Multi-national Reception,' in *Travelling Theories: Travelling Theorists*, ed. James Clifford and Vivek Dhareshwar (Santa Cruz, Calif., 1989). pp. 1–23.

15 See Kwame Anthony Appiah, 'Is the Post- in Postmodernism the Post- in Post-colonial?', *Critical Inquiry* 17 (Winter 1991), p. 353.

16 Achille Mbembe, 'Prosaics of Servitude and Authoritarian Civilities,' trans. Janet Roitman, *Public Culture* 5 (Fall 1992), p. 137.

17 See Edward W. Said, foreword, in *Selected Subaltern Studies*, pp. v–x.

18 For a sampling of essays, see *Confucianism and Modernization: A Symposium*, ed. Joseph P. L. Jiang (Taipei, 1987). Scholars such as Tu Wei-ming and Yu Ying-shih have played a major part in efforts to revive Confucianism, while the quasi-fascist regime of Singapore (especially under Lee Kuan Yew) also has been a major promoter of the idea.

19 For a discussion of this problem in detail, see Dirlik, 'Mao Zedong and "Chinese Marxism," ' *Encyclopedia of Asian Philosophy* (forthcoming).

20 Althusser recognized this problem with specific reference to Mao Zedong Thought. See Louis Althusser, 'Contradiction and Overdetermination,' *For Marx*, trans. Ben Brewster (New York, 1970), pp. 87–128. For the molding of ideology, see his 'Ideology and Ideological State Apparatuses,' *Lenin and Philosophy and Other Essays*, trans. Brewster (New York, 1971), pp. 127–86. Mani gives a good (personal) account of the contextual formation of ideology in Mani, 'Multiple Mediations.' The risk in contextual ideological formation, of course, is that a problem may be transformed into a celebration – or game playing. This is evident in Spivak's 'playfulness' throughout *The Post-Colonial Critic* as well as in, say, James Clifford's approach to the question of ethnography and culture. For a brief example of the latter see, among his many works, Clifford, 'Notes on Theory and Travel,' *Travelling Theory: Travelling Theorists*, pp. 177–88. My objection here is not to the importance of immediate context in the formation of ideology (and the variability and transpos-ability of roles that it implies) but to the way such emphasis on the local mystifies the larger contexts that differentiate power relations and that suggest more stable and directed positions. No matter how much the ethnographer may strive to change places with the native, in the end the ethnographer returns to the First World academy and the native back to the wilds. This is the problem with postcoloniality and is evident in the tendency of so much postcolonial criticism to start off with a sociology of power relationships only to take refuge in aesthetic phraseology.

21 Appiah, 'Is the Post- in Postmodernism the Post- in Postcolonial?', p. 353.

22 See the example Shohat gives of her experiences at CUNY ('NP,' p. 99).

23 Anne McClintock, 'The Angel of Progress: Pitfalls of the Term "Post-Colonialism," ' *Social Text* 31/32 (1992), p. 86.

24 Rosalind O'Hanlon and David Washbrook, 'After Orientalism: Culture, Criticism, and Politics in the Third World,' *Comparative Studies in Society and History* 34 (Jan. 1992), p. 166; hereafter abbreviated 'AO.'

25 See Carl E. Pletsch, 'The Three Worlds, or the Division of Social Scientific Labor, circa 1950–1975,' *Comparative Studies in Society and History* 23 (Oct. 1981), pp. 565–90.

26 See Fernando Coronil, 'Can Postcoloniality Be Decolonized? Imperial Banality and Postcolonial Power,' *Public Culture* 5 (Fall 1992), pp. 99–100.

27 See David Harvey, *The Condition of Postmodernity: An Enquiry into the Origins of Cultural Change* (Oxford, 1989), and Fredric Jameson, 'Postmodernism, or the

Cultural Logic of Late Capitalism,' *New Left Review* 146 (July/Aug. 1984), pp. 53–92.

28 Folder Fröbel, Jürgen Heinrichs, and Otto Kreye, *The New International Division of Labour: Structural Unemployment in Industrialised Countries and Industrialisation in Developing Countries*, trans. Pete Burgess (Cambridge, 1980). 'Disorganized capitalism' comes from Claus Offe, *Disorganized Capitalism: Contemporary Transformations of Work and Politics*, ed. John Keane (Cambridge, Mass., 1985), while *global capitalism* is the term used by Robert J. S. Ross and Kent C. Trachte, *Global Capitalism: The New Leviathan* (Albany, NY, 1990). Other noteworthy books on the subject are Leslie Sklair, *Sociology of the Global System* (Baltimore, 1991), which spells out the implications of global capitalism for the Third World, and, especially in light of what I say below, of the new presidency of the United States, Robert B. Reich, *The Work of Nations: Preparing Ourselves for Twenty-First Century Capitalism* (New York, 1991). Reich's book incorporates his contributions to the *Harvard Business Review*, that have such suggestive titles (in the present context) as 'Who is US?' and 'Who is Them?' For 'subcontracting,' see Gary Gereffi, 'Global Sourcing and Regional Divisions of Labor in the Pacific Rim,' *What Is in a Rim? Critical Perspectives on the Pacific Region Idea* (forthcoming).

29 See Riccardo Petrella, 'World City-States of the Future,' *New Perspectives Quarterly* 24 (Fall 1991), pp. 59–64. See also William E. Schmidt, 'A New Hanseatic League? In a Post-Cold War Era, Scandanavia Rethinks Itself,' *New York Times*, (23 Feb. 1992), p. E3.

30 See Kenichi Ohmae, 'Beyond Friction to Fact: The Borderless Economy,' *New Perspectives Quarterly* 23 (Spring 1990), p. 21. See also Masao Miyoshi, 'A Borderless World? From Colonialism to Transnationalism and the Decline of the Nation-State,' *Critical Inquiry* 19 (Summer 1993), pp. 726–51.

31 This phenomenon is addressed in most of the works cited above in note 28.

32 See Ohmae, 'Beyond Friction to Fact.' See also James Gardner, 'Global Regionalism,' *New Perspectives Quarterly* 25 (Winter 1992), pp. 58–9.

33 William Taylor, 'The Logic of Global Business: An Interview with ABB's Percy Barnevik,' *Harvard Business Review* 69 (Mar.–Apr. 1991), p. 91.

34 See Mbembe, 'The Banality of Power and the Aesthetics of Vulgarity in the Postcolony,' trans. Roitman, *Public Culture* 4 (Spring 1992), pp. 1–30; previously published as 'Provisional Notes on the Postcolony,' *Africa* 62. 1 (1992), pp. 3–37. See also the discussion provoked by this essay in *Public Culture* 5 (Fall 1992), pp. 47–145.

35 See Jameson, 'Cognitive Mapping,' in *Marxism and the Interpretation of Culture*, pp. 347–57. Jameson has been a forceful advocate of the necessity of retaining a sense of totality and structure in a socialist politics. His own totalization of the global structure has come under severe criticism. See Ahmad, 'Jameson's Rhetoric of Otherness.' I should stress here that it is not necessary to agree with his particular mode of totalization to recognize the validity of his argument.

36 Appiah, 'Is the Post- in Postmodernism the Post- in Postcolonial?', p. 348.

My being (more or less) one of the Third World intellectuals in First World academe does not privilege the criticism of postcolonial intellectuals that I offer below, but it does call for some comment. It is not clear to me how important the views I discuss (or the intellectuals who promote them) are in their impact on contemporary intellectual life. *Postcolonial* has been entering the lexicon of academic programs in recent years, and over the last two years there have been a number of conferences and symposia inspired by related vocabulary (postcolonialism, 'after Orientalism,' and so on), as well as special issues devoted to the subject in periodicals such as *Social Text* and *Public Culture*. But given the small number of intellectuals directly concerned with post-coloniality and the diffuseness in their use of the concept, it might make more sense to study the reception of the term *postcolonial*. Such a study is particulary important, I argue here, because the ideas associated with postcoloniality are significant and widespread as concerns, even if they predate the term *postcolonial* itself. It is not the importance of these ideas that I question, in other words, but their appropriation for postcoloniality. Otherwise, there is a Third World sensibility and mode of perception that has become increasingly visible in cultural discussions over the last decade. I myself share in the concerns (and even some of the viewpoints) of postcolonial intellectuals, though from a somewhat different perspective than those who describe themselves as such. For a recent example of this kind of work, see my 'Post-socialism/Flexible Production: Marxism in Contemporary Radicalism,' *Polygraph* 6/7 (1993), pp. 133–69.

While relieving them of any complicity in my views, I would like to thank Harry Harootunian, Masao Miyoshi, Roxann Praziak, Rob Wilson, and Zhang Xudong for their comments and assistance with sources.

16

Ella Shohat

Notes on the 'Post-Colonial'＊

The academic opposition to the Gulf War mobilized a number of familiar terms – 'imperialism,' 'neo-colonialism,' 'neo-imperialism' – in a verbal counter-strike against the New World Order. But conspicuously absent from the discussion was the term 'post-colonial,' even from speeches made by its otherwise prominent advocates. Given the extraordinary circulation of the term in recent academic conferences, publications and curricular reformulations, this sudden invisibility was somewhat puzzling. Was this absence sheer coincidence? Or is there something about the term 'post-colonial' that does not lend itself to a geopolitical critique, or to a critique of the dominant media's Gulf War macro-narratives? When lines drawn in the sand still haunt Third World geographies, it is urgent to ask how we can chart the meaning of the 'post-colonial.' It is from my particular position as an academic Arab-Jew whose cultural topographies are (dis)located in Iraq, Israel/Palestine, and the U.S.A. that I would like to explore some of the theoretical and political ambiguities of the 'post-colonial.'

Despite its dizzying multiplicity of positionalities, post-colonial theory has curiously not addressed the politics of location of the very term 'post-colonial.' In what follows, I propose to begin an interrogation of the term 'post-colonial,' raising questions about its ahistorical and universalizing deployments, and its potentially depoliticizing implications. The rising institutional endorsement of the term 'post-colonial' and of post-colonial studies as an emergent discipline (evident in MLA job announcements calling for specialization in 'post-colonial literature') is fraught with ambiguities. My recent experience as a member of the multicultural international studies committee at one of the CUNY branches illustrates some of these ambiguities. In response to our proposal, the generally conservative members of the college curriculum committee strongly resisted any language invoking issues such as 'imperialism and third worldist critique,' 'neo-colonialism and resisting cultural practices,' and 'the geopolitics of cultural exchange.' They were visibly relieved, however, at the sight of the word 'post-colonial.' Only the diplomatic gesture of relinquishing the terrorizing terms 'imperialism' and 'neo-colonialism' in favor of the pastoral 'post-colonial' guaranteed approval.

＊ From *Social Text* 31/32 (1992), pp. 99–113.

My intention here is not merely to anatomize the term 'post-colonial' semantically, but to situate it geographically, historically and institutionally, while raising doubts about its political agency. The question at stake is this. Which perspectives are being advanced in the 'post-colonial?' For what purposes? And with what slippages? In this brief discussion, my point is neither to examine the variety of provocative writings produced under the rubric post-colonial theory, nor simply to essentialize the term 'post-colonial,' but rather to unfold its slippery political significations, which occasionally escape the clearly oppositional intentions of its theoretical practitioners. Here I will argue for a more limited, historically and theoretically specific, usage of the term 'post-colonial,' one which situates it in a relational context vis-a-vis other (equally problematic) categories.

The 'post-colonial' did not emerge to fill an empty space in the language of political-cultural analysis. On the contrary, its wide adaptation during the late eighties was coincident with and dependent on the eclipse of an older paradigm, that of the 'Third World.' The terminological shift indicates the professional prestige and theoretical aura the issues have acquired, in contrast to the more activist aura once enjoyed by 'Third World' within progressive academic circles. Coined in the fifties in France by analogy to the third estate (the commoners, all those who were neither the nobility nor the clergy), the term 'Third World' gained international currency in both academic and political contexts, particularly in reference to anti-colonial nationalist movements of the fifties through the seventies as well as to the political-economic analysis of dependency theory and world system theory (André Gunder Frank, Immanuel Wallerstein, Samir Amin).

The last decade has witnessed a terminological crisis around the concept of the 'Third World.' The three worlds theory is indeed, as many critics have suggested, highly problematic.[1] For one thing, the historical processes of the last three decades offered a number of very complex and politically ambiguous developments. The period of so-called 'Third World euphoria' – a brief moment in which it seemed that First World leftists and Third World guerrillas would walk arm in arm toward global revolution – has given way to the collapse of the Soviet Communist model, the crisis of existing socialisms, the frustration of the hoped-for tricontinental revolution (with Ho Chi Minh, Frantz Fanon, and Che Guevara as talismanic figures), the realization that the wretched of the earth are not unanimously revolutionary (nor necessarily allies to one another), and the recognition that international geo-politics and the global economic system have obliged even socialist regimes to make some kind of peace with transnational capitalism. And despite the broad patterns of geo-political hegemony, power relations in the Third World are also dispersed and contradictory. The First World/Third World struggle, furthermore, takes place not only between nations (India/Pakistan, Iraq/Kuwait), but also within nations, with the constantly changing relations between dominant and subaltern groups, settler and indigenous populations, as well as in a situation marked by waves of post-independence immigrations to First World countries (Britain,

France, Germany, and the U.S.) and to more prosperous Third World countries (the Gulf states.) The notion of the three worlds, in short, flattens heterogeneities, masks contradictions, and elides differences.

This crisis in 'Third World' thinking helps explain the current enthusiasm for the term, 'post-colonial,' a new designation for critical discourses which thematize issues emerging from colonial relations and their aftermath, covering a long historical span (including the present.) Dropping the suffix 'ism' from 'post-colonialism,' the adjective 'post-colonial' is frequently attached to the nouns, 'theory,' 'space,' 'condition,' 'intellectual,' while it often substitutes for the adjective 'Third World' in relation to the noun 'intellectual.' The qualifier 'Third World,' by contrast, more frequently accompanies the nouns, 'nations,' 'countries' and 'peoples.' More recently the 'post-colonial' has been transformed into a noun, used both in the singular and the plural ('post-colonials'), designating the subjects of the 'post-colonial condition.'[2] The final consecration of the term came with the erasure of the hyphen. Often buttressed by the theoretically connoted substantive 'post-coloniality,' the 'post-colonial' is largely visible in Anglo-American academic (cultural) studies in publications of discursive-cultural analyses inflected by post-structuralism.[3]

Echoing 'post-modernity,' 'post-coloniality' marks a contemporary state, situation, condition or epoch.[4] The prefix 'post,' then, aligns 'post-colonialism' with a series of other 'posts' – 'post-structuralism,' 'post-modernism,' 'post-marxism,' 'post-feminism,' 'post-deconstructionism' – all sharing the notion of a movement beyond. Yet while these 'posts' refer largely to the supercession of outmoded philosophical, aesthetic and political theories, the 'post-colonial' implies both going beyond anti-colonial nationalist theory as well as a movement beyond a specific point in history, that of colonialism and Third World nationalist struggles. In that sense the prefix 'post' aligns the 'post-colonial' with another genre of 'posts' – 'post-war,' 'post-cold war,' 'post-independence,' 'post-revolution' – all of which underline a passage into a new period and a closure of a certain historical event or age, officially stamped with dates. Although periodizations and the relationship between theories of an era and the practices which constitute that era always form contested terrains, it seems to me that the two genres of the 'post' are none the less distinct in their referential emphasis, the first on disciplinary advances characteristic of intellectual history, and the latter on the strict chronologies of history *tout court*. This unarticulated tension between the philosophical and the historical teleologies in the 'post-colonial,' I would argue, partially underlies some of the conceptual ambiguities of the term.

Since the 'post' in the 'post-colonial' suggests 'after' the demise of colonialism, it is imbued, quite apart from its users' intentions, with an ambiguous spatio-temporality. Spreading from India into Anglo-American academic contexts, the 'post-colonial' tends to be associated with Third World countries which gained independence after World War II. However, it also refers to the Third World diasporic circumstances of the last four decades – from forced exile to 'voluntary' immigration – within First World metropolises. In some post-colonial texts, such as *The Empire Writes Back: Theory and Practice in*

Post-Colonial Literatures, the authors expand the term 'post-colonial' to
include all English literary productions by societies affected by colonialism:

> ... the literatures of African countries, Australia, Bangladesh, Canada, Caribbean
> countries, India, Malaysia, Malta, New Zealand, Pakistan, Singapore, South Pacific
> Island countries, and Sri Lanka are all post-colonial literatures. The literature of the
> USA should also be placed in this category. Perhaps because of its current position
> of power, and the neo-colonizing role it has played, its postcolonial nature has not
> been generally recognized. But its relationship with the metropolitan centre as it
> evolved over the last two centuries has been paradigmatic for post-colonial literature
> everywhere. What each of these literatures has in common beyond their special and
> distinctive regional characteristics is that they emerged in their present form out of
> the experience of colonization and asserted themselves by foregrounding the tension
> with the imperial power, and by emphasizing their differences from the assumptions
> of the imperial centre. It is this which makes them distinctively post-colonial.[5]

This problematic formulation collapses very different national-racial formations – the United States, Australia, and Canada, on the one hand, and Nigeria,
Jamaica, and India, on the other – as equally 'post-colonial.' Positioning
Australia and India, for example, in relation to an imperial center, simply
because they were both colonies, equates the relations of the colonized white-
settlers to the Europeans at the 'center' with that of the colonized indigenous
populations to the Europeans. It also assumes that white settler countries and
emerging Third World nations broke away from the 'center' in the same way.
Similarly, white Australians and Aboriginal Australians are placed in the same
'periphery,' as though they were co-habitants vis-a-vis the 'center.' The critical
differences between the Europe's genocidal oppression of Aboriginals in
Australia, indigenous peoples of the Americas and Afro-diasporic communities, *and* Europe's domination of European elites in the colonies are leveled
with an easy stroke of the 'post.' The term 'post-colonial,' in this sense, masks
the white settlers' colonialist-racist policies toward indigenous peoples not
only before independence but also after the official break from the imperial
center, while also de-emphasizing neocolonial global positionings of First
World settler-states.

I am not suggesting that this expanded use of the 'post-colonial' is typical or
paradigmatic.[6] The phrase 'post-colonial society' might equally evoke Third
World nation-states after independence. However, the disorienting space of
the 'post-colonial' generates odd couplings of the 'post' and particular geographies, blurring the assignment of perspectives. Does the 'post' indicate the
perspective and location of the ex-colonized (Algerian), the ex-colonizer
(French), the ex-colonial-settler (*Pied Noir*), or the displaced hybrid in First
World metropolitans (Algerian in France)? Since the experience of colonialism and imperialism is shared, albeit asymmetrically, by (ex)colonizer and
(ex)colonized, it becomes an easy move to apply the 'post' also to First World
European countries. Since most of the world is now living after the period of
colonialism, the 'post-colonial' can easily become a universalizing category
which neutralizes significant geopolitical differences between France and
Algeria, Britain and Iraq, or the U.S. and Brazil since they are all living in a

'post-colonial epoch.' This inadvertent effacement of perspectives, I should add, results in a curious ambiguity in scholarly work. While colonial discourse refers to the discourse produced by colonizers in both the colony and the motherland and, at times, to its contemporary discursive manifestations in literature and mass-mediated culture, 'post-colonial discourse' does not refer to colonialist discourse after the end of colonialism. Rather, it evokes the contemporary theoretical writings, placed in both the First and Third Worlds generally on the left, and which attempt to transcend the (presumed) binarisms of Third Worldist militancy.

Apart from its dubious spatiality, the 'post-colonial' renders a problematic temporality. First, the lack of historical specificity in the 'post' leads to a collapsing of diverse chronologies. Colonial-settler states, such as those found in the Americas, Australia, New Zealand, and South Africa, gained their independence, for the most part, in the eighteenth and nineteenth centuries. Most countries in Africa and Asia, in contrast, gained independence in the twentieth century, some in the nineteen thirties (Iraq), others in the nineteen forties (India, Lebanon), and still others in the nineteen sixties (Algeria, Senegal) and the nineteen seventies (Angola, Mozambique), while others have yet to achieve it. When exactly, then, does the 'post-colonial' begin? Which region is privileged in such a beginning? What are the relationships between these diverse beginnings? The vague starting point of the 'post-colonial' makes certain differentiations difficult. It equates early independence won by settler-colonial states, in which Europeans formed their new nation-states in non-European territories at the expense of indigenous populations, with that of nation-states whose indigenous populations struggled for independence against Europe, but won it, for the most part, with the twentieth century collapse of European Empires.

If one formulates the 'post' in the 'post-colonial' in relation to Third Worldist nationalist struggles of the fifties and sixties, then what time frame would apply for contemporary anti-colonial/anti-racist struggles carried under the banner of national and racial oppression, for Palestinian writers for example, like Sahar Khalifeh and Mahmoud Darwish, who write contemporaneously with 'post-colonial' writers? Should one suggest that they are pre-'post-colonial?' The unified temporality of 'post-coloniality' risks reproducing the colonial discourse of an allochronic other, living in another time, still lagging behind us, the genuine post-colonials. The globalizing gesture of the 'post-colonial condition,' or 'post-coloniality,' downplays multiplicities of location and temporality, as well as the possible discursive and political linkages between 'post-colonial' theories and contemporary anti-colonial, or anti-neo-colonial struggles and discourses. In other words, contemporary anti-colonial and anti-neocolonial resistant discourses from central America and the Middle East to Southern Africa and the Philippines cannot be theoretically dismissed as epigons, as a mere repetition of the all too familiar discourses of the fifties and sixties. Despite their partly shared discourses with Third World nationalism, these contemporary struggles also must be historicized, analyzed in a present-day context, when the 'non-aligned' discourse of revolutions is no longer in the air. Such an approach would transcend the implicit suggestion of a temporal 'gap' between 'post-colonial' and the pre-'post-colonial' discourses, as exemplified in the melange of resistant discourses and struggles in the Intifada.[7] What has to be negotiated, then, is the relationship of difference and sameness, rupture and continuity.

Since, on one level, the 'post' signifies 'after,' it potentially inhibits forceful articulations of what one might call 'neo-coloniality.' Formal independence for colonized countries has rarely meant the end of First World hegemony. Egypt's formal independence in 1923 did not prevent European, especially British, domination which provoked the 1952 revolution. Anwar Sadat's opening to the Americans and the Camp David accords in the seventies was perceived by Arab intellectuals as a reversion to pre-Nasser imperialism, as was Egyptian collaboration with the U.S. during the Gulf war.[8] The purpose of the Carter Doctrine was to partially protect perennial U.S. oil interests (*our* oil) in the Gulf, which, with the help of petro-Islamicist regimes, have sought the control of any force that might pose a threat.[9] In Latin America, similarly, formal 'creole' independence did not prevent Monroe Doctrine-style military interventions, or Anglo-American free-trade hegemony. This process sets the history of Central and South America and the Caribbean apart from the rest of the colonial settler-states; for despite shared historical origins with North America, including the genocide of the indigenous population, the enslavement of Africans, and a multi-racial/ethnic composition these regions have been subjected to political and economic structural domination, on some levels more severe, paradoxically, than that of recently independent Third World countries such as Libya and even India. Not accidentally, Mexican intellectuals and independent labor unions have excoriated the Gringostroika[10] of the recent Trade Liberalization Treaty. Formal independence did not obviate the need for Cuban or Nicaraguan-style revolutions, or for the Independista movement in Puerto Rico. The term 'revolution,' once popular in the Third World context, specifically assumed a post-colonial moment, initiated by official independence, but whose content had been a suffocating neo-colonial hegemony.

The term 'post-colonial' carries with it the implication that colonialism is now a matter of the past, undermining colonialism's economic, political, and cultural deformative-traces in the present. The 'post-colonial' inadvertently glosses over the fact that global hegemony, even in the post-cold war era, persists in forms other than overt colonial rule. As a signifier of a new historical epoch, the term 'post-colonial,' when compared with neo-colonialism, comes equipped with little evocation of contemporary power relations; it lacks a political content which can account for the eighties and nineties-style U.S. militaristic involvements in Granada, Panama, and Kuwait-Iraq, and for the symbiotic links between U.S. political and economic interests and those of local elites. In certain contexts, furthermore, racial and national oppressions reflect clear colonial patterns, for example the oppression of blacks by Anglo-Dutch Europeans in South Africa and in the Americas, the oppression of Palestinians and Middle Eastern Jews by Euro-Israel. The 'post-colonial' leaves no space, finally, for the struggles of aboriginals in Australia and indigenous peoples throughout the Americas, in other words, of Fourth World peoples dominated by both First World multi-national corporations and by Third World nation-states.

The hegemonic structures and conceptual frameworks generated over the last five hundred years cannot be vanquished by waving the magical wand of the 'post-colonial.' The 1992 unification of Europe, for example, strengthens cooperation among ex-colonizing countries such as Britain, France, Germany and Italy against illegal immigration, practicing stricter border patrol against infiltration by diverse Third World peoples: Algerians, Tunisians, Egyptians, Pakistanis, Sri Lankans, Indians, Turks, Senegalese, Malians, and Nigerians. The colonial master narrative, meanwhile, is being triumphantly re-staged. Millions of dollars are poured into international events planned for the quincentenary of Columbus's so-called voyages of discovery, climaxing in the Grand Regatta, a fleet of tall ships from 40 countries leaving from Spain and arriving in New York Harbor for U.S. Independence Day, the Fourth of July. At the same time, an anti-colonial narrative is being performed via the view-from-the-shore projects, the Native American commemorations of annihilated communities throughout the U.S. and the American continent, and plans for setting up blockades at the arrival of the replicas of Columbus's caravels, sailing into U.S. ports. What, then, is the meaning of 'post-coloniality' when certain structural conflicts persist? Despite different historical contexts, the conflict between the Native American claim to their land as a sacred and communal trust and the Euro-American view of land as alienable property remains structurally the same. How then does one negotiate sameness and difference within the framework of a 'post-colonial' whose 'post' emphasizes rupture and deemphasizes sameness?

Contemporary cultures are marked by the tension between the official end of direct colonial rule and its presence and regeneration through hegemonizing neo-colonialism within the First World and toward the Third World, often channelled through the nationalist patriarchal elites. The 'colonial' in the 'post-colonial' tends to be relegated to the past and marked with a closure – an implied temporal border that undermines a potential oppositional thrust. For whatever the philosophical connotations of the 'post' as an ambiguous locus of continuities and discontinuities,[11] its denotation of 'after' – the teleological lure of the 'post' – evokes a celebratory clearing of a conceptual space that on one level conflicts with the notion of 'neo.'

The 'neo-colonial,' like the 'post-colonial' also suggests continuities and discontinuities, but its emphasis is on the new modes and forms of the old colonialist practices, not on a 'beyond.' Although one can easily imagine the 'post-colonial' travelling into Third World countries (more likely via the Anglo-American academy than via India), the 'post-colonial' has little currency in African, Middle Eastern and Latin American intellectual circles, except occasionally in the restricted historical sense of the period immediately following the end of colonial rule. Perhaps it is the less intense experience of neo-colonialism, accompanied by the strong sense of relatively unthreatened multitudes of cultures, languages and ethnicities in India, that allowed for the recurrent usage of the prefix 'post' over that of the 'neo.' Now that debt-ridden India, where 'post-colonial discourse' has flourished, has had to place itself under the tutelage of the International Monetary Fund, and now that its non-aligned foreign policy is giving way to political and economic cooperation with the U.S., one wonders whether the term 'neo-colonial' will become more pervasive than 'post-colonial.'[12]

The 'post-colonial' also forms a critical locus for moving beyond anti-colonial nationalist modernizing narratives that inscribe Europe as an object of critique, toward a discursive analysis and historiography addressing decen-tered multiplicities of power relations (for example, between colonized women and men, or between colonized peasantry and the bourgeoisie). The sig-nificance of such intellectual projects stands in ironic contrast to the term 'post-colonial' itself, which linguistically reproduces, once again, the centrality of the colonial narrative. The 'post-colonial' implies a narrative of progression in which colonialism remains the central point of reference, in a march of time neatly arranged from the pre to the 'post,' but which leaves ambiguous its relation to new forms of colonialism, i.e. neo-colonialism.

Considering the term 'post-colonial' in relation to other terms such as 'neo-colonial' and 'post-independence' allows for mutual illumination of the con-cepts. Although 'neo-colonial,' like 'post-colonial,' implies a passage, it has the advantage of emphasizing a repetition with difference, a regeneration of colonialism through other means. The term 'neo-colonialism' usefully desig-nates broad relations of geo-economic hegemony. When examined in relation to 'neo-colonialism,' the term 'post-colonial' undermines a critique of contem-porary colonialist structures of domination, more available through the repeti-tion and revival of the 'neo.' The term 'post-independence,' meanwhile, invokes an achieved history of resistance, shifting the analytical focus to the emergent nation-state. In this sense, the term 'post-independence,' precisely because it implies a nation-state telos, provides expanded analytical space for confronting such explosive issues as religion, ethnicity, patriarchy, gender and sexual orientation, none of which are reducible to epiphenomena of colo-nialism and neo-colonialism. Whereas 'post-colonial' suggests a distance from colonialism, 'post-independence' celebrates the nation-state; but by attributing power to the nation-state it also makes Third World regimes accountable.

The operation of simultaneously privileging and distancing the colonial narrative, moving beyond it, structures the 'in-between' framework of the 'post-colonial.' This in-betweenness becomes evident through a kind of com-mutation test. While one can posit the duality between colonizer/colonized and even neo-colonizer/neo-colonized, it does not make much sense to speak of post-colonizers and post-colonized. 'Colonialism' and 'neo-colonialism' imply both oppression and the possibility of resistance. Transcending such dichoto-mies, the term 'post-colonial' posits no clear domination, and calls for no clear opposition. It is this structured ambivalence of the 'post-colonial,' of positing a simultaneously close and distant temporal relation to the 'colonial,' that is appealing in a post-structuralist academic context. It is also this fleeting quality, however, that makes the 'post-colonial' an uneasy term for a geopolitical critique of the centralized distribution of power in the world.

Post-colonial theory has dealt most significantly with cultural contradictions, ambiguities, and ambivalences.[13] Through a major shift of emphasis, it accounts for the experiences of displacement of Third World peoples in the metropolitan centers, and the cultural syncretisms generated by the First/Third Worlds intersections, issues less adequately addressed by Third World nationalist and world systems discourses, more rooted in the categories of political-economy. The 'beyond' of post-colonial theory, in this sense, seems most meaningful when placed in relation to Third World nationalist discourse. The term 'post-colonial' would be more precise, therefore, if articulated as 'post-First/Third Worlds theory,' or 'post-anti-colonial critique,' as a movement beyond a relatively binaristic, fixed and stable mapping of power relations between 'colonizer/colonized' and 'center/periphery.' Such rearticulations suggest a more nuanced discourse, which allows for movement, mobility and fluidity. Here, the prefix 'post' would make sense less as 'after' than as following, going beyond and commenting upon a certain intellectual movement – third worldist anti-colonial critique – rather than beyond a certain point in history – colonialism; for here 'neo-colonialism' would be a less passive form of addressing the situation of neo-colonized countries, and a politically more active mode of engagement.

Post-colonial theory has formed not only a vibrant space for critical, even resistant scholarship, but also a contested space, particularly since some practitioners of various Ethnic Studies feel somewhat displaced by the rise of post-colonial studies in North American English departments. If the rising institutional endorsement of the term 'post-colonial' is on the one hand a success story for the PCs (politically correct), is it not also a partial containment of the POCs (people of color)? Before PO-CO becomes the new academic buzz-word, it is urgent to address such schisms, specifically in the North American context,[14] where one has the impression that the 'post-colonial' is privileged precisely because it seems safely distant from 'the belly of the beast,' the United States. The recognition of these cracks and fissures is crucial if ethnic studies and post-colonial studies scholars are to forge more effective institutional alliances.

Having raised these questions about the term 'post-colonial,' it remains to address some related concepts, and to explore their spatio-temporal implications. The foregrounding of 'hybridity' and 'syncretism' in post-colonial studies calls attention to the mutual imbrication of 'central' and 'peripheral' cultures. 'Hybridity' and 'syncretism' allow negotiation of the multiplicity of identities and subject positionings which result from displacements, immigrations and exiles without policing the borders of identity along essentialist and originary lines. It is largely diasporic Third World intellectuals in the First World, hybrids themselves, not coincidentally, who elaborate a framework which situates the Third World intellectual within a multiplicity of cultural positionalities and perspectives. Nor is it a coincidence, by the same token, that in

Latin America 'syncretism' and 'hybridity' had already been invoked decades ago by diverse Latin American modernisms, which spoke of neologistic culture, of *créolité*, of *mestizaje*, and of anthropophagy.[15] The culturally syncretic protagonists of the Brazilian modernists of the nineteen twenties, the 'heroes without character' coined by Mario de Andrade, might be seen as 'postcolonial hybrids' *avant la lettre*. The cannibalist theories of the Brazilian modernists, and their elaborations in the Tropicalist movement of the late nineteen sixties and early nineteen seventies, simply assumed that New Worlders were culturally mixed, a contentious amalgam of indigenous, African, European, Asian, and Arab identities.

At the same time, the problematic spatio-temporality implicit in the term 'post-colonial' has repercussions for the conceptualization of the past in post(anti)colonial theory. The rupture implicit in the 'post' has been reflected in the relationship between past and present in post-colonial discourse, with particular reference to notions of hybridity. At times the anti-essentialist emphasis on hybrid identities comes dangerously close to dismissing all searches for communitarian origins as an archaeological excavation of an idealized, irretrievable past. Yet, on another level, while avoiding any nostalgia for a prelapsarian community, or for any unitary and transparent identity predating the fall, we must also ask whether it is possible to forge a collective resistance without inscribing a communal past. Rap music narratives and video representations which construct resistant invocations of Africa and slavery are a case in point. For communities which have undergone brutal ruptures, now in the process of forging a collective identity, no matter how hybrid that identity has been before, during, and after colonialism, the retrieval and reinscription of a fragmented past becomes a crucial contemporary site for forging a resistant collective identity. A notion of the past might thus be negotiated differently; not as a static fetishized phase to be literally reproduced but as fragmented sets of narrated memories and experiences on the basis of which to mobilize contemporary communities. A celebration of syncretism and hybridity per se, if not articulated in conjunction with questions of hegemony and neo-colonial power relations, runs the risk of appearing to sanctify the *fait accompli* of colonial violence.

The current metropolitan discursive privileging of palimpsestic syncretisms must also be negotiated vis-a-vis Fourth World peoples. It may account, for example, for the paradoxical situation of the indigenous Kayapo in the Amazon forest who, on the one hand, use video-cameras and thus demonstrate their cultural hybridity and their capacity for mimicry, but who, on the other, use mimicry precisely in order to stage the urgency of *preserving* the essential practices and contours of their culture including their relation to the rainforest and the communal possession of land. The defacto acceptance of hybridity as a product of colonial conquest and post-independence dislocations as well as the recognition of the impossibility of going back to an authentic past do not mean that the politico-cultural movements of various racial-ethnic communities should stop researching and recycling their pre-colonial languages and cultures.[16] Post-colonial theory's celebration of hybridity risks an anti-essentialist condescension toward those communities obliged by circumstances to assert, for their very survival, a lost and even irretrievable past. In such cases, the assertion of culture prior to conquest forms part of the fight against continuing forms of annihilation. If the logic of the post-structuralist/post-colonial argument were taken literally, then the Zuni in Mexico/U.S. would be censured for their search for the traces of an original culture, and the Jindywor-obak in Australia criticized for their turn to Aboriginal language and culture as part of their own regeneration. The question, in other words, is not whether there is such a thing as an originary homogeneous past, and if there is whether it would be possible to return to it, or even whether the past is unjustifiably idealized. Rather, the question is: who is mobilizing what in the articulation of the past, deploying what identities, identifications and representations, and in the name of what political vision and goals?

Negotiating locations, identities, and positionalities in relation to the violence of neo-colonialism is crucial if hybridity is not to become a figure for the consecration of hegemony. As a descriptive catch-all term, 'hybridity' per se fails to discriminate between the diverse modalities of hybridity, for example, forced assimilation, internalized self-rejection, political cooptation, social conformism, cultural mimicry, and creative transcendence. The reversal of biologically and religiously racist tropes – the hybrid, the syncretic – on the one hand, and the reversal of anti-colonialist purist notions of identity, on the other, should not obscure the problematic agency of 'post-colonial hybridity.' In contexts such as Latin America, nationhood was officially articulated in hybrid terms, through an integrationist ideology which glossed over institutional and discursive racism. At the same time, hybridity has also been used as part of resistant critique, for example by the modernist and tropicalist movements in Latin America. As in the term 'post-colonial,' the question of location and perspective has to be addressed, i.e. the differences between hybridities, or more specifically, hybridities of Europeans and their off-shoots around the world, and that of (ex)colonized peoples. And furthermore, the differences among and between Third World diasporas, for example, between African American hybrids speaking English in the First World and those of Afro-Cubans and Afro-Brazilians speaking Spanish and Portuguese in the Third World.

'Hybridity,' like the 'post-colonial,' is susceptible to a blurring of perspectives. 'Hybridity' must be examined in a non-universalizing, differential manner, contextualized within present neo-colonial hegemonies. The cultural inquiry generated by the hybridity/syncretism discourse needs re-linking to geopolitical macro-level analysis. It requires articulation with the ubiquity of Anglo-American informational media (CNN, BBC, AP), as well as with events of the magnitude of the Gulf War, with its massive and traumatic transfers of populations. The collapse of Second World socialism, it should be pointed out, has not altered neo-colonial policies, and on some levels, has generated increased anxiety among such Third World communities as the Palestinians and South African Blacks concerning their struggle for independence without a Second World counter-balance.

The circulation of 'post-colonial' as a theoretical frame tends to suggest a supercession of neo-colonialism and the Third World and Fourth World as unfashionable, even irrelevant categories. Yet, with all its problems, the term 'Third World' does still retain heuristic value as a convenient label for the imperialized formations, including those within the First World. The term 'Third World' is most meaningful in broad political-economic terms, and becomes blurred when one addresses the differently modulated politics in the realm of culture, the overlapping contradictory spaces of inter-mingling identities. The concept of 'Third World' is schematically productive if it is placed under erasure, as it were, seen as provisional and ultimately inadequate.

At this point in time, replacing the term 'Third World' with the 'post-colonial' is a liability. Despite differences and contradictions among and within Third World countries, the term 'Third World' contains a common project of (linked) resistances to neo/colonialisms. Within the North American context, more specifically, it has become a term of empowerment for inter-communal coalitions of various peoples of color.[17] Perhaps, it is this sense of a common project around which to mobilize that is missing from post(anti)colonial discussions. If the terms 'post-colonial' and 'post-independence' stress, in different ways, a rupture in relation to colonialism, and the 'neo-colonial' emphasizes continuities, 'Third World' usefully evokes structural commonalities of struggles. The invocation of the 'Third World' implies a belief that the shared history of neo/colonialism and internal racism form sufficient common ground for alliances among such diverse peoples. If one does not believe or envision such commonalities, then indeed the term 'Third World' should be discarded. It is this difference of alliance and mobilization between the concepts 'Third World' and the 'post-colonial' that suggests a relational usage of the terms. My assertion of the political relevance of such categories as 'neo-colonialism,' and even that of the more problematic Third and Fourth World peoples, is not meant to suggest a submission to intellectual inertia, but to point to a need to deploy all the concepts in differential and contingent manners.

In sum, the concept of the 'post-colonial' must be interrogated and contextualized historically, geopolitically, and culturally. My argument is not necessarily that one conceptual frame is 'wrong' and the other is 'right,' but that each frame illuminates only partial aspects of systemic modes of domination, of overlapping collective identities, and of contemporary global relations. Each addresses specific and even contradictory dynamics between and within different world zones. There is a need for more flexible relations among the various conceptual frameworks – a mobile set of grids, a diverse set of disciplinary as well as cultural-geopolitical lenses – adequate to these complexities. Flexible yet critical usage which can address the politics of location is important not only for pointing out historical and geographical contradictions and differences but also for reaffirming historical and geographical links, structural analogies, and openings for agency and resistance.

Notes

1 See, for example, Aijaz Ahmad, 'Jameson's Rhetoric of Otherness and the "National Allegory," ' *Social Text* 17 (Fall 1987); Arjun Appadurai, 'Disjuncture and Difference in the Global Cultural Economy,' *Public Culture* 2.2 (1990); Robert Stam, 'Eurocentrism, Afrocentrism, Polycentrism: Theories of Third Cinema,' *Quarterly Review of Film and Video* 13, 1–3 (Spring, 1991); Chandra Talpade Mohanty, 'Cartographies of Struggle: Third World Women and the Politics of Feminism', in *Third World Women and the Politics of Feminism* ed. by Chandra Talpade Mohanty, Ann Russo, Lourdes Torres (Indiana University Press, 1991).

2 Does that condition echo the language of existentialism, or is it the echo of postmodernism?

3 The relationships between 'post-colonial,' 'post-coloniality,' and 'post-colonialism' have yet to be addressed more rigorously.

4 For a reading of the relationships between post-modernism and post-colonialism, see Kwame Anthony Appiah, 'Is the Post- in Postmodernism the Post- in Postcolonial?,' *Critical Inquiry* 17 (Winter 1991).

5 Bill Ashcroft, Gareth Griffiths, Helen Tiffin, *The Empire Writes Back: Theory and Practice in Post-Colonial Literatures* (London: Routledge, 1989), p. 2.

6 For a radical formulation of resistant post-colonial see Gayatri Chakravorty Spivak, 'Poststructuralism, Marginality, Postcoloniality and Value,' in *Literary Theory Today*, Peter Collier and Helga Geyer-Ryan, eds. (London: Polity Press, 1990).

7 Read for example, Zachary Lockman and Joel Benin, eds., *Intifada: The Palestinian Uprising Against Israeli Occupation* (Boston: South End Press, 1989), specifically Edward W. Said, 'Intifada and Independence,' pp. 5–22; Edward W. Said, *After the Last Sky* (Boston: Pantheon Books, 1985).

8 This perspective explains the harsh repression of movements in opposition to the U.S.–Egypt alliance during the war. In fact, the Camp David treaty is intimately linked to the Open Door economic policy with its dismantling of the Egyptian public sector. Referred to as the shadow government of Egypt, USAID is partly responsible for the positions Egyptian and most Arab governments took during the Gulf War.

9 The rigid imposition of Islamic law in Saudi Arabia is linked to efforts to mask the regime's anti-regional collaboration with imperial interests.

10 'Gringostroika' in the coinage of Mexican multi-media artist Guillermo Goméz-Penã.

11 For discussions of the 'post,' see for example, Robert Young, 'Poststructuralism: the End of Theory,' *Oxford Literary Review* 5, 1–2 (1982); R. Radhakrishnan, 'The Postmodern Event and the End of Logocentrism,' *Boundary 2*, 12.1 (Fall 1983); Geoffrey Bennington, 'Postal Politics and the Institution of the Nation,' in Homi K. Bhabha, ed., *Nation and Narration* (London and New York: Routledge, 1990).

12 As these notes on the 'post-colonial' are on their way to print, a relevant article appeared in *The Nation*, Praful Bidwai, 'India's Passage to Washington,' (20 January 1992).

13 See for example, Homi K. Bhabha, 'The Commitment to Theory,' in *Questions of Third Cinema*, ed. by Jim Pines and Paul Willemen (London: British Film Institute, 1989); Trinh T. Minh-ha, *Woman, Native, Other* (Bloomington: Indiana University Press, 1989).

14 The 'post-colonial' replacement of the 'Third World' is ambiguous, especially when post-structuralist/post-colonial theories are confidently deployed with little

understanding of the historical-material legacy of colonialism, neo-colonialism, racism, and anti-colonial resistance. These slippages have contributed to facile dismissals of Frantz Fanon's formulations as vulgar.

15 On the Brazilian modernists and the concept of anthropophagy, see Robert Stam, *Subversive Pleasures: Bakhtin, Cultural Criticism and Film* (Baltimore: Johns Hopkins University Press, 1989).

16 For another critical consideration of hybridity and memory see also Manthia Diawara, 'The Nature of Mother in *Dreaming Rivers,*' *Third Text* 13 (Winter 1990/1991).

17 Aijaz Ahmad in his ' "Third World Literature" ' and the Nationalist Ideology,' *Journal of Arts and Ideas* 17–18 (June 1989) offers an important critique of the usages of Third World in the U.S. academy. Unfortunately, he ignores the crucial issue of empowerment taking place under the rubric Third World among diverse peoples of color in North American intellectual and academic communities.

17

Sara Suleri

Woman Skin Deep: Feminism and the Postcolonial Condition*

Given the current climate of rampant and gleeful anti-intellectualism that has overtaken the mass media at the present time, both literary and cultural interpretive practitioners have more than ample reason to reassess, to reexamine, and to reassert those theoretical concerns that constitute or question the identity of each putatively marginal group. There are dreary reiterations that must be made, and even more dreary navigations between the Scylla and Charybdis so easily identified in journalism as a conflict between the 'thought police' on the one hand and the proponents of 'multiculturalism' on the other. As readers of mass culture, let us note by way of example the astonishing attention that the media has accorded the academy: the Gulf War took up three months of their time, whereas we have been granted over a year of headlines and glossy magazine newsworthiness. Is our anathema, then, more pervasive than that of Saddam Hussein? In what fashion is the academy now to be read as one of the greatest sources of sedition against the new world order? The moment demands urgent consideration of how the outsideness of cultural criticism is being translated into that most tedious dichotomy that pits the 'academy' against the 'real world.' While I am somewhat embarrassed by the prospect of having to contemplate such a simplistic binarism, this essay seeks to question its own cultural parameters by situating both its knowledge and its ignorance in relation to the devastating rhetoric of 'us and them' that beleaguers issues of identity formation today. Grant me the luxury, then, of not having to supply quotation marks around several of the terms employed, and – since the time of life is short – an acknowledgement that the 'we' to which I am forced to take recourse is indeed very, very wee.

The sustained and trivializing attack on what is represented as academic self-censorship cannot be segregated from current reformulations of cultural identities: the former will continue to misconstrue deliberately questions of marginality into solutions of frivolity, or cultural criticism into tyrannical cliches about the political correctness of the thought police. And, if the debate on multiculturalism simply degenerates into a misplaced desire for the institution of rainbow coalition curricula, its shadow will fall in all heaviness on those disciplines most responsible for producing the kind of rhetoric that is presently

* From *Critical Inquiry* 18 (Summer 1992), pp. 75–69.

castigated for its political rectitude. Discursive formations that question canonical and cultural censors, in other words, are precisely the ones to be singled out
as demonstrative of the academy's spinelessly promiscuous submission to
'correctness.' The list of public enemies thus produced is hardly surprising: our
prostitution is repeatedly characterized by intellectual allegiances to the identity of postcolonialism, of gender, of gay and lesbian studies, and finally, of the
body. The academy has subcultured itself out of viable existence, we are told,
and the subtextual moral that attends such journalistic cautionary tales is
almost too obvious to merit articulation: if thy left hand offendeth thee, cut it
off.

Since none of us is partial to being lopped, the only resort appears to be a
two-tiered response to the anti-intellectualism that is our 'fin de siècle' fate.
First – as has been clear for at least the last year – the world lies all before us;
we have and must continue to respond. While much of the material that has
appeared in the popular press is so low-grade as to disqualify itself as discourse,
the academy must persist in making a resolute attempt to present some firm
alternative opinions within those very columns. On a very simplistic and
pragmatic level, if we must be freaks, let us be freaks with a voice. It may well
be that this effort at articulation will yield some useful readings of the peculiar
identity of the professional academic: how plural are we in our constructions of
singularity; and how singular in our apprehensions of the plural? The second
tier of any sustained response consists of an attempt to engender within the
academy an overdue exchange about the excesses and the limitations that
marginal discourses must inevitably accrue, even as they seek to map the
ultimate obsolescence of the dichotomy between margin and center. For until
the participants in marginal discourses learn how best to critique the intellectual errors that inevitably accompany the provisional discursivity of the
margin, the monolithic and untheorized identity of the center will always be on
them. The following readings seek an alignment with the second strategic tier
to contain anti-intellectualism – that is, an essay into the methodology through
which contemporary academic discourse seeks to decontaminate itself of
territorial affiliations and attempts instead to establish the proliferating and
shifting locations of the margins of cultural identities.

I

The specific margin that is my subject is one most virulently subjected to
popular parodies and to the label of irrational rectitude: the work conducted
around theoretical intersections of feminism and gender studies. It would be
unproductive to demonstrate that journalists are shoddy readers, or that the
'elevation' of Camille Paglia's words to the pages of a soft-core porn magazine
is in fact quite apposite with her discourse. An alternative margin might be
found in the tensions incipient within the critical practice itself: are the easy
pieties that emanate from the anti-thought-police press in any way implicit in
academic discourse on this keen cultural problem? Is girl talk with a difference,
in other words, at all responsible for the parodic replays that it has engendered

in the scurrilous imaginations of North American magazines? If the academy chooses to be the unseen legislator through which cultural difference is regulated into grouped identities of the marginal, then an urgent intellectual duty would surely be to subject not merely our others but ourselves to the rigors of revisionary scrutiny.

If you will allow me some further space-clearing generalizations, I would claim that while current feminist discourse remains vexed by questions of identity formation and the concomitant debates between essentialism and constructivism, or distinctions between situated and universal knowledge, it is still prepared to grant an uneasy selfhood to a voice that is best described as the property of 'postcolonial Woman.' Whether this voice represents perspectives as divergent as the African-American or the postcolonial cultural location, its imbrications of race and gender are accorded an iconicity that is altogether too good to be true. Even though the marriage of two margins should not necessarily lead to the construction of that contradiction in terms, a 'feminist center,' the embarrassed privilege granted to racially encoded feminism does indeed suggest a rectitude that could be its own theoretical undoing. The concept of the postcolonial itself is too frequently robbed of historical specificity in order to function as a preapproved allegory for any mode of discursive contestation. The coupling of *postcolonial* with *woman*, however, almost inevitably leads to the simplicities that underlie unthinking celebrations of oppression, elevating the racially female voice into a metaphor for 'the good.' Such metaphoricity cannot exactly be called essentialist, but it certainly functions as an impediment to a reading that attempts to look beyond obvious questions of good and evil. In seeking to dismantle the iconic status of postcolonial feminism, I will attempt here to address the following questions: within the tautological margins of such a discourse, which comes first, gender or race? How, furthermore, can the issue of chronology lead to some preliminary articulation of the productive superficiality of race?

Before such questions can be raised, however, it is necessary to pay some critical attention to the mobility that has accrued in the category of postcolonialism. Where the term once referred exclusively to the discursive practices produced by the historical fact of prior colonization in certain geographically specific segments of the world, it is now more of an abstraction available for figurative deployment in any strategic redefinition of marginality. For example, when James Clifford elaborated his position on travelling theory during a recent seminar, he invariably substituted the metaphoric condition of postcoloniality for the obsolete binarism between anthropologist and native.[1] As with the decentering of any discourse, however, this reimaging of the postcolonial closes as many epistemological possibilities as it opens. On the one hand, it allows for a vocabulary of cultural migrancy, which helpfully derails the postcolonial condition from the strictures of national histories, and thus makes way for the theoretical articulations best typified by Homi Bhabha's recent anthology, *Nation and Narration*.[2] On the other hand, the current metaphorization of postcolonialism threatens to become so amorphous as to repudiate any locality for cultural thickness. A symptom of this terminological and theoretical dilemma is astutely read in Kwame Anthony Appiah's essay, 'Is the Post- in Postmodernism the Post- in Postcolonial?'[3] Appiah argues for a discursive space-clearing that allows postcolonial discourse a figurative flexibility and at the same time reaffirms its radical locality within historical exigencies. His discreet but firm segregation of the postcolonial from the postmodern is indeed pertinent to the dangerous democracy accorded the coalition between postcolonial and feminist theories, in which each term serves to reify the potential pietism of the other.

In the context of contemporary feminist discourse, I would argue, the category of postcolonialism must be read both as a free-floating metaphor for cultural embattlement and as an almost obsolete signifier for the historicity of race. There is no available dichotomy that could neatly classify the ways in which such a redefinition of postcoloniality is necessarily a secret sharer in similar reconfigurations of feminism's most vocal articulation of marginality, or the obsessive attention it has recently paid to the racial body. Is the body in race subject or object, or is it more dangerously an objectification of a methodology that aims for radical subjectivity? Here, the binarism that informs Chandra Mohanty's paradigmatic essay. 'Under Western Eyes: Feminist Scholarship and Colonial Discourses,' deserves particular consideration. Where Mohanty engages in a particular critique of 'Third World Woman' as a monolithic object in the texts of Western feminism, her argument is premised on the irreconcilability of gender as history and gender as culture. 'What happens,' queries Mohanty, 'when [an] assumption of "women as an oppressed group" is situated in the context of Western feminist writing about third world women?' What happens, apparently, begs her question. In contesting what she claims is a 'colonialist move,' Mohanty proceeds to argue that 'Western feminists alone become the true "subjects" of this counterhistory. Third World women, on the other hand, never rise above the debilitating generality of their "object" status.'[4] A very literal ethic underlies such a dichotomy, one that demands attention to its very obviousness: how is this objectivism to be avoided? How will the ethnic voice of womanhood counteract the cultural articulation that Mohanty too easily dubs as the exegesis of Western feminism? The claim to authenticity – only a black can speak for a black; only a postcolonial subcontinental feminist can adequately represent the lived experience of that culture – points to the great difficulty posited by the 'authenticity' of female racial voices in the great game that claims to be the first narrative of what the ethnically constructed woman is deemed to want.

This desire all too often takes its theoretical form in a will to subjectivity that claims a theoretical basis most clearly contravened by the process of its analysis. An example of this point is Trinh Minh-ha's treatise, *Woman, Native, Other*,[5] which seeks to posit an alternative to the anthropological twist that constitutes the archaism through which nativism has been apprehended. Subtitled *Writing Postcoloniality and Feminism*, Trinh's book is a paradigmatic meditation that can be essentialized into a simple but crucial question: how can feminist discourse represent the categories of 'woman' and 'race' at the same time? If the languages of feminism and ethnicity are to escape an abrasive mutual contestation, what novel idiom can freshly articulate their radical inseparability? Trinh's strategy is to relocate her gendering of ethnic realities on the inevitable territory of postfeminism, which underscores her desire to represent discourse formation as always taking place after the fact of discourse. It further confirms my belief that had I any veto power over prefixes, *post-* would be the first to go – but that is doubtless tangential to the issue at hand. In the context of Trinh's methodology, the shape of the book itself illuminates what may best be called the endemic ill that effects a certain temporal derangement between the work's originary questions and the narratives that they engender. *Woman, Native, Other* consists of four loosely related chapters, each of which opens with an abstraction and ends with an anecdote. While there is a self-pronounced difference between the preliminary thesis outlined in the chapter 'Commitment from the Mirror-Writing Box' to the concluding claims in 'Grandma's Story,' such a discursive distance is not matched with any logical or theoretical consistency. Instead, a work that is impelled by an impassioned need to question the lines of demarcation between race and gender concludes by falling into a predictable biological fallacy in which sexuality is reduced to the literal structure of the racial body, and theoretical interventions within this trajectory become minimalized into the naked category of lived experience.

When feminism turns to lived experience as an alternative mode of radical subjectivity, it only rehearses the objectification of its proper subject. While lived experience can hardly be discounted as a critical resource for an apprehension of the gendering of race, neither should such data serve as the evacuating principle for both historical and theoretical contexts alike. 'Radical subjectivity' too frequently translates into a low-grade romanticism that cannot recognize its discursive status as *pre-* rather than *post-*. In the concluding chapter of Trinh's text, for example, a section titled 'Truth and Fact: Story and History' delineates the skewed idiom that marginal subjectivities produce. In attempting to proclaim an alternative to male-identified objectivism, Trinh-as-anthropologist can only produce an equally objectifying idiom of joy:

> Let me tell you a story. For all I have is a story. Story passed on from generation to generation, named Joy. Told for the joy it gives the storyteller and the listener. Joy inherent in the process of storytelling. Whoever understands it also understands that a story, as distressing as it can be in its joy, never takes anything away from anybody (*WNO*, p. 119).

Given that I find myself in a more acerbic relation both to the question of the constitution of specific postcolonialisms and of a more metaphoric postcolonial feminism, such a jointly universalist and individualist 'joy' is not a term that I would ordinarily welcome into my discursive lexicon. On one level, its manipulation of lived experience into a somewhat fallacious allegory for the reconstitution of gendered race bespeaks a transcendence – and an attendant evasion – of the crucial cultural issues at hand. On a more dangerous level, however, such an assumption serves as a mirror image of the analyses produced by the critics of political rectitude. For both parties, 'life' remains the ultimate answer to 'discourse.' The subject of race, in other words, cannot cohabit with the detail of a feminist language.

Trinh's transcendent idiom, of course, emanates from her somewhat free-floating understanding of 'postcoloniality': is it an abstraction into which all historical specificity may be subsumed, or is it a figure for a vaguely defined ontological marginality that is equally applicable to all 'minority' discourses? In either case, both the categories of 'woman' and 'race' assume the status of metaphors, so that each rhetoric of oppression can serve equally as a mirrored allegory for the other. Here, *Woman, Native, Other* is paradigmatic of the methodological blurring that dictates much of the discourse on identity formation in the coloring of feminist discourse. To privilege the racial body in the absence of historical context is indeed to generate an idiom that tends to waver with impressionistic haste between the abstractions of postcoloniality and the anecdotal literalism of what it means to articulate an 'identity' for a woman writer of color. Despite its proclaimed location within contemporary theoretical – not to mention post-theoretical – discourse, such an idiom poignantly illustrates the hidden and unnecessary desire to resuscitate the 'self.'

What is most striking about such discursive practices is their failure to confront what may be characterized best as a great enamorment with the 'real.' Theories of postcolonial feminism eminently lend themselves to a reopening of the continued dialogue that literary and cultural studies have – and will continue to have – with the perplexing category known as realism, but at present the former discourse chooses to remain too precariously parochial to recognize the bounty that is surely its to give. Realism, however, is too dangerous a term for an idiom that seeks to raise identity to the power of theory. While both may be windmills to the quixotic urge to supply black feminism with some version of the 'real,' Trinh's musings on this subject add a mordantly pragmatic option to my initial question: 'what comes first, race or gender?' Perhaps the query would be more finely calibrated if it were re-phrased to ask, 'What comes first, race, gender, or profession?' And what, in our sorry dealings with such realisms, is the most phantasmagoric category of all?

According to *Woman, Native, Other*, such a triple bind can be articulated only in order to declare that bonding is all. An opening section of that text is in fact titled 'The Triple Bind'; it attempts to outline the alternative realism still to be claimed by the postcolonial feminist mentality:

> Today, the growing ethnic-feminist consciousness has made it increasingly difficult for [the woman of color who writes] to turn a blind eye not only to the specification of the writer as historical subject ... but also to writing itself as a practice located at the intersection of subject and history – a literary practice that involves the possible knowledge (linguistic and ideological) of itself as such (*WNO*, p. 6).

Here the text evades the threat of realism by taking recourse to the 'peaceable' territory of writing, on which all wars may be fought with each discursive contingency in deployment. While writing may serve as a surrogate for the distance between subject (read self) and history, Trinh unwittingly makes clear her academic appreciation of alterity: the female writer, or the third person 'she' that haunts her text, 'is made to feel she must choose from among three conflicting identities. Writer of color? Woman writer? Or woman of color? Which comes first? Where does she place her loyalties?' (*WNO*, p. 6). The hierarchy of loyalties thus listed illustrates the danger inherent in such cultural lists: the uneasy proclamation with which *Woman, Native, Other* sets out to be the 'first full-length study of post-feminism' (according to the book's jacket) is a self-defeating project, for feminism has surely long since laid aside the issue of an individualized female loyalty as its originating assumption. If race is to complicate the project of divergent feminisms, in other words, it cannot take recourse to biologism, nor to the incipient menace of rewriting alterity into the ambiguous shape of the exotic body.

The body that serves as testimony for lived experience, however, has received sufficient interrogation from more considered perspectives on the cultural problems generated by the dialogue between gender and race, along with the hyperrealist idiom it may generate. Hazel Carby helpfully advocates that

> black feminist criticism [should] be regarded critically as a problem, not a solution, as a sign that should be interrogated, a locus of contradictions. Black feminist criticism has its source and its primary motivation in academic legitimation, placement within a framework of bourgeois humanistic discourse.[6]

The concomitant question that such a problem raises is whether the signification of gendered race necessarily returns to the realism that it most seeks to disavow. If realism is the Eurocentric and patriarchal pattern of adjudicating between disparate cultural and ethnic realities, then it is surely the task of radical feminism to provide an alternative perspective. In the vociferous discourse that such a task has produced, however, the question of alternativism is all too greatly subsumed either into the radical strategies that are designed to dictate the course of situated experience, or into the methodological imperatives that impell a work related to *Woman, Native, Other* such as bell hooks's *Talking Back: Thinking Feminist, Thinking Black.*

While the concept of 'talking back' may appear to be both invigorating and empowering to a discourse interested in the reading of gendered race, the text *Talking Back* is curiously engaged in talking to itself; in rejecting Caliban's mode of protest, its critique of colonization is quietly narcissistic in its projection of what a black and thinking female body may appear to be, particularly in the context of its repudiation of the genre of realism. Yet this is the genre, after all, in which African-American feminism continues to seek legitimation: hooks's study is predicated on the anecdotes of lived experience and their capacity to provide an alternative to the discourse of what she terms patriarchal rationalism. Here the unmediated quality of a local voice serves as a substitute for any theoretical agenda that can make more than a cursory connection between the condition of postcolonialism and the question of gendered race. Where hooks claims to speak beyond binarism, her discourse keeps returning to the banality of easy dichotomies: 'Dare I speak to oppressed and oppressor in the same voice? Dare I speak to you in a language that will take us away from the boundaries of domination, a language that will not fence you in, bind you, or hold you? Language is also a place of struggle.'[7] The acute embarrassment generated by such an idiom could possibly be regarded as a radical rhetorical strategy designed to induce racial discomfort in its audience, but it more frequently registers as black feminism's failure to move beyond the proprietary rights that can be claimed by any oppressed discourse.

As does Trinh's text, hooks's claims that personal narrative is the only salve to the rude abrasions that Western feminist theory has inflicted on the body of ethnicity. The tales of lived experience, however, cannot function as a sufficient alternative, particularly when they are predicated on dangerously literal professions of postcolonialism. *Yearning: Race, Gender, and Cultural Politics*, hooks's more recent work, rehearses a postcolonial fallacy in order to conduct some highly misguided readings of competing feminisms within the context of racial experience. She establishes a hierarchy of color that depressingly segregates divergent racial perspectives into a complete absence of intellectual exchange. The competition is framed in terms of hooks's sense of the hostility between African-American and Third World feminisms:

> The current popularity of post-colonial discourse that implicates solely the West often obscures the colonizing relationship of the East in relation to Africa and other parts of the Third World. We often forget that many Third World nationals bring to this country the same kind of contempt and disrespect for blackness that is most frequently associated with white western imperialism. ... Within feminist movements Third World nationals often assume the role of mediator or interpreter, explaining the 'bad' black people to their white colleagues or helping the 'naive' black people to understand whiteness. ... Unwittingly assuming the role of go-between, of mediator, she re-inscribes a colonial paradigm.[8]

What is astonishing about such a claim is its continued obsession with a white academy, with race as a professional attribute that can only reconfigure itself around an originary concept of whiteness. Its feminism is necessarily skin deep in that the pigment of its imagination cannot break out of a strictly biological reading of race. Rather than extending an inquiry into the discursive possibilities represented by the intersection of gender and race, feminist intellectuals like hooks misuse their status as minority voices by enacting strategies of belligerence that at this time are more divisive than informative. Such claims to radical revisionism take refuge in the political untouchability that is accorded the category of Third World Woman, and in the process sully the crucial knowledge that such a category has still to offer to the dialogue of feminism today.

The dangers represented by feminists such as hooks and Trinh is that finally they will represent the profession as both their last court of appeal and the anthropological ground on which they conduct their field work. The alternative that they offer, therefore, is conceptually parochial and scales down the postcolonial condition in order to encompass it within North American academic terms. As a consequence, their discourse cannot but fuel the criticism of those who police the so-called thought police, nor is it able to address the historically risky compartmentalization of otherness that masquerades under the title of multiculturalism. Here it is useful to turn to one of the more brilliant observations that pepper Gayatri Spivak's *The Post-Colonial Critic*. In concluding an interview on multiculturalism, Spivak casually reminds her audience that

> if one looks at the history of post-Enlightenment theory, the major problem has been the problem of autobiography: how subjective structures can, in fact, give objective truth. During these same centuries, the Native Informant [was] treated as the objective evidence for the founding of the so-called sciences like ethnography, ethnolinguistics, comparative religion, and so on. So that, once again, the theoretical problems only relate to the person who knows. The person who *knows* has all of the problems of selfhood. The person who is *known*, somehow seems not to have a problematic self.[9]

Lived experience, in other words, serves as fodder for the continuation of another's epistemology, even when it is recorded in a 'contestatory' position to its relation to realism and to the overarching structure of the profession.

While cultural criticism could never pretend that the profession does not exist, its various voices must surely question any conflation of the professional model with one universal and world historical. The relation between local and given knowledge is obviously too problematic to allow for such an easy slippage, which is furthermore the ground on which the postcolonial can be abused to become an allegory for any one of the pigeonholes constructed for multiculturalism. Allow me to turn as a consequence to a local example of how realism locates its language within the postcolonial condition, and to suggest that lived experience does not achieve its articulation through autobiography, but through that other third-person narrative known as the law.

2

I proffer life in Pakistan as an example of such a postcolonial and lived experience. Pakistani laws, in fact, pertain more to the discourse of a petrifying realism than do any of the feminist critics whom I have cited thus far. The example at hand takes a convoluted postcolonial point and renders it nationally simple: if a postcolonial nation chooses to embark on an official program of Islamization, the inevitable result in a Muslim state will be legislation that curtails women's rights and institutes in writing what has thus far functioned as the law of the passing word. The Hudood Ordinances in Pakistan were promulgated in 1979 and legislated in 1980, under the military dictatorship of General Mohammad Zia-ul-Haq. They added five new criminal laws to the existing system of Pakistani legal pronouncements, of which the second ordinance – against *Zina* (that is, adultery as well as fornication) – is of the greatest import. An additional piece of legislation concerns the law of evidence, which rules that a woman's testimony constitutes half of a man's. While such infamous laws raise many historical and legal questions, they remain the body through which the feminist movement in Pakistan – the Women's Action Forum – must organize itself.

It is important to keep in mind that the formulation of the Hudood Ordinances was based on a multicultural premise, even though they were multicultural from the dark side of the moon. These laws were premised on a Muslim notion of *Hadd* and were designed to interfere in a postcolonial criminal legal system that was founded on Anglo-Saxon jurisprudence. According to feminist lawyer Asma Jahangir,

> the Hudood Ordinances were promulgated to bring the criminal legal system of Pakistan in conformity with the injunctions of Islam. . . . Two levels of punishments are introduced in the Ordinances. Two levels of punishment and, correspondingly, two separate sets of rules of evidence are prescribed. The first level or category is the one called the 'Hadd' which literally means the 'limit' and the other 'Tazir', which means 'to punish'.[10]

The significance of the *Hadd* category is that it delineates immutable sentences: *Tazir* serves only as a safety net in case the accused is not convicted under *Hadd*. These fixed rules are in themselves not very pretty: *Hadd* for theft is amputation of a hand; for armed robbery, amputation of a foot; for rape or adultery committed by married Muslims, death by stoning; for rape or adultery committed by non-Muslims or unmarried Muslims, a hundred public lashes (see *HO*, p. 24). While I am happy to report that the *Hadd* has not yet been executed, the laws remain intact and await their application.

The applicability of these sentences is rendered more murderous and even obscenely ludicrous when the immutability of the *Hadd* punishments is juxtaposed with the contingency of the laws of evidence. If a man is seen stealing a thousand rupees by two adult Muslim males, he could be punished by *Hadd* and his hand would be amputated. If an adult Muslim stole several million rupees and the only available witnesses were women and non-Muslims, he would not qualify for a *Hadd* category and would be tried under the more free-floating *Tazir* instead. 'A gang of men can thus rape all the residents of a women's hostel,' claims Jahangir with understandable outrage, 'but [the] lack of ocular evidence of four Muslim males will rule out the imposition of a Hadd punishment' (*HO*, p. 49). Such a statement, unfortunately, is not the terrain of rhetoric alone, since the post-Hudood Ordinance application of the *Tazir* has made the definition of rape an extremely messy business indeed.

Here, then, we turn to *Zina*, and its implications for the Pakistani female body. The Hudood Ordinances have allowed for all too many openings in the boundaries that define rape. Women can now be accused of rape, as can children; laws of mutual consent may easily convert a case of child abuse into a prosecution of the child for *Zina*, for fornication. Furthermore, unmarried men and women can be convicted of having committed rape against each other, since a subsection of the *Zina* offense defines rape as 'one where a man or a woman have illicit sex knowing that they are not validly married to each other' (quoted in *HO*, p. 58). In other words, fornication is all, and the statistics of the past few years grimly indicate that the real victims of the Hudood Ordinances are women and children, most specifically those who have no access to legal counsel and whose economic status renders them ignorant of their human rights.

Jahangir cites the example of a fifteen-year-old woman, Jehan Mina, who, after her father's death, was raped by her aunt's husband and son. Once her pregnancy was discovered, another relative filed a police report alleging rape. During the trial, however, the accused led no defense, and Mina's testimony alone was sufficient to get her convicted for fornication and sentenced to one hundred public lashes. That child's story is paradigmatic of the untold miseries of those who suffer sentences in Muslim jails.

Let me state the obvious: I cite these alternative realisms and constructions of identity in order to reiterate the problem endemic to postcolonial feminist criticism. It is not the terrors of Islam that have unleashed the Hudood Ordinances on Pakistan, but more probably the United States government's economic and ideological support of a military regime during that bloody but eminently forgotten decade marked by the 'liberation' of Afghanistan. Jehan Mina's story is therefore not so far removed from our current assessment of what it means to be multicultural. How are we to connect her lived experience with the overwhelming realism of the law? In what ways does her testimony force postcolonial and feminist discourse into an acknowledgement of the inherent parochialism and professionalism of our claims?

I will offer a weak bridge between the two poles of my rhetorical question: a poem by the feminist Pakistani writer, Kishwar Naheed. Her writing has been perceived as inflammatory, and she has been accused of obscenity more than once. The obscenity laws, or the Fahashi laws, are another story altogether. Once they were passed, they could not be put in print because the powers that be declared them to be too obscene. The poem below, however, is one that could easily earn the poet a prison sentence in contemporary Pakistan:

> It is we sinful women
> who are not awed by the grandeur of those who wear gowns
> who don't sell our lives
> who don't bow our heads
> who don't fold our hands together.
>
> It is we sinful women
> while those who sell the harvests of our bodies
> become exalted
> become distinguished
> become the just princes of the material world.
>
> It is we sinful women
> who come out raising the banner of truth
> up against barricades of lies on the highways
> who find stories of persecution piled on each threshold
> who find the tongues which could speak have been severed.
>
> It is we sinful women.
> Now, even if the night gives chase
> these eyes shall not be put out.

For the wall which has been razed
don't insist now on raising it again.

It is we sinful women.
who are not awed by the grandeur of those who wear gowns
who don't sell our bodies
who don't bow our heads
who don't fold our hands together.[11]

We should remember that there remains unseen legislation against such poetry, and that the *Hadd* – the limit – is precisely the realism against which our lived experience can serve as a metaphor, and against which we must continue to write. If we allow the identity formation of postcolonialism to construe itself only in terms of nationalism and parochialism, or of gender politics at its most narcissistically ahistorical, then let us assume that the media has won its battle, and the law of the limit is upon us.

Notes

1 James Clifford's course, 'Travel and Identity in Twentieth-Century Interculture,' was given as the Henry Luce Seminar at Yale University, Fall 1990.
2 See *Nation and Narration*, ed. Homi K. Bhabha (New York, 1990).
3 See Kwame Anthony Appiah, 'Is the Post- in Postmodernism the Post- in Post-colonial?' *Critical Inquiry* 17 (Winter 1991), pp. 336–57.
4 Chandra Talpade Mohanty, 'Under Western Eyes: Feminist Scholarship and Colonial Discourses,' *Third World Women and the Politics of Feminism*, ed. Mohanty, Ann Russo, and Lourdes Torres (Bloomington, Ind., 1991), p. 71.
5 See Trinh T. Minh-ha, *Woman, Native, Other: Writing Postcoloniality and Feminism* (Bloomington, Ind., 1989); hereafter abbreviated *WNO*.
6 Hazel V. Carby, *Reconstructing Womanhood: The Emergence of the Afro-American Woman Novelist* (New York, 1987), p. 15.
7 bell hooks [Gloria Watkins], 'On Self-Recovery,' *Talking Back: Thinking Feminist, Thinking Black* (Boston, 1989), p. 28.
8 hooks, *Yearning: Race, Gender, and Cultural Politics* (Boston, 1990), pp. 93–4.
9 Gayatri Chakravorty Spivak, 'Questions of Multiculturalism,' interview by Sneja Gunew (30 Aug. 1986), *The Post-Colonial Critic: Interviews, Strategies, Dialogues*, ed. Sarah Harasym (New York, 1990), p. 66.
10 Asma Jahangir and Hina Jilani, *The Hudood Ordinances: A Divine Sanction?* (Lahore, Pakistan, 1990), p. 24; hereafter abbreviated *HO*.
11 Kishwar Naheed, 'We Sinful Women,' in *Beyond Belief: Contemporary Feminist Urdu Poetry*, trans. Rukhsana Ahmad (Lahore, Pakistan, 1990), pp. 22–3.

18

Ruth Frankenberg and Lata Mani

Crosscurrents, Crosstalk: Race, 'Postcoloniality' and the Politics of Location *

This paper had its immediate point of origin in the invitation to contribute to a lecture series on 'Postcoloniality and California' in the spring of 1991. Commonplace as the term 'postcoloniality' has rapidly become in literature, anthropology and Cultural Studies in recent times, the title begged a number of questions, about the notion of 'postcoloniality' and its efficacy, either in relation to California in particular, or to the United States in general. If the concept of 'post-coloniality' is spreading like brushfire through the terrain of cultural theory, what we propose by way of remedy is a carefully strategized 'controlled burn' approach that begins by posing the following questions.

What does 'postcoloniality' mean, for whom does it resonate, and why? What are the risks and effects of too hastily globalizing the concept?[1] In what senses, for example, are India, Britain or the United States 'postcolonial' locations? What are the multiple implications of 'post-ness' in relation to 'colonialism', in context, for example, of the persistence and current escalation of racism? We will argue that rigorous attention to that which neo-Gramscians and Althusserians call 'conjuncture', and some feminists describe as a 'politics of location', is critical to specifying both the limits and value of the term 'postcolonial'. In this paper we sketch the beginnings of what we call a 'feminist conjuncturalist' approach to the issue of which spaces and subjects might be conceived as 'postcolonial', and in what senses such a description might hold.[2]

Notes on the term 'postcolonial', or what we think it means, anyway

INDIA: 'postcolonial' implies independence from Britain; birth of the nation-state; end of territorial colonialism; inauguration of a path of economic development characterized by the growth of indigenous capitalism; neo-colonial relationship to the capitalist word; aid from socialist countries and horizontal assistance from other Third World countries non-aligned to either the First or Second World.

* From *Cultural Studies* 7.2 (May 1993), pp. 292–310.

BRITAIN: 'postcolonial' signals loss of most, though not all, former colonies – bear in mind Hong Kong, N. Ireland, the appearance on British landscapes of a significant number of people from the former colonies: 'We are here because you were there.' The transition from a society of predominantly white ethnic groups to one that is multiracial. The 'Other' no longer geographically distanced, but within, and over time significantly shaping landscape and culture. Samosas at the National Theatre café. Race riots.

USA: Here, the term 'postcolonial' sticks in our throats. White settler colony, multiracial society. Colonization of Native Americans, Africans imported as slaves, Mexicans incorporated by a border moving south, Asians imported and migrating to labor, white Europeans migrating to labor. US imperialist foreign policy brings new immigrants who are 'here because the US was/is there', among them Central Americans, Koreans, Filipinos, Vietnamese and Cambodians. The particular relation of past territorial domination and current racial composition that is discernible in Britain, and which lends a particular meaning to the term 'postcolonial', does not, we feel, obtain here. Other characterizations, other periodizations, seem necessary in naming for this place the shifts expressed by the term 'postcolonial' in the British and Indian cases: the serious calling into question of white/Western dominance by the groundswell of movements of resistance, and the emergence of struggles for collective self-determination most frequently articulated in nationalist terms.

'Post-Civil Rights' is a possible candidate for signalling this double articulation in the United States context. Let us emphasize at the outset that we use the term 'post-Civil Rights' broadly, to refer to the impact of struggles by African American, American Indian, La Raza and Asian American communities that stretched from the mid 1950s to the 1970s, movements which Michael Omi and Howard Winant have credited with collectively producing a ' "great transformation" of racial awareness, racial meaning, racial subjectivity'.[3] However, the name, 'post-Civil Rights'; would only grasp one strand of our description of the US. The term would have to be conjugated with another, one that would name the experience of recent immigrants/refugees borne here on the trails of US imperialist adventures, groups whose stories are unfolding in a tense, complicated relation – at time compatible, at times contradictory – with post-Civil Rights USA.

Post-*what*?!

We are quite aware that the terms 'postcolonial' and 'post-Civil Rights' are in important senses, incommensurable. First, 'colonial' refers to a system of domination while 'Civil Rights' designates collective struggle *against* a system or systems of domination. Strictly speaking, the analogous term to 'post-Civil Rights' would be 'post-decolonization struggle'. Conversely, the term analogous to 'postcolonial' at its most literal would be 'post-racist'. This in turn underscores the dangers of a literalist reading of the word 'postcolonial'. It seems to us that placing the terms 'postcolonial' and 'post-Civil Rights' alongside one another immediately serves to clarify some of the temporal and conceptual ambiguities of the 'post' in both cases. From the vantage point of the US today, it draws attention to the unfinished nature of the processes designated by both terms. It undermines, specifically, the sense of completion often implied by the 'post' in 'postcolonial', and which, if political conservatives could have their way, would settle upon the 'post' in 'post Civil Rights'. In doing so it helps to clarify that the 'posts' in both cases do not signal an 'after' but rather mark spaces of ongoing contestation enabled by decolonization struggles both globally and locally. Finally, 'post-Civil Rights' has not, to our knowledge, been used to name or claim identity. Questions of subject formation have on the other hand been integral to a consideration of the 'postcolonial'.[4] Accordingly, in this paper we move between considering 'postcolonial' as periodization and axis of subjectivity. By contrast, 'post-Civil Rights' is developed here as a form of periodization that we believe to be particularly helpful in coming to terms with the ideological and political landscape of the US today.[5]

Postcolonial(ity?): a state of being?

Taking the word apart, with the help of the dictionary, we find that 'post', in the sense that it interests us here, means variously 'after in time', 'later', 'following', or 'after in space'. Without the benefit of the dictionary, we take it that 'colonization', and 'colonialism' indicate a system of domination, in particular one involving geographical and/or racial distanciation between the rulers and the ruled, and one which, like all systems of domination, has interlinked political, economic and discursive dimensions. The suffix, 'i-t-y', in English 'ity', in French 'ité', in Latin 'itas' is said to mean 'character', 'condition' or 'state', with 'state' defined as 'a set of circumstances or attributes characterizing a person or thing at a given time', a 'way or form of being'. This confirms the suffix, 'ity' in 'postcoloniality' as connoting a condition that is evenly developed rather than internally disparate, disarrayed or contradictory.

Dictionary explorations, of course, mean little, in the sense that there is no collective unconscious, nor even a common Spellcheck and Thesaurus in the hard-drive, by means of which cultural critics continually confirm their intended meanings by reference to Webster's. But it seems to us that this staged form of attention to both prefix and suffix dramatizes the crux of what is problematic in the concept of 'postcoloniality'. The first problem lies with the 'post'. 'Post' means 'after in time'. But what happened during that time – presumably in this instance a time between 'colonialism', or 'coloniality', and now? In what senses are we now situated 'after' 'coloniality' in the sense of 'coloniality' being 'over and done with'? What, about 'the colonial', is over, and for whom? This is not a rhetorical but a genuine question, for it seems to us that, in relation to colonialism, some things are over, others transformed, and still others apparently unreconstructed. What, by the way happened to 'neo-colonialism' in all of this talk of the colonial and the post? In short, what do we too hasily elide when we involve the 'postcolonial', especially as an 'ity', as a condition, state, way or form of being spread evenly over an area without specified borders or unevenness or contradiction?

Autobiographical riff: Lata

As things go, I qualify rather well for the appellation 'postcolonial'. Born and raised in post-independence Bombay, singing the Indian national anthem in school assemblies, standing to it in movie theatres, submitting endless unsuccessful entries to essay competitions on the theme 'India's unity lies in her diversity'. In my youth the colonial period was just that – a demarcatable historical phenomenon. Its greatest significance, we learnt, lay in its incitement and provocation of a national liberation movement whose heroes we encountered, sometimes daily, as street names, as marble busts in school yards or as statues presiding over busy intersections, home to pigeons and the poor. Yes, I think there *is* a way in which my sense of self, my subject position, if you will, takes shape within a 'postcolonial' context, one also constituted among other things by my gender, class and thoroughly urban upbringing.

And yet there is something about the privileging of the concept of 'postcoloniality', the particular way in which it is globalized, either as a description of the world or of identity, that makes me exceedingly anxious. I think about Native American friends who rightly cringe at the suggestion that the Americas are 'postcolonial'. I ponder the fact that Black and Chicano critics have in the main not rushed to embrace the term as adequate to their present condition. I wonder if it is significant that the theorists most associated with the term – Edward Said, Gayatri Spivak and Homi Bhabha are themselves first-generation diasporic intellectuals, displaced to the US and UK from an elsewhere that shaped them in fundamental ways. At this point in my musings, I recognize two strategies that I could adopt in pursuing the question further. I could explore the historico-intellectual and political biographies of Said, Spivak and Bhabha in relation to their theoretical production, tracing the disjunctions between their own formulation of the issues and the politics of their reception within the Western academy. Alternately, I could explore my disquiet about 'postcoloniality' in relation to stories that narrate my own experiences and those of others with whom I debate such things.

> Identity is neither continuous nor continuously interrupted but constantly framed between the simultaneous vectors of similarity, continuity and difference.[6]

Stuart Hall's formulation, which charts a path between an essentialist and a rigorously poststructuralist conception of identity, captures the complex and dynamic interplay of modes of Othering and racialization within and against which, for instance, my own sense of self and construction by others can be understood.

Incident 1

It is dark and pouring with rain and I curse, unprepared as I am for the downpour and for the fact that buildings on campus are locked at 5.00 p.m. for reasons of safety. I am keeping a colleague waiting and there is no phone nearby. I decide to knock on the window of the office closest to the entrance. The gentleman, white and in his mid forties, is on the phone and gestures impatiently for me to wait. Although he is less than a minute, it feels much longer and I hop from foot to foot in the vain hope of dodging the raindrops. Placing the receiver on the cradle, he comes to the door. Opening it a crack, he asks me irritatedly what it is that I want. Surprised that he needs an explanation, I ask to be let in, stating that I am to meet someone in the building and had forgotten that the doors were locked at 5.00 p.m. Refusing to open the door any further, he states flatly that he cannot let anyone in off the street, god knows what I might do. I stand there gaping at him, shocked and taken aback.

Incident 2

Later that same week I am hurrying to my car loaded down with books. I hope that luck is on my side and that some kindly soul will let me into the building that borders the parking lot, thereby saving me the trouble of walking all the way around it. I dare not assume too much given my experience earlier in the week. As I approach the door I notice a Filipina woman at work cleaning the corridor. She looks up at me, smiles, and without a word opens the door for me.

Occurring as they did back to back, these incidents illustrated for me that which we otherwise experience in more undramatic ways: that identity is both relational and situated. Not having interviewed either the professor or the cleaning lady, I cannot claim to have their account of the incidents. My comments therefore are to be understood as my account of their constructions of me. In the first case my colleague refused to let me in, presumably concluding that I did not look like someone who had legitimate business in a university building at that time of the evening. I did not, I suppose, look like an authority figure. My clothes or books which could have signified either class or profession were clearly not sufficient clues as to who or what I might be. Race appears to have overriden class. In the latter incident, however, it took the Filipina worker less than 30 seconds to size me up. With similar visual clues and no request from me, she appears to have deemed it safe or appropriate to allow me to enter the building. Class appears to have determined her decision.

These incidents clarified for me a general confusion I had been experiencing in my institutional life in the contrast between the warm response to me of people who explicitly knew what my business was at the university, and the wariness of those who did not, and whose suspicions required explanations or ID cards in order to be allayed. I should stress here that I am not singling out any particular institution as an especially reprehensible site of racism, but am drawing on some of my experiences to think through my inscription into racist as well as colonial and postcolonial discourses.

My initial naïveté and surprise in response to such incidents as I have just described speaks to my own 'postcolonial' and class identity. Not having grown up as the Other of my society, I do not expect to be positioned as such. Indeed, this fundamental difference in life experience has led to my own sense of the importance of specifying the differences between those of us from the geographical Third World and those of us who came to adulthood as people of color in the West. Attention to such differences is crucial if we are not to falsely equalize groups with very different relations to the US power structure. We need to be wary of the possibility that university affirmative action or diversity agendas might be met by filling positions with people trained elsewhere, a strategy common in the business world, and one further enabled by the 1991 Immigration Act. In sum, as many have pointed out, the Other is not a homogeneous entity.

Having said that, however, what has been instructive to me is the extent to which modes of racialization specific to the history of certain Others are available for extension to other Others. The best instance of this comes from a story of an Arab woman who was told by a prospective employer in the midst of job negotiations that 'I will not haggle over your head.' As she put it, she felt dumbstruck as the discourse of slavery, of the trade in human beings as property, re-emerged in context of the bargaining that is an integral part of all hiring and is usually assumed to be a process that is at least nominally one among equals, not between master and slave.

The eruption in unexpected places of elements of the discourse of slavery or of the Other as trespasser or potential thief does not in any way undo the specificities of our positionings, but does point to the necessity that any consideration of 'postcolonial' identity must necessarily engage the vectors of similarity, continuity and difference. For the 'postcolonial' we will argue, is no unifying moment. Not only are we positioned differently in relation to that which is called up by that term, but disjunction must be central to our understanding of it.[7]

Autobiographical riff: Ruth

Like Bombay, India, *my* home – Manchester, England – has a Victoria Station. Two ends of the same imperial line. My first twenty years were shaped both by British imperialism, and by the diasporas that sprang from its demise. Thus in my childhood in the late 1950s and 1960s, some of my toys, clothes and combs were marked 'Empire Made'. Colonial encounters marked the English language: I used and still use words transformed from Hindi and other Indian languages – shampoo, dungarees, pyjamas, cushy. As a small girl my favorite bedtime stories were about Epaminondas, the 'naughty picanniny' who lived on a plantation, and who according to his mother, illustrated in the books as large, cheerful, wearing bright dresses, a white apron and headscarf, 'didn't have the sense he was borned with'. Among my dolls was a black, cuddly 'Gollywog', Sambo crossed with Teddy Bear. In one of my proudest moments, my sister and I marched down the aisle of our Unitarian Chapel dressed in feathered headdresses and fringed tunics made of old curtains and, beating out a rhythm on drums that my father had brought back from Kenya, sang to the assembled congregation something that claimed to be 'The Huron Indian Christmas Carol'. It began, 'Twas in the moon of wintertime/when all the birds had fled ... '[8]

Postcolonial times brought imperialist nostalgia, crudely slapstick TV shows like *Up the Jungle, It Ain't 'Alf Hot, Mum* and *The Black and White Minstrel Show*, in which white men went into blackface as South Asians and African Americans, and the more recent, more upscale *Jewel in the Crown* serial drama in the early eighties.

For many white Britons, the Other was more palatable confined within the white imaginary than in person. During my teens, Enoch Powell made his infamous 'rivers of blood' speech, marshalling the white population's fear and hatred of immigrants of color, as South Asians, transported to East Africa by the British at the height of Empire, were caught in the crossfire of Ugandan and Kenyan nationalism and came to the 'mother country'. There, they found themselves joining African-Caribbeans in, among other things, selling bus tickets and emptying hospital bedpans. I remember newspaper articles about Indian and Pakistani 'multi-occupied houses', where new immigrant families would work, and sleep, in shifts. The moral of these stories was not, however, that the UK was less than hospitable to its new arrivals, but rather that South Asians were dirty and uncivilized. There were court cases, about whether turbans were or were not an appropriate adjunct to a bus conductor's uniform, an adequate substitute for a motorcyclist's helmet.

Raised left-wing, my first involvements as a student activist were with 'Rock against Racism' and the 'Anti-Nazi League', massive youth movements in response to an upswing of racist violence and electoral success by neo-Nazi parties around the country. Our chants of 'Black and White, Unite and Fight!' and 'Never Again!' scrambled together a 'Just Say No!' approach to racism with another 'moment of glory' in British popular memory – World War II and the fight against Hitler.

This is, of course, a partial and idiosyncratic history. But my point here is that, in my own and, most likely, my white compatriots' subject formation, a tangle of images and practices, colonial and 'postcolonial', from the relatively benign to the brutal, are jostling for position. This has several implications for the present re-examination of 'postcoloniality'. First, it suggests that period-izing colonialism and its 'posts', is not a simple task. There is no evidence here of a smooth march-in-formation, such that, as the economics and politics of domination are transformed, the discursive aspects of colonization follow along and change from colonial to 'postcolonial' forms. The white subject, in short, remains enamoured of colonial imagery long after the heyday of direct rule, in ways that are both different and the same, changed, and not changed much at all.

Second, it is in this context that colonial discourses can plausibly be hauled out apparently unchanged, and redeployed. Telling examples of this, so to speak, renewable energy source, were British *and* US descriptions of Saddam Hussein, his army and Arab people in general, during the recent period of military engagement with Iraq. Here, the rhetoric of colonialism and racism were so evident as to require few if any skills in cultural criticism. The British press, for example, referred to the Iraqi army as, amongst other things, 'hordes' and to the troops as 'bastards of Baghdad', 'mad dogs', 'blindly obedient', 'ruthless' and 'fanatical'. Meanwhile, the British forces were 'lionhearts', 'heroes', 'dare-devils' and 'young knights of the skies'.[9] In Bellevue, Washington, a Republican State Senator insisted on local radio that 'there's no such thing as a moderate Arab.' And on National Public Radio, during the period of US bombing of Iraq, a white woman American 'expert' on the Arab world confidently described '*the*' Arab psyche as fundamentally narcissistic and yet low in self-esteem. This tragic contradiction, she felt, explained both why Saddam Hussein had gone to war, and why future wars, future Saddam Husseins, were an inevitability for which the US and its allies must be prepared. In short, although the period of the build-up to armed conflict between the US-European Allied force and the Iraqi army was relatively brief, it provided ample time for a dramatic resurgence of elements of colonial discourse, premised for their *form* on notions of essential, ontological difference between the Other and the Western 'self' (extremist and irrational versus calm and rational, infantile narcissism versus maturity), and for their *content* on Orientalist categories (ruthlessness, fanaticism, Oriental despotism, etc.)[10]

Moreover, colonial discourses in the white imaginary are dispersed across space as well as time, evoking images from British colonization of India and Africa, as well as from the history of the United States as a settler, slave-owning colony. As in the incidents and events Lata Mani has described here, my own psyche and material experiences have been and continue to be assailed both by my own country's engagements with colonialism and those of others.

All of this suggests that white, Western 'postcolonial' subjects are still interpellated by classical colonialism itself. Which raises a question – when does 'colonial' become 'post'? And what, in this context, does 'post' mean? This kind of 'bricolage' cannot, we feel, be fully explained by reference to 'postmodernity' and thence by extension to the 'postcolonial'. For even in the heyday of direct-rule colonization, colonial fiction, museum exhibits, travel accounts and even 'discoveries' at times shared this same disrespect for location and veracity.[11]

Stuart Hall makes an observation about time and social transformation that is helpful here. Hall argues that history consists of

> processes with different timescales, all convened in the same conjuncture. Political time, the time of régimes and elections, is short: 'A week is a long time in politics.' Economic time, sociological time, so to speak, has a longer durée. Cultural time is even slower, more glacial. All human action has both its subjective and its objective side.[12]

This observation certainly confirms one part of what I am claiming here about white subject formation and cultural context in Britain: both form and content continue to echo colonialism well after the decline, if not demise, of the British Empire. However, we would add some further observations to those of Hall, beginning by noting in passing that we take it that 'culture' here refers to structures of thinking, not to 'style' – for style, as we know, changes rapidly. We would suggest that perhaps cultural time is paced differently according to one's location in relation to systems of domination. Thus, the 'afterlife' of colonial discourse is very different for the colonizer and for the colonized. Finally, perhaps for each of us there are multiple time-pathways, variously paced, so that cultural change is simultaneously slow and fast, not just across communities, but within socially and historically positioned selves.[13]

Something 'postcolonial' is happening – but what, where and to whom?

It is this notion of a political, economic and discursive shift, one that is decisive without being definitive, that we would like to argue regarding the term 'postcolonial'. For it enables us to concede the shift effected by decolonization without claiming either a complete rupture in social, economic and political relations and forms of knowledge (an end to racial inequality, economic self-sufficiency for new nations, 'the end of History') or its opposite, admittedly argued by few, that the present is nothing more than a mere repetition of the past.

The distinction between 'decisive' and 'definitive' seems to us important given the enabling status accorded to decolonization in discussions of the new ethnography, contemporary cultural theory, the crisis in the Humanities, and more recently, in Robert Young's important discussion of the emergence of poststructuralism.[14] While we are generally in sympathy both with the direction of such discussion and with the ethical impulses that motivate it, we are wary of certain tendencies within the debate.[15] We would like to note two concerns in particular.

Robert Young's *White Mythologies: Writing History and the West* is a fine example of a project that embodies both the promises and some of the problems of the rethinking currently underway. Young makes a compelling argument for considering the impact of the Algerian War of Independence on French political and philosophical thought. However, his powerful critique of ethnocentrism is undermined by his general tendency to read anti-colonial movements as primarily engaging the logic of Western philosophy. Thus it seems, at times, that a key object and achievement of the Algerian War of Independence was the overthrow of the Hegelian dialectic! An argument that a critique of colonial discourses is implicitly a critique of the West becomes in effect an argument that a critique of colonial discourses is primarily and fundamentally a critique of the West. In failing to specify and delimit its own project, *White Mythologies* ironically ends up universalizing and thus compromising its own critique. One is tempted to wonder whether we have merely taken a detour to return to the position of the Other as resource for rethinking the Western Self, only this time, it is not the Other as 'ourselves undressed' so much as 'ourselves disassembled'.[16]

We would also urge a greater awareness than is sometimes evident in such debate that, despite the impact in certain quarters of the critique of specific textual practices and philosophical presumptions, elsewhere much remains the same – it's business as usual. The integrity of the Subject may have been exposed as a ruse of bourgeois ideology by philosophers and cultural critics, but law, to take one powerful institution, still operates as though this were not the case. To cite only one example, the legitimacy of land-rights claims of indigenous or Fourth World peoples turns on ahistorical conceptions of culture and essentialist notions of identity. An American anthropologist, having recently discovered Benedict Anderson,[17] can unwittingly create complications for Maori land claims in arguing that Maori traditions are 'invented'.[18] The point here is not so much that anti-essentialist conceptions of identity are reactionary, as that, so long as other conceptions of identity have effectivity in the world, we necessarily need to engage them.[19] A position of abstract theoreticism that adjudicates between positions solely on the basis of 'theoretical correctness' seems to us to aggrandize theory, while failing to grasp the complex and contradictory workings of power/knowledge.

Returning to our conception of the term 'postcolonial' then, we would like to accent the ambiguity of the 'post' in 'postcolonial' and underscore the *twin* processes that are evoked by it, namely colonization/decolonization. We would argue that 'postcolonial' marks a decisive, though not definitive shift that stages contemporary encounters between India and Britain and between white Britons and their non-white Others, though not always in the same way or to the same degree.

Location is in many respects key in determining the importance of the 'postcolonial' as an axis staging cross-racial encounters. In Britain at least, it seems to us that the 'postcolonial' is an axis with effectivity. The memory and legacies of colonization/decolonization form one axis through which social relations and subjectivities are shaped. The operation of the 'postcolonial' axis – of the memories and legacies of colonization/decolonization – may be either explicit or implicit. When we argue that the axis of colonization/decolonization stages cross-racial encounters in Britain, we suggest that whether through negation, denial, affirmation, repression or evasion, the history condensed in the sentence 'We are here because you were there', is necessarily engaged. To say this is not to indicate anything about *how* this history of colonization/decolonization is engaged. One need only point to the positions taken on *Satanic Verses*[20] by Salman Rushdie himself, the Bradford fundamentalists, the irate white conservatives, the confused and then outraged white liberals, and the feminist group Women Against Fundamentalism, to note something of the range of possible ways of negotiating this history.[21] The example of *Satanic Verses* also serves to clarify another point. It is also not our claim that colonization/decolonization is the only axis with effectivity in the British context. For, obviously, positions on the Rushdie controversy were equally shaped by other axes, among them gender, race, religion, sexuality, political orientation.

The 'postcolonial' as an axis of subject formation is constructed not simply in dialogue with dominant white society, but is an effect of engagement between particular subjects, white society, region of origin and region of religious and/or political affiliation, what Paul Gilroy describes as 'the dialectics of diasporic identification'.[22] Thus, many African or South Asian Muslims in Britain, would include in this matrix the home of their religion, the Middle East. Similarly, the films of Isaac Julien and the Black film collective Sankofa, for instance, *Passion of Remembrance* and *Looking for Langston*, are transatlantic meditations on African-Caribbean political and sexual identity. The struggle of African Americans in the USA becomes a political resource for forging imagined diasporic communities. The engagement of colonization/decolonization thus has transnational dimensions, its local expressions multiply inflected by regional and global affinities and considerations, in turn crosscut by class, race, gender, sexuality, etc.

Not all places in this transnational circuit are, however, similarly 'postcolonial'. The active, subjective, inescapable, everyday engagement with the legacies of colonization/decolonization that is part of the British matrix for reggae, bhangra rap, Hanif Kureshi's screenplays, or Homi Bhabha's conception of 'hybridity',[23] are not the terms of theoretical, artistic or political endeavors in India. As noted earlier and argued more fully elsewhere,[24] in India it is the nation state and its failure to represent anything other than narrow sectional interests that provides grist for the mill of politics and theory. We are not claiming here that India is not 'postcolonial', that would be an absurd proposition; rather that it is not 'postcolonial' *in the same way*. The hand of the past in the shape of the present is multiply refracted such that the term 'postcolonial' fails to grasp the ways in which people are driven to apprehend the world and their relation to it.

Meanwhile back at the ranch in the good old USA

We suggested at the very beginning of this paper that 'post-Civil Rights' may be to the USA what 'postcolonial' is to Britain: a name for a decisive though hardly definitive shift that implicitly or explicitly structures, whether through affirmation, negation, denial, repression or evasion, relations between the races in this country. We use the term 'Civil Rights' here to signal a range of struggles including those against segregation, for voting rights and political representation, for institutional and economic equality, as well as the cultural renaissance and cultural nationalisms of the late 1960s and early 1970s. Like 'postcolonial', 'post-Civil Rights' retains the ambiguity, perhaps more immediately telling given this is our back yard, of the 'post' in relation to Civil Rights: the way it simultaneously signals both the fight against entrenched institutional and cultural racism, and the need for continued struggles for racial equality. Whether one is left or right on the political spectrum, for or against affirmative action, for or against an ethnic studies requirement, it seems to us that we all necessarily do battle on a discursive and political terrain that is distinctly 'post-Civil Rights'. This was abundantly evident in the debates surrounding the nomination of Clarence Thomas to the Supreme Court and the challenge to it presented by Anita Hill's allegations of sexual harassment. Indeed, the concerted effort over the last decade by the Reagan and Bush administrations to dismantle the gains of the Civil Rights movement is testimony to the shifts effected by it and to the power of the term to signify both the history of colonial and racist domination and collective resistance to it.

The history of 1950s and 1960s civil rights movements is, however, the narrative of the domination and resistance of established communities of color in this country: the original Native Americans, African Americans, Latino/ Chicanos, Asian Americans. To this we must add the tales of recent immigrants/refugees, who rather more like Asians and African-Caribbeans in Britain represent the return of the repressed on the borders of the imperialist center. They also negotiate a 'post-Civil Rights' US landscape. Their travel to the US has been occasioned by a history related to, but distinct from, that of people of color already here. Their historical experiences stretch existing categories – 'Hispanic', 'Asian' – inflecting them with new meanings. Relations between recent immigrants/refugees and those already here, whether whites or people of color, are constituted through discourses that draw heavily on colonial and racist rhetoric both in form and content. Such mutual ignorance and parochialism in context of economic depression and state supported nativism can be, and has been, explosive. Nothing but the most complex and historically specific conceptions of identity and subjectivity can sufficiently grasp the present situation and articulate a politics adequate to it.

Multiple axes, conjunctures, and politics of location

Thus far in this paper, we have attempted to situate the term 'postcolonial' in time and space, pointing to differences in its effectivity in a range of contexts. In this final section of the paper, we wish to take our argument a step further, suggesting that it is also necessary to view colonial/postcolonial relations as co-constructed with other axes of domination and resistance – that the 'postcolonial' is in effect a construct internally differentiated by its intersections with other unfolding relations. We propose here the value of what we will term a 'feminist conjuncturalist' approach, drawing tools and inspiration from both Marxist cultural criticism and US Third World feminism.[25] We believe such a framework serves well our goal of benefiting from the analytical space opened up by the term 'postcolonial' while avoiding the dangers of failing to delimit it. It enables us to argue that at given moments and locations, the axis of colonization/decolonization might be *the* most salient one, at other times, not so.

In the past two decades, there has been underway in feminism, a process of decentering the white/Western subject (whether male *or* female) which has been at times similar to, enabling of, and indebted to, but most often separate from, the projects of poststructuralist and 'postcolonial' cultural criticism. Since the late 1960s, US women of color, frequently speaking simultaneously from 'within and against' *both* women's liberation and anti-racist movements, have insisted upon the need to analyse and challenge systems of domination, and concomitant constructions of subjecthood, not singly, but multiply.[26] More recently and following their lead, US white feminists have made parallel arguments.

From the inception of second-wave feminism in the late 1960s and early 1970s, Black women activists like Frances Beale, Toni Cade, Florynce Kennedy and later the Combahee River Collective argued that race and gender domination (and in Combahee's case, class and sexuality also) were inseparably involved in their experience of subordination.[27] And as Norma Alarcon argues in her 1990 essay on the 1981 anthology *This Bridge Called My Back: Writings by Radical Women of Color*:

> As speaking subjects of a new discursive formation, many of *Bridge's* writers were aware of the displacement of their subjectivity across a multiplicity of discourses: feminist/lesbian, nationalist, racial, socioeconomic, historical, etc. The peculiarity of their displacement implies a multiplicity of positions from which they are driven to grasp or understand themselves and their relations with the 'real' in the Althusserian sense of the word.[28]

Parallel with Alarcon, and exemplifying for our purposes the move by some white feminist critics to follow the analytical direction proposed by US Third World feminisms, Teresa de Lauretis writes:

> What is emerging in feminist writings is [...] the concept of multiple, shifting, and often self-contradictory identity [...] an identity made up of heterogeneous and heteronomous representations of gender, race, and class, and often indeed across languages and cultures; an identity that one decides to reclaim from a history of multiple assimilations, and that one insists on as a strategy.[29]

What is significant to us here is the emphasis, within feminist theorizing, on the complexity of effective links between intersecting axes of domination, and the concomitant complexity of subjectivity and political agency. Moreover, as de Lauretis adds, axes of domination and of representation at times clash or contradict, while at other times they may be mutually supporting or mutually irrelevant. Each axis involves the unfolding of both material and discursive relations. To this list we would add that this unfolding, this displacement of subjectivities is 'variously and contradictorily paced'. For we have argued that the discursive legacy of 'colonization/decolonization' is radically non-diachronic. We have also indicated the interplay of different axes of domination/resistance and history, as for instance when US race and class relations, and Indian 'postcolonial' relations, may hail the same subject in mutually contradictory or supportive ways.

Although not the direction or intent of any of the feminists named and quoted above, it should be recognized that notions of 'multiplicity' have at times led critics down the very problematic path of what one might call 'neo-relativism', such that it is sometimes argued that 'we' are all decentered, multiple, 'minor' or 'mestiza' in exactly comparable ways. It becomes critical, then, to maintain a sharp analysis of the relationship between subjectivity and power, subjectivity and specific relations of domination and subordination. In this regard, some feminist theorists have argued for attention to the 'politics of location', to 'the historical, geographic, cultural, psychic and imaginative boundaries which provide the ground for political definition and self-definition. [...] [L]ocation forces and enables specific modes of reading and knowing the dominant.[30]

However, these problems *do* in a sense arise out of the current state of feminist theorization of subjectivity and systems of domination. For feminist theory – by no means a unified terrain – has vacillated over how to analyse the relationships between the multiple axes of oppression that it names. Thus, feminism seems to comprise at least four tendencies. First we can distinguish a white feminist 'rearguard' that continues to argue for the primacy of gender domination, as well as a second, so to speak, 'neo-rearguard' tendency, again especially by white feminists, to reabsorb notions of multiply determined subjectivity under the single 'mistress narrative' of gender domination.

Thirdly, other theorists and activists, frequently but not exclusively women of color, responding *both* to the prioritization of gender in 'hegemonic' feminism, and to the pervasive sexism and/or heterosexism and/or racism of other movements, insist on the 'simultaneity' of the workings of axes of domination.[31] This insistence on a non-hierarchical analysis of how oppression works was born of political practice and has been critical to coalition building. It is, in fact, articulated in response to prior elisions and erasures in analyses of subject and social formation, whether in feminism, La Raza, Black Power, the Marxist left, or elsewhere. There is finally a fourth tendency which is in fact an outgrowth of the third. This builds on and further complicates the ideas of 'simultaneity' and 'multiplicity' to examine how oppression may be experienced in specifiably complex and shifting relationships to different axes of domination.[32] Lest this four-part map be taken to describe a straightforward diachronic unfolding, it is important to point out that, in fact, the editors and contributors to *This Bridge Called My Back*, the 1981 anthology to which Alarcon's article refers, were already practitioners of the fourth tendency, that of complex, multiply engaged yet locally focused analyses.

Building complex analyses, avoiding erasure, specifying location: feminist analysts of this kind share a great deal, some consciously and others not, with 'postmodern conjuncturalism' as described by Lawrence Grossberg in his avowedly partial intellectual history of the Birmingham Centre for Contemporary Cultural Studies during Stuart Hall's tenure as Director. We find postmodern conjuncturalism helpful to our current project for, like the feminist developments just noted, it firmly centers the analysis of subject formation and cultural practice within matrices of domination and subordination. Moreover, it does so in a way that neither conceives domination in single-axis terms ('Even at their most concrete, relations of power are always multiple and contradictory') nor falsely equalizes the effects of these relations on subjects:

> A conjunctural theory of power is not claiming [...] that all such relations of power are equal, equally determining, or equally liveable; these are questions that depend on the analysis of the specific, concrete conjuncture.[33]

Also key for our purposes, postmodern conjuncturalism asserts that there is an effective but not determining relationship between subjects and their histories, a relationship that is complex, shifting and yet not 'free'. The concept of articulation links subjects and structures dynamically, such that practices, meanings and identities 'are forged by people operating within the limits of their real conditions and the historically articulated "tendential lines of force"'.[34]

This framework intersects with feminist appropriations of Althusser, such as de Lauretis's insistence on 'an identity that one *decides* to reclaim', (emphasis ours) and, stating even more succinctly the dialectic of agency and context, Alarcon's conceptualization of subjects 'driven to grasp' their subject positions across a shifting, though not *randomly* shifting, field.

> The concept of articulation within postmodern conjuncturalism foregrounds the production of contexts, the ongoing effort by which particular practices are removed from and inserted into different structures of relationships, the construction of one set of relationships out of another, the continuous struggle to reposition practices within a shifting field of forces.[35]

This brings us full circle to one of our arguments about the term 'postcolonial'. For we have noted the complex temporal and spatial repositioning and recombining of practices and signifiers from the histories of racism and colonization, in the construction of contexts and identities in the USA and Britain. We have emphasized the ways practices may be given new meanings, and create 'new subjects', in different locations.

Finally, postmodern conjuncturalism's call for attention to the 'tendential lines of force', its insistence that the meanings and effectivity of particular practices and relations of power are dependent on historical moment and locale, underscores our other central argument about the term 'postcolonial'. For we have argued that the concept must be carefully specified, used to describe moments, social formations, subject positions and practices which arise out of an unfolding axis of colonization/decolonization, interwoven with the unfolding of other axes, in *uneven, unequal* relations with one another.

The affinities between US feminist developments we have described and a conjuncturalist approach to Cultural Studies are all the more interesting once one notes the context in which the latter came into being. For, in fact, the theoretical appropriations of Althusser and Gramsci we draw on here, like US Third World feminism, were not developed as part of an abstract 'race for theory'. Rather, they were generated out of the endeavor of a group of scholar-critic-activists (including amongst others, Stuart Hall and Paul Gilroy) to analyse racial domination and resistance in 1970s Britain – a Britain in which, to adapt the title of a book published by Birmingham Centre scholars in 1982, 'the Empire struck back'.[36] In short, British conjuncturalist analysis emerges from and speaks to a postcolonial Britain, just as US Third World feminism develops out of and addresses a post-Civil Rights USA.

What we have attempted in this paper is to sketch in outline a feminist conjuncturalist reading of the term, 'postcolonial' in three locations – India, Britain and the USA. We wish to emphasize once again that we have not undertaken here a general reading of the 'postcolonial' that is applicable to all places at all times. Not only are we inadequately placed to undertake such a task, but we would argue against the idea that there is such a thing as '*the*' 'postcolonial' in any simple sense. This does not mean, however, that we are against theorizing the term, nor that it is without utility. Rather, as we have said, we would argue that the notion of the 'postcolonial' is best understood in context of a rigorous politics of location, of a rigorous conjuncturalism. There are, then, moments and spaces in which subjects are 'driven to grasp' their positioning and subjecthood as 'postcolonial'; yet there are other contexts in which, to use the term as the organizing principle of one's analysis, is precisely to 'fail to grasp the specificity' of the location or the moment.

Notes

1 In his analysis of artistic and literary production in sub-Saharan Africa and the reception of the former in the US, Kwame Anthony Appiah makes a persuasive argument about the importance of circumscribing the postcolonial and specifying its relation to postmodernism. See 'Is the Post- in Postmodernism the Post- in Postcolonial?' *Critical Inquiry* 17 (Winter 1991), pp. 336–57.

2 We note with pleasure the publication of *Social Text* 31/32 on questions of the postcolonial, which appeared whilst our article was under review. Many of the concerns authors raise there intersect with our own. On questions about the efficacy of the term postcolonial see especially Anne McClintock, ' "The Angel of Progress": Pitfalls of the Term "Postcolonialism" ', *Social Text* 31/32 (Spring 1992), pp. 84–98, and Ella Shohat, 'Notes on the Postcolonial', *Social Text* 31/32 (Spring 1992), pp. 99–113.

3 Michael Omi and Howard Winant, *Racial Formation in the United States: From the 1960s to the 1980s* (New York: Routledge, 1986), p. 90. Omi and Winant state that the phrase 'great transformation' is taken from Karl Polyani, and is deployed by them to indicate the epochal nature of the transformation under consideration in their text (p. 172, note 2).

4 See, for example, Edward Said, 'Intellectuals in the Post-Colonial World', *Salmagundi* 70/71 (1986), pp. 45–64; Homi Bhabha, 'Location, Intervention, Incommensurability: a Conversation with Homi Bhabha', *Emergences* 1 (Fall 1989), pp. 63–88; and Sarah Harasym, ed., *The Post-Colonial Critic: Interviews, Strategies Dialogues: Gayatri Chakravorty Spivak* (New York: Routledge, 1990).

5 The terms 'postcolonial' and 'post-Civil Rights' as we use them, are periodizations that name the *initiation* of particular struggles. These struggles were, of course, to develop in heterogeneous directions, for example, socialism and bourgeois nationalism in the case of India, cultural nationalism and revolutionary race-class struggle in the example of the US.

6 Stuart Hall, in Angie Chabram and Rosa Linda Fregoso, 'Chicano/a Cultural Representations: Reframing Alternative Critical Discourses', *Cultural Studies* 4.3 (October 1990), p. 206.

7 For an analysis of contemporary culture that proposes the centrality of disjuncture see Arjun Appadurai, 'Disjuncture and Difference in the Global Cultural Economy', *Public Culture* 2.2 (Spring 1990), pp. 1–24.

8 ' 'Twas in the moon of wintertime/when all the birds had fled/That mighty Gitcheemanitou/Sent angel choirs instead/Before their light the stars grew dim/And wandering hunters heard the hymn/ "Jesus, your king is born/Jesus is born/In excelsis gloria." ' Huron Christmas carol.

9   *Guardian Weekly* (3 February 1991), p. 4.

10 Edward Said, *Orientalism* (New York: Vintage, 1979).

11 See, for example, Peter Hulme, *Colonial Encounters* (New York: Methuen, 1986); Mary Louise Pratt, 'Scratches on the Face of the Country; or What Mr Barrows Saw in the Land of the Bushmen', *Critical Inquiry, Special Issue on 'Race' Writing and Difference* 12.1 (Autumn 1985), pp. 119–43; Haryette Mullen, 'The Psychoanalysis of Little Black Sambo', Santa Cruz, California: Occasional Papers, Group for the Critical Study of Colonial Discourse, University of California at Santa Cruz; and Inderpal Grewal, 'The Guidebook and the Museum: Imperialism, Education, and Nationalism in the British Museum', *Bucknell Review, Special Issue on Culture and Education in Victorian England* (1990), pp. 195–217.

12 Stuart Hall, 'Brave New World: the Debate about post-Fordism', *Socialist Review* 21.1 (1991), p. 61.

13 For a fuller discussion of this point with respect to white American female subjectivity, see Ruth Frankenberg, *White Women, Race Matters: The Social Construction of Whiteness* (Minneapolis: University of Minnesota Press, 1993).

14 Robert Young, *White Mythologies: Writing History and the West* (New York: Routledge, 1990).

15 See also Lata Mani, 'Cultural Theory, Colonial Texts: Reading Eyewitness Accounts of Widow Burning', in Lawrence Grossberg, Cary Nelson and Paula Treichler, eds., *Cultural Studies* (New York: Routledge, 1992), pp. 392–408.

16 We refer here to Michele Rosaldo's essay, 'The Use and Abuse of Anthropology: Reflections on Feminism and Cross Cultural Understanding', *Signs* 5.3 (1980), pp. 389–417. In it Rosaldo argues that 1970s feminist anthropologists frequently viewed their studies of the status of women in 'non western' societies as occasions to examine themselves 'undressed', that is, to analyse world cultures in explicitly or implicitly evolutionary terms.

17 Benedict Anderson, *Imagined Communities: Reflections on the Origin and Spread of Nationalism* (London: Verso, 1983).

18 Allan Hanson, 'Probably Not: a Reply to Jean Jackson's "Is There a Way to Talk About Making Culture Without Making Enemies?" ' American Ethnological Society, 113th Annual Spring Meeting, Charleston, SC (15 March 1990).

19 James Clifford, 'Identity in Mashpee', in *The Predicament of Culture*, (Cambridge: Harvard University Press, 1988), pp. 277–346 and Evelyn Legaré, 'Native Indian Identity: the Need to be Other', American Ethnological Society, 113th Annual Spring Meeting, Charleston, SC (14 March 1990).

20 Salman Rushdie, *Satanic Verses* (New York: Viking, 1989).

21 For a sense of the debate see Lisa Appignanesi and Sara Maitland, eds., *The Rushdie File* (London: ICA, 1989); Women Against Fundamentalism, Press Statement, 1989) p. 9 March 1989, in *Feminist Review* 33 (Winter 1989) p. 110; Clara Connelly, 'Washing our Linen: One Year of Women Against Fundamentalism', *Feminist Review* 37 (Spring 1991), pp. 68–77; and for Rushdie's shifting position, Rushdie, *Imaginary Homelands: Essays and Criticism 1982–1991* (London: Viking, 1991).

22 Paul Gilroy, 'It Ain't Where You're From, It's Where You're At: The Dialectics of Diasporic Identification', *Third Text* 13 (Winter 1990/91), pp. 3–16.

23 Homi Bhabha, 'Signs Taken for Wonders: Questions of Ambivalence and Authority Under a Tree Outside Delhi, May 1817', *Critical Inquiry* 12.1 (1985), pp. 144–85.

24 Lata Mani, 'Multiple Mediations: Feminist Scholarship in the Age of Multinational Reception', *Feminist Review* 35 (Summer 1990), pp. 24–41.

25 For one definition of the latter, see Chela Sandoval, 'U.S. Third World Feminism: The Theory and Method of Oppositional Consciousness in the Postmodern World', *Genders* 10 (May 1991), p. 18, note 3.
26 Parallel debates have also gone on in Britain. See the journals *Spare Rib* and *Outwrite*, and also Valerie Amos *et al.*, eds., *Many Voices, One Chant*, Special Issue, *Feminist Review* 17 (Summer 1984); Kum Kum Bhavnani and Margaret Coulson, 'Transforming Socialist-Feminism: The Challenge of Racism', *Feminist Review* 23 (Summer 1986), pp. 81–92; and Shabnam Grewal *et al.*, eds., *Charting the Journey: Writings by Black and Third World Women* (London: Sheba, 1988).
27 Frances Beale, 'Double Jeopardy: To Be Black and Female', in Toni Cade, ed., *The Black Woman: An Anthology* (New York; Mentor, 1970), pp. 90–100; Toni Cade 'On the Issue of Roles', in Cade, *Black Woman*, pp. 101–10; Florynce Kennedy, 'Institutionalized Oppression vs. the Female', in Robin Morgan, ed., *Sisterhood is Powerful: An Anthology of Writings from the Women's Liberation Movement* (New York: Vintage, 1970), pp. 492–50; Combahee River Collective, 'A Black Feminist Statement, April 1977', in Zillah R. Eisenstein, ed., *Capitalist Patriarchy and the Case for Socialist Feminism* (New York: Monthly Review Press, 1979), pp. 362–72.
28 Norma Alarcon, 'The Theoretical Subjects of *This Bridge Called My Back* and Anglo-American Feminism', in Gloria Anzaldua, ed., *Making Face, Making Soul/Haciendo Caras: Creative and Critical Perspectives by Women of Color* (San Francisco: Aunt Lute Foundation, 1990), p. 356.
29 Teresa de Lauretis, 'Feminist Studies, Critical Studies: Issues, Terms and Contexts', in de Lauretis, ed., *Feminist Studies/Critical Studies* (Bloomington: Indiana University Press, 1986), p. 8.
30 Chandra Talpade Mohanty, 'Feminist Encounters: Locating the Politics of Experience', *Copyright* 1.1 (1987), pp. 31, 42.
31 Combahee River Collective, 'A Black Feminist Statement'; Patricia Zavella, 'The Problematic Relationship of Feminism and Chicana Studies', *Women's Studies* 17 (1988), pp. 123–34.
32 Cherrie Moraga and Gloria Anzaldua, eds., *This Bridge Called My Back: Writings by Radical Women of Color* (Watertown, Mass: Persephone Press, 1981; republished 1984 by Kitchen Table Women of Color Press); Sandoval, 'U.S. Third World'.
33 Lawrence Grossberg, 'The Formation of Cultural Studies: An American in Birmingham', *Strategies* 2 (1989), p. 138.
34 Grossberg, 'The Formation of Cultural Studies', p. 136.
35 Grossberg, 'The Formation of Cultural Studies', p. 137.
36 Centre for Contemporary Cultural Studies, *The Empire Strikes Back: Race and Racism in 70s Britain* (London: Hutchinson, 1982).

We would like to thank Chetan Bhatt, Avtar Brah, Rosa Linda Fregoso, Lisa Lowe, Ted Swedenburg and Kamala Visweswaran for their comments on earlier incarnations of this paper.

19

Rosemary Jolly

Rehearsals of Liberation: Contemporary Postcolonial Discourse and the New South Africa *

> With the mutilation and decline of the conquered tribe a new shaman or artist struggles to emerge who finds himself moving along the knife-edge of change. He has been, as it were, cross-fertilized by victor and victim and a powerful need arises to invoke the lost generations, in a new creative, visionary light. It is a task which is profoundly personal (and archetypal) and, therefore, accompanying an enormous potency for change – for vision into resources – runs the danger of self-enchantment or hubris.[1]
>
> Wilson Harris, *Explorations*

Since its rise with the election of the Nationalist Party in 1948 and especially during its halting fall, apartheid has drawn eloquent condemnations from the international community. Yet if the atrocities that characterized South Africa before the April 1994 election are to make any sense at all, moral outrage must be supplemented by critical evaluation of the terms used to phrase condemnations of racism in the age of (semiconscious) late colonialism. This activity needs to take place in various intersecting spheres – economic, social, political, and cultural – in numerous different localized contexts, but it must also proceed with an awareness of its international implications. Such a massive critique will require a communal effort; I attempt to contribute to that critique by questioning the effects of some contemporary constructions of postcolonial criticism on the current formation of South African cultural discourse. What, then, is the nature of postcolonialism's contribution to a postapartheid future?

My particular concern is the extensive postcolonial critical discourse about South Africa that thrives in the academy outside that country and that plays a role in envisaging a postapartheid South Africa. The international community's material effect on South African life has already been demonstrated in condemnations of apartheid and, more effectively, in related economic sanctions.[2] My goal is not to congratulate Western governments on their (notoriously intermittent) dedication to the antiapartheid cause, however, but to interrogate the limits of the discourse that resulted in the formulation of official antiapartheid policies and that in turn limited the scope of those

* From *PMLA* 110.1 (January 1995), pp. 17–29.

policies. Thus I investigate how criticism of apartheid that is phrased in current postcolonial terms can become atrophied, constituting a reactionary measure at a historical moment in which the break from apartheid and its constructions requires a profoundly different strategy. Correlatively, the terms of an act of liberation – a concept postcolonial critics use to characterize their practice – can be inadequate to the task. My interrogation of postcolonial criticism begins with Homi Bhabha's work on the stereotype and colonial narratives. I then examine the co-optation of antiapartheid theater in its migration from the South African township to the international metropolis, as well as Jacques Derrida's antiapartheid appeal in 'Racism's Last Word.' The co-optation of both these scenes of resistance, I argue, rests on staging apartheid as the international stereotype of racism, but the stereotype, Bhabha points out, has crippling limitations as a trope of dissidence.

In 'The Other Question,' Bhabha discusses the extent to which colonialist discourse depends on 'the concept of "fixity" in the ideological construction of otherness,' and he identifies the primary strategy of this discourse as the stereotype.[3] To displace the racist, sexist identifications of colonialist discourse, Bhabha argues, it is necessary to eschew the temptation to present counteridentifications, since the very mode of such representation – this battle between 'fixed' images of the positive and the negative – requires interrogation:

> My reading of colonialist discourse suggests that the point of intervention should shift from the identification of images as positive or negative, to an understanding of the processes of subjectification made possible (and plausible) through stereotypical discourse.[4]

Bhabha points out that the Western addiction to securing 'fixed' points of identification, even when deployed in nominally anticolonialist arguments, always functions within the poles of a Manichaean opposition – white (positive)/black (negative) – which are constituted as 'natural' in order to produce pleasure for the colonizer and to deny the colonial subject 'knowledge of the construction of that opposition.'[5]

This observation has special relevance to a particular kind of anticolonialism. In a text that can be identified as neocolonial because of its nominal rather than structural anticolonialism, not only are colonial subjects denied knowledge of the construction of the Manichaean opposition but also, more important, colonizers can induce themselves to forget the artificiality of that construction. Nominal dissidence becomes the stage for the colonizers to disguise their complicity in constructing the opposition from colonial subjects and from themselves. This strategic forgetting can be rendered visible only when the split between the stereotype and the discourse that constitutes it is shown to feed colonialist desire at the precise moment that it claims to do the opposite.

The ability of colonialist discourse to conceal its oppressive operations in institutions that appear to tolerate dissidence is evident in the period of so-called reform (from 1980 on) that followed the phase of extreme censorship in

South Africa. During the last decade of its rule the Nationalist government increasingly allowed the performance of banned plays in contexts that it correctly judged would not significantly threaten its authority.[6] Thus in 1984 Maishe Maponya, who had written two plays about the security police, was informed by the Publications Control Board that permission had been granted for his plays to be presented in small venues such as the Laager at the Market Theatre in Johannesburg but that he would have to request further permission to stage them in the townships.[7] The predominantly white South African audience that could afford Market Theatre tickets might have been reminded of the plight of fellow South Africans by performances but was unlikely to demonstrate or to riot. It can be argued that during the states of emergency declared in the eighties, such forms of civil disobedience were crucial in registering protest against both the Nationalist government and the politics of surrogate representation.[8]

The same careful calculation of political consequences can be seen in the government's decision to permit certain kinds of antiapartheid theater to flourish overseas by allowing the actors to work without severe police harassment and to travel internationally. The shift in the context of *Woza Albert!* – from various locations in the townships to the Market Theatre and finally to off Broadway – progressively removed the play's political effect from the local audience for whom the play was first performed.

The reviews that *Woza Albert!* elicited when it was staged at the Lucille Lortel Theater, in New York, seem to reflect varying degrees of understanding of the play's aims and original production site. For example, Howard Kissel's comment about the improvisational aspect of the performance ('how much more imaginative and meaningful ... it might be had half this effort gone into writing a real play') suggests that he has not considered the demands of a township setting, in which a staging of 'a real play' would have been impracticable and unlikely to reach its intended audience.[9] In contrast, Clive Barnes, who praises the performance, recognizes that South African dissident theater performed in institutionalized settings both within South Africa and abroad may operate simply as an outlet for liberal sentiment: 'But as Mtwa and Ngema raise our safe Liberal enthusiasm with their encantation, we must not forget what we have learned of Soweto, Albert Street, Robben Island and other placenames in the topography of man's inhumanity to man.'[10]

The desire of antiapartheid cultural workers to create theater that will succeed overseas may cause that theater to lose its dissidence by conforming to the expectations of the liberal enthusiasts Barnes describes. The demands of this overseas market inevitably affect playmaking in South Africa. The exported theater that results, Ian Steadman points out, 'might even be viewed as an instrument of ruling-class hegemony, for the image of South African culture prepared for outsiders is highly selective and often reinforces the very stereotypes it seeks to undermine.'[11] In this context, Douglas Watt's complaints about the difficulty of the actors' accents for the New York audience of *Woza Albert!* testify to one aspect of the international performance of the play that refuses co-optation: the actors' accents, together with dialogue in a number of

South African languages other than English, create a barrier between performer and audience that resists easy consumption of the plight of black South Africans by liberal overseas theatergoers.[12]

Resistance, then, is not a quality inherent in a cultural product but rather an effect of the process of that product's creation and reception. Like exported South African dissident theater, critiques of apartheid have often been blunted by audiences who receive them as gratifying spectacles that displace the imperialist conquests sustaining the development of Western capitalism onto a canvas that paints South Africa as the atavistic other. Such displacement reinvokes a narrative of progress that resurrects – however subtly – Western hubris. Ignoring the relation between what the argument says and the particular discursive space in which it performs its antiapartheid work has crucial consequences.

I single out Derrida's condemnation of apartheid in 'Racism's Last Word' for particular scrutiny because its rhetorical effects, analyzed in the context of the text's performance, are radically at odds with its stated goal, the condemnation of racism. 'Racism's Last Word' entreats its readers to recognize apartheid as a 'crime against humanity,' as 'the ultimate racism.'[13] This plea certainly invites readers to be complicit in the text's condemnation of apartheid, but it does so by appealing to South Africa as spectacularly other. The text's performative context prevents the recognition, which 'Racism's Last Word' apparently calls for, of apartheid South Africa as both a product and a symptom of the West's continued dependence on an economy that is colonial in its inextricably linked ideological and financial interests. Moreover, Derrida's identification of South Africa as the most spectacular criminal in a broad array of racist activity turns the reader's critical gaze away from American and European colonialism and thus displaces the actions of the colonizer countries both geographically and chronologically onto the colony – South Africa. Exhibiting 'the ultimate racism in the world, the last of many,'[14] South Africa becomes the 'last' place where the racism of the imperial West, assumed to be past, still flourishes; it becomes the atavistic other in a neocolonialist gesture that once again, albeit unwittingly, disguises colonialist imperatives.

The context of 'Racism's Last Word' sheds some light on the problem. The essay was originally published in the catalog for Art *contrel* against Apartheid, a traveling exhibition that was to be given to the first democratically elected government of South Africa. Derrida locates the power of the artworks to cast an accusatory gaze at apartheid in a 'silence [that] is just.'[15] The artworks represent the atrocity of apartheid, thus presenting apartheid as a spectacle to be condemned. The notion of exhibition as just condemnation – both in the exhibition and, more important for this discussion, in 'Racism's Last Word' – depends on the viewer or reader's assumption of an authority, an objectivity, that enables condemnation.

As a part of a catalog for a museum exhibition, 'Racism's Last Word' cannot help invoking, and contributing to, the authority of the institutional space of which the exhibition is a part. 'Racism's Last Word' unwittingly draws on and thus replicates the politics of traditional museum performance.[16] Exhibitions have historically constituted a primary locus for the exercise of an imperialist anthropological gaze on exoticized and objectified native subjects.[17] Derrida's condemnation of apartheid as 'the ultimate racism in the world, the last of many,' deploys the authoritarianism of the Western subject–object binarism that is an integral part of the imperialist history of the Western academy, including the institution Derrida seeks to use counterdiscursively. The authority of the art exhibition, once used to construct the other, must now deconstruct it.[18]

The effect of 'Racism's Last Word' thus proves to be neocolonial rather than counterdiscursive. The text calls on the (non-South African) audience to be subjects who perceive racism as a global problem and simultaneously poses apartheid as a (South African) object that is unfit by virtue of its spectacular otherness. Here apartheid is an exhibition that readers attend at Derrida's request in order to condemn the performance and to dissociate themselves from it. Yet Derrida seems anxious not to provide readers with the comforts of such dissociation. As he points out, apartheid has been sustained by European complicity, indeed by Western economic imperialism:

> Since the Second World War, at least if one accepts the givens of a certain kind of calculation, the stability of the Pretoria regime has been prerequisite to the political, economic and strategic equilibrium of Europe. . . . Whether one is talking about gold or what are called strategic ores, it is known to be the case that at least three-fourths of the world's share of them is divided between the USSR and South Africa. Direct or even indirect Soviet control of South Africa would provoke, or so think certain Western heads of state, a catastrophe beyond all comparison with the malediction . . . of *apartheid*. And then there's the necessity of controlling the route around the cape, and . . . the need for resources or jobs that can be provided by the exportation of arms and technological infrastructures. . . .
>
> Apartheid constitutes, therefore, the first 'delivery of arms,' the first product of European exportation.[19]

Derrida describes Western complicity in apartheid, but his rhetorical strategy counteracts his readers' recognition of that complicity. Through the active voyeurism and displacement that the notion of apartheid as 'the ultimate racism' invites, through the exoneration it promises, Derrida persuades readers to condemn racism. Yet the readers are also supposed to see themselves as complicit in apartheid. Comforted by their separation, as perceiving subjects, from the evil object of apartheid, they are also to see themselves as part of that object. They are to collapse the gap between subject and object, against the basic structure of the exhibition, to perceive themselves as perpetuators of apartheid.

The trajectory Derrida would have readers follow to accomplish their conversion reproduces the fault that Bhabha identifies:

> To judge the stereotyped image on the basis of a prior political normativity is to dismiss it, not to displace it, which is only possible by engaging with its *effectivity*; with the repertoire of positions of power and resistance, domination and dependence that constructs the colonial subject (*both coloniser and colonised*) [second emphasis mine].[20]

The complexity of enacting the radical critique Bhabha describes implies envisioning a different future while remaining loyal to the present and aware of its historical production, whereas 'Racism's Last Word' constitutes 'an appeal, a call to condemn, to stigmatize, to combat, to keep in memory.'[21] Anne McClintock and Rob Nixon argue that

> Derrida ... blurs historical differences by conferring on the single term *apartheid* a spurious autonomy and agency: 'The word concentrates separation. ... by isolating being apart in some sort of essence or hypostasis, the word corrupts it into a quasi-ontological segregation.' ... Is it indeed the word, *apartheid*, or is it Derrida himself, operating here in 'another regime of abstraction' ... , removing the word from its place in the discourse of South African racism, raising it to another power, and setting separation itself apart? Derrida is repelled by the word, yet seduced by its divisiveness, the division in the inner structure of the term itself which he elevates to a state of being.
>
> The essay's opening analysis of the word apartheid is, then, symptomatic of a severance of word from history.[22]

The debate illustrates the difficulty of forging a critical language that can move from a colonial or neocolonial past and present into a genuinely postcolonial future, that uses the past as a resource for a different future. Defending his position, Derrida rebukes McClintock and Nixon: 'If you had paid attention to the context and the mode of my text, you would not have fallen into the enormous blunder that led you to take a *prescriptive* utterance for a *descriptive* (theoretical and constative) one.'[23] Can the relation between the hortatory and the theoretical remain as distinct as Derrida's defense suggests, specifically within the context of contemporary literary constructions of postcoloniality?

Without sufficient interrogation, the construction of South African literature as postcolonial can also reproduce the contradictions in the production and reception of South African theater abroad and in Derrida's 'Racism's Last Word.' The term *postcolonial* can play an important role in introducing students to literatures that have been marginalized by traditional canonical imperatives, but current theoretical constructions of postcoloniality that describe the processes of change in South Africa can be co-opted into the often conservative context of academic critique.

Symptomatically, in the influential introduction to postcolonial writing *The Empire Writes Back*, Bill Ashcroft, Gareth Griffiths, and Helen Tiffin carefully maintain differences among the various literatures they identify as post-colonial, particularly for South African literature, since, as they point out, South Africa falls between, or out of, D. E. S. Maxwell's categories of settler and nonsettler colonies.[24] Yet this identification of South African literature as postcolonial exhibits a nostalgia for the very categories that the preoccupation with apartheid, which Ashcroft, Griffiths, and Tiffin suggest is the distinctive feature of South African writing, emphasizes. These authors point out that because of the legacy of apartheid the literatures of South Africa cannot be identified as settler colony literatures, like those of Australia, New Zealand, or Canada, or nonsettler colony literatures, like that of Nigeria. Nevertheless, the terms *The Empire Writes Back* uses to define South African literatures as postcolonial depend on what Bhabha calls '*secure* point[s] of identification':[25]

> Maxwell did not include South Africa in his category of settler colonies, but white South African literature has clear affinities with those of Australia, Canada, and New Zealand. Black South African literature, on the other hand, might more fruitfully be compared with that of other African countries. But the contemporary racist politics of South African apartheid creates a political vortex into which much of the literature of the area, both Black and white, is drawn. The common themes of the literatures of settler colonies – exile, the problem of finding and defining 'home', physical and emotional confrontations with the 'new' land and its ancient and established meanings – are still present in literature by white South Africans, but are muted by an immediate involvement in race politics. Pervasive concerns of Nigerian or Kenyan writing, dispossession, cultural fragmentation, colonial and neo-colonial domination, postcolonial corruption and the crisis of identity still emerge in writing by Black South Africans, but again are necessarily less prominent than more specific and immediate matters of race and personal and communal freedom under an intransigent and repressive white regime.[26]

Placing South African literature within the (modified) terms of Maxwellian cartography as a way of bringing it within the postcolonial curiously necessitates the bracketing of apartheid, as the phrases beginning with 'but' suggest. The location of black South African writing as like or not like nonsettler colony literatures and of white South African writing as like or not like settler colony literatures may be convenient, but it limits the emancipatory project of postcolonialism and its possibilities for liberation. That approach not only describes but also requires maintenance of the binary colonizer/colonized as an essentially racial opposition in contemporary South African literatures. As critics, teachers, and students, we need to forge a language beyond apartheid that refuses to hypostatize South Africa as the model in which the colonized black and the settler white eternally confront each other in the 'ultimate racism.'

The pervasiveness of such categorization, despite its problematic relation to South African apartheid, is equally evident in Vijay Mishra and Bob Hodge's criticism of *The Empire Writes Back*. These reviewers share my concern about the totalizing potential of the postcolonial as a field of study whose successes in the academy encourage its exponents not to examine their own complicity with the colonial imagination. Despite approaching other categories attached to postcoloniality with caution, however, Mishra and Hodge promote Maxwell's categories. Indeed, in Mishra and Hodge's vocabulary, the settler-nonsettler distinction is explicitly racial:

> [I]t is especially important to recognize the different histories of the White settler colonies which, as fragments of the metropolitan centre, were treated very differently by Britain. ... What an undifferentiated concept of postcolonialism overlooks are the very radical differences in response and the unbridgeable chasms that existed between *White and non-White* colonies (emphasis mine).[27]

Mishra and Hodge use the distinction between settler, or 'white,' and nonsettler, or 'black,' colonies to stress the vast differences in the material resources of the two groups, and they therefore criticize Ashcroft, Griffiths, and Tiffin's marginalization of theories of postcolonial affirmation based on race, such as negritude and aboriginality.[28] But an allegiance to Maxwell's categories or, in broader terms, to racial identity as a prerequisite for the work of liberation in South Africa may, on the one hand, overlook the specific need of the new South Africa to triumph over the history of apartheid and, on the other, limit unnecessarily the variety of resources available for this struggle.[29]

One aspect of the ideological history of South Africa that is overlooked by the Maxwellian settler-nonsettler terms – one that has dominated South African politics for at least the last fifty years – is underscored in Annamaria Carusi's 'Post, Post, and Post; or, Where Is South African Literature in All This?' Carusi explains that while apartheid has meant the suspension of a postcolonial era for the majority of South Africans, postcolonial liberation was a fact for Afrikaner nationalists before 1990,[30] since independence from Britain was won with the 1961 establishment of the republic under the leadership of Hendrik Verwoerd. Afrikaner nationalists believed that they were defending this independence and accepted the isolation that resulted from international antiapartheid policies as the price of freedom. It is impossible to understand the psychology of nationalist Afrikaners as colonizers without understanding that they continued to see themselves as victims of English colonization and that the imagined continuation of this victimization was used to justify the maintenance of apartheid. In this view, which is not unique,[31] Afrikaner nationalists have always seen themselves as true postcolonials. Nostalgia for the homeland and reflections on the colony as the new land, which, according to Ashcroft, Griffiths, and Tiffin and to Mishra and Hodge, characterize the settler imagination and which do in fact characterize the English settler imagination in South Africa, are strikingly absent from Afrikaner narratives of the last two centuries. For Afrikaner nationalists South Africa was the homeland, even before the Anglo-Boer War.

The bifurcated vision of the Maxwellian model of South African literature obscures heterogenous elements that can contribute to a postapartheid era. The 'english' construction of postcoloniality facilitates this exclusion of multiple differences among and within racial groups.[32] English-speaking colonists were far more likely than Afrikaans-speaking whites were to refer to Britain as 'home.' There are also marked differences within the black community of South Africa, which includes the Xhosa, the Sotho, the Zulu, immigrants of Indian heritage, and the Cape 'coloreds' of Malay heritage, to name but a few. The differences among these groups are elided, and the hegemony of apartheid maintained, when the groups' literatures are consigned to the monolithic category 'Black South African literature.'

The construction of black South African literatures in English as the postcolonial opposition to an Afrikaner apartheid points up the plight of the black writer of Afrikaans, who must work to decolonize a language that carries a seemingly indelible stain not only in other countries but also among other black South Africans. Black authors who use Afrikaans or the Kaaps dialect have been so stigmatized that a significant number have considered ceasing to write in their native tongue.[33] Their position is analogous to that of Afrikaner antiapartheid figures such as Breyten Breytenbach, for whom writing against apartheid in his first language seems impossible. Thus alliances among dissident speakers of Afrikaans on both sides of the color bar, which may seem strange in the light of the binarism dictated by apartheid, may yet prove to be a considerable resource in the creation of a new South Africa.

The issues of Afrikaner nationalism and the challenges facing both South African dissident theater and international critiques of apartheid suggest that positioning oneself in opposition to the hegemonic forces of a particular historical moment can be a truly postcolonial act. Yet these issues and challenges also demonstrate that maintaining such a stance in relation to a declining regime may mean siding with forces both reactionary and paralytic. The discourse of Afrikaner nationalism as analyzed by André Brink contributes a historic example of this particular strategic error. Brink has pointed out that the Afrikaner nationalists have wrongly interpreted their resistance against the colonial power as the source of an essential unity; thus they have always participated in the colonialist identification of an other against which to establish themselves.[34] The struggle of the Dutch and French Huguenot settlers against the Dutch East India Company (and particularly against Governor Willem Adriaan van der Stel) in the early eighteenth century; the settlers' rebellion against the British in the Cape, which preceded the Great Trek of 1834–40; and the Anglo-Boer War (1899–1902) have all been fetishized by Afrikaners as moments of extreme nationalist achievement and unity. Apartheid and, in the present, the rhetoric of the Afrikaner *Weerstandbeweging*[35] have constructed the black as the necessary other, an essentially reactionary paradigm, in the absence of sustained communal development. Thus, Brink argues, the oppositional origins of the Afrikaner people have been lost as a resource for future self-determination; the community's disparate composition has been eclipsed by the myth of homogeneity, of cultural and linguistic purity.

The inability to envisage process evident in a static model based on binary oppositions can result in cultural bankruptcy, as Steadman observes of current South African drama. He argues that the conventions of antiapartheid theater that developed during the states of emergency were radical in that context but are in danger of becoming atrophied as South Africa moves toward a post-apartheid era. An overwhelming preoccupation with the evils of the apartheid regime during the height of Nationalist power may thus obscure the possibility the theater offers for rehearsals of the desired liberation. Steadman sees critical theory as capable of maintaining the vitality of counterdiscursive strategies by constantly recognizing dissident practices in the context of change. Speaking of current theater practices in relation to the decline of apartheid, he comments:

> The conventions of anti-apartheid theater, now more than ever, need to be re-evaluated and *theorized* in new contexts lest they harden into dogma. Convention becomes dogma when practice is undertaken in ignorance of the theory which once informed it.[36]

Similarly, postcolonial theory will live up to expectations only if it constantly reevaluates its own biases and makes an effort to dispel them. The developments in South Africa provide one example of a situation in which such reevaluation is necessary for delineating how postcoloniality's stake in the future can be strengthened.

In this effort, the academy needs to accept as its crucial project the task of promoting a language that ruptures the division between the prescriptive and the descriptive on which Derrida's defense of 'Racism's Last Word' rests. The acceptance of such a language would mean that the theoretical would no longer be confined to the descriptive and opposed to the prescriptive, as it is in Derrida's formulation; as Steadman has pointed out, the creative, pedagogical role of the critical would be recognized. In this scenario, it would no longer be acceptable for critics to make what could be called, after its American exemplar, the 'Fishy' maneuver: claiming, in the name of pragmatism, that literary theory is always descriptive, never prescriptive (even if it is meant to be), and that it therefore can have 'no consequences.'[37] This point of view finds its South African counterpart in those white academics who assume that their position of relative privilege renders them politically disabled and hence claim that their work is futile, since it does not affect the 'masses.' This stance, as Carusi has pointed out, is profoundly irresponsible:

> This argument, arising from the political urgency of opposition, is, however, a specious argument. Foucault provides us with the tools to understand strategies and counter-strategies of power. Although power may be everywhere and therefore inescapable, he has also shown that no one is completely without power. Grassroots activists in the townships do not need Foucault, or any theorist to tell them this, but academics working in university institutions perhaps do.[38]

Like the artist that Wilson Harris describes, the postcolonial critic has the potential to negotiate between peoples in the context of the 'knife-edge of change,' though this potential carries the risk of 'self-enchantment or *hubris*.'[39] How can the visionary role of the postcolonial critic be realized in a time of crucial change? What specific form could Harris's 'hubris' take in postcolonial criticism and practice, and how can that fault be avoided?

If the analytical and the visionary, the past and the future, are to be fused creatively in contemporary postcolonial criticism, it is necessary for those of us who work in academic institutions to reject the form that the imperialist self-other binary takes in the academy: the division between studying subject and (archaeological) object. This problem is acute when the studying subject – and possibly the subject's students as well – belongs to a privileged group and the 'objects' of study belong to a disenfranchised people. And the problem is not confined to South Africa; anthropologists have been attempting to deal with it for at least two decades, as collections such as Dell Hymes's *Reinventing Anthropology* indicate.[40]

One way that white North American critics have addressed the dilemma of how to engage aboriginal culture in an academic setting whose modes of understanding can mirror imperialist paradigms is by choosing not to work on aboriginal texts at all. But in certain institutions, such as my own, the absence of aboriginal faculty members means that if all faculty members were to respond that way, the texts would not be taught, and the opportunity for a noncolonizing, heterogenous engagement between aboriginal text and the nonaboriginal subjective imagination would be lost. It is a form of arrogance for us as students of aboriginal texts to assume that we do not need the encounter both with the texts and with the difficulties the texts produce for us as teachers. Disengagement from aboriginal texts – as a refusal to violate the politics of identity – can mask the academy's refusal to confront the demands of an indigenous vision and can withhold engagement with that vision from all potential scholars, students and teachers alike. The institutionalization of such relativism may not represent an infallible admission of historical complicity with imperialism but conceivably may signal 'the bad faith of the conqueror, who has become secure enough to be a tourist.'[41]

There is, I think, a critical alternative that neither constitutes appropriation nor relinquishes the opportunity for syncretic dialogue with texts originating from communities other than one's own. This criticism would involve a resurrection of the scholar's 'I,' but not as a self-authorizing gesture or as a fetishization of self-consciousness, which, as Bob Scholte notes, 'involv[es] us in an unproductive paradox of infinite regress and self-doubt at the expense of matters of political ... urgency.'[42] Both positions are examples of Harrisian self-enchantment. Instead, I recommend reference to the self that does not simply authorize or silence critics on the basis of the 'adequacy' of their experience but rather promotes awareness of the institutional context and the limitations inherent in that context. Recognition of this kind of partiality enables, in turn, recognition of the communality of the critical act, of its heterogeneity and reciprocity. Here 'the critical act' refers both to critical writing and reading and to the processes of teaching and learning in the classroom. In both contexts, postcolonial criticism can articulate difference as it rehearses communal liberation.

The Jamaican writer and social worker Erna Brodber describes the mode of criticism I suggest here as the principle of operation necessary for a social worker, steeped in the Eurocentric, Cartesian tradition of research, to practice effectively in Jamaica. She writes as a social worker who has educated herself through fiction writing and communicated her experience to her students, therapists, and clients in an effort to achieve cultural liberation at a personal level:

> Boredom with a social science methodology devoted to 'objectivity' and therefore distancing the researcher from the people and spurning the affective interaction between the researcher and the researched led me into fiction. ...
> Accountability has not been to the people researched but to fellow academics. ... Thus although *Jane and Louisa Will Soon Come Home* [Brodber's first novel] was intended to provide such information as Erikson, Mead et al. had given to students of culture and personality, I felt that my examination of Jamaican society could not be written down from the standpoint of the objective outside observer communicating to disinterested scholars. It had to incorporate my 'I' and to be presented in such

a way that the social workers I was training saw their own 'I' in the work, making this culture-in-personality study a personal and possibly transforming work for the therapists and through them the clients with whom the therapists would work.[43]

Despite Brodber's focus on social work, her strategy offers a model combination of what Derrida calls the prescriptive and the descriptive in the fictive, a model that suggests the task of postcolonialism. Her use of the self, together with her exploitation of the critical possibilities of fiction, recalls Steadman's vision of South African drama as a crucial testing ground for postapartheid conceptions of liberation and demonstrates one of Harris's key concepts, 'infinite rehearsal.' Harris uses this phrase to indicate fiction's potential to dramatize that there is no 'final performance' of the kind assumed by Cartesian concepts of knowledge, by certain essentialist modes of narrative realism, and by the rhetoric of defense required by traditional academic performance. Here fiction has a responsibility to be 'a privileged rehearsal pointing to unsuspected facets and the re-emergence of forgotten perspectives in the cross-cultural and the universal imagination.'[44]

Such a critical-fictive practice offers possibilities similar to those suggested by Arnold Krupat's notion of cross-cultural translation. Anti-imperial translation, Krupat argues, is a practice in which the translator examines the norms underlying the language into which she or he is translating a text of aboriginal origin:

> [A] *critical* practice that seeks to undo its largely imperial history – its claim to speak for those who have no eloquent language of their own, its domination of the foreign figure of speech ... by domesticating it, siting-by-citing it within one's own discourse.[45]

Krupat's translation as critical practice, like the 'rehearsal' that Harris outlines, can interrogate the past and situate it so that the fictive imperative – the revision of the transition to a nonimperialist, genuinely multicultural future – is fulfilled. Harris's own critical fiction (*The Infinite Rehearsal* is indeed a novel) conforms to his vision of an ethical postcolonial practice that depends on 'an art of memory which dislocates, in some measure, an idolatrous plane of realism by immersing us in a peculiar kind of ruined fabric, [one that] may help to free us from a consensus of bestiality, monolithic helplessness, monolithic violence.'[46]

The practice of such cross-cultural criticism requires the existence and recognition of many kinds of native experience at all levels within the academy. Otherwise, what Biodun Jeyifo (who is now at an American university) says of Africanist studies will remain true for all postcolonial work undertaken in academic settings that lack aboriginal authority:

> Whatever genuine 'truths' our studies and readings generate, there is always the uncomfortable, compromising 'falsehood' of its massive displacement from the true center of gravity on the African continent, there is always the harrowing 'falsehood' involved in the production and reproduction of Africa's marginalization from the centers of economic and discursive power in an inequitable capitalist world system.[47]

Like Jeyifo, I recognize the challenge that the institutionalization of post-colonial work faces. Academics working outside South Africa have an almost parasitic relation to apartheid that evokes the last lines of the C. P. Cavafy poem from which the South African writer J. M. Coetzee took the title *Waiting for the Barbarians*: 'Now what's going to happen to us without barbarians? / Those people were a kind of solution.'[48]

The task that postcolonial scholars face in the academic context, if the stake in the oppressive present is to be relinquished, is analogous to the one faced by apartheid South Africa: the redistribution of resources and power necessary to realize an international postapartheid future. The noncolonizing mutual exploration of difference that I have attempted to outline as a strategy for postcolonial work resembles what Albie Sachs proposes in a paper entitled 'Preparing Ourselves for Freedom.'[49] Sachs describes the moment of intense change in which South Africans find themselves today as providing an opportunity for 'moving out of the phase of – you can call it defensive affirmation, survival strategies, survival based on a vision of the future – towards affirmative positions.'[50] Sachs is concerned that South African dissidents will make the error that Brink outlines as the historical fault of Afrikaner nationalists: continuing to define themselves as a community only within the framework of a Manichaean opposition. If a community with the potential to inaugurate a postapartheid era remains exclusively focused on white oppression, Sachs asserts, the conditions of that era will be dictated yet again by the disempowering lack of options of the apartheid age rather than by the kind of self-exploration Harris proposes:

> *The oppressor stalks our vision.* We should be speaking more about *ourselves* and exploring ourselves. It's another form of domination if you like, where the whites dominate the image, even if it's the image of the enemy and the focus of our artistic endeavour is trying to dispel – to reduce to size – this overwhelming presence of the oppressor. ... Even if the oppressor is there, physically is there, and is trying to penetrate our minds and to push us, and even to tell us how we should win our freedom. ... We should also not be afraid to enter into our own contradictions and difficulties, because we have sufficient confidence to do that. If we can reach down to our roots – and not invented roots, *real* roots – with all the tragedy of contradiction, the interest, the variety, the surprise that's involved in that, then I think that will do more to destroy the domination of the oppressor than simply putting the oppressor up as a target all the time.[51]

Perhaps the targets of postcolonialism have too often been the easy ones, such as apartheid. Identifying scapegoats may be delaying the urgent and no doubt painful exploration of the contradictions and difficulties of the postcolonial (ex)community. The fracturing of the self, which postmodernism has taken the dubious liberty of defining as a function of choice – a move that constitutes a dangerously utopian vision of this late colonial age – can be seen, alternatively, as the schizophrenic locus of an imagination that can produce, but that is also produced by, the violence of conquest. If the self is to do the work of what may accurately be called a postcolonial era, those of us who work as scholars may need to risk confessing to a series of awkward complicities and differences – and to our ignorance – in public spheres, including the classroom, the conference, and the published paper. Otherwise, we restrict ourselves by maintaining an allegiance to an obsolete opposition that insists on a homogenous rhetoric of defense, and in so doing we paralyze our resources for the future.[52]

Notes

1 Wilson Harris, *Explorations* ed. Hena-Maes Jelinek (Aarhus: Dangaroo, 1981), pp. 16–17.

2 International condemnation of specific policies of the Nationalist government, together with economic sanctions, contributed to pressures that elicited significant changes. The report of the Independent Expert Study Group for the Commonwealth Secretariat lists as examples of change the withdrawal of South Africa from Angola and Namibia, the release of the Rivonia prisoners, the release of Nelson Mandela, and the reprieve of the Sharpeville Six. See Joseph Hanlon, ed., *South Africa: The Sanctions Report: Documents and Statistics: A Report from the Independent Expert Study Group on the Evaluation of the Application and Impact of Sanctions against South Africa* (London: Currey; London: Heinemann, 1990), p. 142. One example of specifically literary action is France's lobbying on behalf of Breyten Breytenbach, which in 1982 resulted in his early release from imprisonment under the Terrorism Act.

3 Homi Bhabha, 'The Other Question . . . Homi K. Bhabha Reconsiders the Stereotype and Colonial Discourse,' *Screen* 24 (1983), p. 18.

4 Bhabha, 'The Other Question,' p. 18.

5 Bhabha, 'The Other Question,' p. 30.

6 This logic also characterized the decisions of the Publications Appeal Board, which heard appeals against banned publications. During the tenure of J. H. Snyman, chair of the board from April 1975 to April 1980, crude, severe decisions were handed down, obviously to maintain the puritanical and racist interests of the board. The board subsequently introduced a series of 'mitigating' factors, including consideration of 'the likely reader,' 'literary value,' 'research and academic value,' 'historical or period value,' 'satire,' 'limited distribution,' and 'price of publication.' This action has allowed the unbanning of a number of significant texts, such as Can Themba's *The Will to Die*, Todd Matshikiza's *Chocolates for My Wife*, Wole Soyinka's *Aké*, and Ngũgĩ wa Thiong'o's *Petals of Blood*. See Isabel Hofmeyr, ' "Setting Free the Books": The David Philip Africasouth Paperback Series,' *Research in African Literatures* 12 (1985), p. 85, and Louise Silver, *A Guide to Political Censorship in South Africa* (Witwatersrand: Centre for Applied Legal Studies, 1984). The board's later decisions, which may thus appear more liberal than earlier ones, were merely more politically astute. Apart from the question of black illiteracy, if blacks cannot afford to buy unbanned publications, these works can hardly represent a threat to the state and will surely find their way into an exclusive academic context. The furor raised over the banning of works unlikely to reach the black majority has not been worth the board's while. One can only hope that the pioneering work of publishers such as Ravan (with its Staffrider Series) and David Philip (Africasouth Paperbacks) in publishing unbanned works relatively cheaply will bear full fruit once the extraordinarily complex legislation governing the banning of publications in South

Africa has been dismantled and the education system rendered equitable – no small order.

7 Ian Steadman, 'Theater beyond Apartheid,' *Research in African Literatures* 22 (1991), p. 85.

8 The period to which I refer here, which saw the genesis of *Woza Albert!*, followed President P. W. Botha's proposal of a tricameral parliament that would extend elected central-government representation in racially segregated and subordinate parliamentary chambers to 'colored' and Indian South Africans but would continue to deny any central-government representation to the black majority. The states of emergency that Botha subsequently imposed in the middle and late eighties were in part a response to the huge multiracial effort to prevent the success of his 'divide and rule' strategy. Under such conditions, protest against any kind of surrogate representation entailed civil disobedience (the August 1984 elections for the tricameral parliament were widely boycotted). For further information on this period, see Jeremy Seekings, *The United Democratic Front in South Africa, 1983–1991* (Johannesburg: Ravan, forthcoming).

9 Howard Kissel, Review of *Woza Albert!*, by Percy Mtwa, Mbongeni Ngema, and Barney Simon, *Women's Wear Daily* (24 February 1984).

10 Clive Barnes, ' "Albert": Masterpiece out of South Africa.' Review of *Woza Albert!*, *New York Post* (24 February 1984), p. 23.

11 Steadman, 'Theater beyond Apartheid,' p. 84.

12 Douglas Watt, Review of *Woza Albert!*, by Percy Mtwa, Mbongeni Ngema, and Barney Simon, *New York Daily News* (24 February 1984).

13 Jacques Derrida, 'Racism's Last Word,' trans. Peggy Kamuf, *Critical Inquiry* 12 (1985), pp. 295, 291.

14 Derrida 'Last Word,' p. 291.

15 Derrida 'Last Word,' p. 299.

16 That the exhibition is a traveling one does not negate the politics of the museum; if anything, it exacerbates them, since the performance occupies not a single location but a number of international venues.

17 Exhibitions have played a key role in institutionalizing the Western imperialist gaze as 'perceiving' subject of the black, colonized 'object.' The 'Hottentot Venus,' described by Sander Gilman, is the most striking example of displaying South African native peoples in an exhibition with nominal pretensions to (anthropological) scholarship but actual interests in an imperialist voyeurism that is racist and sexist:

> In 1815 Saartje Baartman, also called Sarah Bartmann, or Saat-Jee, a twenty-five-year-old Hottentot female who had been exhibited in Europe for over five years as the 'Hottentot Venus,' died in Paris. ...
>
> For most Europeans who viewed her, Sarah Bartmann existed only as a collection of sexual parts. ...
>
> The audience that had paid to see Sarah Bartmann's buttocks and fantasized about her genitalia could, after her death and dissection, examine both, for Cuvier presented [to] 'the Academy the genital organs of this woman prepared in a way so as to allow one to see the nature of the labia.' ... Sarah Bartmann's genitalia and buttocks summarized her essence for the nineteenth-century observer, as indeed they continue to do for twentieth-century observers, since they are still on display at the Musée de l'Homme in Paris.

See Sander L. Gilman, *Difference and Pathology: Stereotypes of Sexuality, Race, and Madness* (Ithaca: Cornell University Press, 1985), pp. 85–8.

18 In the history of the Western academy, objectification of subjects of study – women, persons of color, nature, or the common collapse of these distinctions in the 'other' – is complicit in a mechanistic approach to the relation of persons to their environment; see Carolyn Merchant, *The Death of Nature: Women, Ecology, and the Scientific Revolution* (New York: Harper, 1980). This mechanistic approach is not universal, however. The beliefs and practices of animistic postcolonial communities, which Merchant considers an alternative to mechanistic philosophy, do not necessarily suffer the gender-biased drawbacks of Western organic thought. From this perspective, it is possible to see how the academy might initiate self-criticism based on philosophies that do not derive from Cartesian assumptions.

19 Derrida, 'Last Word,' p. 295.

20 Bhabha, 'The Other Question,' pp. 18–19.

21 Jacques Derrida, 'But, Beyond. ... ' trans. Peggy Kamuf, *Critical Inquiry* 13 (1986), p. 158.

22 Anne McClintock and Rob Nixon, 'No Names Apart: The Separation of Word and History in Derrida's "Le dernier mot du racisme," ' *Critical Inquiry* 13 (1986), pp. 140–1.

23 Derrida, 'But, Beyond. ... ' p. 158.

24 The settler–nonsettler model discussed in *The Empire Writes Back* is based on an essay by Maxwell. Ashcroft, Griffiths, and Tiffin develop this model, which has been debated by Vijay Mishra and Bob Hodge, among others, through reference to Maxwell, who notes that

[t]here are two broad categories. In the first, the writer brings his own language – English – to an alien environment and a fresh set of experiences: Australia, Canada, New Zealand. In the other, the writer brings an alien language – English – to his own social and cultural inheritance: India, West Africa.

See D. E. S. Maxwell, 'Landscape and Theme,' in John Press, ed., *Commonwealth Literature: Unity and Diversity in a Common Culture* (London: Heinemann, 1965), p. 82. See also Bill Ashcroft, Gareth Griffiths, and Helen Tiffin, *The Empire Writes Back* (London: Routledge, 1989), p. 25.

25 Bhabha, 'The Other Question,' p. 22.

26 Ashcroft, Griffiths, and Tiffin, *Empire*, p. 27.

27 Vijay Mishra and Bob Hodge, 'What Is Post(-)colonialism?' *Textual Practice* 5 (1991), p. 408.

28 Mishra and Hodge, 'What is Post(-)colonialism?' p. 411.

29 For this reason, many artists – perhaps the best-known among them Es'kia Mphahlele and Lewis Nkosi – have rejected negritude as a strategy for South African liberation. These artists' critiques of negritude constitute not what Omafume Onoge calls 'the advocacy of bourgeois individualism' but a recommendation that the antiapartheid community needs, by definition, to be based on something other than, or at least in addition to, black identity. Omafume F. Onoge, 'The Crisis of Consciousness in Modern African Literature,' in Georg M. Gugelberger, ed., *Marxism and African Literature* (Trenton: Africa World, 1986), p. 32. For Nkosi, this something proves to be Marxist-influenced recognition of class; for Mphahlele, humanism replaces 'the ethnic imperative.' See Lewis Nkosi, *Tasks and Masks: Themes and Styles of African Literature* (London: Longman, 1981), and Ezekiel

Mpahlele [Es'kia Mpahlele], 'The Function of Literature at the Present Time: The Ethnic Imperative,' *Transition* 45.9 (1974), p. 47.

30 Annamaria Carusi, 'Post, Post, and Post; or, Where Is South African Literature in All This?' in Ian Adam and Helen Tiffin, eds., *Past the Last Post* (Calgary: University of Calgary Press, 1990), p. 96.

31 For comparisons of the nationalist rhetorics of persecution used to justify the occupation of land in Israel, Ireland, and South Africa, see Donald Harmon Akenson, *God's Peoples: Covenant and Land in South Africa, Israel, and Ulster* (Kingston: McGill-Queen's University Press, 1991).

32 Ashcroft, Griffiths, and Tiffin use a lowercase e for 'postcolonial literatures written in english' to distinguish them from English as a colonialist discipline. Unfortunately, this usage exhibits limitations in the study of South African literatures. For an excellent analysis of the tunnel vision – and arrogance – of the 'english' construction of postcoloniality within the South African academy, see Njabulo S. Ndebele, 'The English Language and Social Change in South Africa,' *Triquarterly* 69 (1987), pp. 217–35.

33 V. A. February points out that Adam Small has been criticized for using Kaaps by his fellow 'colored' writers, who claim that the dialect entrenches the stereotype of the 'colored' as a cultural and linguistic 'buffoon.' V. A. February, *Mind Your Colour* (London: Kegan, 1981), p. 95. Speaking of the generation of black Afrikaans writers to which he belongs, Hein Willemse states that 'after 1976, no black Afrikaans writer [could] be spared the intellectual anguish of rationalizing his choice of language.' Hein Willemse, 'The Black Afrikaans Writer: A Continuing Dichotomy,' *Triquarterly* 69 (1987), p. 242.

34 André Brink, *Mapmakers: Writing in a State of Siege* (London: Faber, 1983), pp. 15–17.

35 The name of the extreme right-wing neo-Nazi movement, which promotes white supremacy, can be translated 'Afrikaner Resistance Movement.'

36 Steadman, 'Theater beyond Apartheid,' p. 77.

37 I have chosen not to review the well-known debates over the 'new pragmatism' here; such a move would risk defining the South African dilemma primarily in terms of a North American debate. Two texts that together offer an adequate history of that debate are W. J. T. Mitchell, ed., *Against Theory* (Chicago: University of Chicago Press, 1982) and Jonathan Arac and Barbara Johnson, eds., *Consequences Of Theory* (Baltimore: Johns Hopkins University Press, 1991). I pick Stanley Fish rather than some other 'pragmatist' as my target because his error mirrors Derrida's, for Fish appears to believe that he has full control over his self-representation, over the implications of his own actions. He claims that, theoretically, his own arguments have 'no consequences' – despite his extraordinarily public persona and his pride in performing his views before audiences both at home and abroad. 'Fish's most characteristic gesture [is] the paradox that his own argument, like theory in general, has "no consequences,"' according to Bruce Robbins, who explains the paradox: 'The traditional role of rhetoric was of course persuasion: winning a verdict of guilty or innocent, seeing a course of action adopted or defeated, having a decisive effect upon one's hearers – what Paul de Man called, with audible displeasure, "actual action upon others." In recognizing its dependence on an audience, rhetoric cannot avoid being kinetic and consequential. All of this is what Fish denies when he affirms that his own words have not after all been for or against anything. In the very act of championing rhetoric, he himself takes a position outside

it; but in championing rhetoric, he also champions the principles of public consequence and constituency which his argument otherwise denies.' See Bruce Robbins, 'Oppositional Professionals: Theory and Narratives of Professionalization,' in Arac and Johnson, *Consequences*, p. 21.

38 Carusi, 'Post,' pp. 105–6.

39 Harris, *Explorations*, pp. 16–17.

40 Dell Hymes, ed., *Reinventing Anthropology* (New York: Random, 1969).

41 Stanley Diamond, 'Anthropology in Question,' in Hymes, *Reinventing*, p. 421.

42 Bob Scholte, 'Toward a Reflexive and Critical Anthropology,' in Hymes, *Reinventing*, p. 442.

43 Erna Brodber, 'Fiction in Scientific Procedure,' in Selwyn R. Cudjoe, ed., *Caribbean Women Writers: Essays from the First International Conference* (Wellesley: Calaloux, 1990), pp. 165–6.

44 Wilson Harris, *The Infinite Rehearsal* (London: Faber, 1987), p. vii.

45 Arnold Krupat, *Ethnocriticism: Ethnography, History, Literature* (Berkeley: University of California Press, 1992), p. 198.

46 Harris, *Explorations*, p. 14.

47 Biodun Jeyifo, 'The Nature of Things: Arrested Decolonization and Critical Theory,' *Research in African Literatures* 21 (1990), p. 46.

48 See C. P. Cavafy, *Collected Poems*, ed. George Savadis, trans. Edmund Keeley and Philip Sherrard (Princeton: Princeton University Press, 1975), p. 33 and J. M. Coetzee, *Waiting for the Barbarians* (London: Secker, 1980). A colleague of mine who works on South African history recently commented in a moment of conscious self-irony, 'What are we to do without apartheid?'

49 Sachs's paper, which he delivered to an African National Congress in-house seminar in 1990, generated a debate on postapartheid writing that is still active. For the text of this paper, together with a number of responses that outline the controversy, see I. de Kok and K. Press, eds., *Spring Is Rebellious* (Cape Town: Buchu, 1990). The discussion is continued in Duncan Brown and Bruno van Dyk, eds., *Exchanges: South African Writing in Transition* (Pietermaritzburg: University of Natal Press, 1991).

50 Albie Sachs, 'An Interview with Albie Sachs,' with Eve Bertelsen, *World Literature Written in English* 30 (1990), p. 104.

51 Sachs, 'An Interview with Albie Sachs,' p. 99.

52 I would like to thank Gary Boire, Ted Chamberlin, Eve D'Aeth, Alan Jeeves, Fred Lock, Margaret Lock, Joan McMullen, Julian Patrick, Dan O'Meara, and the Canadian Research Consortium on Southern Africa for their comments on earlier drafts of this article. I would also like to acknowledge the financial assistance of the Office of Research Services, Queen's University.

BIBLIOGRAPHY

Achebe, Chinua. *Hopes and Impediments*. London: Heinemann, 1975.
—— *Morning Yet on Creation Day*. London: Heinemann, 1975.
Adam, Ian and Helen Tiffin, eds. *Past the Last Post*. Calgary: University of Calgary Press, 1990.
Ahmad Aijaz. *In Theory*. London: Verso, 1992.
—— 'The Politics of Literary Postcoloniality'. *Race and Class* 36.3 (1995): 1–20. (Also in this volume, Chapter 14.)
Ahmed, Leila. 'Western Ethnocentrism and Perceptions of the Harem'. *Feminist Studies* 8 (Fall 1982): 521–34.
—— *Women and Gender in Islam: Historical Roots of a Modern Debate*. New Haven: Yale University Press, 1992.
Aidoo, Ama Ata. 'That Capacious Topic. Gender Politics'. Mariani, 151–4.
Alavi, Hamza. 'The State in Post-Colonial Societies: Pakistan and Bangladesh'. *New Left Review* 74 (July–Aug. 1972).
Alavi, Hamza *et al. Capitalism and Colonial Production*. London: Croom Helm, 1982.
Amos, Valerie and Pratibha Parmar. 'Challenging Imperial Feminism'. *Feminist Review 17* (July 1984): 3–19.
Anderson, Benedict. *Imagined Communities: Reflections on the Origin and Spread of Nationalism*. London: Verso, 1983.
Anzaldúa, Gloria, ed. *Borderlands/La Frontera: The New Mestiza*. San Francisco: Spinsters/Aunt Lute, 1987.
——, ed. *Making Face, Making Soul/Haciendo Caras: Creative and Critical Perspectives by Feminists of Color*. San Francisco: Spinsters/Aunt Lute, 1990.
Anzaldúa, Gloria and Cherrie Moraga, eds. *This Bridge Called My Back: Writings by Radical Women of Color*. Watertown, MA: Persephone Press, 1981.
Appadurai, Arjun. 'Disjuncture and Difference in the Global Cultural Economy'. *Public Culture* 2.2 (Spring 1990): 1–24.
—— 'The Heart of Whiteness'. *Callaloo* 16.4 (1993): 796–807.
—— 'Is Homo Hierarchicus?' *American Ethnologist* 13.4 (1986): 745–61.
—— 'Patriotism and Its Futures'. *Public Culture* 5.3 (1993): 411–29.
—— 'Putting Hierarchy in Its Place'. *Cultural Anthropology* 3.1 (1988): 36–49.
—— 'Theory in Anthropology: Center and Periphery'. *Comparative Studies in Society and History* 28.1 (1986): 356–61.
Appiah, Kwame Anthony. *In My Father's House: Africa in the Philosophy of Culture*. London: Methuen, 1992.
—— 'Is the Post- in Postmodernism the Post- in Postcolonial?' *Critical Inquiry* 17 (Winter 1991): 336–57. (Also in this volume, Chapter 3.)
—— 'Out of Africa: Topologies of Nativism'. *Yale Journal of Criticism* 1.2 (1988): 153–78.

Arac, Jonathan and Barbara Johnson, eds. *Consequences of Theory*. Baltimore: Johns Hopkins University Press, 1991.

Asad, Talal. 'Are There Histories of Peoples Without Europe?' *Comparative Studies in Society and History* 29.3 (July 1987): 594–607.

—— 'A Comment on Aijaz Ahmad's *In Theory*'. *Public Culture* 6.1 (Fall 1993): 31–40.

—— ed. *Anthropology and the Colonial Encounter*. London: Ithaca Press, 1973.

Asad, Talal and John Dixon. 'Translating Europe's Others'. Barker *et al.*, *Europe and Its Others*, volume 1, 170–7.

Ashcroft, Bill, Gareth Griffiths and Helen Tiffin. *The Empire Writes Back: Theory and Practice in Post-Colonial Literatures*. London: Routledge, 1989.

Azim, Firdaus. *The Colonial Rise of the Novel*. New York: Routledge, 1993.

Baker, Houston. 'Caliban's Triple Play'. *Critical Inquiry* 13.1 (Autumn 1986): 182–96.

Baker, Peter. 'Directions in Left Theory'. *Minnesota Review* 41/42 (March 1995): 262–79.

Balibar, E. *Masses, Classes, Ideas: Studies on Politics and Philosophy Before and After Marx*, trans. James Swenson. New York: Routledge, 1994.

—— 'The Nation Form: History and Ideology'. *Race, Nation, Class: Ambiguous Identities*, eds. E. Balibar and I. Wallerstein. London: Verso, 1991, 86–106.

Barkan, Elazar. 'Post-Anti-Colonial Histories: Representing the Other in Imperial Britain'. *Journal of British Studies* 33 (April 1994): 180–203.

Barker, Francis *et al.*, eds. *Colonial Discourse/Postcolonial Theory*. Manchester: Manchester University Press, 1994.

—— *et al.*, eds. *Europe and its Others: Proceedings of the Essex Conference*. 2 vols. Colchester: University of Essex Press, 1985.

Baucom, Ian. 'Dreams of Home: Colonialism and Postmodernism'. *Research in African Literatures* 22 (Winter 1991): 5–27.

Bhabha, Homi. 'Articulating the Archaic: Notes on Colonial Nonsense'. Collier and Geyer-Ryan, 203–18.

—— ' "Caliban Speaks to Prospero": Cultural Identity and the Crisis of Representation'. Mariani, 62–5.

—— *The Location of Culture*. London: Routledge, 1994.

—— 'Of Mimicry and Men: The Ambivalence of Colonial Discourse'. *October* 28 (1984): 125–33.

—— 'The Other Question: the Stereotype and Colonial Discourse'. *Screen* 24.6 (1983): 18–36. (Also in this volume, Chapter 2.)

—— 'Postcolonial Criticism.' Greenblatt and Gunn, 437–65.

—— 'Remembering Fanon – Self, Psyche and the Colonial Condition'. Foreword. *Black Skin, White Masks* by Frantz Fanon. London: Pluto Press, 1986, vii–xv.

—— 'Representation and the Colonial Text: A Critical Exploration of Some Forms of Mimeticism'. *The Theory of Reading*, ed. Frank Gloversmith. Brighton: Harvester, 1984, 93–122.

—— 'Signs Taken for Wonders: Questions of Ambivalence and Authority Under a Tree Outside Delhi, May 1817'. *Critical Inquiry* 12.1 (1985): 144–65.

—— ed. *Nation and Narration*. London: Routledge, 1990.

Bhattacharyya, Gargi. 'Cultural Education in Britain'. *Oxford Literary Review* 13.1/2 (1991): 4–19.

Bilgrami, Akeel. 'What is a Muslim?' *Critical Inquiry* 18.4 (Summer 1992): 821–42.

Boehmer, Elleke. *Colonial and Postcolonial Literature*. Oxford: Oxford University Press, 1995.

Brah, Avtar. 'Re-framing Europe: En-gendered Racisms, Ethnicities and Nationalisms in Contemporary Western Europe'. *Feminist Review* 45 (Autumn 1993): 9–29.

Brantlinger, Patrick. *Rule of Darkness: British Literature and Imperialism 1830–1914.* Ithaca: Cornell University Press, 1988.

Brathwaite, E. K. *Contradictory Omens: Cultural Diversity and Integration in the Caribbean.* Mona, Jamaica: Savacou Press, 1974.

—— *History of the Voice: The Development of Nation Language in Anglophone Caribbean Poetry.* London: New Beacon Books, 1984.

Breckenridge, Carol and Peter van der Veer. *Orientalism and the Postcolonial Predicament, Perspectives on South Asia.* Philadelphia: University of Pennsylvania Press, 1993.

Brennan, Timothy. 'The National Longing for Form'. Bhabha, 44–70.

—— *Salman Rushdie and the Third World.* London: Macmillan, 1989.

Butler, Judith. 'Contingent Foundations: Feminism and the Question of "Postmodernism" '. Butler and Scott, 3–21.

Butler, Judith and Joan Scott, eds. *Feminists Theorize the Political.* New York: Routledge, 1992.

Cabral, Amilcar. *National Liberation and Culture*, trans. Maureen Webster. Syracuse, N Y: Syracuse University Press, 1970.

—— *Unity and Struggle: Speeches and Writings*, trans. Michael Wolfers. London: Heinemann, 1980.

Carby, Hazel. *Reconstructing Womanhood: The Emergence of the Afro-American Woman Novelist.* New York: Oxford University Press, 1987.

—— 'White Women Listen! Black Feminism and the Boundaries of "Sisterhood" '. Centre for Contemporary Cultural Studies, 212–35.

Carusi, Annamaria. 'Post, Post, and Post; or Where is South African Literature in All This?' Adam and Tiffin, 95–108.

Césaire, Aimé. *Discourse on Colonialism.* New York: Monthly Review Press, 1972.

Centre for Contemporary Cutural Studies. *The Empire Strikes Back: Race and Racism in 70's Britain.* London: Hutchinson, 1982.

Chabram, Angie. 'Chicana/o Studies as Oppositional Ethnography'. *Cultural Studies* 4.3 (October 1990): 228–47.

Chakrabarty, Dipesh. 'The Death of History?: Historical Conciousness and the Culture of Late Capitalism'. *Public Culture* 4.2 (Spring 1992): 47–65.

—— 'History as Critique and Critique(s) of History'. *Economic and Political Weekly* 26.37 (September 14, 1991): 2162–6.

—— 'Postcoloniality and the Artifice of History'. *Representations* 37 (Winter 1992): 1–26. (Also in this volume, Chapter 12.)

—— *Rethinking Working-Class History: Bengal, 1890–1940.* Princeton: Princeton University Press, 1989.

Chambers Iain and Lidia Curti, eds. *The Post-Colonial Question: Common Skies, Divided Horizons.* London: Routledge, 1996.

Chatterjee, Partha. 'Colonialism, Nationalism, and Colonized Women: The Contest in India'. *American Ethnologist* 16.4 (November 1989): 622–33.

—— *The Nation and Its Fragments: Colonial and Postcolonial Histories.* Princeton: Princeton University Press, 1993.

—— *Nationalist Thought and the Colonial World.* London: Zed Press, 1986.

Chicago Cultural Studies Group. 'Critical Multiculturalism'. *Critical Inquiry* 18 (Spring 1992): 530–55.

Chinweizu, Jemie O. and I. Madubuike. *Toward the Decolonization of African*

Literature. Washington: Howard University Press, 1983.
Chow, Rey. 'Between Colonizers: Hong Kong's Postcolonial Self Writing in the 1990s'. *Diaspora* 2.2 (1992): 151–70.
—— 'Postmodern Automatons'. Butler and Scott, 101–17.
—— 'Rereading Mandarin Ducks and Butterflies: A Response to the "Postmodern" Condition'. *Cultural Critique* 5 (1986–87): 69–93.
—— 'Violence in the Other Country: China as Crisis, Spectacle, and Woman'. Mohanty *et al.*, 81–100.
—— *Woman and Chinese Modernity: The Politics of Reading Between West and East.* Minneapolis: University of Minnesota Press, 1991.
✓ —— *Writing Diaspora*. Bloomington: Indiana University Press, 1993.
Chowdhury, Kanishka. 'Theoretical Confrontations in the Study of Postcolonial Literatures'. *Modern Fiction Studies* 37.3 (Autumn 1991): 609–16.
—— *Black Feminist Criticism*. New York: Pergamon, 1986.
Christian, Barbara. 'The Race for Theory'. JanMohamed and Lloyd, 37–49. (Also in this volume, Chapter 8.)
Clausen, Christopher. ' "National Literatures" in English: Toward a New Paradigm'. *New Literary History* 25.1 (Winter 1994): 61–72.
Clifford, James. 'Diasporas'. *Cultural Anthropology* 9.3 (August 1994): 302–38.
—— 'On Ethnographic Allegory'. Clifford and Marcus, 98–121.
—— 'On Ethnographic Authority'. *Representations* 1.2 (Spring 1983): 118–46.
—— 'On Ethnographic Self-fashioning: Conrad and Malinowski'. *Reconstructing Individualism*, eds. T. C. Heller *et al.* Stanford: Stanford University Press, 1986, 140–62.
—— *The Predicament of Culture*. Cambridge MA: Harvard University Press, 1988.
—— 'Travelling Cultures'. *Cultural Studies*. Grossberg *et al.*, 96–112.
Clifford, James and Vivek Dhareshwar, eds. *Traveling Theories: Traveling Theorists. Inscriptions* 5 (1989).
Clifford, James and George Marcus, eds. *Writing Culture*. Berkeley: University of California Press, 1986.
Collier, Peter and Helga Geyer-Ryan, eds. *Literary Theory Today*. Ithaca: Cornell University Press, 1990.
Copek, Peter. 'Imperial Affiliations'. *Minnesota Review* 41/42 (March 1995): 253–61.
Coronil, Fernando. 'Can Postcoloniality be Decolonized? Imperial Banality and Postcolonial Power'. *Public Culture* 5.1 (Fall 1992): 89–108.
Curthoys, Ann. 'Identity Crisis: Colonialism, Nation, and Gender in Australian History'. *Gender and History* 5.2 (Summer 1993): 165–76.
Dallmayr, Fred, ed. *Colonialisms*. Special issue of *Nineteenth-Century Contexts*. 18.1 (1994).
Dash, Michael. 'Marvellous Realism: The Way Out of Négritude'. *Caribbean Studies* 13.4 (1974): 57–77.
✓ Davies, Carol Boyce. *Black Women, Writing and Identity*. New York: Routledge, 1994.
Deane, Seamus, ed. *Nationalism, Colonialism, and Literature*. Minneapolis: University of Minnesota Press, 1990.
de Lauretis, Teresa. *Feminist Studies/Critical Studies*. Bloomington: Indiana University Press, 1986.
Dhareshwar, Vivek. 'Marxism, Location Politics, and the Possibility of Critique'. *Public Culture* 6.1 (Fall 1993): 41–54.
—— 'Toward a Narrative Epistemology of the Postcolonial Predicament'. *Inscriptions* 5 (1989): 135–58.

Diawara, Manthia. *African Cinema: Politics and Culture.* Bloomington: Indiana University Press, 1992.

—— Englishness and Blackness: Cricket as Discourse on Colonialism'. *Callaloo* 13.4 (1991): 830–44.

—— 'The Nature of Mother in *Dreaming Rivers*'. *Third Text* 13 (Winter 1990/91): 73–84.

—— 'On Tracking World Cinema'. *Public Culture* 5.2 (Winter 1993): 339–43.

Dirks, Nicholas B. 'History as a Sign of the Modern'. *Public Culture* 2.2 (Spring 1990): 25–33.

Dirks, Nicholas B., ed. *Colonialism and Culture.* Ann Arbor: University of Michigan Press, 1992.

Dirlik, Arif. 'The Postcolonial Aura: Third World Criticism in the Age of Global Capitalism'. *Critical Inquiry* 20 (Winter 1994): 328–56. (Also in this volume, Chapter 15.)

Dominguez, Virginia R. 'A Taste for the "Other" '. *Current Anthropology* 35.4 (August–October 1994): 333–48.

Donaldson, Laura. 'The Miranda Complex: Colonialism and the Question of Feminist Reading'. *diacritics* 18.3 (Fall 1988): 65–77.

Driver, Felix. 'Geography's Empire: Histories of Geographical Knowledge'. *Environment and Planning D: Society and Space* 10 (1992): 23–40.

During, Simon. 'Postmodernism or Postcolonialism?' *Landfall* 39.3 (1985): 366–80.

—— 'Postmodernism or Post-colonialism Today'. *Textual Practice* 1.1 (1987): 32–47.

—— 'Waiting for the Post: Some Relations Between Modernity, Colonization, and Writing'. Adam and Tiffin, 23–45.

Fabian, Johannes. 'Presence and Representation: the Other and Anthropological Writing'. *Critical Inquiry* 16.4 (Summer 1990): 753–72.

—— *Time and the Other: How Anthropology Makes its Object.* Cambridge, MA: Harvard University Press, 1983.

Fanon, Frantz. *Black Skin, White Masks.* New York: Grove Press, 1967.

—— *A Dying Colonialism.* New York: Monthly Review Press, 1965.

—— *The Wretched of the Earth.* New York: Grove Press, 1963.

Ferguson, Moira. *Subject to Others: British Women Writers and Colonial Slavery, 1630–1874.* London: Routledge, 1992.

Foucault, Michel. *Discipline and Punish*, trans. Alan Sheridan. London: Allen Lane, 1977.

—— *The Order of Things.* London: Tavistock Publications, 1970.

—— *Language, Counter-Memory, Practice*, ed. Donald F. Bouchard. Ithaca: Cornell University Press, 1980.

Fraiman, Susan. 'Jane Austen and Edward Said: Gender, Culture, and Imperialism'. *Critical Inquiry* 21.4 (Summer 1995): 805–21.

Frankenberg, Ruth. *White Women, Race Matters: The Social Construction of Whiteness.* Minneapolis: University of Minnesota Press, 1993.

Frankenberg, Ruth and Lata Mani. 'Crosscurrents, Crosstalk: Race, "Postcoloniality" and the Politics of Location'. *Cultural Studies* 7.2 (May 1993): 292–310. (Also in this volume, Chapter 18.)

Gates, Henry Louis. 'Critical Fanonism'. *Critical Inquiry* 17 (Spring 1991): 457–70.

—— *The Signifying Monkey.* New York: Oxford University Press, 1989.

—— 'Tell Me Sir, What is Black Literature?' *PMLA* 105.1 (January 1990): 11–22.

—— ed. *'Race', Writing, and Difference.* Special issue of *Critical Inquiry* 12.1 (Autumn 1985).

Gellner, Ernest. *Nations and Nationalism*. Oxford: Basil Blackwell, 1983.

Gilman, Sander. *Difference and Pathology: Stereotypes of Sexuality, Race and Madness*. Ithaca: Cornell University Press, 1985. *Picturing Health & Illness 1995*

Gilroy, Paul. *The Black Atlantic: Modernity and Double Consciousness*. Cambridge, MA: Harvard University Press, 1993.

—— 'Cultural Studies and Ethnic Absolutism'. Grossberg *et al.*, 187–98.

—— 'It Ain't Where You're From, It's Where You're At: The Dialectics of Diasporic Identification'. *Third Text* 13 (Winter 1990/91): 3–16.

—— 'Nationalism, History, and Ethnic Absolutism'. *History Workshop Journal* 30 (Autumn 1990): 114–20. *Small Acts 1993*

—— *There Ain't No Black in the Union Jack*. London: Routledge, 1991.

Giroux, Henry A. 'Academics as Public Intellectuals'. *Minnesota Review* 41/42 (March 1995): 310–23.

Glissant, Edouard. *Caribbean Discourse*, trans. Michael Dash. Charlottesville: University of Virginia Press, 1989.

Gordon, Deborah, ed. *Feminism and the Critique of Colonial Discourse. Inscriptions* 3/4 (1988).

Gramsci, Antonio. *Selections from the Prison Notebooks*, trans. Quentin Hoare and Geoffrey Nowell Smith. London: Lawrence & Wishart, 1971.

Greenblatt, Stephen and Giles Gunn, eds. *Redrawing the Boundaries*. New York: MLA, 1992.

Grewal, Shabnam *et al. Charting the Journey: Writings by Black and Third World Women*. London: Sheba, 1988.

Griffiths, Gareth. 'Imitation, Abrogation and Appropriation: the Production of the Post-Colonial Text'. *Kunapipi* 9.1 (1987): 13–20.

Grossberg, Lawrence *et al.*, eds. *Cultural Studies*. New York: Routledge, 1992.

Guha, Ranajit, ed. *Subaltern Studies*, 5 vols. New Delhi: Oxford University Press, 1982–6.

—— 'On Some Aspects of the Historiography of Colonial India'. Guha and Spivak, 37–44.

Guha, Ranajit and Gayatri Spivak, eds. *Selected Subaltern Studies*. New Delhi: Oxford University Press, 1988.

Gunew, Sneja. 'Australia 1984: A Moment in the Archaeology of Muticulturalism'. Barker *et al.*, *Europe and Its Others*, volume 1, 178–93.

—— 'Authenticity and the Writing Cure: Reading Some Migrant Women's Writing'. *Poetics* 17.1/2 (April 1988): 81–97.

—— 'Denaturalizing Cultural Nationalisms: Multicultural Readings of "Australia"'. Bhabha, 99–120.

—— 'Framing Marginality: Distinguishing the Textual Politics of the Marginal Voice'. *Southern Review* 18.2 (July 1985): 142–56.

Gunew, Sneja and Kateryna O. Longley, eds. *PMT (Post Modernist Tensions): Reading for (Multi) Cultural Difference*. Sydney: Allen & Unwin, 1992.

Gupta, Akhil and James Ferguson. 'Beyond "Culture": Space, Identity, and the Politics of Difference'. *Cultural Anthropology* 7.1 (February 1992): 6–23.

Haberly, David T. 'The Search for a National Language: A Problem in the Comparative Study of Postcolonial Literatures'. *Comparative Literature Studies* 11.1 (1974): 85–97.

Hall, Stuart. 'Brave New World: the Debate About Post-Fordism'. *Socialist Review* 21.1 (1991): 57–64.

—— 'Cultural Identity and Diaspora'. Rutherford, 222–37. (Also in this volume, Chapter 6.)

—— 'Cultural Studies and Its Theoretical Legacies'. Grossberg *et al.*, 277–86.

—— 'Culture, Community, Nation'. *Cultural Studies* 7.3 (October 1993): 349–63.

—— 'The Emergence of Cultural Studies and the Crisis of the Humanities'. *October* 53 (Summer 1990): 11–23.

—— *The Hard Road to Renewal: Thatcherism and the Crisis of the Left*. London: Verso, 1988.

—— 'Minimal Selves', in *The Real Me: Postmodernism and the Question of Identity*. London: ICA Documents 6 (1987): 44–6.

—— 'New Ethnicities', in *Black Film/British Cinema*. London: ICA Documents 7 (1988): 27–30.

—— 'Recent Developments in Theories of Language and Ideology: a Critical Note'. *Culture, Media, Language: Working Papers in Cultural Studies*, eds. Hall *et al.* London: Hutchinson, 1980.

—— 'The Toad in the Garden: Thatcher Among the Theorists'. Nelson and Grossberg, 35–73.

—— 'When Was 'The Post-Colonial'? Thinking at the Limit'. Chambers and Curti, 242–60.

Hammond, Dorothy and Alta Jablow. *The Africa That Never Was: Four Centuries of British Writing About Africa*. New York: Twayne Publishers, 1970.

Harlow, Barbara. *Resistance Literature*. New York: Methuen, 1987.

Harris, Wilson. *The Womb of Space: The Cross-Cultural Imagination*. Westport, CT: Greenwood Press, 1983.

Hassan, Ihab. 'Pluralism in Postmodern Perspective'. *Critical Inquiry* 12 (1986): 503–20.

Hobsbawm, E. J. *Nations and Nationalism Since 1780*. Cambridge: Cambridge University Press, 1990.

Hobsbawm, E. J. and Terence Ranger, eds. *The Invention of Tradition*. Cambridge: Cambridge University Press, 1983.

Hodge, Bob and Vijav, Mishra. *Dark Side of the Dream: Australian Literature and the Postcolonial Mind*. North Sydney, NSW: Allen & Unwin, 1991.

Holt, Thomas C. 'Marking: Race, Race-making, and the Writing of History'. *American Historical Review* 100.1 (February 1995): 1–20.

Homans, Margaret. ' "Women of Color" Writers and Feminist Theory'. *New Literary History* 25.1 (Winter 1994): 73–94.

hooks, bell. *Talking Back: Thinking Feminist, Thinking Black*. Boston: South End Press, 1989.

—— *Yearning: Race, Gender, and Cultural Politics*. Boston: South End Press, 1991.

Huggan, Graham. 'Anthropologists and Other Frauds'. *Comparative Literature* 46.2 (Spring 1994): 113–28.

—— 'Decolonizing the Map: Post-Colonialism, Post-Structuralism and the Cartographic Connection'. Adam and Tiffin, 125–38.

Hulme, Peter. *Colonial Encounters: Europe and the Native Carribbean 1492–1797*. London: Methuen, 1986.

—— 'Hurricanes in the Caribbees: The Constitution of the Discourse of English Colonialism'. *1642: Literature and Power in the Seventeenth Century*. Essex: University Essex Press, 1981, 55–83.

—— 'Polytropic Man: Tropes of Sexuality and Mobility in Early Colonial Discourse'. Barker *et al.*, *Europe and its Others*, volume 2, 17–32.

—— 'A Response to Myra Jehlen'. *Critical Inquiry* 20.1 (Autumn 1993): 179–91.

Hutcheon, Linda. ' "Circling the Downspout of Empire": Post-colonialism and Post-modernism'. *Ariel* 20.4 (1989): 149–75.

—— *A Poetics of Postmodernism: History, Theory, Fiction*. London: Routledge, 1988.

Iavawardena, Kumari. *The White Woman's Other Burden: Western Women and South Asia during British Colonial Rule*. London: Routledge, 1995.

Inden, Ronald. 'Orientalist Constructions of India'. *Modern Asian Studies* 20.3 (1986): 401–46.

Jacoby, Russell. 'Marginal Returns: The Trouble With Post-Colonial Theory'. *Lingua Franca* (September/October 1995): 30–7.

James, C. L. R. *Beyond a Boundary*. Durham: Duke University Press, 1993.

—— *The Black Jacobins: Toussaint L'Ouverture and the San Domingo Revolution*. New York: Vintage Books, 1989.

—— *The C. L. R. James Reader*, ed. Anna Grimshaw. Oxford: Basil Blackwell, 1992.

Jameson, Fredric. 'Postmodernism, or the Cultural Logic of Late Capitalism'. *New Left Review* 146 (1984): 53–92.

—— 'Third-World Literature in the Era of Multinational Capital'. *Social Text* 15 (Fall 1986): 65–88.

JanMohamed, Abdul R. 'Humanism and Minority Literature: Toward a Definition of Counter-hegemonic Discourse'. *boundary 2* 12 (Spring/Fall 1984): 281–99.

—— *Manichean Aesthetics: The Politics of Literature in Colonial Africa*. Amherst: University of Massachusetts Press, 1983.

JanMohamed, Abdul R. and David Lloyd, eds. *The Nature and Context of Minority Discourse*. New York: Oxford University Press, 1990.

Jayawardena, Kumari. *Feminism and Nationalism in the Third World*. London and Atlantic Highlands, NJ: Zed Books, 1986.

Jehlen, Myra. 'History Before the Fact: or, Captain John Smith's Unfinished Symphony'. *Critical Inquiry* 19 (Summer 1993): 677–92.

Jeyifo, Biodun. 'Determinations of Remembering: Post-Colonial Fictional Genealogies of Colonialism in Africa'. *Stanford Literature Review* 10.1/2 (Spring/Fall 1993): 99–116.

—— 'The Nature of Things: Arrested Decolonization and Critical Theory'. *Research in African Literatures* 21 (1990): 33–47. (Also in this volume, Chapter 9.)

—— 'On Eurocentric Critical Theory: Some Paradigms From the Texts and Sub-Texts of Post-Colonial Writing'. *Kunapipi* 11.1 (1989): 107–18.

Joshi, Svati, ed. *Rethinking English: Essays in Literature, Language, History*, New Delhi: Trianka, 1991.

Kanneh, Kadiatu. 'Place, Time, and the Black Body: Myth and Resistance'. *Oxford Literary Review* 13.1/2 (1991): 140–63.

Katrak, Ketu. 'Decolonizing Culture: Toward a Theory for Postcolonial Women's Texts'. *Modern Fiction Studies* 35.1 (1989): 157–79.

Keddie, Nikki. 'Problems in the Study of Middle Eastern Women'. *International Journal of Middle Eastern Studies* 10 (1979): 225–40.

Kiernan, Victor. *The Lords of Human Kind: European Attitudes Towards the Outside World in the Imperial Age*. Boston: Little, Brown & Co., 1969.

—— *Marxism and Imperialism*. New York: St. Martin's Press, 1975.

Kim, Elaine H. 'Defining Asian American Realities Through Literature'. Jan, Mohamed and Lloyd, 146–70.

Kroller, Eva-Marie. 'Postmodernism, Colony, Nation: the Melvillean Texts of Bowering and Beaulieu'. *University of Ottawa Quarterly* 54.2 (1984): 53–61.

Laclau Ernesto and Chantal Mouffe. *Hegemony and Socialist Strategy: Towards a Radical Democratic Politics*, trans. Winston Moore and Paul Cammack. London: Verso, 1985.

Landes, Joan. 'Women and the Public Sphere: A Modern Perspective'. *Social Analysis* 15 (August 1984): 20–31.

Lazarus, Neil. *Resistance in Postcolonial African Fiction*. New Haven, CT: Yale University Press, 1990.

Lazreg, Marnia. 'Feminism and Difference: The Perils of Writing as a Woman on Women in Algeria'. *Feminist Studies* 14.1 (Spring 1988): 81–107.

—— 'Gender and Politics in Algeria: Unraveling the Religious Paradigm'. *Signs* 15.4 (Summer 1990): 755–80.

Lim, Shirley Geok-Lin. *Nationalism and Literature: English Language Writing from the Philippines and Singapore*. Quezon City, Philippines: New Day Publishers, 1993.

—— 'Semiotics, Experience, and the Material Self: An Inquiry Into the Subject of the Contemporary Asian Woman Writer'. *Women's Studies* 18 (1990): 153–75.

Lim, Shirley Geok-Lin and Amy Ling, eds. *Reading the Literatures of Asian America*. Philadelphia: Temple University Press, 1992.

Loomba, Ania 'Overworlding the Third World'. *Oxford Literary Review* 13 (1991): 164–91.

Loomba, Ania and Suvir Kaul, eds. *On India: Writing History, Culture, Post-Coloniality*. Special issue of *Oxford Literary Review* 16.1/2 (1994).

Lyotard, Jean-François. *The Differend: Phrases in Dispute*, trans. Georges Van Den Abeele. Minneapolis: University of Minnesota Press, 1988.

Majeed, Javed. *Ungoverned Imaginings: James Mill's* The History of British India *and Orientalism*. Oxford: Clarendon Press, 1992. ✓

Makdisi, Saree. 'The Empire Renarrated: *Season of Migration to the North* and the Reinvention of the Present'. *Critical Inquiry* 18 (Summer 1992): 804–20.

—— ' "Postcolonial" Literature in a Neocolonial World: Modern Arabic Culture and the End of Modernity'. *boundary 2* 22.1 (Spring 1995): 85–115.

Mannoni, O. *Prospero and Caliban*. Ann Arbor: University of Michigan Press, 1990.

Mani, Lata. 'Contentious Traditions: The Debate on *Sati* in Colonial India'. *Cultural Critique* (1987): 119–56.

—— 'Multiple Mediations: Feminist Scholarship in the Age of Multinational Reception'. *Inscriptions* 5 (1989): 1–23.

—— 'The Production of an Official Discourse on *Sati* in Early Nineteenth-Century Bengal'. Barker *et al.*, *Europe and Its Others*, volume 1, 107–27.

Marcus, George and Michael Fischer. *Anthropology as Cultural Critique*. Chicago: University of Chicago Press, 1986.

Marcus, George and Dick Cushman. 'Ethnographies as Texts'. *Annual Review of Ethnography* 11 (1982): 25–69.

Mariani, Philomena, ed. *Critical Fictions. The Politics of Imaginative Writing*. Seattle: Bay Press, 1991.

Maxwell, Anne. 'The Debate on Current Theories of Colonial Discourse'. *Kunapipi* 13.3 (1991): 70–84.

Mbebe, A. 'The Banality of Power and the Aesthetics of Vulgarity in the Postcolony'. *Public Culture* 4.2 (Spring 1992): 1–30

—— 'Prosaics of Servitude and Authoritarian Civilities'. *Public Culture* 5.1 (Fall 1992): 123–45.

McClintock, Anne. 'The Angel of Progress: Pitfalls of the Term "Post-colonialism"'. *Social Text* 31/32 (1992): 84–98.

—— *Maids, Maps and Mines: Gender and Imperialism*. New York: Routledge, 1993.

—— *Imperial Leather: Race, Gender and Sexuality in the Colonial Contest*. London: Routledge, 1994.

Memmi, Albert. *The Colonizer and the Colonized*. New York: Orion Press, 1965.

Menon, Nivedita. 'Orientalism and After'. *Public Culture* 6.1 (Fall 1993): 65–76.

Mercer, Kobena. 'Black Art and the Burden of Representation'. *Third Text* 10 (Spring 1990): 61–78.

—— *Welcome to the Jungle: New Positions in Black Cultural Studies*. New York: Routledge, 1994.

Miller, Christopher. *Blank Darkness: Africanist Discourse in French*. Chicago: University of Chicago Press, 1985.

Minh-ha, Trinh T. *Woman, Native, Other*. Bloomington: Indiana University Press, 1989.

Mishra, Vijay and Bob Hodge, 'What is Post(-)Colonialism?' *Textual Practice* 5.3 (1991): 399–414.

Moghadam, Valentine M., ed. *Identity Politics and Women. Cultural Reassertions and Feminisms in International Perspective*. Boulder: Westview Press, 1994.

Mohanty, Chandra Talpade. 'Feminist Encounters: Locating the Politics of Experience'. *Copyright* 1.1 (1987): 30–44.

—— 'On Race and Voice: Challenges for Liberal Education in the 1990s'. *Cultural Critique* 14 (Winter 1989–1990): 179–208.

—— 'Under Western Eyes: Feminist Scholarship and Colonial Discourses'. Mohanty *et al.*, 52–80. (Also in this volume, Chapter 10.)

Mohanty, Chandra Talpade, Ann Russo and Lourdes Torres, eds. *Third World Women and the Politics of Feminism*. Bloomington: Indiana University Press, 1991.

Mohanty, S. P. 'Us and Them: On the Philosophical Bases of Political Criticism'. *Yale Journal of Criticism* 2.2 (1989): 1–31.

—— ed. *Colonialism and the Postcolonial Condition*. Special issue of *PMLA* 110. 1 (1995).

Mudimbe, V. Y. *The Idea of Africa*. Bloomington: Indiana University Press, 1994.

—— *The Invention of Africa: Gnosis, Philosophy and the Order of Knowledge*. London: James Currey, 1988.

—— ed. *The Surreptitious Speech: Présence Africaine and the Politics of Otherness, 1947–1987*. Chicago: University of Chicago Press, 1992.

Mukherjee, Arun P. 'The Exclusions of Postcolonial Theory and Mulk Raj Anand's "Untouchable": a Case Study'. *Ariel* 22.3 (1991): 27–48.

—— 'Whose Post-colonialism and Whose Postmodernism'. *World Literature Written in English* 30.2 (1990): 1–9.

Mutman, Mahmut and Meyda Yegenoglu, eds. *Orientalism and Cultural Differences. Inscriptions* 6 (1992).

Nasta, Susheila, ed. *Motherlands*. London: The Women's Press, 1991.

Nelson, Cary and Lawrence Grossberg, eds. *Marxism and the Interpretation of Culture*. Urbana: University of Illinois Press, 1988.

Ngũgĩ wa Thiong'o. *Decolonizing the Mind*. London: Heinemann, 1986.

—— *Homecoming*. London: Heinemann, 1972.

—— *Writers in Politics*. London: Heinemann, 1981.

Nicholson, Linda. 'Feminism and the Politics of Postmodernism'. *boundary 2* 19.2 (1992): 53–69.

Obeyesekere, Gananath. *The Apotheosis of Captain Cook*. Princeton: Princeton University Press, 1992.

—— ' "British Cannibals": Contemplation of the Event in the Death and Resurrection of James Cook, Explorer'. *Critical Inquiry* 18.4 (Summer 1992): 630–54.

Ochoa, Maria *et al.*, eds. *Enunciating Our Terms: Women of Color in Collaboration and Conflict. Inscriptions* 7 (1994).

Odeh, Lama Abu. 'Post-Colonial Feminism and the Veil: Thinking the Difference'. *Feminist Review* 43 (Spring 1993): 26–37.

O'Hanlon, Rosalind. 'Recovering the Subject: *Subaltern Studies* and Histories of Resistance in Colonial South Asia'. *Modern Asian Studies* 22.1 (February 1988): 189–224.

O'Hanlon, Rosalind and David Washbrook. 'After Orientalism: Culture, Criticism, and Politics in the Third World'. *Comparative Studies in Society and History* 34.1 (January 1992): 141–67.

Ong, Aihwa. 'Colonialism and Modernity: Feminist Re-Presentations of Women in Non-Western Societies'. *Inscriptions* 3/4 (1988): 79–93.

—— *Spirits of Resistance and Capitalist Discipline: Factory Women in Malaysia.* New York: SUNY Press, 1987.

Owens, Craig. 'The Discourse of Others: Feminists and Postmodernism'. *The Anti-Aesthetic*, ed. Hal Foster. Port Toursont: Bay Press, 1983, 57–82.

Pandey, Gyanendra. 'In Defense of the Fragment: Writing About Hindu–Muslim Riots in India Today'. *Representations* 37 (Winter 1992): 27–55.

Parker, Andrew *et al.*, eds. *Nationalisms and Sexualities.* New York: Routledge, 1991.

Parry, Benita. 'Current Problems in the Study of Colonial Discourse'. *Oxford Literary Review* 9.1/2 (1987): 27–58.

—— 'Resistance Theory/Theorizing Resistance, or Two Cheers for Nativism'. Barker *et al.*, *Colonial Discourse/Postcolonial Theory.* 172–96. (Also in this volume, Chapter 5.)

Pathak, Zakia and Rajeswari Sunder Rajan. 'Shahbano'. *Signs* 14.3 (Spring 1989): 558–82.

Pathak Zakia, Saswati Sengupta and Sharmila Purkayastha. 'The Prisonhouse of Orientalism'. *Textual Practice* 5.2 (Summer 1991): 195–218.

Pease, Donald. 'Toward a Sociology of Literary Knowledge: Greenblatt, Colonialism, and the New Historicism'. Arac and Johnson, 107–53.

Peterson, Kirsten Holst and Anna Rutherford, eds. *A Double Colonization: Colonial and Post-Colonial Women's Writing.* Mundelstrup, Denmark: Dangaroo Press, 1986.

Pletch, Carl. 'The Three Worlds, or the Division of Social Scientific Labor, Circa 1950–75'. *Comparative Studies in Society and History'.* 23.4 (1981): 565–90.

Prakash, Gyan. *Bonded Histories: Genealogies of Labor Servitude in Colonial India.* Cambridge: Cambridge University Press, 1990.

—— 'Can the "Subaltern" Ride? A Reply to O'Hanlon and Washbrook'. *Comparative Studies in Society and Histories* 34.1 (January 1992): 168–84.

—— 'Postcolonial Criticism and Indian Historiography'. *Social Text* 31/32 (1992): 8–19.

—— 'Subaltern Studies as Postcolonial Criticism'. *American Historical Review* 99.5 (December 1994): 1475–90.

—— 'Writing Post-Orientalist Histories of the Third World: Perspectives from Indian Historiography.' Comparative Studies in Society and History 32.2 (1990): 383–408.

Pratt, Mary Louise. *Imperial Eyes: Travel Writing and Transculturation.* New York: Routledge, 1992.

—— 'Women, Literature and National Brotherhood'. *Nineteenth-Century Contexts* 18

(1994): 27–47.

—— ' "Yo Soy La Malinche": Chicana Writers and the Poetics of Ethnonationalism'. *Callaloo* 16.4 (Fall 1993): 859–73.

Radhakrishnan, R. 'Postcoloniality and the Boundaries of Identity'. *Callaloo* 16.4 (Fall 1993): 750–71.

—— 'Toward an Effective Intellectual: Foucault or Gramsci?' Robbins, 57–99.

Retamar, Roberto Fernandez. 'Caliban: Notes toward a Discussion of Culture in our America', trans. Lynn Garafola, David Arthur McMurray, and Robert Marquez. *Massachussetts Review* 15 (Winter/Spring 1974): 7–72.

Robbins, Bruce. 'The Politics of Theory'. *Social Text* 18 (Winter 1987/8): 3–18.

—— 'Secularism, Elitism, Progress, and Other Transgressions: On Edward Said's Voyage In'. *Social Text* 40 (1995) 25–37.

—— 'Othering the Academy: Professionalism and Multiculturalism'. *Social Research* 58.2 (Summer 1991): 355–72.

—— ed. *Intellectuals: Aesthetics, Politics, Academics*. Minneapolis: University of Minnesota Press, 1990.

Robinson, Pearl T. 'The National Conference Phenomenon in Francophone Africa'. *Comparative Studies in Society and History* 36.3 (July 1994): 575–610.

Rosaldo, M. A. 'The Use and Abuse of Anthropology: Reflections on Feminism and Cross-Cultural Understanding'. *Signs* 5.3 (Spring 1980): 389–417.

Rosaldo, Renato. *Culture and Truth: The Remaking of Social Analysis*. Boston: Beacon Press, 1989.

—— 'Ideology, Place, and People Without Culture'. *Cultural Anthropology* 3.1 (1988): 77–87.

—— 'Politics, Patriarchs, and Laughter'. *Cultural Critique* 6 (1987): 65–86.

Rutherford, Jonathan, ed. *Identity: Community, Culture, Difference*. London: Lawrence & Wishart, 1990.

Said, Edward. *Culture and Imperialism*. New York: Vintage, 1994.

—— 'Figures, Configurations, Transfigurations'. *Race & Class* 32.1 (1990): 1–16.

—— 'Identity, Negation and Violence'. *New Left Review* 171 (September/October 1988): 46–62.

—— 'Intellectuals in the Post-Colonial World'. *Salmagundi* 70/71 (Spring/Summer 1986): 44–64.

—— 'Narrative, Geography, and Interpretation'. *New Left Review* 180 (March/April 1990): 81–97.

—— *Orientalism*. New York: Vintage, 1979. (Also in this volume, Chapter 1.)

—— '*Orientalism*, an Afterword'. *Raritan* 14.3 (Winter 1995): 32–59.

—— 'Orientalism Reconsidered'. *Literature, Politics and Theory*, eds. Francis Barker *et al*. London: Methuen, 1986. 210–29.

—— 'The Politics of Knowledge.' *Raritan* 11.1 (Summer 1991): 17–31.

—— 'Representing the Colonized: Anthropology's Interlocutors'. *Critical Inquiry* 15.2 (Winter 1989): 205–25.

—— 'Third World Intellectuals and Metropolitan Culture'. *Raritan* 9.3 (1990): 27–50.

—— *The World, the Text, and the Critic*. Cambridge, MA: Harvard University Press, 1983.

Sanchez, Rosaura. 'Ethnicity, Ideology, and Academia'. *The Americas Review* 15.1 (Spring 1987): 80–8.

Sandison, Alan. *The Wheel of Empire: A Study of the Imperial Idea*. London: Macmillan, 1967.

Sandoval, Chela. 'U.S. Third-World Feminism: the Theory and Method of Oppositional

Consciousness in the Postmodern World'. *Genders* 10 (May 1991): 1–24.

Sangari, Kumkum. 'The Politics of the Possible'. Jan Mohamed and Lloyd, 216–45.

Sangari, Kumkum, and Sudesh Vaid, eds. *Recasting Women: Essays in Colonial History.* New Delhi: Kali for Women, 1989.

Sarkar, Sumit. 'Orientalism Revisited: Saidian Frameworks in the Writing of Modern Indian History'. *Oxford Literary Review* 16.1/2 (1994): 205–24.

Senghor, Léopold. *The Foundations of 'Africanite' or 'Négritude' and 'Arabite'*, trans. Mercer Cook. Paris: Présence Africaine, 1971.

—— *Nationhood and the African Road to Socialism*, trans. Mercer Cook. Paris: Présence Africaine, 1962.

—— *Négritude et humanisme.* Paris: Seuil, 1964.

—— *On African Socialism*, trans. Mercer Cook. New York: Praeger, 1964.

—— *Poems of a Black Orpheus*, trans. William Oxley. London: Menard Press, 1981.

Sharpe, Jenny. 'Figures of Colonial Resistance'. *Modern Fiction Studies* 35.1 (1989): 137–55.

Shohat, Ella. 'Imaging Terra Incognita: The Disciplinary Gaze of Empire'. *Public Culture* 3.2 (Spring 1991): 41–70.

——'Notes on the Post-Colonial'. *Social Text* 31/32 (1992): 99–113. (Also in this volume, Chapter 16.)

Simeon, Dilip. 'Tremors of Intent: Perceptions of the Nation and Community in Contemporary India'. *Oxford Literary Review* 16.1/2 (1994): 225–44.

Slemon, Stephen. 'Magic Realism as Post-Colonial Discourse'. *Canadian Literature* 116 (Spring 1988): 9–24.

—— 'Modernism's Last Post'. *Ariel* 20.4 (October 1989): 3–17.

—— 'Monuments of Empire: Allegory/Counter-Discourse/Post-Colonial Writing'. *Kunapipi* 9.3 (1987): 1–16.

—— 'Post-Colonial Allegory and the Transformation of History'. *Journal of Commonwealth Literature* 23.1 (1988): 157–68.

—— 'The Scramble for Post-Colonialism'. Tiffin and Lawson, 15–32.

—— 'Unsettling the Empire: Resistance Theory for the Second World'. *World Literature Written in English* 30.2 (1990): 30–41. (Also in this volume, Chapter 4.)

Slemon Stephen and Helen Tiffin, eds. *After Europe: Critical Theory and Post-Colonial Writing.* Sydney: Dangaroo Press, 1989.

Soja, Edward. *Postmodern Geographies: The Reassertion of Space in Critical Social Theory.* London: Verso, 1989.

Spivak, Gayatri Chakravorty. 'Acting Bits/Identity Talk'. *Critical Inquiry* 18 (Summer 1992): 770–803.

—— 'The Burden of English'. Breckenridge and Van der Veer, 134–57.

—— 'Can the Subaltern Speak?' Nelson and Grossberg, 271–313.

—— *In Other Worlds: Essays in Cultural Politics.* London: Methuen, 1987.

—— 'The Making of Americans, the Teaching of English, and the Future of Culture Studies'. *New Literary History* 21 (1990): 781–98.

—— 'Neocolonialism and the Secret Agent of Knowledge'. *Oxford Literary Review*, 13.1 (1991): 220–51.

—— *Outside in the Teaching Machine.* New York: Routledge, 1993.

—— *The Post-Colonial Critic: Interviews, Strategies, Dialogues*, ed. Sarah Harasym. New York: Routledge, 1990.

—— 'Poststructuralism, Marginality, Postcoloniality and Value'. Collier and Geyer-Ryan, 219–44. (Also in this volume, Chapter 11.)

—— 'The Rani of Sirmur: An Essay in Reading the Archives'. *History and Theory* 24.3

(1985): 247–72.

—— 'Scattered Speculations on the Question of Value'. *diacritics* (Winter 1985): 73–93.

—— 'Subaltern Studies: Deconstructing Historiography'. Guha and Spivak, 3–32.

—— 'Teaching for the Times'. *Journal of the Midwest MLA* 25.1 (1992): 3–22.

—— 'Theory in the Margin: Coetzee's *Foe* Reading Defoe's *Crusoe/Roxana*'. Arac and Johnson, 154–80.

Spivak, Gayatri Chakravorty *et al*. 'Who Needs the Great Works?: A Debate on the Canon, Core Curricula, and Culture'. *Harper's* 279 (September 1989): 43–52.

Sprinker, Michael. 'The National Question: Said, Ahmad, Jameson'. *Public Culture* 6.1 (Fall 1993): 3–29.

—— 'The War Against Theory'. *Minnesota Review* 39 (Fall/Winter 1992/3): 103–21.

Stoler, Ann. 'Making Empire Respectable: The Politics of Race and Sexual Morality in 20th Century Colonial Cultures'. *American Ethnologist* 16.4 (November 1989): 634–60.

—— 'Rethinking Colonial Categories: European Communities and the Boundaries of Rule'. *Comparative Studies in Society and History* 31.1 (January 1989): 134–61.

—— 'Sexual Affronts and Racial Frontiers: European Identities and the Cultural Politics of Exclusion in Colonial Southeast Asia'. *Comparative Studies in Society and History* 34.3 (July 1992): 514–51.

Stoler, Anne and Frederick Cooper. 'Tensions of Empire: Colonial Control and Visions of Rule'. *American Ethnologist* 16.4 (November 1989): 609–21.

Strathern, Marilyn. 'An Awkward Relationship: The Case of Feminism and Anthropology'. *Signs* 12.2 (Winter 1987): 276–92.

—— 'Intervening'. *Cultural Anthropology* 2 (May 1987): 255–67.

Strobel, Margaret and Nupur Choudhry, eds. *Western Women and Imperialism*. Bloomington: Indiana University Press, 1992.

Suleri, Sara. *The Rhetoric of English India*. Chicago: University of Chicago Press, 1992.

—— 'Woman Skin Deep: Feminism and the Postcolonial Condition'. *Critical Inquiry* 18 (Summer 1992): 756–69. (Also in this volume, Chapter 17.)

Sunder Rajan, Rajeswari. *Real and Imagined Women*. London: Routledge, 1993.

—— ed. *The Lie of the Land: English Literary Studies in India*. New Delhi: Oxford University Press, 1992.

Taiwo, Olufemi. 'Colonialism and Its Aftermath: The Crisis of Knowledge Production'. *Callaloo* 16.3 (1993): 891–908.

Tharu, Susie. 'Thinking the Nation Out: Some Reflections on Nationalism and Theory'. *Journal of Arts and Ideas* 17/18 (June 1989): 81–9.

Tiffin, Chris and Alan Lawson, eds. *De-Scribing Empire*. London: Routledge, 1994.

Tiffin, Helen. 'Post colonial Literatures and Counter-Discourse'. *Kunapipi* 9.3 (1987): 17–34.

—— 'Post-colonialism, Post-modernism and the Rehabilitation of Post-colonial History'. *Journal of Commonwealth Literature* 23.1 (1988): 169–81.

Trivedi, Harish. *Colonial Transactions*. Calcutta: Papyrus, 1993.

Tsing, Anna Lowenhaupt. 'From the Margins'. *Cultural Anthropology* 9.3 (August 1994): 279–97.

Tucker, Judith. 'Problems in the Historiography of Women in the Middle East: The Case of Nineteenth-Century Egypt'. *International Journal of Middle East Studies* 15.3 (August 1983): 321–36.

Tyler, Stephen. 'The Vision Quest in the West, or What the Mind's Eye Sees'. *Journal of Anthropological Research* 40 (Spring 1984): 23–40.

Vaughan, Alden T. 'Caliban in the "Third-World": Shakespeare's Savage as Sociopolitical Symbol'. *Massachusetts Review* 29 (Summer 1988): 289–313.

Vieux, Steve. 'In the Shadow of Neo-liberal Racism'. *Race and Class* 36.1 (1994): 23–32.

Viswanathan, Gauri. 'The Beginnings of English Literary Study in British India'. *Oxford Literary Review* 9.1/2 (1987): 2–26.

—— *Masks of Conquest: Literary Study and British Rule in India.* London: Faber & Faber, 1989.

Ware, Vron. *Beyond the Pale: White Women, Racism, and History.* London: Verso, 1992.

Wolf, Eric R. 'Perilous Ideas: Race, Culture, People'. *Current Anthropology* 35.1 (February 1994): 1–12.

Woodcock, Bruce. 'Post-1975 Caribbean Fiction and the Challenge to English Literature'. *Critical Quarterly* 28.4 (Winter 1986): 79–95.

West, Cornel. 'Black Culture and Postmodernism'. *Remaking History*, eds. B. Kruger and Phil Mariani. New York: DIA Foundation, 1989, 87–96.

—— 'Minority Discourse and the Pitfalls of Canon Formation'. *Yale Journal of Criticism* 1.1 (Fall 1987): 193–202.

Young, Robert. 'The Politics of "The Politics of Literary Theory"'. *Oxford Literary Review* 10.1/2 (1988): 131–57.

—— 'Poststructuralism: the End of Theory'. *Oxford Literary Review* 5.1/2 (1982): 3–20.

—— *White Mythologies: Writing History and the West.* London: Routledge, 1991.

Zavella, Patricia. 'The Problematic Relationship of Feminism and Chicana Studies'. *Women's Studies* 17 (1988): 123–34.

INDEX